KENYA

THE ROUGH GUIDE

THE ROUGH GUIDES

OTHER AVAILABLE ROUGH GUIDES
ZIMBABWE & BOTSWANA • WEST AFRICA • MOROCCO
TUNISIA • EGYPT • PERU • GUATEMALA & BELIZE • BRAZIL
MEXICO • CALIFORNIA & THE WEST COAST USA
SAN FRANCISCO • NEW YORK • FRANCE • PARIS
BRITTANY & NORMANDY • PROVENCE & COTE D'AZUR
THE PYRENEES • SPAIN • PORTUGAL • GERMANY • BERLIN
HOLLAND, BELGIUM & LUXEMBOURG • AMSTERDAM
ITALY • VENICE • SICILY • GREECE • CRETE • TURKEY
EASTERN EUROPE • YUGOSLAVIA • HUNGARY • POLAND
CZECHOSLOVAKIA • SCANDINAVIA • IRELAND • NEPAL
HONG KONG • ISRAEL & THE OCCUPIED TERRITORIES
MEDITERRANEAN WILDLIFE • WOMEN TRAVEL
NOTHING VENTURED

FORTHCOMING
USA • CANADA • EUROPE • THAILAND • WORLD MUSIC
TUSCANY & UMBRIA • ROMANIA • FLORIDA

ROUGH GUIDE CREDITS

Series Editor: Mark Ellingham
Editorial: Martin Dunford, John Fisher, Jack Holland, Jules Brown,
    Jonathan Buckley, Richard Trillo, Greg Ward
Production: Susanne Hillen, Kate Berens, Andy Hilliard
Typesetting: Gail Jammy

Many thanks to everyone on the production team, in particular to Susanne Hillen and Gail Jammy for all their help (and patience) and to Catherine Mulvenna for another excellent proofreading job.

To Doug Paterson my gratitude as always for musical enlightenment, to Dave Warne at *STA Travel* and Alan Dixson at *Let's Go Travel* all my thanks for speedy faxing of fiddly details; and my thanks to Tony Zurbrugg at the *Africa Book Centre* for publication details in the books section; to Phil ("Songa kidogo") Bunce for record reviews and to Stephen Hunt, for last-minute information for disabled travellers.

For aid, ideas, and encouragement in diverse forms on the first edition, my continuing indebtedness to Jeremy Torr (for the bike), Graeme Ewens, Werner Graebner, Jackie Switzer, Rosie Mercer, Robert Gordon and family and all the Khans in Kisii.

And, lastly and mostly, to my wife Teresa and to Alexander the small, all my love.

Dedicated to the memory of **Jim Allen**, whose knowledge and enthusiasm for Swahili culture were a real inspiration.

Contributors acknowledgements – those who helped update
The long list of the readers whose letters were sifted for this edition appears on p.455, together with details about writing to us for the next edition.

Illustration credits
"Basics": Jane Smith
"Contexts": Henry Iles
Incidental illustrations in Part One and Part Three: Edward Briant

Published by Harrap Columbus, Chelsea House, 26 Market Square, Bromley, Kent BR1 1NA.

Typeset in Linotron Univers and Century Old Style to an original design by Andrew Oliver.
Printed by Cox & Wyman, Reading, Berks.
480pp.
Includes index.

British Library Cataloguing in Publication Data
Trillo, Richard
Kenya: the rough guide. – (The rough guides)
1. Kenya – Visitors' guides
I. Title II. Trillo, Richard III. Series
916.76204

ISBN 0-7471-0255-4

KENYA
THE ROUGH GUIDE

WRITTEN AND RESEARCHED BY

RICHARD TRILLO

With additional research by
Jill Bitten, Marc Dubin, David Else,
Werner Graebner and
Doug Paterson

Edited by

Richard Trillo

HARRAP COLUMBUS ■ LONDON

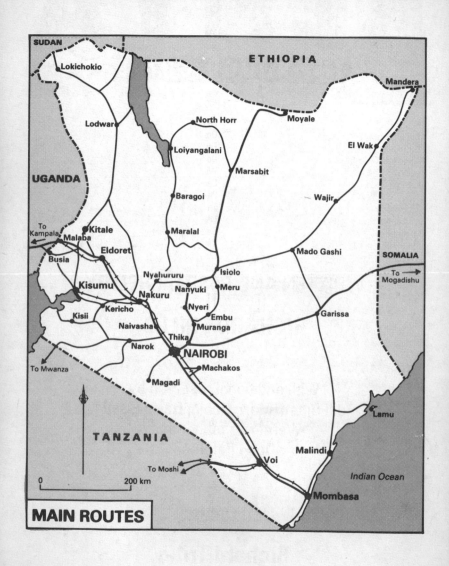

MAIN ROUTES

CONTENTS

Introduction vi

INTRODUCTION

With its long, **tropical beaches** and dramatic **wildlife parks**, **Kenya** has an exotic tourist image. Justifiably, for this is one of the most beautiful lands in Africa and a satisfyingly exciting and relatively easy place to travel – whether on a short holiday or an extended stay. And while the glossy hype of the brochures ignores the country's less salubrious images – its share of post-colonial poverty and mounting political tension – it is true in its way and a valid enough reason for visiting.

Treating Kenya as a succession of tourist sights, however, is neither the best nor the most enjoyable way of experiencing the country. **Travelling independently**, or at least with eyes open – which this book is designed to facilitate – you can enter the more genuine and very different world inhabited by most Kenyans – a ceaselessly active, contrasting landscape of farm and field, of streams and bush paths, of wooden and corrugated-iron shacks, teashops and lodging houses, of crammed buses and pick-up vans, of overloaded bicycles, and of streets wandered by goats and chickens and toddlers.

You'll find a rewarding degree of warmth, openness and curiosity in these **towns and villages**, especially off the more heavily-trodden tourist routes. And out in the wilds, there is an abundance of authentic scenic glamour – vistas of rolling savannah dotted by **Maasai** and their herds, high **Kikuyu** moorlands prowled by shaggy lions, dense **forests** bursting with birdsong and insect noise and, in the north and east, stony, shimmering **desert** – all of which comes crisply into focus when set in its intense, Third World context. On the **coast**, the palm-shaded strands of beach and an almost continuous, reef-protected lagoon are even better than the holiday brochures would have you imagine – no photo can really do justice. And, of course, everywhere you go, Kenya's **wildlife** adds a startling and rapidly addictive dimension.

Shape and divisions

Physically, Kenya consists mostly of broad plateaux. The majority of the population live in the rugged highland areas in the **southwest** quarter of the country, where the ridges are a sea of *shamba* smallholdings and plantations. Ripping through the heart of these highlands sprawls the **Great Rift Valley**, an archetypal East African scene of dry, thorntree savannah, splashed with lakes and hot springs and studded by volcanoes. The walls of the Rift, and **Mount Kenya** itself, dominate the horizon for much of the time. **Nairobi**, the capital, feels like the centre of Kenya, but it lies at the highlands' southeastern edge, only a three-hour drive from the Tanzanian border. The famous **game parks**, watered by seasonal streams, are mostly located in savannah country on the highland fringes.

Kenya's **area** of 582,000 square kilometres makes it about two and a half times the size of Britain. The **population**, which is growing faster than any other country in the world at about four percent per year, is now around twenty-four million.

Further west, towards **Lake Victoria,** lies a gentler rural countryside, less often visited. And in the **north** the land is **desert** or semi-desert – a surprise for many visitors – broken only by the natural highlight of **Lake Turkana,** almost unnaturally blue and gigantic in the wilderness.

East of the highlands, separating the interior from the coast, there are further arid lands – the **Taru Desert** – a barrier which in large part accounts for the very different shifts of history and culture. **The coast** – which is at once satisfyingly predictable in its palms, white sands and warm sea – shelters a surprising and quite distinct Islamic **Swahili** civilisation and carries a long historical record in its mosques and tombs and the ruins of ancient towns cut from the jungle.

Where to go and when

Where to travel clearly depends on your personal interests, and the time you have available. The **Coast** and **Game Parks** are the most obvious targets; and if you come to Kenya on an inclusive tour you're likely to have your time divided between these two attractions. If you like the idea of walking or climbing, there are the high forests and moors of the **Central Highlands** and the hot, dry **Rift Valley.** For serious adventure, the **North** is one of the most spectacular and memorable of all African regions.

More detailed rundowns on the specific character and appeal of each region are given in the **chapter introductions.** There too, and at times within the main text, you will find brief backgrounds on the various **Kenyan peoples.** The ten main language groups cannot any longer be wholly identified with the regions (and moves towards the cities and intermarriage are blurring distinctions) but some understanding of cultural differences is worth achieving. See also "Kenya's People and Religions", in *Basics.*

As far as **climate** is concerned, Kenya has complicated and unpredictable shifts. Broadly, the pattern is that January and February are hot and dry, while from March to May it is hot and wet – this period is known as the "long rains". From June until October the weather is warm and dry, and then come the "short rains", making November and December warm and wet.

Temperatures, though, are determined largely by altitude. Nairobi's are surprisingly moderate compared with, say, London's (see box, overleaf). You can reckon on a drop of 6°C (or 11°F) in temperature for every 1000m you climb from sea level. The low-lying coast and the north remain hot all year round, while the highlands (which range to over 4000m and peak above 5000m) are generally warm or mild during the day but much cooler at night. Nairobi, higher than the Cairngorms, can drop to 5°C (41°F).

At the highest altitudes, it may **rain** at almost any time. Western Kenya, too, has a more scattered rainfall pattern influenced by Lake Victoria. Temperatures tend to climb towards the end of the dry seasons, particularly in late February and early March, when it can become very humid before the rains break. It's worth noting that Kenya's climate has been drying out in recent years and the charts overleaf paint a slightly rainier picture from the 1970s.

The main **tourist seasons** tie in with the **rainfall** patterns: the biggest influxes are in December and January and, to a lesser extent, July and August. **Dry season** travel does have a number of advantages, not least a greater visibility of wildlife as animals concentrate along the diminishing watercourses. July and August are probably the **best months,** overall, for game-viewing. October to January are the months with the clearest seas for goggling – especially November.

In the "long rains", the mountain parks are sometimes closed, as tracks become undriveable. But the **rainy seasons** shouldn't deter travel unduly: the rains usually come only in short afternoon or evening cloudbursts, and the landscape is strikingly green and fresh even if the skies may be cloudy. There are bonuses, too, in the lack of tourists: hotel and often car hire prices are reduced and people generally have more time for you. Kenya is not a country where you need slavishly follow established seasons, any more than itineraries.

KENYA'S CLIMATE

	JAN	FEB	MAR	APR	MAY	JUN	JUL	AUG	SEPT	OCT	NOV	DEC
NAIROBI (Alt 1661m)												
Av day temp (°C)	25	26	25	24	22	21	21	21	24	24	23	23
Av night temp (°C)	12	13	14	14	13	12	11	11	11	13	13	13
Days with rainfall	5	6	11	16	17	9	6	7	6	8	15	11
Rainfall (mm)	38	64	125	211	158	46	15	23	31	53	109	86
MOMBASA (sea level)												
Av day temp (°C)	31	31	31	30	28	28	27	27	28	29	29	30
Av night temp (°C)	24	24	25	24	24	23	22	22	22	23	24	24
Days with rainfall	6	3	7	15	20	15	14	16	14	10	10	9
Rainfall (mm)	25	18	64	196	320	119	89	66	63	86	97	61
KISUMU (Alt 1135m)												
Av day temp (°C)	29	29	28	28	27	27	27	27	28	29	29	29
Av night temp (°C)	18	19	19	18	18	17	17	17	17	18	18	18
Days with rainfall	6	8	12	14	14	9	8	10	8	7	9	8
Rainfall (mm)	48	81	140	191	155	84	58	76	64	56	86	102

LONDON'S CLIMATE

	JAN	FEB	MAR	APR	MAY	JUN	JUL	AUG	SEPT	OCT	NOV	DEC
LONDON (Sea level)												
Av day temp (°C)	6	7	10	13	17	20	22	21	19	14	10	7
Av night temp (°C)	2	2	3	6	8	12	14	13	11	8	5	4
Days with rainfall	15	13	11	12	12	11	12	11	13	13	15	15
Rainfall (mm)	54	40	37	37	46	45	57	59	49	57	64	48

THE
BASICS

GETTING THERE

Flying to Kenya is invariably the cheapest way of getting there, and London the best departure point, both for price and choice of airlines. Other – more esoteric – locations for cheap flights include Athens, Cairo and Tel Aviv, if you plan to take in Kenya as part of wider travels.

Alternatively, buying a package holiday can make a lot of sense if your time available, rather than money, is the limiting factor, and prices have plummeted in recent years. If you choose carefully, you shouldn't feel too packaged. Some of the tour brochures contain quite interesting safari itineraries and a number of independent companies specialise in adventure packages.

Another option, of course, is to make your way to Kenya overland.

If you're considering taking a bicycle to Kenya, see p.9 and 26.

FLIGHTS FROM BRITAIN

In London, and increasingly in other cities, travel agents offer tickets for scheduled flights at substantially **discounted rates** – well below the official fares agreed by *IATA*, the association to which most airlines belong. In the past, airlines prepared to sell off their tickets through these agents were generally the less reputable carriers left with the most unsold seats. But more and more major carriers are cashing in – though some admittedly are doing so as part of a "restricted eligibility" arrangement where the passenger has to be a **student**, for example, or under a certain **age**. There are also a number of short-stay, "flight only" package deals on **charter flights** to Mombasa (see box on p.7).

BOOKING SEATS AND BUYING TICKETS

The so-called **"bucket shops"** are, almost without exception, respectable travel agents, even if first impressions sometimes indicate otherwise. If you phone around, you quickly get an idea of the set-up by throwing a few destinations at them.

When booking, note whether the agent reserves seats to Nairobi directly with the airline by telephone or on a computer system, or has to go through another agent. Fraud isn't a problem but confusion and delays are common enough. Don't expect to see your ticket until you've paid in full. While many agents have ticketing agreements with certain airlines and can write tickets on the premises, they may have to order some tickets from the nominated "consolidator" of the airline concerned – that usually means another agent.

Always ask what **refund** you'll get if anything goes wrong and find out how easy it will be to **change your reservation dates** once you've got your ticket. You can sometimes leave a return ticket "open-dated" on its return portion, but in that case you'll have to make a seat reservation yourself with the airline. It's just as easy, and safer, to have a confirmed seat and change the date if necessary (and if seats are available). Note that if you book through a discount agency, you cannot deal direct with the airline on your booking until you have your ticket, though you can always quote them the details and ask them to check the reservation is held under your name. If it's not, don't panic. It will probably be held under the agent's block seat allocation. Remember, seat reservations and tickets are two quite separate matters.

Airline "seasons" for Kenya vary a little but generally departures in July, August and December will be the most expensive and most airlines have low season rates from February to June, and often again from October to early December. This also ties in with student and youth fares which are always more in summer and Christmas holiday periods.

DISCOUNT AGENTS IN BRITAIN AND IRELAND

Africa Travel Centre, 4 Medway Court, Leigh St, London WC1H 9QX (☎071 387 1211, Fax 071 383 7512). Helpful and resourceful.

Campus Travel, 52 Grosvenor Gardens, London SW1W 0AG (☎071 730 8111). Student/youth specialists.

Campus Travel, 39 Queen's Rd, Bristol BS8 1QE (☎0272 292494).

Campus Travel, 5 Emmanuel St, Cambridge CB1 1NE (☎0223 324 283).

Campus Travel, 5 Nicholson Sq, Edinburgh EH8 9BH (☎031 668 3303).

Campus Travel, 13 High St, Oxford OX1 4DB (☎0865 242 067).

Sam Travel, 14 Broadwick St, London W1V 1FH (☎071 434 9561) and 805–7 Romford Rd, London E12 5AN (☎081 478 8911). Specialists in flights via Moscow.

Soliman Travel, 233 Earl's Court Rd, London SW5 (☎071 370 6446). Particularly good on flights via Cairo.

South Coast Student Travel, 61 Ditchling Rd, Brighton BN1 4SD (☎0273 570226). A good agent with plenty to offer non-students as well.

STA Travel, 74 Old Brompton Rd, London W7 (☎071 937 9962, autoqueue). Large range of fares and airlines for Kenya, from 20 offices in the UK and 120 worldwide. Special fares for students and young people as well as a specialist Africa Desk at 117 Euston Rd (☎071 465 0486, Fax 071 388 0944).

STA Travel, 25 Queens Rd, Bristol BS8 1QE .

STA Travel, 38 Sidney St, Cambridge CB2 3HX.

STA Travel, 75 Deansgate, Manchester M3 21BW.

STA Travel, 19 and 48 High St, Oxford, OX1 4AH.

Trailfinders, 42–48 Earl's Court Rd, London W8 6EJ (☎071 938 3366). Respected discount flights agency with a convenient range of other services. Some reasonable fares, but not especially geared up for Africa.

USIT, O'Connell Bridge, 19/21 Aston Quay, Dublin 2 (☎01 778 117). Student and youth specialist.

Wexas, 45 Brompton Rd, London SW3 1DE (☎071 589 3315). If you're unable to visit others, this membership-only organisation handles everything competently by post. Detailed brochures and fare and airline information.

Book as far in advance as you can. Six months isn't too long. Some airlines are full to capacity at peak periods, especially Christmas, and discounted seat availability is often snapped up quickly. On the other hand, if you find early on that flights seem to be "full", check the same outlets again nearer your departure date – assuming you haven't got something by then – for reservations not taken up and released allocations.

TYPES OF TICKET

Return tickets are generally of three types – short excursions (usually one month), three month excursions and one year (never more). A **one-way** fare (valid a year) is normally half the relevant "yearly" fare. You may be able to fly out to Nairobi and back from somewhere else (an "open jaw"), depending on the airline and the agent's contract.

In rare cases, you may also be able to purchase **tickets *back* from East Africa** before you leave – useful if you're travelling out overland. *Egyptair* tickets can be bought like this, though the ticket is collected from their office in the city in question. Such arrangements, known as *PTA*s, are often surprisingly reliable.

STUDENT AND YOUTH FARES

If you're **a student, academic or under 32**, ask if the agent has special fares – some of the better airlines (including *British Airways* – the only airline flying non-stop), *KLM* and *Pan Am* grant various **restricted eligibility fares** to certain, selected agents which are not available in theory to the general public. Note that the advantage of some of these discretionary fares may lie more in the length of stay they offer and an easing of booking regulations than purely in their price. They are not automatically cheaper than anthing else.

It's worth remembering that *KLM* fly from regional airports in Britain, as well as from Heathrow and Gatwick. All flights are through Amsterdam.

DISCOUNTED AGENTS' FARES

As regards **discount prices**, you can pay anything from a shade under £400 return to over £700 for a discounted return ticket. One-ways will always be over £200. The **airlines to watch** for the cheapest fares are *Egyptair* and *Aeroflot*. Neither has any student–youth deals.

On a one-way, **Aeroflot** is by far the cheapest, and their tickets are always valid a full year. Weekly flights connect through Moscow, with a current lay-over of about six hours (or a basic hotel at their expense). Some agents won't deal with *Aeroflot* because they're slow to make refunds.

Egyptair excursion fares (three-month maximum) can also be found from little over £400. They give you the chance of a stop-over in Cairo for as long as you like at no extra cost. One-ways, though, are relatively expensive. There are daily flights to Cairo, with Thursday and Sunday connections through to Nairobi.

Sudan Airways – whose flights to Nairobi were suspended at the time of writing – have competitive prices, but you must be prepared for a medley of delays and setbacks. Avoid if possible.

Lastly, you might ask about **Saudia** and **Ethiopian Airlines**, both of which are reputable carriers with good fares, but often forgotten by agents. *Saudia* may have seats at Christmas when everything else is full.

AIRLINES' OWN FARES

For an idea of the saving over the **airlines' own fares**, make a few calls to their fares departments (see the "Airlines" box on the following page). In principle, they should all be about the same.

Current **British Airways** and **Kenya Airways** apex fares to Nairobi (minimum 21 days advance booking; 14 day minimum stay, 90 day maximum) go for £517 (April–May), £642 (Feb–Mar, June, Oct–Nov) or £742 (Dec–Jan, July–

RESERVATIONS-SPEAK

Apex Advance purchase excursion fare. Usually the cheapest return deal an airline will offer to you direct.

Charter A flight chartered from an airline by a tour operator to ferry tourists.

Classes Every seat has its class. The common ones are F (first), J (business) C (club) and Y (economy). Any other class is likely to be an economy seat with a special price.

Confirmed (OK) What your reservation has to be to get a seat (written as "OK" on the ticket), a guarantee in Europe, not always in Africa.

Direct flight A flight that takes you from departure point to destination without your having to leave the plane (not necessarily a non-stop flight, as you'll discover if you fly *Aeroflot*).

Flight number Every scheduled flight has one, made up of the two-letter airline code and three digits. It's unique to the airline, the route and the day of the week, but not specific to the date.

MCO Miscellaneous Charges Order. A refundable receipt for funds held in your name by an airline, no longer of any use in immigration situations where you need an onward ticket.

Pax Passengers.

PTA Passenger ticket advice. Prepayment for a ticket back home to be collected in the city of departure.

Reconfirm What some airlines insist you do direct with them within 48 hours of departure. It's vital to do this in Africa or you may find your seat bumped. Note that your ticket nearly always remains a valid travel voucher even if you miss your confirmed travel reservation or lose your seat.

Requested (RQ) A booking which has this status isn't even on the waiting list.

Scheduled A flight operated by the airline to a regular timetable regardless of demand. In Africa these are sometimes cancelled, diverted or simply unknown.

Stop-over A voluntary stay in a city/country en route to your destination where you would otherwise stay in the plane or make a simple connection.

Waitlisted (WL) On a waiting list for cancellations in a particular class, or for empty seats from other agents' expired allocations.

TICKET CONSIDERATIONS

When buying, try to avoid a flight which arrives at night – definitely not the best time for a first encounter with Nairobi. If that isn't possible, don't be alarmed: it's worth seeing how much a pre-booked hotel room would cost (*STA* can be helpful here).

If you want to travel onwards from Kenya and only need a one-way flight, check the cancellation charge for cashing in the unused half of a return ticket. While it doesn't apply much to the land borders, passing through immigration at the airport is always smoother if you have a flight out again.

AIRLINES

The following airlines currently fly London to Nairobi. Departures are given as overnight (meaning arrival the next morning) or by day (meaning arrival same evening).

Aeroflot (SU) 70 Piccadilly, London W1 (☎071 355 2233). Out overnight Fri; back overnight Sat; change in Moscow.

Air France (AF) 158 New Bond St, London W1 (☎071 499 9511 or ☎0345 581393). Out daily overnight except Tues, Sat; back daily overnight except Wed, Sun; change in Paris.

Alitalia (AZ) 205 Holland Park Ave, London W11 (☎071 602 7111). Out by day Fri, Sun (and Wed, but no same day connection); back Mon, Sat by day, Wed overnight; change in Rome.

British Airways (BA) 75 Regent St, London W1 (☎081 897 4400/4000). Out and back daily overnight non-stop.

Egyptair (MS) 31 Piccadilly, London W1 (☎071 734 2395 or ☎437 6426). Out overnight Thurs, Sun; back by day Fri, Mon; change in Cairo.

El Al (LY) 185 Regent St, London W1 (☎071 437 9255). Out Mon and Thurs, overnight; back Tues and Sun overnight; change in Tel Aviv. Outbound, no same day connection from London.

Ethiopian Airlines (ET) 85 Jermyn St, London SW1 (☎071 930 9152). Out overnight Fri, Sat; back by day Fri, Sat; change in Addis Ababa.

Gulf Air (GF) 10 Albemarle St, London W1 (☎071 408 1717). Out overnight Wed, Fri; back by day Thurs, Sat; change in Muscat or Abu Dhabi.

Kenya Airways (KQ) 16 Conduit St, London W1 (☎071 409 0277, fares ☎071 409 0185). Out and back daily overnight, via Rome, Paris, Athens, or Cairo. No plane change.

KLM Royal Dutch Airlines (KL) 8 Hanover St, off Regent St (☎081 750 9000). Out overnight Mon, Thurs, and by day Sat; back overnight Tues, Fri, Sat; change in Amsterdam.

Lufthansa (LH) 23–26 Piccadilly, London W1 (☎071 355 4994). Out overnight Tues, Thurs, Sat, Sun; back overnight Mon, Fri, and by day Sun, Wed; change in Frankfurt.

Olympic Airways (OA) Trafalgar House, Chalkhill Rd, London W6 (☎081 846 9080). Out overnight Wed; back overnight Fri; change in Athens. On the outbound journey, Wed night in Athens at the airline's expense.

Pan American World Airways (PA) 193 Piccadilly, London W1 (☎081 759 8888). Out Thurs, Sun morning; back same night; change in Frankfurt.

Sabena (SN) 36 Piccadilly, London W1 (☎081 780 1444). Out overnight Tues, Fri, Sun; back overnight Mon, Wed, Sat; change in Brussels.

Saudia (SV) 171 Regent St, London W1 (☎081 995 7777). Out Fri; back Sat; change in Jeddah; long layover.

Sudan Airways (SD) 12 Grosvenor St, London W1 (☎071 499 8101). Out overnight Thurs, Sun; back overnight Thurs and by day Sun; change in Khartoum. *Nairobi flights currently suspended.*

Swissair (SR) 10 Wardour St, London W1 (☎071 734 6737 or ☎439 4144). Out overnight Tues, Fri, Sun; back overnight Wed, Sun, Mon; change in Zurich.

DEPARTURE TAX

When leaving Kenya by air there's a **departure tax** of $20. This does not have to be paid in US dollars, but must be paid in hard currency – not Kenyan shillings. If you don't have the right money, change will be given only in Kenyan shillings, which cannot be exported, though if you have time you will be able to change them to hard currency. Departure tax on domestic flights is Ksh50. Some airlines (*BA* for example) will collect this payment in Nairobi on the day of departure if you prefer. If you're booked on a package, check these taxes are included in the price.

Sept). A book-anytime, non-seasonal fare is £449 one way, £898 return for a stay of up to one year (no stop-overs allowed).

If you want to have stop-overs en route (eg, on *BA* flights, in Cairo, Kampala or anywhere on the *BA* network), you can do so for £740 one way, £1156 for a 14–90 day excursion (book anytime, non-seasonal) or £1286 for a one year ticket. Once ticketed, these fares are fixed, but all are liable to change through 1991 and 1992.

If you want to do some detective work, ask the airline to give you details of their **consolidators**. Some are only too happy; others refuse (see box above).

WARNING: TRANSATLANTIC PASSENGERS

North American passengers who expect to use **transatlantic baggage quotas** – two unweighed pieces of hold luggage – will have problems flying on to Kenya from Europe where a **20-kilo weight limit** applies. This rule is even enforced for *Pan Am's* New York-to-Nairobi return passengers *when they check in at Nairobi to fly home via Frankfurt.* Two "excess baggage payment" counters have been set up and they charge around $15 per kilo. . .

"FLIGHT-ONLY" CHARTER PACKAGES

If you're happy to fly into Mombasa, there are now several charter operations with which you can get seats from £330. The three main charter operations to Kenya are *Air 2000, Caledonian Airways* and *Kenya Airways* themselves. *Tropical Places* is the cheapest outlet for these seats, but you should also try *STA, Africa Travel Centre,* and *Kuoni.* It's important to realise that these are strictly holiday flights, not scheduled services.

There's usually a maximum stay of four or six weeks, price depends on the number of days you stay and you won't be able to change your dates.

PACKAGE HOLIDAYS

With the charter flights operating out of London's Stanstead and Gatwick airports to Mombasa, **packages** of flight and half board in a beach hotel have crashed in cost to prices as low as

PACKAGE TOUR OPERATORS

Package tour operators come in a number of shapes and sizes. Below are listed both the mainstream operators whose brochures are likely to be found in every high street travel agent together with several more unusual companies. If you're considering a package, look also at the companies in the "Overland and Adventure Tour Operators" box.

Abercrombie and Kent, Sloane Square House, Holbein Place, London SW1 (☎071 730 9600). Very upmarket, with unusual offerings and a dedicated and very flexible manner. Busy Nairobi operation.

African Safari Club, 35 Thayer St, London W1M 5LH (☎071 486 4595, Fax 071 487 3966). Swiss-based company offering very cheap beach packages. Flights out of London Stanstead on their own planes.

Art of Travel, 268 Lavender Hill, London SW11 1LJ (☎071 738 2038, Fax 071 924 3661). Innovative travel stylists with a personal approach, specialising in tailor-made holidays at prices chosen by the customer.

Flamingo Tours (☎071 409 2229). Maintain a big operation in Nairobi.

Hayes and Jarvis (☎071 245 1051). Some cheap beach self-catering and safari combinations.

Kuoni, (☎0306/ 885 717 or 0306 740 500). Most recommended of the mainstream operators, with a flexible approach and lots of experience. Excellent value and a wide choice from a good brochure.

Select (☎0992 554 144). Good value.

Silk Cut Faraway (☎0730 65211). Upmarket and glamorous (little change from £1500 for anything) but a very limited programme.

Speedbird, 152 King St, London W6 0QU (☎071 741 8041). *British Airways* holiday offshoot. Similar to *Thomson*, but uses more expensive coast hotels and has a proper safari programme.

Thomson (☎071 387 1900). Basically, competitive beach holidays with 1–4 day Tsavo safaris available.

Tropical Places, Freshfield House, Lewes Rd, Forest Row, East Sussex RH18 5ES (☎0342 82 4011, Fax 0342 822364). Basically a tele-booking operation (ITV Oracle p.359), particularly good value for people looking for a bit of packaged independence – charter flights from London Gatwick to Mombasa (max. 28 day stay) from £330, coast hotels from £17/day and good value short safaris from £80 for 2 days in Tsavo.

Twickers World, (☎081 892 8164). Original and environmentally sensitive operator, with an excellent (though not cheap) Kenya tour, using some exclusive and private accommodation.

Wildlife Safari, The Old Bakery, South Rd, Reigate, Surrey, RH2 7LB (☎0737 223903). Individual operator with a firm emphasis on high quality safaris using good accommodation. Two weeks safari including BA flight and professional guides from £1430.

£400 or even less. It really makes sense to consider this option for a short holiday. You don't have to stick with the crowd all the time – or even stay at the hotel – and you could do several short independent trips around the country if you wanted.

Coast hotels can vary greatly in price. Find out as much as possible about the establishment and beware of spending hundreds of pounds more on a place that isn't actually a lot nicer than the one next door. The tropical beach environment is so all-encompassing that much of what you're paying extra for (staff in smarter uniforms, pricier furniture, carpets) is likely to be almost irrelevant to your enjoyment. As any experienced Kenya traveller will tell you, some of the nicest places are also the most reasonable.

It's important to realise, too, that a **safari** component in a package tour always knocks the price up a lot: a week on the beach may look cheap, but add a week's safari and £650 will be the absolute minimum cost, inclusive of flight – and that's in April or May, and Tsavo only (*Kuoni*). Nor should you be misled about the length or style of inexpensive safaris if you do elect to go for the full works. All too often a couple of nights are wasted in Nairobi and the rest of the "safari" consists of Amboseli and a night in *Treetops*.

OVERLAND AND ADVENTURE TOUR OPERATORS

The **"overland tour"** catch-all covers most of the organised holidays that don't feel like packages. Not many of them are *overland* the entire way. The fly out, tour around by truck, fly back option is an increasingly popular one. Note that operators sometimes run trips "in association" with each other and the number of long, ex-UK trips offered each year is actually quite small. Most run occasional evening slide and video sessions when you can decide if a packaged adventure is for you. A number of other, smaller operators also advertise regularly in *BBC Wildlife* magazine. As well as the operators listed here, check the "Package Tour Operators" and "Discount Agents" boxes. Most of the latter are agents for companies below.

Africa Travel Centre, 4 Medway Court, Leigh St, London WC1H 9QX (☎071 387 1211, Fax 071 383 7512). Offers a good selection of inexpensive trips in Kenya, bookable in advance (eg Turkana £230, Camel Safari £205, both excluding flight), plus trips starting in Kenya (eg 25 days camping Kenya, Tanzania, Rwanda, Zaire, Uganda from £720, excluding flight) and more luxurious trips (eg 21 days coach trip Nairobi–Harare from £2140).

Dragoman, Camp Green, Kenton Rd, Debenham, Suffolk IP14 9LA (☎0728 861133). Personal and creative operators with notably good trucks and competitive prices. Regular trans-African departures.

Exodus Expeditions, 9 Weir Rd, London SW12 0LT (☎081 675 5550). Run several trips a year between Nairobi and London via West Africa. And also a good selection of trips inside Kenya, including trekking on Mt Kenya and the Aberdares (18 days, £1740 including flight) and an unusual Maasai Mara, Mt Elgon and Kakamega trip (16 days from £1330 including flights).

Explore Worldwide, 1 Frederick St, Aldershot, Hampshire, GU11 1LQ (☎0252 319448, Fax 0252 343170). Highly respected small groups operator with a creative safari – 16 days from £1190 (including flight).

Guerba Expeditions, 101 Eden Vale Rd, Westbury, Wiltshire BA13 3QX (☎0373 827046, Fax 0373 858351). The acknowledged African experts, running a string of Kenya trips, including a top-value 3 week safari from £1335 (including flight) and a coast-based diving trip – with lessons – from £610 (without flight) plus several London to Nairobi journeys.

Individual Safaris Ltd, West Dunster, Cadeleigh, Tiverton, Devon, EX16 8HR (☎088 45 452). Low key and non-glossy by conviction, this is not an operator but an enthusiastic agent for many adventure travel companies in Kenya (*Let's Go, Just the Ticket, Brusafaris*) and very useful for their personal approach to specific requests.

Kumuka Africa, 42 Westbourne Grove, London W2 5SH (☎071 221 2348). One week safaris from £195 (Maasai Mara, Nakuru, Baringo, camping) and cottages on Diani beach at £12/night/person. Their Kenyan partner is *Ferian*, 2nd Floor, Arrow House, Koinange St, Nairobi (☎228107).

Tracks Africa, 12 Abingdon Rd, London W8 6AF (☎071 937 3028-30). Offers a London-to-Nairobi (or vice versa) and a number of short, well-priced safaris in Kenya (eg 9 day Highlights of Kenya from £370, 15 days bird-watching £975, both excluding flight).

TAKING CHILDREN

Kenya is a tremendously exciting country for children, but you need to bear one or two concerns in mind. Most people worry first about **health and sanitation**. Babies should not be exposed to **malaria** risk if it's avoidable (and remember the pills only limit or subdue an attack of the disease). And you wouldn't want to take a child in nappies on safari — four is probably the youngest age for even the shortest trip like this.

But there's no reason why small children shouldn't go to **the coast** — the hotels are on sandy beaches facing a warm sea, safely protected by the reef, and dining rooms provide easily adapted food as well as snack and children's menus. On safaris, most children of five or six will probably fare very well so long as they get adequate explanations of what's going on, can see properly, and get lots of drinks and snacks. Most **hotels, lodges and tented camps** do not specifically exclude children of any age (indeed,if you book yourself you'll find the vast majority give huge **reductions**), but a number of organised tours have a **minimum age** of 7, while several of the more exclusive tented camps and all four of the "tree hotels" have minimum ages of seven, eight or even ten.

If you're still undecided about whether to take a child to Kenya, remember how many healthy second generation expatriate children have been brought up there. The biggest health problem for Kenyan children is poverty.

TYPES OF SAFARI

Before arranging the details, think about whether you want comfort or a more authentic experience. Internal flights (an **"air safari"**) will add enormously to the cost and comfort of your trip and give you spectacular views but a much less intimate feel of Africa. On the other hand, **long bumpy drives** to meet the demands of an itinerary can be completely exhausting while hours of your time may be eaten away in a cloud of dust.

Many safaris take you from one game park hotel (known as **lodges**) to another, using **mini-buses** with lift-up roofs for picture taking. Make sure you have a window seat and ask about the number of passengers and whether the vehicle is shared by several operators or is for your group only. More details about the food and accommodation you can expect from a package are covered in relevant sections further on.

The alternative to a standard lodge safari is a true **camping safari**, where the crew — or you — put up your tents at the end of the day and you spend all your time in the open air. With this kind of trip you have to be prepared for a degree of discomfort along with the self-sufficiency — insects can occasionally be a menace, you may not get a shower every night, the food won't be so lavish and the beer not as cold.

Camping, you normally travel in a fairly **rugged vehicle** — a four-wheel drive Landcruiser or even an open-sided lorry — giving more flexibility about where you go and how long you stay. The more expensive camping safaris come very expensive indeed and tend to model their style on images culled from *Out of Africa*; they can easily cost over £200 a day. At the other end of the scale, you can pre-book a week-long camping safari from the UK for hardly any more than this — without flights. Decide where and how you want to go, and find a tour to fit.

Most high street travel agents can fix you up with brochures for the more **mainstream tour operators** whose packages generally (though not always) fall into the lodge and minibus category. For more **off-beat adventure trips**, or a better selection of camping safaris, you should contact the operator directly. Note that the **single person supplement** tends to be high on conventional beach and safari packages and somewhat less (or you can share) on the more adventure-spirited trips. For both genres, see the boxes (on p.7 and 8). And a last vital tip: **leave the coast until the end of your holiday**.

HOMESTAY HOLIDAYS

If you're interested in **living with a Kenyan family** as a guest, contact *Experiment in International Living*, Upper Wyche, Malvern, Worcestershire (☎06845 62577). This is a non-profit friendship organisation, offering home-stays of one to four weeks: write well in advance.

CYCLING HOLIDAYS

And if nothing so sedentary interests you, you might like to try an organised **bicycle tour** of Kenya. *Paradise Bicycle Tours*, PO Box 1726 Evergreen, Colorado, 80439, USA (☎303 670 1842) offer twelve-day mountain bike trips from US$1195, plus US$150 bike hire, with full board accommodation in lodges and a Maasai Mara safari included (flights excluded). You can fix up similar arrangements in Kenya through *Safari Seekers*, their local partners, and book much shorter jaunts to Hell's Gate and Lakes Naivasha, Nakuru, Baringo and Bogoria. In Nairobi too, *Gametrackers* are now offering mountain bike safaris (addresses in "Nairobi Directory" on p.89).

Also see the section on cycling independently in Kenya, on p.26.

FLIGHTS FROM AUSTRALASIA

If you're **approaching Kenya from the east**, you'll find there are no direct flights from Australia or New Zealand. The main service, **Sydney-Bombay-Nairobi**, on *Alitalia* and *Kenya Airways*, twice weekly, is prohibitively expensive at A$2800 upwards for a return.

Alternative options – a great deal cheaper – include flying **via Bangkok**, and then on to Nairobi with *Pakistan International Airlines*; going **via London** and buying a Nairobi ticket there; or, if you're happy to start your travels in **Zimbabwe**, using *Qantas'* twice weekly flight to Harare from Sydney and Perth. If you don't want to take the train through Zambia and Tanzania, there are four flights a week from Harare to Nairobi, economy fare about £160. Among recommended agents for deals on the Harare and other routes, *STA* is probably most reliable. They have offices all across Australia and New Zealand. Head offices are:

STA Travel, 1a Lee St, Sydney 2000 (☎2/212 1255).

STA Travel, 64 High St, Auckland (☎9/390 458).

FLIGHTS FROM AFRICAN CITIES

Within Africa, direct (but rarely non-stop) flights to Nairobi are available from Abidjan, Accra, Addis Ababa, Bujumbura, Brazzaville, Cairo, Dakar, Dar-es-Salaam, Douala, Entebbe, Gaborone, Harare, Johannesburg, Khartoum, Kigali, Kinshasa, Lagos, Lusaka, Mahe, Mogadishu, Monrovia, Moroni, Tananarive and Zanzibar. Flights from other capitals connect through these cities, often with long delays.

Fares, which are rarely discounted, can seem a little high – over £300 one-way Accra–Nairobi for example, and around £400 for a one month excursion. If you're planning on taking Nairobi in as part of broader air travel in Africa, you may well find some saving in making separate trips out of London. The big transcontinental carriers in Africa are *Ethiopian Airlines* and *Air Afrique*. There are also twice-weekly flights on *Cameroon Airlines* between Douala and Nairobi.

OVERLAND TO KENYA

Opportunities to **travel overland** to Kenya from Europe are liable to change as Africa's borders open and close in the wake of political and military conflicts. There's been, however, a **general improvement**, overall, in conditions over the last decade and there's no shortage of expedition operators promising the journey of a lifetime. There's more information in "Onward: African Travel Options" in the *Contexts* section.

OVERLAND VIA EGYPT AND SUDAN

At the time of writing – and since 1984 – the **Nile route through Sudan** is impassable, with the countryside in the south entirely controlled by the anti-government forces of the Sudanese Peoples' Liberation Army. Sudan is shaky at present, and visas not issued routinely. Unless you find something discounted, the necessary flight from Khartoum to Nairobi will cost over £200. If the route is reopened, Nile steamers ply upriver as far as Juba in the rainy season (April–Oct) from where a road, hopefully soon to be surfaced, connects with Lodwar in Kenya.

For the very determined only, a possible route may still exist **via Nyala**, a four- or five-day lorry ride southwest of Khartoum north of the war zone, to Birao in the Central African Republic. The route then goes via Zaire, Uganda and into Kenya. One or two UK-based overland operators have recently used the Birao route.

OVERLAND VIA NORTH AND WEST AFRICA

The jouney **across the Sahara and via West Africa** is a long one but Kenya's attractions make it a good destination after all that travel. The main route is through Niger and Nigeria, thence south through Cameroon, east across the Central African Republic, southeast through Zaire and –

now that Uganda has become safe for travel again – east over the highlands to Kenya. For the West African portion of this trip (including the Algerian Sahara, Niger, Nigeria and Cameroon) you would surely want a copy of the encyclopaedic and invaluable *West Africa: the Rough Guide* (Harrap Columbus, 1232 pages, £9.95).

OVERLAND EXPEDITIONS

For a number of years, **operators of overland expeditions** have been following the West Africa route as far as Zaire and then cutting south around Lake Victoria and through Tanzania, taking in some of the rich scenic and faunal variety of that country's northwest region. Most organised trips finish in Nairobi. See the box on p.8 for tour operators' addresses.

If you're interested in one of the more **inexpensive expedition companies** – sometimes regrettably one-off outfits – that advertise in the classified columns, it's worth paying them a visit. It seems unfair to throw blanket disapproval over them, but even more unfair on you if things go disastrously wrong. Scrutinising their blurb gives a good indication of their probable preparedness and real know-how. And if the blurb looks cheap or hasty you should forget it.

GOING UNDER YOUR OWN STEAM

The other option – **driving yourself**, or entering into partnership with others (sometimes located through classified ads) to fix up a vehicle and head off to Africa – is obviously peppered with potential pitfalls. It's perfectly feasible though – thousands do it every year – as is setting off alone, or with a companion, using **public transport**, hitching lifts and walking. Don't go into an overland trip on your own via North and West Africa if you've less than six months. The adventure, otherwise, becomes a race.

BY SHIP TO KENYA

It is still possible to get to East Africa **by ship**, but you can expect to pay considerably more for a berth for the twenty-day passage than you would for an air ticket. The *Strand Cruise Centre*, Charing Cross Shopping Concourse, The Strand, London WC2N 4HZ (☎071 836 6363, Fax 071 497 0078) is the main agent in Britain for **passenger-carrying cargo ship voyages**. They can fix you up on one of the **Mediterranean Shipping Line's** monthly sailings from Felixstowe, through the Med and the Suez Canal to Mogadishu, Dar-es-Salaam, Tanga and Mombasa from £1950 one way. Or you could start the trip in Genoa, and go via Livorno and Naples for £150 less.

RED TAPE AND VISAS

Obvious, but still worth stating, check that your passport is current. And check that it will remain valid for at least six months beyond the end of your projected stay in Kenya. If you're travelling further afield in Africa, you'll need to allow for this, and ensure your passport has plenty of spare pages for stamps. British citizens (except those of Indian, Bangladeshi or Pakistani origin) need no visa to enter Kenya. Nor do most other Commonwealth citizens – with the exceptions of Australians, Sri Lankans and Nigerians – or passport holders from Eire, Germany, Denmark, Finland, Ethiopia, Sweden, Spain, Turkey and Uruguay, all of whom can enter Kenya freely, with just a Visitor's Pass, issued routinely on arrival.

VISAS AND VISITORS' PASSES

Visas can be obtained in advance from any Kenyan embassy, consulate or high commission, or from a British embassy in countries where Kenya has no diplomatic representation. Visas

KENYAN EMBASSIES, CONSULATES AND HIGH COMMISSIONS

AUSTRALIA: 33 Ainslie Ave, PO Box 1990, GPO Canberra (☎062 47 46 66).

AUSTRIA: Rotenturmstrasse 22, 1010 Vienna (☎1 63 32 42).

BELGIUM: Av Joyeuse Entrée 1–5, Brussels (☎2 230 30 65).

CANADA: Gillia Building, Suite 600, 141 Laurier Ave, West Ottawa, Ontario K1P 5J3 (☎613/563-1773).

EGYPT: 8 Medina Munawara St, PO Box 362, Dokki, Cairo (☎85946 or 859455).

FRANCE: 3 rue Cimarosa, 75116 Paris (☎1 45 53 35 00).

WEST GERMANY: Villichgasse 23, 5300 Bonn 2 (☎228 35 30 66 or 35 60 41).

INDIA: 66 Vasant Marg, Vasant Vihar, New Delhi (☎11 670963).

ITALY: Consulate, CP 10755, 00144 Rome.

JAPAN: 24–20 Nishi-Azabu 3-Chome, Minato-Ku, Tokyo (☎3 479 4006).

NETHERLANDS: Konninginnegr. 102, The Hague (☎703 50 42 15).

NIGERIA: PO Box 6464, 53 Queen's Drive, Ikoyi, Lagos (☎1 682768).

SWEDEN: Birger Jarlsgatan 37, 2st 11145 Stockholm (☎8 21 83 00).

UNITED KINGDOM: 45 Portland Place, London W1N 4AS (☎071 636 2371).

USA: Embassy, 2249 R St. NW, Washington, DC 20008 (☎202/387-6101 or 6104). Consulate, 9100 Wilshire Blvd, Beverly Hills, CA 90212 (☎213/274-6635); 424 UN Mission, Madison Ave, New York, NY 10017 (☎212/486-1300).

USSR: Bolshaya Ordinka, Dom 70, Moscow (☎095 231 87 33 or 231 68 46).

ZAIRE: Plot 5002, ave de l'Ouganda, BP 9667, Zone Gombe, Kinshasa (☎12 30117).

ZAMBIA: Harambee House, 5207 United Nations Ave, PO Box 50298, Lusaka (☎1 212531).

ZIMBABWE: 95 Park Lane, PO Box 4069, Harare (☎790847).

normally take 24 hours to process, require two passport-size photos and usually an **air ticket** out of the region (not just to Uganda or Tanzania). This requirement is usually waived if the embassy is satisfied of your alternative arrangements or financial responsibility. South African stamps in your passport used to be a problem. It seems the government's attitude to this is changing, as *South African Airways* have recently been granted landing rights at Nairobi. Remember that Kenyan diplomatic missions are **closed on Kenyan public holidays** (see p.38 for a list).

Visas are normally valid for six months from date of issue. On arrival in Kenya, however, various factors will determine the length of stay actually granted to you, including your appearance, how much money you have and (fortunately) how long you want to stay. They normally give visitors' passes of up to three months.

You can also get a **visa on arrival** at the airport (US$26) but this may cause delays. If you're arriving at night it's best avoided.

If you're planning on visiting Tanzania out of Kenya, you can cross the border freely within the validity of your Kenya visa (assuming of course you have a visa for Tanzania if you need one), but for other trips outside Kenya, you should make sure you obtain a Kenyan **multiple entry visa**.

EXTENDING YOUR STAY

It's important to know just how long a stay you've been granted in Kenya, particularly, perhaps, if you don't require a visa. There have recently been a number of cases of travellers **overstaying** the limits of their visitors' passes by a few days and finding themselves invited to spend the night behind bars while a suitable fine was discussed – anything from Ksh1000 to Ksh4000. The problem can arise if, for example, you can't decipher KVP5W/H ("Kenya Visitors' Pass 5-Week Holiday" of course). Ask what's been stamped when you arrive and renew well in advance. You will certainly have to renew after three months.

Extensions to visitors' passes and **visa renewals** can theoretically be done at any provincial capital (Nairobi, Mombasa, Nakuru, Kisumu, Embu or Garissa) but it's easiest done at Nyayo House near the old post office in Nairobi (Mon–Fri 8.30am–12.30pm & 2–3.30pm).

If your passport requires a visa and you have stayed a total of **six months** in the country and don't have resident's status, you will have to leave not only Kenya, but East Africa, in order to obtain a new visa to allow you to return.

For **neighbouring countries' embassies** in Nairobi see "Nairobi Directory" (p.84).

MONEY AND COSTS

Kenya's currency, the Kenyan shilling (Ksh), is a colonial legacy based on the old British currency. A soft currency with no value outside the country, it's now worth a lot less than its original 5 pence sterling – one shilling – equivalent (though only ten years ago it was worth considerably more than 5 pence). The current rate of exchange is around Ksh45: £1. People occasionally talk in "pounds", meaning Ksh20, and often in "bob", meaning shillings. You'll also hear "quids" (meaning "dough") for pounds. There are Ksh500, 200, 100, 20 and 10 notes and coins of Ksh5, 1, 50 cents (half a shilling), 20 cents, 10 cents and 5 cents. Kenyan shillings may not be imported or exported and will be confiscated if found at customs. Never destroy Kenyan currency. You will be arrested and fined if you do. Give it away if you haven't spent or exchanged it by the time of your departure.

MONEY

All funds are supposed to be declared on arrival. Whenever you exchange hard currency for Kenyan, your **currency declaration form** will be stamped. This is sometimes forgotten, and in

any case, the forms are rarely checked when you leave the country. At some border crossings, you may not be given one, but pick one up as soon as possible from the Bank of Kenya building in Nairobi to avoid problems later; if you want to reconvert money, you'll have to produce it and everything will have to add up.

BANKS

You can **exchange** hard currencies in cash or travellers' cheques at banks all over the country, and at most large hotels for a marginally poorer rate. Dollars and British sterling are always the most acceptable and will cause the least delay where the rates aren't immediately to hand; always ask first what commission and charges will be deducted. *Barclays* are normally fastest. **Banks** are usually open Mon–Fri 8.30am–1pm and Sat 8.30–11am. Saturday openings, however, are often only on the first and last Saturday of each month.

CARRYING IT AND KEEPING IT

Travellers' cheques are the obvious way to carry your funds. There's really little advantage to **cash** and it can't be replaced if lost or stolen. It's definitely worth **shopping around** for the cheapest travellers' cheques, as some banks levy large charges.

You should have some hard currency in cash – preferably US dollars – and remember, if you're flying out, you need US$20 cash or the exact equivalent in any other hard currency for departure tax.

It's wise to carry valuable cash (as opposed to Kenyan shillings) in a very **safe place**, ideally in a leather pouch under your waistband, looped to your belt. You may not have a waistband, but ingenuity counts. Pouches hanging around your neck aren't too great and ordinary wallets are a disaster. As for Kenyan shillings, you'll be carrying around large quantities of coins and paper money. Be aware that, except in the towns,

HAVING MONEY SENT TO KENYA

Try to avoid **sending home for money**. It's expensive and even telexed draft orders can take weeks to reach you at the counter even though the normal delay should be four or five working days. You should be able to receive **hard currency** if you're leaving the country.

Ksh500, 200 and even 100 bills can be hard to change (few people have that sort of money) – so make sure you have a safe purse or secure zip pocket to stuff all the small denominations in.

CREDIT CARDS

If you're into **plastic**, *VISA* and *American Express* are widely accepted for tourist services such as upmarket hotels, flights, safaris, car hire; *Mastercard/Access* is more limited. There's usually a two- to five-percent mark-up on top of the price, but, as establishments are charged a fixed percentage of their transactions, this is obviously negotiable. A credit card can be very useful for leaving a deposit for car hire (frequently thousands of shillings). *Barclays Bank* will give you **cash advances** in US dollars on *VISA* cards – a useful service, but expensive.

THE BLACK MARKET

Cash can make you a profit if you change it on the **black market**, but it seems unfair on a strangled economy to squeeze it even harder for the sake of a ten or fifteen percent bonus to your purchasing power. Less altruistically, it needs to be said, whatever else you do in Kenya, *do not change money on the street*. You risk (a) being immediately ripped off, (b) getting a hefty fine, and (c) being deported. You might suffer all three.

COSTS

Prices in the book are given as a basis for comparison as much as anything else but as far as possible all were correct for the 1990/91 high season. **Inflation** has been creeping up as the Kenya shilling steadily loses value against hard currencies like the dollar and the pound. It currently stands at over twenty percent so you could expect prices given here in Kenya shillings to have risen by perhaps a third by the beginning of 1992 and by probably fifty percent by the end of the year.

BARGAINING

You'll need to get into **bargaining** quickly (see p.37), but be cautious, at first, over your purchases, until you've established the value of things. Once you start, it's surprising how little is sold at a strictly fixed price. It's nearly always worth making an offer. In places that see tourists and travellers, prices sometimes vary considerably through the year. This "seasonal factor" seems to be increasing in importance, too.

SEASONS

If you're planning a trip to Kenya using moderate or expensive accommodation, it's useful to know that a lot of money can be saved by not going in the high season. With slight variations on date, **resort hotels and safari lodges** have separate low, mid- and high season rates (it applies much less to town hotels).

Low season:1 April to 30 June or 15 July.
Mid-season: 1 or 16 July to 30 Nov or 15 Dec.
High season: 1 or 16 Dec to 31 March.

Typically, in recent years, the mid season rate has been the same as the previous high season, which gives you some predictability about costs in the future. Low season rates are discounted by anything from a third to almost a half of the high season tariff just past.

TRAVELLING CHEAPLY

Kenya can clearly be expensive if you want to hire a car or go on organised safaris. But it doesn't need to be. By staying in the more economical hotels, eating in local places and using public transport, you can get by easily enough on around Ksh500 (say **£10** a day), or less if you camp and buy your own food (many Kenyans survive on an average of around Ksh80 a week). On a daily average budget of Ksh1000 (**say £20** or a little more), you would be living very well most of the time, even staying in the occasional more luxurious tourist hotel.

Staying put for a while you'll find it much easier to live cheaply: a week or so in Lamu on the coast or Lake Naivasha in the Rift Valley need not cost you much more than Ksh200 a day.

Travel costs

For people on low budgets, **travel** is probably still the biggest expense. Getting around by **bus and pick-up van** (*matatu*) is cheap, but the crucial disadvantage is that they can't drive you around the game parks. In order to do that, **hiring a vehicle** – and paying for petrol – will add at least £40 a day to your costs, though shared between two or more this isn't cripplingly expensive for a week or so. You could also find all-inclusive camping safaris from around £30 a day, sometimes less.

Lodgings

Rooms in local "Boarding and Lodgings" start at about Ksh50 for a single, Ksh80 for a twin or double (abbreviated to Ksh50/80 throughout the book), and rarely go much above Ksh200 for a twin room. Prices depend largely on whether the room is self-contained (s/c) with a shower and toilet. Tourist hotels, lodges and tented camps are very much more expensive. See "Sleeping" (p.28).

Food costs

As for **food**, the prices of many basic commodities – including soft drinks, cigarettes, bread, cornmeal (*ugali*), sugar, milk and tea – are fixed

and low (though **beer**, which used also to be price controlled, now varies from around Ksh15–30 for a large bottle).

Eating out is not a Kenyan tradition and few Kenyans would consider it cheap. Still, in the most basic local restaurant, decent **meals** can be had for less than Ksh40 and sometimes for half that. For fancier meals in touristy places, expect to pay up to £4–10 (Ksh180–Ksh450) – rarely more – for a three- or four-course meal of international-style dishes.

HEALTH AND INSURANCE

For arrivals by air from Europe, Australia, or North America, Kenya no longer has any required inoculations. Entering overland, though, you may well be required to show both yellow fever and cholera International Vaccination Certificates and a cholera jab is, in any case, a good precaution – there are occasional outbreaks in Kenya. If you fly on an airline that stops en route in Africa, you should have both shots before you leave. You may otherwise be subjected to them at the airport. Plan ahead and start organising your jabs at least six weeks before departure. Remember that a first-time cholera inoculation needs at least two weeks between the two injections of the course; and a yellow fever certificate is only valid ten days after you've had the jab.

OTHER JABS

Doctors usually recommend **typhoid** jabs and you should have **tetanus** and **polio** boosters. Opinion

is divided about gamma-globulin shots against **hepatitis A**. The disease itself is debilitating, taking up to a year to clear up, but the injection is only effective for a few months, sometimes it seems not at all. A new vaccination is currently being developed – your doctor may be able to advise you.

Whether you have the jab or not, be extra careful about cleanliness and in particular about contamination of water – a problem wherever a single cistern holds the whole water supply in a cockroach-infested toilet/bathroom, as often happens in Lamu.

MALARIA

Protection against **malaria** is absolutely essential. The disease – caused by a parasite carried in the saliva of some mosquitoes – is endemic in tropical Africa; many people carry it in their bloodstream and get occasional bouts of fever. It has a variable **incubation period** of a few days to several weeks so you can get it long after being bitten. If you get malaria, you'll probably know: the fever, shivering and headaches are something like severe flu and come in waves. Malaria is not infectious but it can be very dangerous and sometimes even fatal if not treated quickly. The destruction of red blood cells by the *falciparum* type of malaria parasite can lead to **cerebral malaria** (blocking of the brain capillaries) and is the cause of a nasty complication called **blackwater fever** in which the urine is stained by excreted blood cells.

PREVENTION

It is vital therefore to take **anti-malaria tablets**. Doctors can advise you on which kind – it's

GOING DOWN WITH MALARIA

If you go down with malaria, you'll need to take a cure. Don't compare yourself with local people who may have considerable immunity. The priority, if you think you might be getting a fever, is **treatment**. Delay is very risky.

First, confirm your diagnosis by getting to a doctor and having a blood test to identify the strain. If this isn't possible, **quinine tablets** are recommended as the best treatment – 600mg twice a day for five days, and then three Fansidar tablets. Or, take chloroquine tablets at the rate of 10mg per kilo body weight up to a maximum of 600mg (usually four tablets) immediately, then half as much (usually two tablets) eight hours later. Take this second dose again on the second and third days.

If you notice no improvement after the initial dose, try again to see a doctor or take three Fansidar tablets if you have them; your malaria is chloroquine-resistant.

generally the latest anti-resistant creation – but you can buy them without prescription at a chemist. It is equally important to keep a routine, and cover the period before and after your trip with doses. Once in Kenya, the chloroquine-based tablets (eg Nivaquin, Aralen and Resochin), as well as Paludrin and Daraprim, can be bought everywhere, but Maloprim, Fansidar and some of the newer drugs to which *falciparum* malaria (one of the common East African strains) is less resistant, are only available in big towns.

Chloroquine is safe during pregnancy but Maloprim and Fansidar sometimes have side effects. The latter isn't recommended (whether you're pregnant or not) as a prophylaxis. Mefloquine, a safer variation on Fansidar which is only taken once a week, is worth asking your doctor about.

Sleep under a **mosquito net** when possible – they're not expensive – and burn **mosquito coils** (readily available in Kenya) for a peaceful night. Don't use *Cock Brand* or *Lion*, which are said to contain DDT and are banned in many countries.

Female *Anopheles* mosquitoes – the aggressors – prefer to bite in the evening. They can be distinguished from other mosquitoes by their rather eager, head-down position. Wherever the mosquitoes are particularly bad – and that's not often – cover your exposed parts with something strong. Pure *Deet* (the insecticide DT) works well; citronella oil is a help and smells better. Strangely, the best mosquito repellent of all is said to be *Avon* bath oil – but they don't market it as such. In the highlands the malaria risk is low, but you should under no circumstances break your course of pills as it's vital to keep your parasite-fighting level as high as possible.

OTHER DISEASES

Bilharzia is a bit of a bogey. The usual recommendation is never to swim in, wash with, or even touch, lake water that can't be vouched for. In fact, while various lakes and rivers harbour the disease – in places – the only inland water you would probably want to swim in is Lake Turkana, which is bilharzia-free.

Bilharzia, the medical name of which is **schistosomiasis**, comes from tiny flukes (the schistosomes) that live in freshwater snails and which, as part of their life cycle, leave their hosts and burrow into animal (or human) skin to multiply in the bloodstream. The snails only favour stagnant water and the chances of picking up bilharzia are small. Of course, if you pass blood – the first symptom – see a doctor: it's curable.

The only other real likelihood of your encountering a serious disease is if it's **sexually transmitted**. Venereal diseases are widespread, particularly in the larger towns, and the **HIV virus** which can cause Aids is alarmingly prevalent and spreading all the time (see p.46). It's very easily passed between people suffering relatively minor, but ulcerous, sexually transmitted diseases, and the very high prevalence of these is thought to

HOSPITALS

If you need serious treatment in Kenya, you'll discover a frightening lack of well-equipped **hospitals**. The *Consolata Sisters' Hospitals* (one outside Nairobi and another in Nyeri) are reassuring exceptions that we're aware of. Nairobi itself is reasonably well equipped.

IMMUNISATIONS AND ADVICE

In Britain your first source of advice and probable supplier of jabs and prescriptions is your general practitioner. Family doctors are often well informed and some won't charge you for routine injections. For yellow fever and other exotic shots you'll normally have to visit a specialist clinic, often in a county town health authority headquarters.

In London, advice and low-cost **inoculations** are available from the **Hospital for Tropical Diseases**, 4 St Pancras Way, London NW1 0PE (☎071 388 8989). They produce a series of useful fact sheets and you can get most jabs without prior appointment any weekday morning. With a referral from your GP, the Hospital for Tropical Diseases will also give you a complete **check-up** on your return if you think it may be worth it.

Also in London, the *British Airways Travel Clinic*, 75 Regent St, London W1 (☎071 439 9584/5) is open Monday to Friday 9am–7pm. They can provide a wide variety of unusual shots like plague, anthrax and rabies as well as the usual ones, anti-malarial tablets and various hardware.

If you can't make it to London, you may want to check out the services of *MASTA* (Medical Advisory Services for Travellers Abroad, Bureau of Hygiene and Tropical Diseases, Keppel St, London WC1E 7HT) who provide very detailed, personalised "Health Briefs" for whichever country you're visiting. They advise on which inoculations you need and when to get them, give rundowns on all the diseases you're (not) likely to fall victim to and include up-to-date health news from the countries concerned. The "Concise Brief" seems pretty complete but the "Comprehensive" one is amazingly so and a delight for hypochondriacs (students half-price). *MASTA* also sell Neat Deet insect repellant (brilliant stuff), various mosquito nets and *Sterile Emergency Kits* – basically sterile needles and drip. These, sometimes called **Aids Kits** are more useful as a reassurance to anxious relatives. If you're in such a bad way that you need a blood transfusion in Africa, you'll probably die anyway, never mind catching Aids. But it can do no harm to have the kit if you're set on it.

Other major tropical disease centres in the UK are:

Liverpool School of Tropical Medicine, Pembroke Place, Liverpool L3 5QA (☎051 708 9393).

Communicable Diseases Unit, Ruchill Hospital, Glasgow G20 9NB (☎041 946 7120).

Department of Communicable and Tropical Diseases, East Birmingham Hospital, Bordesley Green Rd, Birmingham B9 5ST (☎021 772 4311).

account for the high incidence of heterosexually transmitted HIV. So there you have it: not exactly an incitement to throw caution to the winds.

WATER AND BUGS

In most places, the **water** you drink will have come from a tap and is supposed to be pure. Since bad water is the most likely cause of **diarrhoea**, you should be fairly cautious about drinking rain or well water if you can't get clean tap water. Endless cups of super-heated *chai* are the obvious solution, if your teeth can stand it.

In truth, **stomach upsets** don't afflict many travellers. If you're only staying a short time, it makes sense to be very scrupulous: either using purifying tablets or boiling (or both) kills most things. For longer stays, think of **re-educating your stomach** rather than fortifying it; it's virtually impossible to travel around the country without exposing yourself to strange bugs from time to time. Take it easy at first, don't overdo the fruit (and wash it in clean water), don't keep food too long, and be very wary of salads (not often served in cheap places anyway).

GENERAL HEALTH TIPS

Some people **sweat** heavily and lose a lot of salt. If this applies to you, sprinkle extra salt on your food. Salt tablets are a waste of money but you do need to keep a healthy salt balance. About **papaya**: these fruit, if you like them, can be eaten as a kind of tonic. They contain excellent supplies of invigorating minerals and vitamins, and are reckoned to help the healing process and to aid digestion. Papaya seeds, which taste like watercress, are good for you, too. If you're not wild about lowland papayas, try the smaller and much more fragrant **mountain** variety.

MEDICINE BAG

There's no need to take a mass of drugs and remedies you'll probably never use – and best not to plan a pharmaceutical relief number and give away a lot of miscellaneous pills. Various items, however, are immensely useful, especially on a long trip, and well worth buying in advance.

On a local level, if you're interested in herbal and other natural remedies, you'll find a wealth of examples in markets. Intuition, common sense and persistent enquiries are all you need to judge whether they're worth trying.

Paracetamol Safer than aspirin for pain and fever relief.

Water purifying (chlorine) tablets Taste horrid but do the trick. Shop around – they vary greatly in price.

Anti-malaria tablets Enough for prophylactic use plus several courses of *Fansidar* and/or quinine tablets in case of attack.

Codeine phosphate This is the preferable emergency antidiarrhoeal pill but is on prescription only. Some GPs may oblige. *Lomotil* is second best.

Antibiotics *Flagyl* is good in a lower bowel crisis. *Amoxil* is a broad spectrum antibacterial drug useful against many infections. Neither should be used unless you cannot see a doctor.

Zinc oxide powder Useful anti-fungal powder for sweaty crevices.

Antiseptic cream *Cicatrin* is good but creams invariably squeeze out sooner or later so avoid metal tubes. Bright red or purple *mercurochrome* liquid dries wounds.

Alcohol swabs *Medi-swabs* are invaluable for cleaning wounds, insect bites and infections.

Sticking plaster, steri-strip wound closures, sterile gauze dressing, micropore tape You don't need much of this stuff. If you use it, supplies can be replenished in Nairobi.

Lipsalve/chapstick Invaluable for dry lips.

Thermometer Very useful. Ideally you'll be 37.5°C. A *Feverscan* forehead thermometer is unbreakable and gives a ready reckoning (from chemists).

Lens solution If you wear contact lenses you'll need a good supply of solution.

Should you have a **serious attack**, 24 hours of sweet, black tea and nothing else may rinse it out. The important thing is to replace your lost fluids. If you feel the need, you can make up a **rehydration mix** with four heaped teaspoons of sugar or honey and half a teaspoon of salt in a litre of water. If it seems to be getting worse – or, horrifically, you have to travel a long distance – any chemist should have name brand anti-diarrhoea remedies. These – *Lomotil, Codeine phosphate,* etc – shouldn't be overused. Stay right away from *Kaomycin* and *Immodium,* neither of which is safe to use and can even encourage diarrhoea. And avoid jumping for antibiotics at the first sign of trouble: they annihilate what's nicely known as your "gut flora" (most of which you want to keep) and will not work on viruses. Most upsets resolve themselves. If you continue to feel bad, you should really seek a doctor.

TRAVELLER'S HEALTH

Edited and regularly updated by Richard Dawood *Traveller's Health* (OUP) is a sane, detailed and well written guide to tropical health, with something for just about every imaginable symptom.

INJURIES AND ATTACKS

Take more care than usual over minor **cuts and scrapes**. The most trivial scratch can become a throbbing infection if you ignore it. Take a small tube of antiseptic with you – bacitracin is recommended.

Otherwise, there are all sorts of potential **bites**, **stings** and **rashes** which rarely, if ever, materialise.

Dogs are usually sad and skulking, posing little threat. Scorpions and spiders abound but are hardly ever seen unless you turn over rocks or logs: scorpion stings are painful but almost never fatal, while spiders are mostly quite harmless. **Snakes** are common but, again, the vast majority are harmless. To see one at all, you'd need to search stealthily; walk heavily and they obligingly disappear. To allay fears of larger beasts, see the "Wildlife" section on p.40.

Many people get occasional **heat rashes**. A warm shower, to open the pores, and cotton clothes should help. And, on the subject of heat, it's important not to overdose on **sunshine** in the first week or two. The powerful heat and bright light can mess up your system. A hat and sunglasses are really recommended.

TEETH

Get a thorough **dental** check-up before leaving home and take extra care of your teeth while in Kenya. Stringy meat, acid fruit and sugary tea are some of the hazards. You might start using a freshly cut "toothbrush twig" (*msuake*), as local people do. Some varieties contain a plaque-destroying enzyme. You can buy them at markets.

If you lose a filling and aren't inclined to see a dentist in Kenya, try and get hold of some gutta-percha – a natural, rubbery substance – available from some chemists, or from your dentist. You heat it and then pack it in the hole as a temporary filling. Using chewing gum is a bad idea.

INSURANCE

Insurance, in the light of all these medical possibilities, is too important to ignore. Before you purchase special **travel insurance**, whether for medical or property mishaps, check to see that you won't duplicate the coverage of any **existing plans** which you may have or be covered by. Travel facilities paid for with **credit cards** are routinely insured, but this doesn't help you if your camera is stolen or your jeep is rammed by a rhino (the former instance about a million times more likely than the latter).

Home insurance may cover theft or loss of documents, money and valuables while overseas, though exact conditions and maximum amounts vary from company to company. Students may even be covered by their parents' policies.

You should, however, be most interested and concerned about insuring your **health** and being certain that if you have to spend time in hospital, or even have to be repatriated, you'll be covered.

Premiums vary widely – from the very reasonable ones, offered primarily through student and youth travel agencies (though available to anyone), to ones so expensive that the cost for anything more than two months of coverage will probably equal the cost of the worst possible combination of disasters. You should note also that few – if any – insurers will arrange on-the-spot payments in the event of a major expense or loss; you will usually be reimbursed only after going home.

If you want insurance cover against theft, *ISIS* travel insurance, available through branches of *STA Travel* or *Endsleigh* (in London, 71 Old Brompton Rd, London SW7 3JS ☎071 589 6783) – is one of the cheapest available in Britain. £20–30 per month will cover you against all sorts of calamities as well as lost baggage, flight cancellations and hospital charges.

If you need to claim, you *must* have a police report in the case of theft or loss, and supporting evidence in the case of hospital and medication bills. Keep photocopies of it all and don't allow months to elapse before informing the insurer. Write immediately. You can usually claim later.

FLYING DOCTORS

Kenya's **Flying Doctor service** (which also operates in Tanzania) offers free evacuation by air to a medical centre. This is very reassuring if you'll be spending time out in the wilds – it costs around £10 for a month or £20 for a year. The income goes back into the service and the *African Medical Research Foundation* behind it. You can contact them in advance (PO Box 30125, Nairobi, ☎501301) or buy their insurance on arrival at the airport.

FOR WHEELCHAIR USERS

British Airways offer the only **non-stop flights** to Kenya – more costly, but less physically demanding than the cheapies. You may need the extra energy for Nairobi airport, where accessibility means how well you cope in a scrum. A **city centre hotel** with lifts (like the *Six–Eighty*) is probably the best plan. Attitudes to disabled people are generally good – there are always willing hands to help you over any obstacle.

Safari trucks have superb springing, but taking a pressure cushion is a wise precaution. Even then, off-road trips can be very arduous. It's perhaps better to use Nairobi as a base, and go on one of the many one-day excursions, to Nakuru, Naivasha or the *Outspan* for example. **Let's Go Travel** gives good advice here.

The all-night **sleeper train** to Mombasa sounds improbable but is possible. On arrival at Mombasa station haggle for a taxi. Loading up a wheelchair never diminishes the drivers' smiles. Drivers will also find you a suitable hotel room, with enough space for you and your companion/helper to operate in – the *Splendid* is recommended. In this sunny, surprising city everything is easy going except crossing the street – beware! The tourist beaches and bars are reachable and Fort Jesus even boasts a row of vacant wheelchairs for the needy at the gate! *Steven Hunt*

MAPS AND ADVANCE INFORMATION

Kenya Tourist Offices abroad tend to be thin on useful maps and information (the Ministry of Tourism relies on the private sector to promote Kenya), but they are always worth visiting if you're nearby. Try to buy maps in advance – with the exception of Kenya Survey maps they're usually cheaper. If you're going to Kenya for some time, there's a growing list of libraries, resource centres and journals which can give you some insight into the country before you touch down.

In Nairobi, there's a good selection of maps at the **Public Map Office** (see "Nairobi Directory" for details on how to obtain the survey maps) and it's really worth getting hold of the Survey of Kenya park maps (three of which have now been superseded by *Macmillan's* publica-

tions for Tsavo, Amboseli and Masai Mara) before taking off for the wilds. In the parks themselves they're usually either out of stock or twice the price. With the aid of the numbered junctions, you can actually find your way around.

MAP AND BOOK SUPPLIERS

Stanford's, 12–14 Long Acre, Covent Garden, London WC2E 9LP (☎071 836 1321). Centrally located and one of the world's best map and guide book suppliers.

Africa Bookcentre, 38 King St, London WC2E 8JT (☎071 240 6649). Located in the Africa Centre, Mon–Sat 11am–5.30pm. A very wide selection of books from and about the continent, with an emphasis on African writers and academic works.

The Travellers Bookshop, 25 Cecil Court, London WC2N 4EZ (☎071 836 9132). New shop, with enthusiastic, well-travelled staff and "buyback" offer on used books.

Daunt Books for Travellers, 83 Marylebone High St, W1M 4AL (☎071 224 2295). A huge selection of guides and maps, plus history, novels and more.

LIBRARIES AND RESOURCE CENTRES

Africa Centre, 38 King Street, London WC2E 8JT (☎071 836 1973). Office and reading room open Mon–Fri 9.30am–6pm. Britain's best independent charity institute for African affairs, open to all – reading room with magazines and newspapers, exhibitions, music, theatre, cinema, language teaching. Bar and restaurant open seven days. A good place to meet people.

KENYA TOURIST OFFICES ABROAD

FRANCE: 5 rue Volney, Paris 75002 (☎1 42 60 66 88).

GERMANY: Hochstrasse 53, 6000 Frankfurt 1 (☎69 28 25 51).

HONG KONG: 1309 Liu Chong Hing Bak Building, 24 Des Voeux Rd, Central GPO Box 5280, Hong Kong (☎5 236053).

JAPAN: RM 216 Yurakucho Building, 1–10 Yurakucho, 1-Chome, Chiyoda-Ku, Tokyo (☎3 214 4595).

SWEDEN: Birger Jarlsgatan 37, 11145 Stockholm (☎8 21 23 00).

SWITZERLAND: Bleicherweg 30, CH-8039 Zurich (☎1 202 22 44).

UNITED KINGDOM: 25 Brooks Mews, London, W1 (☎071 355 3144).

USA: 424 Madison Ave, New York, NY 10017 (☎212 486-1300).

9100 Wilshire Blvd, Doheny Plaza Suite 111, Beverly Hills CA 90121 (☎213 274-6634).

MAPS

You'd do well to buy a good, large-scale **map of Kenya** before leaving. Other, locally useful, maps, are mentioned in passing through the guide.

Bartholomew This offering makes all the roads look the same so can't be recommended for travelling with.

Shell Accurate Kenyan AA-approved map – if new editions are updated – but tends to fall apart quickly.

Macmillan Clear and fairly tough, but less detailed (and irritatingly devoid of distances) though it has Nairobi and Mombasa plans on the reverse. They also do park maps for Amboseli, Tsavo and Maasai Mara.

Nelles Verlag German, but published in English, and detailed (though poor on minor road numbers and a number of recently built highways). Includes a good chunk of Northern Tanzania and some inserts, together with mostly accurate annotations.

If you're doing more in Africa than visiting Kenya alone, you probably want one or more of the **Michelin** series, nos. 953, 954, or 955, still the best all-purpose travel maps for Africa – Kenya comes out small at this scale but with surprising detail.

School of Oriental and African Studies Library, Thornhaugh St, Russell Square, London WC1H 0XG (☎071 637 2388). A vast collection of books, journals and maps in a modern building. Day visits are allowed but membership to borrow costs £10 with a £50 deposit and a reference.

Commonwealth Institute, Kensington High Street, London W8 6NQ (☎071 603 4535) Large centre offering library and resource services, shop, exhibitions, workshops. Performance venue.

Royal Geographical Society, 1 Kensington Gore, London SW7 2AR (☎071 581 2057). Helpful Expedition Advisory Service provides a wealth of information, including maps and technical guides.

MAGAZINES AND PERIODICALS

Worthwhile Africa-centred magazines, worth checking through for news before you go, and not likely to be available once you're there, include:

Africa (Kirkman House, 54a Tottenham Court Rd, London W1P 0BT, ☎071 637 9341). Mainstream news and business magazine.

Africa Confidential (Miramoor Publications, 73 Farringdon Rd, London EC1M 3JB, ☎071 584 9141). Fortnightly eight-page newsletter with solid inside info. Subscription only.

Africa Events (Abercorn Commercial Centre, Bridgewater Rd, Alperton, Middlesex HA0 1BD ☎081 902 7972). Comment and analysis with a Muslim flavour.

African Business (IC Publications, PO Box 261, Carlton House, 69 Great Queen St, London WC2B 5BN, ☎071 404 4333). Good general coverage.

Africa Report (833 UN Plaza, New York, NY 10017, ☎212 949 5666). Bi-monthly American serious newsmag published by African-American Institute. Good analyses and in-depth reporting.

GETTING AROUND

A quick reference roundup of regional travel details is given at the end of each chapter. Details refer both to routes within the chapter and to routes from towns covered in the chapter to places in other chapters. Hence, details of getting to the coast are covered in the Nairobi chapter. Bus and train telephone booking numbers are also given.

BUSES, MATATUS AND TAXIS

There's a whole range of vehicles on Kenya's roads. Alongside the flashy **"video coaches"** tearing up one or two of the main highways, you'll find smaller **"country bus"** companies operating a single battered Leyland. In towns of any size, a whole crowd of **minibuses**, **pick-up vans** and **Peugeot taxis** hustle for business constantly. The transport scene is always a screaming hive of confusion, but somehow you'll always arrive.

Fares vary a great deal according to the competition and the condition of the road. KSh0.50–KSh1.00 per kilometre is normal and rarely will you be charged more than the going rate. **Baggage charges** are usually supplementary, however, and have to be bargained over. Never pay more than half your fare for luggage – it should be a lot less – and always talk to other passengers to find out how much they paid.

BUSES

Ordinary **buses** cover the whole country, getting you close to almost anywhere. Some, on the main runs between Nairobi and Mombasa, and to a lesser extent the west, are fast, comfortable and keep to schedules: you generally need to **reserve** seats on these **a day in advance**. The large companies – in particular *OTC* and *Akamba* – have ticket offices near the bus stations in most towns, where they list their routes and prices. But their parking bays are rarely marked and there are no published timetables. The easiest procedure is to mention your destination to a few people at the bus park and then check out the torrent of offers. Keep asking – it's virtually impossible to get on the wrong bus. Once you've acquired a seat, the wait can be almost a pleasure if you're in no hurry; as you watch the throng outside and field a continuous stream of vendors proffering wares through the window. (If you want something, ask one of them to get it for you; there'll be a tiny mark-up.)

A fairly recent addition to the bus system is a network of green **Nyayo buses**, government-run and operating on short-haul routes. They have uniformed drivers and usually two or three uniformed conductors. Modern, comfortable, they're about the cheapest form of transport available.

MATATUS

Public vehicles at the smaller end of the spectrum have a gruesome safety record and their drivers, on the whole, a breathtaking lack of road sense; this is especially true of *matatus* – usually pick-up vans fitted with wooden benches and a canvas roof. But *matatus*, whose name has something to do with "three" (room for three more? we still have three wheels? more likely three ten cent coins a ride – but no longer) are often the most convenient and sometimes the only means of transport to smaller places off the main roads. If there's any choice, take a larger vehicle – *Nissans* are the best – even if this does mean a longer wait for places to fill. Be warned, however, that minibus **kombi vans** tend to have low windows, so you don't get much of a view. Best are the small, **25-seater coaches** which are fairly roomy and have good visibility.

Some of the *matatus* are clearly falling apart: they break down often and travel terrifyingly fast when they're able to. But on occasions they can be an enjoyable way of getting about, giving you close contact (literally) with local people, and some hilarious encounters. The best places in a *matatu* are right at the back by the door or up near the cab, but it's a good idea to wear sunglasses if your face is near a front window – they sometimes shatter. . .

TAXIS

Peugeot taxis – more comfortable, business-like and expensive – usually drive directly from one point to another with a full complement of passengers. Always choose a vehicle that's full and about to leave or you'll have to wait inside until they are ready to go – sometimes for hours. Beware of being used as bait by the driver to encourage passengers to choose his car. Competition is intense and people will lie unashamedly to persuade you the vehicle is going "just now".

In particular, don't hand over any money before you set off; or, if the taxi does get going, wait until you've left town. This isn't a question of being ripped off (though discreetly noting the licence

---

URBAN TRANSPORT

Nairobi and Mombasa have municipally run **local bus** services (*KBS*) and city **taxis**. The taxis are about the only means of getting around late at night, but always settle on a fare before getting in because the meters hardly ever work.

TRAIN BOOKINGS

It's important to **make bookings** for the trains, especially if you want a first-class compartment, but above all during the busy Christmas and New Year period when trains are invariably full. Ticket offices at the stations in Mombasa and Nairobi are open mornings and afternoons, and will take bookings weeks ahead. **Travel agents** will usually do the work for you, sometimes for a fairly hefty supplement. A number of overseas agents will handle first-class train bookings, too, though you can expect to pay a little more. To travel first class, you have to take a private two-berth compartment. Second-class compartments are shared by four people and single sex, though, with the consent of the occupants, this can sometimes be disregarded. One-way fares are Ksh420 first class, Ksh220 second class. Nairobi bookings ☎21211. Note that you can't reserve Mombasa–Nairobi berths in Nairobi (and vice versa). **Couples** thinking of travelling first class should note a couple of other things: 1) that first class compartments have rather small windows, compared with second class; and 2) that it's perfectly allowable to book a whole second class compartment for two adults and two children (who only pay half price), with no binding obligation that the children show up.

plate of the vehicle is never a bad idea) but too often the first departure is just a cruise around town rounding up passengers and buying petrol, with your money, and then back to square one.

It is worth considering your general direction through the trip and which side will be shadier. This is especially important on dirt roads when the combination of a slow, bumpy ride, dust and fierce sun through closed windows can be horrible.

TRAINS

Although the **railways** aren't used a great deal by travellers (most trains go by night, there are no great savings over road travel unless you go hard-seated third class, and they're fairly slow) an extremely popular exception is the **Nairobi–Mombasa run**. This is a travelling experience in its own right and one of the world's great railway journeys.

The two trains each way leave with shocking punctuality at 5pm and 7pm, arriving at 7.30am and 8am respectively. Most people take the later, fast train, but the slower, stopping train is often less crowded and gives you a couple of hours of evening light to watch the passing scene: from Nairobi, the animals on the Athi Plains; from Mombasa, the sultry crawl up from the ocean to the Taru Desert. Taking the train to Nakuru over the fantastic escarpment route is worthwhile too, since it leaves Nairobi at 3pm.

There was an experiment on the Nairobi–Mombasa line recently, with a **daytime train** replacing the 5pm, and leaving at 7.30am. But the advantage of being able to watch the changing landscape was outweighed by the inconvenience of arriving well after dark. Like the "Steam Safari" which operated every Sunday between Nairobi and Naivasha, with a return uphill by diesel loco, the day train seems to have been dropped. Nairobi and Mombasa travel agents have the latest details.

There are some other **branch lines**, including two lines to the west, terminating at Malaba on the Uganda border and Kisumu on Lake Victoria. There are also two small branch lines with infrequent services in the south: one down to Lake Magadi from Konza (mostly freight), the other from Voi to Taveta on the Tanzania border. Some maps mark **misleading branch lines**: Kitale, Thika and Nyahururu no longer have passenger services.

PLANES

Kenya has a number of reasonably priced **internal air services** and it's well worth seeing the country from the eagle's point of view at least once. There are details of schedules and fares at the end of each chapter. Daily flights on *Kenya Airways* from Jomo Kenyatta Airport connect **Nairobi** to Kisumu and Mombasa. *Air Kenya Aviation* and *Equator* between them fly from Wilson Airport to the Maasai Mara lodges, Malindi, Lamu and Kiwaiyu, among other destinations. Occasionally, you can pick up non-scheduled flights at Wilson by being rightly placed and timed – to towns in the northern deserts, for example – and you might even hitch a ride if you're persuasive.

Along the **coast**, *Eagle Aviation* is the recommended air service, with daily scheduled flights between Mombasa, Malindi and Lamu (details in Chapter Six); the flight to Lamu is an exotic and exhilarating one over reefs and jungle up to the islands. Airlines' details are given in the appropriate town "directories".

Baggage allowances on internal flights, apart from *Kenya Airways'*, are usually under 20kg and may be as little as 10kg. Be prepared.

Lastly, note that ordinary **connecting times** shouldn't be relied on if you're flying to catch an international departure. Domestic services are often delayed and many cheaper flight tickets to Europe or the USA cannot be endorsed to another airline if you miss your flight.

FERRIES

Travel by boat, in a country with few large rivers, is rarely a functional way of getting around. On the coast, the only regular ferries of any importance are those connecting the islands of the Lamu archipelago, and the ferry-bridges across the Tana River and the coastal creeks. Lake Victoria, which used to have a network of steamer routes, is beginning to pick up the pieces again after the break-up of the East African Community. Small ferries, operated by *Kenya Railways*, churn around the Winam Gulf and out to a couple of the islands. There are international passenger steamers, in theory, to Musoma, Mwanza and Bukoba in Tanzania, and to Kampala in Uganda, from Kisumu. And there's a high speed ferry service between Mombasa and Zanzibar.

HITCHING

This is how the majority of rural people get around – by **waving down a vehicle** – but they invariably pay, whether it's a bus, a *matatu*, a lorry or a private vehicle with a spare place. Private vehicles, except on the main Kisumu–Nairobi–Mombasa artery and one or two through routes, are comparatively rare and usually full. Because of the cheapness of buses, travellers don't try it much, but hitching can be a good change of pace, enabling you to cover distances fast and usually in safety. Along the coast, where there are relatively fewer *matatus* and more private cars, it's often easy. More calculatingly, if you're on a low budget, hitching rides with private cars can throw you in with Asians and Europeans, often resulting in opportunities to visit national parks and reserves.

Hitching **techniques** need to be fairly exuberant; a modest thumb is more likely to be inter-preted as a friendly, or rude, gesture than a request for a lift. Beckon the driver to stop with your palm. And if you can't afford to pay, say so right away; generosity will often provide you a lift anyway.

CAR HIRE AND DRIVING

Hiring a car is the opposite extreme, with petrol comparable to Britain's, but it does have advantages over any other means of transport which make it seriously worth considering for a week or two. All the parks and reserves are open to private and hired vehicles (as well as organised tours), and there's a lot to be said for the freedom of choice that having your own wheels gives you. Unless there are more than two of you, though, it won't save you money over one of the cheaper camping safaris. You're also required to leave a hefty deposit, roughly equivalent to the expected cost. Credit cards are useful for this.

CHOOSING A VEHICLE

Four-wheel drive (4WD) *Suzuki* **jeeps** are ideal safari vehicles: light, rugged and capable of amazing feats of negotiation. Don't expect them to top more than 80kmph (50mph), however, and beware their notorious tendency to fall over on bends. Those equipped for camping may have only two seats, and so work out more expensive. Land Rover rates are unrealistic.

The cheapest compromise is to fill a *Peugeot 504* or something similar with four or five people, but non-4WD hired cars are not allowed into the parks. Hiring a car is often cheaper by the week if you do enough miles, and many firms are prepared to negotiate a little as well, especially off season. Reckon on driving an average of 1000 kilometres per week (or around 100 miles per day).

There are one or two rent-a-car places in the smaller towns and along the coast but the only real choice is in Nairobi and Mombasa. Some **recommendations** are given on p.84. Minimum age is usually 23. Foreign driving licences are okay for up to three months; you're supposed to have them validated at a provincial headquarters, but few people seem to bother. Check the insurance details and always pay the daily **collision damage waiver** premium: even a small bump could be very costly otherwise. Have a look at the engine and tyres, and don't set off without checking the spare (preferably two) and making sure

BOOKING CAR HIRE IN ADVANCE

It's quite easy to book a vehicle before you even set foot in Kenya, pay for it at home, then pick it up when you arrive. It costs more to do this than tracking down a good deal locally – and prices are extremely variable – but if time is short you may find it preferable. The prices quoted here are guidelines (full cost including collision damage waiver) for a *Suzuki* jeep in January 1991.

Avis UK Central Reservations (☎081 848 8733); £420/week, then £60/day.

Budget UK Central Reservations (☎0800 181 181); £287/week, then £41/day.

Europcar UK Central Reservations (☎081 950 5050); £315/week, then £45/day.

Hertz UK Central Reservations (☎081 679 1799); £505/week, then £72/day.

you have a few vital tools. Don't automatically assume the vehicle is roadworthy; have a look at the comments in the Nairobi "Directory" section. **Four-wheel drive** (4WD) is always useful but, except in mountainous areas and on some of the marginal dirt roads during periods of heavy rain, not essential. However, few, if any agencies will hire out non-4WD vehicles for use in the parks, and most park rangers will turn away such cars at the gate, regardless of season. This does depend on the park: Maasai Mara, Amboseli, Tsavo, Samburu and the mountain parks (Mount Elgon, Mount Kenya and the Aberdares) are the most safety-minded.

DRIVING IN KENYA

When **driving**, beware of unexpected rocks and ditches – and animals and people – on the road; it's accepted practice to honk your horn stridently to warn pedestrians. Kenya drives on the left, though in reality vehicles often keep to the best part of the road until they have to pass each other. Left- and right-hand signals are conventionally used to say "Please overtake" or "Don't overtake!" but you shouldn't assume the driver in front can really see. In fact, never assume anything about other drivers. Driving-test examiners aren't incorruptible and Kenya's road death statistics are horrifying.

On the question of **driving etiquette**, it's common practice to flash oncoming vehicles at night, and to signal left to indicate your width. You may find both practices a little disconcerting at first.

Should you have the misfortune to break down on the road, or have an accident, the first thing to do is pile **bundles of sticks or foliage** fifty metres or so behind and in front of the car. These are the universally recognised "red warning triangles" of Africa, and their placing is always scrupulously observed (as is the wedging of a stone behind at least one wheel).

Although you're unlikely to be stopped by the police, you should know that you may be asked to produce evidence that your hired car has a **PSV licence** as a "passenger service vehicle". You should have a sticker on the windscreen for this and you're strongly advised to check it out with the company before you leave.

Beware of the **"sleeping policemen"** that stripe the road through many towns and villages. Occasionally you'll see a sign like "Rumble strips ahead", but more usually the first you'll know of them is when your head hits the roof. Anticipate. The Nairobi suburb of Banana Hill had, at one time, thirteen "Speed Bumbs [*sic*]" each about a foot high, but only on the downhill side of the road – to slow the coasting *matatus*. . . The result was chaos as drivers swerved to avoid them.

On most of the main paved highways you can make good time, but as soon as you leave them, **journey times** are very unpredictable. We've tried to give some idea of road conditions in various places throughout the book, but they can change radically in half a year. The north and highland regions (everywhere) are the worst, particularly during periods of heavy rain when districts do become virtually cut off.

Except on the main highways, it's important to keep jerry cans of petrol and water on board. As for **breakdowns**, local mechanics are usually brilliant and can apply creative ingenuity to the most disastrous situations. But spare parts, tools and proper equipment are rare off the main routes. Always settle on a price before the work begins. Note, also, that a new scam has started operating in several places, basically involving the appearance of drops of oil under your vehicle while you were away, and the fortuitous arrival of a team of mechanics keen to repair it at once.

BUYING A CAR SECOND-HAND

Lastly, if you're going to be in Kenya for some time, or you're planning to travel some more, **buying** a second-hand vehicle in Nairobi, though prices are inflated, is a realistic possibility if you're confident about engines. Hire companies sometimes have vehicles to dispose of, and the *Nation* and *Standard* carry lots of ads. The *Sarit Centre* in Nairobi has a weekly used car sale, and you can sell back fairly easily in Nairobi.

CYCLING

Kenya's climate and varied terrain make it challenging **bicycling** country. If it appeals to you – whether you're a lycra-laminated pro or just use a bike once in a while – it's one of the best ways of getting around. With a bike, given time and average determination, you can get to parts of the country that would be hard to visit by any other means except perhaps on foot. And what would take several days to hike can be cycled in a matter of hours. It's also one way you will get to see wildlife outside the confines of the game parks.

BUYING LOCALLY

Almost nothing other than old-fashioned 28-inch **roadsters** is sold in Kenya. If you buy one of these three-speed heavyweights in Nairobi (see "Nairobi directory") you can then sell it at the end of your trip. There's a ready market for second-hand ones.

BIKES BY AIR

Bringing your own bicycle by air is easier than it seems. As long as it's a lightweight tourer and you keep your baggage weight down, you needn't go much above 20kg – and it's remarkable how much weight you can get in a small bag as cabin luggage. Airlines are unpredictable about bicycles, sometimes making an exception of them, other times scrupulously charging one percent of the first-class fare for every kilo overweight. It's worth asking them, though they'll usually just give you the rule book, and checking if there are any packing requirements for your bike.

Few airlines will insist your bike be boxed or bagged. But it's best to turn the handlebars into the frame and tie them down, invert the pedals and deflate the tyres. Probably the most helpful airline for bikes (so long as you don't take them for granted) is *KLM*.

You should do everything to facilitate your transit from check-in desk to plane: write in advance to the ground operations manager of the airline, pack as many heavy items into your hand luggage as possible and arrive several hours before the flight to get to know the check-in staff. It's rare that you'll be obliged to pay.

It's much harder, as a rule, to avoid excess fees on charter flights. Let them know in advance and plead your case. The 20kg weight allowance, which your bike and luggage is likely to exceed, is a notional figure with no bearing on air safety, used to extract more profit from the passengers.

If you can solve the weight problem, the heavier, all-terrain **mountain bikes** are ideal, giving you a really wide measure of freedom far off the main roads and sparing you some punctures and spoke breakages.

PRACTICAL CONSIDERATIONS

Whatever you take, it will need low gears and strongly built wheels and you should have some essential **spare parts**.

If you're taking a bike with you, then you'll probably want to **carry your gear** in panniers. These are fiendishly inconvenient when not attached to the bike, however, and you might consider sacrificing ideal load-bearing and streamlining technology for a backpack you can lash down on the rear carrier. An arrangement like this is probably what you'll have to do if you buy a bike in Kenya. With light wood, or the kind of cane used to make cane furniture, plus lashings of inner tube rubber strips you can create your own highly unaerodynamic **carrier**, with room for a box of food and a gallon of water underneath.

With a bike from home, do take a battery **lighting system** (dynamo lighting is a pain) – it's surprising how often you'll need it. The front light doubles as a torch and getting batteries is no problem.

Also take a **U-bolt cycle lock**. In situations where you have to lock the bike, you'll always find something to lock it to. Out in the bush it's less important. Local bikes can be locked with a padlock and chain in a length of hosepipe which you can buy and fix up in any market.

If you have a sympathetic local bike shop, you might consider leaving a deposit with them so they could send you **spare parts** if and when necessary. A combination of telex and courier service could get you the necessary in a couple of days.

CYCLING

Cycling won't restrict your travel options. Buses and *matatus* with roof-racks will always **carry** bicycles for about half fare — even if flagged down at the roadside — and lorries will often give a lift. The trains take bikes, too, at a low, fixed fare.

You do need to consider the seasons however; you won't make much progress on dirt roads during the rains when chain sets and brakes become totally jammed with sticky mud.

Obviously, you also need to be cautious when **cycling on main roads**. A mirror is essential and, if the pavement is broken at the edge, give yourself plenty of space and be ready to leave the road if necessary. That said, cycle tourists are still a novelty in Kenya: drivers often slow down to look and you'll rarely be run off the road.

OUTDOOR ACTIVITIES

Kenya is a country with untapped potential for outdoor activities. Safaris are covered in a separate section further on. The following brief notes suggest the possibilities for walking, riding, fishing, climbing, caving, and rafting. Cycling is covered under "Getting There" and above.

WALKING

Walking, if you have plenty of time and the relevant *Survey of Kenya* maps, is highly recommended and gives you unparalleled contact with local people. In isolated parts, it's often preferable to waiting for a lift, while in the Aberdares, Mau and Cherangani ranges, and on Mounts Kenya and Elgon, it's the only practical way of moving away from the main tracks. You will sometimes come across animals out in the bush, but buffalo and elephant, unless solitary or with young, usually move off. Don't ignore the dangers, however, and stay alert. *Mountain Walking in Kenya*, by David Else (McCarta) is a useful book. For walking you'll need to carry several litres of water much of the time (which means several *kilos*), especially in lower, drier regions.

Before plunging off into the bush, though, you might prefer to go on an organised walking safari, at least as a starter. Walking safaris are offered by *Kentrack, Bataleur* and *Tropical Ice* (addresses in "Nairobi Directory").

RIDING

The are good **riding opportunities** in the Central Highlands and an active equestrian community in Nairobi. *Safaris Unlimited* (address in "Nairobi Directory") offer riding safaris near the Maasai Mara National Reserve.

Camel safaris are increasingly popular. *Yare Safaris* (PO Box 63006 Nairobi, ☎559313, Fax 331756) do one out of Maralal. And, again, check the "Nairobi Directory".

FISHING

Many of the highlands streams are well stocked with trout, imported early this century by the settlers. Local fishing associations are still active and the usual rules about season and licences apply. *Naro Moru River Lodge, Thomson's Falls Lodge* and the *Tea Hotel* are three places that offer rods for hire. But the Fisheries Department headquarters, next to the National Museum can supply details. *Safaris Unlimited* ("Nairobi Directory") offers fishing trips.

CLIMBING

Apart from **Mount Kenya**, the **Aberdares**, **Cheranganis**, **Matthews Range**, **Hell's Gate** and **Rift valley volcanoes** offer climbing at all grades. If you have time to get acquainted with them, the *Mountain Club of Kenya* (PO Box 45741 Nairobi; clubhouse at Wilson Airport) is a good source of advice and **contacts**, not just for climbing, but for outdoor pursuits in general. If you intend any serious climbing in the country, you should make early contact in writing. Don't expect them to answer detailed route questions, however. Leave that until you arrive.

CAVING

Caving, which has a large following, is organised around the *Cave Exploration Group of East Africa*, whose address is *Kenya Caverns and Lodges*, PO Box 47363, Nairobi, Kenya (☎60438 Nairobi). Avid cavers arriving in Nairobi can also contact the Caving Equipment Officer on ☎582257 Nairobi.

RAFTING

Both the Tana and Athi rivers have sections which can be rafted when they're in full spate.

Approximate dates are 1 November to 15 March and 15 April to 31 August. *Let's Go Travel* (see "Nairobi Directory", p.90) is running trips from 1991.

SLEEPING

Accommodation in Kenya exhibits a fine diversity, ranging from campsites and local lodging houses for a pound or two a night to genuinely excellent, luxury hotels costing fifty or a hundred times as much. Beds can also be found in "tented camps" and "tree hotels" at the expensive end of the spectrum and *bandas* and a clutch of youth hostels at the budget end.

BOARDING AND LODGINGS

In any town, down to the very smallest, you'll always find **Boarding and Lodgings** (for which we've coined the abbreviation "B&Ls"). These can vary from a mud shack with water from the well, to a little multistorey building of self-contained rooms (s/c) with washing facilities, a bar and restaurant. B&Ls tend to be noisy, sometimes stuffy and often double unofficially as brothels, but the better ones are clean and homy.

Prices of rooms (say, Ksh50–100 single and Ksh 80–200 twin) aren't always a good indication of the standard and it's worth checking several places, testing the hot water (if any), and asking to see the toilets; you won't cause offence by saying no thanks. Some places actually seal the doors of rooms as a kind of guarantee of fresh-

ness: if they won't let you look because they'd have to reseal, it's suggested you move on. And if it seems noisy in the afternoon, it will probably become cacophonous during the night, so ask for a room away from the source of the din. And try to bargain for a good price.

Boarding and Lodgings are covered in some detail through the regional chapters; there's nearly always at least one good example in every town. As yet, there isn't an official body to represent them or to set standards and prices.

If you're driving, some lodgings have lock-up yards where you can park – an important consideration unless you bring all your equipment into the room.

HOTELS

More **expensive hotels** are a variable commodity. At the top end in this price range are the big tourist establishments, many in one of the country's four or five chains. In the game parks, they are usually called **lodges**. Some are extremely good value and a night in a good hotel can be tremendously fortifying if you're usually roughing it. Others are shabby and overpriced. Check carefully before splurging. If possible you should try to reserve the more popular establishments in advance (see box), especially for the busiest season from December to February. As a rule expect to pay from Ksh700 to Ksh2500 for two sharing, and not much less for a single occupancy. Out of the towns, prices at the top end of the scale are normally quoted on a full board basis, and prices can go right into orbit. Most of these hotels cut their prices in the low season, April–June (see "Costs" p.14), and many have lower rates for Kenyan *residents* (sometimes *citizens*) which you might get if you're convincing.

Between the hotels featured in the glossy brochures and the cheap lodging houses come all the **medium-priced**, middle-class places. Some of them were once slightly grand, others are old settlers' haunts that don't fit modern Kenya, and

ACCOMMODATION TERMS AND ABBREVIATIONS

AC – air conditioning, usually only on the coast or in lodges.

banda – basically a thatched cottage or chalet, sometimes round and dubbed *rondavel*, generally cheap, occasionally furbished into upmarket "bush" accommodation for tourists.

B&B – bed and breakfast.

B&L – a boarding and lodging house.

cube – sometimes used to refer to a small room in a B&L.

FB – full board, meaning all meals included.

HB – half board, meaning dinner, bed and breakfast.

hoteli – a cheap restaurant or greasy spoon, rarely a hotel.

lodge – designer hotel or country house, usually in the game parks.

long-drop – self-explanatory; the kind of non-flushing toilet found in some B&Ls, and in most bandas and campsites.

s/c – self contained, with private shower and toilet.

tented camp – hotel in the bush, or in a game park, using large tents and *bandas*, often now with all the usual hotel facilities plumbed into a solid bathroom at the back.

tree hotel – an animal-viewing hotel in the trees, or on stilts, after the style of *Treetops*.

Ksh150/200 – means (for example) Ksh150 for a single room, Ksh200 for two people sharing, usually a twin-bedded room.

some newer ones are catering for the black middle class. A few are fine – delightfully decrepit or bristlingly smart and efficient. Most are boozy and uninteresting; it adds more colour to your travels to mix the cheapest lodgings with the occasional night of luxury.

COTTAGES AND VILLAS

Increasingly, it's possible to book self-catering apartments, villas or cottages, especially on the coast. *Kenya Villas*, PO Box 57046, Westminster House, Kenyatta Ave, Nairobi (☎010 254 2 338072) are agents for many holiday homeowners. Try writing, but they may need a phone call.

YOUTH HOSTELS

Disappointingly, Kenya's **youth hostels** are few indeed. Nairobi and Malindi have one each, International Youth Hostel Association (IYHA) affiliated, and well run if rather claustrophobic. For members, the rate is Ksh60. Non-members normally have to join the Association first. Mount Kenya's youth hostel was the best, the very epitome of the species, with cold water, log fires and glorious, nurturing air and scenery. But it burned to the ground in August 1988 and it's hard to predict whether and when a replacement will rise from the ashes. Others, at Mount Elgon and Kitale, have effectively closed, but the "YMCA" at Lake Naivasha is perennially popular and always a nice place to stay. There are **YM/YWCAs** in

Kisumu, Nairobi and Mombasa, with church-run hostels and dormitories in a number of small towns. In these, the atmosphere can be a cloying contrast to the sleazier lodging houses.

CAMPING

While a **tent** is dead weight whenever you sleep in a hotel, Kenya has enough campsites to make it worthwhile carrying one, and camping rough is very often a viable option, too. Bring the lightest tent you can afford or consider **making your own**. A few weekends with a sewing machine, rip-stop nylon and some netting should see the job done if you have any dexterity at all: make a scale model in paper first, and test the tent under wet conditions before taking it to Kenya. Camping in the rain doesn't make much sense (whatever the protection, you're likely to get wet); the main point of a tent is to keep insects out, but it's still good to be protected against unexpected showers. Nylon netting with a sewn-in groundsheet is the basic tent. A rip-stop nylon flysheet adds privacy. Outside poles back and front can be used for guys and tension, but you'll probably resort to trees if there are any.

If you'd rather **buy a tent**, here's the best. It's called the *Skeeter*, made by *The North Face (Scotland) Ltd*, PO Box 16, Industrial Estate, Port Glasgow, PA14 5XL (☎0475 41344), sold through branches of *Alpine Sports* in the UK and costs most of £300. But it uses "no-see-um" mosquito netting in a geodesic design to give you ample

HOTEL RESERVATIONS

Addresses and telephone numbers for most larger hotels covered are included in the guide. Many are part of chains or management groups; rooms can be reserved by phoning or writing to the head offices.

AFRICAN TOURS AND HOTELS (AT&H)

Partly state-owned chain, generally high quality. Information and bookings in Kenya through travel agents or *AT&H*, PO Box 30471, Nairobi (☎336858, Fax 336961); counter bookings at City Hall Way office, Nairobi (☎21855). UK bookings can be made through high street travel agents or *LRI/Lawson*, 113–119 High St, Hampton Hill, Middx TW12 1PS (☎081 941 7200). Bookings in Germany can be made through *LRI/Lawson*, Kleine Hoschstrasse 9, 6000 Frankfurt 1 (☎069 28 99 71).

Lodges
Mountain Lodge, Mount Kenya
Buffalo Springs Tented Lodge, Buffalo Springs Reserve
Kilaguni Lodge, Tsavo West National Park
Ngulia Safari Lodge, Tsavo West National Park
Voi Safari Lodge, Tsavo East National Park
Olkurruk Mara Lodge, Maasai Mara National Reserve

Town Hotels
Panafric Hotel, Nairobi
Milimani Hotel, Nairobi
Kabarnet Hotel, Kabarnet, near Lake Baringo
Sirikwa Hotel, Eldoret
Tea Hotel, Kericho
Sunset Hotel, Kisumu

Coast Hotels
Mombasa Beach Hotel, North Coast
Two Fishes, Diani Beach
Trade Winds, Diani Beach
Whispering Palms, Mombasa, North Coast

SERENA LODGES AND HOTELS

PO Box 48690, Nairobi (☎338656 or 339800 or 339840, Telex 22878).

Lodges
Amboseli Serena Lodge, Amboseli National Park
Mara Serena Lodge, Maasai Mara National Reserve
Samburu Serena Lodge, Samburu National Reserve

Nairobi
Serena Hotel

Coast
Serena Beach Hotel, Mombasa north coast

MSAFIRI INNS

PO Box 42013, 11th floor, Utalii House, Uhuru Highway, Nairobi (☎330820, Telex 23009). A group formed to look after some of *AT&H*'s less successful hotels. Standards vary, but the lodges, at least, are in fine locations.

Lodges
Mount Elgon Lodge, Mount Elgon
Marsabit Lodge, Marsabit
Meru Mulika Lodge, Meru National Park

Town Hotels
Golf Hotel, Kakamega town
Homa Bay Hotel, Homa Bay, Lake Victoria
Izaak Walton Inn, Embu, Mount Kenya

THORN TREE SAFARIS

PO Box 42475, Nairobi (☎225951 or 225641)

Lodges
Maralal Safari Lodge, Maralal
Maasai Lodge, Nairobi National Park

BLOCK HOTELS

Consistently good, state-of-the-art, package-tour establishments, popular with Kenya residents, too. Information and bookings in Kenya through travel agents or with *Block Hotels*, PO Box 47557, Rehema House, Standard St, Nairobi (☎335807, Telex 22146). UK bookings through high street travel agents or through: *Tourism International Ltd*, Paramount House, 71–75 Uxbridge Rd, Ealing Broadway, London W5 5SL (☎081 566 2606).

Lodges
Keekorok Lodge, Maasai Mara National Reserve
Lake Baringo Club, Lake Baringo, Rift Valley
Lake Naivasha Hotel, Lake Naivasha
Samburu Lodge, Samburu National Reserve
Outspan Hotel, Nyeri
Treetops, Aberdare National Park, near Nyeri
Shimba Hills Lodge, Shimba Hills National Park, near Mombasa

Nairobi
Norfolk Hotel, Harry Thuku Rd
Jacaranda Hotel, Westlands

Coast
Nyali Beach Hotel, Mombasa, Nyali beach
Hemingways, Watamu

SIGNET HOTELS

PO Box 59749, First Floor, Silo Park House, Mama Ngina St, Nairobi (☎335900 or 335887 or 221318). Highly recommended group of hotels if money is no object.

Lodges

Aberdare Country Club, Mweiga, north of Nyeri
The Ark, Aberdares National Park tree-hotel
Mount Kenya Safari Club, Nanyuki, north flank of Mount Kenya

SAROVA HOTELS

PO Box 30680, New Stanley Hotel, Nairobi (☎333233, Telex 22223).

Lodges

Sarova Mara Camp, Maasai Mara National Reserve
Lion Hill Camp, Nakuru National Park

Nairobi

New Stanley Hotel
Hotel Ambassadeur

Coast

Whitesands Hotel, Mombasa, north coast
Sindbad Hotel, Malindi

ALLIANCE HOTELS

PO Box 84616, Mombasa (☎01261 2021, Telex 21189); counter bookings in Nairobi PO Box 49839, 1st Floor, College House, University Way, Nairobi (☎337501-8 or 229961). Highly rated group with pleasant hotels.

Lodges

Naro Moru River Lodge, Naro Moru, west flank of Mount Kenya

Coast

Jadini Beach Hotel, Diani Beach
Africana Sea Lodge, Diani Beach
Safari Beach Hotel, Diani Beach
Castle Hotel, Mombasa town

WINDSOR HOTELS

Prudential Building, Wabera St, PO Box 74957, Nairobi (☎726707, Fax 726328). UK bookings through Windsor Hotels International Ltd, Sloane Sq, Holbein Place, London SW1 8NS (☎071 730 8702).

Lodges

Kichwa Tembo, Maasai Mara National Reserve
Cottars Camp (*Siana Springs*), Maasai Mara
Island Camp, Ol Kokwe Island, Lake Baringo

HILTON HOTELS

PO Box 30624, Nairobi (☎334000, Telex 22252).

Nairobi

Hilton International

Lodges

Taita Hills Lodge, Taita Hills Game Sanctuary
Salt Lick Lodge, Taita Hills Game Sanctuary

AFRICAN SAFARI CLUB

PO Box 46020, Moi Avenue, Nairobi (☎28760 or 891861). This group's hotels are all managed or owned by *ASC* and are only available to travellers booked on *ASC* packages (see "Getting There").

Lodges

Mara Buffalo Camp, Maasai Mara Reserve
Tsavo Inn Lodge, Mtito Andei, near Tsavo West National Park

Coast

Seahorse Hotel, Kilifi
Mnarani Club, Kilifi
Watamu Beach Hotel, Watamu
Coral/Palm Beach Hotels, Mombasa, north coast
Shanzu Beach Hotel, Mombasa, Shanzu beach
Silver Beach Hotel, Mombasa, north coast
Silver Star Hotel, Mombasa, north coast
Bahari Beach Hotel, Mombasa, Nyali beach
Dolphin Hotel, Mombasa, Shanzu beach
Malaika Hotel, Mombasa, Shanzu beach

---

room for two, total **insect protection** and all-round visibility when the flysheet is off, and it only weighs 3kg.

The *Camping Guide to Kenya*, by David Else (Brandt, 1989) is a useful aid for fans of canvas.

CAMPSITES

Campsites, wherever they exist, are mentioned in the main body of the guide and listed in the index. Those in the parks are always very cheap and equally basic. A handful of privately owned

sites have more in the way of facilities. In rural areas, hotels are often amenable if you ask to camp discreetly in their grounds.

Camping rough depends on whether you can find a suitable space. In the more heavily populated and farmed highland districts, you should ask someone before pitching in an empty spot. Out in the wilds, hard or thorny ground is likely to be the only obstacle. During the dry seasons, you'll rarely have trouble finding wood for a fire so a stove is optional, but don't burn more fuel than you need. You're not allowed to collect firewood in the mountain parks. Camping gas cartridges and packaged, dried food is available in variety in Nairobi, but the easiest and cheapest camping food is *ugali* (see "Eating and Drinking" below) – flavoured with curry powder or sauce mixes if you like.

SAFETY

Camping out is pretty safe. A fire may worry local people and delegations armed with *pangas* sometimes turn up to see who you are, and might want to stay and chat. But there is undoubtedly less chance of being attacked or robbed than if you were to camp rough in Europe or North America. Camping right by the road, in dried-out riverbeds, or on trails used by animals going to water are all, obviously, unwise. On the subject of **animals**, if you're way out in the bush, lions and hyenas are very occasionally curious of fires, but will never attack you unless provoked.

An important exception to the safety of rough camping is the Indian Ocean coast. Almost anywhere between Malindi and the Tanzanian border, **sleeping out on the beaches** should be counted as an invitation to robbery. North of Malindi, there are few tourists and the risks are correspondingly less. But to be camping out on these deserted shores, you'd probably need a vehicle anyway.

LANGUAGE AND MEDIA

Kenya's main languages are English and Swahili, a simplified version of the older coastal Kiswahili. English tends to predominate; higher education and Parliament get by almost exclusively on it, and the media use it heavily. You'll always find English speakers in the towns. Out in the country, local languages come to the fore, with Swahili used as a lingua franca where strangers have to communicate – on the road, at markets, in official business. While it's helpful, and not difficult, to speak some Swahili (see "Language" in Contexts), you'll rarely have problems without it – just more demonstrative conversations.

RADIO AND TV

Voice of Kenya (VOK) radio has three services, broadcasting in English, Swahili and vernacular languages. Kenyan television, much of it imported, is in English and Swahili.

With a short-wave set, you can also pick up the *BBC World Service* and *Voice of America*.

BBC wavelengths are as follows (all times GMT): 21.47mHz (09.00–15.15), 17.885mHz (04.00–17.45) and 15.07mHz (15.15–21.15).

VOA wavelengths are as follows: 621, 3990 and 11835 kHz (03.00–04.30); 9525 kHz (03.00–05.00); 6035, 7280 and 9575 kHz (03.00–06.00); 9540 kHz (05.00–06.00); 9575 and 11920 kHz (16.00–19.00); 15445, 15600 and 17870 kHz (16.00–22.00); and 621 kHz (17.30–22.00).

THE PRESS

Kenyan **newspapers** are limited: the *Standard* – Lonrho-owned and the settlers' rag – is dull, lightweight and eclipsed now by the *Nation*, owned by the Aga Khan, which has meatier news coverage and a letters page full of insights into Kenyan life. The *Kenya Times* is a stodgy KANU organ which has just received the unlikely attentions of Robert Maxwell's *Mirror Group Newspapers* (to the tune of a 45-percent stake). All are available just about anywhere. Other papers, *Taifa Leo* and *Kenya Leo*, are in Swahili. The occasionally critical *Weekly Review* is always worth picking up (or used to be). *Drum* and the women's magazine *Viva* also carry interesting articles from time to time.

Of the **foreign press**, the *Daily Telegraph* gets to all sorts of settler-ish bastions. British Sunday and daily papers (such as the *Times*, *Express* and *Mail* and more occasionally *The Guardian* and *The Independent*) and the *International Herald Tribune* can usually be found in Nairobi or, a few days old, at one or two stores around the country. They tend, however, to be unavailable when Kenya's internal affairs make international news.

Time and *Newsweek* are hawked widely and, together with old *National Geographic*s and copies of *The Economist*, filter through many hands before reaching the second-hand booksellers.

POST AND TELEPHONES

than 105cm long and the sum of the three sides less than 200cm, and must be wrapped in brown paper and tied with string. They are usually examined in advance, so everything has to be checked, in the post office, before you wrap it.

Stamps are bought only at post offices and large hotels. There are main post offices in all the towns and, except in the far north, sub-post offices throughout the rural areas. Prepaid **"aerograms"** are the cheapest way of writing home, but they tend to sell out quickly. If you want speedy delivery, pay a little extra for *express*. The internal service, like the international one, is pretty efficient.

Keeping in touch by mail and telephone is generally easy. Mail takes a few days to Europe and perhaps ten days to Australia and New Zealand; slightly longer times from these places to Kenya. Kenya's telephone system is improving. Area codes are used for exchanges and these are given after "travel details" at the end of each chapter. To telephone Kenya from the UK the code is 010 254, then the local area code omitting the 0. Lines are often busy. Fax can be easier and international directory enquiries (153 in the UK) can give fax numbers.

RECEIVING MAIL

Poste restante is free, and fairly reliable in Nairobi, Mombasa, Malindi and Lamu. Have your family name marked clearly but look under any combination of initials and be ready to show your passport. Address mail: *Name, Poste Restante, GPO, Town.* Smaller post offices will also hold mail but your correspondent should mark the letter "To Be Collected". Parcels can be received, too (in Nairobi at the separate Parcels Office), but expect to haggle over import duty payment when they're opened. Ask the sender to mark packages "Contents To Be Re-exported From Kenya".

When posting things home, out of Kenya, airmail packages are expensive but **surface mail** (up to a maximum of 20kg) is good value, reliable and worth considering if you've accumulated things on your travels. Parcels must be no more

TELEPHONES

The local **telephone service** is generally dependable and inexpensive, though outside the big towns, old-fashioned wind-up phone booths are still the norm and you can spend a long time waiting for a connection or passing the time of day with the operator.

To make **local telephone calls**, look up the area code at the back of the relevant chapter in this book (or in the pink section of the directory), or dial 900 for the operator. When you pick up any pay phone you'll hear a sustained tone and, in the background, a series of beeps. After five beeps you dial (you can dial before that, but you might lose your money). You line the shillings up at the top and put the one that's to go into the machine at an angle – it drops in when the call is answered. The engaged tone is more rapid than the ringing tone.

For **international calls**, it's always easiest to go to a main post office. You prepay for your conversation and get your money back if you fail to get through. Note that, unless you need to speak to a specific person, and only that person, you should ask for "station to station" rather than "person to person" which is much more expensive. The number for the international operator is ☎0196. There are substantial reductions for calls made between 10pm and 10am. And for international calls within East Africa, there's a fifty percent discount after 6pm. There are also now IDD (international direct dialing) facilities and **cardphones** (the prepaid, credit-card-sized plastic tokens used in them can usually be bought at newsstands as well as post offices) at the GPOs in Nairobi, Mombasa, Kisumu and Nakuru.

Reverse charge (collect) calls can be made, but the bills are reduced if you call your correspondent briefly and ask them to call you back.

Post office **opening hours** are usually 8am–1pm and 2–4.30 or 5pm on weekdays; larger ones are open on Saturday. Otherwise, you can usually phone from large hotels, but you'll pay extra for this facility.

EATING AND DRINKING

Not surprisingly, perhaps, Kenya has no great national dishes: the living standards of the majority of people don't allow for frills and food is generally plain and filling. For culinary culture, only the coast's long association with Indian Ocean trade has produced distinctive regional cooking, where rice and fish, flavoured with coconut, tamarind and exotic spices, are the dominant ingredients.

FOOD

But if meals are unlikely to be a lasting memory, at least you'll never go hungry. In any **hoteli** (a small restaurant, not a hotel), there's always a number of predictable dishes intended to fill you up at the least cost. Potatoes, rice and especially *ugali* (a stiff, cornmeal porridge) are the national staples, eaten with chicken, goat, beef, or vegetable stew, various kinds of spinach, beans or sometimes fish. Portions are usually gigantic: half-portions (ask for *nusu*) aren't much smaller. But even in small towns, more and more **cafés** are appearing where most of the menu is fried — eggs, sausages, chips, fish, chicken and burgers.

Snacks which can easily become meals include samosas, chapatis, miniature kebabs, roasted corn cobs, *mandaazi* and egg-bread.

Mandaazi – sweet, puffy, deep-fried dough cakes – are made before breakfast and served until evening time, when they've become cold and solid. *Egg-bread* (misleadingly translated from the Swahili *mkate mayai*) is a light wheatflour "pancake" wrapped around fried eggs and minced meat, usually cooked in a huge frying pan. While you won't find it everywhere, it's a delicious Kenyan response to the creeping burger menace.

Indian restaurants in the larger towns generally offer something more exciting. Locally, there's often a strong Indian influence in *hoteli* food as well.

If you **splurge**, it will usually be in a tourist hotel or lodge, on something barely distinguishable from what you might be served in a hotel restaurant at home (exceptions are mentioned through the guide). It will rarely cost more than Ksh200 a head, though there's a handful of classy establishments which take delight in charging, for Kenya, exorbitant prices for lavish meals – up to Ksh500 – generally with some justification. The lodges usually have buffet lunches at Ksh100–150, which can be great value if you're really hungry, with table-loads of salads and cold meat.

Vegetarians don't have an easy time because meat is the conventional accompaniment to any kind of special meal – in other words, any meal not eaten at home – and *hotelis* seldom have much else to accompany the starch. Even vegetable stew is normally cooked in meat gravy. Nor are salads and green vegetables served much in the cheaper *hotelis*. Eggs, at least, can be had almost anywhere, and fresh milk is distributed widely in waxpaper tetra-packs. With bread and tinned margarine, two more staples available everywhere, you won't starve. Look out for **Indian vegetarian restaurants** where you can often eat remarkably well at very low cost.

Fruit, of course, is the main delight, whether you eat meat or not. Bananas, avocados, papayas and pineapples are in the markets all year,

MENU AND FOOD TERMS

The lists below should be adequate for translating most Swahili menus and explaining what you want: spelling may vary – see "Language" in *Contexts*.

BASICS

Food	*Chakula*	Spoon	*Kijiko*	Pepper	*Piripiri*	Egg/Eggs	*Yai/Mayai*
Water, juice	*Maji*	Knife	*Kisu*	Bread	*Mkate*	Fish	*Samaki*
		Fork	*Uma*	Butter, margarine	*Siagi*	Meat	*Nyama*
Ice	*Barafu*	Bottle	*Chupa*			Vegetables	*Mboga*
Table	*Meza*	Bill	*Hesabu*	Sugar	*Sukari*	Sauce	*Mchuzi*
Plate	*Sahani*	Salt	*Chumvi*	Milk	*Maziwa*	Fruit	*Matunda*

SNACKS

Chapati	Unleavened, flat wheat bread, baked on a hot plate or in an oven (*tandoor*)	*Maziwalala*	Yogurt
		Mkate Mayai	"Egg-bread": soft thin dough wrapped around fried egg and minced meat
Keki	Cake		
Kitumbuo	Deep-fried rice bread	*Samosa*	Deep-fried triangular case of chopped meat and vegetables
Mandaazi	Deep-fried sweet dough, some-times flavoured with spices, known as *mahamri* on the coast	*Tosti/Slice*	Slice of bread
		Halwa	Sweetmeat; Turkish delight

MEAT

Kuku	Chicken	*Ngombe*	Beef
Mushkaki	Kebab, small pieces of grilled, marinated meat on or off the skewer	*Nguruwe*	Pork
		Steki	Steak, grilled meat
		Mbuzi	Mutton, goat meat

DISHES

Irio/Kienyeji	Potato, cabbage and beans mashed together (Mount Kenya region)	*Sukuma wiki*	Green leaves boiled, usually a kind of spinach
Kima	Mince	*Ugali/Sima*	Corn meal boiled to a solid porridge with water, occasionally milk; yellow *ugali* is considered inferior to white but is more nutritious
Matoke	Mashed plantain		
Mboga	Vegetables: usually potatoes, carrots and onions in meaty gravy		
Mchele	Plain white rice	*Uji*	Porridge or gruel made of millet; good for chilly mornings
Michicha	Spinach cooked with onions and tomatoes	*Wali*	Rice with added fat and spices; almost *pilau*
Pilau	Rice with spices and meat		

TERMS

Choma	Roast (*Nyama Choma* – roast meat – is the food for parties and celebrations)	*Chemka*	Boiled	*Baridi*	Cold
		Kaanga	Fried	*Nusu*	Half
		Moto	Hot	*Ingine*	More, another

FRUIT

Limau	Lime	*Matopetope*	Custard apples	*Papai*	Papaya/Pawpaw
Machungwa	Oranges	*Nanasi*	Pineapple		
Madafu	Green coconuts	*Nazi*	Coconuts	*Parachichi*	Avocado
Maembe	Mangoes	*Ndimu*	Lemon	*Pera*	Guava
Mastafeli	Soursops	*Ndizi*	Bananas	*Sandara*	Mandarins

VEGETABLES			
Maharagwe	Red kidney beans, often cooked with coconut	Muhogo	Cassava
Mahindi	Corn	Ndizi	Bananas or plantains (often served with meat dishes)
Mbaazi	Pigeon peas, small beans	Nyanya	Tomatoes (also means grandmother)
Mtama	Millet (made into a gruel for breakfast)	Viazi	Potatoes
		Vitunguu	Onions

DRINKS			
Chai, chai kavu, chai strungi	Tea, black tea, strongly spiced tea	Kahawa	Coffee
Maziwalala	Fermented milk/almost-yogurt (literally "sleeping milk")	Bia	Beer
		Pombe	Home-brewed "beer"
		Soda	What else?
		Tembo	Coconut palm wine

mangoes and citrus fruits more seasonally. Look out for passion fruit, cape gooseberries, custard apples and guavas – all highly distinctive and delicious. On the coast, roasted cashew **nuts** are cheap, especially at Kilifi where they're grown and processed, while coconuts are filling and nutritious, going through several satisfying changes of condition (all edible) before becoming the familiar hard brown nuts.

DRINKS

As to **drinking**, the national beverage is *chai* – tea. Universally drunk at breakfast (often *for* breakfast) and as a pick-me-up at any time, it's a weird variant on the classic British brew: milk, water, lots of sugar and tea leaves, brought to the boil in a kettle and served scalding hot. It must eventually do diabolical dental damage but it's curiously addictive and very reviving. Instant **coffee** – rarely fresh – is normally available in *hotelis* as well, but it's expensive (ironically, in Kenya), so not as popular as tea.

Kenyan **lager beer** is generally good, though sadly no longer sold at fixed prices according to the grade of the bar. It now varies from around Ksh12–35 a large bottle. *Tusker*, *White Cap* and *Pilsner* are the main brands, sold in half-litre bottles (or "export" one-third-litre sizes of the first two). I adopted *Pilsner*, but eventually realised I couldn't reliably tell the difference between any of them. *Premium*, however, in a small bottle, is noticeably stronger.

Other alcoholic drinks, *Kenya Cane* (white rum) and *Kenya Gold* (a gooey, coffee-flavoured liqueur), deserve a try perhaps, but they are expensive and nothing special.

More interesting is **papaya wine**, Kenya's desperate solution to its shortage of vineyards. This – in medium dry, white and rosé – is certainly an acquired taste, but it's one you might acquire quickly: the stuff is potent and much cheaper than imported wine. A whole range of fruity wines have recently appeared, including passion and mango. There are now several quite drinkable **white wines** made from Kenyan grapes – notably the products of *Naivasha Wineries*.

Soft drinks ("sodas") are very cheap (about Ksh4) and crates of *Coke*, *Fanta* and *Seven-up* find their way to the wildest corners of the country where, uncooled, they're pretty disgusting. *Krest*, a bitter lemon, is a lot more pleasant. Sometimes you can get *Vimto*, which is supposed to do you some good, and occasionally plain soda water, which can't do you any harm. There are fresh **fruit juices** in the towns, especially on the coast. Passion, the cheapest, is excellent. Some places serve a variety: you'll sometimes find carrot juice and even tiger milk – from tiger (chufa) nuts.

Ordinary bottled **mineral or spring water** is expensive (KSH15–40) and only available in large towns or major hotels. Tap water (see "Health and Insurance" above) is usually quite drinkable.

There are a battery of laws against **home brewing and distilling** – perhaps because of the loss of revenue in taxes on legal booze – but these are central aspects of Kenyan culture and they go on. You can sample *pombe* (beer) under many different names all over the country. It is as varied in taste and colour as its ingredients: basically fermented sugar and millet or banana, with herbs and roots for flavouring. The results are frothy and deceptively strong, and can cause you to change your plans for the rest of the day.

On the coast, where the coconuts grow, merely lopping off the growing shoot produces a naturally fermented **palm wine** (*tembo*), which is indisputably Kenya's finest contribution to the art of self-intoxication. Eat your heart out, *Malibu*. Though there's usually a furtive discretion about *pombe* or *tembo* sessions, nobody ever seems to get busted.

Not so with **spirits**. Think twice before accepting a mug of *chang'aa*. It's treacherous firewater, and is also frequently contaminated, regularly killing drinking parties *en masse*, and filling a niche in the Kenyan press currently taken by crack in the USA. Sentences for distilling and possessing *chang'aa* are harsh, and police raids common.

OPENING HOURS AND SHOPPING

Standard opening hours, where there are any, follow familiar patterns: in larger towns, the major stores will be open from 8am to 5 or 6pm, offices and museums at similar times, though perhaps with a break for lunch. In rural areas and out in the bush, small shops can be open at almost any hour, and may double as hotelis or chai kiosks.

What constitutes **things worth buying** is really up to you: sculptures and carvings in **wood** and **soapstone** (*Kisii-stone*) are cheap and ubiquitous, as are **sisal baskets** (*chondo/vyondo*) which are functional, too. Beadwork (*ushanga*, *mkufu*) and tribal regalia – **weapons**, **shields**, **drums** (ngoma), **musical instruments**, **stools**, **headrests** and **metal jewellery** – are common as well but much more expensive when authentically used rather than made for the tourist industry. **Masks** are mostly imported; they're not a feature of traditional Kenyan art. Textiles, notably a profusion of printed women's wraps in cotton – **kanga** – and heavier-weave men's loincloths – **kikoi/vikoi** – are really good buys on the coast, and older ones represent collectable items worth seeking out. Local specialities are mentioned through the guide.

Ivory, fashioned any which way, is illegal and most countries have recently banned all ivory imports. Ivory will be seized and, in the USA, the carrier is subject to a fine of $5000.

BARGAINING

Bargaining is an important skill to get into. Every time you pay an unreasonable price for goods or services, you contribute to local inflation. You're expected to knock most negotiable prices down by at least half and the bluffing on both sides is part of the fun; don't be shy of making a big scene. Where prices are marked, they are generally fixed – which you'll quickly discover if you walk out and aren't called back. Once you get into it, you'll rarely end up paying more than the going rate for food, transport or accommodation, and, ironically, hospitality and pride will quite often see you getting a better deal than local people.

FESTIVALS AND HOLIDAYS

Both Christian and Muslim holidays are observed, as well as secular national holidays. Local seasonal and cyclical events, peculiar to particular ethnic groups, are less well advertised.

THE RALLY AND SHOWS

The only regular national event that gets much international attention is the Easter **Safari Rally**. From the beginning of the year, the Kenyan papers wax eloquent about this "toughest motor rally in the world", the teams and drivers who will be entering, and the cost of their preparations. Asian

and European entrants predominate; while the
whole country seems gripped with rally fever, the
costs are prohibitive for most Kenyans and no
African driver has yet won.

The rally usually takes place from Good Friday
to Easter Monday and the route seems to circle
Kenya about three times, most of it on appalling
roads, often in heavy rain. Stone-throwing and
road-sabotaging take place every year – usually,
it seems, the actions of frustrated onlookers;
there have been many fatal accidents, of course.
Kisumu may be left out of the route in the future.

If you'd like to be in the right place at the right
time, information can be had from the *Automobile
Association* at their Hurlingham headquarters (PO
Box 40087, Nairobi, ☎720382). Be warned: drivers
tend to do practice legs all over the country in
March – an additional and unexpected road
hazard if you're driving around at that time.

AGRICULTURAL SHOWS

The annual **agricultural shows** put on by the
Agricultural Society of Kenya (ASK) are lively,
revealing occasions, borrowing a lot from the
British farming show tradition, but infused with
Kenyan style. As well as stock and produce
competitions, and the usual beer and snack tents,
there are often some less expected booths:

PUBLIC HOLIDAYS

Public holidays when all official doors are
closed are: Christmas Day and Boxing Day
(December 26), New Year's Day, Good Friday
and Easter Monday, May 1 (Labour Day), June 1
(Madaraka Day, celebrating the granting of self-
government in 1960), October 10 (Moi Day),
October 20 (Kenyatta Day, the anniversary of his
imprisonment) and December 12 (Jamhuri Day,
or Independence Day).

ASK SHOWS

Eldoret	First week in March.
Nanyuki	First week in May.
Meru	Second week in June.
Nakuru	Last week in June.
Kisii	First week in July.
Nyeri	Fourth week in July.
Kisumu	First week in Aug.
Embu	Second week in Aug.
Mandera	Last week in Aug.
Mombasa	Last week in Aug.
Nairobi	First week in Oct.
Kitale	First week in Nov.
Kakamega	Last week in Nov.

women's groups, family planning, beekeeping,
soil conservation, herbalism. . . . Large towns have
an *ASK* fairground (sometimes reasonable places
to camp, incidentally) and the shows happen at
roughly the same time each year. Many smaller
towns have annual district shows as well.

THE ISLAMIC CALENDAR

On the coast, throughout the northeast, and in
Muslim communities everywhere, the lunar
Islamic calendar is followed, parallel to the
Gregorian one. The Muslim year has 355 days,
with 354 days eleven times every thirty years, so
dates recede against the Western calendar by an
average of eleven days each year. Only the month
of fasting called **Ramadan** and *Id ul Fitr* – the
feast of relief at the end of it which begins on the
first sighting of the new moon – will have much
effect on your travels. During Ramadan, most
stores and *hotelis* are closed through the daylight
hours in smaller towns in Islamic districts. Public
transport and official business continue as usual.
Maulidi, the celebration of the prophet's birthday,
is worth catching if you're on the coast at the right
time, especially if you'll be in Lamu.

ISLAMIC FESTIVALS – APPROXIMATE DATES

	1991	1992	1993
Beginning of Ramadan (1st Ramadan)	Mar 18	Mar 7	Feb 24
Id ul Fitr/Id al-Saghir (1st Shawwal)	Apr 17	Apr 6	Mar 26
Tabaski/Id al-Kabir (10th Dhu'l Hijja)	Jun 26	Jun 15	Jun 4
New Year's Day (1st Moharem)	Jul 9	Jun 29	Jun 18
Ashoura (10th Moharem)	Jul 19	Jul 8	Jun 28
Maulidi/Mouloud (12th Rabial)	Oct 3	Sep 23	Sep 12

DANCE, MUSIC, THEATRE AND SPORTS

Kenya's espousal of western values has belittled much traditional culture, so only in remote areas are you likely to come across traditional dancing and drumming which doesn't somehow involve you as a paying audience. If you're patient and reasonably adventurous in your travels, however, you'll be able to witness something more authentic sooner or later – though most likely only by accident or if you stay somewhere off the beaten track long enough to make friends. Kenyan popular music and spectator sports are more accessible.

DANCE

Best known are **Maasai and Samburu dancing**: hypnotic swaying and military displays of effortless leaping. Similar dance forms occur widely among other non-agricultural peoples. Foremost among exponents of drumming are the Akamba and the Mijikenda. Mijikenda dance troupes (notably from the Giriama people) perform up and down the coast at tourist venues. As with the Maasai dancing, it's better to ignore any purist misgivings you might have about the authenticity of such performances and enjoy them as distinctive and exuberant entertainments in their own right.

MUSIC

As for **popular music**, apart from what your ears pick up on the street and in buses (often amaz-

ingly loud), the live spectacle is limited to Nairobi and coastal entertainment spots, with a fair scattering of up-country discos and "country clubs". The indigenous music scene seems overshadowed by foreign influences: British and American soul and jazz-funk, reggae (especially in the sacred image of Bob Marley) and a vigorous contribution from Zaire predominating on *VOK* radio and in record shops. Zairean music has had a pervasive influence on local sounds, too. The guide to the **Nairobi club and music scene** includes a detailed run-down on where to hear the home-grown product. The pieces in *Contexts* at the end of the book give a condensed **history of music** in Kenya and a current **discography**.

If you're lucky enough to be invited to a coastal Swahili wedding with all the trimmings, a *tarabu* band may be playing. *Tarabu* music is hauntingly beautiful, the effervescent result of blending African, Arabic and Indian musical influences. Steady drumbeat, tambourines, accordions, an instrument called the *udi* – like a lute – and plaintive Swahili lyrics are the traditional components; electric guitars, fiddles and microphones are modern additions.

THEATRE AND FILM

Films and **theatre** in Kenya revolve almost entirely around imports. The big towns have cinemas and a few drive-ins, smaller towns may have one cinema with the occasional screening. British, American and Indian box-office hits are the staple fodder. Theatre is effectively limited to one or two semiprofessional clubs in Nairobi and Mombasa. African actors and scripts are rare.

Indigenous theatre was dealt a severe blow in 1978 when the innovative *Kamiriithu Community Education and Cultural Centre* in Limuru put on a Kikuyu language play by Ngugi wa Thiongo and Ngugi wa Mirii (*I will Marry When I Want*), which, after seven weeks of playing to packed houses, was banned. The authorities mistrusted the play's power to mobilise people and question the status quo in Kikuyu rather than English; Ngugi wa Thiongo was detained without trial for a year as a result. In such a climate – which doesn't appear to have altered much – the notion of popular, issue-raising theatre gets labelled automatically as subversive and hasn't much hope of emerging again. *Kamiriithu*'s brief but spectacular success only shows the potential.

SPORTS

Sports received encouragement from Kenya's much-vaunted — if financially disastrous — hosting of the 1987 All Africa Games. The country's successes at the 1988 Seoul Olympics were indisputable, with a clutch of gold and silver in the track events. Kenyan athletes — notably John Ngugi, Paul Ereng and Henry Rono — are the continent's leaders and you'll find evidence of keen amateur involvement — joggers, martial arts tourneys and road cyclists in training. Kenya has possibly the most successful athletics training school in the world in St. Patrick's High School, Iten, in the Rift Valley, which has produced such stars as Peter Reno.

But **football**, especially, is wildly popular. The national team, *Harambee Stars*, win the East and Central Africa Challenge cup frequently and, in Division One, Nairobi's *AFC Leopards* and *Gor Mahia* rank with the best clubs on the continent. Crowds are pretty well behaved, perhaps because forking out for the modest gate fee precludes getting drunk as well.

WILDLIFE AND NATIONAL PARKS

Despite the tremendous losses this century and the continued decimation of the elephant and rhino populations, Kenya really does teem with wildlife and you can hardly fail to be impressed. In one place or another, even outside the protection of the forty-odd parks and reserves, it is possible to see almost all of Kenya's big animals.

WILDLIFE

If you expect to do some camping, you're likely to see various **gazelle** and **antelope**, **zebra**, **giraffe**, **hippo**, **buffalo**, **crocodile** and even **elephant**. This list needn't worry you unduly. Where wild animals compete with domestic herds, they are usually timid and tend to move off when they smell or hear humans. Outside the parks, the **big cats** are hardly seen except far from centres of population. Man-eating **lions** and enraged **elephants** are not a realistic cause for concern; the few remaining **rhinos** live entirely within the parks, while **buffalos** (a more serious threat because so numerous) are only dangerous when solitary. For lonely hikes, hiring a guide/companion is sometimes a good idea.

In the **smaller range**, you'll see **monkeys** in all the moister parts of Kenya — troops of them live in City Park in the centre of Nairobi — and baboons often hang around at the side of the road.

Underfoot (or preferably not), spiders and scorpions and, on the coast, the harmlessly trundling **giant millipedes** will always do their best to get away from you, while the **butterflies** are all you could wish for in a butterfly. **Lizards** are common everywhere, harmless and often colourful: the biggest, **Nile monitors**, are often seen near water and from a distance look, as they race off, something like speeding baby crocodiles. In coastal lodgings at night, the translucent little aliens on the ceiling are **geckoes**, catching moths and other insects, and worth encouraging, while in the highlands you may come across prehistoric-looking **chameleons**, too.

Kenya's **birdlife** is astonishingly diverse, attracting ornithologists from all over the world and converting many others as well. Superb starlings, iridescent relatives of our own subtler species, are everywhere. Other birds — over 1200 species in all, from the thumb-sized red-cheeked cordon bleu to the ostrich — as well as mammals and reptiles, appear throughout this book.

SWAHILI ANIMAL NAMES

Bweha	Jackal	Nigri	Warthog
Bweha masigio	Bat-eared fox	Nsya	Duiker
Choroa	Oryx	Nungu	Porcupine
Chui	Leopard	Nyamera	Topi
Dondoo	Steinbok, grysbok	Nyani	Baboon
Duma	Cheetah	Nyati	Buffalo
Fisi	Hyena	Nyegere	Ratel
Fisi maji	Otter	Nyoka	Snake
Fungo	Civet cat	Nyumbu	Wildebeest
Kalasinga	de Brazza's monkey	Paa	Suni antelope
Kamandegere	Springhare	Paka	Cat
Kanu	Genet	Pala hala	Sable antelope
Kiboko	Hippopotamus	Pimbi	Rock hyrax
Kifaru/Faru	Rhinoceros	Pofu	Eland
Kima	Monkey	Punda	Horse, ass
Komba	Bushbaby	Punda milia	Zebra
Kongoni	Hartebeest	Sange	Elephant shrew
Korongo	Roan antelope	Sibamangu	Caracal
Kuru	Waterbuck	Simba	Lion
Mbega	Colobus monkey	Sunguru	Hare, rabbit
Mbwa mwitu	Hunting dog	Swala pala	Impala
Mdudu	Insect, bug	Swala granti	Grant's gazelle
Mondo	Serval	Swala tomi	Thomson's gazelle
Mamba	Crocodile	Swala twiga	Gerenuk
Muhanga	Aardvark	Tandala	Kudu
Ndege	Bird (also means plane)	Taya	Oribi
Ndovu	Elephant	Tohe	Reedbuck
Nguchiro	Mongoose	Tumbili	Vervet monkey
Nguruwe	Pig, Hog	Twiga	Giraffe

PARK GENERALITIES

The **National Parks** are administered by the Parks Authority in Nairobi as total sanctuaries where human habitation (apart from the tourist lodges, of course) is prohibited. **National Reserves**, run by local councils, tend to be less strict on the question of human encroachment. Parks and reserves are not fenced in (except Nakuru National Park and the north side of Nairobi National Park), and the animals are free to come and go, but they tend to stay within the boundaries, especially in the dry seasons when cattle outside compete for water.

Entrance fees for the parks and reserves are mostly standardised at Ksh220 each for "tourists" and Ksh30 per car. Kenya *citizens*, but no longer resident expatriates, are officially eligible for reduced rates. With a **student card** (ISIC), you may also get substantial, if variable, reductions, but this seems to be increasingly uncommon.

Fees in the national parks are usually **one-off** for the visit, regardless of how long you stay, but Samburu, Buffalo Springs, Shaba and Maasai Mara national *reserves* charge the entrance fee for **every day** you're inside. Mount Kenya National Park also has daily charges. Additionally, unless you have booking vouchers for a lodge, you will usually have to pay **camping fees** at the gate – widely standardised at Ksh50 per person per night.

In the past, a **"National Parks Pass"** (Ksh500, obtainable from the Park HQ at Nairobi National Park) was available for residents. Residents' eligibility for this apparently remains unchanged: you simply have to give the registration of your private car. It is valid for six months and allows free entry to the National Parks (but not National Reserves) for a car and passengers.

The parks and reserves are all open to private visits. A few have been really developed for tourism with graded tracks, signposts, lodges and the rest, but none has any kind of bus service at the gate for people without their own transport. The largest and most frequently visited are covered in depth in Chapter Five. Details

about smaller and lesser-known parks and reserves, some of which can be visited on foot, are included in the regional chapters. For books on wildlife, see the "Books" section in *Contexts*.

CAMPING SAFARIS

Once in Kenya, choosing a safari company to spend your money on can be fairly hit-or-miss. Unless you have the luxury of a long stay, your choice will probably be limited by the time available. Remember, though, that you may be able to use this to your advantage; if you ask, many companies are willing to discount a trip in order to fill unsold seats if you're buying at the last minute. Some outfits will also give student discounts – again, if you remember to ask.

A number of **recommended operators** are given in the "Nairobi Directory" but it's notoriously difficult to find a company that's absolutely consistent. (Members of *KATO* – see below – should be reliable.) Group relations among the passengers can assume surprising significance in a very short time and other **unpredictables** such as weather, illness and visibility of animals all contribute to the degree of success of the trip. More **controllable factors**, like breakdowns, food, camping equipment and competence of the drivers and tour leaders, really determine reputations. The companies listed on p.89 all have pretty good records and get regularly mentioned in readers' letters, but even they turn up the occa-

sional duff trip. Give them a try unless an alternative sounds especially good. The Nairobi grapevine is probably your most reliable guide on this.

If anything goes wrong, reputable companies will do their best to compensate on the spot (an extra day if you broke down, a night in a lodge if you didn't make it to a camp site, partial refunds without demur. . .). But, these days, there's a great deal of competition and corners do get cut. If your grievance is unresolved, you might want to contact the *Kenya Association of Tour Operators (KATO)*, PO Box 48461, Kaunda Street, Nairobi (☎225570), who can certainly intercede with their members. If this fails, try *Tourist's Kenya*, PO Box 40025, corner of Mama Ngina Street and Moi Avenue (☎337169), who publish the fortnightly pamphlet of the same name. They may well be able to help if the company concerned advertises with them. It should be noted that some operators – presumably less honorable ones – claim to have an exclusion clause relating to food poisoning . . . It is suggested you check before buying.

An introduction to the main game parks, giving you some idea of what to expect from them and when is the best time to visit, is given on p.231.

PHOTOGRAPHY

Kenya is immensely photogenic and with any kind of camera you'll get beautiful pictures. If you take photography seriously, you will probably want a single-lens reflex (SLR) camera and two or three lenses; but remember, these are heavy, relatively fragile and eminently stealable. Except in the game parks (where some kind of telephoto is essential if you want pictures of animals rather than savannah), you don't really need cumbersome lenses. It's often easier and less intrusive to take a small compact and keep your money for extra film.

Whatever you decide to take, **insure it** (if ordinary travel insurance won't cover it, check the insurers who advertise in photo magazines) and make sure you have a dust-proof bag to keep it in, as film in the camera gets scratched otherwise. Take spare **batteries** – they can be outrageously expensive in Nairobi. **Film** is no longer especially expensive, but try to bring all you'll need just the same, partiularly if you use colour transparency film or black and white. Try to keep it cool by stuffing it inside a sleeping bag and, if you'll be away for some time, posting it home seems a good idea; packages rarely go astray if registered. Processing in Kenya tends to be hit-or-miss – and certainly is expensive – but one or two places in Nairobi have a decent enough reputation (see "Nairobi Directory").

SUBJECTS

As for subjects, **animal photography** is a question of patience and not taking endless pictures of nothing happening: if you can't get close enough, don't waste your film. While taking photos, try keeping both eyes open and, in a vehicle, always turn off the engine.

The question of **photographing people** is more prickly. Every two seconds, somebody in Kenya has their photo taken by a tourist – and they're getting pretty fed up with it. Considering the reality of the situation, in fact, most people are amazingly tolerant of the camera's harassment. The Maasai and Samburu – Kenya's most colourful and photographed people – are usually prepared to do a deal, and in some places, you'll even find professional posers making a living at the roadside. If you're motivated to take a lot of pictures of people, you might seriously consider lugging along a Polaroid camera and as much film as you can muster. And you could have a lot of photos of you and your family printed up with your address on the back, which should at least raise a few laughs when you try the exchange.

One thing is certain: if you won't accept that some kind of interaction and **exchange** are warranted, you won't have many pictures. Taking the subject's name and address and sending a print when you get home is an option that some people prefer, but it is decreasingly popular with subjects who look on the photo call as work. Blithely aiming at strangers is arrogant; it won't make you any friends and it may well get you into trouble.

On the subject of sensitivity, it's a bad idea to take pictures of anything that could be construed as strategic, including any military or police building, prisons, airports, harbours, bridges and His Excellency the President. . . It all depends on who sees you, of course – protesting your innocence won't appease small-minded officials.

TECHNICAL BUSINESS

Getting (slightly) **technical**, use skylight or UV filters to block haze and protect your lens. Take several speeds of film (don't let anyone tell you it's unnecessary to have fast film) in rolls of twenty, so you don't get stuck at the wrong speed too long. And if you feel it's worth taking a camera bag of lenses for your SLR, then it really makes no sense not to take two camera bodies as well – less lens changing, more film speeds available, and you could shoot the same subject in (say) fast black and white and slow, fine-grain colour.

Early morning and late afternoon are the **best times for photography**. At midday, with the sun almost directly overhead, the light is flat and everything is lost in a formless glare. In morning and evening, the contrast between light and shade can be huge, so be careful to expose for the subject and not the general scene. And remember, as you negotiate for your next Maasai masterpiece, that black skin usually needs a little more exposure (think of people as always back-lit); a half stop is normally enough.

The **rainy seasons** are rewarding, especially when the first rains break: months of dust are settled, greenery sprouts in a few hours, the country has a lush, bold sheen, and the sky is magnificent.

TROUBLE

There are places in Kenya where you can leave an unattended tent for the day and find it untouched when you return in the evening. And there are a few spots where walking alone after dark is almost guaranteed to get you mugged. As a general rule, though, you have a far higher chance of being a victim in touristy areas. On an encouraging note, the eight months of research for this book (including a month in Nairobi) produced not a single first-hand experience.

AVOIDANCE

After arriving by air for the first time, an incredible number of people get ripped off during their **first day or two in Nairobi**. You should at first be

TROUBLE FROM MISUNDERSTANDINGS

It's very easy to fall prey to misunderstandings in your relations with people (usually boys and young men) who offer their services as guides, helpers or "facilitators" of any kind. You should absolutely never assume anything is being done out of simple kindness. It may well be, but, if it isn't, you must expect to pay something. If you have any suspicion, it's invariably best to confront the matter head on at an early stage and either apologise for the offence caused by the suggestion, or agree a price. What you must never do, as when bargaining, is enter into an unspoken contract and then break it by refusing to pay for the service. If you're being bugged by someone whose help you don't need, just let them know you can't pay anything for their trouble. It may not make you a friend, but it always works and it's better than a row and recriminations.

acutely conscious of your belongings, never leave anything unguarded even for fifteen seconds, never take out cameras or other valuables unless absolutely necessary, and be careful of where you walk, at least until you've got the pack off your back and you're settled in somewhere.

The only substantial risks otherwise are down at the coast (where valuables often disappear from the beach or occasionally get grabbed), in the other big towns (Nakuru and, to a lesser extent, Kisumu), and in some of the game parks – Samburu and Maasai Mara have had a number of incidents in recent years.

If you're **driving**, it's never a good idea to leave even a locked car unguarded if it has anything of value in it. In towns, there's usually someone who will volunteer to guard it for you for a few shillings.

All of this isn't meant to induce paranoia. But if you flaunt the trappings of wealth where there's urban poverty, somebody will want to remove them. There's always less risk in leaving your valuables in a locked hotel room or – judiciously – with the management, than in taking them with you. If you clearly have nothing on you, you're unlikely to feel, or be, threatened. In Nairobi, the rush hour at dusk is probably the worst time, but it's a good idea to be alert getting off a night bus early in the morning, too. It's also worth tuning into the monthly cycle of poverty and wealth among urban Kenyans; there are always more pickpockets about at the end of the month, when people are carrying the salaries they've just been paid.

When you have to **carry money**, put it in several places if possible. Avoid socks, though; it seems thieves are on to that and people have had their footwear literally ripped off. *Velcro* pocket closures seem a good idea. And see "Money and Costs", p.13.

THIEF GRIEF

If you get mugged, it will be over in an instant and you're unlikely to be hurt. But the hassles, and worse, that gather when you try to do anything about it make it imperative not to let it happen in the first place. Thieves caught red-handed are usually mobbed – often killed – so when you shout "Thief!" ("*Mwizi!*" in Swahili), be ready to intercede once you've retrieved your belongings.

Usually you'll have no chance, or desire, to catch the thief and the first reaction is to go to the **police**. Unless you've lost a lot of money (and cash is virtually irretrievable) or irreplaceable property, however, think twice about doing this. They rarely do something for nothing – even stamping an insurance form will probably cost you – and secondly you should consider the ramifications if you and they set off to try and catch the culprits. This kind of scenario, with you in the back of a police car expected to point out the thief in the crowds, is a complete waste of time. And, whatever you do, never agree to act as a decoy in the hope that the same thing will happen again in front of a police ambush. Police shootings take place all the time and you may prefer not to be the cause of a cold-blooded murder. As angry as you may feel about being robbed, the desperation that leads men and boys to risk their lives for your things gives a lot of support to the idea that capital punishment is no deterrent.

If you have to visit the police in Nairobi, go to the main police station (marked on the map), not any of the smaller posts and offices.

DEALING WITH THE POLICE

Kenyan police are probably no worse than most others. There are few possible generalisations and stories do sometimes get recounted of extraordinary **kindness** at times of trouble and of occasional bursts of **efficiency** that would do credit to any police force. But, badly educated and poorly paid as the police mostly are, you would be wise to steer clear as far as possible. If you have **official business** with the police, then polite-ness, smiles and handshakes always help. If you're expected to give a bribe — as you usually are — wait for it to be hinted at and haggle over it as you would any payment; Ksh30 or 50 is often enough to oil small wheels.

In **unofficial dealings**, the police, especially in remote outposts, can go out of their way to help you with food, transport or accommodation. Try to reciprocate. Police salaries are low — often counted in hundreds of shillings a month — and they rely on unofficial income to get by. Only a brand new police force and realistic salaries could alter a situation which is now entrenched.

IN TROUBLE WITH THE POLICE

Common ways of exciting police interest are infringements of currency laws and drug posses-sion, either of which will land you a large fine and deportation at least — don't expect to buy yourself out of this kind of trouble. Driving offences are less serious; drivers (at any rate white drivers) are rarely stopped at the fairly frequent checkpoints. It's worth knowing, though, that some forces have speed-trap radar equip-ment which they set up outside towns: drive with caution as speed limits are often vague.

UNSEEMLY BEHAVIOUR

Be warned that failure to observe the following points of **Kenyan etiquette** can get you arrested or put you in a position where you may be obliged to pay a bribe. Stand in cinemas and on other occasions when the national anthem is playing. Stand still when the national flag is being raised or lowered in your field of view. Don't take photos of the flag or H.E. the president (often seen on state occasions in Nairobi). Pull off the road completely when a hundred motorcycle outriders appear, then get out and stand by your vehicle (for it is he). Never tear up a banknote, of any denomination. And don't urinate in public.

WOMEN'S KENYA

Machismo, in its full-fledged Latin varieties, is rare in Kenya and male egos are usually softened by reserves of humour. Women's groups flourish across the country, but are concerned more with improvement of incomes, education, health and nutrition than social or political emancipation.

SEXUAL HARASSMENT

Women, whether travelling alone or together, may come across occasional **persistent hass-lers** but seldom much worse. Universal rules apply: if you suspect ulterior motives, turn down all offers and stonily refuse to converse, though you needn't fear expressing your anger if that's how you feel. You will, eventually, be left alone. Really obnoxious individuals are usually on their own, fortunately. These tactics are hardly neces-sary except on the coast, and then particularly in **Lamu**. Avoid walking alone down beach access roads north or south of Mombasa, however, as there's a danger of violent robbery for either sex.

Blonde women suffer more, though cutting your hair short or dyeing it seem drastic and rather prejudicial steps. There is already enough discou-ragement in the world to women wanting to travel without the company of men — and Kenya is prob-ably easier in this respect than most countries.

BROADER ISSUES

Despite the International Women's Decade conference held in Nairobi in 1985, Kenya's

Women's Movement is still embryonic. The *National Council of Women of Kenya* lobbies hard in the campaign for the legalisation of abortion and, with government support, in education for contraception and efforts to abolish the practices of female genital mutilation — known, in a classic bit of male anthropologese, as "female circumcision".

Kenya, tragically, is still used as a contraceptive testing ground; Depo-provera, high oestrogen pills and the Dalkon shield have all been foisted on Kenyan women. For more information and contacts, get in touch with the *NCWK* (see "Nairobi Directory"). You might also try writing to the *Pan-African Women's Trade Union*, PO Box 61068, Nairobi.

SEXUAL ATTITUDES

Sexual mores in Kenya are refreshingly hedonistic and uncluttered, nor is prostitution the rigid, secretive transaction of the West. Unfortunately, sexually transmitted diseases, including the HIV virus, are rife. Attitudes in Kenya are waking up to this reality, but you should be aware of the very real risks should you accept a proposition. Surveys have revealed up to one in four Nairobi prostitutes are HIV-positive. It goes without saying that casual sex without a condom is a deadly gamble and you should assume any sexual contact to be HIV-positive.

Despite this, female **prostitution** flourishes enthusiastically everywhere and a remarkable number of the cheaper hotels double as brothels, or at least willingly rent their rooms by the hour. Gigolos and male prostitutes — far fewer — are limited mostly to Nairobi and the coast. Among tourists, enough arrive expecting sexual adventures to make flirtatious pestering a fairly constant part of the scene, irritating or amusing as it strikes you. And if you're here looking for a holiday affair, Lamu seems to be the place.

As for attitudes to **gay life**, they're rather hard to pin down. While there is no gay scene as such, male homosexuality is an accepted undercurrent on the coast, where it finds most room for expression in Lamu. The Lake Victoria region has a fairly relaxed attitude, too. *Msenge* is Swahili for gay man. Elsewhere, Nairobi aside, homosexuality is scarce enough not to be an issue. On the statute books, however, it remains illegal.

KENYA'S PEOPLE, LANGUAGES AND RELIGIONS

Whether called peoples, ethnic groups or tribes, Kenyans have a multiplicity of racial and cultural origins. **Distinctions would be simple if similarities in physical appearance were shared by those who speak the same language and share a common culture: the term "tribe" tends to imply this kind of banal stereotype. But "tribes" have never been closed units, and appearance, speech and culture have always overlapped. Families, for instance, often contained members of different tribes. In the last fifty years, tribal identities have broken down still further as broader class, political and national ones have emerged.**

The most enduring ethnic distinction is language. A person's "mother tongue" is still important as an index of social identity and a tribe is best defined as people sharing a common first language. But, in the towns and among afflu-

AFRICAN LANGUAGE GROUPS IN KENYA

This, broadly, is the breakdown of Kenya's language groups into separate ethnic identities. You'll find variations on these spellings, and inconsistencies in the use of prefixes (ie Kamba instead of Akamba, Agikuyu instead of Kikuyu, and so on).

BANTU-SPEAKING
Western Bantu: Luyia, Gusii, Kuria.
Central Bantu: Akamba, Kikuyu, Embu, Meru, Mbere, Tharaka.
Coastal Bantu: Swahili, Mijikenda, Segeju, Pokomo, Taita, Taveta.

NILOTIC-SPEAKING
Lake-River Nilotic: Luo.
Plains Nilotic: Maasai and Samburu (Maa-speakers), Turkana, Teso, Njemps, Elmolo
Highland Nilotic: Kalenjin group including Nandi, Marakwet, Pokot, Tugen, Kipsigis, Elkony.

CUSHITIC-SPEAKING
Southern Cushitic: Boni.
Eastern Cushitic: Somali, Rendille, Orma, Boran, Gabbra ("Galla" is often used to describe all these language groups except the Somali).

ent families, even language is increasingly unimportant. Many people speak three languages (their own, Swahili and English) or even four if they have mixed parentage. And for a few, English has become a first language.

There are pieces throughout the book on aspects of the history and cultures of the main language groups in each region.

NAMES AND GROUPS

Books continue to use various unwieldy terms: *Bantu* and *Nilotic* are language groups (like Indo-European or Semitic) and, restricted to a linguistic sense, fair enough. But *Hamitic*, which still pops up occasionally, is almost meaningless and hedged with racist overtones. "Hamitic influence" has been credited with many technological, social and political innovations in the past. The Biblical origins of the word give it away: it reflects the early European presumption that lighter-skinned people with thinner lips and straighter noses were more intelligent than other Africans. The origins of these people in northeast Africa and their implied association with the well-springs of Mediterranean civilisation were further "evidence" of this. The term "Nilo-hamitic" (often used to refer to the Maasai and other pastoralists admired by the Europeans) just confuses the issue further; it implies the cross-cutting cultural, linguistic and racial overlays that most Kenyans have inherited, without abandoning the idea of racially superior influences from the north.

Biologically, of course, Negroid inheritance predominates among Africans, with Caucasoid elements clear enough in many regions. But physiology doesn't have much to do with language or

culture. Travelling around Kenya, you become aware of just how far off the mark the old racist doctrines really were.

Apart from the African majority, who make up about 99 percent of the population, Kenya has a considerable and diverse **Asian** population – perhaps over 150,000 – most of whom live in Nairobi, Mombasa, Kisumu and Nakuru. Descendants in part of the labourers brought over to build the railway, they also number many whose parents and grandparents came in its wake, to trade and set up businesses. And some families, notably on the coast, have lived in Kenya for centuries. Predominantly Punjabi and Gujerati speakers from northwest India and Pakistan, they are overwhelmingly dominant in business. There's a dispersed Christian Goan community, too, who tend to have less formalised relations with other Kenyans. And a persistent, but diminishing **Arab**-speaking community remains on the coast.

Lastly, there are still an estimated 10,000 **European** residents – a surprisingly motley crew from British ex-servicemen to Italian aristocrats – scattered through the highlands and the rest of the country, some 4000 of whom hold Kenya citizenship. Some maintain a scaled-down version of the old planter's life; a few still hold senior civil service positions; and there's even one white member of parliament. Increasingly, though, the community is turning to the tourist industry for a firmer future – and a life beyond Kenya if necessary.

RELIGION

In the matter of **religion**, broad-based, non-fundamentalist **Sunni Islam** dominates the coast and the northeast, and is in the ascendant throughout the country. Many towns have several mosques (or dozens on the coast), but one usually serves as the focal **Friday mosque** for the whole community. Shiite fundamentalism is almost unknown among African believers, but the Aga Khan's Ismaili sect is an influential Asian constituency with powerful business interests. Hindu and Sikh temples are found in most large towns, and there are adherents of Jainism and the Bahai faith, too. Varieties of **Catholicism** and **Protestantism** are present more in the highlands and westwards. In the far west, especially towards Lake Victoria, are many minor **Christian sects** and churches, many based around the teaching of local prophets and preachers.

Indigenous religion (mostly based around the idea of a supreme god) continues to play a large part in many people's lives, however, with sacrifices and appropriate rituals performed from time to time; belief in Christianity or Islam is rarely watertight.

ETIQUETTE

Islamic moral strictures tend to be generously interpreted. On the question of **dress**, on the coast, it's always best to wear loose-fitting long sleeves and skirts or trousers in the towns, but shorts and T-shirts won't get you into trouble: people are far too polite to admonish strangers. Malindi, in particular, is very relaxed. Lamu calls more for *kikoi* and *kanga* wraps for both sexes and, because it's so small, more consideration for local feelings. Suitably dressed and hatted men, and often women, can enter **mosques**. Few are very grand, however, and you rarely miss much by staying outside.

DIRECTORY

Addresses All addresses in Kenya have a post office box number except out in the sticks, where some are just given as "Private Bag", or "PO", followed by the location of the post office. In large towns, business and office addresses are usually identified by the "House" or "Building" in which they're situated.

Beggars are fairly common in the touristy parts of Nairobi and Mombasa. Most are visibly destitute; many are cripples, lepers or homeless mothers with children. Some have regular pitches, others keep on the move. They are harassed by police and often rounded up. Kenyans often give to the same beggar on a regular basis and, of course, alms-giving is a requirement of Islam believed to benefit the donor.

Books Less than fifty percent of Kenyans are literate but books and reading material have a high profile. Bookstores in Nairobi, Mombasa and in the tourist hotels have imported paperback selections. Second-hand book stalls are often worth looking over, too. Or ask other travellers: bring one book and keep exchanging. For suggestions on reading matter, see "Books" in *Contexts*.

Clothes Particularly if you're only coming for a short stay, it's important to bring what you need to be comfortable. Take cotton clothes and good quality tennis or sports shoes, plus at least one warm sweater or, better still, a soft-lined jacket with pockets. (See the "Mount Kenya" section for advice on that.) A grey cotton jersey tracksuit is ideal for early morning game runs when you'll quite often set off before sunrise. And, even if you're doing everything on a shoestring, take some nicer clothes to wear in lodges: access is often difficult for the ragged.

Con-men Approaches in the street from "schoolboys" with sponsorship forms (only primary education is free, and even then, books, uniforms, even furniture have to be bought) and from "refugees" with long stories are not uncommon and probably best shrugged off. Some, unfortunately, may be genuine.

The latest scam involves an approach by such a "student", followed by a request for a small sum of money. As you leave with a sigh of relief, a group of heavies surround you and claim to be police, interested in the discussion you've been having with that "subversive", and the funds you provided him. A large fine is demanded. You can tell them to go to hell, or suggest you all go the police station. Such aggressions are never the real thing.

Lastly, an old one that still catches people out: if you're grabbed by a man who has just picked up a wad of money in the street and seems oddly willing to share it with you in a convenient nearby alley, you'll know you're about to be robbed.

Contraceptives Condoms are available from town chemists. Family planning clinics are helpful and will sometimes provide them and – with a prescription – oral contraceptives, free or for a small charge. If you use pills, though, it's far wiser to bring all you'll need.

Drugs Grass (bhangi) is widely cultivated and smoked and is remarkably cheap. Officially illegal, the authorities do make some effort to control it. Use and attitudes vary considerably but you should be very discreet if you're going to indulge. The ruling KANU party's "Youth Wingers" have broadened their operations from political thuggery to snooping on tourists – especially on the coast. Watch out who you get high with. Official busts result in a shakedown by the police, a heavy fine and deportation at the very least. Your embassy will not be sympathetic. Anything harder than marijuana is rarely sold and will get you in worse trouble if you're caught. Miraa, a mild herbal stimulant chewed with bubble gum, is legal and widely available, especially in Nairobi, Mombasa and in the north. It's the East African lorry driver's "upper" and something of an acquired taste.

Electricity When there is some, 220–240V. Only fancier hotels have outlets or shaver points in the rooms.

Emergencies Try not to have them. Ambulance is 999 but the police usually take ages.

Gifts Ballpoint pens and postcards are about the only small items worth taking and can always be given to children. Off the beaten track, they'll be appreciated by many adults, too, though few people will have an exaggerated idea of their real value. If you'll be travelling or staying for some time and really want to prepare, get a large batch of photos of you and your family with your address on the back. You'll get lots of mail.

"Kenya" or "Keenya"? Although you'll hear "Kenya" most of the time, the second pronunciation is still used, and not exclusively by old colonials. It seems that the colonial pronunciation was closer to the original name of the mountain, Kirinyaga. This was early on shortened to Kinya and spelled, Englishly, "Kenya" (as in "key"). With the arrival of modern African orthography, this spelling came to be pronounced with a short "e" and, when Kenyatta became president, the coincidence of his name was exploited.

Laundry There are no launderettes in Kenya and it's usually easiest to wash your own clothes: you can buy packets of Omo laundry soap, and things dry fast. Otherwise, there's often someone wherever you're staying who will be prepared to negotiate a laundry charge. Don't spread clothes on the ground to dry: they might be infested by the tumbu fly, which lays its eggs in them for the larvae to hatch and burrow into your skin. Not desirable.

Place names Place names all over Africa (not just Kenya) are remarkably confusing to outsiders. In some parts every town or village seems to have name starting with the same syllable. In the Kenya highlands, you'll find Kiambu, Kikuyu, Kiganjo, Kiserian, Kinangop etc. Further west you confront Kaptagat, Kapsabet, Kabarnet, Kapsowar. . . As soon as you detect a problem like this, just get into the habit of ignoring the first syllable, "de-stressing" it. A more practical problem all over rural Kenya is the vague use of names to denote a whole district and, at the same time, its nucleus, be it a small town, a village, or just a cluster of corrugated iron shops and bars. Sometimes there'll be two such focusses. They often move in a matter of a few years, so what looks like a junction town on the map, turns out to be away from the road, or in a different place altogether. The main "centre" is usually called just that. Ask for the "shopping centre" and you'll usually find the local hive of activity and the place with the name you were looking for.

Snorkelling If you plan to do a fair bit of goggling, try to bring your own mask and snorkel. They aren't highly expensive, or particularly heavy, and you'll benefit from having equipment that fits and works and save money you'd spend hiring it otherwise. Don't forget although certain parts of the coast have exceptional stretches of reef, you can have a rewarding dip under the waves almost anywhere.

Student cards If you qualify, get hold of an International Student Identity Card (ISIC) from student unions or branches of *STA Travel* or *Campus Travel*. In Kenya, it's no passport to automatic cheap deals, but it can be worth waving for discounted park and museum entry fees, though rarely so in the popular parks – at least in the high season.

Tampax Available in town chemists but expensive, so bring supplies.

Time Kenya is three hours ahead of Greenwich Mean Time all year round. With slight variations east and west, it gets light at 6am and dark at 6pm. If you're learning Swahili, remember that "Swahili time" runs from dawn to dusk to dawn rather than midnight–midday–midnight. 7am and 7pm are both *saa moja* (one o'clock) while midnight and midday are *saa sita* (six o'clock). It's not as confusing as it first sounds – just add or subtract six hours to work out Swahili time.

People and things are usually late in Kenya. That said, if you try to anticipate, you're generally caught out. Trains nearly always leave right on time; buses often have punctual departures as well. In more remote areas though, if a driver tells you he's going somewhere "today", it doesn't necessarily mean he expects to arrive today. . .

Toilets Carry toilet paper – which you can buy in most places – as few cheap hotels provide it. Town public toilets (*Wanawake* = Women's; *Wanaume* = Mens) are invariably disgusting. Public buildings and hotels are unlikely to turn you away if you ask.

Work Unless you've lined up a job or voluntary work before leaving for Kenya, you have little chance of getting employment. Wages are extremely low (university lecturers, for example, start at not much more than the equivalent of £150 per month) and there's serious unemployment in the towns. Particular skills are sometimes in demand – mechanics at game-park lodges, for example – but the employer will need good connections to arrange the required papers. It's illegal to obtain income in Kenya while staying on a visitor's pass.

ODD ESSENTIALS

In no particular order, and not all essential:

● **Binoculars** (the small, fold-up ones) are invaluable for game-watching. Without them you'll miss half the action.

● **Sunglasses** are a health precaution worth bringing even if you're not used to them, and they're expensive to buy in Kenya.

● **Plastic bags** are invaluable: large bin-liner bags to keep dust off clothes, small resealable ones to protect cameras and film.

● Take a multipurpose **penknife**, a **torch**, a small **alarm clock** (handy for pre-dawn starts) and a **padlock** – vital in lodgings where doors don't lock properly.

● **Camping-gas stoves** are light and useful even if you're not camping. The cylinders can be bought in Nairobi (see "Directory") and a number of other places.

● A tube of **ant-killer** comes in handy if you're camping, particularly on the coast.

● Down on the coast, too, **plastic sandals** are best for walking on the reef: you can buy them cheaply in Kenya.

● You might want to take your own **flip-flops/ thongs** for cheap hotel bathrooms (though a pair is often provided).

● **Earplugs** are a help in some lodgings if you're a light sleeper.

● A **sheet sleeping bag** (sew up a sheet) is essential for low-budget travel.

● If you shave bring a supply of disposable **razors**.

● For driving around the parks and hiking, a **compass** is immensely useful.

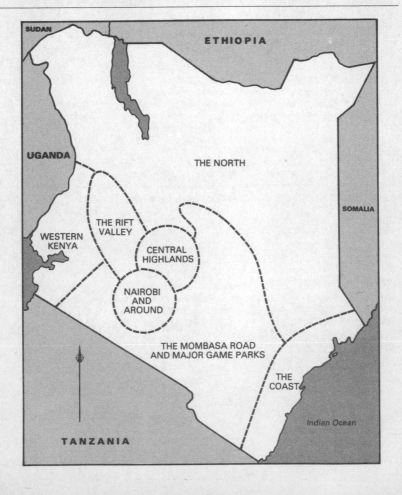

CHAPTER ONE

NAIROBI AND AROUND

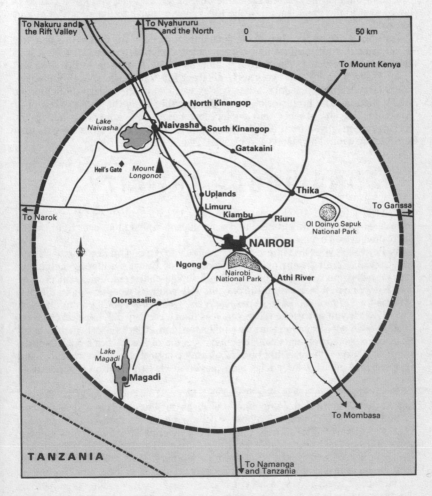

Easily the largest city in East Africa, **Nairobi** is also the youngest, the most modern, the fastest growing and the highest (1700m). The superlatives could go on forever. "City in the sun," runs one tour brochure sobriquet, "City of flowers" another. Less enchanted visitors growl "Nairobbery." The city catches your attention at least. This is no tropical backwater.

Most roads, particularly paved ones, lead to Nairobi and, like it or not, you're bound to spend some time here. But walking down Kenyatta Avenue at rush hour, or up Tom Mboya Street after dark, when the security men cluster around their fires on the pavement, it's perhaps easy to forget how quickly you can leave the city and be in the bush. Apart from being the safari capital of the world, Nairobi is an excellent **base for travel**, just six hours by road to the coast, or an overnight train journey, about the same time to the far west, and just a couple of hours west to the great trough of the Rift Valley or north to the slopes of Mount Kenya.

For **shorter trips**, worthwhile destinations, covered at the end of this chapter, lie all around, with the first and closest target **Nairobi National Park**, a wild attraction where you'd expect to find suburbs. **Lake Naivasha** to the west and **Lake Magadi**, south, are two utterly different Rift Valley lakes, each just a few hours away from the capital – a day trip by car, two or three days if hitching or taking the bus. The prehistoric site of **Olorgasailie** is on the way to Magadi. If you're looking for greener and cooler destinations, an interesting hiking (or biking) route is given from **North Kinangop to Thika**. For higher heights turn north to the central highlands and Chapter Two.

NAIROBI – THE CITY

NAIROBI is one of Africa's major cities: the UN's fourth "World Centre", East Africa's commercial and aid hub, and a significant capital in its own right, with a population of well over a million.

As a traveller, your first impressions are likely to depend on how – and where – you arrived. Coming here overland, from one of Kenya's suffering neighbour states, some time resting up among the fleshpots can seem a pleasant proposition. Newly arrived by air from Europe, though, you may wonder – amid the rash of signs for *California Cookies, Brunchburgers, Woolworth's* and *Oriental Massage* – just how far you've travelled. Nairobi, less than a century old, has real claims to western-style sophistication but, as you'll soon find, it lacks a convincing heart. Apart from some lively musical attractions – some of East Africa's busiest **clubs** and best **bands** – there's little here of magnetic appeal, and most travellers stay long enough only to take stock – and maybe to visit the **National Museum** – before moving on.

Which is a pity in a way. For if you're interested in getting to know the real Kenya, then Nairobi is as compelling a place as any and displays enormous vitality and buzz. The controlling ethos is commerce rather than community, and there's an almost willful superficiality in the free-for-all of commuters, shoppers, police, hustlers and tourists. It's hard to imagine a city with a more fascinating variety of people, and almost all of them newcomers. Most are immigrants from rural areas, drawn to the presence and opportunities of money, and Nairobi, on the surface at least, seems to accept everyone with complete tolerance. On any downtown pavement you can see a complete cross section of Kenyans, plus every variety of tourist. Young Maasai and Samburu men in the warrior-age grade don't get away with spear-carrying in town, but you'll occasionally see more supercilious individuals risking police harassment by cruising the streets in ochre and beads (more background on p.256).

Nairobi's rapid growth inevitably has a down side however (talk to any resident and you'll hear some jaw-dropping stories of crime and police shootings), and you should certainly be aware of its reputation for **bag-snatching and robbery**, frequently directed at new tourist arrivals (see the "Security" box overleaf). If you plan to stay for any length of time, learn the art of survival; with the right attitude, you're unlikely to have problems. For the few days that most people spend – if initial misgivings can be overcome – it's a stimulating city.

Some history

Nairobi came into being in 1899, an artificial settlement created by Europeans at Mile 327 of the East African railway line, then being systematically forged from the coast into the interior. It was initially a supply depot, switching yard and campsite for the thousands of Indian labourers employed by the British. Its site, bleak and swampy, was simply the spot where operations came to a halt while the engineers figured out their next move, namely getting the line up the steep slopes that lay ahead. The name came from the local Maasai term for the valley, *Ewaso Nairobi*, "Stream of Cold Water".

Unexpectedly, the unplanned **settlement** took root. A few years later it was totally rebuilt after an outbreak of plague and the burning of the original town compound. By 1907, it was so firmly established that the colonists took it as the capital of the newly formed "British East Africa" (BEA). Europeans, encouraged by the authorities, settled in large numbers, while Africans were forced into employment by tax demands or onto specially created **reserves** – the Maasai to the Southern Reserve and the Kikuyu to their own reserve in the highlands.

The capital, lacking development from any established community, was somewhat characterless – and remains so. The **original centre** retains an Asian influence in its older buildings, but today it is shot through with glassy, high-rise blocks, indistinguishable from those in any western city. Surrounding the commercial hub are thousands of acres of **suburbs**: wealthiest in the west and north, increasingly poor to the south and especially the east, where they become, in part, out-and-out slums.

Names of these suburbs – Parklands, Lavington, Eastleigh, Shauri Moyo among others – reflect the jumble of African, Asian and European elements in the Kenyan population, none of whom were local. The term "Nairobian" isn't in circulation because it would scarcely apply to anyone. Although it has a predominance of Kikuyu, the city is not the preserve of a single ethnic group, nor is it built on any distinctively tribal land. Standing as it does at the meeting point of Maasai, Kikuyu and Kamba territories, its choice as capital, accidental though it may have been (Kikuyu **Limuru** and Kamba **Machakos** were also considered), was a fortunate one for the future of the country.

Arrival

Getting into central Nairobi presents few problems, and once you're there, you'll have little trouble finding your way around. The city has widespread suburbs but its inner area is relatively small: a triangle of stores, offices and public buildings, with the railway station on the southern flank and the main bus stations on the east.

Arriving by air

Arriving by air, you'll find yourself at **Jomo Kenyatta International Airport**, 15km out of town to the southeast on the Mombasa highway. Check your **luggage** is intact as soon as you get if off the carousel. If anything appears to be missing go straight to the "Lost Luggage" desk before passing through customs. (If you're really concerned, or your bags are insecure, you might, as one traveller suggested, stuff dirty underwear behind all the zips to deter riflers).

There's a **24-hour bank**, which you should try to get to as soon as possible, and an office of the **Flying Doctors** organisation, where you can buy their special brand of life-saving insurance if you expect to be out in the wilds a lot.

Invariably, hordes of taxi drivers assail you outside the airport (if you want to be met, try contacting *Save Taxi Service* – address under "Taxis" on p.58). **Taxi rates** to any Nairobi city destination run between Ksh200 and 400 – they don't have meters, so bargain firmly. For the yellow taxis there's a fixed price however – Ksh243 at the last check. Otherwise there are two kinds of buses: the *Kenya Airways* bus, which operates hourly until 8pm for Ksh40 and can drop you at any of the pricier hotels, or the Kenya Bus Services (KBS) bus #34, which operates only until 6pm and costs just Ksh5. It enters the city through the eastern suburbs (rather than running straight up the proud artery of **Uhuru Highway**) and stops at the central KBS terminal before continuing to the **Youth Hostel** on Nairobi Hill. See the warning below in the "Security" box about robbery on the #34 bus.

SECURITY

An alarming number of new arrivals have to deal with a **robbery** in their first day or two in Nairobi, before they've adjusted to the city's pace and ways. A lot of people get ripped off on the **#34 bus** on their way from the airport to the youth hostel. It's a joke really, and the secret is to clock the thieves – usually pretty young – and let them know you've seen them. Surprisingly enough, this usually stops them, and you can all have a (nervous) laugh.

Victims get distracted in conversation or have their hands grabbed and shaken by strangers. If you want to avoid being victimised, you should take exaggerated care of your valuables, keep your hands out of reach and be – rationally – suspicious of everyone until you've caught your breath. It doesn't take long. Every rural Kenyan coming to the city for the first time goes through exactly the same process, and many are considerably less streetwise than you, having never been in a city before.

Beware also that certain areas have acquired local notoriety. In particular **Uhuru and Central parks** look peaceful enough, but you should avoid walking through them on your own at any time of day and after dark it would be absolute lunacy. The whole area between the centre and Nairobi Hill, where the youth hostel is located, is dangerous after dark – take a bus, *matatu* or taxi. Similarly, the area **near the Museum and Casino** is generally unsafe at night. The post office building on Kenyatta Avenue used to be the scene of phenomenal pickpocketing and bag-snatching. It's too early to say whether the new General Post Office (GPO) on Haile Selassie Avenue will have better security.

These are all parts of the city where tourist pickings are fairly rich – and there are always a few who haven't read a guidebook. If you head **out from the centre** to poorer districts there seems to be less of a threat. The River Road district, although it may seem heavy at first, probably poses no more of a threat to your security than a stroll down Kenyatta Avenue. If Nairobi fills you with trepidation, read the section entitled "Trouble" in *Basics* on p.43.

You will be obliged to take a taxi if your plane arrives **late at night**. You may well feel intimidated by a night-time first contact with central Nairobi and you'll find many of the cheapest hotels are already closed before midnight. An obvious alternative is simply to curl up in a corner of the arrivals hall until the first bus in the morning. Remember, though, this isn't a large airport: comforts and even basic facilities are very limited and dossing in a corner is only barely tolerated. Not much help, but on a more upbeat note, the *Simba Restaurant* at the top of the arrivals building is surprisingly good and reasonably priced.

Arriving by train
Arriving by train from Mombasa or western Kenya, you'll find yourself virtually in the city centre. From the **railway station** (forewarned about the taxi drivers and porters who, once again, more or less kidnap your luggage if allowed), just walk straight out through the concourse and follow Moi Avenue into town.

Arriving by bus
Most **bus companies** have their booking offices or termini in the urban sprawl along the south banks of the Nairobi River (these days more of a ditch) and, again, this is just a short walk from the city centre. If you've been following the map and know where you are, however, you can generally ask to be dropped off anywhere along the bus route into town.

Orientation

The triangle of **central Nairobi** divides into three principal districts divided by the main thoroughfares of **Kenyatta Avenue** and **Moi Avenue**.

The grandest and most formal part of town is the area around **City Square**, in the southwest. This square kilometre is Nairobi's heart, as government buildings, banks and offices merge (to the north and east) with upmarket shopping streets and luxury hotels. Its big landmark is the extraordinary **Kenyatta Conference Centre**, Kenya's most monumental building, visible from certain points miles outside the city.

North of Kenyatta Avenue, there's a shift to smaller scale and lesser finance. The **City Market** is here, surrounded by a denser district of shops, restaurants and hotels. **Jeevanjee Gardens** are a welcome patch of greenery and, a little further north is Nairobi's oldest establishment, *The Norfolk*, contemporary with the original rebuilding of the city.

East of Moi Avenue, the character changes more radically. Here, and down towards the Nairobi River, is the relatively poor, inner-city district identified with **River Road**, its main thoroughfare. The River Road quarter is where all long-distance buses and *matatus* start and terminate, and it's where you'll find the capital's cheapest restaurants and hotels, as well as the highest concentration of African-owned businesses. It is also a somewhat notorious area with a traditional concentration of sharks and pickpockets – a reputation that's undoubtedly over-played. Some unwary *wazungu* (white people) consider themselves likely victims here; you can meet European residents who work five minutes' walk away and in all their years in Nairobi have never been to this part of town. If you stay reasonably awake, don't display valuables, and preferably don't carry anything you wouldn't like to lose, you should have little trouble. Violence against tourists is very rare.

Transport

Getting around central Nairobi is straightforward. By day, most visitors **walk**; by night, they take a **taxi**. Unless you're only here for a day or two, though, it's certainly worth getting to know the city's **public transport** systems.

Taxis

Nairobi's **taxis** are overpriced by Kenyan standards. At night, however, when certain parts of the city are definitely not recommended for pedestrians, you'll almost certainly want to make use of them. Hordes of brand-new, grey, London-style taxis crowd around key spots in the city – notably the Hilton area – and cost the same as the other, yellow perils. Whichever you choose, you need to bargain. Ksh50 is about the bottom-line fare for any trip in the city. Keep this in mind, work out how much you want to pay and then offer about two-thirds of that, so you can come up in price.

The *Save Taxi Service* (PO Box 10148, ☎22953 ext. 6, *Ambassadeur Hotel*) obviates all this messing about by promising fixed fares to all destinations, at a shade over the lowest bargainable rates. They're good for early morning airport runs and similar requirements and they should be able to meet you at the airport.

Wheels of the wananchi

Public transport – buses or *matatus* – used by the ordinary people (the *wananchi*) of Nairobi saves money on getting around, certainly for longer trips out of the city centre, but it takes some figuring out. The **KBS buses** roar around Nairobi all day, usually packed far beyond capacity. They're cheap and very unpredictable. Buses are numbered but bus stops aren't and routes change frequently. For points recommended in this chapter, appropriate buses (#34 and so on, and where to board them) have been indicated.

Matatus can be slightly easier. They tend to take the same routes as buses and often display the same route numbers. They're generally faster, if more dangerous. The confusion in Nairobi is occasionally exacerbated by clumsy police sweeps in which *matatu* and bus drivers are "netted" for overloading their vehicles, leaving their passengers stranded – usually at rush hour when they cause maximum chaos.

The main KBS city **bus terminus** is off the bottom end of River Road, behind the bizarre-looking Siri Guru Singh Sabha Temple on Uyoma Street. Other principal bus and *matatu* stops include Ambassadeur Hotel/Hilton (on Moi Ave), Nation House (top of Tom Mboya St) and the old post office on Kenyatta Avenue.

Finding accommodation

Finding a place to stay in Nairobi isn't usually difficult. Hotels are rarely full even during the peak season (exceptions noted below), and it's only during the occasional large international conferences that you may have problems finding a room. The main question is which area fits your needs: the city lacks a long established focus, so travellers end up congregating at a number of different spots. The following listings are arranged by approximate location, and then roughly in ascending order of price. If you're arriving in town very early, beware that most places won't allow you to take a room before 10am.

OMETHING COMPLETELY DIFFEREN

For a total change of atmosphere, you might think about taking a bus out to EASTLEIGH (the main KBS depot is there, so an endless stream of buses goes there from the centre). Eastleigh is low-rise, dusty, scruffy, with its parallel streets fading east into dry scrub and no-man's-land, north to the slum wilderness of Mathare Valley. Eastleigh is also the focus for Ethiopian and Somalian refugees in Nairobi, and offers an entirely different cultural milieu from the one you may have grown used to around River Road. Not very promising perhaps. Yet the *New Paradiso Hotel* (corner of First Ave and Tenth St, very near the bus depot) is one of the nicest in Kenya. Accommodation is in itself nothing special (Ksh40/bed in triple rooms), but the owner is charming and the Ethiopian food in the restaurant delicious: many varieties of *wat* with *njera*, with great Amharic music in the background and no shortage of interesting conversation.

East Nairobi and the River Road area

The **very cheapest lodgings** are around River Road, the main drag through the city's poorest quarter. In most of the following you can expect to run into other travellers, but numerous others, particularly towards the country bus station, may be as good as – or even better than – these. For a different experience, or if you're genuinely broke, you might try the welcoming **Sikh temple** on Gaberone Road. Rooms and meals are free, though you are expected to leave a donation.

Cheap lodgings

Iqbal Hotel (PO Box 11256, ☎220914), Latema Rd. Number one in the travellers' popularity stakes for several years now: secure, with hot water available every day, and cleaner than you might expect (Ksh75/bed in a dormitory or triple room, Ksh150/double room). They do a good laundry service (charges per item, no underwear!) and there's a safe, lock-up store for daytime use if you check out in the morning. The lobby area has a vast, dark hall of a restaurant with reliable, tasty food: a good rendezvous. Go early and put your name on the room waiting list for a day or so if necessary. It's worth making a booking by phone.

Sunrise Lodge (PO Box 48224, ☎330362), Latema Rd. Small, secure and well kept, but lacks communal areas; some rooms are exceptionally noisy due to its location next to the *Modern Green Bar* (Ksh130/single, Ksh180/double bed, Ksh270/twin beds). Don't dawdle after dark in the alley between them.

New Kenya Lodge (PO Box 43444, ☎222202), River Rd, end of Latema Rd. Although it has a popular communal terrace, security is very iffy – roof sleepers have nowhere to keep their bags. Friendly, cheap, and unhygienic, sporadically cliquey, no hot water (Ksh30/roof, Ksh65/dormitory bed, Ksh130/double room).

Naseem's B&L (PO Box 42341, ☎20038), River Rd, just west of Latema Rd. Very clean and safe (Ksh180/double s/c B&B).

Hotel Bujumbura, Dubois Rd off Latema Rd. A very ordinary place but utterly dependable.

New Safe Life B&L (PO Box 10035, ☎221578), Dubois Rd, directly opposite the Bujumbura. Lives modestly up to its name, with large rooms, a splash of hot water and average hygiene (Ksh100/120).

West View Hotel, Kijabe St, off the roundabout at the north end of River Rd. Basic rooms, but good value and secure (Ksh 120/room).

Abbey Hotel (PO Box 75260, ☎331487), Gaberone Rd. Not bad either but rowdier (Ksh140/210 B&B, Ksh 200/single s/c B&B).

Dolat Hotel (PO Box 45613, ☎22797), Mfangano St. Exceptionally clean, friendly and excellent value (Ksh180/240 s/c B&B). Highly recommended – the best of the cheapies.

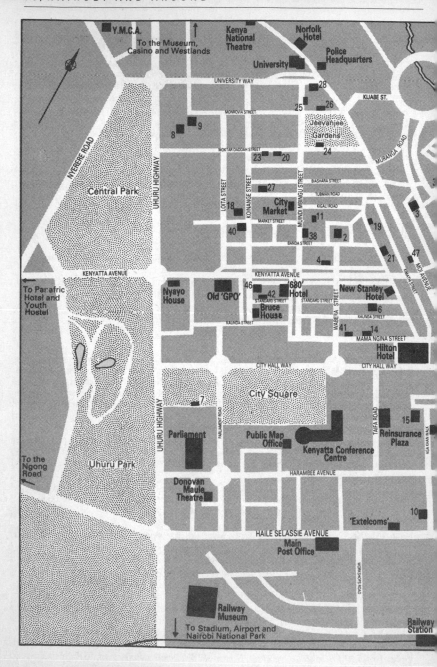

Y.M.C.A.

To the Museum,
Casino and Westlands

Kenya
National
Theatre

Norfolk
Hotel

University

Police
Headquarters

UNIVERSITY WAY

28

KIJABE ST.

MONROVIA STREET

25

26

MURANGA ROAD

9

8

Jeevanjee
Gardens

24

INYERERE ROAD

MOKTAR DADOAH STREET

23

20

BASHARA STREET

UHURU HIGHWAY

Central Park

LOITA STREET

KOINANGE STREET

27

City
Market

MUINDI MBINGU STREET

TUBMAN ROAD

KIGALI ROAD

18

11

3

MARKET STREET

40

38

2

19

BANDA STREET

KENYATTA AVENUE

4

21

47

KENYATTA AVENUE

To Parafric
Hotel and
Youth
Hostel

Nyayo
House

Old 'GPO'

46

'680'
Hotel

New Stanley
Hotel

STANDARD STREET

42

STANDARD STREET

WABERA STREET

MOI AVENUE

TAIFA STREET

Bruce
House

6

KAUNDA STREET

KAUNDA STREET

41

14

MAMA NGINA STREET

Hilton
Hotel

CITY HALL WAY

CITY HALL WAY

UHURU HIGHWAY

7

City Square

To the
Ngong
Road

Uhuru Park

Parliament

PARLIAMENT ROAD

Public Map
Office

Kenyatta Conference
Centre

TAIFA ROAD

15

Reinsurance
Plaza

AGA KHAN WALK

HARAMBEE AVENUE

Donovan
Maule
Theatre

10

'Extelcoms'

HAILE SELASSIE AVENUE

Main
Post Office

DUBOIS ROAD

Railway
Museum

To Stadium, Airport and
Nairobi National Park

Railway
Station

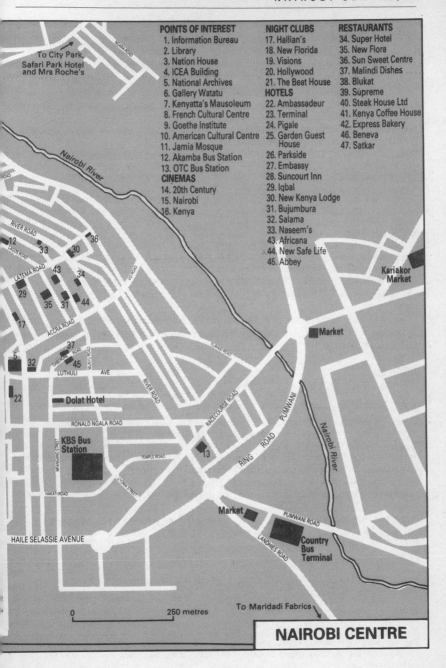

POINTS OF INTEREST
1. Information Bureau
2. Library
3. Nation House
4. ICEA Building
5. National Archives
6. Gallery Watatu
7. Kenyatta's Mausoleum
8. French Cultural Centre
9. Goethe Institute
10. American Cultural Centre
11. Jamia Mosque
12. Akamba Bus Station
13. OTC Bus Station

CINEMAS
14. 20th Century
15. Nairobi
16. Kenya

NIGHT CLUBS
17. Hallian's
18. New Florida
19. Visions
20. Hollywood
21. The Beat House

HOTELS
22. Ambassadeur
23. Terminal
24. Pigale
25. Garden Guest House
26. Parkside
27. Embassy
28. Suncourt Inn
29. Iqbal
30. New Kenya Lodge
31. Bujumbura
32. Salama
33. Naseem's
43. Africana
44. New Safe Life
45. Abbey

RESTAURANTS
34. Super Hotel
35. New Flora
36. Sun Sweet Centre
37. Malindi Dishes
38. Blukat
39. Supreme
40. Steak House Ltd
41. Kenya Coffee House
42. Express Bakery
46. Beneva
47. Satkar

To City Park, Safari Park Hotel and Mrs Roche's

Nairobi River

RIVER ROAD

LATEMA ROAD

ACCRA ROAD

LUTHULI AVE

Dolat Hotel

RONALD NGALA ROAD

KBS Bus Station

TEMPLE ROAD

MFANGANO STREET

HAKATI ROAD

HAILE SELASSIE AVENUE

Kariakor Market

Market

RACECOURSE ROAD

RING ROAD

PUMWANI ROAD

Nairobi River

Market

Country Bus Terminal

LANDHIES ROAD

To Maridadi Fabrics

0   250 metres

NAIROBI CENTRE

Pricier lodgings

Paris Rest House and **Mecca**, both on Mfangano St. Reasonable abodes and both in the Ksh200–300 bracket.

Hotel Africana (PO Box 47827, ☎20654), Dubois Rd. Recommended if you want to be near the Latema Rd area but need a little more luxury, this is clean, shiny, comfortable (Ksh275/ 350 s/c B&B). They do an excellent breakfast here – and good coffee at all hours.

Hotel Salama (PO Box 28675, ☎225898), Luthuli Ave. Sometimes used by travellers (Ksh360/420 s/c B&B).

Sagret Hotel (PO Box 18324, ☎333395), corner of River and Gaberone Rds. Comfortable and rooms even have phones (Ksh300/400 s/c B&B).

Hotel Hermes (PO Box 62997, ☎340066), corner of Moi and Haile Selassie Aves, close to the American embassy. New, well located and good value for home comforts, if a little noisy (Ksh385/550 B&B).

Solace Hotel (PO Box 48867, ☎331277), Tom Mboya St. At Ksh445/665 s/c, this feels overpriced.

City centre

There are a number of **medium-priced places** on the west side of Moi Avenue up near Jeevanjee Gardens and City Market. For the faint-hearted, this may be a better prospect than the River Road area – quieter and possibly safer (at least more salubrious). The listings below include a couple of useful, more outlying addresses.

Central Nairobi also has over twenty real **luxury places** and many more trailing close behind. Some are a rip-off. These recommended places all have private facilities (fully s/c).

Mid-range

Terminal Hotel (PO Box 43229, ☎228817), Moktar Daddah St, across from the *Kenya Airways* terminus. Reasonable rooms (Ksh220/265 s/c B&B) and the adjoining *Fransae Bar & Restaurant* is an excellent curry place and bar.

Hotel Pigale, Moktar Daddah St. Very variable – sometimes fine and other times lousy – literally (Ksh220/260 s/c). Peace corps volunteers get special rates.

Garden Guest House (PO Box 56301, ☎335742) (Ksh220/270 s/c B&B) and **Parkside Hotel** (PO Box 39695, ☎333445) (Ksh 220/300 s/c B&B), both across Jeevanjee Gardens on Monrovia St. Both okay, the second slightly the better of the two.

Hotel Embassy (PO Box 47247, ☎24087), Tubman Rd, right behind the City Market. Scruffy but clean and quite decent, with ancient telephones lovingly preserved in some rooms – they don't all work (Ksh350/480 s/c B&B).

Suncourt Inn (PO Box 51454, ☎21413/8), University Way. Seems a touch expensive but it's not at all bad, right on top of the *Norfolk* and totally unpatronised by tourists – plus the phones work (Ksh425/620 s/c B&B).

New Ainsworth Hotel, top of Museum Hill. Attractively decrepit and excellent value (around Ksh300/400 s/c B&B), across from the casino, regrettably in an area dubious after dark.

Plums 1977 Hotel, Ojijo Rd, Parklands. A pleasant establishment, with good car security if you're driving (Ksh500/600).

Upmarket

Meridian Court Hotel (PO Box 30278, ☎333916), Murang'a Rd, off the top of River Rd, on the way out to Parklands. From around Ksh500/800, with volunteer's rates much reduced (peace corps rate Ksh800/triple). Rooms with kitchenettes, nice staff, underground car park, rooftop pool.

Hotel Ambassadeur (PO Box 30399, ☎336803), Moi Ave. Another modern, all-amenities hotel, but surprisingly noisy. If possible get a double-glazed, top floor room (Ksh720/1200).

Oakwood Hotel (PO Box 40683, ☎20592), Kimathi St across from the *Thorn Tree*. An older place with a low profile but good facilities and unbeatable convenience (Ksh950/1150).

Hotel Boulevard (PO Box 42831, ☎27567), Harry Thuku Rd by the Museum. Well cared-for, in a pleasant setting and with a good pool (Ksh980/1360), this is perhaps the best mid-range address in the city.

680 Hotel (PO Box 43436, ☎332680), corner of Kenyatta Ave and Muindi Mbingu St (Ksh995/1515). Dependable, comfortable and right in the heart of the city. Safe car park and convenient for shopping, but soulless.

New Stanley (PO Box 30680, ☎333233), Kimathi St. Complete with its famous Thorn Tree rendezvous, an (originally) Edwardian hotel and a popular downtown base for American package tours. Reports vary greatly, but at Ksh1800/1950, it's not bad value at this level.

The Norfolk (PO Box 40064, ☎335422 or 24201), Harry Thuku Rd. The usual haunt of celebrities visiting Nairobi – unless they're ensconced in the stratospheric reserve of the *Nairobi Safari Club* not far away – and one of the few expensive places really worthy of major outlay. You may not choose to throw it all away on a room (although in harsh international terms, Ksh2480/3710 seems fair for what you get), but a drink on the hotel's Lord Delamere terrace is always fun, though costs rather more than it would in a Day & Night Club on River Road.

Out of central Nairobi

Two of the city's main **travellers' focuses** are not downtown and both have their devotees. Fortunately the suburbs are only a short journey out of the city centre. Also somewhat out of the centre are some of the city's nicest hotels.

Travellers' Roosts

The **Nairobi Youth Hostel** (PO Box 48661, ☎723012), on Ralph Bunche Rd (many buses including #34 from the airport), is a gentle introduction to the city, full most of the time (Ksh60/bed in dorm, some private rooms for married couples). You have to have IYHA membership (Ksh175 here) and put up with usual YH rules. The small compound can get claustrophobic, and it's a bad idea to walk into town after dark. Still, it's a well-run place with lots of other hostellers to talk to and an informative **visitor's book and notice board**.

Also cheap and out of town, but tending to cater to a different brand of traveller, is **Mrs Roche's Guest House**, Third Parklands Avenue, opposite the Aga Khan Hospital in the predominantly Asian suburb of Parklands (bus #107 or ask a *matatu* for Aga Khan). Take a bed either in one of the cabins or in Mrs Roche's bungalow (Ksh50–70), or else camp in the garden or sleep on the veranda (Ksh40 each). The meditative ambience is popular with worn-out motorised overlanders and travellers who really loathe Nairobi. Fall into either category and you should love it. It is a good place to meet people and it's often possible to fix up shared arrangements to drive to the game parks. There's also a convenient lock-up store (Ksh20/week) to leave surplus gear while you travel.

Out of centre hotels

Among a number of places in a **wide range of prices**, within easy reach of the centre by public transport:

Hurlingham Hotel (PO Box 43158, ☎721920 or 723001), Argwings Kodhek Rd (buses #46, #56). An inexpressible pre-war feeling lingers here: highly recommended if you can get a room and well worth making a booking (Ksh360/575 non s/c B&B).

The Fairview (PO Box 40842, ☎723210), Bishops Rd behind the functional *Panafric Hotel* (many buses). Peaceful – and very popular, so reserve ahead – country-style place with a refreshing lack of uniformity (B&B Ksh700/1100 s/c, with some cheaper rooms). Guests can use the pool at the *Panafric*.

The Jacaranda, Westlands (PO Box 14287, ☎742272). A popular base for some of the expedition-type package tours, and getting expensive these days (Ksh1580 per person B&B); free bus service to the city centre.

Utalii Hotel (PO Box 31067, ☎802540), 6km out on the road to Thika (buses #43, 44, 45 and #143, 144, 145, plus hotel buses for guests). This offers something different, with unbeatable standards. It's run by the Utalii ("tourism") College, so you get impeccable, if slightly hesitant, service (Ksh1045/1360 s/c B&B). Facing it, across the banana tops, sprawls one of Nairobi's worst slums – Mathare Valley.

Camping

If you have your own transport and *Mrs Roche's* is full, try:

Rowallen Scout Camp (PO Box 30176, ☎566655), a long-dormant, but now up-and-running site in Jamhuri Park, just off Ngong Road before the racecourse. Facilities are basic – Ksh40 a night – and unfortunately you can't safely leave your gear for the day.

Long stays

For long stays in Nairobi, check out the central **YMCA** (PO Box 63063, ☎724066), on State House Road, on the west side of Uhuru near the university. Monthly rates are around Ksh10,500 for a single room, Ksh13,200 sharing a double, on a full board basis only. There's a *YWCA* (PO Box 40710, ☎558982) on Mamlaka Rd, off Nyerere Avenue (Ksh135 per person or Ksh95 in dorms). There are other *YMCA*s in Muhoho Avenue (☎504896), off the Langata Road in South "C" and on Ambira Road (☎558383) in Shauri Moyo district. You won't run into many other *wazungu* travellers at these latter two.

Heron Court Apartment Hotel (PO Box 41063, ☎720740), Milimani Road, much used by volunteers and their kin, is fine, especially if self-catering appeals (s/c rooms Ksh390/450, double self-catering apartment Ksh480, with long-stay discounts: Ksh8600/9600 per month). There's a pool and two restaurants.

Lastly, cheap **flats, rooms and studios** are advertised in the classified columns of the *Nation* and the *Standard*. Remember, if the place has no *askari* (security guard), the danger of burglary is very real.

Around central Nairobi

Kenyatta Avenue is the obvious place to start looking around Central Nairobi. A good initial overview of it – and lots else besides – can be had from the vertigo-inducing, glass-walled lifts in the **ICEA building**, on the northwest corner of Wabera Street. If the guards at the bottom need an excuse, tell them you're visiting the Japanese Embassy on the 17th floor; they may even be persuaded to escort you onto the roof.

Kenyatta Avenue

Kenyatta Avenue was originally designed to allow a twelve-oxen-team to make a full turn. Broad, multi-laned and planted with flowering trees and shrubs, it remains (along with the Kenyatta Conference Centre) the capital's favourite tourist image. The avenue is smartest – and most touristy – on its south side, with would-be moneychangers and itinerant souvenir hawkers assailing you from every direction, and shoeshiners inspecting each passing pair of feet from their stands. The focus of the avenue's eastern end is the *New Stanley Hotel's* (PO Box 30680, ☎333233)*Thorn Tree Café*, opposite *Woolworth's* on the corner of Kimathi Street. The *Thorn Tree* is Nairobi's one proper pavement café and, despite irritatingly slow service ("we are stocktaking"), an enduring meeting place. Around the imposing thorn tree in question is a message board, intended for personal notes but always worth scanning for vehicle-sharing deals, unused air tickets for sale, and so on.

Proceeding to the other end of Kenyatta Avenue, you come to the site of the old General Post Office and, just before it, **Koinange Street**, named after the Kikuyu Senior Chief Koinange of the colonial era. Here, too, is the peculiar Galton-Fenzi memorial, a monument to the man who founded, of all things, the Nairobi branch of the *Automobile Association*. Fenzi was also the first motorist to drive from Nairobi to Mombasa, back in 1926.

City Square and Parliament

Head down Koinange Street and on to Kaunda Street, passing the *Intercontinental* (PO Box 30667, ☎335550) on your right and, crossing City Hall Way, enter **City Square**. This is Nairobi's showplace. Jomo Kenyatta's statue sits benevolently, mace in hand, on the far side of the wide, flagstoned court; his mausoleum, with flickering eternal flames, is on the right as you approach the Parliament building. When the flags are out for a conference it all looks very bright and confident.

Kenya's parliament is open to the public. Talk to the guards at the gate, who will tell you when the next session is taking place or, when it's not in session, how to get a tour of the building. If you're assigned a guide make sure both parties are clear about how much you'll pay.

To sit in the public gallery you must first register at the gatehouse on the corner of Parliament Road and **Harambee Avenue**, leaving all your belongings with the attendant outside. Once seated, be on your best behaviour. The gallery tends to be full (of very well-behaved school children), which of course is more than can be said for the chamber (or the members of parliament). Don't expect any startling revelations: the tone of debate is aptly suggested by the legend over the main doors, "For a Just Society and the Fair Government of Men". But try to get hold of a copy of the Orders of the Day; there may be a juicy question or two worth anticipating.

Kenyatta Conference Centre

From Parliament, walking down Harambee Avenue along the shady pavement, you come to Nairobi's pride and joy – the **Kenyatta Conference Centre** and its tall brother, "KANU tower", the party headquarters (all enquiries ☎332383). This, the tallest building in Kenya, is capped by a spacey-looking, mile-high, revolving restaurant (a mile above sea level that is). Confusion has always arisen on the *ground* floor about whether anyone was allowed up to the 28th. It now seems the restaurant has closed anyway, but it's worth making an effort to get as high as possible; try talking to the security staff in the foyer. Assent is given for ascent possibly only on weekdays. The view of Nairobi is without equal and a firm reminder of the vastness of Africa. Just 4km to the south, you see the Mombasa Road leave the suburbs behind and take off across the yellow plains. Northwards, hills of coffee – and, at higher altitudes, tea – roll into the distance. If you pick a good day in December or January you really can see Mount Kenya in one direction and Kilimanjaro in the other. Immediately below, the traffic swarms and Jogoo House is suddenly seen to be built remarkably like a Roman villa.

National Archives

Straight down Harambee Avenue, cut across Moi Avenue and up to the **National Archives** (PO Box 49210, ☎749341). Housed in the striking old Bank of India building on the bend of Moi Avenue across from the Hilton, they amount to a **museum/art gallery** which few visitors to Nairobi seem to know about: entry is free and a look around should take an hour or so (Mon–Fri 8am–4.30pm).

The ground floor is a public gallery with Joseph Murumbi's (briefly vice-president under Kenyatta) oddball collection of paintings dominating the walls. The collection, sold to the government in 1966, ranges from uninteresting dabbles to some beautiful drawings and striking collages, but in a city that's not exactly cluttered with art collections, it does deserve a look. It's a shame there doesn't seem to be any information available about the artists, many of whom were students. In the centre of the floor there's also a fair amount of anonymous ethnographia – musical instruments, weapons, domestic artefacts – all catalogued but unlabelled. The actual archives are closed to the public, though if you're determined you can pay a small fee for six months' membership.

More rewarding, and immediate, is the second-floor collection of black-and-white press photos, highly revealing as a record of the early part of Daniel Arap Moi's presidency, with foreign tours figuring prominently. There's also a number of fascinating portraits of tribal elders, mostly from the colonial era.

Cultural venues

To get an idea of the image the United States would like to project to Kenyans, call in at the **American Cultural Centre** (PO Box 30143, ☎337877, back along Harambee, then turn right up Aga Khan Walk), on the main floor of the National Bank building. On Thursday and Friday at 11am you can see excerpts from the previous week's ABC news. A well-stocked library and a periodicals room are available for the purpose of letting "ideas contest in an open marketplace", as the leaflet prosaically puts it. Perhaps more palatable are the two or three feature films shown every month (details in monthly programmes).

Apart from occasional exhibitions, the only art galleries deserving the name (other than the National Archives) are the two **Gallery Watatu** exhibition spaces on Standard Street (PO Box 41855, ☎28737). The work here, usually by East African artists, is often a lot better than the popular elephants-in-a-dustbowl school of painting. The gallery is also the venue for occasional "alternative" events.

With a few exceptions, things to do north of Kenyatta Avenue have a commercial bent. Two slightly out-of-the-way places which you might not otherwise notice are the **French Cultural Centre** (PO Box 49415, ☎336263), and the **Göethe Institut** (PO Box 49468, ☎24640), both of which pursue their activities rather less chauvinistically than the US of A. Both places are at the top of Loita Street near Uhuru Highway. The *Göethe Institut* puts on art exhibitions (German and Kenyan) and has a monthly programme of subtitled German films. The *French Cultural Centre* operates a more dynamic and better-financed programme, offering a space for Kenyan dance and theatre as well as staging events and activities derived from France. Currently the most active cultural and intellectual focus in Nairobi, it's well worth checking out during your stay and has a good restaurant – see p.75.

The Jamia Mosque

If you've never been inside a mosque, have a look around the **Jamia mosque** across from the City Market. The ornate green and white exterior is a striking contrast to the simple interior. The inside is typically roomy and uncluttered, with the large central dome appearing much bigger from beneath than it did from the courtyard outside. Although most Kenyan towns now have at least one mosque, often financed by Saudi Arabia, few are as large or as beautiful as the Jamia in Nairobi. For a bird's-eye view of the mosque, the top of the ICEA building is (again!) a good vantage point.

The museums and parks

Covered here are the handful of parks and museums in Nairobi itself. Nairobi National Park gets separate coverage in the Nairobi Province section later in this chapter (see p.91), as do the *Bomas of Kenya*, the *Karen Blixen Museum* and the *Langata Giraffe Centre*. Unless you have your own wheels you may be better off joining a tour for them. The following sites, however, are all easily walkable.

The National Museum

Open daily 9.30am–6pm; Ksh100 for non-Kenyans, Ksh10 for Kenyans; guides available on request, free (PO Box 40658, ☎742161).

The National Museum is without a doubt the city's prime sightseeing attraction but surprisingly few travellers make the small effort to get to it. You should: it's the best possible prelude to any tour around the country, and it's only about a half-hour walk from Kenyatta Avenue – less by bus (#119 from Moi Ave or #23 from the *Hilton*). If possible, allow yourself a morning or afternoon to look around thoroughly.

Natural history

The museum's most extensive collections are **ornithological**, with most of Kenya's thousand-plus species of birds represented. Kenya's birdlife usually makes a strong impression, even on non-birders. Look out for the various species of hornbills, turacos and rollers, and for the extraordinary standard-wing nightjar, which frequently has people doing a double-take the first time they see it flutter-ing low over a swimming pool at dusk in its hunt for insects. There's also a multi-tude of stuffed game heads, dioramas of Kenyan mammals, casts of fish, even a whale skeleton, as well as a fibreglass replica of the famous elephant from Marsabit, "Ahmed".

Human prehistory

The special interest of Nairobi's museum, however, lies in the human (and quasi-human) and cultural exhibits. The room where the **palaeontology** exhibits are housed has walls disguised with stunning reproductions of a series of Tanzanian rock paintings. Ahead, on the floor, is a cast of wide-splayed, human-looking footprints – the small pair following in the prints of the larger one – which were discovered at Laetoli in Tanzania. They belong, almost certainly, to *Homo erectus*, believed to be the direct ancestor of our own species. They were squeezed into the mud about fifteen hundred *thousand* years ago. Down the hall, brilliant and eerily life-sized reconstructions of a family of *erectus* wolfing down an antelope carcass, as well as other dioramas of the more primitive (and ultimately unsuccessful) australopithecines, bring the story of human evolution vividly to life. Notice the nearby photographic wall display entitled "From Space Age to Stone Age", subtitled "Cities, Dancing, Space Craft, Industry, Farming, Starvation . . .", etc.

Ethnography and history

In contrast, the rather dry second-floor cases of **ethnographic** odds and ends aren't awfully illuminating. It's not that the exhibits are uninteresting in themselves, and the beadwork jewellery is certainly magnificent, it's just that, on the whole, they're unimaginatively displayed. But if you're planning on travelling through any of the areas inhabited by pastoral peoples (especially Samburu, Maasai or Turkana), then seeing some old and authentic handicrafts beforehand is a good idea. This will also be a big help when you find yourself faced with, for example, an urgent salesman offering you a dozen different carved headrests – not an uncommon experience. The collections indicate the tremendous diversity of Kenya's cultures, a quality also impressively evoked by Joy Adamson's series of ethnic portraits, despite the fact that these have to be flipped through like a rack of posters (her beautiful **botanical paintings** are better displayed).

The **photographic exhibition** of the **struggle for independence** is compelling – not just for its content but because this is almost the only public place where Kenyans can be reminded of the period in their history euphemistically called "The Emergency".

A final museum recommendation is the **Swahili room** on the main floor, which contains an excellent exhibition of work being carried out for the Lamu Conservation Project. If you're going there, this mustn't be missed.

The Snake Park and Aquarium
Same prices and times as the museum.

Opposite the museum and going downhill (in both senses of the word) is the **Snake Park**. It's only fair to say that you'd have to be very enthusiastic about reptiles to find this interesting, and very insensitive to find it enjoyable. Exhibits take in East African and American snakes, a crocodile or two, some murky terrapins, emaciated monitor lizards and some boring fish tanks. There are much better (and cheaper) snake parks on the coast.

The Railway Museum

Open daily 8.30am–4.45pm (closes 3.30 Sat); Ksh10.

Underrated and almost unnoticed, Nairobi's **Railway Museum** is a natural draw for rail fans and of passing interest for anyone else. Signposted, ten minutes' walk from the station, it's a drag to report several grab-and-run robberies down here of late: perhaps go in a group, or a taxi, or without valuables.

The main hall contains a mass of memorabilia: photos of early stations, of the line being built, and the engineering feats involved in getting the carriages up and down the escarpment, drawings of the plans, and strange pieces of hardware, such as the game-viewing seat mounted at the front of the train. Passengers who risked this perch were reminded that "The High Commissioner will not be liable for personal injury (fatal or otherwise)". In the museum annex, the motorised bicycle inspection trolley is quite a sight but, as the write-up explains, the experiment in the 1950s "was not really successful", as the wheels kept slipping off the rail.

The engines
Outside, rustingly exposed to the elements, is the museum's collection of old **locomotives**. Most of what you see was built in England. You can clamber inside any of the cabs to play with the massive levers and switches. The restriction of forward visibility on some of the engines seems incredible: the driver of the Karamoja Express couldn't have had any idea what was in front of him while steaming down a straight line. If it fills you with nostalgic delight, this is a good place to tell you that Nairobi and Mombasa stations both have locomotive grave-yards which, with enthusiastic persistence, you should be able to look around.

Lions figure prominently in the early history of the Uganda railway: look in the shed for first-class coach no. 12 to learn the story of Superintendent C. H. Ryall. He was dragged from this car and devoured by a lion: he'd dozed off while waiting for the beast to appear so he could shoot it. The coach, together with the repainted loco no. 301, took part in the filming of *Out of Africa* at Kajiado.

The city's parks

A colour map of Nairobi suggests a multitude of cool green spaces around the city. The parks aren't always very inviting, but several are pleasant places to retreat to for a while. Biggest and best is **City Park** in the north, a half-hour stroll from the National Museum down Forest Road and Limuru Road, or by bus #107 from Nation House or #19 from the *Iqbal*. City Park has a wealth of tropical trees and birdlife, several troops of vervet monkeys, a small stream with wooden bridges, gravel paths, shady lawns, and, on weekends, families everywhere. During the week it's delightful, though not for women alone. And as usual, hang onto your possessions.

The Arboretum (bus #48, Hilton) is less frequented and in a predominantly European, as opposed to Asian, district. Somewhat overgrown, almost jungly in parts, it is still a lovely place to wander or picnic, and, of course, a must if you're botanically inclined. You may be reassured – or unnerved – by the officious plain clothes policemen who stalk the glades.

Uhuru and Central parks, on the western side of Uhuru Highway, have the city's worst reputation for muggings, particularly after dark. They're unfenced and never closed but to walk across either park after 6pm is, to put it mildly, asking for trouble. It's probably safe to take a rowing boat out on the lake in Uhuru Park on a Sunday afternoon.

In a more reputable part of the city, try **Jeevanjee gardens**, especially during a weekday lunchtime when you can picnic on a bench and chat with the office workers who aren't thronging the nearby restaurants. You can listen, too, to the preachers who have recently made Jeevanjee their church and the bemused picnickers their congregation.

Markets and shopping

It doesn't take long to realise that commerce is Nairobi's *raison d'être*. Disappointingly perhaps, the form trade takes here is not always very exotic. But Nairobi is the best place in East Africa to buy **handicrafts**, with the widest (if not the cheapest) selection and the best facilities for posting the stuff home. The city also has some lavish **produce markets**, enjoyable even if you only want to browse.

Bargaining is expected at all Nairobi's markets and most shops, with the exception of supermarkets and stores selling imported goods.

Produce markets and food

It doesn't offer the city's lowest prices, but for a colourful and high-quality range of fruits and vegetables the **City Market** is the obvious target. If you're buying, the best-value stalls are in the outside aisle flanking the main hall on the right. Fish and meat are on either side of the main building, and the supermarket at the entrance has a good variety of Kenyan cheeses.

The other large produce markets are the **Wakulima** (farmers) market, a cavernous and dank hall at the bottom of River Road, just before the country bus station (fruit and vegetables are pretty cheap here), and a good, open-air one at the end of Racecourse Road, just across the Nairobi River. If you're staying at *Mrs Roche's*, the fruit stalls on the corner of Limuru and Forest roads are handy and inexpensive. And there are usually dozens of children and young women selling a few oranges, mangoes, whatever, on street corners. Blink, and they may be gone, tipped off that city *askaris* are about to "swoop". So buy from them while you have the chance.

There are **supermarkets and groceries** all over the city. Better than most, with a fast turnover, is *K & A* on Koinange Street, right by the old post office. An excellent **bakery**, with daily supplies of fresh rye and wholegrain bread, is *Express Bakery*, just around the corner on Standard Street.

Crafts and fabrics

For the exhausting business of **buying crafts and curios**, it's advisable to decide what you want before stepping into a shop or looking at a stall. At some of the more pretentious places you can browse for ages undisturbed, but at the cheaper outlets dilly-dallying is not encouraged and the pressure may be on to part with your "quids". So, purely for browsing, visit *African Heritage* (PO Box 17871, ☎3233157), on the north side of Kenyatta Avenue, which has (some) beautiful things at absurd prices. It's the largest curio shop in Nairobi, with eager suppliers in many parts of Africa, not only Kenya.

Elsewhere, there are dozens, maybe hundreds, of **artefact shops** and, depending on any number of factors, you might get a good deal at almost any of them. Clearly, however, the cheaper prices will usually be at places where they don't have to pay a shop rent – street stands and market booths. Once again the booths at the City Market are an obvious choice, especially for soapstone, batiks and, to the back, off Koinange Street, basketwork, but the whole area is something of a tourist trap. Better deals are found at a handful of stands in the square between the City Market and Jamia Mosque, and in clusters south of Kenyatta between Muindi Mbingu and Kimathi. If you have any skill at bargaining, you should get a good deal at all these stands. Be aware, however, that the "last price" will vary seasonally and can skyrocket when a major conference hits town.

For Maasai traditional and tourist gear, the **Maasai Market** every Tuesday from 9am to 3pm is a hot recommendation. Twenty or thirty Maasai women set up stalls in the empty lot behind Chester House, between Loita Street and Uhuru Highway. You'll find prices here well below those in any tourist mart, or even in the Narok/Mara area.

A real artisan's market is **Kariakor Market** (buses #6, #7, #8, #9, *Ambassadeur* plus others), and this is undoubtedly the place in Nairobi to buy *vyondo* (sisal bags). Inside and outside the market there are thousands of baskets available, and since many are made here, you can buy just the basket without the leather pieces or straps which raise the price. Long sisal straps can be bought separately for a few shillings. *Vyondo* come in sisal, coloured with natural or artificial dyes, in garish plastic, or in cord manufactured from the bark of the baobab tree. Some of these last baskets are truly exquisite, occasionally quite old, with tiny beads included in the tight weave.

Kariakor, (named after the wartime "Carrier Corps") is closer to an oriental bazaar than most markets in Kenya, with permanent booths for the traders. Inside, there's as much manufacture and finishing going on as selling – sisal weavers, leather workers, makers of tire-rubber sandals, carpenters, tailors, hairdressers and a row of good, very cheap, amazingly clean eateries, popular at lunchtime with local workers. A number of booths sell vaguely pharmaceutical oddities – snuff, remedies, charms, amulets, etc – where you can pick up anything from feathers to snakeskin.

Buying curios from strolling vendors is generally unwise. You're not going to get a good deal from a cruising hawker, whose wares are almost bound to be low quality. Furthermore, while you're being distracted on one side, you may be being ripped off on the other. The "elephant hair" bracelets, incidentally, often are just that – collected, they say, not poached. When lit, strands should smell of burnt hair. Some smell of burnt grass, which is what they are.

For everyday **general merchandise stores**, the eastern part of the City Market district is the most worthwhile area. Biashara (Commerce) Street is the street for fabrics and the best place to buy a mosquito net; Tubman Road and Kigali Road have a lot of open-fronted (and tight-fisted) groceries with dry food in sacks. As it happens, this part of the city has retained its earlier character fairly well. The upper part of Moi Avenue is Nairobi's busiest ordinary shopping street, all colonnaded shop-fronts and antiquated name-boards, fun to wander past.

ELEPHANT HAIR

These accounts come from bracelet salesmen asked about how they obtained the hair: "We follow the animal softly and when it goes to sleep we sneak up quietly and cut off the tail hair with scissors." "We follow the animal, then when it goes to sleep all the hairs fall out and then we collect them in the morning when the animal has gone away". Suggestions that they shot the elephants between the eyes with an elephant gun were met with convincingly reproachful tongue-clicking. Maybe it's all true.

CHARITY CRAFT SHOPS

Nairobi has a growing number of crafts shops with charitable status, or based on development projects. Although sometimes a little expensive – and you can't bargain – they are worthy of support, and often have unusual, and well-made stock (some of which finds its way into the Christmas charity catalogues overseas). *Maridadi* and *Undugu* are both a little way out of town, but well worth making special journeys to visit – both of them good tonics if you're suffering from shopper's fatigue.

Cottage Crafts Phoenix Arcade, Standard St. Run by *Jisaidie* (self-help) *Cottage Industries*, this crafts and clothing shop always has good stuff at fair prices, supplied directly by various self-help groups around the country.

The Spinner's Web, behind the Norfolk Hotel. A large shop, with a Germanic influence detectable, selling a lot of good stuff – crafts, textiles, woollen goods and jewellery much of it made by self-help groups, and much like *Cottage Crafts*, more extensively displayed.

Spin 'n' Weave Shop, corner of Mama Ngina and Wabera Sts. A sumptuous selection of woollen goods; expensive, but produced by self-help weaving projects in Eastleigh and Nanyuki (where a branch is located), so your money is well spent.

Undugu, Woodvale Grove, Westlands, behind the shopping centre (☎745207 open Mon–Fri 8.30am–5pm). This is the *Undugu* (brotherhood) society's retail outlet, helping raise funds for a rapidly expanding list of development and community self-help programmes, notably for the homeless and jobless, young men in particular. With its roots in the church, *Undugu* is the most vigorous society of its kind in Kenya, and, by promoting cooperation, goes some way to patching up the worst effects of the struggle for existence in Nairobi. The shop sells a good selection of well-priced, **high-quality crafts** with some unusual items as well, such as **Ethiopian jewellery and basketwork**. A free **booklet** about the Undugu society is available and you may be able to have a look around the workshops.

Maridadi Fabrics, city stadium roundabout, a kilometre past the main entrance to the country bus station (PO Box 16254, ☎554288, Mon–Fri 8am–5pm). Take a bus #21, #22, #34, #36 from *Ambassadeur*. Church-based, like *Undugu*, *Maridadi* was created in 1966 as an income-generating community project for women in one of Nairobi's oldest slum areas – Pumwani and Shauri Moyo. It's a delight for people who are into making their own clothes. A large screen-printing workshop (on view from the visitors' gallery) produces the wide range of prints for sale in the shop; the bark cloth prints are especially appealing. **Bark cloth**, a natural weave obtained from beneath the outer bark of certain trees, is soaked, stretched, hammered before use, and was used for clothing by many East African peoples until the end of the last century.

In the district around Maridadi, there's a tremendous diversity of enterprises, with two distinctive market areas – **Gikomba** (clothes) and **Landhies Mawe** (scrap metal processing) – both recommended to visit. The latter is deafeningly unmistakable, the place to go to get your handmade tin suitcase.

Eating and drinking

Nairobi has no shortage of **eating places**. Their diversity is one of the city's best points and eating out, in default of much else in the way of entertainment (but see the next section), is an evening pastime which never dulls. Admittedly, African food is generally not highlighted in the more expensive hotels and restaurants. What stands out in these places, gastronomically speaking, is a range of Indian and European food, and spectacular quantities of meat.

This bias isn't really a problem. You can save money *and* eat African and Indian food in hundreds of unpretentious places, though to catch the cheap eats you'll have to go out early: by 8pm most of the cheaper restaurants have finished the day's food. And if you must have a burger or a pizza or a huge steak or totally vegetarian salad, it's all available – and with few time limits.

Bottom line eateries

The **River Road area** has all the very cheap places with one *hoteli* (cheap restaurant) after another on most streets. A couple at the end of this list are further out, but special. You should be able to eat hugely for under Ksh50.

New Flora, Tsavo Rd. Used to be extremely popular among locals and travellers alike for very good budget meals with tandoori bread. But the sometimes terrible service is a drawback.

Prestige, Tsavo Rd, opposite *New Flora*. Much better, with delicious fish and even a few vegetarian dishes, and outstandingly friendly waiters.

Super Hotel, River Rd (closes 7pm). Good, all-you-can-eat vegetarian meals – basically curries with excellent chapatis and lassi.

Sun Sweet Centre, bottom of Ngariama Road (open late). Another vegetarian Indian place, bright and appetising, with tempting sweets and for once open late.

Bull Café, Ngariama Road, off River Road. Right by the *New Kenya* and Ksh50 for a huge meal.

Iqbal, Latema Rd (until 11pm). Long menu of cheap, African dishes (*ugali*, *karanga*, greasy *chapatis*, *mboga*, rice) and really tasty *mkate mayai* with salad.

Afro-Arab Restaurant, Ronald Ngala Rd. Good cheap *mushkaki* with reggae accompaniment.

Slush's, Kigali Rd, between Moi Ave and Muindi Mbingu St. Good variety of snacks and takeaways.

Booggy café, Aga Khan Hospital grounds, 3rd Parklands Ave. Usually a popular place for those staying at *Mrs Roche's*.

Bahati Njema, Shauri Moyo district (see map), about 10 minutes' walk up from Maridadi fabrics on the corner of Lamu and Digo roads near the Nairobi River. A great little place (the name means "Good Luck") for very cheap Swahili food.

BREAKFASTS

Get up for breakfast. It's the only time of the day to really enjoy *mandaazi* and *chai*. You can get fried eggs and bread in many cheap places, too (look for Swahili menus saying something like *Mayai kukaanga* or sometimes "Eggs fly"). None of it's healthy, or aiming to do anything but inject you with hot calories. But it tastes good on a chilly Nairobi morning.

You can get an excellent **continental breakfast** at the *Goldstar Restaurant*, on Koinange Street near the *Terminal Hotel*. A good place for **something more hearty** is the *Y-Not* on Tom Mboya St, near the small post office there – stacks of well prepared eggs, sausages, beans, toast and the rest for under Ksh40. The big hotels do lavish breakfast buffets (the *Ambassadeur*'s is around Ksh90) and, if you wake up in a certain frame of mind, you might go down to the *Hilton* for theirs: it's pretty highly rated.

Coffee and snack bars

Coffee and snack bars are mostly situated in the upmarket business district north of City Hall Square and most are closed on Sundays (one which stays open is on the corner of Wabera and Mama Ngina Sts).

Al-Momin's, Banda St. Excellent samosas and other Indian snacks.

Express Bakery, Standard St. Always crowded at lunchtime but otherwise a good place to sit and recoup your energy.

Beneva Coffee House, Koinange St. Across from the old post office, this is a further recommendation – clean, cheap and popular with office workers.

Kenya Coffee Board, Mama Ngina St. The KCB's *Coffee House* does the best cup in town. Faded murals on the walls hark back to a not so distant era of African coffee estate labourers, white overseers and continental café-loungers. You can also buy the house blend by the kilo.

STREET FOOD

Strictly, **street food** is limited to **roasted corn cobs** (which take so long to eat you'll feel you've had a whole meal) and **fruit**. But places like the booths lining the road down to the railway station and the wooden shacks near the country bus station can fill you up with tea and *mandaazi* for next to nothing. Off the street, but still on your feet, you can eat at **fish and chip shops**, as ubiquitous in Nairobi as they used to be in Britain, and at prices that compare favourably with 1970s London, too – Nile perch 'n' chips for twenty shillings. *Reata*, on the corner of Taveta and Accra Rds, is a renowned purveyor.

Restaurants

The following listings are mostly of more upmarket eating houses, some of which it's a good idea to book (many are closed on Sundays or Tuesdays). Most of Nairobi's medium-priced restaurants specialise in **curries**. Very notable exceptions are one or two good **Swahili restaurants** and the ever popular *African Heritage*. Prices should work out at Ksh100–150 a head, though you can certainly eat more cheaply at *Malindi Dishes* and several of the curry houses, and you'll pay more at *African Heritage*. In the more international league, specialising mainly in meat, prices are higher (Ksh150–300 a head). The city has famously good beef and other fleshy delights so, if you enjoy it, indulge here, as the rest of the country is much less well endowed.

Swahili and African

Malindi Dishes (☎333191), Gaberone Rd. Excellent Swahili cooking – tasty chicken, fish and vegetable dishes with coconut rice and good *maziwalala*.

African Heritage (☎333157), Kenyatta Ave. Quite expensive, but worth it, is the Ethiopian buffet on Friday evenings at the eating half of the swanky gallery-cum-crafts shop, with accompaniment from the band of the same name (though, for culinary and budgetary balance, compare it with the *New Paradiso* in Eastleigh – see box p.59).

Mostly Indian

The New Three Bells (☎20628), Utalii House (mezzanine floor), near the French Cultural Centre. Quite classy and very good value.

Satkar (☎337197), Moi Avenue near Kenyatta Avenue. South Indian vegetarian, very popular and exceptionally good value.

Curry Pot (☎28684), top of Moi Avenue. Less polished but always busy.

Fransae (☎335368), Moktar Daddah Street. Good value, and especially fine *chapatis*, with the bonus of a bar.

Maharajah (☎27880), top of Muindi Mbingu St. A very extensive Parsee menu and usually packed. Closed on Tuesdays.

Dhasa, Ngariama Rd. A Punjabi restaurant, with wonderful "Teeka-takka Jeera chicken".

Blukat (☎229418), corner of Muindi Mbingu and Banda Sts. Best features are its pavement patio, unusual in Nairobi, and self-serve salad bar.

Safeer (☎336803), at the *Hotel Ambassadeur*, is an excellent Mughal restaurant with a rich and spicy South Indian menu.

Mayur at the *Supreme Hotel* (☎25241), corner of Kilome and Ngariama Rds at the top of River Rd. In a class of its own, this presents, in sheer magnificence, a real challenge to any prospective restaurateur in Nairobi. The food is, again, South Indian vegetarian, but so delicious and so well presented that to miss eating at the *Mayur* would be a shame. The buffet upstairs (at Ksh95, an absolute bargain even with a large tip expected) is worth starving all day for – in fact it's advisable – and the waiters are too polite to say anything if they notice you dropping Indian sweetmeats into a napkin. Downstairs, in the cheaper *Supreme* itself, there's a less lavish choice, but substantially the same dishes. Open after 7pm, closed on Tuesdays.

Mainly meat

Steak House Limited (☎23093), 3rd floor, Chester House, Koinange St, next to *The New Florida* nightclub. Their 1.2-kilo T-bone is very large indeed and probably the best quality you'll find anywhere in the country.

Carnivore (☎501775), out on Langata Road towards the national park entrance (bus #14, #15 from *Hilton*). Grossly named and yes, there is a connection – the all-you-can-eat menu (Ksh250) includes charcoal-grilled game meat, often impala. A trip to the *Carnivore* has become part of every package itinerary and it's often tacked onto the tour outfits' excursions to Nairobi National Park. It's touristy, with discos at weekends, but very few people (vegetarians among them perhaps) seem to dislike it. See also the *Carnivore*'s listing under "Live music venues".

Meateater's Den (☎331189), top end of Tom Mboya Street. Endless supplies of the fauna you thought was carefully protected, served as you like it (rare?). The game meat comes largely from private farms. Shares premises with the *Lobster Pot*, a seafood restaurant.

Red Bull, (☎335717), Silopark House, Mama Ngina St. Wonderful food.

Porter House, corner of Mama Ngina and Wabera Sts. Great steaks.

Chinese

Hong Kong (☎28612), corner of Koinange and Monrovia Sts. Excellent Chinese for around Ksh150/head.

Italian

Trattoria (☎340855), corner of Wabera and Standard Sts. Usually gets enthusiastic notices from low-budget travellers having a splurge, though it's sometimes too busy for its own good. The pasta dishes and pizzas are the real thing (bills work out around Ksh80–100 a head) and the cakes and ice cream – when they come – *magnifico*.

Marino's (☎27150) Reinsurance Plaza. Better, quieter and, as you'd expect, more expensive than the *Trattoria*.

French

French Cultural Centre (☎336263), Loita St. Though sometimes open only for morning tea and lunch (phone to check), the restaurant here offers a fairly classy night out, with occasional live music and an interesting range of really good food.

Salads

Jax Restaurant (☎23427), Mutual Building, Kimathi St, just down from the *Thorn Tree*. Good salads, in this city of meat and sugar, are somewhat hard to find. Very healthy salad buffets (about Ksh80).

Blukat (see above, under "Mostly Indian") also has help-yourself salads if you're fed up with the high-carb diet.

Bars

Sooner or later, a drink at the *Norfolk Hotel* (see p.63) is a must, though it's no longer the bargain entertainment in **people-watching** that it was when beer prices were fixed. At times, too, it can feel unengagingly close to a pub in the City of London. For more local – and less vicarious – city centre experiences you might try the *Blukat Restaurant*'s bar (see above) or the *680 Hotel*'s *The Pub* on Standard Street, which isn't very pub-like except in its 11pm closing, but can be a good place to meet local people. The Hilton's effort, *The Jockey Club* on City Hall Way next to *Egyptair*, has a more traditional pubby feel, though perhaps not one you'd choose.

Otherwise, unless you go to unmemorable hotel bars, central Nairobi is a bit of a dead loss after office hours. It's more fun to venture out, suitably stripped down (the clothes on your back and a little cash), to the land of **"Day and Night Clubs"**. The River Road district vibrates from dawn to dusk and back to dawn again with the sound of beery mayhem and jukeboxes – see the "Nightlife" section.

Film and theatre

Nairobi has twelve **cinemas**, including two drive-ins, but **theatre** in the city is embryonic.

Screen

The *20th Century* (☎27957), on Mama Ngina St (twin screens), the *Nairobi* on Nkrumah Lane just off Harambee Ave, the *Kenya* (☎26981) on Moi Ave, and the *Fox Drive-In* (☎802293) on the Thika Road screen fairly recent mainstream releases – usually blockbusters or award winners. Others tend to show Kung Fu, vintage James Bond, old Westerns and, of course, Indian movies which you don't need to understand to enjoy. Seats are around Ksh40. The *Embassy* and the *Odeon* on Latema Rd and the *Cameo* on Kenyatta Ave are popular for weekend matinees. Daily programmes can be found in the *Nation* and the *Standard* newspapers.

Stage

The small theatre at the *Professional Centre*, at the end of Parliament Rd (box office and enquiries ☎25506) has now assumed the old *Donovan Maule Theatre*'s mantle as Nairobi's leading playhouse. Its repertory company, the Phoenix Players, has now churned, rather grimly, through more than 500 plays since they were formed in 1948. Performances usually feature British or American actors, rarely a Kenyan script. They aim to put on a new show – farces, thrillers, variety – at least once a month.

The crowning irony for years was the *Kenya National Theatre*, where you could sometimes catch opera or ballet, but hardly ever anything home grown. This has happily changed with the appointment of a dynamic new Kenyan director, Joyce Mulinge, and the *National Theatre* now gives considerable emphasis to Kenyan drama and African theatre in general.

If you're interested in the state of the theatre in Kenya, the *French Cultural Centre*, the *Göethe Institut*, or even *Gallery Watatu* may be able to tell you more, and the first two sometimes host productions. Thursday editions of the *Standard*, and the *Sunday Nation* carry theatre pages.

Nightlife and music

With that range of cultural activities available, it's not surprising that **drinking and dancing** are what a night out in Nairobi is usually about. Entrance fees are low by international standards and prices for drinks are much the same as you'll pay everywhere in the country. Be warned, however that, male or female, if you're not accompanied by a partner of the opposite sex, you soon will be.

Live music venues

Given the volatile nature of the music business in Kenya, **venues and bands** change at a moment's notice. Although there are a few downtown music places, much of Nairobi's live music action takes place on the perimeter of the city. The following listings include all the places that have been around for some time, plus the latest information on new ones.

STARTING TIMES

Starting times vary considerably for all the clubs. On weekdays, 7.30 or 8pm wouldn't be too early, while weekend warm-ups usually begin around 9–10pm, and some may not get really rolling until midnight. But don't judge any band by their **first hour**. Many run through some pretty dreadful warm-up material to begin with. Remember, too, that many clubs have Sunday afternoon matinees – convenient if you don't want to be taxiing around the city late at night.

City centre venues

Garden Square (☎720425), City Hall Way near Parliament Rd, across from the *Intercontinental*. Not frantically raunchy, but relaxed and a good place to bop, this is less intimidating than most spots if you're not part of a couple and don't wish to be – and it's one of the few places in Nairobi where you can catch live music on a Wednesday night, from about 7.30–10pm. On Fridays and Saturdays, the music starts at 9.30pm and runs on into the early hours. At lunchtime, and some evenings, the "African Buffet" is pretty good value, and it's not a bad place to hang out with a beer at any time. Samba Mapangala and Orchestra Virunga have been playing the *Garden Square* for a couple of years, with time off now and then for recording in Europe.

Foresta Magnetica (☎728009/728518), Corner House, Kimathi St, opposite the *Hilton* (closed Sunday). This restaurant generally features a mix of the sort of pop, reggae, souk-ous, and "chakacha beat" often found in the coastal tourist hotels. Sometimes something more interesting.

Visions, Kimathi St (see the disco listings). Occasional live music in similar, "sophisticated" vein to *Foresta Magnetica*.

African Heritage gallery and restaurant (☎333157) on Kenyatta Avenue (2.30–5pm). An easy-going, informal, Saturday afternoon mix of reggae and soukous.

Galileo's Private Members' Club (☎742600/744477) at the International Casino, Westlands Road at Museum Hill. Has recently been showcasing live music on Thursdays, Fridays, and Saturdays – no guarantees about its merits, or whether it will continue.

Sirona Hotel, Parklands. Within easy striking distance if you're staying at *Mrs Roche's*. Sunday afternoons have featured the Zairean/Kenyan music of the group Zaiken and, most recently, the reggae sounds of Mpendo Moja.

Suburban and out of town

Bombax Club (☎565691), Ngong Rd, across from the Kenya Science Teachers College at Dagoretti Corner in the southwest of the city (see "Nairobi Area" map). A small, friendly bar with live music Thursday to Sunday and tasty, though not lightning fast, food. There's always a happy, relaxed crowd at the club and low entrance fees. Take a bus #1, #2, #3, #4 or any bus that passes Dagoretti Corner from the old GPO (but plan on taking a taxi back to town).

Carnivore (☎501775), off the Langata Road on the way to Nairobi National Park. A success-ful meld of live music and disco in a pleasant, outdoor environment. If you can resist all the food, it's definitely a bargain on Wednesday evenings with a happy hour before the music begins and a lower entry fee than at weekends. The Wednesday and Saturday house band is always good entertainment, with visiting groups often taking the Sunday afternoon slot (see the Sunday papers for the line-up). Buses #14 and #15 from Gill House, opposite the *Kenya*

NAIROBI BANDS

Most of these groups are around Nairobi much of the time, but it's hard to be sure where to find them. Current, or recent residencies are given in brackets. And there's more background in the "Music in Kenya" section in *Contexts* at the back of the book.

THE BIG NAMES

Samba Mapangala and Orchestra Virunga Zairean soukous at its best – high energy dance music, with soaring vocals (*Garden Square*).

Les Wanyika Twelve years of the finest Swahili pop from these Tanzanian transplants – ecstatic stuff, with John Ngereza on lead guitar and Professor Omari on rhythm (*Bombax Club*).

Zaiken Good, solid Zairean dance music (*Sirona Hotel*, *African Heritage*).

Ibeba System Former house band at *JKA Resorts* and the *Carnivore*, and definitely worth seeing if they resurface somewhere.

Maroon Commandos The Army group that's hard to find.

Popolipo Moments of greatness from Lessa Lassen's Zairean group (*Gringos*).

Simba Wanyika Tanzanian Swahili pop – fantastic guitar and vocal sound but just one six-hour tune (*New Kibigori Day and Night Club*, Eastleigh).

Muungano All Stars Great guys with a wonderful hybrid Swahili-Benga-Zairean sound (*Muungano Point*, Eastleigh).

Mavalo Kings Cousins to Les Wanyika and just as gorgeous-sounding (no fixed abode).

Africa Jambo Jambo Led by vocalist Sammy Kasule of Shauri Yako fame (*Carnivore*).

Professor Naaman and the Nine Stars Band Up and coming Zairean sounds – used to be called Super Rumba – led by the gargantuan Naaman (*New Congoni*).

The Pressmen New young group – formed out of a former tourist circuit band – that's caused quite a stir with the release of their first album, "Musenangu"; the wave of the future? (*Foresta Magnetica*).

Cinema on Moi Ave, will drop you at the *Carnivore*'s entrance road, where someone is bound to give you a lift.

Gringos (☎521231), Limuru Road, Ruaka, one kilometre past Runda Estates (on the road signed "To Limuru & Naivasha" on the "Greater Nairobi" map). A Tex-Mex restaurant that's been known to have some pretty good Zairean soukous on Fridays and Saturdays – and a nice spot to go on a Sunday afternoon.

Hillock Inn (☎3558685/553682), Enterprise Rd near the Ngong River bridge (between Likoni Rd and Mombasa Rd, buses #109 and #110). This is a place to go when their house band is *not* playing. Give them a call to see if anything special is coming up – they often host some of the top Kikuyu names (for example Joseph Kamaru and Julius Kang'ethe with his Kiru Stars) on their guest nights.

JKA Resorts Club (☎822066) Mombasa road, just beyond the airport turn-off from Nairobi. Although some way out of town and a little difficult to get to unless you have your own vehicle, *JKA Resorts* features a regular band on Friday and Saturday nights and Sunday afternoons into the evening. Watch the papers, too, for announcements of special *JKA* entertainment events often coinciding with holidays. The club area has a pleasant, garden setting and, at cooler times of the year, they light fires in hearths on either side of the dance floor. Buses #109 and #110 (both to Athi River) from Tusker House bus terminal can get you there, but only about once an hour. And, while it's easy enough to hitch back in daylight, after about 9pm (when the last bus returns) a taxi is your only option. Given taxi fares these days, an overnight at the *JKA Hotel* attached to the club, while not very cheap, might be worth considering.

COASTAL AND HOTEL POP BANDS

Them Mushrooms, Safari Sound, Forest People Competent musicians, playing flawlessly, and lots of fun – but too bland to be really exciting (play Nairobi all the time).

SLEEPING GIANTS

Bands that have slipped from the top into oblivion but occasionally regroup to put on a good show.

Super Mazembe Many of the original Mazembe musicians are still around in other groups and a reincarnation may be starting up on the coast.

Les Mangelepa A Zimbabwean offshoot is doing quite well in Harare.

Wanyika Stars Tanzanian Swahili sounds from the remains of Issa Juma's band.

Vundumuna Former champs at the *Carnivore* who pop in every so often and surprise people with some fine dance music.

MUSICIANS SINGING IN KENYAN LANGUAGES

KIKUYU

Joseph Kamaru and the Kamaru Superstars The grand master of Kikuyu pop music.

Mbiri Stars and **Kiru Stars** Both groups have strings of hits.

KAMBA

Kalambya Boys with **Kalambya Sisters** Brace yourself for a wild evening – who said they sing like high school girls on speed?

Original Kilimambogo Brothers/OKB Stars One line of descent of the most famous Akamba band.

Peter Mwambi and the Kyanganga Boys Perennial favourite of the Akamba people.

LUO

D.O. Misiani and Shirati Jazz The most famous name in Benga music, a must if they're around (try the *River Yala Club*, Kariobangi)..

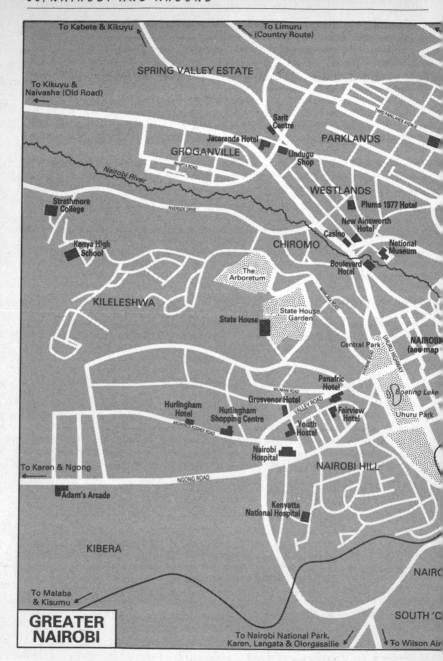

To Kabete & Kikuyu

To Limuru
(Country Route)

SPRING VALLEY ESTATE

To Kikuyu &
Naivasha (Old Road)

Sarit
Centre

PARKLANDS

Jacaranda Hotel

GROGANVILLE

RHAPTA ROAD

Undugu
Shop

Nairobi River

WESTLANDS

Strathmore
College

RIVERSIDE DRIVE

Plums 1977 Hotel

New Ainsworth
Hotel

Casino

National
Museum

Kenya High
School

CHIROMO

Boulevard
Hotel

The
Arboretum

KILELESHWA

State House
Garden

State House

Central Park

NAIROBI
(see map

Panafric
Hotel

Boating Lake

Grosvenor Hotel

VALLEY ROAD

Uhuru Park

Hurlingham
Hotel

Hurlingham
Shopping Centre

Fairview
Hotel

BROWNING KODHEA ROAD

MILIMANI ROAD

Youth
Hostel

Nairobi
Hospital

To Karen & Ngong

NGONG ROAD

NAIROBI HILL

Adam's Arcade

Kenyatta
National Hospital

KIBERA

To Malaba
& Kisumu

NAIR

GREATER
NAIROBI

To Nairobi National Park,
Karen, Langata & Olorgasailie

SOUTH 'C

To Wilson Air

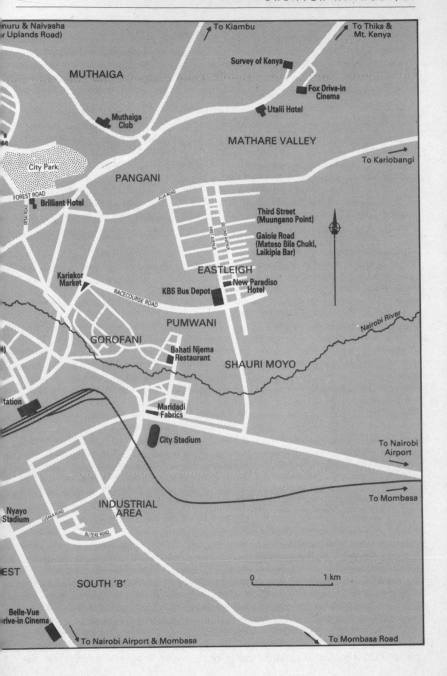

To Kiambu

To Thika &
Mt. Kenya

MUTHAIGA

Survey of Kenya

Fox Drive-in
Cinema

Utalii Hotel

Muthaiga
Club

MATHARE VALLEY

City Park

To Kariobangi

PANGANI

FOREST ROAD

JUJA ROAD

Brilliant Hotel

Third Street
(Muungano Point)

Galole Road
(Mateso Bila Chuki,
Laikipia Bar)

SECOND AVENUE

FIRST AVENUE

EASTLEIGH

Kariakor
Market

New Paradiso
Hotel

RACECOURSE ROAD

KBS Bus Depot

PUMWANI

GOROFANI

Nairobi River

Bahati Njema
Restaurant

SHAURI MOYO

Station

Maridadi
Fabrics

City Stadium

To Nairobi
Airport

To Mombasa

INDUSTRIAL
AREA

Nyayo
Stadium

LUSAKA ROAD

BUTERE ROAD

0   1 km

EST

SOUTH 'B'

Belle-Vue
Drive-in Cinema

To Nairobi Airport & Mombasa

To Mombasa Road

Sportview Hotel (☎803890), Thika Road, near the Moi Sports Complex at Kasarani. From time to time, this relatively new entrant to the club scene books some interesting groups (such as the 47-stone Professor Naaman and his Nine Stars Band). Call ahead to see if there's live music at the weekend. You can get there on buses #45 and #145 from Tusker House – last run at 8pm – but you'd be better off sharing a taxi for the evening in a group.

Discos

Reggae is the popular staple sound of the **cheap discos**, often not much more than Day & Night Clubs. The government's anti-rasta drive of a year or two back faded away and reggae music is back on the airwaves and in the street. Of course, the capital also has a fair number of **disco palaces** complete with flashy interiors and the latest dance hits from Europe and America. If this style appeals, try one of the established places below. In the glitzy places, men usually pay more – around Ksh150 – than women. In the rootsier discos, entrance is free or very cheap.

Reggae Discos

Brilliant Hotel (☎23124), Forest Rd at Desai Rd (on the south side of City Park – 20 minutes' walk from *Mrs Roche's* if you're staying there): inconvenient by bus but not too expensive in a taxi.

New Congoni Day & Night Club (☎331789) Reggae discos on Sunday afternoons. Unpredictable live music, predictably smelly toilets.

Cantina, Wilson Airport.

Disco Palaces

The New Florida (☎334870), Koinange Street. Irresistible for its tackiness, this big orange mushroom of a building is always full of hookers and rather desperate-looking business types. But the atmosphere is merely steamy, not heavy, and there's an excellent sound system.

Florida 2000, Moi Ave near the *Kenya Cinema*. The *New Florida*'s sister establishment attracts similar clients and offers equally unambiguous entertainment.

Visions (☎332331), top of Kimathi St (closed Mon). Bathes in a lavish design with video monitors and a slick mix of music.

Hollywood (☎27949), Moktar Daddah St. Less stylish, mostly reggae.

Bubbles, International Casino, Museum Hill. Nairobi's current fave rave (and they use that language), this is going down a hurricane with young ex-pats and white Kenyans and has become something of a meat market. Incredibly popular, incredibly tacky.

The big discos all put on floor shows for those who stay late enough – gyrating trios, limbo dancing, frank contortions . . .

Local dives – city centre

Meanwhile, on **Latema Road**, people are doing contortions just to get into the *Modern Green Day and Night Club*. Here, entrance is free, cold beer is not the fashion – though you can get it, from the barman in his security cage – and the floor show is you and the rest of the customers. Just why the place is so popular is hard to say. For the girls it's partly because of the steady trickle of potential customers from the *Iqbal* and other lodgings nearby. For some of the men it's a place to chew *miraa* all night for the price of a soda. From the outside, with the usual arguments and hustle going on in the doorway, it might appear a place to avoid. But squeeze inside, drink a beer or two, and soak up the elevated atmosphere. People make friends quickly here, though having a conversation over the racket of the throng and the din of the jukebox is exhausting.

If you can't take the pace, try the *New Congoni Day and Night Club* (☎331789), on River Road, off Lithuli Ave (see "Discos"). Admission is dirt cheap. Bear in mind the *Modern Green* and the *New Congoni* are only two of dozens of similar places in Nairobi. There's nothing to keep you from checking out others – plenty of people do. Try, for example, the local *pombe* at the *Mlachahe Bar & Restaurant* opposite *Malindi Dishes* in Gaberone Road.

Local dives – Eastleigh music

Aside from the city centre clubs and the fairly touristy places which draw their custom from a wide area, there are plenty of other nightspots catering for a more local clientele in the outlying communities. One of the livelier of such communities, musically or otherwise, is **Eastleigh**. Although only a ten-minute bus ride from town, it has a completely different look and feel from the modern centre.

Quite a number of bars in Eastleigh feature **live music** (another reason to think of staying out there), if not necessarily on a regular weekly schedule. Check out *Mateso Bila Chuki* and *Laikipia Bar* along Galole Rd (between Fifth and Fourth streets, a short walk from the big *KBS* bus depot), both interesting nightspots that sometimes feature bands. For more adventurous music-seekers, there's the *New Kibigori Day and Night Club* on Juja Road (#28, #32, #42, #48 from *Ambassadeur*) where Simba Wanyika Original may still have a residency.

One place in Eastleigh that's been quite consistent is *Muungano Point*, currently home to a tight and newly assembled band called **Muungano All Stars**, formed from members of the veteran Orchestra Mazadijo and Simba Wanyika, as well as Super Wanyika musicians and others. *Muungano Point* is definitely a one-of-a-kind sort of place, literally a drive-in bar. It might be worth the low price of admission just to see it, but the music is pretty agreeable as well. After you pay to get inside the corrugated iron fence, you walk into a big car park with a covered dance floor at the far end and a tiny space for the band. From central Nairobi take bus #6 or #9 on Tom Mboya St, hop out at Second Ave and Third St in Eastleigh, and walk along Third St for a few hundred metres.

Catching Luo, Kikuyu and Kamba bands

"**Vernacular music**" – as opposed to songs in Swahili – is performed in and around Nairobi, sometimes quite frequently, but the gigs are most often one-night stands. Doyens of this catch-all non-genre are Owino (D.O.) Misiani and his **Shirati Jazz**, the Luo-speaking, "Benga beat" stars whose recent international tours have been resoundingly successful. They usually play most weekends at *River Yala Club* in Kariobangi shopping centre (though you may find a certain Orchestre Mazadijo currently in residency). But Kariobangi isn't the greatest place to wander at night so go first on a Sunday afternoon. Buses #14, #15 and #28 among others go to Kariobangi from *Ambassadeur*. Once on Kamunde Road – the one that encircles Kariobangi – get off at the first stop, then backtrack to the first cross street and follow it to the shopping centre.

These detailed instructions are worth it because Shirati Jazz, equipped with new instruments from Britain, sound superb – light and danceable, with chattering rhythm and busy bass, Congolese influences (derived from the amazing 1950s guitarist Jean Bosco Mwenda), and traditional Luo women's singing called "bodi".

Another place to venture boldly – though with less rewards – is *Althusi Bar and Restaurant*, behind the *OTC* bus station (see "Nairobi Centre" map). They have recently had Kamba bands playing here.

Otherwise, if you'd like to catch a Kamba, Kikuyu, or Luo group, your best bet is to look around the River Road area for **posters** announcing forthcoming appearances.

Nairobi directory

American Express *Express Kenya*, PO Box 40433, c/o *Silver Spears Tours*, Consolidated House, Standard St is the main office (☎556688 or 334722). They'll hold card-holders' mail.

Area code Nairobi's code is ☎02.

Automobile Association Main office at Hurlingham Shopping Centre (PO Box 40087, ☎720382) – buses #46–9, #56 from *GPO*. Six-month membership Ksh200.

Banks *Barclays*, corner Kenyatta Ave and Moi Ave (Head Office: Bank House, PO Box 30120, Nairobi). Main branch is Kenyatta Ave (PO Box 30616). Foreign exchange centre is fairly efficient and open 9am–4.30pm Mon–Sat (PO Box 47278). Money can be cabled to this address from abroad.

Bicycles Indian three-speed models can be bought at *Kenya Cycle Mart*, Moi Ave. Unfortunately, no bicycle hire available yet.

Books The main bookshops are: *Nation*, corner of Kenyatta Ave and Kimathi St; *Select*, Kimathi St; *Heritage*, Wabera St; *Book Corner*, Mama Ngina St; *Prestige*, Mama Ngina St. All these sell imports as well as Kenyan publications. There's a pretty good **secondhand bookshop** on the corner of Market St and Koinange St, across from the City Market. It doesn't appear to have a name; above the door a sign reads "We buy and sell almost anything". They also exchange books.

Camping gas Available at a number of places including *Woolworth's* from Ksh40 or more – but it's twice the price anywhere else in Kenya so buy it while in town.

Car hire *Avis* (PO Box 49795, ☎334317) and *Hertz-UTC* (PO Box 42196, ☎331960) are steep. The following are recommended:

Budget Rent A Car, Parliament La, Haile Selassie Ave (PO Box 59767, ☎337154).

Rasul's, Butere Rd, Industrial Area (PO Box 18172, ☎558234 or 541355); not convenient to get to (taxi to Mater Misericordiae Hospital or bus #68 and #116, which go right by Butere Rd), but some of the cheapest prices in town, often used by the big companies;

Let's Go Travel, Caxton House, Standard St (PO Box 60342, ☎29539);

Central Hire-A-Car, Fedha Towers, Standard St (PO Box 49439, ☎22888 or 332296);

Ebra Tours and Safaris, 4th floor, Standard Building, Standard St (PO Box 43457,☎331494 or 334937);

Concorde Car Hire, Agip Garage, Westlands (PO Box 25053, ☎743008);

The Chequered Flag Ltd, Westlands Shopping Centre (PO Box 14483,☎743155 or 745946);

Glory Car Hire, Tubman Road (PO Box 49095,☎25024/24428/767571);

Habib's Cars, Agip House, Haile Selassie Ave (PO Box 48095, ☎20463/23816, Fax 339357): new fleet of Suzukis;

Intasun, Kenwood House, Kimathi Street (PO Box 42977, ☎24037 or 334438).

AIRLINE OFFICES

Aeroflot (☎20746), Corner House, Mama Ngina St

Air Canada (☎339755), Kimathi House, Kimathi St

Air France (☎726265), Chai House, Koinange St

Air India (☎334788), Jeevan Bharati Building, Harambee Ave

Air Kenya Aviation (☎501601), Wilson Airport

Air Madagascar (☎25286), Hilton, City Hall Way

Air Malawi (☎333683), Cotts House, corner City Hall Way and Wabera St

Air Mauritius (☎29166), Union Towers, corner Mama Ngina St and Moi Ave

Air Tanzania (☎336397), Kimathi St

Air Zimbabwe (☎339499), Koinange St

Air Zaire (☎25626), Kimathi St

Alitalia (☎24361), Hilton, City Hall Way

British Airways (☎334440), 11th floor, International House, Mama Ngina St

Cameroon Airlines (☎337788), Kenyatta Ave

Egyptair (☎26821), Shankardass House, Moi Ave

El Al (☎28123/4), Sweepstake House, Mama Ngina St

Equator Airlines (☎21177/501399), Wilson Airport

Ethiopian Airlines (☎330837), Bruce House, Muindi Mbingu St

Gulf Air (☎728401/3), Global Travel, International House, Mama Ngina St

Iberia, Hilton, Mama Ngina St (☎331648/338623)

Kenya Airways (☎332750/29291), Airways Terminal, Koinange St;

KLM (☎332673/7), Fedha Towers, Muindi Mbingu St

Lufthansa, Kimathi St (☎26271)

Olympic Airlines (☎338026), Hilton, Watalii St and Moi Ave

Pakistan International Airlines (☎333901), ICEA Building, Banda St

Pan Am (☎23582/23226/28379), Hilton

Royal Swazi National Airways (☎729475), Taifa Rd

Sabena (☎22185), International House, Mama Ngina St

Saudia (☎331456), Jamia Mosque, Banda St

Scandinavian Airlines System (☎338347), Grindlays Building, Kimathi St

Somali Airlines (☎335409), Bruce House, Muindi Mbingu St

Sudan Airways (☎25129), UTC House, General Kago St

Swissair (☎340231/2/3), Mama Ngina St

TWA, Ryan International (☎24036), Rehema House, Standard St

Uganda Airlines (☎21354), Phoenix House, Kenyatta Ave

Zambia Airways (☎21007), Hamilton House, Kaunda St

It's sometimes possible to negotiate a price but expect to pay around Ksh500 per day plus Ksh6–7 per km for a Suzuki 4WD jeep, the most popular vehicle. Minimum age is usually 23 and, remember, you'll need to pay a deposit plus extra for insurance. Do not assume your vehicle is roadworthy; the best companies sometimes send out vehicles in a terrible state. Check it as carefully as you can.

Car repairs Always bargain hard before work begins. In Nairobi the *Undugu Society* workshop (☎540187) is recommended (near *Maridadi Fabrics* by the city stadium roundabout).

Chartering a plane *Air Kenya Aviation*, Wilson Airport (☎501421), (bus #34, GPO) has three-seaters from around Ksh40/mile plus airstrip fees. Or try *Africair*, Z Boskovic Air Charters Ltd, PO Box 45646 (☎501210).

Cheap flights There's been a proliferation of discounted, "bucket shop" ticket agencies in recent years and you'll only find the cheapest seat by checking them out one by one. You can expect: one-ways to London from Ksh6000, to Bombay Ksh5000, Bangkok Ksh10,000 and New York Ksh12,000. Seats are purchased by the shops at the airline's unofficially discounted rate so variations entirely depend on their mark-ups. You'll generally have to provide bank receipts in Kenya shillings equal to the normal fare (about twice the discounted fare). Beware of *Sudan Airways*: even assuming they're flying again, passengers with confirmations are forever being bumped. Most people survive *Aeroflot* okay. Fares tend to be lowest if you book in a group. Shop around.

Hanzuwan El Kindiy Tours and Travel (PO Box 49266, ☎335615), Tom Mboya St, is the best known, though not necessarily the best: the famous Eddy used to send his passengers Christmas cards;

Crocodile Travel (PO Box 20380, ☎335250/28910),Tom Mboya St;

Kambo Travel corner of Tom Mboya St/Latema Rd, offers cheap flights to London on *Saudia*;

Somak Travel (PO Box 48495, ☎20557), Corner House, 5th Floor, Mama Ngina St;

Bankco Travel (PO Box 11536, ☎331874/26736), Latema Rd, is a newer outfit offering very competitive deals;

Prince Travel, ground floor of the Kenyatta Conference Centre, may still be the cheapest;

Jujofreight (PO Box 60058, ☎340866), Tom Mboya St, opposite the *Ambassadeur*, has "courier tickets" to London – worth checking out.

Chemists Those open late include: *Saga Chemists* on Koinange Lane off Koinange St, near the *Kenya Airways* terminus (Mon–Sat 8.30am–10pm), and *Rawan Chemists*, Loita St, opposite the old post office (open Sun).

Contraceptives Oral contraceptives are available from the Family Planning Clinic in Phoenix Arcade, Standard St.

Doctors Dr Belcher, corner of Rhapta and Church roads (in Westlands, bus #50), is recommended (☎725904/60363); or ask your embassy for a list.

Flight information ☎822111 or 822206 Jomo Kenyatta Airport.

Freight Air freight is cheaper than sea freight except for very large items. *Express Kenya*, Standard St, is helpful.

Gemstones For loose gems try *Treasures and Crafts Ltd*, Kaunda St.

Hair braiding If you've enough of your own, and want a laugh, there's a place called *Mike's* opposite the petrol stations on Accra Rd where you can have it done for thirty shillings or so – or up to a hundred with hair pieces added.

Horse racing Frequent buses on race days (usually Sunday) to Ngong Road Race Course from the *KBS* bus station.

Hospitals The *Consolata Sisters' Nazareth Hospital*, (Karurui ☎40875), Riara Ridge Rd, near Limuru about 25km from Nairobi, bus #117 from bus station, charges reasonable rates and is highly recommended if you need to be in for some time. *The Nairobi Hospital* (PO Box 30026, ☎722160) is reckoned to be the best one in the city. Or ask your embassy.

Language schools *Kingozi Language Services*, PO Box 21394, corner of Joseph Kangethe/ Suna Rds, Adam's Arcade, off Ngong Rd (☎569316) (buses #1–5, #8 from *Hilton*), offers Kiswahili courses individually and in groups. Other languages are also available. *The Language Centre*, Ndemi Close and *Trans Africa*, Joseph Kangethe Rd, are both near Adam's Arcade. *LACOP* (Language and Cultural Orientation Programmes), 4th floor, Cargen House, Harambee Ave (☎26850), is similar. Also check out *Makioki Language Services*, Kijabe St. For private teaching, check the notice board at *Gallery Watatu*.

Laundry There are no launderettes in Nairobi. If you really can't face it, hotels and lodgings will always do it for you at prices appropriate to the room charges. Some indeed will insist you don't wash your own.

Left Luggage Bags can be left safely at the railway station left luggage office for a small fee. It's open 8am–noon, 2–6pm.

EMBASSIES AND HIGH COMMISSIONS

Algeria, PO Box 53902 (☎724634 or 724663), Matungulu House, Mamlaka Road

Austria, PO Box 30560 (☎28281), City House, corner of Standard/Wabera Sts

Australia, PO Box 47718 (☎334666), Development House, Moi Ave

Belgium, PO Box 30461 (☎20501), Silopark House, Mama Ngina St

Burundi, PO Box 44439 (☎338721), Development House, Moi Ave

Canada, PO Box 30481 (☎334033), Comcraft House, Haile Selassie Ave

Denmark, PO Box 40412 (☎331088),Rehani House, Kenyatta Ave

Egypt, PO Box 30285 (☎25991/2), Harambee Plaza, corner Uhuru Highway, Haile Selassie Ave

Ethiopia, PO Box 45198 (☎723035), State House Ave, Nairobi Hill

Finland, (☎334777)International House, Mama Ngina St

France, PO Box 41784 (☎339978 or 48037), Embassy House, Harambee Ave

Germany PO Box 30180 (☎26661 or 27069), Embassy House, Harambee Ave

Ghana, PO Box 48534 (☎749615), Muthaiga Road

India, PO Box 30074 (☎22566), Jeevan Bharati Building, Harambee Ave

Israel, PO Box 30354 (☎20429), Mama Ngina St

Italy, PO Box 30107 (☎337356), Prudential Assurance House, Wabera St

Japan, PO Box 60202 (☎332955), ICEA Building, Kenyatta Ave

Lesotho, PO Box 44096 (☎337493 or 24876), International House, Mama Ngina St

Madagascar consular office at *Air Madagscar* (see above)

Morocco, PO Box 61098 (☎22361), Moi Ave

Netherlands, PO Box 41537 (☎27111), Uchumi House, Nkrumah Ave

Nigeria, PO Box 30516 (☎564116), Lenana Road, Hurlingham

Norway, PO Box 46363 (☎337121), Rehani House, Kenyatta Ave

Pakistan, PO Box 30045 (☎61666), St Michael's Rd, off Rhapta Rd (bus #50)

Portugal, PO Box 34020 (☎338990 or 339853) Reinsurance Plaza

Rwanda, PO Box 48579 (☎334341), International House, Mama Ngina St

Somalia, PO Box 30769 (☎24301), International House, Mama Ngina St

Spain, PO Box 45503 (☎335711 or 26568), Bruce House, Standard St

Sudan, PO Box 74059 (☎720853), Minet ICDC House, Mamlaka Rd, Central Park

Sweden, PO Box 30600(☎29042), International House, Mama Ngina St

Swaziland, PO Box 41887 (☎339231)

Switzerland, PO Box 30752 (☎28735), International House, Mama Ngina St

Tanzania, PO Box 47790 (☎331056), 5th Floor, Continental House, corner of Uhuru Highway/City Hall Way

Thailand, PO Box 58349 (☎62742), Grevillea Grove

Turkey, PO Box 30785 (☎520404), Gigiri Road

Uganda, PO Box 60853 (☎330801), Phoenix House, Kenyatta Ave

United Kingdom, PO Box 30465 (☎335944), Bruce House, Standard St

USA, PO Box 30137 (☎334141 or 48313), Moi Ave

Zaire, PO Box 48106 (☎29771), Electricity House, Harambee Ave

Zambia,PO Box 48741 (☎724796 or 725938), Nyerere Rd

Zimbabwe, PO Box 30806 (☎721045), Minet ICDC House, Mamlaka Rd, west of Central Park

Libraries *British Council*, ICEA Building, Kenyatta Ave. (Tues–Fri 10am–5pm, Sat 9am–noon). British newspapers and magazines. *McMillan Memorial Library*, Banda St (Mon–Fri 9am–5pm, Sat 8.30am–1pm; small weekly fee). Many books, plus the "Africana" reading room.

Maps Game park maps (some of which are now terribly out of date), *City of Nairobi*, and *Nairobi and Environs* are available from bookshops; so, too, are the city-wide A-Z of Nairobi (pub. *Kenway Publications*) and general maps of Kenya. For *Survey of Kenya* maps, you first visit the Public Map Office, Harambee Ave (just west of the Conference Centre), to find out which of the sheets you want are available and note their numbers (they sell all the game park maps, too). Then you go to the Director of Surveys, Adhi House, Ngong Rd (buses, #1, #2, #3 from *GPO*), armed with your "request for clearance", which you write on the way. Once it is stamped, you return to the PMO for your maps. Note: you may have to go to the *Survey of Kenya* headquarters opposite the *Fox Drive-In* on the Thika road (bus #43/4/5 and #143/4/5), so check at the PMO which office you need. For some sheets (notably border regions), you may be refused clearance.

Massages *Topos Massage*, Cabral Street, behind the *Lobster Pot*, is reckoned the best value for a real massage – Ksh150 for an hour of tenderising.

Newspapers and magazines Foreign papers such as the *International Herald Tribune* are available from several newsstands around Kenyatta Ave. Also *Newsweek* and *Time*. Or, if you're really counting the pennies, you can sometimes rent a paper for a small charge.

Notice boards The obvious and best known one is the Thorn Tree at the *New Stanley Hotel*. The *Iqbal* and *Mrs Roche's* have more budget-traveller-oriented notice boards, as does the Youth Hostel, which also maintains a "Hostellers' Comments Book" of lively and up-to-date news and revelations on travelling in East Africa. The *Fairview Hotel* maintains a slightly more upmarket notice board, used by travellers. *Gallery Watatu* has a board likely to be of more interest to long-stay visitors.

Ornithology The Museum Ornithology Society organises bird walks/drives around Nairobi. Enthusiastic non-members are welcome if they make a donation. Meet at the museum on Wednesdays at 8.30am.

Parachuting If you're trained and would like to jump in Kenya, telephone H Trempeneau ☎882292. The Kenya Parachute Club has its club room at Wilson Airport.

Photo booths There's a "Photo-Me" on Kenyatta just west of Kimathi St.

Photocopiers For some reason Nairobi is abundantly endowed with photocopiers, with prices as low as Ksh2 per copy.

Photography For **camera repairs**, try *Camera Clinic*, Biashara St (☎22492/22327). For **camera batteries**, *Ebrahim Camera House* , corner of Kimathi and Standard Sts, is cheap.

Buying a camera is approximately twice as expensive as in Europe. Instead, check the notice boards at the *Thorn Tree* and the *Iqbal*. To **rent camera and binoculars,** the main outlet is *Elite Camera House*, Kimathi St, south of Kenyatta. For **film developing and printing** there are lots of places but variable quality. *Elite Studios*, corner of Banda and Muindi Mbingu streets, is recommended for cheap *Ektachrome* processing; *Expo Camera*, Mama Ngina St, offer a fast, reliable service for prints and slides. *Woolworth's* is also reckoned to be good.

Photo studios Five-minute passport photo service at *Studio One*, corner of Moi/Nkrumah Aves.

Post Poste Restante is at the newly moved General Post Office, Haile Selassie Ave by the pedestrian footbridge (Mon–Fri 8.30am–5pm, Sat 9am–noon). Letters normally take 3–6 days from Europe. The **parcels** office is upstairs (open for posting Mon–Fri 8am–5pm, Sat 9am–noon; open for collecting Mon–Fri 8am–1pm, 2–5pm). Parcels from home can be addressed to Poste Restante. You'll get a note from the Parcels Section. Note that if you're over on the northeast side of town, and just want to post mail, there's a small, and quicker, post office on Tom Mboya St. If you have **valuable items to send home**, *DHL* courier service has an office on the ground floor of International House, Mama Ngina St. *TNT Skypak* (PO Box 41520, ☎723554), on Nyerere Rd is slightly cheaper.

Records and cassettes Street sellers in Lithuli Ave and River Rd probably have the best selection of 45s, especially for vernacular music. For LPs and tapes, try one of the big three: *Assanand's*, Moi Ave, *Ebrahim Camera Shop*, Kimathi St, or *Woolworth's*. Or check out *City Sounds*, next to to *Zahra Lodge* in River Rd. Look out for names in the "Discography" in *Contexts*, and also **Peter Mwambi, Mbiri Stars** and **James Mbugua & the Karura Brothers**. There are some fine old Swahili language collections around, too: get the *Marashi ya River Road* LP/cassette. Also popular in Nairobi are current Kiswahili recordings by Tanzanian-based bands like **Mlimani Park, Maquis Original, Vijana Jazz** and **Orchestra Safari Sound International**. Pirated cassettes may seem a good deal at around Ksh60 but quality and durability are so bad they're practically worthless. Identify them by plastic wrapper and absence of labels on the cassette itself. See also the discography in *Contexts*.

Safari operators Before calling at the operators themselves, shop around some of the names under "Travel Agents". Every other shop seems to belong to a safari outfit and it's obviously impossible to mention more than a few. With so much to go wrong, spotless reputations are hard to maintain (read the section on "Camping Safaris" in *Basics*) but the following, who run **camping trips mostly by lorry or land-cruiser**, are good value and only rarely come in for criticism :

Best Camping, Nanak House, corner of Kimathi St and Banda St. Highly recommended by some.

Exotic Safaris, PO Box 54483, Uniafric House, Koinange Lane (☎33811). Again, have been highly praised by some travellers.

Safari Camp Services, PO Box 44801 (☎28936/330130/891348), corner of Moktar Daddah and Koinange Sts. Reputable operators of the original "Turkana Bus" and also of a "Wildlife Bus" trip emulated by many others.

Gametrackers, PO Box 62042 (☎338927/22703), Finance House, corner of Banda and Loita Sts. Popular, consistently good and now offer cycling safaris.

Savuka, PO Box 20433 (☎225108), Pan-Africa Ins. Bldg, Kenyatta Ave. Recommended.

Special Camping Safaris (☎338325/566142), PO Box 51512, Gilfillan House, Kenyatta Ave. Noted for their long Turkana trip.

Safari Seekers, PO Box 32834 (☎26206/334585), Room 544, 5th floor, Jubilee Insurance Exchange Building, Kaunda St, next to the *20th Century* cinema. Now offer mountain bike safaris in cooperation with an American company, *Paradise Bicycle Tours* (see *Basics*).

Scenic Safaris, PO Box 49188 (☎26526/29092/25833), 1st floor, Westminster House, Kenyatta Ave, by the *New Stanley*. Run a wide range of shorter trips and reasonably priced lodge safaris as well.

The following are recommended because they offer unusual, if more expensive, trips – notably **safaris on foot and using pack animals**:

Bateleur Safaris, PO Box 42562, Mezzanine floor, Hilton, Mama Ngina St (☎27048). Specialise in walking safaris for ornithologists.

Camel Trek Ltd, c/o Lewa Downs, Private Bag, PO Isiolo. Conducts camel trips and has a long-established reputation; bookings through *Flamingo Tours* (see "Travel Agents", below);

Ewaso River Camel Hikes Conducts slightly cheaper, "camel-assisted" walking safaris along the Ewaso Nyiro River in Northern Kenya; contact Simon Evans, *Just the Ticket*, PO Box 14845, Nairobi, ☎741755.

Kentrak, PO Box 47964 (☎27311/339094) Offers backpacking safaris.

Let's Go Travel (see under "Travel Agents") offer unique white-water rafting on the Tana and Athi rivers.

Safaris Unlimited Ltd, PO Box 20138, Jubilee Insurance Exchange, Mama Ngina St (☎332132). Run horse and foot safaris, in pursuit of photos and fish.

Tropical Ice, 5th floor, Jubilee Insurance Exchange, Mama Ngina St (☎23649). Offers walking safaris along the Tsavo and Galana rivers.

Selling things Many of the safari companies are often on the lookout for good, used, camping equipment, especially two-person tents.

Sunglasses The small clothing and bric-a-brac shops on the east side of Moi Ave, south of the *Ambassadeur*, have cheap (and not very good) sunglasses for which you'll pay around Ksh100.

Swimming pools The best pool is at *Hotel Boulevard*, a nice setting and delightful water. Another welcoming pool is the one at the *YMCA* on the west side of Uhuru Highway, near the university. The pool at Nyayo Stadium is now open to the public. The pool at the *Grosvenor Hotel* is handy if you're staying at the *Youth Hostel*, over on the other side of Valley Road. The pool at *Silver Springs Hotel* in Valley Rd, behind the YH, is even better. A day by the pool is usually around Ksh50.

Telephone, Telegrams, Telex You can send **telegrams** from the 24-hour International Telecommunications (*Extelcoms*) centre on Haile Selassie Ave, situated next to the US Embassy. **International phone calls** are made from the same place, but it's easier – once you've bought a card – to use the IDD card phones. If all else fails, you can make them from large hotels, though you pay through the nose for this. The public **telex** is efficient and open 24 hours. Three minutes' worth (say 100 words) costs less than a phone call and you can receive telexes here, too.

Tent and equipment hire *Atul's*, Biashara St (PO Box 43202, ☎25935, open 8.30–12.30pm and 2–5.30pm, closes 4.30pm Sat), charges around Ksh100/day for a two-person tent with a deposit of Ksh1500. They do a large range of equipment – especially useful if you're going to Mount Kenya. *Habibs Cars* (see *Car Hire* above) rents gear, too, as does *Let's Go Travel* (see below) – a full set for under Ksh300/day. Always open tents and examine equipment before heading off for the wilds.

Tourist information The information bureau outside the *Hilton* has basically become a safari shop. Which means that Kenya has no official tourist information service – a lamentable state of affairs. The free and widely circulated *Tourist's Kenya* and *What's On in Kenya*, the first fortnightly, the second monthly, are always worth a glance, though they often carry outdated information. *Tourist's Kenya*, 1st Floor, Union Towers, Moi Ave (PO Box 40025, ☎3387169 or 331274), offers free practical and legal advice on tourist matters. The *Standard* newspaper is a useful source of current info and special offers.

Travel agents Recommended general travel agents are:

Let's Go Travel (PO Box 60342, ☎340331; fax 336890), Caxton House, Standard St, opposite Bruce House. Outstanding, providing complete lists of hotel tariffs and helpful, not pushy advice, they can make bookings for just about anything – including self-catering parks *bandas* – and also offer some specially negotiated deals on certain, more expensive, hotels, and their own Mara, Amboseli and Shaba camping safaris.

Nilestar (PO Box 90090, ☎226997/21426), Kenyatta Ave, opposite *680 Hotel* .

Bunson Travel Service (PO Box 45456, ☎337712), Pan Africa House, Standard St.

Flamingo Tours Ltd (PO Box 44899, ☎228961/2/3), 10th floor, Harambee Plaza, corner of Uhuru Highway and Haile Selassie Ave.

Yare Safaris Ltd (PO Box 63006, ☎725610), Union Towers, opposite *Hilton*.

Vaccinations Cholera, yellow fever, typhoid and hepatitis jabs can be obtained from City Hall, City Hall Way, or from Dr Sheti, 3rd floor, Bruce House, Standard St, who can also advise about malaria.

Visitor's passes/visas Visitor's pass extensions can be obtained at Nyayo House, Posta Rd, behind the old post office (Mon–Fri 8.30am–12.30pm, 2–3.30pm). This is usually done while you wait.

Women's movement *The National Council of Women of Kenya (NCWK)*, at the top of Moi Ave, is the organising body for women's groups in Kenya (☎24634). The *Maendeleo ya Wanawake* organisation has its main office in Maendeleo House on Monrovia St, top of Loita St (PO Box 44412, ☎22095 or 27033). The *MYWO* also has a shop on Muindi Mbingu St, selling crafts without the middlemen.

NAIROBI PROVINCE

Nairobi Province stretches way beyond the city suburbs, taking in an area of some 690 square kilometres (270 square miles) that ranges through agricultural and ranching land to jungle and national park.

For visitors, most of the interest lies to the **south**, in the predominantly Maasai land that begins with **Nairobi National Park** and includes the watershed ridge of the **Ngong Hills**. It's a striking landscape which you may find familiar from Karen Blixen's *Out of Africa*.

North of the city, the land is also distinctive: narrow valleys twisting down from the Kinangop plateau, some still filled with jungle and, it's said, leopards. In spite of that, the steep slopes here are high value real estate, in the process of development as exclusive suburbs, planted with shady gardens and festooned with security signs. To the **west**, the railway cuts through largely Kikuyu farmland, densely cultivated with corn, bananas and the cash-crop insecticide plant, pyrethrum. **East**, beyond the shanty suburb of Dandora, are the wide Athi plains, which are mostly ranching country.

Nairobi National Park

Open daily, dawn to dusk; Ksh220, Ksh30 cars.

If you don't think you'll be able to see any of the big Kenyan game reserves, try at least to spend a morning or afternoon in Nairobi's own **National Park**. Despite the hype, it really is remarkable that this 28,000-acre (113 square kilometre) patch of plains and woodland should exist almost uncorrupted – complete with more than eighty species of large mammals – literally within earshot of the downtown traffic. The park has no elephants but this is a small deficiency among a surprisingly high concentration of animals. For all the low-flying planes, tourist buses and lines of kombi vans, you have a greater chance of witnessing a kill here than in any of the other parks.

Practical information

The park gates open each morning at 6.15am and the first hours of the day are always best for game-watching. Without your own transport, the cheapest and most adventurous **way in** is to **hitch a ride** at the main gate. This is probably easiest on a Saturday or Sunday morning, when Kenyans are most likely to visit. The weekends are also by far the busiest time; during the week you'll find it very quiet. Take bus #125 at 5.40am or bus #24 at 6.40am from Nairobi's main bus station. Bus #11 also comes this way.

Alternatively, you should be able to swing a good deal on a **hired car** for a single day – you won't need anything more than a saloon car (the park roads are tarred) and kilometre charges won't amount to much. You could compare the cost with that of hiring a taxi for a few hours; if you do that, be dead sure of what you'll get for the agreed price – petrol will cost you.

Lastly, most of the safari shops in town sell three- to four-hour **trips around the park** for Ksh400 or so. *Nilestar* (see "Travel Agents" opposite) is one of the cheapest. The problem here is that they normally leave at 10am and 2pm, which

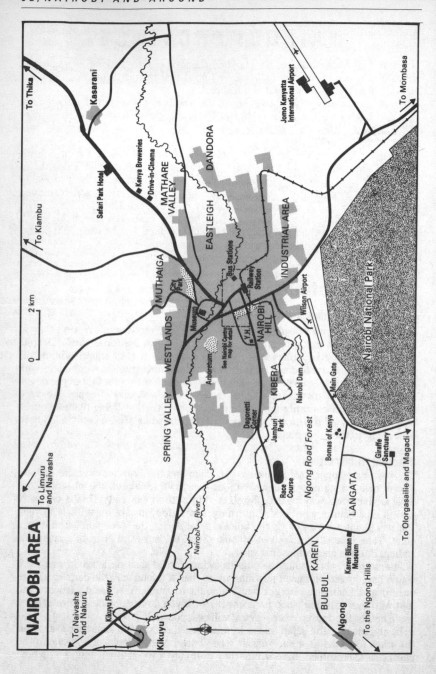

NAIROBI AREA

To Limuru and Naivasha

0   2 km

To Thika

Kasarani

To Kiambu

Kenya Breweries
Drive-in-Cinema
Safari Park Hotel

MATHARE VALLEY

DANDORA

Jomo Kenyatta
International Airport

To Mombasa

EASTLEIGH

INDUSTRIAL AREA

MUTHAIGA

City Park

Bus Stations
Railway Station

Wilson Airport

Nairobi National Park

Museum

WESTLANDS

Arboretum

See Nairobi Centre
map for detail

NAIROBI HILL

Y.H.

KIBERA

Nairobi Dam

Main Gate

SPRING VALLEY

Degoretti Corner

Jamhuri Park

Ngong Road Forest

Bomas of Kenya

Giraffe Sanctuary

To Olorgasailie and Magadi

Race Course

LANGATA

Nairobi River

KAREN

BULBUL

Karen Blixen Museum

Ngong

To the Ngong Hills

Kikuyu Flyover

To Naivasha and Nakuru

KIKUYU

To Limuru

are not ideal times – though late afternoon is better than midday. A trip like this doesn't guarantee anything, but your chances of sighting most of the animals are high. (Note: open-topped minibuses provide better vantage points than cars, though a recent rule, following a lion attack, forbids opening them in this park.)

Seeing the animals

If you're driving around independently, go to the western end, near the main entrance, where most of the woodland is concentrated. This is where you are most likely to see giraffe and, just after dawn, if you're very lucky, a leopard. The highest point here, known as **Impala Hill**, is a good spot to scan the park with binoculars, but lions, usually found in more open country, are more easily located by checking with the rangers at the gate. There are literally only two or three cheetahs in the park at present. You have to be lucky.

It's not that difficult to see some of the park's **rhinos**, however, most often found in the forest glades in the west. **Hippos** can usually be viewed at a pool in the **Mbagathi River** in the east. The Mbagathi forms the southern boundary of the park and is the only permanent river. It's fringed with the yellow acacias that early explorers and settlers dubbed "fever trees" because they seemed to grow in the areas where fever (malaria) was most common. Several of the park's seasonal streams are dammed to regulate the water supply: in the dry season, these **dams** – all located on the northern side of the park where the streams come down off the Empakasi plain – draw the heaviest concentrations of animals. Many of the herds cross the Mbagathi every year and disperse across the Athi plains as the rains improve the pasture, returning to the park during the drought. Before 1946, when the park was opened, only the physical barrier of Nairobi itself diverted the northward migration. The erection of fences along the park's northern perimeter has changed that, but the occasional lion still finds its way up as far as the suburb of Karen.

Although the western end has the best cross section of wildlife, there are two gates out onto the Mombasa road in the east, so you don't have to retrace your route. This gives you a chance to drive through the open savannah country favoured by **zebra and antelope**. There are large herds of introduced **buffalo** which you can see – they're hard to miss – out here and almost anywhere in the park.

Birdlife in the park is staggering – a count of more than 400 species. Enthusiasts won't need priming, and will see rarities from European latitudes as well as the exotics. Even if you're fresh off the plane and ornithologically illiterate, the first glimpses of ostrich, secretary bird, crowned crane and the outlandishly hideous marabou stork never fail to impress.

An orphanage, not a zoo

If you don't go straight out onto the Mombasa road, return by an alternative route to the main gate and have a look in at the moderately interesting – if it's open – **animal orphanage** (4–6pm daily; Ksh33). Here, a motley and shifting collection of waifs and strays, protected from nature, have, for some years been allowed to regain strength before being released. That anyway was the idea, though many of the inmates seemed to be established residents and it always appeared doubtful whether "This orphanage is not a zoo," as the sign claimed. Presumably they didn't rescue the two tigers. At least it's a zoo with a difference: there are as many wild monkeys outside the cages as in them. It's been closed for some months, however, pending a reopening.

David Sheldrick Wildlife Trust and orphanage

The **elephant and rhino orphanage** run by Daphne Sheldrick on the trust fund set up in memory of her husband (for three decades the indomitable warden of Tsavo) is a very worthwhile side trip when you're at the park. Telephone before you visit (☎891996, PO Box 15555) and leave a donation towards the work – there's no charge as such.

Daphne Sheldrick has spent twenty-five years perfecting the delicate techniques of **hand-rearing** baby elephants and, in the process of trial and error, has produced a mass of scientific data on their developmental biology and psychology. They require the sort of twenty-four hour attention devoted to human babies and, only by treating them as such, do they pull through the severe grief of losing their families to poachers. By the time a calf is nine months old it is consuming twenty-eight litres of special milk formula a day – though only when its trunk is in contact with a suitable substitute for a mother's flank, usually a tent or piece of tarpaulin, but sometimes the armpit or neck of a human attendant. The work occupies a group of dedicated keepers full-time in the care of a handful of babies and the visit is quite moving.

Daphne Sheldrick aims to bring up elephant orphans to the age of about two when, as "toddlers", they can safely be delivered to the care of a foster matriach elephant in Tsavo park. **Rhino orphans**, less sensitive and much less intelligent, are an easier task to rear, and several young rhinos have been accepted by the resident rhino community in Nairobi National Park.

The Bomas of Kenya

Forest Edge Road, 2km past National Park main entrance, open Mon–Fri, 9am–5pm, Sat and Sun 1–6pm, Ksh100 (PO Box 40689, ☎891801).

The **Bomas of Kenya** were originally an attempt to create a living museum of indigenous Kenyan life, with a display of traditional homesteads (*bomas*) and an emphasis on regional dances. Unfortunately the place seems to suffer from a lack of proper funding. Its vitality is channelled mainly into souvenir-selling: the homesteads, representing the architectural styles of Kenya's people, are for the most part sadly unkempt. Even so, if you're looking to fill an afternoon, or you want a change from the National Park, they can be enjoyable enough, particularly on weekends when they're crowded and a disco follows the dance show.

Surprisingly, perhaps, the dances (weekdays at 2.30pm, weekends at 3.30pm) are not performed by the appropriate Kenyan nationalities – the Harambee dancers doing fast costume changes between acts and presenting the nation's traditional repertoire as professionals rather than participants. If the sound system were good, the acoustics bearable and the whole place less of an amphitheatre, the impression would undoubtedly be better. As it is, most people find the spectacle somewhat degrading, and one hour quite enough of the two-hour show. At least you do get a very comprehensive taste of Kenyan dance styles, from the mesmeric jumps and sinuous movements of the Maa-speaking peoples to the wild acrobatics of some of the Mijikenda dances. But this is a theme park, not a living museum.

Karen, Langata and the Ngong Hills

KAREN is the quintessential white suburb – five-acre plots spaciously set on eucalyptus-lined avenues amid fields grazed by ponies. African homes are few. *Karen Dukas*, the shopping centre, includes a mock-Tudor restaurant and an arty riding-tack and gift shop. Still separated from Nairobi by a dwindling patch of dense, bird-filled woodland – the Ngong Road Forest – Karen is a reminder of how completely the settlers visualised and created little Europes for themselves. In Karen you could almost be in the English shires – or, for that matter, northern California. Buses to Karen include the #111 (fast) and the interminable #24 (a large red *matatu* from the KBS bus station).

From the National Park/Bomas, bus #24 cuts through the equally pleasant and alien suburb of LANGATA to the crossroads at *Karen Dukas*, where you can either turn left and catch the #111 up to Ngong, or right and head back to Nairobi.

A good place to focus on for a visit in Karen is the *Kazuri Bead Centre* (☎882362) near Hillcrest School and close to the Blixen museum. This employs nearly a hundred women (mostly unsupported or destitute) to make an extraordinary variety of handmade jewellery and beads, principally ceramic.

Karen Blixen Museum

Karen Road; open 9.30am–6pm daily; Ksh100, Ksh10 for Kenyans

Bus #24 (a large red matatu from the KBS bus station) can also drop you at the **Karen Blixen National Museum**, the house where much of the action of Karen Blixen's *Out of Africa* took place. The Danish government presented it to Kenya as an Uhuru gift along with the Agricultural College built in the grounds. It's a beautiful, well-proportioned house with square, wood-panelled rooms. The restoration of its original appearance and furnishings has evidently been very thorough.

On weekends you may be suffocated by Mozart and tour groups complaining about how little Denys Finch Hatton resembles Robert Redford, but come during the week and it's more peaceful, though still not especially worthwhile since you can view the rooms through the windows. The gardens, laid out as in former times, are delightful: they have a Nature Trail marked out now, and a replica 1920s coffee factory is being built in the grounds. If you're a true fan, you can come on an organised tour from town – often including the *Giraffe Centre* (below).

The fake-1920s Nairobi that was built, not far away, for the shooting of the movie would have been a more magnetic attraction than the Bogani house. Strangely, political dictates ensured its demolition once the film crews left.

The Langata Giraffe Centre

Gogo Falls Lane, 1km from Hardy Shopping Estate (continue past National Park main entrance, leaving Magadi Rd to the left, then turn left down Langata South Rd; follow signs); bus #24; open, in school term time, Mon–Fri 4–5.30pm, 10am-5.30pm weekends, and during holidays, 11am–5.30pm. Ksh80, children free (PO Box 15004, ☎891658).

Although promoted as a children's outing, the **Langata Nature Education Centre**, run by the AFEW (*African Fund for Endangered Wildlife*), has serious intentions: it has successfully boosted the population of the rare Rothschild's giraffe and educates children about conservation. The original nucleus of giraffes here came from the wild herd near Soy. "Daisy Rothschild", among others, is still fluttering her eyelashes, and you'll get some good mug shots from the giraffe-level observation tower.

The Ngong Hills

NGONG village is 8km past *Karen Dukas* (bus # 111, 111A every 30 min.; every 20 min. at weekends) but, if you have the chance, stop on the way at BULBUL and take a look at the pretty mosque of this largely Muslim village. As often happened in Kenya, Islam spread through the settlement of discharged troops from other British-ruled territories – this time Sudanese Nubia.

The **Ngong Hills** are revered by the Maasai, who have several traditional explanations of how they were formed. The best known says that a giant, stumbling north with his head in the clouds, tripped on Kilimanjaro. Thundering to the ground, his hand squeezed the earth into the Ngongs' familiar, knuckled outline. An even more momentous story explains the Ngongs as the bits of earth left under God's fingernails after he'd finished creating.

The **walk along their sharp spine** was once a popular day's hike and picnic outing. The views, of Nairobi on one side and the Rift Valley on the other, are magnificent, and the forested slopes are still inhabited by buffalo and antelope. Unfortunately, the number of attacks and robberies of unwary walkers has discouraged people. The route up from the village is now patrolled by police on weekends – small fees are usually levied per car and per person, and the whole excursion is not encouraged. It's better to go in a group. Check things out at Ngong police station, where they'll probably provide you with an escort if you go on a weekday when there are fewer visitors. Women travelling without men are, as usual, at a disadvantage. All this is a great pity as the walk, even simply up to the radio relay station above Ngong village, is a fine one.

With a **4WD vehicle**, in the dry season, you can get to the summit, Point Lamwia (2459m), and shouldn't normally need a guard with you. There are 360 degrees of view. Down on the lower ridges, almost due east of the highest point, is the **Finch Memorial,** Karen Blixen's tribute to the man who took her flying.

FURTHER AFIELD

Once they decide to leave Nairobi, many travellers overlook the attractions of the surrounding area. **Naivasha**, a strange and lovely Rift Valley lake, is the most obvious example: a highly recommended first staging post, with birdlife and hikes enough to keep you busy for several days. On from here (a short bus ride) is the wilder and spectacular country around Kinangop, again rewarding for walkers.

To the south, **Magadi**, a soda lake, is a harsh and fiercely hot place, virtually ignored by Nairobi. If you're driving, this is a possible day's excursion from the capital. But it's best taken more slowly, allowing time to see the prehistoric site at **Olorgasailie** on the way.

Thika, to the east, has little of the romance of its name, but the **Fourteen Falls** and **Ol Doinyo Sapuk National Park** nearby are worth the short drive. Reaching them by public transport is harder.

Lake Naivasha and around

NAIVASHA, like so many Kenyan place names, is a corruption of a local (Maasai) original: *E-na-iposha* (heaving waters), a pronunciation still used by Maa speakers you'll meet in the vicinity. The grassy shores of the lake were traditional Maasai grazing land for centuries, prior to its "discovery" by Joseph Thomson in 1884. Before the nineteenth century was out, however, the "glimmering many-isled expanse" had seen the arrival, with the railway, of the first European settlers. Soon after, the Maasai *laibon* Ole Gilisho, whom the British had appointed chief of the Naivasha Maasai, was persuaded to sign an agreement ceding his people's grazing rights all around the lake – and the country houses went up. Today the Maasai are back, though many of the properties here are still owned by Europeans.

The lake, a slightly forbidding but highly picturesque waterscape with its floating islands of papyrus, has some curious physical characteristics. It's fresh water – with Lake Baringo the only other example in the Rift – and the water level mysteriously fluctuates. It has dropped quite considerably in recent years to enlarge the variable acreage of lakeside terrain, though not enough to regain the areas of shore that were cultivated in the 1950s when the lake was half its present area. The outer edge of the fringing band of papyrus marks the shoreline the settlers knew and you can still see fence posts sticking up. Perhaps of more immediate and visible interest though, is the lake's protected hippo population and extraordinary **birdlife**: all kinds from the grotesque marabou storks to pet shop lovebirds in pairs. These, and the area's climate, with a light breeze always drifting through the acacias, make Naivasha a hard place to beat as a first stop out from Nairobi.

Naivasha town: orientation and arrival

Coming **from Nairobi** on the older, lower road (see map, p.100) you could ask to be dropped off at the lake road turning. If you're hitching or in a private vehicle, you're more likely to arrive on the faster Uplands road and might be dropped at the junction, uphill behind the town.

It's possible to catch a *matatu* or bus straight down to the lake, but if you plan to stay any time in the area, you should go into the town of **Naivasha** first to stock up on essentials. Most travellers tend to do their own cooking and there's a much wider choice of supplies in town than at the lake itself.

For **food supplies**, the fruit stalls on the main road are good; there's not much added choice at the market. The *Multiline Supermarket* opposite the stalls has the best selection of groceries. An excellent **hoteli** is the *North Kinangop* – inexpensive fish and chips and amazingly filling *mandaazi*. Or try the unusual *La Belle Inn* (PO Box 532, ☎20116, restaurant closed Tuesdays), which serves barbecued tilapia and has a nice line in pizzas, vegetarian pies and real croissants. You can **stay the night** at *La Belle Inn*, too (B&B Ksh800/1200) and it's a popular stopover between Maasai Mara and Nairobi. There are a number of less comfortable places, especially near the bus station. Tops is *Top Lodge* (PO Box 1164, ☎20121; Ksh80/100 non s/c), a safe but insanely noisy abode, where you're advised to choose a courtyard-side room if you want any sleep. Naivasha town, as a place to stay, has little to offer; unless you arrive late in the day, you may as well head on down to the lake.

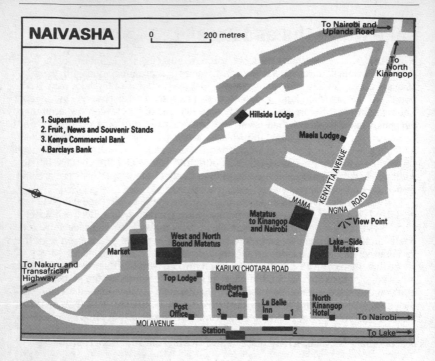

NAIVASHA

0   200 metres

To Nairobi and
Uplands Road

To
North
Kinangop

1. Supermarket
2. Fruit, News and Souvenir Stands
3. Kenya Commercial Bank
4. Barclays Bank

Hillside Lodge

Maela Lodge

KENYATTA AVENUE

MAMA
NGINA ROAD

View Point

Matatus
to Kinangop
and Nairobi

Lake-Side
Matatus

West and North
Bound Matatus

Market

To Nakuru and
Transafrican
Highway

KARIUKI CHOTARA ROAD

Top Lodge

Brothers
Cafe

La Belle
Inn

North
Kinangop
Hotel

To Nairobi

Post
Office

3

1

MOI AVENUE

Station

2

To Lake

Lakeside practicalities

Getting to the lake, there's a regular shuttle of *matatus*, a bus every hour or so, and easily hitchable traffic. But if you have time, walking at least part of the way down the **lake road** is delightful. Distances below refer back to the lake road junction with the main Nairobi road, 3km from Naivasha town itself.

Camping on the east shore: or staying in luxury

After a couple of kilometres, you reach the first camping site at the house marked "Burch", next to the defunct *Thitavo Shop & Hotel*. Burch's (PO Box 40, ☎20154) has camping in the garden (Ksh50), boats pulled ashore as accommodation (plenty of room for two, Ksh100), hot showers and farm produce for sale. Nice people, too; they offer water-skiing and parascending, a recent addition. The place tends to be jammed with Nairobi weekenders but is empty most of the week. A kilometre or so further down the road, you pass the *Lake Naivasha Hotel* (PO Box 15, ☎20013, *Block Hotels* stateliness at around Ksh4000/double HB but more than 50 percent discount April–June); opposite its entrance, is a scruffy little staff village it has generated.

After that it's just acacias, tall grass, prickly pears and the occasional walking companion until, some 10km from the junction, you arrive at the *Safariland Lodge* (PO Box 72, ☎331960 – similar prices to the *Lake Naivasha*). This is by far the nicer of the two lake hotels, set amid glorious gardens, with horse riding, tennis, fishing and boat trips all on hand. You can occasionally see giraffes around here,

DANGER: LAKE NAIVASHA

Beware, out on the lake. The possibility that underground springs may feed it, its location on the floor of the Rift Valley, and its shallowness combine to produce notoriously fast changes of mood and weather: grey and placid one minute, suddenly green and choppy with whitecaps the next. Watch out, too, for hippos, who can overturn a small boat easily enough if frightened or harassed. Naivasha shouldn't be underestimated, as boating mishaps are all too common, but swimming, with the hippos distant, is said to be safe enough and bilharzia absent.

floating blithely through the trees, taking barbed wire and gates in their stride. The lodge allows camping on a small site, for a stiff Ksh100 per person (which includes use of the pool and all facilities), but there's further discouragement in that it doesn't offer much in the way of specific campers' requirements, and may also involve the companionship of a couple of hundred British soldiers on R&R. There's a *duka* (on the left opposite the hotel entrance) for basic supplies.

The YMCA

Most travellers, though, press on further, to the *YMCA* or to *Fisherman's Camp* (PO Box 370, ☎20370). If this is your plan, you may well want to get a lift: the first is 14km along the road, the second 17km, and the walking is made somewhat less than idyllic by vehicles kicking up dust from the outrageously bumpy track. The so-called **YMCA** – or youth hostel – is the lake's cheapest place to stay, either camping in the acacia grove or hiring out one of the spartan bandas (camping Ksh30, beds Ksh50, cheaper for IYHA members). When there's a group of people there, evenings around the fire make it arguably the best place to stay, and it's certainly easiest if you're planning an early morning hike into Hell's Gate National Park, as the entrance is just up the road. Firewood, eggs, tinned food, lake fish and milk, warm from the cow, are sporadically available. Hot showers depend on you lighting and stoking the fire under the water tank.

The *YMCA* is separated from the shore by woodland and scrub, an uncontentious grazing patch for hippos, and one to which the unfortunate beasts are regularly driven from neighbouring farms. The dull earth tremors you sometimes feel if you're camping down there add considerably to the already exciting African night. Despite their bulk, hippos seem to be remarkably sensitive creatures, and they must be able to see in the dark, too, for nary a guy-line is twanged.

Fisherman's Camp and around

The advantage of **Fisherman's Camp**, 3km further, is its site right on the lakeshore, so you could, if you wished, lie in your tent with your toes in the water. At least, you could if a rampant growth of reeds hadn't recently spread along the shore, cutting the whole area off from the water. You also get free use of their **boats** (otherwise hireable). Rowing along the papyrus-fringed shore just after the sun has come up, drifting among the pelicans and past other people's back gardens, is a rare pleasure – though large areas are now filled with a rank growth of weed and lilypads which makes it an exhausting one too. With luck (and a rod), you'll catch a tilapia. *Fisherman's Camp* charges Ksh40 to camp and also has *bandas* at various altitudes – and prices (Ksh100–150 per person) – on the slopes behind. You can rent double tents for Ksh110.

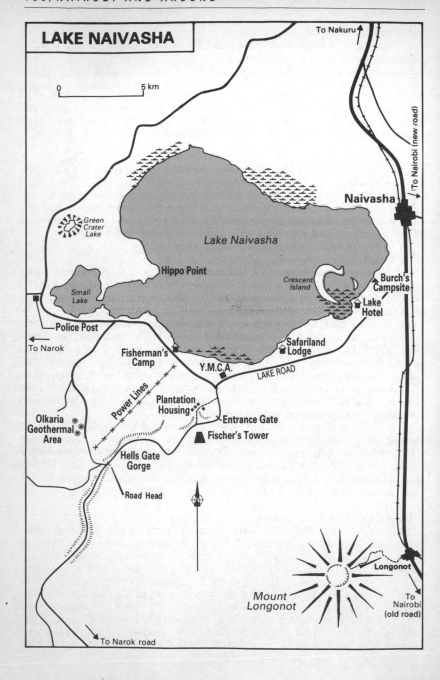

LAKE NAIVASHA

To Nakuru

To Nairobi (new road)

0   5 km

Green
Crater
Lake

Lake Naivasha

Hippo Point

Small
Lake

Naivasha

Crescent
Island

Burch's
Campsite

Lake
Hotel

Police Post

To Narok

Fisherman's
Camp

Safariland
Lodge

Y.M.C.A.

LAKE ROAD

Power Lines

Plantation
Housing

Olkaria
Geothermal
Area

Entrance Gate

Fischer's Tower

Hells Gate
Gorge

Road Head

Longonot

*Mount
Longonot*

To
Nairobi
(old road)

To Narok road

Between the *YMCA* and *Fisherman's Camp* lie the beginnings of what will surely become, in time, a new town. The big Sulmac Plantation here employs about 4000 people, producing flowers for the world market. There are several *dukas* and *hotelis* in the small "shopping centre" and, nearby, a little street market for fruit and vegetables.

If you're staying at the *YMCA* and looking for transport into Naivasha, it's generally better to walk towards the Sulmac stores. If you wait at the *Y*, you could be stuck some time as many vehicles are already full by that point. There's a **bus** back to Naivasha every day from *Fisherman's Camp* at 8am and 1pm.

Out and about: Crescent Island and around the lake

A very popular short trip is a visit to the **private game sanctuary** on **Crescent Island**. The crescent is the outer rim of a volcanic crater which forms a deep bay, the deepest part of the lake. The island is attached to the shore by a narrow causeway but don't try to enter there; go instead to *Lake Naivasha Hotel* and ask at the reception desk about a boat. The fixed price is Ksh115. You're left to wander over the island and taken back to the shore when you're ready. At first you may think there's nothing there, but the island, barely two square kilometres, is home to hundreds of species of birds as well as gazelle, waterbuck (caution – they can be dangerous), and some startlingly large, though harmless, pythons.

Circumnavigating the lake by road is difficult unless you have wheels. Very few vehicles have reason to go beyond *Fisherman's Camp* and it's not really worth trying to go the whole way. It is worth walking a little further, however, up to the superb viewpoint overlooking the **Small lake**. *"Elsamere"*, former home of Joy Adamson, is now a Conservation Centre and open to the public in the afternoons (video, followed by civilised afternoon tea on the lawn). If you have a genuine interest in wildlife conservation and would like to do some research in the Naivasha area, it's possible to stay at the centre (for Kenya residents around Ksh500/day FB, for others Ksh900). Contact Elsamere Conservation Centre, PO Box 4, Naivasha or PO Box 30029, Nairobi (☎742121 Nairobi). Amazingly, a troop of colobus monkeys lives in the grounds: they're normally found only in moist forests.

If you can get to it, the mysterious (because so few people do) **Green Crater Lake** is said to be beautiful, and the Maasai consider its deep alkaline waters good for sick cattle. It's some 6km past the SOUTH LAKE police post, between the shore of the main lake and the road. See if you can arrange a ride, though, before setting off on foot.

Hell's Gate National Park

Ksh220 (student reductions possible; ask), Ksh50 to camp.

The best expedition in the Naivasha area is the hike through the Njorowa gorge – **Hell's Gate**. This is a spectacular and exciting area, the gorge's red cliffs and undulating expanse of grassland providing one of the few remaining places in Kenya where you can walk among the **herds of plains game** without having to go a long way off the beaten track. Buffalo, zebra, eland, hartebeest, Thomson's gazelle and baboons are all usually seen; lions and leopards hardly ever, but you might just see a cheetah, and you'll certainly come across their pug marks if you scan the trail. There are servals, one of the most delicate cats, and, high on the cliffs, small numbers of *klipspringer* (cliffjumper) antelope. Njorowa is a fairly small area and the quantity of wildlife varies seasonally. The gorge is occasionally rather empty of animals.

The entrance to Hell's Gate is just south of the *YMCA* but the park gate is a further 1.5 km along this track. If you're wheel-less you should ideally get there as early as possible in the day: it's 25km to the end and back and, while the occasional Land Rover goes up there, this is unlikely during the week, making your chances of a lift somewhat slim. Still, hitching to the end and walking back is the standard way of doing Hell's Gate. You can camp in the gorge but if you want to come back the same day then the heat away from the lakeshore means trying to avoid the midday hours. You'll need to carry plenty of water and some food.

Through the gorge

The **National Park** is a recent creation. The track used to pass first through plantation workers' housing (cramped and fairly squalid but considerably better than some you can see), then through a narrow defile, echoing with the screaming of baboons, and out into the gorge proper. The baboon ravine has now been wired off at the lakeside end. It's still accessible from within the park. People who attempt to get into Hell's Gate without paying the fees are usually nabbed by a ranger equipped with binoculars, stationed by the gate.

From the entrance gate, take a look first at the rock known as **Fishcher's Tower**, after the German explorer who arrived at Lake Naivasha via Hell's Gate. The rock is a volcanic plug, the hard lava remaining from an ancient volcano after the cone itself has been eroded away. It's now the home of a colony of very astute hyrax, like large, shaggy guinea pigs, who expect to be fed.

Continuing through the gorge, more and more animals are visible on the slopes leading up to the sheer cliffs. Ornithologists probably don't need reminding that at least one pair of rare **lammergeier eagles** nest on the cliffs – or used to. They haven't been seen since 1986. More obvious are the secretary birds: these you'll always see, mincing carefully through the grass at a safe distance.

Hell's Gate is somehow a very authentic-looking part of East Africa. Its colours and acoustics give it a distinct sense of place. It has been used several times as a film location, most recently for that stirring epic *Sheena – Queen of the Jungle*, and a number of fibreglass rocks still litter the otherwise primaeval scene. The gorge's more enduring significance is as the one-time outlet for the prehistoric freshwater lake that stretched from here to Nakuru and, it's believed, would have supported early human communities on its shores.

At the southern end of the gorge (12km from the entrance), a second rock tower – **Ol Basta** – marks its transition into tangled ravine. If you've come equipped for a night out and you have the *Survey of Kenya* map for the area, you can press on, to emerge after a further (and difficult) 12km at the end of the canyon – still 15km short of the NAROK road. For orientation, aim for **Mount Suswa** – itself an area of great exploring interest, only properly documented in the last few years.

Otherwise, either turn back and retrace your path to the gate, or else climb up through the bushes on the right towards the noise and steam of the new Olkaria geothermal station. Here on the cliff top you can look out over the gorge and a Maasai enkang below, with your back to the first productive **geothermal installation** in Africa. The underground temperature of the super-heated, pressurised water is up to 304°C, one of the hottest sources in the world, and the station is eventually expected to supply half of Kenya's energy requirements.

Heading for the main buildings through the scrub, and the maze of pipes and hissing steam jets, you eventually meet a perfect new **tarmac road**: from here, you shouldn't have any problem getting a ride with plant workers down to the lake road at a point several kilometres past *Fisherman's Camp*. The road emerges near the Oserian farm where they produce dried carnations. If you hike it, allow about three hours to complete this section; you could also follow the power lines down to the road near the *Sulmac* stores. There are fine views of the Small and Crater lakes.

Mount Longonot

Ksh220, student reductions; local guides available.

Mount Longonot is worth climbing. It is there. And, if the season's right, there are fabulous views in every direction as you circle the rim. Don't try to make the ascent from the lake road or Hell's Gate, however – it's further and steeper than it looks, and is covered in dense bush on its north slopes. Head instead for Longonot police station, just outside the village of the same name on the old Nairobi road. Here you can leave valuables and enquire, if you like, about a **guide** (Ksh60). If you're alone this isn't a bad idea, as much for company as security: furthermore, there's only one straightforward route up to the crater rim – and the guides know it. Longonot was recently given national park status, but the standard fees can sometimes be negotiated downwards.

If you're **driving**, there's a driveable road that leads the six or seven kilometres to the base of the mountain from the main road, and you can now leave your car there safely and get a drink. For **overnight stays** in the village, the *First and Last Hotel* is recommended – very basic but friendly, around Ksh60.

Up the mountain

Longonot's name comes from the Maasai *oloonong'ot,* "mountain of many spurs" or "steep ridges", and you soon find out why. The cone is composed of very soft volcanic deposits that have eroded into deep gulches and narrow ridges. The **hike to the rim** takes about an hour. At the top you can collapse (the last section is rather steep), and look back over the Rift Valley on one side and the enormous, silent crater on the other. Thomson, the first *mzungu* up here, was overcome:

> *The scene was of such an astounding character that I was completely fascinated, and felt under an almost irresistible impulse madly to plunge into the fearful chasm. So overpowering was this feeling that I had to withdraw myself from the side of the pit.*

If you feel the same urge, you can now walk, or scramble, down a steep **crater path**; you turn left from the gravelly landing on the rim and find the path after about ten minutes' walk. Exciting encounters with buffalo on the crater-floor aren't uncommon: a 1937 guidebook observes that "any attempt to descend into the crater is accompanied by hazard". Preferably you should take a guide.

The walk **around the crater rim** is what most climbers do. The anti-clockwise route is easier because the climb to the summit on the western side is quicker and steep sections more negotiable. It doesn't look far, but allow two to three hours. Much of the path is over crumbly volcanic tufa and has been worn, by a combination of walkers and rain, into a channel so deep and narrow that it's almost impossible to put one foot in front of the other.

Until recently, Longonot's crater was famous for its steam jets. Although their pockmark-like vents are still visible in several places around the rim and on the crater walls, their emissions of steam have decreased since the Olkaria plant went on line, though the hot-air thermals are said to be still sufficient to deflect light aircraft. Another rumour is the existence of a tunnel running from the inside base of the crater on the south side and out onto the plain beyond. It's supposed to be too hot to go the whole length, so no one really knows.

From Kinangop to Thika

If you're serious about hiking, mountain biking, or fairly adventurous expeditionary driving, **the route from North Kinangop to Thika** is a dramatic and attractive one. It cuts up from the Rift Valley and right over the southern flank of the Nyandarua (Aberdare) range – still, in large part, untouched mountain jungle.

The approach from NAIVASHA is quite straightforward, as frequent *matatus* make the journey up to NORTH KINANGOP. Routine though it may be, this part of the journey is still spectacular. The road climbs constantly towards the **Kinangop Plateau**, with the Rift Valley and Lake Naivasha way below. The land hereabouts is Kikuyu farming country, once widely settled by Europeans, who were lured by the wide open moors, rocky outcrops and gushing streams. Sheep and cattle graze everywhere.

NORTH KINANGOP is nowadays a rather isolated rural community, a village of big rubber boots and raggy sweaters (it can freeze here at night), whose road becomes nearly impassable during the long rains. Transport onwards from here outside the rainy season, though, is usually little problem – at least as far as South Kinangop. Tractors will pick you up and there are a few old lorries, too, trundling around. **SOUTH KINANGOP** is livelier than its northern counterpart, a small trading centre with a paved road straight to Naivasha (look out for the quaint, red-tiled colonial buildings which are now a *Caltex* station).

Beyond here – heading towards Thika – you're pretty much down to walking. A murram road (the C67) does continue, but there's very little traffic as it switchbacks in descent, across a series of streams flowing south from the Aberdares to the Chania River. The road follows the river, with tremendous scenic variation, though almost always through forest; sometimes wild, sometimes conifer plantation. But after the turn-off for **Kimakia forest station**, the occasional *shambas* and all signs of habitation stop completely: from here down, the forest is untouched mountain jungle, trees with huge dark green leaves, birds shrieking in alarm, the crashing of colobus monkeys, chameleons wobbling across the road. In the wrong season the road becomes an appalling quagmire, really just for tractors (I saw only one), but on foot, or even by mountain bike, there's no danger of getting stuck.

You reach tarmac and human population again at **GATAKAINI**, and, just before you do, there's the very pleasant *Kimakia Fishing Camp* (*bandas*, toilets and running water), unsupervised but a good place to spend the night with your own tent. The camp is run by the Fisheries Department (headquarters next to the National Museum in Nairobi). At Gatakaini you can also find *matatus* and buses to get you down to the relative metropolis of Thika. Irritatingly, towards evening public transport thins out and the country bus may leave you stranded at GATURA. If you have no luck hitching, give the excellent, but no longer appropriately named, *Tarmac End Inn* a try; a clean B & L with hot water at Ksh70/cube.

South Kinangop to Gatakaini is a thirty-kilometre stretch, taking seven or eight hours on foot. It's also a great mountain bike trip. It proves, again, how many exhilarating areas there are close to Nairobi – and how many more there must be.

Thika and nearby

Despite the literary connections (Elspeth Huxley, *The Flame Trees of Thika*), **THIKA** is a dull little town – suitably humdrum if you've just arrived from the wilds of the Kinangop or GARISSA – not even redeemed by the profusion of flame trees you might expect. It's best thought of as a satellite town of Nairobi.

Pineapples, introduced in 1905, are Thika's contemporary claim to fame. Thousands of acres flourish here, easily confused with the sisal that is also grown in the area. Until 1968, most of the valuable export crop was produced on *shambas*; since then Del Monte has held the lion's share of the plantations.

Thika is off the tourist route – or at least the main road to Mount Kenya – so you're not very likely to stay the night. The bus station, oddly, seems to be full of rastas – a real Jah-ville. If you stay, the rooms at the *December Hotel* (s/c) are reasonable enough, but cheaper and fairly acceptable is the *White Line Hotel* – occasional hot water and a good restaurant. Just out of town on the road north is the *New Blue Posts Hotel* (PO Box 42, ☎32241), which is older than the town itself and boasts of "overlooking both Thika and Chania Falls". Although you might expect a certain quaint shabbiness, the old place has recently been refurbished and is now smartly comfortable (rooms from around Ksh300/400).

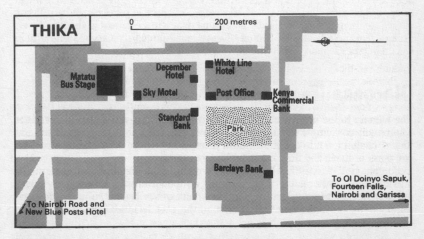

The Fourteen Falls and Ol Doinyo Sapuk National Park

From Thika, the trip out to tiny **Ol Doinyo Sapuk** National Park and the Fourteen Falls on the Athi River is a popular one with motorised travellers and Nairobi weekenders. The falls are genuinely impressive when heavy rains flood them into a single, red, thundering cataract. But a vague, obnoxious smell hangs in the air, presumably caused by effluent from Thika's emerging industries.

To get to either site, head for KILIMA MBOGO village – also known as Ol Doinyo Sapuk – some 20km down the GARISSA road. There are *matatus* from Thika to this village located 4km off the main road. The *Fourteen Falls Hotel* is close to the main road; the **turning to the falls** 2.5km down the murram road, on the left, before you reach the actual village. A rash of robberies at the Fourteen Falls car park, ten minutes' walk away, explains the presence of two policemen every day till 5pm.

Ol Doinyo Sapuk National Park

The **national park gate** is reached by crossing the Athi river, then taking a right turn in Kilima Mbogo village. The gate is 3km from the village and, while usual park fees apply, you get an armed guard to protect you from animal and human dangers. You're not allowed in on foot. The quantity of buffalo is enough dissuasion but the usual population of thugs and bandits is said to pose a terrific threat as well (they must be immune to the buffalo). You'd probably catch a ride if you waited at the gate (especially on a weekend). Ordinary camping (Ksh50) is possible at two sites, just inside the gate and a kilometre up the track; there's also a "special campsite", reservable by the week.

The park contains just the mountain of **Ol Doinyo Sapuk** (Maasai: "big mountain"), known to Kikuyu speakers as *Kilima Mbogo* (buffalo mountain). Visiting it consists basically of driving 8km up the steep dirt road to the top. At the six-kilometre mark, you come to the grave of Sir William Northrop McMillan, the fattest of famous settlers, whose intended burial place on the summit had to be abandoned when the modified tractor-hearse's clutch burned out. Views from here are tremendous and you're not likely to get further, even with four-wheel drive, because the final couple of kilometres of track is particularly bad. If you make it to the top, the 360-degree panorama over a huge oxbow in the Athi River, Thika's pineapple fields and Mounts Kenya and Kilimanjaro can be wonderful in December and January, when the air is really clear.

Olorgasailie and Lake Magadi

The journey to the prehistoric site at **Olorgasailie** takes you instantly out of the commotion of Nairobi and down into a hot, sparsely inhabited part of the Rift Valley. Hitching a ride could be a slow process but the country bus (10am, noon and 2pm) is cheap and the Maasai are lovely company.

The bus halts at KISERIAN for a few minutes – your chance to buy last-minute provisions, as further south there's almost no food available. The scenery opens out dramatically as you skirt the southern flank of the Ngong Hills and descend steeply down the escarpment. Try to get a front seat, as giraffe and other animals are often seen.

Olorgasailie

Ksh150, open daily.

OLORGASAILIE Prehistoric Site is signposted, 1.5km from the main road. You need to bring all requirements apart from water. The **accommodation** and **museum** are just above the excavations on a ridge overlooking what was once a wide, shallow lake. Double *bandas* are Ksh80/night or you can camp (book *bandas* in advance at the National Museum in Nairobi to be sure of beds). Do-it-yourself showers and free firewood are also available. Olorgasailie is a peaceful place to stay, while the **guided tour** around the excavations (included in the entrance charge) is fascinating and not to be missed.

The hand axe site

Between 400,000 and 500,000 years ago the lake shore was inhabited by "people", probably *Homo erectus*, of the **Acheulian culture** (after St. Acheul in France, where it was first discovered). They made a range of identifiable stone tools: cleavers for skinning animals; round balls for crushing bones, perhaps for hurling or possibly tied to vines to be used, à la gaucho, as *bolas*; and heavy hand axes, for which the culture is best known, but for which, as Richard Leakey writes, "embarrassingly, no one can think of a good use". The guides tell you they were used for chopping meat and digging. This seems reasonable but some are very large, while hundreds of others, particularly at the so-called factory site, seem far too small. The story here is that they were made by children practising . . . At least it's almost plausible. The great thing about places like Olorgasailie is that the answers are not cut and dried. There's plenty of room for the imagination to construct scenarios of how it *might* have been.

Mary and Louis Leakey's team did most of the unearthing here in the 1940s. Thousands of the stone tools they found have been left undisturbed, *in situ*, under protective roofs. Maybe most impressive is the fossilised leg bone of a gigantic extinct elephant, dwarfing a similar bone from a modern elephant placed next to it. It was long hoped that human remains would also be uncovered at Olorgasailie, but despite extensive digging none have been found – more scope for speculation.

Staying on

Although you could conceivably look around the site before the next bus passes two hours later, and then ride down to MAGADI, it's much better to give yourself a day and a night. Sitting in the shade of the open-sided picnic *bandas* with a pair of binoculars and looking out over what used to be the lake can yield some rewarding animal-watching, especially in the brief dusk. Go for a walk out past the excavations towards the gorge and you'll see more: gerenuk, duiker, giraffe, eland and baboons.

Contacts with Maasai are good here, too. If you'd like to take pictures, food is a more acceptable payment than money. There's usually some jewellery for sale as well. And if you're enchanted with the peace and presence of Olorgasailie, and stay longer than you'd anticipated, you can cultivate further friendships – and collect some scant provisions – at the cluster of desolate *dukas* at **OLTEPESI**, 3km back along the Nairobi road, where they also have warm beer and soft drinks.

Lake Magadi and west to the Nguruman escarpment

Heading south and descending, **LAKE MAGADI** is a vast shallow pool of soda, a sludge of alkaline water and crystal trona deposits lying in a Rift Valley depression a thousand metres below Nairobi. This is one of the hottest places in the country. On a barren spit of land jutting out across the multicoloured soda, the *Magadi Soda Company*, an ICI interest, has built the very model of a company town. Everything you see, apart from the homes of a few Maasai on the shore, is owned and run by the corporation. You pass a company police barrier and enter over a causeway, past surreal pink saltponds. Now on company territory, a sign tells visitors to report their arrival to the town police station "in their own interest". You should do so. Though the formalities are not taken seriously, there's a useful map of the area on the wall.

Making do in Magadi

Having arrived, you might wonder how you'll fill the time until the bus leaves for Nairobi the next morning. Behind the police station, which stands on the highest point of the peninsula, the lake glows unnaturally in the afternoon sun. Looking the other way (that's west), the road to the left leads to the "European" end of town, where a dozen or so managers live and where there's a strange, barren golf course; to your right, **the town** slopes gently down to a crusty shore where most of the Kenyan employees live. The less snobbish of five staff clubs (bars) are located here, and there are two or three stores and something which might, at some times of the year, pass as a market.

The company has built blocks of apartments, a church, a mosque and schools and, with a touch of inspiration, a large, glittering **swimming pool** that used to be public, free, and open daily from 10am to 2pm and 5 to 11pm. Recent reports indicate you shouldn't assume automatic access, but the pool is the town's only real focus and probably your target after the bus ride, anyhow. The pool itself is rarely used, but the poolside bar and *nyama choma* kiosk are popular in the evenings. On weekends, there are even a few picnickers from Nairobi. Magadi has no hotel or lodgings, though you can pitch a tent almost anywhere – the golf course would probably be a good place – and it's likely you'll be invited home by employees.

The atmosphere here, somewhat surprisingly because of the harshness of environment and nature of the work, is relaxed and welcoming. People tend to get drunk a lot: by comparison with the rest of Kenya, the company pays high wages, and accommodation and services are free.

The lake

Many visitors come to Magadi specifically for its **birdlife**. There's a wealth of avifauna here including, usually, large numbers of flamingos at the southern end of the lake. At this end, there are also freshwater swamps which attract many species.

The **lake** itself is fascinating to walk across (on the causeways: in practice only the inlet between Magadi and the eastern shore). On the eastern side, where you first arrive, you can watch the sweepers in rubber boots shovelling the byproduct, sodium chloride (common salt), into ridges on the technicolour "fields". Sodium chloride crystallises on top of the sodium carbonate (the "soda") and is loaded on to tractor-drawn trailers and taken away to be purified for human and animal consumption.

But the company is primarily concerned with extracting the soda. Magadi is the second largest source of sodium carbonate in the world. ICI's investment here is guaranteed – hot springs gush out of the earth's crust to provide an inexhaustible supply of briney water for evaporation. The dried soda is exported, first by rail to Mombasa via KAJIADO and KONZA, thence, much of it, to Japan. Magadi soda, used principally for glass-making, is Kenya's most valuable mineral resource after oil. But, despite the "high" wages, you wonder how anyone can be persuaded to work in this lurid inferno: the first rains here are usually "phantom rain", the ground so hot that the raindrops evaporate before hitting the surface. It's important to wear sunglasses and a hat while out in the sun.

Across from the town, on the eastern shore, Maasai will sell you *pombe* made from a base of roots and herbs, and fermented with honey. It's a lot cheaper than beer, and stronger, too. Asked if there was another name apart from the generic *pombe* they said "We just call it 'Ups". Drinking it in the middle of the day is not advisable.

Onwards or back

Returning to Nairobi from Magadi, the bus leaves at 6am, or you could ask about hitching a ride on the **train** to KONZA and Mombasa if you're headed that way. There's supposed to be a passenger service on Wednesday.

But with your own vehicle, you can drive on from the town, across the lake to the hot springs on the western side. Check the map in the police station first. From the **hot springs**, you can drive further (but you'd never hitch a ride), at least as far as the Ewaso Ngiro River at the foot of the Nguruman escarpment. Here you can pitch a tent near the local game warden's camp. Maasai and the rangers will keep you occupied, but although there are some *dukas*, you should bring what you can. They get no visitors here – it's another good place to meet untouched Kenya. In the right season, you should be able to four-wheel-drive it through to Narok. Good luck.

travel details

Getting out of Nairobi by public transport is normally a fairly haphazard business. The following is intended to lend a degree of structure to a chaotic scene, but to make it comprehensive would be a never-ending task. If in doubt, ask. You'll always get where you want to somehow.

Buses

OTC (bookings office, Racecourse Rd, PO Box 30475, ☎26155) and **Akamba Bus** *Service* (bookings office, Lagos Rd, PO Box 40322, ☎340430) have cheap fares and the **widest route coverage**. Both specialise in destinations west of Nakuru and around Mount Kenya. In addition they both do some runs to Mombasa, and *Akamba* covers Machakos and Kitui. Buses leave from the bus station behind the *OTC* bookings office, and from Lagos Rd in front of the *Akamba* office. Most routes have several day and night services daily.

Principal up-country destinations, in order of frequency of service, are: Nakuru, Kisumu, Kericho, Nyeri, Kisii, Kakamega, Meru, Eldoret, Machakos, Isiolo, Kitale, Embu, Nyahururu. Most

services will sell seats to towns on the way, when space permits.

To the northeast: you can get straight out to Garissa, daily, in the early morning, and around noon, from the *Garissa Express* terminus opposite the *KBS* depot in Eastleigh. From Garissa, onwards, there are connections for Wajir and Mandera, Liboi (for Somalia) and Mpeketoni (for Lamu). See "travel details" in Chs. 6 and 7.

To the coast: *Goldline* (bookings, Cross Road, PO Box 20861, ☎25279), and *Coastline* (bookings, bottom of Accra Rd, PO Box 16030, ☎29494), compete on the Kisumu–Nairobi–Mombasa route, undercutting the train, but it's a tedious ride. Both are fairly comfortable.

For express journeys: *Rift Valley Peugeot* (*RVP*) (Duruma Rd, PO Box 48817, ☎26374), runs minibuses non-stop, daytime only, to: Mombasa (3 daily, 6hr); Nakuru (3 daily, 2hr), calling at Naivasha (90min); Kisumu (3 daily, 5hr), calling at Kericho (4hr); Eldoret (3 daily, 5hr); Kitale (2 daily, 6hr). *MPS*, Duruma Rd, operates a similar schedule.

Tickets for all the above should, if possible, be reserved in advance at the company's own office.

For trips to places in this chapter, or just for fairly unstructured travel, you should head for the melée of the **country bus station**. A continual stream of buses leaves for Thika and destinations in Kiambu district. Many buses call at Naivasha en route for points west (Ch. 4). Others go to Magadi (10am with Akamba, plus noon and 2pm by country bus, 4hr, via Olorgasailie, 3 hr), to Machakos, Namanga, Narok (Ch. 6) and the Central Highlands (Ch. 2).

Matatus

If you decide to take a *matatu* out of Nairobi, you'll find that vehicles for different destinations congregate in certain areas of town (for example, *matatus* for Machakos wait by the market of the same name, in the car park just north of the country bus station; for Meru and Embu, try in the central reservation of Accra Rd, etc). You can take your choice – and rather yours than mine – of ordinary pick-ups, battered Berlins, Hiaces and the rest. But remember, the reputation attached to *matatus* isn't entirely the result of paranoia.

Hitching

Here are some **jumping-off points** to get you started:

To Naivasha (and destinations in Chs. 1, 3, 4, 7) take bus #103, 104, or 105 from the central *KBS* bus station or the railway station as far as the "Kikuyu flyover".

To Thika (and Chs. 2, 7), take bus #144/5 from *KBS* bus station as far as *Kenya Breweries.*

To Mombasa (or Amboseli, Tsavo), take bus #12 from Gill House on Moi Ave to Nairobi South "C" on the Mombasa highway.

Trains

Bookings on ☎21211, and see *Basics*, p.23.

To Mombasa: Daily at 5pm and 7pm arriving at 7.30 and 8am.

To Malaba (Uganda Border): Tues, Fri, Sat, at 3pm (arr. 9am) via Naivasha (6.50pm), Nakuru (8pm) and Eldoret (3am).

To Kisumu: Daily at 6pm, arriving at 8am via Naivasha (9pm) and Nakuru (10.50pm).

Planes

Booking desk addresses are given in Nairobi "Directory" in the Airlines box.

Kenya Airways flies at least 6 times daily from Jomo Kenyatta International to **Mombasa** (50–135min depending on routing and aircraft), with extra flights at weekends and in high season. First flight at 7am, last flight at 8–11pm. Flights via **Malindi** 1 or 2 times daily (85min). Flights to **Kisumu** 1 to 3 times daily (65min). Economy class fares (given in sterling): Mombasa, £28; Malindi £28; Kisumu £19. Always check in in good time – overbookings are commonplace.

Air Kenya Aviation flies out of Wilson Airport on the following routes, most of which operate only on demand. Check with the airline. To **Lamu** daily at 1.15pm (105min); to **Kiwaiyu** daily at 1.15pm (105min); to **Eldoret** Tues and Thurs at 7am and 3.45pm (60min); to **Amboseli Lodges** daily at 7.30am (roughly 30min depending on lodge); to the **Maasai Mara Lodges** daily 10am and 3pm (roughly 45min depending on lodge); to **Kalokol/Lake Turkana** Wed and Sun at 12.30pm (120min); to **Nyeri**, **Nanyuki** and **Samburu** daily at 9.15am (25, 50 and 85min respectively).

Economy class fares (one-way/return):
Lamu Ksh3000/5700;
Kiwaiyu Ksh4400/8500;
Eldoret Ksh1840/3430;
Amboseli Ksh1550/2720;
Mara lodges Ksh1960/3400;
Kalokol, Lodwar, Loiyangalani Ksh3580/6800;
Nyeri and Nanyuki Ksh1490/2600;
Samburu Ksh2300/4020.

Equator Airlines also flies out of Wilson. Their fares are a little lower but schedules no more guaranteed than *Air Kenya*'s, so check with them. To **Lamu** daily at 10am (90min); to Maasai Mara Lodges daily at 10am and 2pm (approximately 45min); and to **Garissa**, **Wajir** and **Mandera** at 7am (50, 150 and 255min respectively).

Economy class fares (one way/return):
Lamu Ksh2200/4250;
Mara lodges Ksh1300/2250;
Garissa Ksh2100/4000;
Wajir Ksh2400/4400;
Mandera Ksh3000 one-way.

TELEPHONE AREA CODES

Nairobi ☎ 02   **Naivasha** ☎0311   **Thika** ☎0151

CHAPTER TWO

THE CENTRAL HIGHLANDS

P olitical and economic heartland of the country, the **Central Highlands** stand at the focal point of Kenyan history. Mount Kenya, Africa's second highest peak, gave the colonial nation its name; the majority of British and European settlers carved their farms from the countryside around it. Later, and as a direct consequence, it was this region which saw the development of organised anti-colonial resistance culminating in *Mau Mau*.

Until independence, the fertile highland soils ("A more charming region is not to be found in all Africa," thought Joseph Thomson, exploring in the 1880s) were reserved largely for Europeans and considered, in Governor Eliot's breathtaking phrase, "White Man's Country". The **Kikuyu peoples** (Kikuyu, Meru and Embu), were skilled farmers and herders who had held the land for centuries before the Europeans arrived and were at first mystified to find themselves "squatters" on land whose ownership, in the sense of exclusive right, had never been an issue in traditional society. They were certainly not alone in losing land, but, by supplying most of the fighters for the Land and Freedom Army, they were placed squarely in the political limelight. In return, they have received a large proportion of what Kenyans call the "Fruits of Independence".

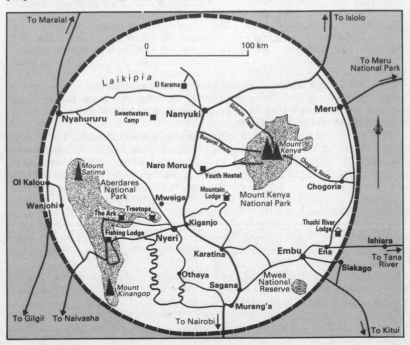

THE KIKUYU PEOPLES: SOME BACKGROUND

The ancestors of **the Kikuyu** migrated into this region over successive generations between the sixteenth and eighteenth centuries, from somewhere to the northeast of Mount Kenya. Stories describe how they found various hunter-gatherer peoples already inhabiting the region they now occupy: the **Gumba** on the plains and the **Athi** in the forests. A great deal of intermarriage, trade and adoption took place; the newcomers cleared the forests and planted crops, giving the hunters gifts of livestock, honey, or wives in return for using the land. As this Bantu-speaking, cultivating, livestock-keeping culture expanded and consolidated in the Highlands, the indigenous peoples gradually lost their old identities.

Between **Maasai** and Kikuyu, relations were less easy. They both placed (and still place) high value on the ownership of cattle, the Maasai depending entirely on livestock. During bad droughts, Maasai might raid their Kikuyu neighbours' herds, with retaliation at a later date being almost inevitable. But such **inter-tribal warfare** often had long-term benefits, as ancient debts were forever being renegotiated and paid off by both sides, thus sustaining the relationship. There was lively trade and **intermarriage** between the two peoples, and married Kikuyu women enjoyed a special immunity enabling them to organise trading expeditions deep into Maasailand, often with the help of a *hinga*, a Kikuyu of Maasai descent, to oil the wheels.

As well as these economic and social relations, the Kikuyu had close **cultural affinities** with the Maasai in the past. Many visitors are surprised when they first see the evidence of this – for example, in traditional dress styles – in museums or old photos. Like the Maasai, the Kikuyu advanced in status as they grew older, through named age-sets, with appropriate rituals at each stage. And although age is figured more chronologically these days, it's still an important social index: a Kikuyu who discovers you're both the same age is likely to say "We're age mates then!"

Circumcision, of young men and women, still marks the most important transition into adulthood for most Kikuyu, though "female circumcision"

Today most of the land is in African hands again, and it supports the country's highest rural population. There is intensive farming on almost all the lower slopes, as well as much of the higher ground, beneath the **National Parks** of **Mount Kenya** and **the Aberdares**.

There are considerable rewards in travel through the Highlands. Above all, if you're into hiking, there's the ascent of **Mount Kenya**. And, while hikes lower down and in the **Aberdare** range are easier, they are scarcely less dramatic, with the bonus of a chance to see some of the highland **wildlife**. If you like **fishing**, the mountain streams are full of trout that were introduced early this century, and most tourist lodges will rent fishing tackle even if you're not staying there. Nor is **travel itself** ever dull in the Highlands, where the range of scenery is a spectacular draw in its own right: primary-coloured **jungle** and **shambas**, pale, windswept **moors** and dense **conifer plantations**, all with a mountain backdrop. People everywhere are friendly and quick to strike up a conversation. Towns are animated and markets colourfully chaotic.

Prospects for **hitching** are well above average, but **public transport** is good, too, and bus journeys invariably packed with interest and amusement. For **accommodation**, you'll find a handful of tourist hotels and lodges – including *Treetops* – that will give fair return for your cash if you're in the mood to splurge. But there's also a wide range of reasonably priced lodgings. *Hotelis* are plentiful and serve gargantuan portions.

(clitoridectomy) is illegal and performed less and less. In the past, the operations were accompanied by changes in dress and ornament. Once circumcised, boys could grow their hair long and dye it with ochre in the style of Maasai warriors (in fact, the Maasai got their ochre from the Kikuyu, so it may really be the other way around). They also wore stacks of glass beads around their necks, metal rings on their legs and arms, and pulled their ear lobes out with heavy weights and cylindrical ear plugs. Women wore a similar collection of ornaments and, between initiation and marriage, a headband of beads and discs, still worn today by most Maasai women.

Traditionally the Kikuyu had no centralised **authority**, no tribal or clan chiefs: "chiefs" were only installed by the colonial administration. When disputes had to be settled or far-reaching decisions made, the elders of a district would meet as a council, usually with a little persuasion in the form of meat or beer from the people summoning them, and the matter would be cleared up in public, with a party to follow. After their deaths, elders – as ancestors – continued to be respected and consulted.

Although Christianity has altered the picture in the last few decades, many church-goers still believe strongly in an **ancestor world** where the dead have powers for good and bad over their living descendants because of their closeness to *Ngai* (God). The Kikuyu traditionally believed that *Ngai*'s most likely abode, or at least his frequent resting place, was **Kirinyaga**, the *Place of Brightness*, Mount Kenya. Accordingly, they built their houses with the door always looking out towards the mountain; hence the title of Jomo Kenyatta's book, *Facing Mount Kenya*.

Today the Kikuyu remain in the forefront of Kenyan development and, despite entrenched nepotism and the growing poverty gap, they are accorded grudging respect as highly successful business people and formidable politicians (though their political power at national level has been much eroded in recent years). There is considerable political rivalry between the **Kiambu Kikuyu**, of the tea- and coffee-growing district north of Nairobi, and the **Nyeri Kikuyu**, who rely on a more mixed economy.

AROUND MOUNT KENYA: THE KIRINYAGA RING ROAD

After the main game areas and the coast, this natural **circuit** is one of the most travelled in Kenya. This isn't to say it's crowded, or even very touristy (such places are few indeed up-country), but there are always a few *kombi* vans somewhere on the road and there are signs (little more as yet) that, with the completion of the paved road between Meru and Embu, the tourist industry up here is beginning to grow.

At present, the whole region is wonderfully untouched by anything but the steady encroachment of *shambas* on the ridges and the burgeoning of small towns into larger ones. Little of this is wild country any more (except Mount Kenya itself), but you have to hand it to them: the Kikuyu, Meru and Embu are amazingly hard workers and they have created an extraordinary spectacle of cultivation on the steep slopes, gashed by the road to reveal brilliant red earth.

As you travel, you're also aware of the looming presence of **the mountain**. Its twin peaks are normally obscured by clouds, but early in the morning and just before sunset, the shroud can vanish suddenly, leaving them magically exposed for a few minutes. With a base 80km across, Mount Kenya is one of the largest free-standing volcanic cones in the world, and the peaks – when you can see them from the road – are always distant. To the east and south, the mountain slopes steeply away to the broad expanse of Ukambani (Akambaland) and the Tana River basin. Westward, it drops more gently to the rolling uplands of Laikipia, drier than the east and for the most part treeless.

Getting here is an easy trip from Nairobi up a busy road: either buy a bus ticket from Nairobi direct to any of the towns in this section, or make Thika or **Murang'a** a first destination before heading clockwise or anticlockwise around the mountain. **Naro Moru**, the usual base for climbing Mount Kenya, lies on the west side some 25km south of **Nanyuki**, an alternative base for a climb from the north. On the eastern slopes, **Chogoria**, between **Meru** and **Embu**, offers arguably the finest route up the mountain.

Murang'a

Leaving Thika behind, **MURANG'A** is the first town of any size you come to. Established as an administrative outpost called Fort Hall in 1900, it has since come to be thought of as the "Kikuyu Homeland" because of its proximity to *Mukuruwe wa Gathanga* (the "Garden of Eden of the Kikuyu"). Here, in Kikuyu mythology, God made husbands for the nine daughters of Gikuyu and Mumbi, spiritual ancestors of all the Kikuyu people. The husbands, who became the ancestors of the nine Kikuyu clans, were found by Gikuyu under a large fig tree. Take a *matatu* to MUGEKA and walk from there if you'd like to see it; there used to be a museum at the site, though this, and apparently the original *mukuruwe* (fig tree), are no longer in evidence.

Fort Hall was never a settlers' town. The district was outside the zone earmarked for white colonisation and most of it comprised the "Kikuyu reserve". Richard Meinertzhagen, an officer in the King's African Rifles posted here in 1902, found the time, when not shooting animals – or people – to write:

If white settlement really takes hold in this country it is bound to do so at the expense of the Kikuyu who own the best land, and I foresee much trouble.

That said, Meinertzhagen helped put down some of this trouble, launching "punitive expeditions" from Fort Hall with his African troops.

Earthly needs and church murals

At the beginning of this century, the town consisted of "two grass huts within a stone wall and a ditch". Present-day Murang'a, perched above the busy main road, remains small, but there are a number of decent B&Ls on the steep hillside if you feel like staying – and it's a happy enough place, bustling energetically. Recommended **lodgings** are *Rwathia Bar* on Market Street (PO Box 243, ☎22527; Ksh50 per cube), basic but clean with a pleasant courtyard; and *Ngurunga Bar Hotel* (Ksh70 a room), right by the bus station. There's no shortage of *hotelis* either; *Kim Muna's* has outstanding samosas and the *New Three Gates* a fine balcony for watching the town.

Murang'a even has a bit of sightseeing. In the **CPK Cathedral** (formerly the Church of St. James and All Martyrs) hangs an unusual *Life of Christ* mural sequence by the Tanzanian artist Elimo Njau. It depicts the Nativity, Baptism, Last Supper, Gethsemane and Crucifixion of an African Christ in an African land-

MURANG'A

To Nyeri, Nanyuki & Embu

To Kiriani, Othaya & Nyeri

Hospital

HOSPITAL ROAD

Open-air Market

Bus & Matatu Station

Covered Market

Kanu Office

MARKET STREET

Rwathia Bar & Restaurant

Ngurunga B & L

Post Office

Kim Muna's Hoteli

UHURU HIGHWAY

Union Bank

Matatu Stage

KENYATTA ROAD

New Three Gates

Police

Barclay's Bank

Caltex

Church of St. James & All Martyrs

KCB Bank

Shell

Bakery

To Koimbi, Aberdares Forest & Nyeri

Total

0   200 m

To Thika & Nairobi

scape. It is interesting, and curiously appropriate for the muddled history of black-white relations here. The murals were painted in 1955, the year the church was founded by the Archbishop of Canterbury as a memorial to the thousands of Kikuyu victims of *Mau Mau* attacks.

Onwards from Murang'a

There are three onward travel options from Murang'a: clockwise around Mount Kenya via Karatina and Naro Moru (see next page); anticlockwise around the mountain via EMBU (see p.130); or up to NYERI and the Aberdares (p.134). Nyeri, a few kilometres off the Mount Kenya circuit, is a recommended detour and one which most public transport on the ring road will include.

Routes west into the Aberdare range

If you want to get up into the **Aberdare forest**, take one of the two minor roads leading out of Murang'a to the west. They join at KIRIANI and dip north to Nyeri via OTHAYA. If you have all day to dawdle, either of them would be a nice, circuitously backwoods route to Nyeri. *Matatu* availability will determine which you take. If you have your own wheels, the longer of the two, via KOIMBI, takes you past the start of a rough, snaking, high-altitude track which climbs as far as TUSHA, just 10km from the Aberdare Park's Kiandongoro Gate, the main park entrance above Nyeri.

Towards Mount Kenya: Mountain Lodge

Bookings for Mountain Lodge: see the box in "Sleeping" in Basics; minimum age for children is eight

You pass through the feverish market town of KARATINA (several B&Ls) and, in the direction of Mount Kenya, the signposted turning up to **Mountain Lodge** – the most accessible of Kenya's three highlands "tree hotels", the other two being *Treetops* and *The Ark* – and the only one on the slopes of Mount Kenya. *Mountain Lodge* (PO Box 123 Kiganjo, ☎4248, Nyeri) is set at an altitude of 2200m, about 30km from Karatina, mostly along good tarmac (the President's Sagana State Lodge is also up this way; be discreet with your camera).

Mountain Lodge has consistently good game-viewing over the floodlit water hole, and larger rooms than either of its competitors. Prices work out a little higher for singles, but less on twin rooms (HB around Ksh2500/3100 s/c). Rooms have private bathrooms and balconies and there's good food. You can stay up all night, with continuous supplies of tea and coffee on hand. Or you can be choosy about your animal-watching, tick off what you're interested in being woken to see, and then slumber through the herds of buffalo and antelope. They wake you at 6am in any case.

North to Naro Moru

After passing the turning to Nyeri, and then KIGANJO (a second road turns left to Nyeri here and then one to the right to *Mountain Lodge*) you emerge from the folded, shambolic landscape of Kikuyu cultivation onto a high, windswept plain. Here, you're crossing one of the great animal migration routes, severed by human population pressure over the last eighty years. Until 1948, when the two mountain parks were created, every few years used to see the mass migration of **elephants** from one side to the other. In 1903, a herd estimated at 700 animals was seen wending across the open country from Mount Kenya to the Aberdares. When the parks were opened, it was decided to keep the elephants away from the crowded farmlands in between, so an eight-kilometre ditch was dug across their route.

Naro Moru

The road climbs gently and steadily (on its appalling surface) to **NARO MORU**, which stands on the watershed between the Tana and the Ewaso Nyiro river basins. The most straightforward **base for climbing Mount Kenya**, or simply exploring the mountain forests lower down, Naro Moru is nondescript, built around its now disused railway station. There's a post office (Mon–Fri 8am–1pm & 2–5pm) but no bank and not a lot in the food department, either, though things are improving. If you plan to spend several days on the mountain, buy any special food you want in Nairobi. Naro Moru's offerings are strictly in the bread and milk, *karanga na chapati*, line.

There are several **accommodation** options should you need a room at the end of the day. Besides the *Naro Moru 82 B&L*, recommended only for the very broke and tentless, there's the ominous-sounding *Silent Lodge*, and the fresh and reasonable *Naro Moru Hotel '86* (Ksh60/90, Ksh80/120 s/c), complete with *Kirinyaga-*

viewing balcony. Out of town, there's a clutch of alternatives. Cheapest and closest is the rather exposed **campsite** at *Naro Moru River Lodge* (about 2km north and signposted): Ksh70/person with freezing showers and expensive firewood. With the B&Ls in town, there's not much point in paying an exorbitant Ksh130 for a hard bunk in one of the bunkhouses. The **lodge** proper (PO Box 18 Naro Moru, ☎22018 Nanyuki) is the only place to indulge yourself if you're in need of creature comforts (Ksh2350 for a twin HB, with self-catering cottages cheaper).

The **youth hostel** was a wonderful old place, a converted farmhouse with log fires and no electricity, rigorously spartan but a homely and peaceful highlands rest stop. Sadly, it burned to the ground in August 1988 and plans to rebuild are still vague. It wasn't owned by the *KYHA* and was uninsured, but the owners hope to rebuild it. You can still camp and there's a clutch of *bandas* with bunk beds (Ksh45 per person). Cooking is done on open fires and cold water and milk are available. Despite the burnt-out ruin nearby, it's still a very nice place.

If you're alone, and on a budget, it's also probably still the best place to **team up with others for the ascent** (campers with their own vehicles tend to use the more expensive set-up at *Naro Moru River Lodge*). The youth hostel site lies about 9km up the well signposted track to Mount Kenya. You may get a lift up from the main road; otherwise break your walk with a *chai* at the *Kariaku Restaurant*: they have a lurid and grisly mural. Three little *dukas* up the track a kilometre or so beyond the youth hostel sell one or two vital commodities, but they're very basic indeed.

Mount Kenya National Park

Ksh220 (students Ksh50) plus Ksh50 per night spent in the park. Entry allowed on foot; minimum group two people except for day hikes (Warden PO Box 69 Naro Moru, ☎2575 Nyeri).

An extinct volcano, with jagged peaks rising to 5200m, **Mount Kenya** is Africa's second highest mountain. Its heart is actually the remains of a gigantic volcanic plug, from which most of the outpourings of lava and ash have eroded away to create the distinctive silhouette. These peaks are permanently iced with snow and glaciers, while on the upper slopes the combination of altitude and a position astride the equator results in forms of **vegetation** that only exist here and at a few other lofty points in East Africa. Seemingly designed by some 1950s science fiction writer, it's hard to believe the "water-holding cabbage", "ostrich plume plant", or "giant groundsel" when you first see them. Mount Kenya is unexpectedly different and, unless your time is very limited, too good to miss.

Europe first heard about the mountain when the missionary Krapf saw it in 1849, but his stories of snow on the equator were not taken seriously. It was only in 1883 that the young Scottish traveller, Joseph Thomson, confirmed its existence. The Kikuyu, Maasai and other peoples living in the vicinity had venerated the mountain for centuries: park rangers still occasionally report finding elderly Kikuyu high up on the moorlands, drawn by the presence of *Ngai*, whose dwelling place this is. It's not known, however, whether anyone had actually scaled the peaks before Sir Halford Mackinder reached the highest, Batian, in 1899. Another thirty years passed before Nelion (10m lower but a tougher climb) was conquered. Both are named after nineteenth-century Maasai *laibon* or ritual leaders.

Climbing Mount Kenya: the practicalities

There are four **main routes**. The **Naro Moru trail** provides the shortest and steepest way to the top. **Burguret** and **Sirimon trails** from the northwest are less well trodden: Sirimon has a reputation for lots of wildlife, while Burguret passes through a long stretch of dense forest. The fourth, the **Chogoria trail**, is a beautiful but much longer ascent up the eastern flank of the mountain.

Batian (5199m) and Nelion are accessible only to experienced, fully equipped mountaineers – they look almost vertical – and the easiest route is Grade IV, making them a lot more testing than most of the routes up the Matterhorn. If you want to climb these peaks, you should join the *Mountain Club of Kenya* (PO Box 45741, ☎501747 Nairobi; their clubhouse is at Wilson Airport, bus #34). They will not only put you in touch with the right people but also give you reductions on hut fees.

Location and climate

Anyone who is reasonably fit can have a crack at **Point Lenana** (4986m). This climb has somehow acquired the reputation of being fairly easy, and lots of people set off up the mountain quite unprepared for high-altitude living. If you try it, forget you're on the equator. The top of the mountain is **freezing cold and windy** – wickedly so after dark; the air is thin, and it rains or snows, at least briefly, almost daily, though most precipitation comes at night. Mount Kenya's **weather** is notoriously unpredictable. Even during the rainy seasons, there are days when it's fairly clear, but driving up the muddy roads to the park gates may be nearly impossible, and if it's really bad, you probably won't be allowed in anyway. The **most reliable months** are February and August, although January and most of July can be fine, too.

Preparations

Above all, it's essential to have a **really warm sleeping bag**. One **thick sweater** at the very least (better still, several thinner ones), and either a **windproof jacket** or a down- or fibre-filled one are absolutely necessary. A **change of foot-wear** is pretty much essential, too, as you're bound to have wet feet by the end of each day. **Gloves** and a **balaclava or woolly hat** will seem vital to some, but are probably not handy in your backpack. A light cagoule or anorak is good to have: judge the season and weather for yourself. Another prerequisite is a **stove**, as you'll be miserable without regular hot fluids: firewood is not available and cannot be collected once you enter the park. For **food**, dehydrated soup and chocolate are perhaps the most useful. Remember, excess baggage can be left for Ksh30/day at *Naro Moru River Lodge*, so take only what you'll need. Here you can also purchase a packaged mountain climb, all-inclusive (PO Box 18, Naro Moru, Central Province; ☎22018 Nanyuki).

The *River Lodge* has a **hire** shop where you can get just about anything, at prices that may make you wish you'd simply bought it in Nairobi (indeed, *Atul's* in Nairobi – see under "Tent and Equipment hire" in the Nairobi Directory – is perhaps the best place to pick things up). The Youth Hostel used to have various items for rent also, a bit shabbier, but at least the charge could be discussed. Be cautious of anyone who approaches you offering to hire out gear.

If you are travelling alone and don't meet a suitable companion, it's usually possible to hire a **guide/porter** at the *Naro Moru River Lodge* or the youth hostel (the latter is a good place to find someone much more cheaply). Expect to pay from Ksh80–100 per day plus all his park fees, but insist on a written agreement showing the wages, the number of days, who's providing the food – everything. You shouldn't pay the full fee until the trip is finished; nor should you entirely *rely* on your guide to make every necessary preparation. Note that you're not likely to find a guide up at the park gate, but one is **obligatory** if you're hiking on your own, so allow time to arrange it. Obviously, single women are generally at a disadvantage as few would want to do this.

For a quick, and not overly expensive **taste of the mountain**, you can fix up a day's hike to *Mackinder's*, inclusive of lifts up to the gate and back down again, for around Ksh400, through one of the caretakers of the youth hostel *banda* site.

Mountain health

Physical fitness is an important consideration; but while being fit certainly won't hinder your climb, the ascent itself is mostly just a steep hike, if rough underfoot in parts. Much more germane than the training programmes that some people embark on is giving yourself **enough time to acclimatise**, so your body has a chance to produce extra oxygen-carrying red blood cells. Above 4000m, you are likely to notice the **effects of altitude** but it's how fast you climb that is critical. Physical symptoms are unpredictable, vary between individuals, and aren't much related to how fit you are. Breathlessness, nausea, disorientation and even slurred speech are all possible, and headaches are fairly normal at first, especially at night. All this can be largely avoided by taking your time over the trek, as minor symptoms gradually disappear. Don't attempt to climb from the base of the mountain to Point Lenana in less than **72 hours**. Keeping your fluid intake as high as possible will also help and, unfortunately, it's best to avoid alcohol. If someone in your group shows signs of being seriously tired and weak, stay at that altitude. Should it develop into unsteadiness on the feet and drowsiness, **descend immediately**. The effects of altitude are remarkable – especially on bodies tuned only to sea level – and can quickly become very dangerous.

Accommodation on the mountain

Taking a **tent** is useful because the only other **accommodation on the mountain** is a handful of basic cabins and mountain huts. For the Naro Moru route, these are supposed to be reserved at the *River Lodge*. In practice, this is rarely necessary unless you want to be sure of getting a bunk at the *Meteorological Station* or *Mackinder's Camp* (also know as *Teleki Valley Lodge*). If you have a tent, you can **camp** anywhere in the park: the only practical advantage of the campsites at the *Met. Station* (3050m) and *Mackinder's* (4175m) being water pipes and "long drops" at each. But most water on the mountain is reckoned to be safe to drink and you're never far from it.

In addition to the park and daily fees, there's a charge of Ksh50 per person to camp out at *Mackinder's* and the *Met. Station*. The *Met. Station bandas* cost Ksh230 per bunk; *Mackinder's* charges Ksh230 "for a bed in a concrete cell" (it does seem to have reached rare heights of exploitation). An informal, and perhaps less certain, alternative to *Mackinder's* is the Rangers' Cabin nearby, with negotiable rates usually costing you about half the *Mackinder's Camp* price. Camping here is allowed and it's altogether a friendlier place to huddle, with a fire burning most nights. Porters around *Mackinder's* will cook up a huge meal (given sufficient notice) for Ksh50–100.

Also available are the small, bare **huts** built by the *Mountain Club of Kenya*, which normally have four walls, a roof, bunks, and nothing else (Ksh50/person). These are located near the peaks, thus making it possible to spend a day or two around the high tarns and glaciers before returning to the base of *Mackinder's camp* (warmer and more oxygen). *Top Hut*, next to *Austrian Hut*, is reserved for *MCK* members. The huts have no facilities or staff – you must be entirely self-sufficient. Most of the foam mattresses are missing, so a closed-cell bed-roll is a great comfort.

GUIDEBOOKS AND MAPS

A new **book** on Kenya's highlands, *Mountain Walking in Kenya* by David Else (McCarta), should prove a usefully detailed companion.

If you're a **climbing** enthusiast, you'll want to get hold of the Mountain Club of Kenya's *Guide Book to Mount Kenya and Kilimanjaro* or the *East Africa International Mountain Guide* by Andrew Wielochowski (West Col Productions, 1 Meadow Close, Goring, Reading, Berks, RG8 9AA), which is adequate on the technical ascents.

As for **maps**, don't expect to find any in the Naro Moru area or at any of the park gates. The recent *Tourist Map of Mount Kenya National Park and Environs* (Ordnance Survey, through regular stockists) is an updated version of an excellent Survey of Kenya map. At 1cm:1.25km, it provides a very useful – and visually pleasing – overview of the whole district, showing all the routes, the region around the base and most of the ring road.

The adequate, topographical map, *Mount Kenya 1:50,000 Map and Guide* by Andrew Wielochowski and Mark Savage (about Ksh120 – or available from Executive Wilderness Programmes, 32 Seamill Park Crescent, Worthing, BN11 2PN, UK) covers just the mountain itself at 1cm:500m and includes a detailed rundown on the huts and technical information for scalers of Nelion and Batian.

There's also a quite user-friendly Survey of Kenya topographical **map of the peak area** at 1cm:250m that's worth getting hold of in Nairobi if you're intending to walk around the peaks.

The Naro Moru route

From the main A2 road to the *Met. station*, where the driveable earth road ends, is a 26-kilometre haul; even from the Youth Hostel it's at least a five-hour walk. *Naro Moru River Lodge* will taxi you up here – for an extortionate price – or you may be lucky and get a lift, but a completely free ride would be a miracle.

Some 9km from the Youth Hostel, you come to the airstrip, the **park gate and HQ**, and usually three or four gigantic buffalo chewing the cud on the lawn. Entry is the usual Ksh200 (though porters, and sometimes student card holders, are charged Ksh50, sometimes less), plus Ksh50 for every night you intend to stay in the park (don't overestimate; there are no refunds). From here, you leave the conifer plantations and occasional *shambas* behind as the road twists and climbs through shaggy forest into a zone of colossal **bamboo**. Look out for elephant and particularly **buffalo** if you walk this stretch, though you'll more often see their droppings and footprints. If you find buffalo on the path, you're supposed to lob stones at them – and they're supposed to move out of the way. But exercise caution if they're about.

The final three kilometres to the *Met. Station* is a series of steep hairpins usually driveable only in 4WD. You start to get some magnificent views out over the plains from up here, while right under your nose you may find a three-horned **chameleon**, stalking cautiously through the foliage like a miniature dinosaur. The high forest is their favourite habitat. A **black panther** – the melanistic form of the leopard found at high altitudes – was also favouring this habitat recently, near the *Met. Station*.

With an early start, it's quite possible to reach *Mackinder's* (4175m) in one day, but unless you're already acclimatised, you'll probably feel well below par by the time you get there. It is far better to take it easy and get used to the *Met. Station*'s 3050m altitude; perhaps stroll a little higher or, if you have a tent, climb an hour or so up to the treeline and camp there. Ready-erected tents can be hired at the *Met. Station* if you can't afford the *bandas*. The mountain's weather is another good reason to stop here: after midday, it often gets foul, and the infamous vertical bog is no fun at all in heavy drizzle and twenty-metre visibility.

Up the Teleki Valley

An early start from the *Met. Station* the next morning should see you to *Mackinder's* by lunchtime, before the clouds start to thicken up. In fair weather, the **vertical bog** is not as daunting as it sounds: you keep to the left of the red and white marker posts where it isn't as wet. As you reach the bog, you enter another vegetation zone, that of **giant heather**. Beyond the bog, the path follows a ridge high above the **Teleki Valley** with the peaks straight ahead, rising brilliantly over a landscape that seems to have nothing in common with the hazy plains below.

This is the land of giant groundsel and lobelia. Identities are confusing: the cabbages on stumps and the larger candelabra-like "trees" are the same species – **giant groundsel** or **tree senecio** – an intermediate stage of which has a sheaf of yellow flowers. They are slow growers and, for such weedy-looking vegetables, they may be extraordinarily old – up to 200 years. The tall, fluffy, less abundant plants are a species of giant **lobelia** discovered by the explorer Teleki and found only on Mount Kenya. The name plaque below one of these (there's a little nature trail along the ridge) calls it an "Ostrich plume plant", and it is the only plant that could fairly be described as cuddly. The furriness which gives it such an animal quality acts as insulation for the delicate flowers.

For **Mackinder's Camp**, you follow the contours across the valley side and jump, or cross by stepping stones, over the snowmelt Northern Naro Moru stream. The camp, virtually at the head of Teleki Valley, is a long stone and concrete bunkhouse with dishevelled tents tacked into the icy ground around it. Certainly no hotel, it does at least provide some warmth and the company of others: climbers, Kikuyu guides and porters. **Batian** and **Nelion** tower magnificently over the valley, with a third pinnacle, **Point John**, even closer. There's usually a fresh icing of snow every morning but early sunlight melts most of it by midday.

Trekking around the peaks

If you want to climb **straight to Point Lenana**, you're likely to find at least one group leaving early the following morning (say around 3am) with a guide, though it's not difficult to find your own way, especially if there's a moon. Leaving this early allows you to get to the top by dawn for a fabulous view (sometimes) from northern Kenya to Kilimanjaro. It's not advisable to rush into this final ascent, however. For most people, day three is better spent getting acclimatised in the Teleki Valley, making the climb to Point Lenana the next morning. And note: spending your third night on the mountain at the *Austrian Hut*, just below Point Lenana, is not a good idea. Sleeping at high altitude unacclimatised is a nightmare.

Though most people head straight up to Point Lenana, **trekking round the peaks** is really a far more exhilarating experience, with the added chance to explore some of the tarns and glacial valleys on the north side. It's supposed to be easier to do this anticlockwise in two or three days. If you want to do it in one, however, set off clockwise from *Mackinder's* via *Two Tarn Hut* by **Hut tarn**, set in a glorious and eerily silent col beneath the glaciers and scree. The walk from here round to Point Lenana is very much a switchback affair but, as long as the mists stay away, the scenery is fairytale. If you're fairly fit and acclimatised, it should take eight to ten hours. *Kami Hut*, on the north side of the peaks, and *Austrian hut* (as well as *Two Tarn*), are suitable night stops, though you may not get much sleep, particularly at *Austrian Hut*, which is the highest.

Incidentally, nights in the mountain huts are normally shared with large numbers of persistent **rodents** which you won't see until it's too late. Remember to isolate your food by suspending it from the roof. The familiar diurnal scavengers are **rock hyrax**, which are especially tame at *Mackinder's Camp*: the welfare service provided by tourists preserves elderly specimens long past their natural lifespan. Hyrax are not rodents but, by virtue of their feet, are somehow distantly related to elephants, a fact reported in all natural history books without imparting any useful information about elephants or hyraxes. You'll come across **other animals** at quite high altitudes, too, notably duiker antelope on the moorlands. And the carcass of an elephant was once found above *Mackinder's*, at an altitude of 4500m.

When you're ready to come down, it doesn't take long. You can do so in one day, right to Naro Moru or further, assuming you've left your vehicle at the *Met. Station*, or else manage to find a lift there.

The Chogoria route

Rather than retrace your steps to Naro Moru, a more exhilarating and less frequently used alternative is to descend by one of the other routes: the **Chogoria trail**, for example. This would mean taking all your gear up with you, as well as extra food. The Chogoria trail is scenically far superior to any of the others, and it's become more popular now that the road around the east side of the mountain has been paved. From the eastern side, the hike to the top can be done in three days, but it's easier to allow four or five if you're setting out from Nairobi.

Up to the park entrance

Following the route from **CHOGORIA** village (where the *Transit Motel* is one of several rudimentary *hotelis* and lodgings), the hamlet of **Mutindwa** lies 4km up the mountain. You can find a porter/guide here for about Ksh100/day (remember, if you're alone you must have one to be allowed to stay in the park overnight). From Mutindwa it's about 26km to the park gate. On weekends, you may stand a better than average chance of getting a lift with a group going up to *Meru Mount Kenya Lodge*, a self-service place just inside the gate, run by the district council (Ksh240; book through *Let's Go Travel* in Nairobi). Normally a lift will cost about Ksh600 for a Land Rover and driver hired in Mutindwa, but it's a good idea not to pay (at least not everything) until you reach the gate – a feat that for much of the year is by no means guaranteed. Be sure to keep receipts for your park fees to satisfy the rangers at the gate on the other side. Once in the park, take the left fork and **Urumandi Hut** is an hour's walk up the track; it costs only Ksh40 and, unlike all the other *MCK* huts, still has its complement of mattresses. If you left Nairobi in the morning, you'll gladly stay here the night, and there's water from the ravine nearby. If you're camping, follow the right fork from the park gate and you'll come to a good site with running water and toilet.

On the mountain

Forty-five minutes' walk beyond *Urumandi* you arrive at the roadhead car park, served by a driveway from the lodge. And from here wheels are abandoned as you slog on foot up to *Minto's Hut*, a six-hour stint away in the high moorlands. The route tracks along the axis of an ascending ridge, then flattens to hug the rim of the spectacular **Gorges Valley**, carved deep by glaciation. There are unobstructed and encouraging views up to the peaks as you hug the contours of the valley wall. Watch out for buffalo.

Minto's, like *Mackinder's*, is three or four hours from Point Lenana. Situated by three small tarns, it's perched above the larger Lake Michaelson at the head of the valley below – a very beautiful place, inspiringly set off by giant groundsel and lobelia plants.

In the morning you have two options. The first is to head up to the ridge west of *Minto's* and follow it to **Simba Tarn**. From there, head due south around the peaks and past little **Square Tarn** before turning right to follow the contours for a tough kilometre to the so-called **Curling Pond** (matches have been held on the ice here) and *Austrian Hut*. Alternatively, from *Minto's* make for the base of the ridge extending east from Point Lenana, then tackle the cruel scree slope to the south for a ninety-minute scramble up to a saddle followed by a straight drop to the head of the **Hobley Valley** with its two tarns. From here, it's just an hour across to the base of Lenana Ridge, behind which, again, is *Austrian Hut*. Mercifully, whichever route you choose, this day's hike is a short one and at this altitude (over 4000m), you'll be glad to spend the rest of the day at one of the huts, recuperating for the final ascent. Considering the altitude, a safer and probably more comfortable option would be to spend a second night at *Minto's*, acclimatising, followed by a pre-dawn assault on Point Lenana.

After the climb to Lenana, you have a ninety-minute **descent** from *Austrian Hut* along the edge of Lewis Glacier, tracking back and forth over miserable scree, to the Teleki tarn at the head of the Naro Moru stream. *Mackinder's*, and the scent of civilisation, is just an hour away down the valley. But if you can resist that lure, and it is still early in the day, *and* if you have enough food, you can continue around the west side of the peaks to Hut Tarn, then up and down over the ridges to *Kami Hut*, at the head of the Sirimon route on the north side.

If you want to do it, there's no problem making it from *Minto's* to Point Lenana and on down to the *Met. Station* in one day.

The Burguret and Sirimon routes

A fairly recent alternative to Naro Moru as a convenient base on the west side is **Mount Rock Hotel** (PO Box 333 Nanyuki, ☎62625 Nanyuki, the former *Bantu Lodge*), about 8km north of Naro Moru. This place aspires to some of *Naro Moru River Lodge's* status as a base lodge for climbers, but using local capital and without the aid of the Kenya tourist machine behind it. The entrance can't be missed, as it's marked by two enormous Kikuyu figures carved out of tree trunks and flamboyantly painted. It has decent and very reasonably priced **rooms** (Ksh350/600) with log fires, and a good restaurant and bar (hearty meals with plenty of fresh veg for Ksh150). You can **camp** in the grounds forKsh80. There's even a small waterhole in the back garden that attracts elephants once in a while, and a resident accordion player who serenades each new guest with Kikuyu tunes.

There are **horses** for rent at Ksh100 per hour (reduced rates for longer periods) for mountain treks. The limited tack needs careful checking, and ask about fodder and water before galloping off. You can also do escorted walks through the forest in the vicinity of the lodge, for around Ksh40.

Mount Rock can fix you up with an inclusive three- or four-day **guided tour** up to Point Lenana from around Ksh3500 per person for a group of four. This includes transport to and from the base of the trail, park fees, all food and equipment, and a last night at *Mount Rock*. It's a good deal if you're unequipped or wary, especially compared with *Naro Moru River Lodge's* tour prices, but it's considerably more expensive for singles or couples.

Mount Rock's route used to follow the **Burguret river** through thick bamboo forest and moorland. A four-wheel-drive vehicle can drive up to 3000m and it terminates at *Two Tarn Hut* behind Teleki Valley. En route, it passes a clutch of caves described as a "*Mau Mau* conference centre". The Hotel has built two huts on the mountainside at the 3000m and 4000m marks, *Bantu Secret Valley Camp* and *Highland Castle Camp*, the former near a natural salt lick, both at Ksh150 per person. The status of these seems uncertain, because *Mount Rock* is no longer offering walking trips along this route, which is closed to the public. Instead they use the Naro Moru and **Sirimon** trails.

This fourth main trail, Sirimon, which is renowned for its wildlife, commences about 14km east of NANYUKI, just before the Sirimon River bridge on the Nanyuki to Meru road. It climbs over the northern moorlands, giving superb views of the main peaks as well as the twin "lesser" peaks of Terere and Sendeyo (4714m and 4704m), which have small glaciers of their own. *Mount Rock Hotel* has put up two more huts – *Judmeier Camp* and *Shipton's Cave Camp* – along the way.

Other routes

The four trails described here represent only a fraction of the mountain's hiking possibilities. All ground above 3200m is within the boundaries of the national park, and if you had time and sufficient food, you could hike the forests and moors for weeks. The southern flanks of the mountain seem to have largely escaped the notice of hikers, but there are several forest stations in the vicinity of Embu and plenty of scope for exploration. Most of the southern slopes were a designated "Kikuyu reserve" during the colonial period, so few European climbers created routes up here.

Over the Equator: Nanyuki and around

From Naro Moru, the road rolls on over yellow and grey downs, scattered with stands of tall gum trees, roamed by cattle and overflown by brilliant blue roller birds. Then it drops to the equator and Nanyuki.

You might be forgiven for expecting something momentous to take place at **the equator**, but there's no "crossing of the line ceremony" here. Still, if you have any control over your transport, you'd have to be pretty cool just to breeze by.

There's a splendid yellow sign, or even two ("This sign is on the EQUATOR"), and, in case there was any doubt, a veritable bazaar of souvenir stalls with salesmen who will go to absurd lengths to entice you ("Hey guy! Want cocaine?"). What they actually offer is all the usual beadwork, carvings, soapstone and bangles at the sort of prices you'd expect.

The town centre is one-and-a-half kilometres down the road, so you could reasonably ask to be dropped at the equator and walk in. Pleasantly situated on the way is the *New Silverbeck Hotel* (PO Box 79 Nanyuki, ☎22710), "new" because the old main building burned down leaving just two freestanding fireplaces (Ksh210/420, B&B in s/c chalets).

Nanyuki

NANYUKI has the dual distinction of being Kenya's air force town (a base which has had a lot of attention lavished on it recently) and the British Army's training and operations centre. Nevertheless it remains in atmosphere very much a country town. A wide, tree-lined main street and the mild climate of 2000m lend an unfamiliar, cool spaciousness that seem to reinforce its oddly colonial character. Shops lining the main road include the *Settlers' Store* (since 1938), the *Modern Sanitary Store* (they sell camping gas), and *United Stores* with its pile of *Daily Telegraphs*.

The first party of settlers arrived in the district in 1907 to find "several old Maasai *manyattas*, a great deal of game and nothing else"; Nanyuki is still something of a settlers' town and European locals are always around.

The animals, sadly, are not. Although you may see a few grazers on the plains, the vast herds of zebra that once roamed the banks of the *Ngare Nanyuki* (Maasai – "Red River") were decimated by hunters seeking hides, by others seeking meat (particularly during World War II, when 80,000 Italian prisoners of war were fed a pound each day), but most of all by ranchers protecting their pastures. As the zebra herds dwindled, so the lions became a greater threat to livestock; they retreated – under fire – to the mountain forests and moors. And the rhinos have just disappeared.

Staying in Nanyuki

For **accommodation in Nanyuki**, you've plenty of options. You're unlikely just to front up at the *Mount Kenya Safari Club's* highly exclusive residence and take a room (prices start from around Ksh3500/4500 FB), but presumably you *could*, and if you're mobile if might be fun to call in anyway, though there's a fairly expensive daily membership (PO Box 35, ☎2141/2 Nanyuki: access near the *Silverbeck*).

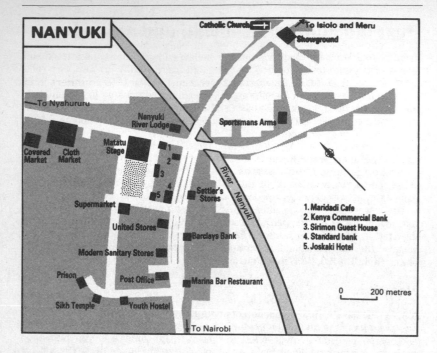

Of more realistic places to put your head down, first mention should be made of the crusty old *Sportsman's Arms* (PO Box 3 Nanyuki, ☎23200), which welcomes **campers** for Ksh120 a head. If you fancy more comfort, the vaguely dilapidated sprawl of wooden cottages gives you a wide choice and you'll probably have the place virtually to yourself (B&B around Ksh260/450 B&B). This used to be the base for visits to *Secret Valley* (a *Treetops*-type establishment) until that burned down – as Kenyan hotels are wont to do – in 1981. Letters and photos smother the walls, reminders of the good old days, but it doesn't look like this one will be renovated.

The tour drivers' favourite digs is *Sirimon Guest House*, sleazy but amiable, with clean rooms and hot water (Ksh100/150 s/c and double beds). Also recommended is *Joskaki Hotel* for its generally excellent food and good rooftop views of the town and Mount Kenya (Ksh80/150 s/c). Trouble is, it's a vast, corridor-riddled warren and can be indescribably noisy when the **bar** is open all night, or there's a disco.

The **"Youth Hostel"** at *Emmanuel Parish Centre* (Ksh60 a bed in single and double rooms) is clean and friendly but cramped, very spartan and makes no concession to privacy – unless you're the only guest, of course, in which case it's not a problem. The toilets are a hazard.

Finally, there's the *Nanyuki Guest House*, useful if you're on your way to Nyahururu, because it is about ten minutes' walk out of town in that direction. Its prison-like exterior belies a good atmosphere, helpful manager and probably the cheapest self-contained rooms in the country.

For a lively **drink**, try the *Marina Bar* opposite the Post Office, a popular hang-out for tourists and soldiers. More wholesome consumables are available at the *Maridadi Café* – a clean place with excellent coffee – and the very nice *Mid Pines Café*, behind the petrol station.

If you have time before leaving, pay a visit to the **Nanyuki Spinners and Weavers** workshop, located about one kilometre out of town on the Nyahururu road, opposite the District Hospital. This women's group provides the *Spin 'n' Weave Shop* in Nairobi with rugs and other articles woven on hand looms, which you can buy here at reduced prices.

Moving on: west to Nyahururu

If you're heading to NYAHURURU, beware of the unpaved road. It's become fiendish of late, even in the dry season; and in periods of heavy rain vehicles get stuck along it for days on end. Despite which setbacks, it's a good road for wild-life spotting: you've every chance of seeing giraffes, gazelles and even elephants if you set off early. And it seems nowadays that even the rhino may make a come-back if the introductions at Laikipia Ranch north of the town prove successful. Here, a herd of black rhinos are part of an experiment in integrated ranching. As browsers, they don't interfere with cattle pasture, and do well in the same envi-ronment as long as the bush isn't cleared. There are several other **game ranches** in the wide country that stretches out north and west of Nanyuki towards the desert. *El Karama*, one of the better known, is open to the public and recom-mended if you have a way to get to it: it's 42km northwest of Nanyuki off the track to MARALAL and on the banks of the Ewaso Nyiro. They provide a small amount of very cheap farmhouse and *banda* accommodation and game rides on horse-back. The AA and *Let's Go Travel* have details (see "Nairobi Directory") or contact the ranch directly at PO Box 172, Nanyuki, ☎34Y2 Laikipia.

Alternatively, if you're up to an **expensive night or two**, the luxury *Sweetwaters Camp* (FB around Ksh2500/3300, children Ksh515) on the private **Ol Pejeta game reserve**, on the south side of the road, some 40-odd kilometres towards Nyahururu, is another excellent chance to see some of the Laikipia region's biggest concentrations of wildlife, again including black rhinos. Ol Pejeta covers some 400 square kilometres, nearly a quarter of which is given over to a rhino sanctuary. The camp specialises in night game drives. Book through *Let's Go Travel* in Nairobi (see under "Travel Agents" in "Nairobi Directory").

Moving on: east to Meru

Leaving Nanyuki eastwards, the ring road skirts closer to the mountain than at any other point in its circumference and the scenery acquires a real grandeur, changing completely yet again before you reach Meru.

The 70km **from Nanyuki to Meru** couldn't illustrate better the amazing variety of climate and landscape in Kenya. The road climbs steeply to almost 3000m, passing alternative routes to the peaks and giving unparalleled views of them in the early morning. But a spectacle you might not have guessed at (until now) is the panorama that spreads out to the north as the road drops once again: on a really clear day, after rain has settled the dust, this is devastatingly beautiful. Even on an average day, you can see as far as the dramatic mesa of **Olokwe**, nearly 100km north in the desert. ISIOLO (p.367) lies out there, too, first stop on the way to the northern wilderness.

Meru

For Meru, the road's straight ahead, suddenly plunging through verdant **jungle**, with glimpses through the trees of the **Nyambeni Hills** and the volcanic pimples dotting the plain. **Meru oak** is the commercial prize of this forested eastern side of the mountain, though judging by the number of active sawmills at the upper end of the town, supplies won't last much longer. The forest still comes right to the town's edge, however, and paths lead off to cleared *shambas* where, for a year or two, just about anything will grow. The moist, jungly atmosphere around Meru, with wood smoke curling up against a background of dark forest, is very reminiscent of parts of West Africa – a total change of mood after the dryish grasslands on the northwest side of the mountain.

Meru town

MERU town is strung out over two or three kilometres, the main road dropping steeply across the hillside to the town centre. It's an unusual place in an interesting location – there are great views from the upper (**Kinoru**) half of town over the densely settled slopes – and well worth a stay. There is even a good, small museum and, in keeping with its market-town functions, no shortage of **accommodation**.

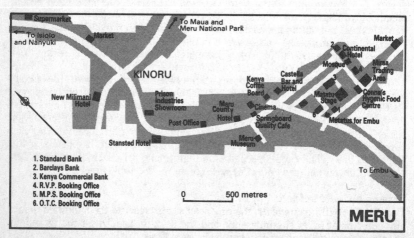

If you have transport, there are a few places you might consider even before you arrive. *Rocky Hill Inn* is some 8km out, an ornate construction among pseudo-Japanese gardens, charging Ksh80 for chalets; it has no proper water supply and is perhaps more a weekend *nyama choma* bar than anything else. Further on is *Forest Lodge*, a wildly optimistic "country club" venture which cost Ksh6 million to build. The cabins are flimsy and outrageously expensive but the swimming pool is worth dropping in for. They'll make good (tourist-priced) meals if you're passing and allow you to use the showers. Unfortunately, "No Picnics" probably also means no camping, though you could ask – because there's nowhere in town.

Lower down, **nearer the town centre** past the prison, is the *Stansted Hotel* (PO Box 1337, ☎20360; note, it's still rather a haul back up the hill if you alight at the main *matatu* stand), with bright rooms at excellent prices (Ksh80/120 s/c B&B). More upmarket is *Meru County Hotel* (PO Box 1386, ☎20427), a fairly metropolitan place with a video lounge and good snack bar (Ksh500/700 s/c B&B). The *Continental* and the *Castella* are basic B&Ls, the latter cheaper and more inviting. For action on weekends, when they have discos – but not during the week, when it's deserted and without water – try the *New Milimani Hotel*. Rooms here are decent and the menu long (specialities – curries and *kinyeji*, the Meru version of *irio*). It's also the cheapest place with safe parking in town (Ksh120/150 s/c B&B).

For **eating**, Meru will treat you well, and cheaply. *Conna's Hygienic* lives up to its name and serves in quantity; the *Kenya Coffee Board* maintains its usual high standards; the *Springboard Quality Café* does good snacks; the *Canopy* (near the *Castella*) is distinctly above average with a large menu, most of which really exists; there's a fresh milk bar next to the *KCB* bank; and a supermarket – the *Super Mart* – at the upper end of town on the Nanyuki road, with a huge range of produce.

Stimulating pastimes

Meru's municipal **market** is a large one and sells a wide range of goods – baskets, clothes, domestic utensils – as well as the agricultural produce of the district. This is cheap and excellent: they grow the best custard apples in Kenya here, and if you like *miraa*, you won't find bigger or better bunches anywhere. Also known as *qat* or *gatty*, **miraa** is a small tree whose bark contains a mild stimulant and appetite suppressant – the freshly plucked twigs and leaves are chewed with bubble gum and, though frequently denounced, it's legal in Kenya. Meru district, where it grows wild but is also now cultivated, is the main source; northeastern Kenya is the biggest home market, and uncounted tons are exported to Somalia, Yemen and Djibouti. There's a trading corner devoted to *miraa* in the town centre. The outdoor market in Kinoru seems reserved largely for small traders offering more wonderful, cheap *shamba* produce.

The tiny but fascinating **Meru museum** (PO Box 592, ☎20482) is also a treat. It occupies the oldest stone building in town, a former District Commissioner's office, where you're likely to be the only visitor (Ksh30), shown around by a guide/ticket-seller who turns the lights on as you go, and off again behind you. Emphasis is on the traditional culture of the Meru people: small ethnographic exhibits, pick-up-and-feel blocks of local stone and timber, stone tools from the Lewa Downs prehistoric site and some woefully stuffed animals.

Outside there's a particularly good **herbal pharmacopoeia**: a collection of traditional medical plants growing in the garden, where you can see what a *miraa* bush looks like, among others. Nearby, several psychotically aggressive monkeys try to get at you through their cage bars. The **Meru homestead** is well presented and feels authentic – you get the impression someone actually lives here on the museum grounds, a feeling accentuated by the escape route in the perimeter fence for fleeing from invaders, which seems to have the well-worn look of years of use.

To Meru National Park

Meru is, of course, the base for visits to **Meru National Park** (p.261). Hitching there can be a frustrating experience. It's better to get to the end of the tarmac before you start trying (take a *matatu* to MAUA but hop out 3km before, at the national park turn-off).

Embu and district

From Meru to Embu the new (and regrettably fast) road swoops around the eastern slopes of Mount Kenya through brilliant, vibrant scenery. Five kilometres south of Meru you cross the **equator line** once again. Hundreds of streams – the run-off from a luxuriant rainfall blown in by the southeast monsoon – cut deeply into the volcanic soil of this eastern flank. As a result, this side has a much broader covering of jungle, which extends, *shambas* permitting, downhill to the level of the road and beyond. You plunge from one green and tan gorge to the next, and whether you enjoy the magnificent landscape or not depends on whether you dare take your eyes off the road. If you take the early morning *OTC* bus (slow, and considered safe), you can relax and admire. Get a seat on the right side for tantalising glimpses of the snow-capped peaks, normally visible at this time of day.

Most public transport stops at **Chogoria**, a base for the eastern Mount Kenya ascent (see p.122). From Embu, too, if you're energetic and resourceful, there's nothing to stop you from hiking up the southern slopes. You'll need the **Ordnance Survey map** (see p.120) for this.

Thuchi River Lodge

If you have independent transport, there's an interesting **accommodation** option to explore on this side of the mountain in the *Thuchi River Lodge*, an establishment left over from the road-building exploits of the French company *Kier*, who constructed the road from KANGONDE (see p.222) to Embu and built their own accommodation. It should still have its complement of pool, squash courts and nice bathrooms. Located a few hundred metres above the Thuchi river, it's exactly 27 km south of Chogoria (29km north of Embu), then 3km south of the main road along the E652 track to nowhere.

Embu town

EMBU, like Meru, is situated at the bottom of a hill: at any rate, the town begins high and descends, with your expectations, to the centre. There's very little to get

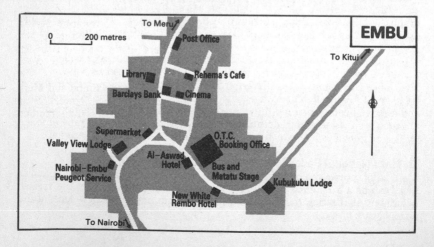

excited about here, though there's talk of a museum – one day. It's not obvious why it was chosen as the capital of Eastern Province. Certainly, without the apparatus of a provincial headquarters, Embu would amount to little.

There is **accommodation**, however, should you need or want to spend the night here. Pleasant if overpriced (Ksh450/550 s/c B&B) is the *Izaac Walton Inn* (PO Box 1, Embu, ☎20128/9), at the top end of town on the way in from Meru. In the centre, *Valley View Lodge* (PO Box 563, ☎20147) has a good location (Ksh325/435 s/c), and the *Kubu Kubu*, on the Kitui road, is clean and comfortable – not a bad place, though the rooms are tiny (Ksh105/190 s/c). The *Al-Aswad* and the *New White Rembo* are cheap B&Ls (Ksh50/100), the former preferable thanks to its popular restaurant, but demand a room with a lock. *Rehema's* café, a little way up the hill, is another busy eatery, well known for excellent spicy samosas.

Onward travel: back to Nairobi or into the wilds

An alternative to the two-hour trip straight **back to Nairobi** (the *Kensilver* bus is fast and safe-ish) is to head on past the huge Tana reservoirs, the Mwea National Reserve and the Mwea rice scheme – a major resettlement area for landless farmers. The ornithologically interesting **Mwea National Reserve** is accessible, in theory, all year from MAVURIA via the Kamburu Dam, but the bridge over the Thiba River on this route is often down. The other way to the reserve, from KAEWA via Masinga Dam, is strictly a dry-season route only, and equally liable to be impassable at any time. On the newly surfaced road between Embu and the Garissa highway (on which you'll swiftly get transport back to Thika or Nairobi) you'll have to rely on fairly infrequent *matatus*. If you cross the highway however, and continue southwards, traffic onwards, to KITUI (p.222) and then back to MACHAKOS (p.218) is heavier.

But there's an intriguing alternative travel option out of Embu – the **Kiangombe Hills**, described next. Their main centre, **Siakago**, can be reached, except in the worst rains, from Embu by *matatu* five or six times daily.

Siakago and the Kiangombe Hills

The relatively modest altitudes of the **Kiangombe Hills** (Kiangombe peak is 1804m) aren't enough to lure climbers – even those willing to go off the beaten track. But the hills, upstaged by Mount Kenya, and ignored by tourists and travellers, are emphatically worth a visit if you retain a romantic view of the world.

The hills are the home of the **Mbere**, related to the Kikuyu, Embu and Meru. The Mbere have a reputation in Kenya as possessors of magical powers. Some villages have elderly sages, **Arogi**, credited with terrifying abilities; though others – the **Ago** – have more beneficent gifts like the ability to foretell the future or find missing goats.

Information is hard to come by; local people either laugh or look blank when directly questioned about such "unprogressive" activities. Numerous cups of tea and endless slices of bread and *Blueband* elicited the story from one local man that a village called Uba-Riri was a place where the *Ago* were active; but he couldn't quite remember where it was, and if he had pointed the way, he explained, legend had it he would have lost the finger he pointed with.

Yet the *Ago* do make their existence known at critical times, as in 1987 when their bush fires are said to have brought on the delayed rains. And the forest rangers on the hills threaten poachers and illegal firewood-cutters with *Arogi* medicine to make their teeth fall out – witchcraft comes to the aid of conservation!

The identity of these "witches" – at best a hazy and mysterious one which people aren't in any hurry to talk about – is further confused by the supposed existence in the hills of a race of **"little red men"** whose small size (estimated at 1.2m) and fleeting appearance and disappearance in the bush have led the odd, dreaming scientist to suppose that they might be *australopithecines* – ape men hanging on into the twentieth century in their remote forest tracts. They, and the *Ago-Arogi*, may be just part of the "old people" mytho-history of central Kenya, which is at least partially based on the real, ancient and probably Cushitic-speaking peoples of two thousand or more years ago.

Such, anyway, are the stories that might draw you from Embu. If you've ever entertained thoughts of seeing a Bigfoot, or a Yeti, or the Loch Ness Monster – and if you kept an eye open for Nandi bears near Eldoret (see p.195) – it's an interesting trip.

Siakago

A bumpy thirty kilometres from Embu, **SIAKAGO** is a one-street town with a few *dukas*, one B&L, a market (main days Thursday and Friday), a *matatu* terminus and a large Catholic mission set amid the huts and *shambas* on the outskirts. Siakago isn't a ki-Mbere word and its derivation is uncertain. It may well have derived from "Chicago", along with a group of American anthropologists who based themselves here in the 1930s and started the ape-men stories.

The anthropologists were appalled at the **poverty** of the district, whose soil barely supports the population with corn and sorghum and sustains only the scrappiest *shambas* of cotton and tobacco as cash crops: their plan was to re-locate the Mbere to better land, a recommendation fortunately never acted upon. The Mbere are still living a tenuous existence, but after the horrific famines and cholera outbreaks of the early 1980s, when the district's proximity to well-off Embu meant that they were largely overlooked, conditions have begun to improve.

In **practical terms**, the *Starehe Restaurant* provides the only accommodation, with a few basic rooms built around a yard with a single tree in the middle to provide some shade (Ksh50/100). They have water and electricity thanks to the dam 25km back along the wires. *New Stanley's Hotel* has to be visited for its name and imaginative murals, if not for the rather limited menu.

Heading for the hills

The Kiangombes rise up behind Siakago town and look deceptively easy to **climb**. From near Siakago's *matatu* stage, one path leads to the smaller community of MISINGETHIO, southeast of **Kiangombe peak**. A better path, but harder to reach, approaches the summit from northwest of the main peaks, from the huts of the forest rangers' station beyond the village of KUNE, 10km from Siakago. Going up to the peaks is really a two-day trip, with a self-contained overnight camp in the hills. Out of Siakago, *dukas* are few and poorly stocked and there's no commercial accommodation.

There's no transport between Siakago and Kune, so you'll probably have to find your way on foot (unless you're driving), asking as you go. The walk should take about three hours. Once at the rangers' huts (thirty minutes' hike beyond Kune), ignore the vehicle track which winds into the hills; it's no longer used and soon becomes difficult to follow. Instead, use the **footpath** leading straight up from behind the huts. At any time but the end of the dry season much of your way is likely to be impeded by thick vegetation. If you're alert to every photographic possibility, you'll find that concentrating on following the overgrown trail is tiresome – especially without a *panga* to trail-blaze with. As you climb, human population quickly thins out; this is red people territory and traditionally feared by the Mbere.

About four hours' hiking from the forest station you reach the peaks area. From the **mountain meadows** just below the forested peaks you can look back over the lower hills and down to the hut- and *shamba*-specked plains beyond. With luck, Mount Kenya and the Aberdares can be seen poking through their respective cloudy wreaths. But you may need help from an *Ago*, as well as luck, to see one of the little red people.

MOUNT KENYA TO LAMU: THE CROSS-COUNTRY ROUTE

From the Mount Kenya region the obvious route to the coast is back to Nairobi, then down via Mombasa. It's perfectly feasible, however – assuming you have some spare time – to **strike out east from the Mount Kenya ring road** and, using a combination of available public transport and foot-slogging, make for Mwingi, Garissa and Lamu.

The easiest departure point on the ring road is the small centre of ENA, 16km northeast of Embu. Ena is at the junction of the new highway with the old "M.A.T. road", the circuitous C92 that used to be the route around the eastern side of the mountain until the tarred highway was completed.

Buses and *matatus* run east along it from Ena to ISHIARA fairly frequently. And Ishiara has a few B&Ls. On Mondays or Tuesdays there's a bus from Ishiara to KATSE. Otherwise, from Ishiara, it's a three-hour walk to the new concrete bridge over the **Tana River**, where there's a *hoteli* and a tailor and not a lot else.

Another three hours' hike downstream on the right bank brings you to KONYU, where you shouldn't have trouble finding somewhere to put up for the night. The primary school may oblige: there are stunning views from here when the air is clear.

You can now proceed by earth road, but on foot, around the **hills east of Konyu** (first heading north, then turning back south) to Katse (at least two days); or else try to find companions in Konyu to walk with you on a more direct **short cut route** to Katse along a watercourse over the baobab-tufted hills (highest peak Mt Mumoni, 1747m). This is about a six-hour walk.

Katse has a pretty **lodging house** and a bus departure at 7am every morning down to MWINGI, on the A3 Nairobi-Garissa highway – only a sixty-kilometre run but it takes hours. You should be able to get to Garissa the same evening and Lamu the next evening.

This is an interesting route to take, virtually unheard-of, full of rewarding encounters and unexplored districts and wilderness. If you plan on walking much of the first part of the route, allow a week for the whole trip.

AROUND THE ABERDARES

The **Aberdare Range**, which peaks at 4000m, is less well known than Mount Kenya. The lower, eastern slopes have long been farmed by the Kikuyu (more recently by European tea and coffee planters), and the dense montane forests covering the higher reaches are the habitat of leopard, bongo, buffalo and elephant. Above about 3500m, lions and other open-country animals roam the cloudy moorlands. Melanistic forms – especially of leopard, but also of serval cat and even bushbuck – are quite common.

The Kikuyu called these mountains *Nyandarua* ("Drying hide", for their silhouette) long before Thomson in 1884 named them after Lord Aberdare, president of the Royal Geographical Society. In their bamboo thickets and tangled forests, **Kikuyu guerrillas** hid out for months and years in the 1950s, living off the jungle and surviving thanks to techniques learned under British officers during the Burma campaign in World War II, in which many of them had fought. Despite the manhunts through the forests and the bombing of hideouts, little damage was done to the natural habitat and Aberdare National Park remains one of Kenya's most pristine forest reserves.

On the western side, the range drops away steeply to the Rift. It was here, in the high **Wanjohi Valley**, that a concentration of settlers in the 1920s and 1930s created the myth of **Happy Valley** out of their obsessive – and unsettled – lives. There's not much to see (or hear) these days. The old wheat and pyrethrum farms were subdivided after independence and the valley's new settlers are more concerned with making their market gardens pay. The memories live on only among veteran *wazungu*.

The Kinangop plateau (p.104) was settled by Europeans, too, but the high forest and moorland here was declared **Aberdare National Park** in 1950. The park, which stretches 60km along the length of the peaks, with the "Treetops Salient" on the lower slopes reaching out east, includes, like Mount Kenya National Park, the worst of the weather. Rainfall up here is high, often closing the Aberdares to vehicles in the wet season, although the game lodges at *The Ark* and *Treetops* stay open all year. Somewhat inaccessible, the park is nevertheless close enough to Nairobi to be worth the effort of getting to **Nyeri**, the usual base.

Nyahururu, the other important town in the region, has **Thomson's Falls** as a postcard attraction, and is also the base for a wild cross-country journey to Lake Bogoria in the Rift Valley, 1500m below (Chapter Three). From here, too, begins one of the four routes into the northern deserts (Chapter Seven), in this case to Maralal and Loiyangalani on the eastern shore of Lake Turkana.

Aberdare National Park

You'll find less transport **travelling** in the lower Aberdares than around Mount Kenya, but it's still relatively easy to get around, with regular bus and *matatu* services between the villages. Heading over the mountains and **through the park**, however, **hitching** is the sole, very uncertain, option if you haven't a vehicle. Determination can pay dividends, but in this case, you could wait for days. If you're going to try, it's suggested you stop at the *Outspan Hotel* in Nyeri and try to arrange a lift.

If you're **driving into the park**, you need four-wheel-drive – it can rain at any time – and it's best to approach from Nyeri rather than Naivasha as the escarpment on the west side is steeper than most people would want to tackle going up. The route across the mountains is closed for several months every year during the rains. But once you're in, it's a beautiful drive, with waterfalls and sensational views more than compensating for comparatively scarce wildlife: buffalo, elephants and colobus monkeys are most often seen. There are a number of basic campsites and you'll certainly have more animal encounters if you stay the night, but you'll need a good sleeping bag to keep out the cold at 3000m.

The high moorlands have some exceptional **walking** and the three peaks – Satima (the highest) in the north, Kinangop in the south, and Kipipiri, an isolated cone above the Wanjohi Valley, in the west – can be climbed relatively easily, given good weather conditions: ask the *Mountain Club of Kenya* in Nairobi for details. Walking in the park is allowed only with the approval of the warden in Nyeri (just outside town on the way to Mweiga – ☎24, Mweiga), though if you drive, it's usually permissible to wander a short distance from your car. The situation changes from time to time: there have been a number of near-misses in recent years with several, apparently human-hungry, lions.

For animals in quantity, and for any real chance of seeing rhinos, giant forest hog, or the Aberdares' prize inhabitant, bongo antelope, you might consider staying a night at one of the two **game-viewing lodges** (*The Ark* or *Treetops*, see overleaf), a recklessly expensive option perhaps, but one you're not likely to forget.

Nyeri and around

Self-styled capital of Kikuyuland – a title the Kikuyu of Kiambu might dispute – **NYERI** is, more prosaically, the administrative headquarters of Central Province and one of the liveliest highland towns. Another former military camp, it emerged as a market town for European coffee growers in the hills and for settlers on the ranching and wheat farms further north. Located beneath the Aberdares, it was on the front line – as much as there was one – during the war for independence.

It is an attractive town and an active trading centre, nestled in green hills where the broad vale between Mount Kenya and the Aberdares drops towards Nairobi. Tumultuous markets, dozens of *dukas*, and even a few street entertainers playing on soda bottles and bottle tops, lend it an air of irrepressible commercialism.

The Outspan

Nyeri's role as rural business centre and major transport crossroads means there are plenty of **places to stay**. Foremost is the *Outspan Hotel* (PO Box 24, ☎2424 Nyeri), twenty minutes' walk (or a Ksh30 taxi ride) from the town centre. The headquarters for *Treetops* – itself some kilometres away in an area of the park known as the Treetops Salient – neither is an obvious choice for accommodation, if you're on any kind of tight budget, though for a night in considerable style – huge rooms, wonderful old baths – you can't do much better than the *Outspan* (Ksh2055). But you'll be very welcome in any case for a meal there, or for tea on the lawn and a swim in the pool. Breakfast and buffet lunch are highly recommended, expensive and worth every shilling, especially if you've just walked down Mount Kenya. There are some good walks along the Chania River bank, though you have to go with a guard from the hotel (small fee).

The extraordinary density of **cultivation** in the tightly spaced *shambas* around Nyeri (maize, beans, potatoes, cassava, bananas, sugar cane, millet, squash and melons, tomatoes, citrus fruit, cabbages and carrots, as well as tea, coffee and macadamia nuts) is partly a hangover of white settlerdom, when a rapidly growing population was deprived of huge tracts of land and forced to cultivate intensively. Partly, too, it's the result of land consolidation: the "rationalisation" of fragmented land holdings into unitary *shambas* that took place in the 1950s and turned people who had held traditional rights into deed-holding property owners. And partly it's the simple consequence of an excellent climate and soil plus a birth rate reckoned (like Kisii's, p.188) to be one of the highest in the world.

There's no doubt that the **changes** which have taken place in Nyeri district have been some of the most profound and rapid anywhere in the country. Even the villages of Kikuyuland are nearly all innovations of the last thirty years, the irreversible effects of The Emergency. Until then, the Kikuyu had mostly lived in scattered homesteads among their crops and herds. British security forces, unable to contain open revolt in the countryside, began the systematic internment of the whole Kikuyu population into fenced and guarded villages, forcing the guerrillas into the high forests. And the villages of today have mostly grown from such places.

On Nyeri's main street, Kimathi Way, is a cenotaph, unusual in the frankness of its inscription: *To the Memory of the Members of the Kikuyu Tribe who Died in the fight for Freedom 1951–1957.*

The *Outspan's Kirinyaga Bar* has good fish and chips, and is okay for a beer in the evening in civilised surroundings, but it's not a hugely stimulating night out. With the right approach at the *Outspan*, though, you might find a lift over the Aberdares – but ask early in the day, when people would be setting off, rather than later.

Lodgings in town

A **bed for the night** can be found, more sparingly, in the town centre, and there are plenty of interesting alternatives. The *Central Hotel* is clean, pleasant and good value (around Ksh400 s/c twin B&B) and the *White Rhino Hotel* (PO Box 30, ☎2189) has reasonable s/c accommodation at Ksh250/400 B&B. For **cheap lodgings**, probably the best bet is *Maru Restaurant & Lodging* with filling meals and clean and efficiently kept rooms (Ksh80/120) – though beware that at weekends it can transform into the sleaziest imaginable pick-up joint. Also good, and well known for its excellent chicken, is *Bahati Restaurant & Lodging* (Ksh90/140 s/c). The *Seremai Hotel* is the place to fuel up on *mandaazi* and the *White Rhino* is for conscientious boozing. Nyeri has a **cheese** factory; lots of it is available locally.

Treetops and The Ark

Bookings for Treetops and The Ark: see the box in "Sleeping" in Basics; minimum age for children 10 at Treetops, 7 at The Ark; prices depend on where you're picked up.

Having invested two thousand-odd shillings for a night in **Treetops** (much less between April and June) and the opportunity to breathe the same air as the rich and/or famous, you might, in retrospect, wish you'd spent your money on a night

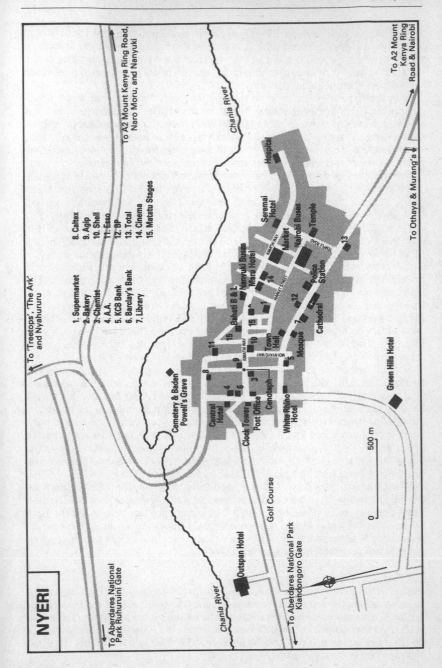

NYERI

To Aberdares National Park Ruhuruini Gate

Chania River

To 'Treetops', 'The Ark' and Nyahururu

To A2 Mount Kenya Ring Road, Naro Moru, and Nanyuki

Chania River

To A2 Mount Kenya Ring Road & Nairobi

To Othaya & Murang'a

1. Supermarket
2. Bakery
3. Chemist
4. A.A.
5. KCB Bank
6. Barclay's Bank
7. Library
8. Caltex
9. Agip
10. Shell
11. Esso
12. BP
13. Total
14. Cinema
15. Matatu Stages

Cemetery & Baden Powell's Grave

Hospital

Seremai Hotel

Market
Nairobi Buses

Temple

TEMPLE ROAD

Nanyuki Buses
Maru Hotel

Police Station

Cathedral

Bahati B & L

Town Hall

KIMATHI WAY

Mosque

MOI NYAYO WAY

MARKET STREET

Central Hotel

Clock Tower
Post Office

Cenotaph

White Rhino Hotel

Green Hills Hotel

Golf Course

500 m

0

Outspan Hotel

Chania River

To Aberdares National Park Kiandongoro Gate

at the *Outspan Hotel* instead. The *Outspan*, set in beautiful gardens, with Mount Kenya rising like a backdrop behind, is the stately base for all visits to *Treetops*. If you're booked to spend a night at "the hotel in the trees", you check in at the *Outspan* for lunch and are driven up in the afternoon, though it's also possible to set out from Nairobi in the morning.

After the hype from the Nairobi tourism machine, *Treetops* is at first a disappointment. The lodge is no longer inside the forest. The original tree-house was looted and burned down in 1955: the present, much larger building is built on stilts among the trees. Down by the **waterhole**, a large area is now virtually bare – red dust and dead wood – the result of foliage destruction by elephants. One patch has even been fenced in, presumably to protect new plant growth.

The problem, as always, is to balance tourist receipts with the needs of wildlife – needs which already conflict with those of farmers on the slopes nearby. Many of the animals that come to *Treetops* are lured by the **salt** which is spread beneath the viewing platform every afternoon before the visitors arrive. This draws large herds of elephant and buffalo nightly, but in the long term seems to ensure the ruination of the environment around the lodge and certainly discourages the appearance of those animals that need plenty of forest cover.

Inevitably rather contrived, the lodge itself remains tremendous fun, with growing branches of cape chestnut twisting through the public rooms. The bedrooms are tiny (the only smaller ones are in *Amigo's Boarding & Lodging* in Nakuru) and without bathrooms. What you pay for is the experience of *Treetops*. Photographs and letters framed on the varnished walls hark back to the 1930s, 40s and 50s, and various Royal and State visits. Princess Elizabeth became Queen Elizabeth II while she was staying in the original Treetops on the other side of the waterhole. All this must instill a sense of elitism in some visitors.

With the rather creaking atmosphere of a wooden ship, and a dining room with trestle tables and polished benches like an officers' mess, this million-dollar-a-year industry is the most exclusive way of living bush. The fact that it's always booked solid, and not just by safari-suited tour groups, affirms its attraction, though this has to do partly with the other fact that you can't check it out beforehand; even if you could find the track up to the park gate, only the accompanied group with bookings is allowed in. Once there, the sense of illusion is never far below the surface. Through the forest, Kikuyu *shambas* and homesteads are visible in every direction: the main Nyeri road passes by just 3km away.

When the sun goes down and the floodlights come on, this can be forgotten; the wildlife below takes over and the cameras start clicking in earnest. Herds of heavyweights can be taken for granted, but leopard are rarely seen and the large **bongo**, that "shy and elusive forest antelope", hasn't put in an appearance for many years – understandably. **Rhino** are fairly common visitors and the curious **giant forest hog** sometimes turns up as well.

The Ark

For better game-viewing, **The Ark**, *Treetops'* upstart competitor, is at a higher altitude, actually in the mountain forest. Here, they do on occasions see leopard and bongo. What's more, the accommodation fits the bill somewhat better. Their base is the *Aberdare Country Club* (PO Box 449, Nyeri, ☎17 Mweiga) near MWEIGA, on the road between Nyeri and Nyahururu. The *Club* is comfortably rural and slightly cheaper than its *Outspan* equivalent.

Out of Nyeri

A signposted route leads **west**, past the *Outspan*, up into the Aberdares and the park's Kiandongoro gate in the high moorland. In the other direction, the road splits out of town, forking **south** to Murang'a via OTHAYA, or continuing **east** to the A2 Mount Kenya ring road and the quickest return route to Nairobi.

A fourth route heads northwest out of town, splitting after 2km. Keep straight on if you want the Mount Kenya ring road, northbound for Naro Moru and Nanyuki via KIGANJO. Fork left and the road sweeps past the track for the Ruhurini gate in the Treetops Salient, then the unmarked tracks for *Treetops* and *The Ark*. It continues, in a pitiful condition, across lonely, forested ridges and wide savannahs to Nyahururu (Thomson's Falls), on the northern fringes of the Highlands.

Tip: be prepared for an argument over the fare if you take a *matatu* from Nyeri to Naro Moru or Nanyuki. It's a dreadful road and they always overcharge *wazungu* on this route.

Nyahururu (Thomson's Falls)

Like Nanyuki, **NYAHURURU** is almost on the equator, and it shares much of Nanyuki's character. It is high (at 2360m, Kenya's highest town), cool, even frosty on January and February mornings, and set on open savannah lands with patches of indigenous forest and plenty of coniferous plantation. Since the new road to Nyeri (see below) was completed, Nyahururu has been less cut off, but still there's an air of slightly wild isolation about it. It's something of a frontier town for routes heading north to Lake Turkana and the desert: a tarred road goes out as far as RUMURUTI and then the fun begins (see p.358). Other roads join Nyahururu with Nanyuki (a dastardly bad road, but good for game-veiwing), GILGIL (p.146) and NAKURU and the remainder of the Northern Rift Valley (p.148).

Joseph Thomson gave the town its original name when he named the nearby waterfall after his father in 1883. Many still call it "T Falls" – and not just the old settlers you might expect. Thomson's Falls was one of the last settler towns to be established. First sign of urbanisation was a hut built by the Narok Angling Club in the early 1920s so its members could fish for trout in the Ewaso Narok, Pesi and Equator rivers. In 1929, when the railway branch line arrived, the town began to take shape. The line has closed now, but the hotel built in 1931, *Thomson's Falls Lodge* is still going strong and Nyahururu remains an important market town. And not, in any sense, a tourist centre. Local people can react rather oddly to the presence of travellers in Nyahururu's lodging houses. Be sensitive to the fact that some think you should stay down by the falls.

Thomson's Falls Lodge

For **accommodation**, most people do head out to the lodge (PO Box 38, ☎22006; bookings in Nairobi on ☎21855) and camp near the falls. The **campsite** is popular with budget safari groups; there are *hot* showers (remind reception to turn on the heater) and ample firewood is included in the price (Ksh40). The lodge itself is very good value, too, offering solid, highlands farmhouse

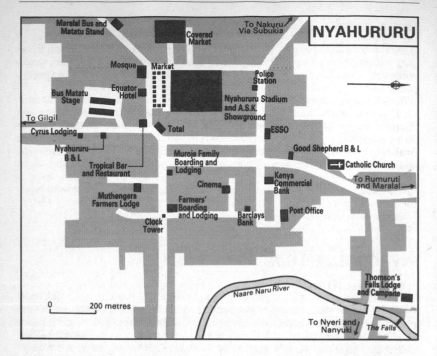

atmosphere with log fires in the rooms, big old-fashioned baths (rooms from Ksh450/620 s/c B&B), decent and reasonably priced **meals** and a good snack menu. Nor does it feel remote from the life of the town itself, as it really doesn't fill its rooms with mainstream package tourists. It's a good place to spend Christmas, but book ahead.

Lodgings in town

If the rooms at the lodge are out of your price range and you don't have a tent, check out the *Baron Hotel*, a newish, "tourist class" establishment (around Ksh300/400 B&B; not marked on the map) on the Gilgil road, just south of the *Tropical Bar*. Below this level, there are a dozen or more **B&Ls** in town (though, note that they tend to be pretty miserable examples, and several don't have doors you could possibly lock). There's not much to choose between them but *Manguo Lodge* (not on the map, behind the *Total* garage), *Cyrus Lodging, Nyahururu B&L,* the *Good Shepherd,* and *Muthengera Farmers Lodge* have the edge (prices around Ksh80–150, some s/c) – the "best" of the rest are marked on our map. The *Silent Fourteen In One Boarding & Lodging* opposite the bus station, alas (for its name alone) is no more. In such a location it would have been anything but silent. Maybe that's why it closed.

For **meals**, the *Cyrus*'s own restaurant, the *Arafa*, comes highly recommended: they do several vegetarian dishes and you get a good view of the bus and matatu stage – so a good place to wait for a connection. For **action** after dark (or quite likely at any time) check out the *Muthengera Bar*, even if you're not staying in their lodging. It jumps.

Thomson's Falls

The Falls themselves are pretty rather than spectacular – though they can be pretty spectacular after heavy rain. They're a popular stop-off for tourists travelling between Samburu and Maasai Mara game reserves (14 kombis at one time is nothing), and the lawns above the falls get crowded with picnickers from town at weekends. At such times, the souvenir sellers on the cliff edge can be a pain. When the crowds leave, they're good company, if you want it.

The path down to the bottom of the 75-metre falls is dangerous when wet. Don't, however, attempt to climb up again by any other route because the cliffs are extremely loose. With several hours to spare, you can search for a longer **walk** down into the forested valley, following the Ewaso Narok River. The spray-laden trees are shaken periodically by troops of colobus monkeys and, as on Mount Kenya, three-horned chameleons are always around if you look hard for five minutes. If you want to try this, cross the bridge first, then look for a way downstream.

A much shorter stroll also takes you over the bridge and past the electricity sub-station, beyond which the first trail leads up to the top of a hill with a communications tower and a rickety lookout post. Excellent views from here stretch south towards OL KALOU and the marshy trough of Lake Ol Bolossat.

Onwards from Nyahururu

There are several buses and *matatus* a day down to NYERI, or you could hitch outside the lodge. The road was built, for most of its length, along a new route, so villages are few; for the most part it either bucks up and down across forested valleys or soars across immense plains of swaying grass. It's already deteriorating, with many potholes. The private, and once easily visited, *Solio Game Ranch* lies off this road before you reach Mweiga. It used to be one of the best places to see rhinos, so if you're independently mobile you could stop in and ask. Many of the relocated rhinos at Nakuru Rhino Sanctuary were bred here. Usually, you'll be referred to the *Aberdare County Club* (PO Box 449 Nyeri, ☎17 Mweiga) who handle bookings. Visits are then made in the estate's own vehicles.

Nyahururu's other transport connections are mentioned below in "travel details". Remember the unsurfaced road to Nanyuki can be treacherous in wet weather. For a **spectacular change of scene**, take the country bus down the scarp to the west as far as SUBUKIA (the fine new road continues to NAKURU) and follow the route described in Chapter Three to Lake Bogoria.

travel details

Buses and *Matatus*
Around Mount Kenya

Unless you have a specific destination in mind, simply **getting to the next town** on the circuit is always easy; *OTC* has offices in all of them. In addition, the country bus services act as shuttles between neighbouring towns. **Nyeri** is something of a break in this "chain" and you may need to rely on *matatus*. **Nanyuki-Nyahururu** and **Nanyuki-**

Isiolo also have limited bus services. Between **Meru** and Nairobi, *OTC*'s new "luxury" service is recommended, dep. Meru 7.30am, 1.30pm (5hr, via Chogoria, 90min, and Embu 150min).

Around the Aberdares
From Nyahururu to Nyeri and vv: daily *OTC* service runs between Nakuru and Nairobi via the *east* side of the Aberdares.

To Rumuruti and Maralal (see Chapter Seven): two daily buses, but the last through bus leaves at 11am (5–6hr).
To Gilgil frequent country bus and *matatu* runs; some go on to Nairobi.

Trains
There is **no longer** a passenger service to any town in this chapter.

Planes
Daily flights on *Air Kenya* from **Nyeri** (departs 9.40am) to **Nanyuki** (10min) and **Samburu**

Lodges (50min) returning same day. Return flight departs Nanyuki 11.30am for Nyeri and **Nairobi** (arrives 12.20pm). Tues, Wed, Thurs flights direct from **Nanyuki to Mara Lodges** at 11.30am.
Fares: Nyeri–Nairobi Ksh1490; Nyeri–Nanyuki Ksh715; Nyeri–Samburu Ksh1080.

Forget about flying Nyeri–Nanyuki no matter what the circumstances: the airstrips are so close together and so far from the towns they serve that you could drive the total 60-km journey faster, even given the state of the road!

TELEPHONE AREA CODES

Burguret Operator connection
Embu ☎0161
Meru ☎0164
Murang'a ☎0156
Mweiga ☎0171
Nanyuki ☎0176
Nyahururu ☎0365
Nyeri ☎0171

CHAPTER THREE

THE RIFT VALLEY

K enya's **Great Rift Valley** is only part of a continental fault system that runs six thousand kilometres clean across Africa from Jordan to Mozambique. It may be Kenya's most important topographical feature, certainly one of the country's great distinguishing marks, a human and natural divide. As such, it has come to be seen as a monumental valley of teeming game and Maasai herders, a trough of grasslands older than mankind. This image is not entirely borne out by reality. The valley certainly is spectacular, a literal *rift* across the country, with all the stunning panoramas and gaunt escarpment backdrops you could wish for, and the plains animals are still abundant in places (I even saw a cheetah with cubs crossing the main highway near Nakuru one morning); nevertheless, much of the game has been dispersed by human population pressure onto the higher plateaus to the southwest, and most of the Maasai nowadays live further south.

At least its **historical influence** cannot be diluted. People have trekked down the Rift Valley, generation after generation, over perhaps the last two or three thousand years, from the wetlands of southern Sudan and the Ethiopian highlands. Some of these immigrants were the forefathers of the **Maasai**, who dominated much of the valley and its surroundings for several centuries before the Europeans arrived. Until the beginning of this century, they lived on both sides, and the northern **Ilaikipiak** group were a constant threat to caravans coming up from the coast. With European settlement, they were forced from their former grazing grounds in the valley's turbulent bottleneck and confined to the Southern Reserve for much of the colonial era. Although many have now returned to the valley, and many towns retain their ancient Maa names, the Maasai are at their most conservative and traditional in southern Kenya; hence more background is included in Chapter Five.

In terms of **travel**, the part of the Rift Valley covered in this chapter offers several exceptional **lakes**, a couple of excellent fast roads, lots of spectacular twisting tracks, and some of the wildest country in central Kenya. (The southern regions of the Rift are covered in chapters One and Five; the north – Turkana – in Chapter Seven.) If you're at all interested in wildlife, especially birds, you'll find it a source of endless fascination, with wonderful **nature reserves** at lakes **Nakuru** and **Bogoria**, and a freshwater ecosystem at **Baringo**.

Apart from **Nakuru** itself, the area covered in this chapter contains few places larger than a village: **lodgings**, strictly speaking, are scarce. Though there usually is somewhere to lay your head, this is a region where a **tent** will be worth its extra weight, and good walking shoes are an added advantage. **Transport** in the higher, agricultural parts of the south is generally good, but northwards, or off the main Nakuru-Baringo-Kabarnet axis, you can expect long waits, next to no buses and infrequent *matatus*. The northern Rift is lower – and consequently hotter – than most up-country regions, so be prepared for some very **high temperatures** and don't underestimate your **water** requirements.

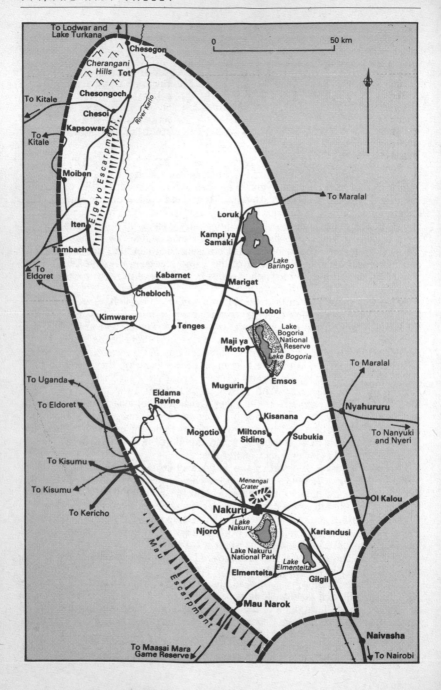

THE KALENJIN

In this part of the Rift Valley, the **Kalenjin** form the majority of the population. Their name, actually a recent adoption by a number of peoples speaking closely related languages, means "I tell you" in all of them. The principal Kalenjin are the Nandi, Terik, Tugen, Elgeyo, Elkony, Sabaot, Pokot, Marakwet and Kipsigis. They are some of the earliest inhabitants of Kenya and probably absorbed the early bushmen or pygmy peoples who were here for hundreds of thousands of years before.

Primarily **farmers**, the Kalenjin have often adapted their economies to local circumstances. It's supposed that the first Kalenjin were herdsmen whose lifestyle has changed over the centuries. The pastoral **Pokot** group, who still spurn all kinds of cultivation and despise peoples who rely on anything but livestock, call the **Marakwet**, living against the western Rift escarpment, *Cheblong* ("the Poor"), for their lack of cattle.

The **Okiek** are another interesting clue to the past: these hunter-gatherers are a Kalenjin-speaking people, living in scattered groups in the forests of the high slopes flanking the Rift. Unlike most hunter-gatherers, though they do very little gathering. Meat and honey from their hives are the traditional staples. They consider wild fruits and vegetables barely palatable, though cornmeal and gardening have now been introduced; they keep some domestic animals, too. They may be the descendants of Kalenjin forebears who lost (or ate) their herds: there are other groups in Kenya who live mostly by hunting – Ndorobo or Wanderoo – for whom such a background is very likely.

Many of the mainstream Kalenjin played key roles in the founding of the Kenya African Democratic Union (*KADU* – now disbanded), but the most famous of their number in recent years has been President Moi, a **Tugen** from Baringo district. Coming from a small ethnic group, his presidency for years avoided the accusations of tribalism levelled so bitterly against Kenyatta, and he still devotes time to touring the country, holding *Harambee* meetings and spurring development. In the last couple of years, however, many senior positions in the civil service do seem to have been occupied by staff with Kalenjin ethnic affiliation.

INTO THE CENTRAL RIFT VALLEY – THE NAKURU DISTRICT

Many travellers' first view of the Rift Valley is from the souvenir-draped shoulders of the **A104 Uplands road**. This, Kenya's best highway, barrels through the forests north of Nairobi, crosses a broad, bleak plateau, then flirts with the precipice before following the contours of the slopes above Naivasha (see p.97) and dropping into the Rift. They sell rhubarb up here, plums, carrots and potatoes. In the wet season, you can find yourself driving over a thick, white carpet of hailstones between gloomy conifer plantations.

All this contrasts dramatically with the endless, dusty plains below. With binoculars, you can pick out herds of gazelle, Maasai with their cattle and, bizarrely, a satellite-tracking station near the grey cone of Mount Longonot.

The Uplands road is a good one to hitch on, and buses and *matatus* often use it; remember to sit on the left for the best views. If you have a car of your own, you can stop at some of the stands on the roadside: small sheepskins are often excellent value, but check they have been properly cured. (And note that the last set of stands in the best location is also the most expensive.) More seriously, if you are driving, treat this road as a continuous **blackspot** – it's only one half of a four-lane highway, as yet unfinished, and overtaking is lethal.

The **"old road"**, built by Italian POWs during World War II, runs parallel to and lower than the Uplands road; it's insanely bumpy and narrow and used by the transcontinental lorries coming from Mombasa. Corresponding to its lower altitude, vegetation down here takes on a more Mediterranean aspect, candelabra euphorbia and spikey agave predominating. The little **chapel**, also Italian-built, seems fitting in this scene. Sadly neglected, it's more often used as a pit-stop picnic site.

Whichever road you use, you pass Naivasha and continue, on Kenya's contribution to the Trans-African Highway (a projected paved ribbon joining Lagos with Mombasa), into the Central Rift Valley – and the area around Lakes Elmenteita and Nakuru.

Gilgil, Elmenteita and Kariandusi

GILGIL – pronounced "Girgir" by many Kenyans – is as dull a town as you could expect to find anywhere. If you are heading north towards Nyahururu and Maralal, however, you may well find yourself hitching or changing buses or *matatus* here. I did, and can safely recommend *Salama Lodge* (PO Box 721) as it was recommended to me: "the best place in town", which in Gilgil is not saying much. Pretty rooms and clean, threadbare beds go from Ksh80–120. Water supplies seemed problematic, but in Gilgil maybe you should just count your blessings. The town has a post office (Mon–Fri 8am–1pm & 2–5pm), but no bank and not much of anything else.

Gilgil War Cemetery

En route to Nyahururu – "T Falls" if it slips off the tongue more easily – you'll pass **Gilgil Commonwealth War Cemetery**. If you've a couple of hours to spare, walk the two or three kilometres out of town into the quiet, breezy savannah and have a look: it's a good place to stop for a picnic and some moments of contemplation before flagging down a vehicle.

There are about 200 graves here from the East African campaign of World War II and from the War for Independence – "the Emergency" – in the later 1950s. Whether by accident (which doesn't seem credible) or design, the African graves are all at the bottom of the slope. They record no personal details apart from name and rank. The graves of British soldiers are higher up and the stones inscribed with family messages. Most are from World War II, but there are also poignant reminders of lives lost between 1959 and 1962, after the British government's futile attempt to prevent the inevitable. The fact that not a single freedom fighter is buried here demonstrates the ambivalent attitude of Kenyans to their struggle for *Uhuru*. The Gilgil cemetery, one of over forty in Kenya tended by the Commonwealth War Graves Commission, is lovingly maintained, one of the most meticulously kept in the country.

The road climbs past *Gilgil Country Club* – "a lethal piss-up on a Friday night" they said, and there can certainly be no competition in town – on through moorland and conifer plantations around the resettlement zone of Ol Kalou, where some of the most violent *Mau Mau* attacks took place, and over the equator to Nyahururu (p.139), Kenya's highest town.

Lake Elmenteita

Beyond the turn for Gilgil, however, the fast new road sweeps the eastern wall of the Rift Valley and pushes up high above **Lake Elmenteita.** This huge white salt pond, which dried up completely in 1985, is more or less inaccessible on a casual visit, since most of it is on private land and is part of the Delamere Estate's *Soysambu* property. But if you take a left towards Elmenteita village shortly after Gilgil and push on down to the shore of the lake, it shouldn't be impossible to take a stroll down there. Clear it with anyone you come across. The lake once had a herd of hippos, which seems incredible now that it's become just a vast salt flat. Around the once-lush shores are a number of prehistoric sites. **Gambles cave** is the most famous; if you're an enthusiast, you can visit it by making arrangements ahead of time – ask first at the National Museum in Nairobi.

Digs and mines: Kariandusi

For an easier shot of prehistory, try a no-fuss visit to **KARIANDUSI,** with a surprising sideshow in the shape of a neighbouring *diatomite* mine. Kariandusi (signposted right, 10 minutes' walk from the highway, open daily 8am–6pm; Ksh15) is an **Acheulian site** characterised, like Olorgasailie, by heavy hand-axes and cleavers. The site is very small, consisting of just two excavated areas cleared by Louis Leakey in 1928, each displaying a scattered assortment of stone tools, many of them made of the black volcanic glass called *obsidian*.

Neither Kariandusi nor Olorgasailie has any signs of permanent habitation and it has been suggested that they were simply **butcheries**, places where the kill was habitually portioned off and consumed, the tools made on the spot and left for the next occasion. But the tools are far from left untouched since they were carefully exposed by Leakey; the obligatory guide climbed a fence and casually passed me a number of stone tools to hold. Nothing much is known about the tool-makers – apart from the fact that they obviously had a formidable grip – but a likely candidate is **Homo erectus**, a primitive early hominid whose remains have been found at Olduvai Gorge in Tanzania beside Acheulian artefacts.

The diatomite industry

Even if you look around the tiny museum, half an hour is plenty of time at Kariandusi. However, right next door is a **diatomite mine** which, once you persuade the gatekeeper to let you in (contact *Diatomite Industries*, PO Box 32, Gilgil, ☎2097 Gilgil, to be sure), is a fascinating complement – as a spectacle, it eclipses the prehistoric site. Diatomite is a light, white, crumbly rock composed of the compressed silica skeletons of microscopic sea organisms (diatoms). The Kikuyu used it as body paint (*karia andus*), but it also makes an excellent filter and it absorbs water like silica gel. Brewers use it for filtration and it makes an effective insecticide in grain silos by dehydrating the weevils without poisoning the grain.

The British manager will gladly tell you more about diatomite, but the real excitement comes when you walk down into the mine itself. A giant bowl has been scooped out of the ground by pick and shovel over the last forty years, with a track spiralling down on the inside. They have now reached a level, about fifty metres down, where a high-grade, brilliant white diatomite is found. Here, a dozen or more **tunnels** dive into the cliffs to form a maze of ghostly subterranean passages, almost architectural in design and home to thousands of fluttering **bats**. The tunnels are wonderfully cool and vents keep the air circulating. You'll be assured that the structure of diatomite makes rock falls extremely unlikely, but a number of shored-up passageways may leave you unconvinced and glad to have along an accounts clerk – or some other conscripted employee – to guide you. You need a torch even though the light goes in a surprisingly long way, but you can't really get lost.

Foreign competition, principally from open-cast pits in California, is gradually forcing this mine out of business. Up on the surface, an ancient, rusting kiln is periodically fired up to dry the diatomite for packing. The whole place has a somewhat archaic air about it – which must have disappointed the group of Romanians once found taking unnecessarily furtive photographs from the main road.

Nakuru and sites surrounding

Were it not that **NAKURU** is a major transport hub and has its own national park closer to its town centre than is Nairobi's, there would be no special reason to visit it. A noisy, incredibly dusty town, Nakuru is Kenya's fourth largest city (though it projects a noticeably busier and more energetic image than Kisumu, the third); it is also capital of the enormous, sprawling Rift Valley Province that stretches from the Sudanese border to the slopes of Kilimanjaro.

The place came into existence on the thrust of the Uganda railway and owed its early growth, at least in part, to **Lord Delamere**, the colony's most famous figure. In 1903, he acquired four hundred square kilometres of land on the lower slopes of the Mau escarpment, followed by two hundred more at Soysambu, on the other side of the lake. Eager to share the empty vistas with compatriots – though preferably with other Cheshire or Lancashire men – he promoted in England the mile-square plots being offered free by the Foreign Office. Eventually, some two hundred new settler families arrived and *Nakuru* – a name which as usual could mean various things, including *Place of the Waterbuck* (Swahili) and *Swirling Dust* or *Little Soda Lake* (Maasai) – became their country capital. It lies on the unprepossessing steppe between the lake and the flanks of Menengai crater. This desolate shelf has a nickname: "the place where the cows won't eat grass" (the pasture was found to be iron-deficient). Farmers near the town turned to the better prospects of pyrethrum, the plant used to make insecticide, as a cash crop.

Nakuru today
Still very much a workaday farmers' town, with unadorned old seed shops and veterinary paraphernalia much in evidence on the main street, Nakuru is a little Nairobi without the flashy veneer, its streets always undergoing ear-shattering repairs. Since it's a stone's throw from **Nakuru National Park**, equally close to the prehistoric settlement site at **Hyrax Hill** and the vast bowl of the **Menengai**

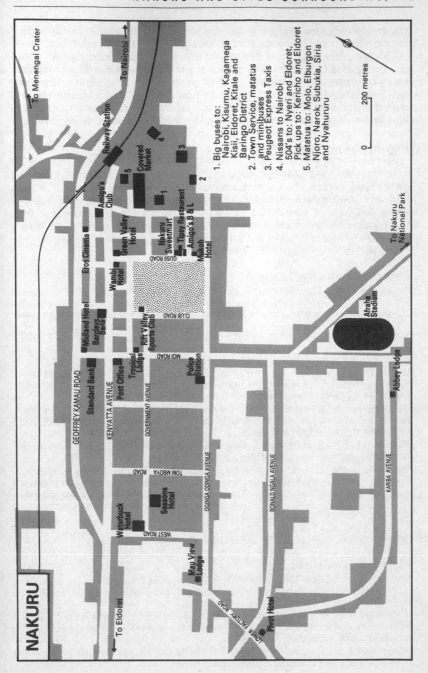

NAKURU

To Menengai Crater

To Nairobi

Railway Station

Covered Market

Amigo's Club

Eros Cinema

Green Valley Hotel

Nakuru Sweetmart

Tipsy Restaurant

Amigo's B & L

Maikoh Hotel

GUSII ROAD

Wambi Hotel

Midland Hotel

Barclays Bank

CLUB ROAD

Rift Valley Sports Club

MOI ROAD

Tropical Lodge

Standard Bank

Post Office

Police Station

GEOFFREY KAMAU ROAD

KENYATTA AVENUE

GOVERNMENT AVENUE

OGINGA ODINGA AVENUE

TOM MBOYA ROAD

RONALD NGALA AVENUE

Waterbuck Hotel

Seasons Hotel

WEST ROAD

Mau View Lodge

KARIBA AVENUE

LOWER FACTORY ROAD

Pivot Hotel

Afraha Stadium

To Nakuru National Park

Abbey Lodge

To Eldoret

1. Big buses to:
   Nairobi, Kisumu, Kagamega
   Kisii, Eldoret, Kitale and
   Baringo District
2. Town Service, matatus
   and minibuses
3. Peugeot Express Taxis
4. Nissans to Nairobi
   504's to: Nyeri and Eldoret,
   Pick ups to: Kericho and Eldoret
5. Matatus to: Molo, Elburgon
   Njoro, Narok, Subukia, Siria
   and Nyahururu

0   200 metres

crater, and the jumping-off point for **trips down into the northern Rift Valley**, you may find yourself passing through Nakuru more often than you'd like.

The town does have some positive aspects, worth emphasising if you're staying. One traveller – an agriculture student – said he found the place compelling for its antiquated **farming supply stores** and the smell of fertiliser on the dusty and fume-laden air. The **market**, certainly, is animated and a pleasure to look around. And if none of this appeals, there's a glimmer of charm still remaining in its colonnaded old streets and the jacaranda-brushed avenues at the edge of town.

Practical matters

At least the town seems to be outstandingly friendly. People will literally take you by the hand to show you the way, and you're never at a loss for long. The **train and bus stations** are packed together at the east end of town with loads of **cheap lodgings** all around. For **cheap rooms**, plenty of other places apart from the following can be found in the centre, though few of them shine. At the **luxury** end, there's nothing at all in Nakuru: most of the thousands of tourists on their way to the park stay in one of the two lodges there.

Cheap and mid-range lodgings

Amigo's B&L (Ksh70/100), Gusii Rd, next to the *Tipsy Restaurant*, and not to be confused with the *Day and Night Club* of the same name off Kenyatta Avenue. One of the most popular cheapies, *Amigo's*, has one toilet and one shower, but they both work and the water, when there is any, is hot.

Tropical Lodge (PO Box 49124, ☎28266), Moi Rd. A presentable, if rather gloomy, alternative, with rooms big enough to swing several cats (Ksh80/110), and incredible noise from the *Tropical Valley Night Club* steaming around the corner.

Wambi Hotel (PO Box 586; it used to be the *Green Ages/Gituamba Lodge*), Gusii Rd. One of the best joints in this quarter of town, with clean and roomy accommodation (Ksh120/170 non-s/c B&B), though again it's raucous on disco nights. Join in.

Carnation Hotel, Mosque Rd (just south of Bus Park 1 on our map, PO Box 1620, ☎43522). A large but well-run and attentive establishment with rooms from under Ksh100 (B&B single, non-s/c) to Ksh220 (B&B twin s/c).

Mukoh Hotel (PO Box 238, ☎4440), Gusii Road, just past the *Sweet Mart*. More expensive, but makes more concessions to sleepers (Ksh240/double s/c).

Mau View Lodge (PO Box 1413, ☎44926), Oginga Odinga Ave, about twenty minutes' walk from the centre. One of the best mid-range lodgings, and useful if you have a vehicle for their really safe parking. Attractive and small, with good rooms, a shady courtyard, bar and restaurant, it's arguably the best value in town, even though some beds need new springs – not surprisingly (from Ksh120/180 s/c and up).

Seasons Hotel (PO Box 3153, ☎45218), Government Ave. A similar set-up to *Mau View*, including the tree-filled garden, but closer to the centre (Ksh275/320 B&B).

More expensive hotels

Midland Hotel (PO Box 908, ☎43953), Geoffrey Kamau Rd. Some unfortunate tourists end up in this over-priced and very average place – basically a huge pub with rooms (Ksh280/505 B&B s/c).

Waterbuck Hotel (PO Box 3327, ☎40081), West Rd. A much better bet if you're looking for real comforts (around Ksh400/600 B&B) plus they do a respectable five-course buffet lunch for Ksh100, and the breakfasts are huge.

Kunste Hotel, on the north side of the road out to Nairobi, just past the State House. A new hotel, that seems very satisfactory (around Ksh900/twin B&B).

Eating, drinking and not much else

Restaurants you should definitely visit include the *Oyster Shell* on the corner of Club Rd and Kenyatta Ave (first floor), where you can eat magnificently for under Ksh100; and the utterly time-warped *Railway Station Restaurant*, where you can have silver service cornflakes and toast for breakfast – and equally immaculately served colonial repasts at lunch and dinner. Otherwise, there's the long-established *Nakuru Sweet Mart*, which does an excellent, and massive, Indian vegetarian *thali*, the cheaper *Tipsy Restaurant* next door (for the less hungry), and *Rose's* in the backstreet parallel to Kenyatta Ave and Geoffrey Kamau Rd. *Gilani's* has been going a long time, too – a supermarket near the post office with a decent video café and restaurant on the first floor.

Aside from the ordinary pursuits of **eating and drinking**, Nakuru has very little to offer. If you find enjoyable and printable **nightlife**, we'd like to know – in detail please. The tourist literature suggests you buy a sheepskin coat (not a very practical addition to the baggage you're bound to feel is already far too heavy) or some flamingo feather flowers – authentically pink and collected, not plucked, but nonetheless in highly questionable taste. This latter industry, mission-inspired, clearly passed its heyday when the flamingoes began mysteriously deserting the lake in the 1970s.

Lake Nakuru National Park

Ksh220, Ksh30 vehicles, Ksh50 to camp. No entry on foot: Warden PO Box 539, Nakuru, ☎2470.

Though not large – some 10km by 25km – **LAKE NAKURU** is a beautiful park, the *terra firma* mostly under light **acacia forest**, well provided with tracks to a variety of hides and lookouts. It's also one of the easiest parks to visit, with or without a vehicle of your own. Towards the end of the dry season in March, the lake is often much smaller than the maps suggest; consequently, water birds are a greater distance from the park roads. The **northern side** of the park is commonly fairly busy with tour vehicles. But the **southern parts** are usually empty, and *Makalia campsite* is an exceptional spot to head for.

The mystery of the vanishing flamingoes

Lake Nakuru has always been considered a flamingo lake *par excellence*; at one time, it was believed up to two million **lesser flamingoes** (perhaps one-third of the world's population) were massing in the warm alkaline water to feed on the abundant algae cultivated by their own droppings. Then, in the late 1970s, a combination of increased rainfall and decreased evaporation (there's no outlet) lowered the lake's salinity and raised the water level. The flamingoes began to disperse, some to lakes Elmenteita, Magadi and Natron (the latter in Tanzania), some up to Turkana, but the majority to Lake Bogoria. Since then, flamingoes have been sporadically seen again in the surreal pink swarms that have become almost a photographic cliché. No one really understands why they left – or returned – though salinity is believed to be a factor. The introduction of a species of *tilapia* fish – partly to control mosquitoes – has encouraged large flocks of white pelicans in recent years and it's likely that their presence is another disruptive element. On Elmenteita a breeding colony of greater flamingoes was forced off by the pelicans. The Nakuru Wildlife Trust has been studying the ecology of Rift Valley lakes since 1971 in an effort to find some of the answers. **Greater flamingoes** can also be

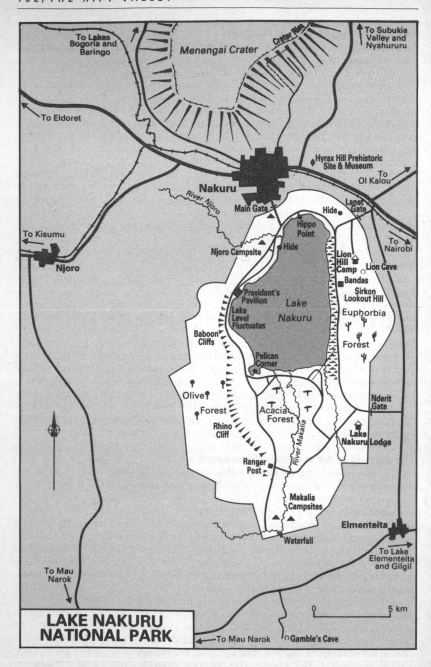

To Lakes Bogoria and Baringo
To Subukia Valley and Nyahururu
Menengai Crater
Crater Rim
To Eldoret
Hyrax Hill Prehistoric Site & Museum
To Ol Kalou
Nakuru
River Njoro
Main Gate
Hide
Lanet Gate
To Kisumu
To Nairobi
Hippo Point
Njoro Campsite
Hide
Njoro
Lion Hill Camp
Lion Cave
Bandas
Sirkon Lookout Hill
President's Pavilion
Lake Nakuru
Euphorbia
Lake Level Fluctuates
Baboon Cliffs
Forest
Pelican Corner
Olive Forest
Nderit Gate
Acacia Forest
River Makalia
Rhino Cliff
Lake Nakuru Lodge
Ranger Post
Makalia Campsites
Elmenteita
Waterfall
To Lake Elementeita and Gilgil
To Mau Narok

LAKE NAKURU NATIONAL PARK

0   5 km

To Mau Narok
Gamble's Cave

seen at Nakuru, though in much smaller numbers than their lesser relations. They're as tall as a small person and have less hooked beaks, with which they sift for small crustaceans and plankton, their heads under water.

Lake Nakuru's other wildlife

Fortunately, in view of the flamingoes' here-today, gone-tomorrow caprice (they have recently been at Nakuru in huge numbers), there is a lot more to the lake's spectacle than the pink flocks. The lake, its multi-faceted shores and the surrounding woodlands are home to some 400 other species of **birds** including, during the northern winter, many migratory European species.

There's a good number of **mammals** here as well. The lake isn't too briny for **hippos**: a herd of a dozen or more snort and splash by day and graze by night at the northern end. Nakuru has become a popular venue for introductions: **Rothschild's giraffe** from the wild herd near Kitale; **lion** and secretive **leopard** from wherever they're causing a nuisance; and more recently rhinos, with the installation of a sanctuary for **black rhinos** relocated from unsafe parts of the country. The intention is to maintain a viable number of rhinos in one well-protected zone, secure from poachers. Electric fencing has been installed around the entire perimeter of the park – the only park in the country to be so enclosed – and a huge investment in money and labour, substantially from the *Worldwide Fund For Nature*, has been expended on this major effort to save the rhino from extinction in Kenya. The cost per rhino, adding up to some £4000 per year, is perhaps twenty times the average income of the people on the other side of the fence. Until recently, the fortunate inmates could generally be seen before dusk near the **Nderit gate**, but word is that several poaching incidents have defeated the rangers' efforts and the rhinos are no longer publicly on display. Plans are being made to set up several more rhino sanctuaries in other parks over the next few years.

The park is also renowned for its very large **pythons**. The patches of dense **woodland** between the lakeshore and the steep cliffs in the southwest are a favourite python habitat. So now you know. One of these huge snakes reportedly dammed up the Makalia stream recently, when it died of internal injuries after swallowing a gazelle.

Lastly, if you tire of the living spectacle, go looking for the **Lion Cave**, beneath Lion Hill ridge in the northeast: it's an excavated prehistoric rock shelter and rarely contains lions.

Practicalities I: visits by taxi, tour or luck

The most straightforward way to see the park if you don't have a vehicle is **by taxi**, especially as some of the taxi drivers around town know the park well. This naturally works out cheaper for a group, but it's suggested you reach an agreement with the driver *before* you're all present. Reckon on some stiff bargaining, then three hours at about Ksh200 an hour. The *Midland Hotel* is as good a place as any to track one down.

Alternatively, you could see what the local *Blackbird Tours* and *Jomima Tours* can offer (they were recently doing "student" tours at about Ksh500 per person for three hours, including park fees). They also have vehicles for hire. *Blackbird Tours*, Carnation Hotel complex, Mosque Rd; *Jomima Tours*: Lake House, Moi Rd, next to *Tropical Lodge* PO Box 2215, Nakuru (☎33012/33018).

An alternative – though admittedly not always a very practical one – is to **hitch at the main gate**, about an hour's walk from the bus stations. The rangers are usually sympathetic to low-budget travellers; they may also help by asking drivers on your behalf, and you'll have no park fees to pay unless you get a lift. You should expect to spend the night in the park once you get a lift, so be prepared for this.

If you're **without a tent as well as on foot**, things look more difficult, but you could always stay the night at the cheery *Florida Day & Night Club B&L* right on the park/town boundary (Ksh50/80). This won't give you a restful night, but you'll want to be up bright and early waiting for a lift in any case; there's the added bonus that you're bound to meet park staff here. A sign across the road reminds you "Patrons are warned it is an offence to wander around in the park stampeding wild animals" – just in case you had this in mind.

Practicalities II: camping or self-catering

There's a specific **backpackers' campsite** (with all facilities) on a pleasant grassy site under fine old yellow acacias – beware the audacious vervets – and two other campsites in the park: **Njoro campsite**, a couple of kilometres down the shore, and the somewhat elusive **Makalia campsite** in a wonderful location at the southern tip of the park, on either side of the stream and close to the waterfall. Very few organised tours come down this way; but should you feel isolated, you may be reassured to know there's a ranger station very close by.

Also check out the *bandas* on the east shore below Lion Hill. There's a couple of "Special Campsites" nearby on the northeast shore – *Kampi ya Nyati* (Buffalo Camp) and *Kampi ya Nyuki* (Bee Camp) – which cost a lot more and will probably have to be booked in advance at the National Parks headquarters in Nairobi National Park.

Practicaliities III: self-drive – and more luxury

The best option has you **driving around in your own vehicle** and stopping where you choose: the park has a number of areas where you can walk. This would allow you to take your pick of the campsites and call in at one of the lodges on the east side for a drink, breakfast, or whatever. Beware of the little scams so popular at the moment, operating between Nakuru town and the park gate, in which local people spot an "oil leak", or some other "problem" with your vehicle, and talk you into having it "repaired" at their garage.

If you're planning on **a night in style** in the bush, *Lake Nakuru Lodge* (around Ksh2000/2700 FB), an old Delamere Estate house on a fabulous site, comes very highly recommended (PO Box 561, Nakuru, ☎5Y6/5Y9 Elmenteita; bookings in Nairobi at Arrow House, PO Box 70559, ☎226778). Try to get one of the larger rooms. At present, this is the one for a flying visit, too – they have a swimming pool and do a stunning buffet lunch. *Lion Hill Camp* (PO Box 30680, ☎2129 Radiocall Nairobi) is not as classy a tented camp as you'd expect for the money (around Ksh2460/2925 FB). Both lodges are bookable through the addresses given on p.30 in *Basics*.

Menengai Crater

Containing an enormous caldera, 12km across and nearly 500m deep in places, the extinct volcanic giant **MENENGAI** rises directly behind Nakuru. Its sloping mass is somehow not especially noticeable from the town. To reach it, head up

Menengai Drive and take the fourth left turn (Crater Climb) through the modestly affluent suburbs above the town. Some 4.5km up the hill you come to a sign referring to a *Campsite and Picnic Area*, but no evidence of either. You could presumably camp by the trees here and get water from nearby houses, but you'd be ill advised to leave your tent unattended and you should bring food. Half a kilometre away is a telecommunications tower: head for this then turn right, following the path through a fragrant forest of gum trees for twenty minutes, to a fire lookout tower on the bare cliff. From the top of this, the massive crater spreads out beneath you, a spectacular sea of bush-covered lava, its black waves frozen solid.

The crater was the site of a battle in which the Ilpurko Maasai defeated the Ilaikipiak, whom they considered upstarts disrespectful to Mbatian, the *laibon* of the time. At intervals throughout the nineteenth century, these **Maasai civil wars** flared up over the issue of true Maasai identity: in this case, it was not simply a matter of honour but also of grazing rights in the Rift Valley, especially around Lake Naivasha and on the scarp slopes. The Ilpurko were herdsmen, while the Ilaikipiak from the north grew crops as well. Both had been preparing for battle for some time and it is said that hundreds of Ilaikipiak *morans* were hurled over the crater rim to their deaths. The place retains a sinister reputation and local people prefer not to go near the edge.

A century later, on the highest point of this windy, doom-laden crest, the Rotary Club erected one of their familiar over-the-top signposts, laden with mutiple pointers. Apart from informing you Nairobi is 140km away and Rome 5997km in the opposite direction, it also pointed out that the crater wall is 2272m above sea level and its area some 90 square kilometres – the whole dramatic extent of which you can see (the sign has apparently disappeared). You'll get fantastic views over Lake Nakuru if you walk down the dirt road along the south side of the gum tree plantation.

From Nakuru town centre it's about an eight-kilometre (three hour) hike to the crater rim; on weekends, you might be lucky and get a lift, but there's no public transport.

Hyrax Hill

9.30am–6pm, Ksh15, students Ksh5.

HYRAX HILL is another easy target, two or three kilometres out of town, just to the left of the Nairobi road. Lanet- and Gilgil-bound *matatus* will drop you at the turn, then it's a short walk to the small museum where you pay your ten bob. The hill, named for the hyrax which once scampered over it, has been a settlement site for a least 3000 years and finds here date from the Neolithic period. It was discovered by Louis Leakey in 1926, excavated by Mary Leakey in 1937–38 and by others in 1965 and 1973. There's an excellent guide booklet on sale in the museum. You can normally **camp** here, free or for a small fee (staff facilities only).

The Northeast Village

The path leading out to the right of the museum winds its way around the north side of the hill to an excavated pit dwelling, or at any rate a "sunken enclosure", with baulks left in place to show the depth of material that was removed during the digging. There are thirteen similar depressions in this **"Northeast Village"** but it's uncertain what they were used for. They have yielded a tremendous quantity of pottery shards, tools made from flakes of obsidian and animal bone fragments, but the absence of post-holes normally needed to support a roof suggests they may have been shelters for livestock rather than humans. Just as plausibly, a roof might have been added whenever needed, leaving no trace, and animals and people may have shared the shelters. The floor of the pit has been left exposed and is littered with stones and obsidian chips. It's easy to convince yourself you've discovered a little knife or part of an arrowhead.

This village has been dated roughly to the fifteenth or sixteenth century AD by its characteristic late Iron Age pottery (the Iron Age in Kenya essentially continued until the twentieth century), several reconstructed examples of which are displayed in the museum. It is believed the inhabitants would have been semi-nomadic Kalenjin herders. Today, Kalenjin-speakers mostly live further west, but they're associated with so-called pit-dwellings elsewhere and, in the case of Hyrax Hill, they may have been forced to flee by an expanding Maasai population from the north.

The fort and burial sites

Following the path towards the top of the hill, you come to an exposed "fort" facing out towards Nakuru. It consists of a circle of hefty boulders enclosing a flattened area. Said to have been an Iron Age lookout post, there's no way of being certain what this actually was, nor even how old it might be, since no artefacts have been found. From the fort, you can scramble over the volcanic boulders – the whole hill is a tongue of Menengai's lava – to the summit, where you get a good view of the southern part of the site and the lake. Now several kilometres away, the lake once extended, probably as fresh water, right to the base of the hill and across much of the Rift Valley, turning Hyrax Hill into a peninsula or even an island.

A hundred metres down the hillside you come to more Iron Age pits and a **trench**. An extraordinary collection of bits and pieces was dug up here in 1974, including some 8000 stone tools and six **Indian coins** between sixty and 500 years old. Whether the oldest of these really implies the very early penetration of overseas foreigners into the interior or whether the coins were simply buried or smothered is another ponderable. Most likely they'd been handed down for generations and were either lost or hidden for safekeeping.

Nearby, in a fenced-in shelter, the massive stone slab which sealed a **Neolithic (New Stone Age) burial mound** has been removed to display part of a skull and some limb bones. The remains of a further nineteen Neolithic skeletons were discovered north of this, beneath a more recent Iron Age occupation area marked by the two stone circles (which were hut foundations). Nineteen Iron Age skeletons were also discovered, overlying the Neolithic graves, mostly young men apparently buried unceremoniously or in a hurry, their skulls and limbs in tangled heaps: possibly the mutilated remains of slain warriors.

These enigmatic graves have further, cultural implications: nine of the Neolithic skeletons are thought to be female and, unlike the male remains, they were found with accompanying **grave goods** in the form of domestic implements – dishes, pestles and flat mortars. The finds pose unanswerable questions. Certainly, many Kenyan peoples remember oral traditions of times when women were more socially and politically powerful than today: the female burials with grave goods might be evidence of this past. But the burials themselves are curious. The coincidence of nineteen skeletons at each level may be just that – coincidence. But did the Iron Age survivors who buried their young men know about the ancient Neolithic graves beneath?

Neolithic recreation

For a less dramatic, but certainly more accessible, impression of life at Hyrax Hill, the **Bau game**, cut into the rock just before you get back to the museum, is a delightfully fresh record. *Bau* is the Bantu name for a game of skill and – depending on the set of rules used – amazing complexity that has been played all over Africa for a very long time. Two people play, moving pieces (cowries, seeds, pebbles) from one hole to another to win. There are a number of these "boards" around the hill; a particularly good one lies very close to the museum. The resident guide who found it, Francis Muli Mulwa, will show it to you, and if you look carefully under the scrub, you may well find others. For me, they were the most fascinating relics on the site.

Onwards from Nakuru

Travel options **from Nakuru** are wide open. You're less than two hours from Nairobi – a journey as easy to hitch as any in the country. The train is inconsiderate of sightseeing and leaves at night, so the climb up the escarpment isn't an attraction.

Heading the other way, the bus lines all run regular services to ELDORET, KISUMU, KISII and points west. Southwards, you can get to NAROK by a smoking *matatu* up the fantastic Mau escarpment (not a great distance but allow the day to arrive). The most obvious destinations – in this chapter – are further north in the Rift Valley, around Lakes Baringo and Bogoria especially, with at least two buses daily to KAMPI YA SAMAKI at Lake Baringo and *matatus* making the run to KABARNET in the hills to the west. There's also a lavishly scenic route to Nyahururu through the Subukia valley, an ascent of the Rift that, for sheer grandeur, comes close to the Naivasha escarpment (daily bus and *matatu* runs).

THE NORTHERN RIFT

North of Nakuru, the Rift Valley drops away gently and, as the road descends, so temperatures rise, the landscape dries and human population becomes sparser. Not far from Nakuru or Nairobi, and no longer a difficult journey, this region has a bright, harsh beauty, quite different from the central Rift: its lakes both make alluring targets, but freshwater **Baringo** scores over **Bogoria** simply because access is easy and you don't need to be self-sufficient to stay there.

It's worth remembering also that this region offers three possible routes up to Lake Turkana (Chapter Seven), two of them joining with the Kitale–Lodwar road west of the lake, the third curving up to Maralal for the east side. Although public transport is virtually nonexistent and the roads pretty rough, the **Kerio valley** route (see below) deserves a special recommendation if you're visiting the west side of Turkana.

Lake Bogoria National Reserve

Ksh220, camping Ksh50; access usually permitted on foot or bicycle; Warden ☎2047 Kabarnet.

One of the least visited lakes in the Rift Valley, **BOGORIA** is a sliver of saline water – unbelievably foul-tasting – entrenched beneath towering hills 60km north of Nakuru. Recently adopted feeding ground of tens of thousands of **lesser flamingoes**, the lake and its shores are a national reserve, and one of the few places where **greater kudu** antelope can, with increasing frequency, be seen. But the reserve is worth visiting as much for its physical spectacle as for the wildlife you may see. It's largely a barren, baking wilderness of scrub and rocks, a series of furious **hot springs** erupting on the western shore and the bleak walls of the Siracho range rising sheer from the east. Even in the far north of the country there are few places so unremittingly severe. Fortunately the rigour of the landscape is relieved by three superb, shady **campsites**, one of which is nearly perfect. The **warden** at Bogoria is quite an authority on **birds** and will happily take you around, or accompany you in your vehicle.

Getting your bearings and getting around

The surfaced road to Baringo skirts Lake Bogoria by a margin of 20km or more. There's reportedly a **bus route** running from MARIGAT via LOBOI to MAJI YA MOTO, but buses on it are assuredly rare, except possibly on Marigat market day (Wednesday). There does seem to be at least one morning *matatu*, from Loboi to Marigat and back, however. Otherwise, unless you're prepared for a long walk or an even longer wait for a lift, the lake can seem effectively off-limits without your own vehicle. Best chances of **lifts** are at the northern end of the reserve (Loboi Gate), where a **new paved road**, intended to encircle the lake, is cutting down along the shore: wait at the Loboi junction a few kilometres south of Marigat, the busiest route down to the reserve. Most vehicles going in will be coming from Lake Baringo rather than directly from Nakuru, so the south (Emsos) and west (Maji ya Moto) gates are used less frequently. (The approach road from the southwest, which starts at Mogotio near Nakuru, is also far longer.) You could also walk from the main B4 road to the Loboi Gate in about four hours, and will normally be allowed into the reserve on foot because there are no large predators. You can certainly camp at the gate, and even leave a pack here if you want. A lodge has long been under construction at this north end. And lastly, if you're into hiking, or off-road cycling, you might like to consider seriously the **cross-country approach** to Bogoria, described next.

Subukia and the cross-country route to Lake Bogoria

An adventurous option to taking the main route from Nakuru to Bogoria is to approach the lake from Nyahururu in the east, crossing the **Subukia valley**. Aside from the pleasure of tackling a road used by very few tourists, this route gives you a special feel for the Rift Valley's striking topography as it drops from one monumental block of land to another, with dramatic changes of climate and scenery. When you reach the plain at the bottom you've an indelible impression of the way the earth has split apart and sunk to form the Rift over the last twenty million years. The first third of this roughly ninety-kilometre trip can be made by country bus or *matatu* (there are several daily runs from Nyahururu to Nakuru via Subukia), but you should be prepared to **hike** the rest if necessary – a good two days. Unless, of course, you have your own vehicle: it's a wonderful **mountain-bike** trip – not too long for a day if you start early.

The new tarmac road leaves Nyahururu, falling in a series of breathtaking steps over the fault lines until it reaches a high scarp above **Subukia**, where it hairpins its way steeply down to the valley. From the cool highlands around Nyahururu, you start to feel the heat building up: fields of sugar cane and bananas seem to grow before your eyes in the hot-house atmosphere and the earth takes on a rich, redolent smell.

This valley was the Maasai's Beautiful Place, *Ol Momoi Sidai*, and its lush pastures their insurance against the failure of the grass up on the Laikipia plateau. But they were evicted in 1911 to the "Maasai Reserve" and the way was clear for the settler families. It's easy to see why they chose this high valley because, despite its isolation (even greater in the 1920s), it has a soft, arcadian beauty far removed from the windy plateaux above or the austere furnace of the Rift Valley floor below.

Cross-country

The village of **SUBUKIA** has a scattering of *hotelis* and a helpful police post where you can go for up-to-date road and route information. Buses and *matatus* stop by the *dukas*. For the cross-country short cut to Lake Bogoria, you can continue (either by public transport for several kilometres or perhaps an hour's walk) past the curious apparition of **St Peter's** – a quaint Anglican church that looks as if it just flew in from England – to the signposted junction where routes to Nakuru and Bogoria fork. From here, the **road to Bogoria** is rough in parts, though normally quite driveable, but very slow hitching from this point on. If you think sixty-odd kilometres is too much to tackle, and what you've seen of the landscape so far doesn't persuade you, then continue on the main highway down to Nakuru, skimming past Menengai crater and joining the Nairobi road near Hyrax Hill. Otherwise, check your emergency water and food supplies, tighten your boot laces/check your brakes and set off west.

The road first climbs another scarp and descends steeply to the SOLAI valley with its disused railway line, which you cross at a place called MILTON'S SIDINGS. If you're in doubt about the precise route – and the tracks crisscross in a number of places down here – there are always people to ask. Over another ledge, across a further wide, dry, pan-flat valley, the route twists over a short rise to reach KISANANA: life-saving *chai* and a suitable place to stop for the night if necessary, though there's no formal accommodation. The closest gate into the Lake Bogoria National Reserve is **Emsos Gate**, about 30km further.

There's another ridge to climb first, where the track winds through dense scrub; then, with the landscape opening out beneath and the road improving to orange dust, a gentle descent northwards towards the lake. On the way, you pass through MUGURIN – almost imperceptibly, so look out for it – where you'll find a solitary *hoteli* with good tea and *chapatis*. From here, you're within the compass of the lake, some 12km away.

Many maps show what looks like a **more direct route** from Kisanana to the lake. If you find it, or if you explore further north in the Subukia or Solai valleys (there's a small *Lake Solai*), we'd like to know for the next edition.

Arriving at the reserve: practicalities

Hidden in its deep bowl, **BOGORIA** – when approached from Mugurin – is only visible when you're almost on top of it. The final stretch of the track down to the Emsos gate is steep, rocky (the sharp bedrock is hard on tyres), and savagely beautiful, the landscape transformed into a strident dazzle of red and blue and splashes of green. The lake itself, a glistening pool of soapy blue and white, has a mirage of pink flamingoes tinting its shores. During the middle hours of the day, the heat is relentless but the unparalleled **Fig Tree Campsite** is the incentive: it's only forty minutes' walk from Emsos Gate and an absolute delight. Except, perhaps, if your visit coincides with a fresh covering of vegetation **after the rains**. Although this makes for an unusually verdant and picturesque scene, you'll also be welcomed by squads of determined tsetse flies. Be prepared to do battle.

You should normally be allowed into the reserve without a vehicle (Ksh200, camping Ksh50) to stay in the campsite , but before heading down to the thickly wooded shore at the south end, ask the rangers at Emsos about **food**; a few basics are usually available nearby to eke out your rations. **Water** is not a problem: a permanent, miniature brook, clear and sweet, runs right through the campsite and provides a natural jacuzzi. Less delightfully, the magnificent glade of giant fig trees which bathe the site in shade is a favourite haunt of baboons who gorge themselves day and night. In the fruiting season (December to February) you should be wary of camping directly beneath any concentrations of figs, for reasons which need no elaboration.

Unless you're ready for another long walk, your best bet for **onward travel** is to wait for a lift from vehicles doing the lake circuit. If you have no luck, you might consider walking the 15km around to the Hot Springs on the western shore, passing *Riverside* and *Acacia Tree* campsites. There's a small picnic site near the Hot Springs, and there have been times recently when camping was allowed in their vicinity. The Bogoria Reserve road has been paved south at least as far as the Hot Springs: this is the junction for the dirt road out to the western, Maji ya Moto, gate.

Hot Springs and kudu

However you enter the reserve, you're bound to want to see the **Hot Springs**: a series of (literally) boiling water spouts on the shore.

They burst up from huge natural cauldrons of super-heated water not far below the surface and drain into steaming rivulets that cut through the crusty ground, continuously collapsing and re-forming their courses down to the lake. Even at midday, when the sun glares like a furnace, clouds of steam drift across this infernal scene: tufts of grass tempt you to sit down and reward you with vicious spines, while, closer to the lakeshore, the macabre bleached skeletons of flamingoes lie strewn in the sand (visions of them landing in the wrong pool), and in the background, the dull thundering of the springs fills the air. It's like some water garden in Hell. It is also **dangerous** and the sinister fascination too merciless for familiarity. Picnickers sometimes think it's fun to boil eggs and heat tins of food in the pools, but the consequences of a slip can be messy and even fatal: a man fell in and died the day after I was there. An *askari* has now been posted to watch out for visitors but if you scald yourself, help might still be a long time coming.

None of which should keep you from going. Although they hardly touch Yellowstone or Rotorua standards, "hot springs" is a tame appellation for this very impressive, terrifying and brilliantly photogenic phenomenon. And the **flamingoes**, for some curious reason – possibly chemical – tend to flock in their greatest numbers to the shallows opposite the hot streams' debouchment. The Bogoria **fish eagles**, incidentally, have made a gruesome adjustment to their fierce, fishless environment: they prey on flamingoes.

The mild and nervous **kudu** live predominantly in the northeastern part of the reserve, but the road around the eastern side of the lake is patchy (possibly non-existent much beyond *Fig Tree*) and you'll need a vehicle with high clearance unless you hike. The greater kudu is a splendidly unmistakable, striped antelope; the bulls have long, spiral horns, shaggy dewlaps and enormous, spoon-like ears. Once widespread, the great rinderpest epidemics of the last century which took such a toll on cattle wiped out much of the kudu population too, leaving pockets only in the least favourable cattle country. Today, Bogoria is the most southerly part of their range in Kenya. Their numbers are increasing, however, and there are now regular reports of kudu being seen in the western parts of the reserve.

Lake Baringo

At one time a barely accessible retreat favoured by just a few weekenders, **BARINGO** now has a fine road from Nakuru. For the present, it remains a peaceful oasis in the dry thorn country, rich in birdlife and with a captivating character entirely its own.

The lake is freshwater (Naivasha is the only other Rift Valley lake that's not saline), so its fish support numerous **birds** less often seen – fish eagles, pelicans, cormorants and herons, for example – and quite a sizeable crocodile population. **Hippos** are common, too. Though you rarely see much more than ears and snout by day, they come ashore after dark, and on a moonlit night, their presence can be unnervingly obvious; even in pitch darkness, they're too noisy to be ignored. The **crocodiles** are reckoned to be quite safe, too small to be dangerous, and rarely provoked by hunters as their skins are undersized – but if you're swimming, you might like to know that a supposed man-eater was shot in 1981.

The **"Njemps"** people of the lakeshore villages live by an unusual mixture of fishing and livestock herding, breaking the taboo on the eating of fish which is the norm among pastoralists. Speaking a dialect of Maa – the Maasai language – these *Ilchumps* fishermen paddle out in half-submerged dinghies made from saplings of the fibrous *ambatch* tree that grow in profusion at the southern end of the lake.

The lake itself is heavily silted with the red topsoil of the region, and it runs through a whole range of colours every day from yellow to coral to purple, according to the sun's position and the state of the sky. Years of drought had reduced it so that a broad swathe of grass and reeds grew between the water's edge and the lakeshore properties. In recent years there have been some heavy rains and lakeside acreage has been cut back once again by the advancing waters.

Baringo travel: Marigat and some practical points

Buses from Nakuru **to Kampi ya Samaki** run twice daily, but Nakuru *matatus* come up only as far as **Marigat**. From Marigat you can hitch or get a local *matatu* to the lake. Kampi ya Samaki is 2km from the main road. Boats to **Ol Kokwe Island** leave on request from the jetty on the other side of Kampi ya Samaki.

Marigat

MARIGAT is a flourishing small town (big market on Wednesdays) and looks set to become the hub of the Baringo–Bogoria tourist circuit. Urban development, though, follows what seems to be an unusual course as, among the tin shacks stands an impressive, bright green and white mosque. With two tiers of large windows and a capacity that obviously exceeds the area's Muslim population, it dwarfs its humble wooden predecessor to the rear. Muslim Nubians from Eldama Ravine, working on the irrigation project south of Marigat, are supposed to explain the building of this mosque, but it seems impossible that the funds could have been local. If you need **to stay** in Marigat, there's a B&L on the main road (Ksh70/ 100), but it's stuffy, and has no electricity, and the water is only sometimes on tap. So you might as well follow the sign at the junction to *Marigat Inn*, 1500m.

Back to Nakuru

Returning to Nakuru, the first bus leaves Kampi ya Samaki at 6.30am but Marigat is an easier departure point. You should find a local vehicle going there. If you have your own vehicle you might stop south of Marigat to investigate a pool to the east of the road, just before the "Nakuru 84" kilometre sign, which was recently home to a pair of quite large crocodiles. How they got to the pool – and what they subsist on assuming they're still there – are unfathomable mysteries.

Beyond Baringo

Travelling north of Baringo is a hit-or-miss affair without your own wheels, so try to arrange something with mobile tourists. Otherwise you'll have to hitch: there's little transport either to MARALAL or to TOT and LODWAR from here.

If you're **driving**, there's a highly recommended and, at the last check, excellent D-road from Lake Baringo towards Maralal (one day) or Samburu National Reserve (best done over two). This route swings up from the lakeshore, leaving tarmac and tourism behind, and takes you into the rugged country of the Lerochi plateau, dotted with Tugen and Pokot settlements. With the right conditions, there are stunning views back over Baringo. You join the terrible RUMURUTI–MARALAL road as far as KISIMA, where you choose between a short journey to Maralal or some inspiring but wheel-shattering driving to Samburu (see p.257). There's **fuel** at Marigat, sometimes at Kampi ya Samaki (and normally at *Lake Baringo Club*), but none after that until Maralal or ARCHER'S POST.

By the lake: practicalities

Low-budget accommodation at Lake Baringo is headed by the *Roberts' Campsite* in a large, acacia-shaded garden. For Ksh60 you get lots of space, showers and firewood bought from the *askari*. There are good *bandas* here, too, with electricity and bedding (around Ksh250/*banda*).

If you'd prefer less of an outdoor atmosphere, there are a couple of B&Ls in **KAMPI YA SAMAKI**, the lake's only, and very small, town. *Hippo Lodge* (ex-*Bahari Lodge*) is on the left as you arrive. There's a good restaurant here; the place is decent and friendly, and even has mosquito nets, but it's also a tour drivers' hangout, so don't expect a quiet night (around Ksh70/110). The *Lake View Lodge* is even cheaper and lacks the nets you'll need except at the driest times of year, but it has nice views.

Lake Baringo Club and Island Camp

In a totally **different league**: if you have Ksh3000 or so for a double with dinner (much cheaper from April to June), you'll be faced with a difficult choice between *Lake Baringo Club* (☎2259 Radiocall Nairobi) and *Island Camp* (PO Box 1141, Nakuru, ☎2261 Radiocall Nairobi). Both are bookable through the addresses listed on p.30 in *Basics*. The first is a sumptuous and unpretentious hotel, the second a no-comfort-ignored tented camp on Ol Kokwe Island in the middle of the lake. If you don't have this kind of money, you can sample both places – and be even more broke – by using the facilities of the *Club* and by taking a motor boat out to *Island Camp*, for the chance to walk around the scenic little island, dense with birdlife.

There used to be a stile by which you gained access to the *Club* from the *Robert's campsite*. This is now closed and stiff **entry fees** (Ksh50 and Ksh100 at weekends, plus the same again to use the pool) are charged as you walk in the gate – unless you're a convincing "guest" and **drive** in, or buy a **meal**. *Island Camp* seems to have lost all sense of proportion, with a Ksh250 return boat fee, Ksh50 "landing fee", and Ksh50 pool fee. They'd obviously rather you stayed – or stayed away completely. It's all a bit of a shame, but understandable (hotels don't make money selling ice-cold beer), and the expense is best rationalised as a necessary luxury: you'll leave Baringo feeling bitter otherwise.

Around the lake: enjoying yourself

Baringo's 448 species of **birds** are one of its biggest draws, and even if you wouldn't know a superb starling from an ordinary one, the enthusiasm of others tends to be infectious. The campsite resounds with birdsong (try responding to some of the calls). Hilary Garland, the resident ornithologist at *Lake Baringo Club*, offers short, informal lecture tours with whom, for Ksh100, you can book a morning or evening bird walk. This goes either along the reedy water margin or out near the main road under some striking red cliffs, an utterly different habitat where, apart from hyrax and baboons, you can see several species of hornbill, sometimes the massive nest of a hammerkop (wonderful-looking birds in flight, resembling miniature pterodactyls with their strange crests) and, with luck, the rare Verraux's eagle, a pair of which nest in the vicinity. You'll have a few dozen species pointed out to you in an hour. The world record "bird watch" for 24 hours is 342 – held by former Baringo ornithologist, Terry Stevenson.

Of course you can do your own bird-watching. There's some interesting bush just beyond the *Club* to the south (accessible by walking back along the road), where you should see some **unusual species** such as the white phase of the paradise flycatcher, grey-headed bush shrike, violet wood hoopoe and various kingfishers. Hippos commonly graze here, too, even in daylight hours.

Baringo trips

Most **other activities** tend to centre around *Lake Baringo Club* or *Island Camp*: boat trips around the shores (Ksh500/hour and room for 1–8 people), water-skiing and wind-surfing, camel rides (the club advertises a "resident camel"), and visits to a nearby Njemps *enkang*. The headman here, Lenjanoi Lekiseku, is paid a retainer by the *Club* and in return allows visitors to look around his compound and freely photograph his wives and children. The visit isn't a particularly comfortable one – you may feel obliged to buy some of the decorated gourds inscribed with planes and ostriches (among other motifs) which the women lay out – but your presence isn't resented. Here's a chance at least to come to terms with your camera's rarely welcome eye. You want photos? Take photos!

There are, again, private, cheaper ways of arranging excursions in the vicinity of the lake. For around Ksh500, you can get a boat trip to Ol Kokwe in the morning and a drive to the small hot springs on the lake's northeast shore in the afternoon. Share this between two or more and it becomes excellent value, but you'll probably need to spend a night or two in Kampi ya Samaki to make the arrangements.

Lastly, two **cancellations**. Jonathan Leakey's widely advertised snake farm has no inmates and is no longer any sort of attraction. And Loimanange, the *Fort Baringo* of British anti-slavery days, is now a mission station on the southern shore. It, too, is distinctly short on spectacle.

Kabarnet and the Kerio Valley

Many people make this trip in reverse order from Eldoret but, in either direction, it mirrors the much harder journey down the eastern side of the Rift from Nyahururu, covered in the "Lake Bogoria" section. If you're setting out from Marigat, frequent *matatus* climb the first stage to Kabarnet.

Kabarnet

KABARNET, for all its piney preamble and zippy new road cutting up the escarpment, is a major letdown. Its setting is superb, perched on the **Kamasia massif** – the slab of rift country that remained upstanding on the brink of the Kerio Valley when the rest of the rift sank. But the town itself could hardly be more dull. Consisting of a small nucleus of *dukas* on the hillside, it has been considerably expanded in every direction in accordance with its newly designated function as capital of Baringo district. The result is a motley scattering of offices and civil servants' housing interspersed with wasteland; the planners must hope this will rapidly fill with enterprising businesses and workshops. President Moi's home town, Kabarnet, is clearly earmarked for development, but is currently expanding in area faster than it's growing in significance. A new **post office** and covered **market** are about all that could interest you, and even then the market's selection is very limited.

Standing above it all, the new and rather impressive *Kabarnet Hotel* (PO Box 42013, Nairobi, ☎2035 Kabarnet, booking address p.30) seems to be jumping the gun, but it's not a bad proposition for the money. Self-contained rooms are Ksh565/690; food is well above average (Ksh100); and there's even a swimming pool – though at this altitude it's not an overwhelmingly tempting prospect. The best alternative in town is the *Sinkoro* (PO Box 256, ☎2245) with s/c rooms at Ksh250/320 B&B.

Into the Kerio valley

The excitement of this route builds only after you leave Kabarnet and plunge **into the Kerio Valley**, a drop of 1000m in not much more than the same distance. Until 1988, travelling across depended a lot on the weather and the condition of the roads. With the completion of the paved **Tambach escarpment road**, you'll now find pretty constant *matatu* traffic across the valley; it has magnificent views as it rolls through CHEBLOCH, with its old bridge over the Kerio River, then turns sharply up to ITEN, and thence to Eldoret. This means that if you want to explore the valley off this now somewhat beaten track, you'll notice a serious dearth of any kind of public transport on the other trans-valley routes. As usual, having your own four-wheel-drive vehicle is insurance against detours or setbacks on the rough tracks: except during the heavy rains (April–May if local people are lucky), high clearance for rocky roads is more important than good traction.

Making your way **on foot and by available transport** off the main road you'll usually get through, though your precise choice of route may be constrained by the direction vehicles are moving. The main alternative to the Tambach–Iten route heads through TENGES and Kimwarer. To Tenges, a surfaced road twists spectacularly south from Kabarnet along the spine of the Kamasia slab, with lovely views across the valley. You'll find some public transport to Tenges from Kabarnet, but very little when you turn right for Kimwarer down in the valley. In the rainy season, in the days before the trans-Kerio road, they used to have to drive from Kabarnet to Eldoret via Nakuru!

Along the valley
KIMWARER is the largest community in the valley, a company town for the **fluorspar mine** at the head of the Kerio. With nothing but bush, Kalenjin herders and the occasional party of honey-hunters round about, Kimwarer's tidy managerial villas and staff quarters come as a surprise, and "Fluorspar Primary School" looks positively progressive in its brilliant paint job, an effect spoiled by the trees in the playground, all neatly labelled with their Latin names.

The town has grown rapidly in the last few years as plans for the production of a thousand tonnes a day of fluorspar have been realised. Fluorspar (calcium fluoride) is used in the manufacture of steel, aluminum, cement – and CFCs . . . If you're interested, arrangements can be made to visit the rock crusher. For the route from Eldoret to Kimwarer, see p.199.

It's possible to **hitch** the length of the Kerio Valley from here, leaving it at TOT and picking up transport on the Lodwar–Kitale road. Most of the time, however, you'll probably be "footing" or waiting by the side of the road. No matter – if you have several days – for this road, following one of the country's most beautiful valleys, is worth a few blisters. It's best in the few months of vivid greenery after the long rains and fiercest in February and March, just before they break. Densely wooded and not much cultivated in the south, for most of the year it resonates with dry heat and the rattle of cicadas and crickets. A new **nature reserve**, the *Kammarok National Reserve*, has been established around the Kerio gorge, but for the time being you can hike everywhere and there are villages at reasonably frequent intervals along the road.

The Tambach escarpment road now provides a quick exit from the southern end of the valley, up the route that used to cause a lot of problems for rally drivers each Easter. The **Torok Falls** near Tambach are said to be worth a visit.

The Elgeyo Escarpment and Cherangani Hills

The Rift Valley is not short of astonishing vistas, but even here few roads match the track up the **Elgeyo escarpment** south of Tot for precipitousness and sheer daring. A thousand, two thousand, metres below, and spreading like a grey-green carpet into the haze, are the scrubby, bush-covered plains of Pokot and south Turkana. Dozens of tiny wisps of smoke from charcoal burners combine to smudge out the distant peaks of Mount Kenya to the southeast. Places where the trees grow thicker mark the passage of temperamental seasonal streams which flood and dry up with the rains: Pokot gold-panners still find enough gold in them to trade with anyone passing through. To add to this distinctive sense of place, the escarpment itself is the location of an **ancient irrigation system**, feeding water from the hills down to the lush cultivation at the foot of the scarp.

Practicalities

Most easily approached on the returning leg of a trip to Turkana (see p.352), the Elgeyo escarpment **road** is diabolical: too rocky for any kind of car and too steep for any but the most steel-nerved of drivers. It's a thrilling, gut-wrenching trip – in someone else's Land Rover, preferably – but think twice before driving up here yourself: it is very, *very* steep. As a walk, getting to the top in one day from Tot is perfectly feasible. You may be lucky and find a ride, if you want it.

TOT, apart from being something of a route focus and a delightfully isolated, peaceful village, offers nothing special, but it's the sort of place where you might happily spend a week doing just that. Camping would probably be okay, but you may also be offered accommodation at the civil servants' quarters on the east side of the road. Leaving again, you'll probably find a lift from Tot to CHESEGON on Sundays (the latter has its market then), going on to SIGOR and the Marich Pass, where you'll soon find transport down to KAPENGURIA and KITALE.

Tot to Chesoi – the Marakwet water channels

From Tot, you can walk or hitch (but don't count on seeing a vehicle, much less on its having space) the twenty-five breathtaking kilometres up to **Chesoi**, turning right halfway at CHESONGOCH for the main ascent. The rocky, almost perpendicular slopes are dotted with **Marakwet** homesteads, the huts unusual in being built of stone (there's a limitless supply up here), which gives them an ancient-looking permanence rarely seen in Kenyan rural architecture.

Stories

The Marakwet may have arrived on these slopes as far back as 1000 years ago. Part of the broadly related Kalenjin group of peoples, they claim to have taken over the **irrigation system** on the escarpment from its previous users. They say the channels were there long before their own forefathers arrived, and it is possible

IN SEARCH OF THE SIRIKWA HOLES

To seek out the **Sirikwa Holes** near MOIBEN, purely for their own sake, would require a certain degree of scholarly dedication, but if you're approaching the Cherangani Hills from the Iten to Eldoret road, or following the route out of the northern Kerio valley, a visit does make an interesting diversion. Perhaps needless to say, it's a lot easier with your own wheels. *Matatus* run daily from Eldoret or Iten to Moiben, and on to CHEBORORWA on the edge of the Cheranganis; you might have to change at the junction where the murram road to Moiben leaves the new paved road. Occasional farm vehicles pass this way, but you could be in for a long wait.

The Sirikwa Holes are some 6km west of Moiben. From the crossroads by the upper primary school and chief's office, follow the dirt track past another school on the left and out into farmland. You may need to ask directions, first for Rany Moi Farm and then for the holes themselves – known locally as "Maasai Holes" or "Maasai Homes". Don't ask for "Sirikwa Holes", as Moiben is the main location of *Sirikwa District* and you'd probably be directed to the district offices.

The holes are a collection of depressions, some circular, about 10m across and a few metres deep, others a longer oval shape, all ringed by large stones. Some holes stand alone, others are joined by passages dug a metre or so into the ground. They closely resemble the pit dwellings at Hyrax Hill near Nakuru. So far, the site is relatively undisturbed, except for gaps in the stone rings where the odd stone has been removed for building. But as the pressure from local farms increases, it seems likely that these enigmatic remains will eventually be demolished and ploughed over.

the original irrigators were a mysterious group called the *Sirikwa*. These people have disappeared, or more likely been absorbed, and the only reminders of them are their name and a lot of curious **holes**, earthworks and cairns (see box) noticed by archaeologists around the Kerio Valley and in other parts of western Kenya.

Marakwet elders still remember stories of a small people called the *Terngeng*, who may have lived in pits in the ground something like those at Hyrax Hill and Moiben. Other stories refer to tall, long-haired, bearded men who roamed the Rift Valley. Either or both of these groups might have been responsible for the building of the irrigation system, but neither sounds very agricultural; perhaps the Marakwets' claim to have inherited the system but not built it is just a way of saying how old it really is.

Looking around

Whatever the truth, **the waterworks** are undeniably impressive in scope, if not especially in appearance, stretching north–south for over 40km to divert water from the Cherangani Hills' gushing streams into a branching layout of furrows and aqueducts. Instead of plummeting straight into the Kerio River, the water gets neatly distributed along the escarpment, with complex, unwritten laws to ensure that each Marakwet sub-clan is fairly provided for. It's a system without parallel anywhere else in the country and the results, as you'll see along the base of the scarp, are spectacular. Indeed, for a considerable distance up the Kerio Valley, there's a band of intensive, luxuriant gardening: tiny *shambas* slotted back-to-back between the spurs and down towards the main river. Magnificent, richly flavoured bananas are on sale everywhere. Many of the irrigation channels now pass under the road, but a few still flow over it and a great deal of ongoing repair work is obviously needed to keep the streams flowing in the right direction.

The best place to see a good furrow is up near **CHESOI** over the crest of the scarp. The land here buckles like a patchwork quilt, with the Cherangani Hills stretching west. "Chesoi canal" is a major water supply a couple of kilometres behind Chesoi centre, a metre-wide channel clinging to the hillside (ask someone to show you). In other places, the irrigation system has become almost a piped water supply, with hollow logs used as aqueducts, but this channel has been built with cement (which sells out everywhere as fast as it becomes available).

There's no **accommodation** advertised in Chesoi but the people up here at the edge of the Cheranganis seem delighted to meet strangers: as a kick-off, ask to see Edward Saina, owner of the *Kosutany hoteli* (a small *chai* shop in Chesoi), who will let you sleep on the floor. You could also camp easily, just about anywhere, if you ask the landowner – and if you can find a flat space.

Onwards from Chesoi: walking in the Cheranganis

If you have the time and inclination, **walking in the Cheranganis** is exhilarating. The thickly forested hills are wild, hardly explored, and still home to bongo antelope. Higher up (Kamelogon peak on Mount Chemnirot is 3517m), they give onto mountain moorland and giant Afro-alpine vegetation: some superb hiking country where you're very unlikely to meet any others doing the same. A couple of days by track will see you over the southern ridges to LABOT, where you'll start to pick up transport to Kitale. More ambitiously, you could get hold of *Survey of Kenya* maps (though the ones covering this area may be restricted) and set off, suitably equipped, northwestwards over the centre of the massif. There are several easily scaled peaks up here.

Chesoi–Kapsowar–Eldoret

Altogether more straightforward, though, is to continue by murram road **towards Eldoret**. To be sure of a *matatu* from Chesoi, you'll need to be up and ready by 6am; one or two other vehicles may come through later in the day but this can't be relied on.

Alternatively, it's a fine and easy twenty-kilometre walk (mostly downhill) around the **highland spurs** to KAPSOWAR. Much of the time you'll seem to be doubling back on yourself – the two villages are only 8km apart as the crow flies. Kapsowar's hospital makes it a local magnet and there's no problem finding onward transport from here.

Beyond Kapsowar, the road changes its mind less often and, after climbing again out of Kapsowar's valley through patches of **forest**, it emerges onto the Uasin Gishu plateau. Then it's all rolling ranchlands, wheatfields and stands of conifers and gum trees as far as ELDORET (p.195).

travel details

Nakuru is the whole region's travel hub. Most other details are given in the appropriate sections.

Trains

Bookings can be made with *Kenya Railways* in Nakuru on ☎40211.

From **Nakuru** to:
Kisumu daily at 12.30am (all stations) and daily from the 1st to the 10th of each month at 10.50pm (express).
Nairobi daily at 2.25am.
Eldoret, Malaba, Tues, Fri, Sat at 12.45am.

Flights
None

Buses (*OTC*)
From **Nakuru** to:
Kisumu 7 daily, 270min.
Nairobi 16 daily, 3hr.
Eldoret 3 daily, 4hr.
Nyahururu 8am, 9pm daily.
Many other lines operate out of Nakuru, e.g. to
Kampi ya Samaki, 2 daily, 3hr.

***Peugeot* taxis**
From **Nakuru** to:
Nairobi, a constant stream, 90min.

Matatus
From **Nakuru** to: **Mau escarpment** towns,
**Subukia, Nyahururu, Narok, Marigat,
Kabarnet** and all over western Kenya.

Hitching
From **Nakuru** to:
Nairobi Stand on the road out of town just past
the railway bridge. Walking further isn't very
helpful.
Westwards Difficult, so take a *matatu* to get out
of town and on the right road, A104.
Northwards Okay as far as Kampi ya Samaki
(Lake Baringo). The paved road stops at the end
of the lake.

TELEPHONE AREA CODES

| Gilgil ☎03751 | Lanet ☎03785 | Kabarnet ☎0328 | Nakuru ☎037 |

CHAPTER FOUR

WESTERN KENYA

Like the tiers of a great amphitheatre, **western Kenya** slopes down to face the stage of Lake Victoria, away from Nairobi, the major game parks and the coast. Cut off by the high Rift wall of the **Mau and Elgeyo escarpments**, the western region of dense agriculture, rolling green valleys and pockets of thick jungle is one of the least-known parts of the country to travellers. Although more accessible than the far north, or even many of the big parks, it has been neglected by the safari operators – and that's all to the good. You can travel for days through lush landscapes from one busy market town to the next and rarely, if ever, meet other tourists or travellers.

It's not easy to see why it has been so ignored. Granted, the disastrous history of Uganda until the late 1980s has discouraged the through traffic that might otherwise thrive. But there's a great deal more of intrinsic interest than the tourist literature's sparse coverage would suggest. What the west undeniably lacks are teeming herds of antelope and zebra, lions at the side of the road and narcissistic warriors in full regalia. What it does offer is a series of delightfully low-key, easily visited attractions. There are **national parks** at **Kakamega Forest**, a magnificent tract of equatorial rainforest bursting with smaller species found nowhere else in Kenya; **Saiwa Swamp**, where pedestrians, for once, have the upper hand; and **Mount Elgon**, a volcano to rival Mount Kenya in everything but crowds. **Lake Victoria**, with the region's major town, **Kisumu**, on its shores, is a draw in its own right, dotted with out-of-the-way islands.

Travel is generally easy: with a high population and many well-paved roads, you'll rarely have long to wait for a bus or *matatu*. If you're inclined to plan ahead, there *is* a vague circuit that begins in Kisumu (as this chapter does) and runs through **Kisii** (of Kisii-stone fame), Kericho, Eldoret, Kitale and Kakamega. You could do this in a couple of weeks . . . or a couple of months. But it's often more rewarding to let events dictate your next move: this area will repay your interest repeatedly if you take time to look around. Much of it, even areas of intensive farming, is ravishingly beautiful: densely animated jungle near **Kakamega** and **Kitale**, regimented landscapes of tea bushes at **Kericho**, dank swamp and grasslands alive with birds by the lake.

There's barely any tourist infrastructure – the west has only a handful of hotels that could by any stretch of the imagination be described as luxurious – but there's no shortage of good, modest **lodgings**. **Food** is as cheap as anywhere and generally excellent; most of Kenya's tea and sugar comes from the west, and agricultural concerns are paramount.

Ethnically, the region is dominated by the **Luo** on the lakeshore lowlands, but other important groups speak Kalenjin languages (principally the **Nandi** around Eldoret and the **Kipsigis** in the Kericho district) and there are Bantu-speaking **Luyia** in the sugar lands north of Kisumu and **Gusii** in the formidably fertile Kisii Hills.

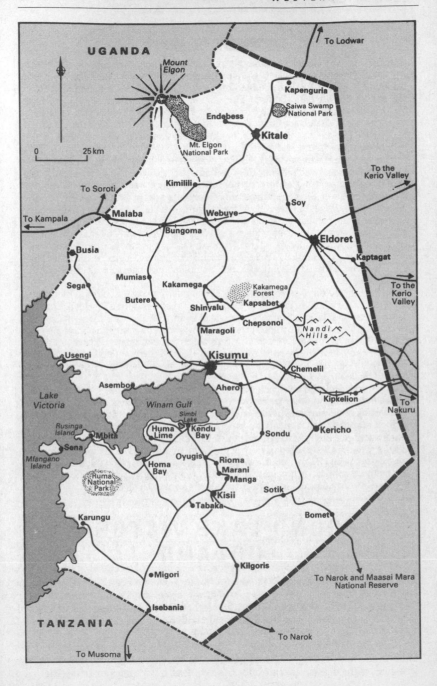

THE LUO

The **Luo** are the third largest ethnic group and one of the most cohesive "tribes" in Kenya. Their language, *Jaluo*, is distinctive and closely resembles the Nuer and Dinka languages of southern Sudan, from where their ancestors migrated south at the end of the fifteenth century. They found the shore and hinterland of Lake Victoria only sparsely populated by hunter-gatherers, scattered with occasional clearings where Bantu-speaking farmers had settled over the previous centuries. Otherwise, the region was wild; untouched grasslands and tropical forest, dense with heavy concentrations of wildlife.

The Luo were swift invaders, driving their herds before them, always on the move, restless and acquisitive. They raided other groups' cattle incessantly, and within a few decades had forced the Bantu-speakers away from the lakeshore. Nevertheless, over the generations, **intermarriage** was common and the pastoral nomads were greatly influenced by their Bantu-speaking in-laws and neighbours, ancestors of the present-day Luyia and Gusii. The Luo today are best known as fishermen but they also cultivate widely and still keep livestock. Culturally, they have remained surprisingly independent. They are one of the few Kenyan peoples who don't practise circumcision. Traditionally, children had six teeth knocked out from the lower jaw to mark their initiation into adulthood: the operation is rarely carried out these days.

Early in the **colonial period**, the Luo benefited from some inspired, if dictatorial, leadership. They had inherited the institution of the *ruoth* (king or chief) from the original immigrants from Sudan. The *ruoth* of Gem, a location northwest of Kisumu, was Odera Akang'o, an ambitious and perceptive young man with an almost puritanical attitude to his duties. He had a private police force to inspect farms and report any idleness to him, and he regularly had his subjects beaten or fined for "unprogressive" behaviour. He introduced new crops and, under British protection, made himself quite a sizeable fortune. He was widely feared.

In 1915, the colonial government sent him, with two other chiefs, to Kampala; he returned full of admiration for the European education and health standards there, and ashamed of Gem and Luoland in general. Fired with enthusiasm, he applied his style of schooling and hygiene, bullying his subjects into sending their children to classes and keeping their shirts clean, while the British turned a blind eye. The results were rapid educational advances in Gem, which is still considered a progressive district today. Odera, unfortunately for him, was employed by the British to use his methods on the Teso people in Uganda, where they singularly failed. He was accused of corruption and sent into internal exile, where he died.

AROUND LAKE VICTORIA: LUOLAND

The lake is the obvious place to make for in the west, and **Kisumu** is the regional centre and transport hub. Rather run-down since the decline of lake traffic destroyed its status as a major port, it nevertheless retains a great deal of tattered charm. It is frustrating that the main roads only rarely get close to the shores of **Lake Victoria**. In order to get a good look at it, take advantage of the ferry services and visit one or two islands. Whatever you do, beware of **bilharzia**: don't swim in the lake and try, as far as possible, to have nothing to do with its water. Instances of the disease are rare after brief contact, but it's not worth the risk.

Of all the ports of call around Victoria's shores, **Mbita** (for **Rusinga** and **Mfangano** islands) is probably the most worthwhile, but you could also disembark at **Kendu Bay** or **Homa Bay** for the short journey inland to Kisii. **Kuwur Bay** is the port for Huma Lime, a village with hot springs nearby at the base of Mount Homa. See the ferry timetables on p.179.

Kisumu

Kenya's third largest town, **KISUMU**, has clearly suffered economically as a result of the East African Community's break-up. Near the port, empty buildings and broken windows are everywhere, and in the expensive residential area at the southern end of town, only the most affluent homes have been kept up. The middle-income timber bungalows are deserted, green paint peeling off the walls and dry grass poking through the driveways. There's a still, sultry atmosphere and a distinctive, pervasive, lake smell – not unpleasant – blows across on a vague breeze from central Africa. One or two small ships still ferry passengers along the Kenyan shore, and services to Tanzania and Uganda have recommenced, but the warehouses are nearly all empty and the trappings of an international port stand in limbo.

Some history

The **railway line** from Mombasa had been stretched as far as the lake by 1901 (pleasing the British public who, after so many years, were beginning to have serious doubts about the project), but the first train only chugged into **Port Florence** station in 1903 when the Mau escarpment viaducts were completed. By that time, European transport had already arrived at the lake in the form of a steamship brought up from Mombasa piece by portered piece, having steamed out from Scotland in 1895 (an obscure sub-plot to the story of European incursion: many of the ship's parts were evidently seized en route from the coast and recycled into Nandi ornamentation and weaponry: it was five years before a complete vessel could be assembled and launched on its maiden voyage across the lake to Port Bell in Uganda).

Kisumu was a pretty disagreeable place in the early years. Apart from endemic sleeping sickness, bilharzia, malaria and the nasty malarial complication blackwater fever, the climate was sweltering and municipal hygiene primitive. But it quickly grew into an important administrative and military base; with the consolidation of the colonies in the 1930s and 1940s, it became a leading East African entrepôt and transport hub, attracting Asian investment on top of the businesses set up at the railway terminus when the Indian labourers were laid off. Since the community's collapse in 1977, however, Kisumu's star has waned so low that even the huge molasses refinery, which would have given a much-needed boost to the region's economy (heavily reliant on sugar cane), has never been finished. Kisumu is a United States Peace Corps and VSO centre, and the volunteers maintain a fairly high profile – at least in relation to the air of stagnation all around.

But the picture isn't entirely bleak. Kisumu does have considerable charm, and it's no small advantage to be one of the few up-country towns with real character (though the slightly time-warped atmosphere of a place that's been treading water for a decade-and-a-half may not be much comfort to its inhabitants). To anyone who's ever travelled in central Africa, it seems to have more in common with that region than with Kenya. It's a distinctly tranquil, easy-going town, the *manambas* in the bus station unusually laid-back, and any anticipation of claustrophobia is quickly soothed by the spacious, shady layout. The contrast with Nakuru, if you're just come from there, is striking.

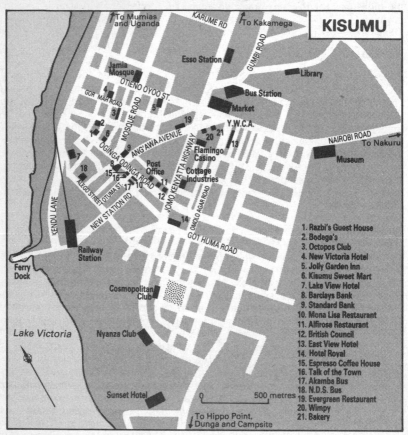

KISUMU

1. Razbi's Guest House
2. Bodega's
3. Octopos Club
4. New Victoria Hotel
5. Jolly Garden Inn
6. Kisumu Sweet Mart
7. Lake View Hotel
8. Barclays Bank
9. Standard Bank
10. Mona Lisa Restaurant
11. Alfirose Restaurant
12. British Council
13. East View Hotel
14. Hotel Royal
15. Espresso Coffee House
16. Talk of the Town
17. Akamba Bus
18. N.D.S. Bus
19. Evergreen Restaurant
20. Wimpy
21. Bakery

Arrival and practicalities

Kisumu is a natural base for exploring western Kenya: half a day's travel should get you to any of the centres in this chapter. The **bus and train stations** are on opposite sides of town, the first by the big junction of the Nairobi and Kakamega roads, the second down the hill in the port area. It is a good idea to install yourself fairly soon and get the pack off your back before starting any energetic wanderings, as it gets tremendously hot here. Try not to arrive on a Sunday. More than most towns, on the "day of rest" just about everything in Kisumu shuts down – even restaurants.

Accommodation

There's a wide choice of **places to stay**, with a good number of modest, mid-range hotels, though prices tend to be somewhat higher than usual. Temperature, humidity and mosquitoes will conspire to give you an uncomfortable night if you don't have a net or a fan (and preferably both), so it's worth paying a little more for the few nights you may be in town. There's a **campsite** at *Dunga Refreshments*, out of town at Hippo Point; see p.177.

BOARDING & LODGINGS

Beograda, close by the bus station (Ksh70/100) has had many thumbs-down of late.

Safari Hotel, next to the Beograda. Better and cheaper.

Jolly Garden Inn *(ex-Lagoon Motel)*, Otieno Oyoo St. Does seem a little jollier than most, but maybe you could ask for a room with the shower adjacent to the squat toilet – rather than directly above it.

Safina, Gor Mah Rd, a block south of the *Jolly Garden Inn* (#5 on the map). A favourite divey hotel – safe and cheap enough (Ksh75/100), but ask for a room away from where the cars pull up at night . . .

New Rozy's Guest House, next to the *Octopus Club* (#3 on the map). Good value (around Ksh120/twin), and clean.

YW/YMCA Offers rather bland good value but it's friendly and cheap (Ksh40/bed in dorms), if erratically supplied with water.

Razbi's Guest House (PO Box 1814, ☎41312), Oginga Odinga St. A well thought of standby – clean and secure, and one of the rooms has a lake view of sorts (Ksh100/160). Popular volunteers' hangout at weekends.

Talk of the Town, Otuma St. Also popular (around Ksh160/twin) with reduced rates for Peace Corps volunteers.

CHEAP HOTELS

Black & Black, Accra Rd. Just down the hill from the *New Victoria* but much smarter (rooms from Ksh150 s/c).

New Victoria (PO Box 2909, ☎41007), Gor Mah Rd. Quite adequate but out of the B&L bracket (around Ksh170/290 s/c B&B).

East View, Omolo Agar Rd. Handy if you've just crawled off the bus. Equally, if you're driving, good for its safe parking (similar prices to the *New Victoria*).

Lake View Hotel (PO Box 1216, ☎45055), Alego St. Getting pricier, but it does have views and, with its corner position, some breeze: comfortable if perhaps a little over-priced (Ksh230/360 s/c B&B).

MID-RANGE HOTELS

Hotel Royale (PO Box 1690, ☎44240; used to go by the name *New Kisumu*). Formerly a good place to meet people and highly rated for its Thursday evening Indian barbecue, the rooms still aren't up to much considering the alternatives (Ksh450/650 B&B, s/c).

Imperial Hotel (PO Box 1866, ☎41485), Jomo Kenyatta Highway. Looks determined to eclipse all opposition, with prices (Ksh880/1100 B&B) and flashiness well ahead of the rest.

Sunset Hotel (PO Box 215, ☎41100/42534). Slightly out of town and these days rather middle-of-the-road, but does include views of beautiful sunsets from every room, for which privilege you pay (Ksh800/1290 B&B). If you retain a sense of proportion and prefer the more soulful places in town, you can still drop in for a whiff of plasticky high-life and the sunsets. The pool is excellent (Ksh25) and the Sunday buffet lunch, at Ksh125, a real blow-out (but check out the buffets in nearby Dunga, below). The *Sunset* is also positioned right above a small **lakeshore park** (inhabitants, a herd of gazelle) and a nearby Wildlife Service **orphanage** which you might care to visit (distressingly small cages).

Eating

Kisumu has a number of good **places to eat** – except on Sundays, when chips are about all that's on offer, and most places are closed anyway. Food is generally heavy on fish but there are some tasty curries around, too:

Kisumu Sweet Mart, Oginga Odinga Rd. Reliable for really cold sodas, bhajias and other snacks, and may be offering vegetarian Indian meals again.

Talk of the Town (closes early), Otuma St. Favourite lodging and food rendezvous.

Espresso Coffee House, Oginga Odinga Rd. Another recommended volunteers' hangout with a long menu from which everything is actually available.

Alfirose (☎41677), Oginga Odinga Rd. Posher but excellent value: most dishes – basically Indian and fish – go for Ksh40–80, and there's a well-stocked bar with excellent fruit juices.

Evergreen Restaurant (☎43504), Ang'awa Ave. Comes with lavish recommendations for its chicken tikka, "the best samosas in Nyanza" and wonderful *mushkaki*.

Mona Lisa, Oginga Odinga Rd (closes 6pm). Highly rated, above all for breakfast.

Chinese Restaurant at the *Flamingo Casino* (PO Box 525, ☎40527). Rather over the top, a self-conscious disco/dining expense that might be fun in a group, but doesn't do enough business to acquire much of a reputation for its mostly tinned menu.

Kisumu after dark

For an enjoyable night out, the *Octopus Bottoms Up Day and Night Club* (PO Box 1329, ☎40835) is more guaranteed than the Casino. It's a pick-up joint of the first order, but relaxed enough if you just want to mingle over a beer or two. Its restaurant is often empty, but the **disco** is always lively and the roof terrace (with barbecue and dart board) is a popular, breezy rendezvous. Nearby, *Bodega's* offers good, if relatively expensive fish, but is best known for its "Happy Hour" from 7–9pm.

You might also try to catch some local music at the *Town Hotel*, 100 metres from the *Beograda* near the bus station. They've recently had **live music** every evening, the group playing "until they get sick of it or sacked". Sounds just right for a long, hot night.

Exploring Kisumu

The **market** by the bus station is the biggest and best in western Kenya, crammed with fruit and vegetables (including some oddities like breadfruit), and all the usual household paraphernalia – pots and plates, reed brushes, wooden spoons . . . it's an absorbing place to wander. For a little more on shopping in Kisumu see "Souvenirs and artefacts" in the "Kisumu Directory" on p.178.

The prayer calls from Kisumu's pastel green and white **Jamia mosque**, not far away down Otieno Oyoo Street, sound odd in this town, but Islam here is well established, and Mumias (see p.214) an important regional influence dating from well into the last century. The orthodox Shafi'ite mosque was built in 1919, though the women's section on the right was only finished in 1984. It currently has two imams, a Tanzanian and a Pakistani. Inside, the long and beautiful mats are from Saudi Arabia.

Kisumu Museum

Open daily, 9.30am–6pm, Ksh30: Curator PO Box 1779, ☎40804.

Clearly foremost among the town's sights is **Kisumu Museum**. New, small and ambitious, this is a highly recommended walk east from the market. Apart from the usual row of game heads around the walls, cases show "Mammals",

"Primates", "Birds" (including two stray bats), "Amphibians and Reptiles", "Fish and Crustaceans from the Sea", and "Insects", all with considerable flair and imagination. The best use appears to have been made of old and moth-eaten exhibits from Nairobi stocks. A free-swinging vulture, for example, spins like a model aircraft over your head as you enter while, best of all, centre stage, is the lion caught in full, savage pounce, leaping onto the back of a hysterical wilde-beest in the most action-packed piece of taxidermy you're ever likely to see (unless, oddly enough, you're ever in Abidjan, where you'll see an identical stuffed attack in the window of *Cath Voyages*).

The **ethnographic** exhibits are uncommonly interesting, too, with some illumi-nating information. The Maasai aren't the only people who take blood from their cattle for food: Kalenjin peoples like the Nandi and the Kipsigis once did the same, and even the Luo lived mostly on cow's blood mixed with milk before they arrived at Lake Victoria and began to plant and fish. There's a good selection of **musical instruments**, including a fine *nyatiti* Luo lyre (the East African equiva-lent of the kora); it is the kind of thing crudely reproduced in a hundred curio shops and now occasionally heard at African gigs in the UK. And look for the disembodied hands pumping the bellows in the metal-working display.

Housed in a series of polygonal halls, infinitely extendable, the museum's plans for the future include a whole compound of halls on the theme of a Luo home-stead layout. Meanwhile, one of them houses a wildly uninteresting **aquarium** where you can see what your curried tilapia looked like before it left the lake, and a **snake house** with a fairly comprehensive collection of venomous species from the Kakamega Forest. Outside, a tortoise pen, a snake pit – one of the pythons was rescued from a hole beneath the tea counter at the bus station – and a croc pond are somehow pointless extras.

In the **"Traditional Luo Homestead"** itself, you may come across the Kisumu Museum drama group rehearsing. An old Luo man used to live in the "First Wife's house", and would tell you in slow Swahili that this is how all the Luo used to live, and indeed how he himself was brought up. He seems to have gone to the ancestors, but the museum is good on guides and often has staff will-ing to show you around with loads of enthusiasm.

Dunga

For a pleasant **walk out of town**, head for **Hippo Point** and the Luo fishing village of **DUNGA**. This is also the way to the **campsite**.

From the *Sunset Hotel* you follow the shoreline south past the *Kisumu Yacht Club*. This, to judge by the number of boats moored, has seen far better days, but it remains strictly members-only: the *askaris* will let you in and kindly turn you straight out again (though see the "Kisumu directory", overpage). Five hundred metres further you come to **Hippo Point**, where you can watch riotous sunsets from the rock-strewn shore. Hippos are still seen here, but cold beers, curries and various vegetarian and non-vegetarian dishes from *Dunga Refreshments* (PO Box 96, ☎42529), half a kilometre beyond the point, are a more certain attraction, making this an evening constitutional popular with Kisumu's large Asian commu-nity. The weekend lunch buffets are popular, too, and good value as long as they keep them below Ksh80. There's a strong, warm breeze at dusk and it's a curi-ously stifling sensation to sit by this giant body of water without a whiff of ozone in the air. They've put in showers and it's a good – in fact the only – place to camp around town (Ksh50) and secure. If you take kids, heed the playground warning on the indescribable piece of machinery labelled *"Children Play at their own Risk"*. And if you fetch up in town and can't face the walk, try giving *Dunga Refreshments* a call and see if someone could come to collect you.

Dunga itself is some 2km further on the headland, a picturesque settlement with the *New Dunga Nam Lich Restaurant* (where you probably won't get a meal). If you'd like to spend a night with the **fishermen** on their boats, Dunga is probably the first place to ask, though you should expect some good-natured negotiations first. Also in Dunga is the impressive residence of a **herbal practitioner** – almost a private hospital – with a strikingly well-kept and decorated front yard of gravel paths with black and yellow kerbstones.

Kisumu Directory

Banks *Standard Bank* Mon–Fri 8.30am–1pm, Sat 8.30–11am; *Barclays Bank* Mon–Fri 8.30am–1pm, Sat 8.30–11am. Both banks are painfully bureaucratic, though recent feedback suggests the *Standard* is determined to out-worse the competition in this respect.

Boat trips Manmit at the Kisumu Yacht Club is able to arrange boat trips on the lake.

British Council (PO Box 454, ☎45004).The library is open Mon–Fri 9.30am–1pm and 2–5pm, Sat 8.30am–12.45pm. British papers and magazines, occasional BBC news videos and films and useful *Survey of Kenya* maps on the wall showing Kisumu district.

Ferries For the domestic service, see the timetable opposite. For international connections (in theory) to Uganda and Tanzania, see the *travel details* section at the end of this chapter.

Golf Temporary membership fee, equipment hire and caddy will set you back around Ksh120/day. Be alert to the rules relating to local difficulties like hippos and pythons in the rough. On the Mumias road.

Immigration Matters The Immigration Department (PO Box 1178, ☎45015) is in a building behind *Alpha House* on Oginga Odinga St, opposite the British Council. They have been known to be exceptionally helpful here, stamping visa and visitor's pass extensions on the spot without objection.

Kakamega Forest There's a daily bus to Eldoret at about 8am, which passes right by the *Forest Rest House*. Get a ticket to Shinyalu – it's just past there.

Kisumu Library Mon–Thurs 9.30am–6.30pm, Fri 9.30am–4.30pm, Sat 9am–1pm.

Kisumu Show Held in the first week of August.

Post Office Mon–Fri 8am–5pm, Sat 9am–noon. Poste restante available.

Souvenirs and artefacts The things to buy here (if you have the space) are heavy, three-legged Luo stools – check near the Post Office. The best are intricately inlaid with beads, and dark brown from repeated oiling. Don't buy Kisii-stone in Kisumu: it's much cheaper at the source. The *NCCK Cottage Industries* shop is worth a browse but its products are not exclusively local. If you don't mind a walk (or a drive), go and visit *Pendeza Weavers* (PO Box 1786), about 3km out of town on the Nairobi road, past the museum, past the chief's camp (on the right in the large field) and indicated with a small white sign on the right. Handwoven *kikois* here are as cheap as you'll find; they turn up later at *Spinner's Web* in Nairobi.

Swimming pools A swim at the *Sunset* is aways a pleasure. You might also take a dip in the *Royale*'s pool. The *Imperial* has a less enticing pool – indoors would you believe . . .

Homa Bay and the Lambwe Valley

Unless you're lucky enough to be travelling after the rains, the approach to the dreary little town of **HOMA BAY** from the landward side is almost bound to be a disappointment after the green, well-watered hills around Kisii. One of the greatest freshwater lakes in the world lies right in front of you, but around are only

THE LAKESHORE AND FERRY TRIPS

Enjoyable as much for the change of pace as anything else, the *Kenya Railways* motor **ferries**, which ply between Kisumu and several lakeshore towns and villages, are a reliable alternative to *matatus* and buses. The timetable given here is as up-to-date as possible: it's been much the same for years and is rigidly adhered to when conditions are favourable, but strong westerly winds at the end of the year can delay the outward legs.

Fares are low. You need to be at the ticket office on the Kisumu wharf by 8am and get on board as soon as you can. The ferries are usually full, but few people bother to buy anything more than a third-class ticket as classes tend to be ignored (second class has softer seats). There's good *chai* and often a few snacks on the boats. You will be welcome enough on the bridge for a chat with the captain if the idea appeals.

TIMETABLES

MV Alestes and MV Reli*				MV Kamongo		
d.	**Kisumu**	9am	Tues	d.	**Kisumu**	10am
a.	Kendu Bay	11am		a.	Kuwur Bay	3.40pm
a./d.	Kuwur Bay	1.10pm		a.	Homa Bay	5.05pm
a.	Homa Bay	2pm	Wed	d.	Homa Bay	7am
d.	Homa Bay	2.30pm		a.	Mbita	10.30am
a.	Asembo Bay	5pm		a.	Mfangano	2.50pm
			Thurs	d.	Mfangano	10am
	Following day:			a.	Mbita	2.05pm
d.	Asembo Bay	8am		a.	Homa Bay	5.20pm
a.	Kuwur Bay	9.50am	Fri	d.	Homa Bay	7am
a.	Homa Bay	10.40am		a.	Mbita	10.30am
d.	Homa Bay	11.10am		a.	Mfangano	2.50pm
a.	Kuwur Bay	11.50am	Sat	d.	Mfangano	10am
a.	Kendu Bay	2pm		a.	Mbita	2pm
d.	Kendu Bay	2.45pm		a.	Homa Bay	5.20pm
a.	**Kisumu**	4pm		d.	Homa Bay	11pm
* Daily except Thursday			Sun	a.	**Kisumu**	5.30am

dusty plains of grass and sisal. Arriving by boat, impressions are slightly less forlorn, but whichever way you look at it, Homa Bay remains scruffy, charmless and barely worth a stay.

If you sacrifice a day in Homa Bay, you can at least rely on two reasonable **B&Ls** – *Nyanza*, opposite *Barclays Bank* on the street across from *Bata* (Ksh60/90, Ksh10 extra for breezier rooms upstairs), and *New Brothers* (Ksh60/90). The latter has mosquito nets (at least in some rooms), which is more than can be said for the *Homa Bay Hotel* (☎22151) down by the lakeshore, which rarely has many guests either (around Ksh400/600). The *Masawa Hotel*, although a little difficult to find, is the best place to check out the local pulse. It's uphill by the right side of the market, then left at the top past the police station and first right, and it's at the top of that street on the right. It's a delightful old colonial-style place with a large, bird-filled garden and rooms at only Ksh60/90. More consistent for **food** is the *Kasongo Hotel* behind the *matatu* stage: good beans, rice and other staples.

The view from Got Asego

Hike up *Got Asego*, the impressive conical hill on the east side of town, and you get a much cheerier view of Homa Bay. The hill is the highest of dozens of volcanic plugs (the cores of old volcanoes) dotted across the plain; from its table-sized summit, you'll have a 360-degree panorama of the lakeshore and surrounding plains. It is remarkable how little of the land is not used for something, as Luo thatched huts are interspersed with tin-roofed homesteads, a patchwork of small plots and agave hedges. Take binoculars and you'll see more: clumps of papyrus drifting across the lake, traffic along the road where it snakes east to Kendu Bay.

It takes about an hour to reach the top from the centre of town (actual ascent 20 min), an easy climb best tackled in the cool of dawn or late in the afternoon. Take the second left after the *Total* petrol station and turn right up the murram road after Homa Bay School. The hill itself is best approached up the northwest ridge, where there's a footpath. Beware of columns of ants.

Leaving Homa Bay

When you decide to flee, *matatus* leave for KENDU BAY, KISII and MIGORI, near the Tanzanian border. Swiftest exit from Homa Bay will probably be aboard a Migori *matatu*, "dropping", as they say, at RONGO on the A1 highway, where you will soon find a Kisii-bound vehicle coming up from Migori.

Lambwe Valley National Reserve/Ruma National Park

If you've come to Homa Bay in search of **Lambwe Valley National Reserve**, you're probably in for another disappointment. The appropriately renamed **Ruma National Park** does exist – in the statute book – but on the ground, it's not easy to find. If you're independently mobile, however, the effort is usually repaid by animal-watching undisturbed by the presence of other visitors; you're virutally guaranteed the place to yourself.

Lambwe Valley's 194 square kilometres of tsetse fly-ridden bush is one of the few places in Kenya where you can see **Jackson's hartebeest** and two opposite extremes of antelope: the enormous, horse-like **Roan** and the miniature **Oribi**. There are about seventy of the beautiful **Rothschild's giraffe** and they're not hard to see above the tall grass; you'll have more difficulty spotting **cheetah** and **leopard**.

Ruma practicalities

To get there, a 34-kilometre drive along the Homa Bay to Mbita road brings you to the northeast gate, where a murram road goes left, 7km, to a signpost for the reserve. Now you know you're on the right track: the Nyatoto Gate is 3km further. You are likely to be greeted by surprised rangers. They get few visitors. Entrance fees are as usual (try to discuss) but there are no facilities of any kind, so although you can camp in the park with your own equipment, you'll need to bring food and water.

At present, Ruma National Park isn't practical without your own transport. If you're dedicated, your only other hope is to see the park warden in Homa Bay. You can find him through the manager of the *BP* petrol station and spare parts store.

Rusinga and Mfangano Islands

Far more practical is a trip to **RUSINGA ISLAND**. This can be accomplished by land, whatever your map may say, since the narrow channel has now been bridged by a **causeway**. But the road from Homa Bay is rough, and *matatus* and buses are always packed, so it's recommended you make at least one journey by ferry. This doesn't take much longer and is a lot more fun.

MBITA, where the ferry docks on the mainland, is very unprepossessing indeed, but things improve once you get on to the island. The building of the causeway – partly over two dump lorries which fell into the lake during the operation and couldn't be recovered – has had some unwanted side effects. Vervet monkeys now move onto the island to raid crops, and fish have become scarce on the Kisumu side of the island because the causeway blocks the current, turning the water there into a stagnant pond. A bridge to replace the old chain ferry would have been the best solution to the island's access problem. As it is, the single bit of civil engineering represented by the causeway has ended Rusinga's slight isolation at what many local people feel is an unacceptable cost.

Mbita practicalities

If you want to get **back as far as Homa Bay** on the same day, you'll need to be in Mbita by 3pm to catch the last transport. You can't **continue to Mfangano** the same day, though you could come to Mbita by road on a Tuesday or Thursday morning and take the *MV Kamongo* the next morning. If you have all the time in the world, spend a night or two in the middle of your cruise at Mbita. There's flourishing birdlife in the vicinity and doubtless a lot more to be uncovered by explorers of the truly non-touristic. The *New Rajus Hotel* (Ksh50/60) is the sort of no-water, no-electricity place you'd expect to find in Mbita, but it's friendly and amenable. The *Mbita Hotel* is said to be not as nice. Try the *Calypso Bar* for good fish.

Rusinga Island

Rusinga is small and austerely pretty, high crags dominating the desolate, goat-chewed centre, and a single dirt road running around the circumference. Life here is difficult, drought commonplace, and high winds a frequent torment. The occasional heavy rain either washes away the soil or sinks into the porous rock, emerging lower down where it creates swamps. Ecologically, the island is in very dire straits; almost all its trees have been cut down for cooking fuel or to be converted into lucrative charcoal. These conditions make harvests highly unpredictable and most people do some fishing to make ends meet, either selling the catch to refrigerated lorries or bartering directly for produce with traders from Kisii. And now the causeway has forced them to make longer fishing trips.

The island does have two significant claims to fame. It is rich in **fossils**, and was the site of Mary Leakey's discovery of a skull of *Proconsul africanus* (a primitive anthropoid ape) which can be seen in the National Museum. And it was the birthplace of **Tom Mboya** (see "Historical Framework" in *Contexts*), civil rights champion, trade unionist and charismatic young Luo politician who was gunned down in Nairobi in 1969, sparking off a crisis that led to over forty deaths in widespread rioting and demonstrations and was a turning point for the worse in Kenya's independent history.

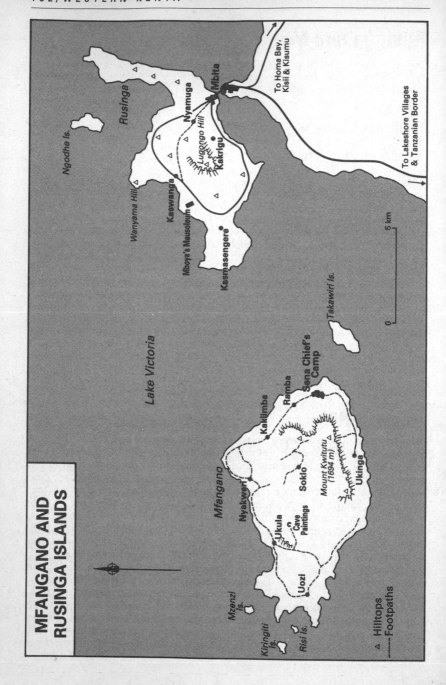

MFANGANO AND
RUSINGA ISLANDS

To Homa Bay,
Kisii & Kisumu

To Lakeshore Villages
& Tanzanian Border

Rusinga

Mbita

Nyamuga

Lugongo Hill

Kakrigu

Ngodhe Is.

Wanyama Hill

Kaswanga

Mboya's Mausoleum

Kasmasengere

Takawiri Is.

Lake Victoria

Sena Chief's
Camp

Ramba

Kakijmba

Mfangano

Nyakweri

Soklo

Mount Kwitutu
(1694 m)

Ukinga

Ukula

Cave
Paintings

Uozi

Mzenzi
Is.

Kiringiti
Is.

Risi Is.

5 km

0

△ Hilltops
—— Footpaths

Mboya's mausoleum

Tom Mboya's mausoleum lies on family land at **Kasawanga** on the north side of the island, about 7km by the dirt road from Mbita, or roughly 5km directly across the island. You might possibly get a lift from Mbita to Kasawanga (in theory there are five *matatus* a day each way), but you must be prepared to walk the whole way there and back if necessary (allow 4 hours and take some water). You're likely to find someone to show you the way but Rusinga is so small you could hardly get lost. Aim for the crags in the centre (if you're feeling energetic, you could climb the tallest to get a view of the whole island), skirt them to the right and walk down to rejoin the road on the other side of the Tom Mboya Memorial Health Centre (which has some European staff). There's a little *hoteli* here with cold sodas. From here, it's less than 2km to Mboya's mausoleum, the white dome clearly visible just off the road. The mausoleum (open most days to visitors) contains various mementoes and gifts Mboya received during his life. The inscription on the grave reads:

> *THOMAS JOSEPH MBOYA*
> *August 15th 1930 – July 5th 1969*
>
> *Go and fight like this man*
> *Who fought for mankind's cause*
> *Who died because he fought*
> *Whose battles are still unwon!*

You don't have to know anything about the man to be impressed. In any other surroundings, his memorial might seem relatively modest. But on this barren, windswept shore, it stands out like a beacon. His family live right next door and are happy to see foreign visitors, who are rare. His mother and father, both very old and proud, died in 1987.

Fifty metres past the Tom Mboya Secondary School, the path to the right takes you through *shambas* of millet and corn to a seasonally grassy lakeside called Hippo Bay. Here you can watch nesting fish eagles as well as – usually – hippos.

Mfangano Island

The diesel ferry to **MFANGANO ISLAND** leaves Mbita dock late on Wednesday and Friday mornings, returning the next day. Said to have been inhabited for centuries, Mfangano is somewhat enigmatic. Out of the range of the smallest fishing boats, and entirely without vehicles, the island is populated by a curious mixture of immigrants from all over Kenya, administered by a chief and three sub-chiefs with the help of a trio of policemen. Monitor lizards swarm on the sandy shores and **hippos** are much in evidence out in the water.

Larger and more populous than Rusinga, with a similarly rugged landscape but better vegetation cover, Mfangano's greatest economic resource is still the lake itself. Traditional **fishing techniques** are unusual: the islanders fish with floating kerosene lamps hauled shorewards, or towards a boat, to draw in the schools to be netted. Of more immediate interest, however, are the island's **rock paintings**, certainly worth the trip if you're into such things and a good excuse to get to know the island in any case.

Mfangano practicalities

Mfangano sees few visitors of any kind and perhaps a handful of travellers each year. Although it seems isolated, access is not really a problem. Large wooden boats with outboard motors run a *matatu* service, shuttling local people and their produce between Mbita and surrounding islands and peninsulas, supplementing *Kenya Railways*' limited service. The Mbita–Mfangano run departs Mbita daily at 9am from the beach on the west side of Mbita causeway. It's a ninety-minute crossing to SENA – the chief's camp (address, PO Mfangano Island Chief's Camp, Sena, ☎3756 Radiocall Nairobi) and the capital of Mfangano.

Because there are no vehicles, Mfangano's people rely on a network of temporary **footpaths** which are constantly changing course. If you arrive at Sena by ferry, you can walk all over the island, though it's always easier if you have a guide – Ksh50 a day is a fair fee. If you come by the smaller taxi-boat, Sena is the first of a half dozen minor ports of call along the north coast. The last one, **UKULA** (pronounced "Wakola"), is closest to the rock paintings, and there's sense in going here first, then working your way back, perhaps over a few days, to Sena.

Sena has a small *duka*, a post office and a government rest house. This **accommodation** is officially free, but you'll need permission from the chief or one of his senior men to use it, so some kind of fee will be called for. Finding places to stay elsewhere on the island is rarely a problem. People have camped wild in the past; at Ukula they've seen the odd traveller before and are more than happy to earn the cost of a B&L for putting you up overnight. You can even be selective, choosing to stay in a house on the lakeshore or up in the hills as the fancy takes you. It's all a bit reminiscent of the Greek islands in the early 1960s – except that here the need for cash is so much greater while the notion that tourism is culturally damaging (a serious concern in other parts of the country) hardly seems to apply. The analogy shouldn't be taken too far; Mfangano is desperately poor, without electricity or a piped water supply, and you should bring with you as many of your requirements as possible.

Rock paintings

From Ukula, an hour or two's walk into the interior (with a guide) brings you to a high, north-facing bluff, with startling views out across the island's north coast. Here, in a gently scooped cave, are the **rock paintings**: reddish spirals and whorls, some with rays, up to half a metre across, that could come from any Von Daniken paperback. People will tell you they're very old; nobody knows who painted them or why, or what they depict. But they exercise a fascination over the islanders, some of whom credit them with peculiar characteristics. It's said that if you go purposefully looking for the paintings, or ask too many questions about them, they'll elude you. But walk as if you didn't care and you'll suddenly come across them. On last check, some of the paintings had got wind of our approach and disappeared from view. Stories like these suggest the paintings were indeed put on the rock by an earlier and distinctive culture, of which people today have no recollection.

Kendu Bay

KENDU BAY's local fame comes from the curiosity of **Simbi Lake** about 4km (45 minutes' walk) from the village. If you arrive by ferry, walk out of the village on the Homa Bay road and pass the turn (left) to KISII. Two kilometres on, over the river bridge, turn right down the path and it's fifteen minutes further.

The lake is unquestionably weird, several bright green but changeable acres of opaque water sunk some twenty or thirty metres below the surrounding land and only a few kilometres from Lake Victoria itself. It has no apparent source and its origins are somewhat mysterious. It looks like a huge meteorite crater with a footpath around the rim.

The story goes that an old woman was refused fire one rainy night at the village that once occupied the site of the lake. A big beer party was going on and she was ignored. Only one woman would allow her to warm herself and the old woman insisted she leave the village with her. The young woman tried to persuade her husband to come with them, fearing the old lady's revenge for her ill-treatment, but in vain. So the two women left alone. And later that night there was a tremendous cloudburst and the rain came down so hard that the village was swamped to become Simbi Lake.*

The little lake's shores are almost devoid of vegetation. Nobody goes out on it in boats and it doesn't look as if they fish there either. According to one local belief, visitors are supposed to throw money in to avoid bad luck. It's usually dubbed with the catch-all "volcanic" and is apparently extraordinarily deep. Whatever the natural explanation, it seems plausible that the area was inhabited when the lake was formed, the disaster accounting for the legends.

If you're heading on to Homa Bay by road, you might like to see the **Oriang pottery centre** in the village of the same name, a few minutes' walk further. It's a new UNDEP-funded programme and ought to be worth checking out. The kilns were apparently broken recently, but bead necklaces are keeping people busy.

Practicalities

Kendu Bay itself is much smaller than Homa Bay and has a good deal more intrinsic charm. The ferry dock (a pier partly made of concrete-filled barges) is about a kilometre from the one-street village. There are four B&Ls but best is the *South Nyanza* (around Ksh70/twin), with a nightly disco. A notable new building is the gorgeous Masjid Tawakal mosque. You can look around it – though there's not much to see – and climb on the roof.

The murram road up to OYUGIS (on the main A1 highway between KISII and Kisumu) is generally firm but it sometimes takes a beating in wet weather and becomes, on occasions, impassable. Normally, though, you'll have no difficulty getting a *matatu* up to Oyugis or west to Homa Bay.

The obvious alternative escape route is the newly tarred **lakeshore road** from Kendu Bay to KATITO and Kisumu.

Siaya District and the road to Uganda

Heading northwest out of Kisumu, down a broad avenue of flame trees, you pass the *Sunni Muslim, Ismailia* and *Hindu* cemeteries, the latter smoking gently, then pass the golf club and emerge into the wide plains of Siaya district. Transport to the border town of BUSIA is fairly constant.

---

* Further variations on the story (I heard many) improve on the theme of drunkenness and debauchery to give a Sodom and Gomorrah ring to the tale. Other lakes in Kenya have similar tales of origin.

The region is pleasantly rural but unremarkable; the one place you might want to spend a night at on the road is the *Jera Inn* (PO Box 14, ☎66 Sega), well sign-posted, near SEGA. This "country club" set-up has rooms, food, discos (Wed, Fri, Sat & Sun; Ksh20 entry) and a general happy ambience that have brought it wide-spread fame in the district. The **rooms** – in fact very smart *bandas* – are self-contained and really good value.

USENGI, a short bus ride from Kisumu, is something of a diversion if you're en route to Uganda, but it's a useful target for an exploration of the district, and a town of pre-colonial historical significance in its own right. The nearby hill, *Got Ramogi*, is by tradition the site where the first Luo arrived at the lake from further north. It's not a hard climb to the top for a satisfying view over the island-dotted lake, the lagoon below (Lake Saru), and the land which the Luo fought for and eventually won from the Bantu-speakers at the end of the fifteenth century. Usengi itself is a pretty town with a causeway over the lake that connects with the Uganda road. Lodgings there are cheap.

Busia

Lastly, **BUSIA**, on the Uganda border, is, as you'd expect, a shark-infested corner, but still a preferable place to cross than Malaba, the busier frontier post on the railway line further north. The formalities are straightforward enough. Busia consists of a line of shacks and bars on the Kenya side and a similar line in Uganda. If you're staying the night, the optimistically named *Silent Lodge* is as cheap as they come, and sometimes even has warm water.

Whether you have a visa for Uganda or not (and Commonwealth passport hold-ers don't need one), you're normally allowed to **cross the border** to look around on the Ugandan side. Unless you're desperate for cheap whisky (Ksh200 a bottle in Uganda), however, there's little point. For further, and encouraging, **information about Uganda**, see "Onwards" in *Contexts*.

From Kisumu to Kisii

If you want it to be, the ride **from Kisumu to Kisii** can be a rapid transition along the main A1 highway from dusty or flooded plain (depending on the season) up into the ample, fecund hills of the Gusii. But there are various minor diversions along the way, if you're independently mobile or enthusiastic enough to make the effort with public transport and your own feet.

There's also a fine **new route from Kisumu to Kisii** along the newly paved **lakeshore road** from KATITO (south of AHERO) to Kendu Bay (see p.184).

Kisumu bird sanctuary

The first place worth investigating off the main A1 road is the **"Heronry"** (Kisumu Bird Sanctuary) near AHERO. From April to July, this is the nesting site of hundreds of pairs not just of herons, but of ibises, cormorants, egrets and storks, the dark and curiously scruffy open-bill stork included. Ornithologically world-famous, this is a must if you're interested in birds.

To get there, you take a right turn (south, towards the lake), nineteen kilome-tres from Kisumu (5km before Ahero), to the school at ORANGO, and from there branch left and follow the track another 2 or 3km. Ask local people, as the best sites and the easiest access to the colony move each year. The site is usually a good place to camp. This low-lying region between Kisumu and the western highlands is known as the **Kano plains** – disablingly hot, humid flat-lands, swaying with sugar cane and rice fields, fertilised by occasional disastrous flooding.

Nyabondo mission: sculpture centre

Next along the highway, near SONDU, there's the Catholic mission where miniature **terra-cotta busts** are sculpted. It's an easy *matatu* journey of some fifteen minutes from the main road to the mission at NYABONDO, whose impressive church was built by Italian POWs. The workshop is normally open to the public (ask in the mission), so you can watch a handful of craftsmen sculpting the heads you may already have seen in Nairobi. Naturally, they're cheaper here and prices are negotiable.

Oyugis "pelicanry"

As you climb into Kisii district's round, picture-book hills, you arrive at the cross-roads town of OYUGIS; like a number of other places, it was originally named *Oyugi's* after a local culture-hero. Apart from the sprawling *matatu* stage (and a good B&L called the *Oyugis Restaurant and Lodge*), Oyugis offers little but its **"pelicanry"**. This is reached by leaving the main road (left, southeast) before the *Caltex* station and walking up the murram in a big two- to three-kilometre arc for half an hour or so, until you reach two huge fig trees on the left.

From August to March, you'll see the parents wheeling in the air from some distance, and when you get closer, there's the distinctive smell of pelican guano to guide you. With binoculars, you can watch the shaggy **chicks** in their tree-top nests ramming their heads down the parents' throats for fish; then, yakking desperately for more, attempting the same manoeuvre on each other.

To Kisii

If you arrive at Oyugis early in the day and are feeling very fit, you can continue on the track past the pelicanry all the way to Kisii, along a route that becomes more and more beautiful as you climb through dense *shambas* and forests, out on to **Manga ridge** above the town (see p.191). You might be lucky and get a lift some of the way – but don't count on it.

THE WESTERN HIGHLANDS

The highlands of the west rise all around Lake Victoria in a great bowl. There's superb walking country throughout, in the **Nandi Hills**, for example, or the little-known **Mau Massif** east of Kericho. But the undoubted highlights are **Saiwa Swamp National Park** and the **Kakamega Forest**, soon to gain National Park status of its own. For serious, sensibly equipped hikers, **Mount Elgon** must also be a major temptation, sharing much of Mount Kenya's flora and fauna but none of its popularity. Highland towns are, on the whole, not arresting. **Kisii** is lively and worth a visit, but **Kericho** ("tea capital of Kenya"), **Eldoret** and **Kitale** are best thought of simply as bases for getting to the real attractions.

Kisii and around

Headquarters of the **Gusii** people, and district town of a region which vies with Nyeri as having the fastest-growing population in the country, **KISII** is a fresh, verdant trading centre in the hills, prosperous and hard working. For its small size, the town creates terrific noise and energy. It has more lodging houses per head than anywhere else in Kenya, and enjoys a profusion of excellent fruit and vegetables all year round, especially bananas and sugar cane. Lavishly fertile, the region gets rain throughout the year, in remarkable contrast to the semi-arid lowlands of the lakeshore just a few kilometres away.

Kisii is also famous for its superb **soapstone**. Surprisingly, there's little of this to be seen in the town itself. Best locality for watching the carvers and making on-the-spot purchases is Tabaka, some way south (see overpage).

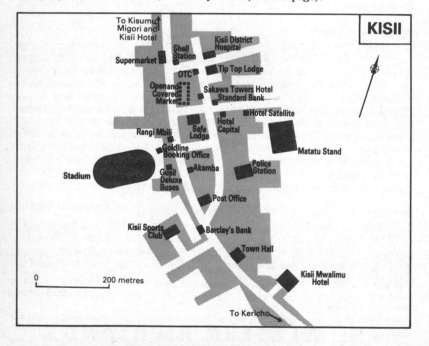

Lodging

You'll find plenty of choices when you look for **somewhere to stay**, although prices have always been a little higher than elsewhere and they have skyrocketed lately. It's worth staying the night, though, as, once you've settled in, there's a number of rewarding local **excursions**:

Safe Lodge (PO Box 156, ☎20945). Must come top of the list, an engaging, flower-bedecked lodging house with an excellent reputation – if sometimes rather noisy. Rooms are small and have a slightly dilapidated air, but over all the place is charming, clean and welcoming (from around Ksh150/200 s/c).

SOME GUSII HISTORY

The Bantu-speaking **Gusii** (after whom the town is named) were only awakened to the brutal realities of British conquest in 1905, when they rebelled – pitching themselves with spears against a machine gun. It was "not so much a battle as a massacre", one of the participants recalled, leaving "several hundred dead and wounded spearsmen heaped up outside the square of bayonets". In 1908, after the District Commissioner was speared in a personal attack, the same thing happened again, only this time the Gusii were trying to escape, not attacking. Crops were burned, whole villages razed to the ground. Churchill telegraphed from the Colonial Office: "Surely it cannot be necessary to go on killing these defenceless people on such an enormous scale."

The Gusii were totally demoralised. In a few brief years, the fabric of their communities had been torn apart, hut taxes imposed, and cattle confiscated to be returned only in exchange for labour. And then came World War I. Kisii was the site of the first Anglo-German engagements in East Africa, and thousands of men were recruited into the hated Carrier Corps by trickery or press gang.

It seems extraordinary that the exceptionally friendly people of Kisii are the grandchildren of the conscripts. The powerful, millennial religious movements which burst among them during the colonial period under the name **Mumboism** may partly account for the very strong ties of community they've maintained against all odds. Prophets and medicine men have always been important here, and even in today's superficially Christianised society, the Gusii have solidly kept their cultural identity. The practice of **trepanning**, for example, which involves tapping a small hole in the skull to relieve headache or mental illness, seems to be as old as the Gusii themselves: it has recently received the ironic laureate of medical journal credibility and the attentions of a German film crew. "Brain operations" are still performed, clandestinely but apparently quite successfully.

Hotel Capital (Ksh120/150 s/c). Other B&Ls don't quite make the same grade but this is perhaps the best of the rest.

Satellite Inn (PO Box 16, ☎21780). A pretty good restaurant and bar, but mediocre ratings for comfort and security (Ksh100/120, or Ksh160 s/c).

Tip Top Lodge Cheapest lodging in town. If nothing else seems worth the money, you might give it a try.

Sakawa Towers (PO Box 541, ☎21218, Ksh200/300). A newish place, the tallest building in town, named after a great Gusii medicine man and prophet. Some lovely views from the roof but it's far too noisy to want to stay.

Kisii Hotel (PO Box 26, ☎20954) on the road out to Kisumu. There's more comfort here and safer parking if you have a car (Ksh200/300 B&B s/c). Preferable out of Kisii's three, slightly upmarket addresses, for its creaking colonial atmosphere and enjoyable dining room.

Kisii Mwalimu Hotel (PO Box 2427, ☎20691, Ksh180/280 B&B s/c). Sightly cheaper and newer, but of a similar standard to the *Kisii Hotel*.

Eating

The overflowing **market** is the first base for hungry travellers, but the lodgings mostly have dining rooms or restaurants of their own.

You might not expect a **bistro** in Kisii, but *Safe Lodge*'s restaurant, with wonderful vegetable curry, comes close. And if you want to **splurge** modestly, the *Kisii Hotel* on the north side of town does very respectable lunches and dinners.

Kisii directory

Banks *Standard* and *Barclays* both Mon–Fri 8.30am–1pm, Sat 8.30–11am. Don't go near the *KCB*: they charge outrageous commission here.

Earth tremors Kisii lies on a fault line and minor earthquakes are not uncommon. Only a slight worry if you're asleep at the top of *Sakawa Towers* hotel at the time.

Kisii Show Held in the first week of July.

Post Office Mon–Fri 8am–1pm & 2–5pm, Sat 9am–noon.

Rangi Mbili (PO Box 532, ☎20318). A very helpful parts store/workshop if your car is in trouble. Helpful anyway, for that matter – they're eager to meet travellers.

Sports Club Swimming pool, tennis, squash, darts, bar, bingo. Saturday discos. A friendly place with temporary membership available.

Stadium Home ground of Kisii's *Shabana FC*, hovering on the brink of Div 1.

Tabaka

This village is one of the most important centres in the world for **soapstone** (*steatite*) production. Strangely enough, it has never become widely known, and the expected sprouting of signposts and tourist shops is nowhere to be seen. Most of the carvings are bought up by buyers from the curio shops in Nairobi and elsewhere, and on first arriving, you might think you've come to the wrong place, it's such a low-key industry.

Getting there

It is best to get a *matatu* directly to **TABAKA**, even if this means waiting around in Kisii. The alternative is hanging around just as long at the halfway point, or a very long walk. If you don't mind the latter, grab any *matatu* heading towards MIGORI and get out at NYACHENGE.

To get to the soapstone carvers and quarries, continue 5km on the murram road, passing the turn for the Tabaka mission hospital on your right; then head downhill from the T-junction. (Last *matatus* from Tabaka back to Kisii leave at 5pm.)

If you're driving to Tabaka from Kisii, head out of town to the north and, after 1km, turn left – south – onto the A1 Migori/Isebania road and proceed 17km to a sign indicating (left) the Tabaka mission hospital and *Kisii Soapstone carvers co-operative society*. From here it's a further 5–6km.

The soapstone quarries and carvers

There are two main **quarries** – one on the left, another further down on the right – but there must be vast reserves of stone under the ground all over the district, which provides almost the entire world supply of soapstone. It emerges in a variety of colours and densities: white is easiest to work, shades of orange and pink harder, and rosy-red the hardest and heaviest. A number of families have become full-time carvers, but for most people it's simply a spare-time occupation after agriculture, a way of making a few shillings. You'll even see children walking home from school carving little animals from chips of stone. The professional carvers often specialise: one in inlaid chessboards, another in chess pieces, others in traditional animals (hippos, elephants, lions, fish) and boxes (square, round, duck, tortoise), vases and cups, ashtrays, candlesticks, snake-boxes, napkin rings, egg-cups, mugs and more recent designs – human figures, soapstone "Makonde" and delightful fruit.

Recommended teams are run by Gabriel Mogendi and his father Alexander, Aloyce Abuya and his wife Queen, and the Obonyo family. They, and others, will happily show you around, sell you their work, and perhaps give you pieces of stone to try carving yourself. It's great therapy. The stone is dampened to bring up the colour and make it easier to work, then waxed to retain the lustre.

Manga Ridge

This dramatic escarpment **cliff** is two or three hours' walk north of Kisii, wonderful in the early morning – or the late afternoon, as long as you can arrange a ride back again.

Leaving Kisii on the Kericho road, you turn left about 500m after the Sports Club, then proceed some 5km till a road slopes off to the left across the valley. After a further 5km you come up behind the ridge (several hundred metres high), now on your left. It's a ten-minute hike up to the edge, where a path follows the cliff for a kilometre or two. Magnificent views out over Kisii and down to Lake Victoria are your reward. It's possible to get *matatus* to Manga from Kisii, but make it clear you want to get off at the ridge.

If you set off early enough, there should be time to walk the whole way around to OYUGIS (see p.187) through the villages of MANGA, MARANI and RIOMA, a total distance of about 40km. From Oyugis, it's a quick *matatu* hop back to Kisii. A fine **walk**, it also makes exuberant **cycling**, travelling through the heart of Gusii-land as the road loops and swerves in a landscape changing magically with every ridge and valley. Up here you'll find dusty lanes, avenues of cypress trees, grassy verges, old women smoking pipes and self-contained, reserved, country hamlets just a few kilometres from the melee of Kisii.

Onwards from Kisii: Kenya's southwest corner

Worthwhile **tips if you're trying to leave Kisii**: try to pick up *matatus*, when nearly ready to go, at the *Shell* station for points north, south and west, and by the *Mwalimu Hotel* for Kericho and points east.

To Maasai Mara

Kisii is something of a route focus, with Kericho and Kisumu each a couple of hours away and a minor, but increasingly popular route to **Maasai Mara** setting out from here. Beware that beyond KILGORIS, the road to the Mara is difficult, even with 4WD, and the section down the Oloololo escarpment can be an impossible quagmire after rain.

South to the border: Migori and around

Heading south, **Tanzania** is accessible by services to the **border crossing**, variously known as Serira/Siria/Isebania/Nyabikaye. MIGORI, down near the border, is an expanding town with a rough reputation. The main centre of activity is the hospital, where the doctors are adept at treating arrow wounds inflicted during land skirmishes between Gusii, Maasai, Kipsigis and the new Kikuyu settlers. Market days are interesting for the variety of peoples and for traditional activities untainted by tourism. The Maasai people here are far less calculating and aloof than many of those further to the east whose lives have been invaded by cameras and minibuses.

The **lakeshore** west of Migori is remote and, in parts, beautiful with KARUNGU BAY a rewarding side-trip. In the other direction, KIHANCHA, on another back-country route to Maasai Mara and on the south bank of the Migori River, is reputedly a pretty area.

Back to Nairobi
If you find yourself in Migori, just arrived from Tanzania, there are "direct" **buses to Nairobi**. From Kilgoris, too, there are regular vehicles to the capital.

Kericho

From Kisii to KERICHO, the road first snakes up through banana gardens, fields of corn, sugar cane and patches of tea. By SOTIK (just off the road to the right, south), you've reached a less abundant high plateau and the start of the rolling swathe of **tea bushes** that stretches for hundreds of square kilometres up towards the crest of the Mau escarpment. On the approach to Kericho itself, the small *shambas* virtually cease, especially on the eastern side of the road where the land shelves to the Kipatriet Valley.

KERICHO is Kenya's **tea capital**, a fact that – with much hype from the tourism machine embellished by the presence of the *Tea Hotel* – is not likely to escape you. Its equable climate and famously reliable, year-round afternoon rain showers make it the most important tea-growing area in Africa. While many of the European estates have been divided and reallocated to small farmers since

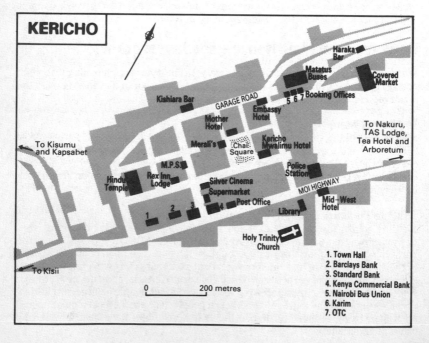

KERICHO

Haraka Bar
Matatus Buses
Covered Market
Kishiara Bar
GARAGE ROAD
5, 6, 7 Booking Offices
Embassy Hotel
Mother Hotel
To Nakuru, TAS Lodge, Tea Hotel and Arboretum
Merali's
Chai Square
Kericho Mwalimu Hotel
To Kisumu and Kapsabet
M.P.S.
Police Station
Hindu Temple
Rex Inn Lodge
Silver Cinema
Supermarket
MOI HIGHWAY
Post Office
1 2 3 4
Library
Mid-West Hotel
Holy Trinity Church
To Kisii
0   200 metres

1. Town Hall
2. Barclays Bank
3. Standard Bank
4. Kenya Commercial Bank
5. Nairobi Bus Union
6. Karim
7. OTC

independence, the area is still dominated by giant tea plantations. Compact and orderly, Kericho itself seems as neat as the serried rows of bushes that surround it. The central square has shady trees and flowering bushes – a bandstand would make it complete – and even the *matatu* park has lawns around it. Clipped, clean and functional, there's little of the shambolic appearance of most up-country towns. And, in many ways, it's an oddity. With so many people earning some sort of salary on the tea plantations or in connection with them, and so few acres under food or market crops, the patterns of small-town life are changed here. Most workers live out on the estates, their families often left behind in the home villages. Kericho is above all an administrative and shopping centre, and a relay point for the needs of the estates: the produce market is small and trading limited.

In town, there's a substantial Asian population. Many of the streets have a strikingly oriental feel – single-storey *dukas* fronted by colonnaded walkways where the plantation "memsahibs" of forty or fifty years ago presumably did their shopping. This curious, composite picture is completed by the grey stone **Holy Trinity Church**, with its small assembly of deceased planters in a miniature cemetery. Straight out of the English shires and entwined with creepers, it tries so hard to be Norman that it hurts to report it was built only in 1952.

The Tea Hotel

The **Tea Hotel** (PO Box 75, ☎20280/2) was also built in 1952. But it belonged to *Brooke Bond* and, now that they've sold it and cut out the plantation tours (photos of the workers and their housing were tarnishing the corporate image), its *raison d'être* is slightly questionable. At Ksh700/850 B&B s/c, it's not unreasonable value, however, and offers fantastic breakfasts.

Cheaper lodging and eating

Kericho isn't overendowed with places to stay – in fact pickings are rather thin as it's not an active market town – but you should find something to suit.

TAS Lodge/Garden Lodge (PO Box 304, ☎21112), just down the road from the *Tea Hotel*. For a realistic place to stay, this is probably the best value around (Ksh115/230 B&B s/c), with a good bar and restaurant and pretty gardens (camping Ksh50). They occasionally break the peace with eruptive discos.

Midwest Hotel (PO Box 1175, ☎20611). A soulless European-style place and popular conference venue (Ksh600/800 s/c B&B); dinner is quite good value if you want to treat yourself.

Kericho Mwalimu Hotel (PO Box 834, ☎20601), in the town centre. Nothing special to recommend it, but a safe bet if you must have a proper hotel room (Ksh180/250 s/c B&B).

Embassy Hotel, Kishiara Bar B&L, and **Rex Inn Lodge**. Ordinary and basic at around Ksh90/120, the first marginally better.

Haraka Bar and Restaurant B&L. Only if you're broke, a totally basic place to crash (Ksh50 per cube). The sheets seemed clean but maybe they were just ironed.

Kericho directory

Banks *Barclays, Standard* and the *KCB* are on Moi Highway at the Kisumu end of town.

Fishing All the gear is available for hire from the *Tea Hotel*.

Hotelis for food The *Mother Hotel* is good: a long menu and *miraa* sold outside. *Merali's* serves non-vegetarian Indian food.

Library By the *Midwest Hotel*. Not bad at all, though they go for quantity rather than diversity, with about ten copies of each title.

Market Much better on Sundays than weekdays, the big day when there's a lively variety of fruit and vegtables, snacks and spices, at lower than expected prices.

Post Office Mon–Fri 8am–1pm & 2–5pm, Sat 9am–noon.

Swimming Pool At the *Tea Hotel*; chilly and Ksh25.

Trappist monastery The Lumbwa Monastery, near Kipkelion Station some 40km from Kericho, is a community of Trappist monks. Several cars go to the monastery each week if you'd like to visit. Check locally for more information.

Around Kericho

Mostly it's **tea**. Kenya is the world's third largest producer after India and Sri Lanka, and the biggest exporter to Britain. Big business as it is, however, and despite the relative prosperity of Kericho, you can't help feeling that the local population would be better served if this fertile land were given over instead to intensive cultivation of food.

The estates are not too anxious for visitors (enquire with Brooke Bond if you like: PO Box 20, ☎20482/20146/7), but the *Tea Hotel* will still provide a **guided tour** if you provide the car, and a reasonable size group might strike it lucky by turning up at the *Kenya Tea Packers (KETEPA)* factory (☎20530/1) and asking to be shown around. Normally, though, you'll be told to apply in writing to PO Box 413, Kericho.

Tea production is not complicated but it is very labour-intensive. Picking continues throughout the year: you'll see the pickers moving through the bushes in their brilliant plastic smocks, nipping off the top two leaves and bud of each bush (nothing more is taken) and tossing them into baskets. Working fast, a picker can collect up to seventy kilos in a day, though half that is a more typical figure; the piece-rate is set at less than a shilling per kilo picked. After withering, mashing, a couple of hours' fermentation and a final drying in hot air, the tea leaves are ready for packing and export. The whole process can take as little as 24 hours.

What the planters left

Down in the **Kiptariet Valley**, behind the *Tea Hotel*, you can get some idea of what the land was like before the settlers arrived. The valley is a deep, tangled channel of sprawling trees and undergrowth, and shafts of sunlight picking out clouds of butterflies. The cold brown waters of the Kiptariet flow down from Chagaik Dam and allegedly harbour **trout**, though the fishermen's footpath marked on the map in the *Tea Hotel*'s lobby seems to have become overgrown. Obtain details there about temporary membership in the *Kericho and Sotik Fishing Association* and about hiring rods.

To get to **Chagaik Dam** and the graceful **Arboretum** nearby, you'll need a lift in the Nairobi direction, past the *KETEPA* buildings to the turn marked "CHAGAIK", about 8km east of town. From there, turn right, then immediately left: it's a five-minute walk to the Arboretum – "Founded by John Grumbley, Tea Planter 1946–75". Acres of beautiful trees from all over the tropical and sub-tropical world lead steeply down through well-tended lawns to a lily-covered lake. There are magnificent stands of bamboo on the banks. Entry to this haven of landscaped tranquillity appears to be unrestricted and you can picnic or rest up as long as you like, though there are gardeners around who will probably insist you don't camp.

Across the lake, thick **jungle** drops to the water's edge. Mysterious splashes and rustles, prolific bird and insect life, and at least one troop of colobus monkeys are a surprising testament to the tenacity of wildlife in an environment hemmed in on all sides by the alien ranks of the tea bushes.

Onward travel from Kericho

Kericho has hassle-free travel options in every direction: **southwest** to KISII, **east** over the Mau escarpment to NAKURU, or **northwest** to KISUMU on the lake and KAPSABET in the Nandi Hills. If you're going east, Nairobi and Nakuru buses generally originate in Kisii and don't depart from Kericho until about midday. Check with the bookings office, but you should have time for a leisurely morning.

The Nandi Hills

The journey **from Kericho to Kapsabet** is one of the most varied and spectacular in the west, through country often far wilder than you'd expect: bleak mountainous scrublands and jungle-packed ravines. Midway, you cross the Kano plains and will normally have to change transport at CHEMELIL, a major crossroads on the flat sugar lands. Beyond that, the road zig-zags into high tea country again, the homeland of the **Nandi**, the fiercest early opponents of the British, and haunt of a zoological mystery known as the **Nandi bear** (see box overleaf).

Kapsabet

KAPSABET is the only town of any size before Eldoret but, even here, unless you arrive at the end of the day, there's little point in stopping. The town has suffered from water shortages recently and supplies may still be arriving by tanker.

There are three **lodgings** if you do stay, all okay. *Kapsabet Hotel* (PO Box 449, ☎2176) is a fairly quiet place but a popular boozer, clean if scruffy (Ksh120 per s/c room) and boasting a restaurant that serves mountainous portions of chips. *Keben Hotel* contains three "lodges" on its three floors, *Tanzania, Kenya* and *Uganda*, with rooms named after towns accordingly. Bar, restaurant, noise and discos make it Kapsabet's main nightspot (Ksh70/90). Lastly, the Somali-run *Bogol Inn*, serves typically tasty and cheap food in its restaurant. Amenities fit the very low prices.

Eldoret

Although more bustling with trade than Kericho, and altogether healthier and more pleasant than Nakuru, **ELDORET** has, in all honesty, hardly anything to do or see that couldn't be done or seen in dozens of other highland centres. Life here is pleasantly humdrum: ordinary occupations and careers are actively but not frenetically pursued; the **Uasin Gishu plateau** all around is fertile, reliable cereal, vegetable and stock-raising country; wattle plantations provide the tannin for the town's leather industry; the *Rivatex* textile factory – one of the country's biggest – provides employment (PO Box 2236, ☎32551–5); and a new educational centre, *Moi University*, has proved a shot in the arm for local schools. In short, this is Kenya's *Middletown*, not very prepossessing perhaps, but with its own momentum for development and, you can be reasonably sure, hardly a tour bus in sight.

HE NANDI . . . AND THE NANDI BEAR

At the end of the nineteenth century, the **Nandi** (one of the Kalenjin-speaking peoples) were probably in the strongest position in their history. Their warriors had drummed up a reputation for such ferocity and daring that much of western Kenya lived in fear of them. Even the Maasai – at a low point in their own fortunes – suffered repeated losses of livestock to Nandi spearmen, whose prestige accumulated with every herd of cattle driven back to their stockades. The Nandi even crossed the Rift to raid Subukia and the Laikipia plateau. They were intensely protective of their own territory, relentlessly xenophobic and fearful of any adulteration of their way of life. Foreigners of any kind were welcome only with express permission.

With the killing of a British traveller, Peter West, who tried to cross their country in 1895, the Nandi opened a decade of guerrilla warfare against the British. Above all, they repeatedly frustrated attempts to lay the railway line and keep communications open with Uganda. They dismantled the "iron snake", transformed the copper telegraph wires into jewellery, and took whatever livestock and provisions they could find. Despite increased security, the establishment of forts, and some efforts to reach agreements with Nandi elders, the raiding went on, often costing the lives of African soldiers and policemen under the British. In retaliation, **punitive expeditions** shot more than a thousand Nandi warriors (about one young man in ten), captured tens of thousands of head of livestock, and torched scores of villages. The war was ended by the killing of Koitalel, the *Orkoiyot* or spiritual head of the Nandi who, having agreed to a temporary truce, was then murdered at a meeting with the British. As expected, resistance collapsed (his people had believed Koitalel to be unassailable); the Nandi were hounded into a reserve and their lands opened to settlers.

Traditionally keepers of livestock, the Nandi have turned to agriculture with little enthusiasm and point instead to their district's milk production: the highest in Kenya. *Shambas*, however, are widespread enough to make your chances of seeing a **Nandi bear** – the source of scores of Yeti-type rumours – remote. Variously said to resemble a bear, a big wild dog, or a very large ape, the Nandi bear is believed to have been exterminated in most areas. But in the less accessible regions, on the way up to Kapsabet, many locals believe it still exists. They call it *Chemoset*. Exactly what it is is another matter, but it doesn't seem to inspire quite the terror you might expect; the occasional reports in the press of savagely mutilated sheep and cattle are probably attributable to leopards. A giant anthropoid ape, perhaps a gorilla, seems the most likely candidate for the *Chemoset* and the proximity of the Kakamega Forest may account for the stories. This is a surviving tract of the rainforest which once stretched in a continuous belt across equatorial Africa and is still home to many western and central African species of wildlife. The *Chemoset* possibly survived up until this century in isolated valleys, even if it is extinct today. Whatever the truth, if you camp out in the Nandi Hills, you won't need to be told twice to zip your fly-sheet.

A little colonial history

Eldoret was a backwoods post office on *Farm 64*, later chosen in 1912 as an administrative centre because the farm's soil was poor and the deeds were never taken up by the owner. The name started as *Eldare* (a river), then Nandi-ised to *Eldaret*, and finally misprinted in the *Official Gazette* as *Eldoret*. Pronunciation is fluid.

Before the town existed, the area was settled by **Afrikaners**; they gave it much of the dour worthiness which seems to have characterised its first half-century and which is perceptible even today, though most of the Boers have long since trekked on. Modern inhabitants are mainly Kalenjin (Elgeyo and Nandi) but there's also a long-established and respected Asian community (Juma Hajee's supermarket is the oldest business in the town); there are Somali-speakers and the remnants of a European community, as well as immigrants from the rest of Kenya. Eldoret's stable prospects seem to make for good relations: if you stay here, there's usually a friendly welcome.

Lodgings and hotels

Eldoret has no shortage of **accommodation**. Cheap places tend to be grubby or clearly intended for "short-term guests". You may have to explain to the management the innocent way you intend to spend the night. There are also one or two quaint old haunts from way back. As in the old days you may still be able to **camp** in the yard of the *New Wagon*. The *Reformed Church Centre*, too, should agree to a tent in the field.

BOTTOM BRACKET

Kabathayu Hotel & Lodging (PO Box 832, ☎22160), Tagore Rd not far from the Post Office. Best of the very cheap places. A simple B&L (Ksh71/95), clean, with a good atmosphere and a roof terrace with a town view.

Top Lodge, corner of Nandi and Oginga Odinga Rds. Will give you a clean room for the whole night for around Ksh80/100.

New Mahindi Hotel (PO Box 1694, ☎31520), Uganda Rd. A bright, fairly new place that allows two to share a single room (Ksh150/200 s/c B&B), though also one of the less restful abodes in town.

Eldoret Valley Hotel, Uganda Rd. For peace and quiet, this is clean and scrupulous but suffers from character loss as a result of its strict no-girls-no-alcohol policy (Ksh100/160 s/c). An excellent Somali-style menu compensates.

Reformed Church of East Africa Conference and Training Centre (PO Box 746, ☎32935), 2km out of town on the Kapsabet road. Be securely accommodated (Ksh60/120) and fed (Ksh45–60), with a minimum of stimulation.

New Lincoln (PO Box 551, ☎22093), Oloo Rd. With original fixtures and fittings, and a creaking charm that seems to augur imminent collapse (Ksh218/315 s/c B&B) this is Eldoret's most interesting hotel.

MIDDLE BRACKET

New Wagon (PO Box 2408, ☎32271), Elgeyo Rd. More expensive (Ksh460/550 s/c B&B), but positively infested with character. Once the *New WagonWheel*, this is newly refurbished and gets quite lively at weekends, with barbecues and games machines.

Highlands Inn (PO Box 2189, ☎22092), Elgeyo Rd. Spacious, presentable and usually quiet place with safe parking (Ksh230/340 s/c B&B).

White Castle (PO Box 566, ☎33095) not on our map (Ksh360/650 s/c B&B). A new place, quite good value.

Sirikwa Hotel (PO Box 3361, ☎31655), Elgeyo Rd. Monolithic and faintly pompous pile (Ksh800/980 s/c B&B) with redeeming features (see "Eldoret directory").

Food

Eldoret has plenty of good places to grab a bite, with a clutch of established snackeries and several places to eat at greater length.

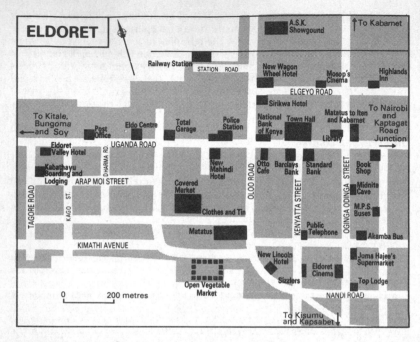

New Wagon Hotel (☎32271), Elgeyo Rd. Good four-course dinners.

Midnite Cave, Oginga Odinga St. Reliable cafeteria fare, day or night.

Eldoret Valley Hotel, Uganda Rd. Good, Somali food and other fare.

Otto Café, Uganda Rd. Another popular *hoteli* with a long and well-priced menu and excellent *mandaazi*, but it closes at 8pm.

Paul's Fresh Bread Bakery, corner of Kimathi Ave and Nandi Rd. Just what's needed on a chilly July morning.

Sizzlers, south of the public phone booths on Kenyatta St. A newish joint, offering a speedy, high quality burger.

Sparks Milk Bar, Oginga Odinga Rd, opposite the Eldoret Cinema. An excellent and venerable establishment – good, inexpensive snack meals and the bonus of decent toilets for once.

Sirikwa Hotel (☎31655), Elgeyo Rd. Fabulous barbecue buffet lunches at weekends for about Ksh120 – worth it if you've just spent three days in the Kakamega Forest or up Mount Elgon.

Eldoret directory

Banks *Barclays* Mon–Fri 8.30am–1pm, Sat 8.30–11am. *Standard* Mon–Fri 8.30am–2pm, Sat 8.30–11am.

Books There's an okay bookshop at the east end of town, a semi-permanent second-hand/exchange stall on Kenyatta Road, and a library with a good African history section. Also a new supermarket at the *Eldo Centre* that stocks a fair range of paperbacks.

Car Hire Try *McNaughtons* (PO Box 717, ☎22464) on Kisumu Rd. Apart from a hefty deposit, their rates for 4WD are reasonable and much cheaper than Kitale if you're headed for Mount Elgon.

Eldoret Show Held in the first week of March.

Kakamega Forest There's a daily, early morning bus to Kisumu via the road leading past the *Forest Rest House*. Ask for a ticket to Shinyalu.

Post Office Mon–Fri 8am–5pm, Sat 9am–noon.

Supermarket *Juma Hajee's* may be historic and all that, but the new one at the *Eldo Centre* is the best in the country outside Nairobi.

Swimming Pool Only at the *Sirikwa Hotel*, Ksh30.

Moving on from Eldoret

Moving on is probably your main concern. Heading directly **towards the Ugandan border**, there's little to delay your progress to MALABA, two or three hours away. BUNGOMA and WEBUYE, en route, are covered on p.209–211.

Uphill and then down again, **eastbound** on the busy A104 road from Eldoret to NAKURU, the sombre scenery is pretty with moors and conifers but the road itself is a fast one. If you discover any interesting detours on the way, let us know. If you arrived in Eldoret early enough in the day, there are two worthwhile **bases outside town** to head to for a night or longer.

Kaptagat and the Kerio valley

The first of these, **Kaptagat Hotel**, is about 20km **towards the Kerio Valley**, a delightful place in the woods, well signposted. Rooms were around Ksh200/330 s/c B&B at last check, but it was closed recently, status uncertain. It seems you can still camp down by the stream with monkeys and chameleons for company, if you tip the *askari*, but if you're tentless, check in Eldoret before you go. You'll have to find a *matatu* in town or, less frustratingly, walk out past the new Eldoret Cathedral to the junction beyond the *Rivatex* factory and wait for a vehicle there.

If you intend to cross the valley to Lake Baringo, you'll find a fair number of *matatus* for KABARNET, using the new Tambach escarpment route. This is a spectacular journey: from the high pastures and wheat fields of the plateau, the valley suddenly yawns out beneath, some 1500m below. However, the route down to the fluorspar mine at KIMWARER, which passes through Kaptagat and used to be the main way across the valley, no longer sees much traffic. Still worth the effort if you have time, or a solid vehicle of your own, it's an incredible hairpin descent that seems to go on forever. Kerio valley route details continue on p.164.

Soy

In the other direction (west) out of Eldoret, there's transport towards Kitale at most times of the day (eg the *Akamba Bus* at 4pm) but the *Soy Country Club*, half-way there, is nice enough to break your journey for. (It is worth pointing out here that the "Youth Hostel" at Blue Skies Farm, 10km before Kitale, has long since ceased to function.) Rooms at the *Club* (PO Box 2, Soy, ☎6 Soy) are good value (Ksh175/260 s/c B&B) and there's a swimming pool and a thoroughly enjoyable country garden ambience. You can camp here, too (Ksh40 and a small charge to use the pool). Guests are very rare except at weekends.

SOY itself is nothing at all – you'll hardly notice it – so if you want **to camp** at the *Country Club* bring supplies.

In the Soy area, look out for the famous herd of **Rothschild's giraffe**, now very rare, and often seen by the road. They stand their ground and, for giraffe close-ups, you won't do better than here, except perhaps at the Langata Sanctuary near Nairobi, where a number of the Soy animals have been moved in recent years.

Kitale

KITALE is smaller than Eldoret, and not much more exciting, but it has more going for it from a traveller's point of view, primarily because it is the base for visits to **Mount Elgon** and the superb, very underrated, hiking country around Kenya's second giant volcanic cone. It is also the most straightforward departure point for trips into the **northern deserts** and the only town with a regular bus service to **Lake Turkana**. There's a **national park** nearby, little known but easily accessible **Saiwa Swamp**, where for once the tables are turned on drivers: you can explore on foot only. And the town itself boasts a good **regional museum.**

The majority of travellers who stop spend just one night in Kitale on the way to Lake Turkana. Unless you're on a tight schedule, however, the museum and Saiwa Swamp add up to a good reason to delay a day. Nor is the road to Turkana so daunting as to make getting a ride there a problem: the buses go early, but there are usually vehicles heading off north until early afternoon.

Beginnings

Originally *Quitale*, a relay station on the old slave route between Uganda and Bagamoyo in Tanzania, the modern town was only founded in 1920, as the capital of *Trans-Nzoia* district. When the first settlers arrived (mostly after World War I), this vale of rich grasslands between Mount Elgon and the Cherangani Hills was apparently almost uninhabited. But just a few years earlier it had been a Maasai grazing area, and a group who refer to themselves as Maasai still live on the eastern slopes of Elgon.

With the arrival of the railway in 1925, the town and the region around it began, literally, to flourish, with a fantastic array of fruit, cereals, vegetables and livestock, and all the attendant settler paraphernalia of agricultural and flower shows, church fetes and gymkhanas. This heady era lasted barely forty years, but the region's **agriculture** is still famous: almost anything, including such exotic fruit as apples and pears, can be grown here. The Kitale Show takes place each year at the end of October or the beginning of November.

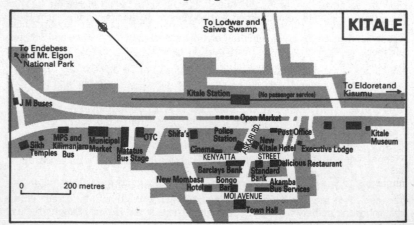

Accommodation and eating

Kitale is a pleasant town for a rest stop, well planted with trees and warm enough, despite its highland location, to hint at the desert which begins not far to the north. Alternatively, if you're heading north out of town anway, you might want to stay at the *Barnley's House* (see p.203). If you don't have your own vehicle, however, allow at least an hour to get there.

Lodgings

There's a number of **cheap lodgings**, the most economical up at the grubby north end of town past the market. The less ornate of the two **Sikh temples** up here also takes travellers; remember to leave a donation.

TOWN CENTRE LODGINGS

Alakara Hotel (PO Box 1984, 20395). A new place, not on the map (Ksh310/360 B&B).

Bismilah B&L, between the market and the *MPS* office. Adequate and dirt cheap.

Bongo Bar Hotel (PO Box 530, ☎20593), Moi Ave. A little expensive, but spacious, properly furnished single rooms without facilities for around Ksh250/340 B&B isn't unreasonable and it comes with the highest praise.

New Kitale Hotel, corner of Askari Rd, Kenyatta St. A vast gloomy warren (some rooms have been hired out as offices and workshops) which has clearly seen better days since it was the region's settler focus; but they are prepared to discuss prices and, while these start high, you can get a decent enough room for around Ksh120/180 s/c.

New Mombasa, Moi Ave. Definitely *not* one to head for.

New Kamburu Silent B&L (Ksh70/100), along the road behind Moi Ave. Excellent value and by no means unpleasant, a basic B&L to practise your Swahili in.

Star Lodge Hotel, again, along the road south of Moi Ave. A highly rated B&L, considering it's only Ksh50/80.

Executive Lodge (Ksh70/140), Kenyatta St. Not only one of the town's best, but one of the best lodgings in Kenya, with excellent rooms, hot showers down the hall, a TV room . . .

KITALE CLUB

Surprisingly reasonable, too, are the accommodations at the *Kitale Club* (PO Box 30, ☎20030) on the way into town from Eldoret. Although you have to pay for temporary membership, you can get a decent room with hot water (log fire under a rusty oil drum gives a nice pink tinge to the water), laundry service and acceptable meals for Ksh416/679 s/c B&B, including membership. If you're just passing by, politeness can earn you a look at their airmail *Daily Telegraphs* and permission to buy a beer. The club, incidentally, is the site of the old slave quarters and the circle of stones in the car park is said to have surrounded a ring to which slaves were chained at night.

Food

As elsewhere, many Kitale restaurants are closed on Sundays. On other days, two **restaurants** worth patronising are the *Black Horse Bar & Restaurant* – cheap and tasty and lots of it – and the *Bongo Bar Take Away and Restaurant*, which is almost as good. See if the *Delicious Restaurant* – the one with the luxuriant tropical garden in the window – is still there, for its ice cream and cold milkshakes; but it's reportedly on its way out of business. The same goes for *Shifa's Fish & Chips*. Wherever you eat, do it early. Many places close after dark.

Kitale Museum

9.30am–6pm, Ksh30; Curator PO Box 1219, ☎20670.

Given its location, the **Kitale Museum** (or Museum of Western Kenya) is a remarkably successful enterprise. Originally the "Stoneham Museum", a collection opened to the public by a Lieutenant Colonel on his Cherangani farm in 1927, it was transferred here in 1972. Most of the early exhibits are now on the right as you enter: the famous **butterfly collection** is sadly diminished and consists largely of fine, empty cases. Keep looking and you'll find the *lepidoptera*. For the most part, Stoneham's other curious collections are just that, collected curiosities: they are a striking contrast to the recent Kenyan additions with more educational motives. The directly exhortatory display at the back of the main hall makes "An Appeal to All Kenyans" on issues of soil conservation, crop rotation and land terracing. Outside, the museum lawn puts the terracing theory into practice.

The **ethnographic displays** on Pokot, Elkony (Elgon), Maasai, Marakwet, Turkana and Luo are interesting, though perhaps more so if you've seen the stuff in real life and now have a chance to return and see it again. The Turkana homestead exhibit, especially, is worth comparing with the realities of present-day Lodwar and the lakeshore villages. The motley wildlife collection on the walls and downstairs is perhaps best ignored. But don't miss the 1916 belt-driven **BSA motorcycle** in the lobby (if it hasn't been absconded with, as rumour suggests). Outside, there's a brand new **snake pit** and the inevitable **tortoise pen**, with its hinged and leopard tortoise inmates. Unless it's the mating season, though, it's as boring for you as it must be for them.

Next to the main building, the octagonal **Museum Hall** has some bold murals of Turkana, Maasai, Nandi and Luo domestic life, commissioned by the National Museum and painted by Maggie Kukler. There's occasionally live music and discos here. The museum also has a craft shop, laboratories and a surprising **nature trail**, which transports you, in a few steps, from suburban Kitale to a chattering, dripping, rainforest where the trees are numbered (the curator apparently has a key of Latin names) and the birds abundant: look out for Ross's turaco, a large, deep purple species with square red crest, commoner here than in other forests. The trail follows a stream with a path and footbridges, but the forest itself is natural and some of the trees stately. The picnic sites near the end of the trail which leads back to the main road are the best places for a picnic in Kitale.

Onwards from Kitale: the Cheranganis and Kapenguria

Looking **to the west**: if you're interested in exploring **Mount Elgon**, it's very much a case of following your nose. ENDEBESS or KIMILILI are the usual starting points, both reached quickly enough by *matatu*; you should get there early in the day if you want to make significant progress up the mountain before dark.

Southwards, Kakamega and Kisumu are, with luck, no more than two or three hours away down the A1, a very busy road.

But most people setting off from Kitale are **heading north**. These days, it's a relatively easy adventure to LODWAR and FERGUSON'S GULF, with several buses each day and a tarred road making hitching a practical option (route details in Chapter Seven). With a tent, it may be more fun to spend the night before at **Saiwa Swamp National Park** rather than in Kitale itself.

Barnley's House

You could also stop off for a day – or quite happily for a week – at **Sirikwa Safaris Guesthouse and Campsite** (bookings through *"Barnley's House"*, PO Box 332 Kitale; no telephone), precisely 23.6km north of Kitale, on a tree-covered hill to the right and sign-boarded with a green-topped frame (if you still can't find it, poor you – try asking for *Bwana Tim's*). There are superb gardens to camp in (hot water and barbecue facilities), and a fine old house with rooms if you're too lazy (Ksh50 to camp, furnished tents Ksh270/390; rooms in the house Ksh390/540; excellent meals Ksh120, big breakfast Ksh90). Staff will undertake your washing – most days. There's exceptional birdwatching in this **Cherangani** foothills area and skilled guides to show you the avifauna if you've caught the bug.

Kapenguria

KAPENGURIA – off the highway, but somewhere else you might find yourself if you're in the district – seems to have no lodgings and nothing much else but a role of minor notoriety in colonial history (background on Kenyatta's trial in *Contexts*). If you turn off the main road to visit, you'll find an immaculately tarred main street leading incongruously up through the hovels of "old Kapenguria" to the smarter new town on the high ground, with its hospital, large police station, huge red octagonal Catholic church (stained glass windows and a spire), and the West Pokot district headquarters.

For accommodation there's a couple of B&Ls down in MAKUTANO – at the Kapenguria intersection. Much more interesting, however, is ORTUM, beautifully positioned beneath the heights of the Cheranganis, close to the **Marich Pass**, and a good locale to start hiking in the hills. There's at least one B&L here and people are pleasantly disinterested in your presence. On Sundays, a constant stream of vehicles to the weekly market at CHESEGON, on the other side of the hills, assures transport into the Kerio valley if you want it (more on that at the end of Chapter Three).

Saiwa Swamp National Park

Ksh220, student discounts, camping Ksh50; car park, entry on foot: Warden PO Box 753, ☎22 Chanira.

Specially created for the protection of a rare and vulnerable semi-aquatic antelope – the **sitatunga** – **Saiwa Swamp National Park** is the country's smallest park. Despite its accessibility – no distance from the *Barnley's House* – it's rarely visited, which is a pity: the requirement that you walk around the two square kilometres of jungle and swamp, plus the virtual guarantee of seeing the antelope as well as various monkeys and birdlife, make it an exciting and interesting goal for a day. If you're staying at the Barnleys', think about hiring a guide there for the trip – not at all expensive, and really worthwhile.

Practicalities

The park lies about 5km to the right of the main Kitale-Lodwar road, near the village of KIPSAIN (also known as Kipsoen). *Matatus* and the *Akamba* bus to Kapenguria (7am only) call at the village, which is some 18km from Kitale and off the main road. From here, if you fail to get a lift, it's a four-kilometre walk to the park gates. For the negotiable Ksh50 camping fee and park fees (once you've been spotted by a ranger), you'll find three good sites, grouped together, but nothing at all in the way of facilities apart from, a clean, piped water supply at the staff village, plenty of firewood and a small *duka*, open sporadically. You will need to make a fire, as the swamp mist makes it very chilly up here at night.

Game watching

The **sitatunga** (pronounced "statunga") is an unusual antelope with strange splayed and elongated hooves. You probably won't see these because the animal lives most of its life partly submerged in water and weed. It's hard to see quite how the hooves help it "to move freely on the surface of boggy swamps": the theory makes sense, but the design needs more work. Otherwise, the sitatunga's appearance is reddish-brown and moth-eaten, with very large, mobile ears and, on the males, horns.

Sitatunga live, in suitable habitats, scattered throughout western and central Africa, and possibly also around Lake Victoria, but only at Saiwa Swamp have they grown used to humans. They can be watched from the **observation platforms** which have been built in the trees at the side of the swamp – one on the east side, three on the west. The best times are early morning and late afternoon, and the farthest platform is less than a kilometre from the campsite. These lookouts are delightful, unmaintained, Tarzanesque structures enabling you to spy down on the life among the reeds. The park shelters plenty of bushbuck, easily distinguished from the sitatunga by their terrified, crashing escape through the undergrowth as you approach. The sitatunga evidently have steadier nerves, as they pick their way through the morass of water weed regardless of human gaze.

A wonderful **early morning walk** takes you across the rickety wooden walkway over the swamp and down a jungle path on the eastern shore: a cinch to follow. Here you're almost bound to see the park's four species of **monkeys**: colobus, vervet, blue and the distinctively white-bearded de Brazza monkey.

Saiwa Swamp is also a great draw for ornithologists, with a number of not-typically Kenyan **bird species**, including several turacos (though the great blue is apparently no longer among them), many kingfishers, and the splendid black-and-white casqued hornbill. But most conspicuous are the crowned cranes, whose lurching flight is almost as risible as their ghastly honking call.

Mount Elgon

The Maasai's *Ol Doinyo Ilgoon* (Breast Mountain) is hidden in clouds most of the time and its precise outline hard to discern. Like Mount Kenya, **Mount Elgon** is an extinct volcano and, around its jagged and much eroded crater rim, the peaks crop up like stumpy fingers of an upturned hand. The two mountains are comparable in bulk, but Elgon is lower (below the snowline) and less precipitous – an encouragement, perhaps, if the thought of tackling the "loneliest park in Kenya" was putting you off. Up near the peaks there's invigorating walking country and the smoothing effects of erosion make hiking relatively easy. The highest peak, **Wagagai** (4321m), is across the caldera in Uganda, but the most evocatively shaped peaks (Sudek/Lower Elgon, 4310m; Koitoboss, 4038m; and Endebess Bluff 2563m) belong to Kenya. The mountain has good rock climbing if you're properly equipped; the best is on the cliffs of Lower Elgon, Sudek and the nearby

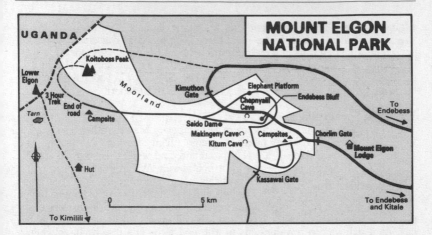

pinnacles. Actually up in the caldera (again, technically in Uganda), the **warm springs** by the Suam River make a delightful bath.

Vegetation here is similar to Mount Kenya's as bamboo and podocarpus forests give way to open moorland inhabited by the strange statues of giant groundsel and lobelia. **Wildlife** isn't easily seen until you get onto the moors but elephant and buffalo do roam the woods. While there are leopards, you're not likely to see one. The lions have long gone.

Elgon's most captivating attraction is the honeycomb of **caves** on the lower slopes, inside the national park boundaries. Some of these were long inhabited by the Elkony, one of the loosely related Kalenjin groups, and used as stock pens at night: at least a few were thought to have been man-made, and an early report refers to "thousands of chisel and axe marks on the walls". It's just as likely, however, that elephants were responsible: **Kitum cave** achieved television fame as the salt fix of local elephants that used to walk into the caves at night to gouge the salty rock from the walls with their tusks.

The Elkony were evicted from the caves by the colonial government, who insisted that they live in the open "where they could be counted for tax". The elephants, though no longer free to migrate back and forth between Elgon and the Cheranganis as they once did, are still occasional troglodytes. There have been cases of them dying under rock falls caused by their over-eager salt mining. Large numbers, however, were wiped out by Ugandan poachers in the turbulent early 1980s and today very few remain.

Part of the east side of the mountain is enclosed within the confines of **Mount Elgon National Park**. Outside this zone, however, you're as free to hike and camp as anywhere in Kenya, subject always to the potentially restricting location of the mountain on what the authorities have often considered a sensitive border.

Practical considerations

In most practical respects, you should treat a trip up Mount Elgon much as you would one to Mount Kenya (many details of which apply here; see p.118). However, **altitude** is much less of a problem on Elgon and, given a couple of days to climb it, few people will be badly affected by the ascent, even near the summits. Access to the mountain can be a little difficult – certainly it's not as straightforward as Mount Kenya – and there is no official permission to enter the park zone without a vehicle. You might think about **hiring a 4WD** for a few days in Kisumu or Eldoret (try *McNaughtons*, see "Eldoret directory"). Car hire in Kitale seems impossible or too expensive. The *Golf Hotel* in Kakamega (part of the same group as *Mount Elgon Lodge*) is helpful with transport.

Timing and companions

The best **season** to visit Elgon is from December to March, rather less good in June and July, with the heaviest rains falling during April–May and August–September. Elgon is a lonely mountain, and while there are no specific restrictions on hiking outside the park boundaries (which enclose less than a quarter of the Kenyan slopes), it's probably better not to go up alone.You aren't likely to see anyone else for a day or two, and if something were to happen to you on the heights you could forget about rescue. Men can find **guide-porters** easily enough in villages around the base: just ask and expect to pay up to Ksh100 per day. As usual, women travelling alone will tend to be at a disadvantage when it comes to such one-to-one arrangements.

Maps

If you plan more than a look into the park by vehicle, it's useful to have at least the *Mount Elgon Map and Guide* by Andrew Wielochowski, obtainable in Nairobi or in the UK from Executive Wilderness Programmes, 32 Seamill Park Crescent, Worthing BN11 2PN. *Survey of Kenya* maps from Nairobi are also available, and the 1.125,000 map can be obtained without clearance, though border sensitivity means some other sheets may be restricted at times.

Equipment

Take a **compass** and your needs for a minimum two to three days of self-sufficiency. Suggestions on clothing and other hardware can be found in the Mount Kenya section. A **tent** will enable you to stay up in the peaks area but you can use the high altitude **hut** as a base for shorter walks. Obviously, if you have a vehicle, preferably 4WD, you can alter these requirements. The park rangers are often willing to accompany drivers.

TWO NOTES OF CAUTION

Elgon's location occasionally makes it a sensitive area. If you plan to go down into the crater and visit the Suam warm springs, remember that they are in Uganda and stories of rebel soldiers were rife throughout the 1980s. Play it by ear – the stories were probably exaggerated.

Hyperbole aside, Elgon has seen a number of violent confrontations between elephant poachers and armed park rangers. The last serious outbreak was in 1988 when they resulted in several deaths. For some time, understandably, Kenyan officials were turning back non-4WD vehicles, even outside the park, and preventing hikers on foot from climbing. Since 1988, the situation has calmed down, but enquiries in Nairobi aren't likely to elicit specifically useful advice, and you'll only find out for sure on the spot – though you could contact *Msafiri Inns* (p.30) who book the *Mount Elgon Lodge*. Assuming you are allowed up, it would indicate it's no longer considered a risk.

The routes

There are basically three **routes** up the Kenyan side of Elgon: one directly into the park and two hikes around either side, passing through fine scenery and neither very severe. You should try, if at all possible, to camp at one of the sites in the lower half of the park – they're highly recommended as some of the most beautiful in the country – and visit the caves. You're going to need a vehicle to do this because, even though the rules appear vague and somewhat contradictory (you are allowed to leave your vehicle but only high up or on designated lower trails), you are supposed to have one if you're in the park.

Mount Elgon Lodge
Mount Elgon Lodge (☎11Y6 Endebess) is located just outside Chorlim Gate, but its status is marginal. While things have recently improved for the hotel, it is running at a loss and isn't certain to be open. Bookings are through *Msafiri Inns* in Nairobi (address in *Basics*, p.30) and latest prices are around Ksh575/1050 B&B s/c. If you're in Kakamega, talk to the deputy manager of the *Golf Hotel*; see p.212). It can be a fabulous place to indulge yourself for the night – superb views and a lovely atmosphere – but can't be counted upon. **Camping** in the grounds is an accepted, and very acceptable alternative to taking a room.

Direct to the Park
Ksh220 per person, Ksh30 vehicle. Ksh50 to camp: Warden PO Box 753 Kitale, ☎11Y11 Endebess.

The most obvious way into the park, and the simplest if you're driving, is through *Chorlim Gate*, the main entrance to the **National Park**, which lies some 10km past ENDEBESS (turn left at Endebess, then right again). The road to Endebess is paved from Kitale and *matatus* make the trip frequently, but getting up to the gate is still a problem without a car and you may have to walk it. Furthermore, you probably won't be allowed in the park until you find a spare seat in a vehicle at the gate; with anywhere from thirty down to as few as ten vehicles per *month* you might be in for a long wait. If you're persuasive – and patient – you *may* be allowed up to the first campsite on foot, accompanied by an armed ranger. But only if you promise not to leave the site (you won't need coercion – there are buffaloes everywhere).

If you have **wheels**, you should be able to negotiate most of the park tracks in dry weather, but in wet conditions be prepared to be refused entry unless you have four-wheel-drive. Once in, the fine campsites not many kilometres from the gate (signposted) are a good target. If you're exceptionally lucky, a night vigil at **Kitum cave** is repaid by a visit from the elephants; the bats and the forest are compensation if you're not. You'll need a good torch. For **Koitoboss Peak** (4038m), follow the driveable track into the moorlands to the trail head outside the park, then walk the final two hours to the summit.

Kimilili and the Western Trail
The **second route** is the most popular with **hikers**. It begins in **KIMILILI**, 45km from Kitale, and, while it's a long trek up to the moorlands (lifts are scarce), there should be a usable **hut** to collapse in at the day's end. In Kimilili, *Jasho Lodging* is recommended for rooms, the *Wanyika Hotel* for meals. It's a lively place on a Thursday, when the **market** attracts rural dwellers from a wide radius. Kimilili Catholic Secondary School, just outside the town, may allow you to **pitch a tent** .

The Headmaster used to be the official key holder for the **Elgon hut**. The key is no longer needed (and the HM has moved on), but it's still worth asking anyone who will listen. The hut was renovated in 1987 with Austrian help – so it's now known as the *Austrian Hut* – and for the time being is in reasonable condition.

The first step **up the mountain** is a *matatu*, as early as possible in the day, to KAPSAKWONY, 7km from Kimilili. (Top up with water here if you forgot in Kimilili.) At the fork above the village, bear left, then after 2km turn right at the sign reading *Forest Station 25km*. You may get a lift from here to the last village, KABERWA (with sign: *Chepkitale Forest Stn 21km*), but from here on, you'll almost certainly have to hoof it. As the mountain hut is 7km past the forest station, this means 28km up; allow eight hours.

Eight kilometres above Kaberwa, the trail gets noticeably worse, as it plunges into the cathedral gloom of a bamboo forest. An hour of this and you break into open stands of moss-enveloped giant podocarpus trees ("podos") with spiralling trunks. The trail rolls upwards, you crest a hill, and the entire southern Elgon Ridge system is spread out before you.

The **forest station** has plenty of abandoned buildings for shelter but uncertain water supplies, so it is worth struggling on the last two hours to the **hut**. Remember to leave time to collect water from the nearby spring and gather firewood – which is scarce. A rough jeep track continues past the hut, but you're unlikely to meet anyone up here.

The trail is well marked with occasional cairns and white blazes: three hours the next morning should see you to the highest peak on the Kenya side. Starting from the hut, a ninety-minute hike brings you to the ridge leading up to the peak of Lower Elgon. (Just beyond is a high valley with the southeast caldera rim, seen from the rear, as its head.) There are duiker antelope bouncing away through the scrub everywhere. Next, climb a false summit, then dip down, parallelling the series of tabular peaks on your right which form the southern crater lip. Shortly before reaching a big **tarn**, the trail swerves cruelly up through a gap in the rock wall to put you on the summit of Lower Elgon.

To get down to the **Suam warm springs**, ignore the ridge just mentioned at the hour-and-a-half mark and, leaving the trail, cut across the valley, following the rim to Koitoboss Peak. This is inside the park. Down in the crater, to the left, are the springs.

Depending on your life support system, you can either turn back to the hut for a second night there or continue around the crater rim to drop down off the mountain on the northeast side, traversing the upper part of the National Park and, ideally, allowing a night camped on the mountain. Note that if you're found in the park, or if you exit through one of the gates, you may have some explaining to do and you'll have to pay park fees at least.

Kimothon route

There's a **third route** which obviates some of the lengthy foot-slogging of the trail from Kimilili. This starts in Endebess and leads up to a second Forest Station at **Kimothon**, about 12km west of the village on the north side of the park. It's recommended that you stay the night here and continue the next day on the well-marked trail to Koitoboss and the Elgon hut. Downhill from there to Kapsakwony (*matatu* connection for the last 7km to Kimilili), it's 37km – a ten-hour knee-wobbler of a hike if you have to walk the whole way.

The Uganda Road – Webuye, Bungoma and Malaba

This is perhaps the least interesting part of western Kenya: largely monotonous, undulating grasslands and sugar fields, dotted with gigantic granite boulders. But it is the route by which the majority of Africa overland travellers enter the country, and the obvious one **out to Uganda**: despite the lack of attractions, it still sees a fair number of travellers passing through.

Webuye and Webuye Falls

WEBUYE certainly offers very little. It's the site of the giant *Panafrican Paper Mills* (visitors' enquiries PO Box 535 Webuye, ☎16/17 Bungoma), which dominate the countryside around with their strong, strange odour as much as anything else. The explanation for the factory's siting is **Webuye Falls**, gushing through rock clefts behind and above the mills, about 5km from the main road. Formerly known as Broderick Falls, Webuye would be a nice spot for a picnic if you have a car, but they're hardly spectacular. To reach them, turn off the main road at the factory and climb (northwards) between housing developments and mills, passing a school. From there, the plant (the largest paper factory in Africa), belching smoke across the hot plains, is a powerful statement about change in Kenya.

Chetambe's Fort

A few kilometres away, on top of the steep scarp that rears up beyond the Kitale road, lies a different kind of monument, the remains of **Chetambe's Fort**. This was the site, in 1895, of a last-ditch stand by the *Bukusu* group of the Luyia tribe against the motley line-up of a British punitive expedition, which had enrolled Ugandan, Sudanese, Maasai and even other Luyia troops. A predictable – Hotchkiss gun – massacre took place, with negligible losses on the attackers' side, but how they managed to storm the scarp in the first place is a mystery: presumably the Bukusu were all inside their walled fort at the top.

With Kenya's historical sites so few, it's worth the scramble up the steep slope if you're interested. Not surprisingly, perhaps, the "Fort" is unimpressive: all that remains is an overgrown, semicircular ditch, perhaps 100m from end to end. A

ELIJA MASINDE'S DINI: THE CULT OF THE ANCESTORS

In the 1940s and 1950s, there was a resurgence of **Bukusu resistance** and nationalism in the *Dini ya Msambwa* (Cult of the Ancestors) movement, spearheaded by the charismatic prophet-rebel, Elija Masinde. The heart of his movement was in the Elgon foothills between Kimilili and the Ugandan border. It called for the eviction of all *wazungu* and the transfer of their property to Africans. As the *Dini* spread, there were violent confrontations with colonial forces and a number of deaths. Masinde was sent into internal exile but, by now a folk hero, his followers kept the sparks of resistance alive throughout the more organised uprising of *Mau Mau* in the Central Highlands, until independence was finally obtained. The movement collapsed in the early years of *Uhuru*, when Masinde was allowed home to Kimilili and his continued denouncements of all authority and claims to divine inspiration began to lose their coherence.

more convincing reason to be there is to talk to some of the people who live nearby – it is really the only way to weave together the threads of history. I was shown the site by people who live around it: the compound is just another field now, but someone told me he used to find bones here when he was young, and women would come to weep in the evenings. There were even animal sacrifices to the dead warriors. Some "awful machine" had killed them.

If you have wheels, a roundabout alternative to the slog up the cliffs is to continue following the road which leads past the falls. The *Nabyole Lodge* up here is quite a good B & L (Ksh70/100), with cold drinks and a restaurant. They'll direct you on to *Chetambe's*, about 8km further on reasonable murram.

Bungoma and into Uganda

The **main road to Uganda** continues west, tarmacked but traffic-attacked. Heavily laden lorries driving to central Africa from Mombasa are the cause of the mangled surface; though, until recently, only the left, west-bound lane was seriously bumpy and pockmarked while the right, heading back to Nairobi was curiously smooth – an ironic comment on Africa's economic state of health, as the side which should have been carrying exports back to Mombasa was little damaged by the empty lorries using it. By the early 1990s, with Uganda's fortunes improving, the road is looking worse than ever and it's hard to find a smooth stretch . . .

Bungoma

Sizeable as it is, **BUNGOMA** manages to be unremittingly dull. Unless you're drawn by the siren calls of the *Bungoma Tourist Hotel's* "sugar belt style" comforts (admittedly unexpected out here), there's scarcely any reason to visit, as it isn't on the main road. The hotel has self-contained rooms (Ksh340/490 B&B) and simple ones (Ksh260/380), and a very helpful and informative manager (PO Box 972, ☎20594/5 Bungoma). Less of a drain on the resources, however, is the new and rather good *Grandma's Hotel* (PO Box 225), just 200m south of the A104 Bungoma junction, before you get into the town, which provides clean, quiet rooms at Ksh50–80/100. If you miss this, or find it full, *Hotel Simba B&L,* has double beds for Ksh80 (Ksh120 s/c) and seems better than the other competition in town.

Apart from noting that Bungoma is experiencing something of a boom – credited by some to its involvement in smuggling coffee out of Uganda in the late 1970s – and suggesting that you eat at the *New Yemeni Hotel*, a superior *hoteli*, Bungoma's interest can't be improved further.

The Ugandan border

MALABA lies at the end of the road and the end of the railway line. Conditions in **Uganda** are changing so rapidly that anything like up-to-date advice and news from the border is next to impossible to provide. However, while there are usually endless lines of lorries waiting on both sides of the border, pedestrians are crossing without difficulty. See "Onwards from Kenya", in *Contexts* for some recent travel information about Uganda.

Arriving in Kenya on a Wednesday, Saturday, or Sunday, you might enjoy collapsing onto the train to Nairobi (departs 4pm, arrives 8.45am) for a good night's sleep and some good, old-fashioned customer relations – such as a man with a bell ringing dinner time. Otherwise, there's no shortage of unappetising **Boarding & Lodgings** along the kilometre of lorry-choked road which is Malaba. And if you're glad to be in Kenya at last, don't make the mistake of relaxing your security routines: many people are robbed soon after arriving.

Kakamega and Kakamega Forest

KAKAMEGA is the headquarters of the **Luyia**, a loosely defined group of peoples whose only clear common denominator is a Bantu language, spoken in more than a score of vernaculars, that distinguishes them from the Luo to the south and the Kalenjin to the east. Numerically, the Luyia (Abaluyia/Luhya) are Kenya's second largest ethnic group, and most are settled farmers.

Kakamega itself was founded as a buying station on the ox-trail known as *Sclater's Road*, which reached here from the coast in 1896. Historically, its only fame came in the 1930s, when gold was discovered nearby and more than a thousand prospectors came to the region. Very few fortunes were made. The town today has little interest for casual visitors and it fails to leave you with much sense of a community.

Conversely, the **Kakamega Forest** is one of western Kenya's star attractions; if you have any interest at all in the natural world, it's worth going far out of your way to see. Fortunately, it's easy to get to from KISUMU or, if you've been in the Mount Elgon region, down the very scenic stretch of the A1 from WEBUYE.

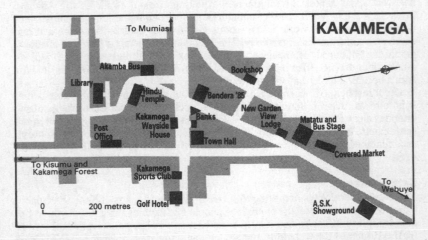

Kakamega town

If you arrive late in the day, you may want to **stay in town** rather than arrive in the forest after dark. The *Bendera 85* is an unexpectedly good B&L – clean and welcoming, with large rooms – while the *New Garden Guest House* matches it on both counts, but is a brothel into the bargain and not for faint hearts. The *Kakamega Wayside House* (PO Box 900, ☎20128) is not unexpected in any way, but at least it's very cheap (eat elsewhere). All are around Ksh50/80. There's really good food at the *Total Service Station* cafeteria and nice vibes in the Somali-run *Soweto* at the *matatu* stage.

If you're feeling expansive (your time in the forest should be very cheap), you could even have a night of relative luxury at the dapper *Golf Hotel* (PO Box 118, ☎20460), where all residents become temporary members of the adjacent Sports Club (golf, squash courts, etc). The place does have some style (Ksh700/850 s/c HB) – easily spoiled by the vultures that hop and flap over the lawns at the back.

Kakamega directory

Books There's a good bookshop with a few foreign paperbacks down at the back of town. The **library** is open Mon–Thurs 9am–6pm, Fri 9am–4pm, Sat 9am–1pm; it should have some background on the Kakamega Forest.

Kakamega Show End of November for three days. The showground is on the Webuye road.

Market A very lively one next to the bus station.

Mount Elgon visits If you're thinking about a trip, contact the deputy manager at the *Golf Hotel* who can provide very helpful information, and arranges for cars to take people up to *Mount Elgon Lodge* and picked up again.

Swimming Pool A small one at the *Golf Hotel*.

The Kakamega Forest

Some four hundred years ago, the tract of rainforest now called **Kakamega Forest** would have been at the eastern end of a broad expanse of forest stretching west, clear across the continent, virtually unbroken as far as the Atlantic. Today, it's a tiny patch of relict equatorial jungle, famous among zoologists and botanists around the world as an example of how an isolated environment can survive cut off from its larger body. The Kakamega Forest is a haven of shadowy gloom for hundreds of species of birds, snakes and butterflies, as well as monkeys and other mammals, many of which are found nowhere else in East Africa because similar habitats no longer exist.

The forest is due to become a national park but entry is free for the time being. It is hard to imagine how it could ever be enclosed: the forest is fragmentary, interspersed with open fields of grassland, cultivated stream margins and small settlements. A part of one of the densest stands is a designated **Forest Reserve** and this is where most visitors come, to the *Forest Rest House* in the glade at its edge.

Getting there

There are several ways of getting to the *Rest House* and maps of Kenya invariably locate the forest incorrectly. Doubtless people in Kakamega can direct you to the quickest route. If you're coming up from Kisumu, a sign points right, off the A1 highway, some 10km before Kakamega, at a location called KHAYEGA or MUKUMA. It's 13km to the *Rest House* from here: take the right branch after 7km at the village of Shinyalu (heading in the direction of ISECHENO) then, after a further 5km, go left at a **signpost**. From there, you have less than a kilometre up a trail to the *Rest House*.

If you're in Kakamega, you can get *matatus*, first to **SHINYALU** and then to the *Rest House* from there, but the area is beautiful for **walking** and you will find plenty of others doing the same for want of wheels (and beware that there's sometimes a bit of a racket with tourists in *matatus* from Kakamega to the forest). Shinyalu has a cattle auction and a major market every Saturday, and if you're here then, it's worth pausing an hour to soak up the atmosphere of cowboys and corrals in the jungle. A good bull can be had for Ksh5000, a cow for Ksh4000, and a calf for a mere Ksh1500.

The best way to arrive is using one of the **buses** that ply, once a day in each direction, between Kisumu and Eldoret via Shinyalu and Kapsabet. Either bus can drop you right by the *Rest House* trail, leaving you a ten-minute walk to it. When you're ready to leave the forest, the buses pass by (no earlier than 9.45am) every morning. If you end up walking out of the forest, eastwards, it takes about three hours, through beautiful forest scenery along the earth road to the tarmac C39 Maragoli (Chevakali)–Kapsabet road.

In the forest

The **Forest Rest House** is a delight. Someone writing in the visitor's book called it a "budget *Treetops*", a description which scarcely does it justice. Ringed by forest, the *Rest House* has just four first-floor double rooms, with a long veranda facing out to the wall of tropical greenery a few metres away. Water supplies are somewhat erratic: when the pump is working, each room has a functioning bathroom and toilet, otherwise you have to fetch water from the pumphouse. The staff can sell you kerosene for the lamps but you should try to bring food with you, as the closest reliable *dukas* are about 3km away on the road to Shinyalu. You can cook on a wood fire in the kitchen beneath the rooms. Alternatively, a small canteen on the way down to the pumphouse sells simple staples and *sometimes* prepares food (*ugali, karanga, chapatis*) morning and evenings (closed Sunday evening), and sporadically has beer and sodas.

To be sure of a room – especially at weekends – you can **reserve in advance** through *The Forester, PO Box 88, Kakamega, Western Province*: Ksh30 per person (or camping on the lawn, but don't leave tents unattended). In dire straits, other arrangements can probably be made locally. Kakamega Forest is becoming popular.

Several of the forest wardens and other staff are knowledgeable guides and their **birdwalks** – for a modest fee of around Ksh40 – are tremendously enjoyable. Expect a three-hour wander on the labyrinthine jungle paths, having birds, monkeys, chameleons and other animals pointed out to you, most of which you would miss on your own – if you didn't quickly get lost. If your guide has John Williams' *Field Guide*, too (see "Books" in *Contexts*), this makes the whole pastime of bird-watching more satisfying. A pair of **binoculars** is more or less indispensable. Among the most common birds are the noisy and gregarious black-and-white casqued hornbill and the very striking, deep violet Ross's turaco. You may also see familiar-looking African grey parrots and, circling above the canopy on the lookout for unwary monkeys, the huge crowned hawk eagle.

But Kakamega's avian stars are the **great blue turacos**, big glossy birds the size of turkeys that look like dowagers in evening gowns. They're most easily located by their raucous calls; a favourite spot at dusk is the grove of very tall trees down by the pumphouse. The flock arrives each evening to crash and lurch among the branches as they select roosting sites.

The forest draws **mammal** watchers as well, particularly for the monkeys: troops are often seen at dusk, foraging through the trees directly opposite the *Rest House* veranda. Apart from the ubiquitous colobus, you can see blue monkeys and the much slimmer black-cheeked white-nosed monkey (so-called, though it's most easily recognised by its red tail). They're often seen milling around with the hornbills. You may also see pairs of giant forest squirrels capering in the treetops: the deep booming call you sometimes hear in the morning is theirs.

At night, with a powerful torch, you might catch a glimpse of bush-babies or a potto, a slow-moving, lemur-like animal whose name aptly conveys appearance and demeanour. The forest is also home to several species of fruit bat, one of which, the hammer-headed fruit bat (*Hypsignathus monstrosus*), is the largest in Africa, with a wingspan of a metre and an enormous head. Other nocturnal Kakamega specialities are the otter shrew, which lives in some of the forest streams, the tree pangolin (a kind of arboreal scaly anteater) and the flying squirrel.

The forest's **reptile life** is legendary, but few people seem actually to see any **snakes** (a local woman on the trail recently said she'd *never* seen a snake!). You're much more likely to meet **chameleons**. Reptiles spend a good deal of time motionless, especially when frightened, and to see any in the dense foliage you have to be well tuned in. Visible or not, however, snakes are abundant and you certainly shouldn't walk in the forest in bare feet or sandals: the gaboon viper, growing to a metre or more in length, and fatter than your arm, is a dangerous denizen of the forest floor. To avoid an encounter simply walk heavily: they're highly sensitive to vibration and will flee at your seismic approach.

Onwards from Kakamega

The obvious routes out lie along the A1 to Kitale or Kisumu. The road **down to Kisumu** is a real roller coaster, with a final 8km descent over the Nyando escarpment that brings Lake Victoria into view. In clear weather it allows fantastic panoramas across the sugar fields of the Kano plains towards the massif of the Mau and the Kisii hills. The florid **church** on the left is the Kenyan headquarters of the Coptic church, originally founded in Egypt in the early years of Christianity.

Alternatively, there's a beautiful road **east to Kapsabet** in the Nandi Hills, starting at the rural centre of Maragoli/Chevakali (also spelled Chyvakali and Kyavakali), along the Kisumu road. Note that Maragoli is the centre on the A1, while Chevakali, effectively part of the same community, is off to the east a kilometre or so.

Lastly, if you have time and inclination for a diversion far off any beaten track, you could visit the small town of **Mumias**, the sugar belt's biggest processing centre and also one of western Kenya's Muslim strongholds. The road from Kakamega is now paved and there's regular transport.

Mumias

MUMIAS was originally *Mumia's*, one of the more important up-country centres, capital of the Luyia-speaking mini-state of **Wanga**, and well established by the middle of the nineteenth century at the head of an important caravan route to the coast. **King Mumia**, who came to power in 1880, was the last King of Wanga. He inherited an army of 10,000 soldiers, half of whom were dispossessed Maasai from the Uasin Gishu plateau known as the *Kwavi*. It was this army which was largely responsible for the smashing of Bukusu resistance at Chetambe's fort fifteen years later.

Even at the beginning of Mumia's reign, Europeans were beginning to arrive in the wake of Arab and Swahili slave-traders, who in turn had been settling in since the 1850s with the full accord of the Wanga royal family. The first was Joseph Thomson in 1883, and by 1894 there was a permanent British sub-commissioner or collector of taxes posted here. Mumia had always welcomed strangers, and he allowed the slavers to continue their work on other groups of the Luyia (notably the Bukusu), but he was unprepared for the swift usurpation of his authority by the British, whom he'd assumed were also there to trade. He was appointed "Paramount Chief" of a gradually diminishing state and then, as an old man, was retired without his real knowledge. He died in 1949, aged 100, and with him Kenya's first (and only) indigenous, up-country state expired, almost without notice.

Mumias today

The present mosque was built in Mumia's honour and its Koran school is just one of about 25 around the town. Mumias has long been a centre of Islam, famous for its coastal ways, but today women in *buibuis* – the long, black coverall of the coast – are rarely seen. According to the chairman of the Mumias Koran Schools Committee, Islam is losing ground to Catholicism because of sectarian quarrelling between Muslim leaders and because, while mission and government education have an equal standing, the *madrassas* must take second place after school hours. If you're interested, Mumias Mission publishes a slim pamphlet outlining their side of the story, and the Catholic church there is quite an impressive old building.

By train from Butere

Leaving Mumias, a paved road leads directly to Kisumu but if you have time to spare you might like to hop on the daily **train** from **BUTERE**, 12km down the road, instead. This branch line was intended to reach Mumias but never did. The daily train service (no longer steam-hauled since 1988, but nearly as slow and one class only) remains a boon to rural-dwellers with more time than money. It leaves Kisumu at 8.45am, arrives in Butere about noon, and returns in the afternoon, taking more than three hours to cover barely sixty kilometres.

travel details

Kisumu is the west's transport centre. Buses and *matatus* run from there to most major centres in this chapter within half a day.

Buses

From **Kisumu** to:
Nairobi numerous daily runs on *OTC, Akamba, Nairobi Deluxe Services (NDS)*, etc. (6–8hr) via **Kericho** (2hr) and **Nakuru** (4–5hr). *MPS* service is fastest (11am and 5pm) and most expensive;
Eldoret several daily runs including one via **Shinyalu** (for **Kakamega Forest**) and **Kapsabet**;

Mombasa 2 daily with *NDS* (14hr).
From **Kisii** to:
Nairobi, at least 6 daily (7–9hr) via Kericho;
Migori 2 (2pm, 4pm) via Homa Bay;
Kisumu numerous daily runs.
From **Kericho** to:
Nairobi 1 morning, 2 evening on *OTC* (7hr) plus many others;
Kisumu 1pm, 2am, (3hr) on *OTC*;
Kisii 12.30am, 12.30pm (2hr) on *OTC*.
From **Eldoret** to:
Nairobi frequent daily runs, eg. *Akamba* (7hr) and *MPS* (6hr);

Kitale (through buses from Nairobi) eg. *Akamba* 4pm;
Kisumu, several daily runs, including one via **Kapsabet** and **Shinyalu** (for **Kakamega Forest**).
From **Kitale** to:
Nairobi several services daily (8–11hr);
Kapenguria on *Akamba* daily, at 7am;
Lodwar at least 2 daily on *JM* and *Kilimanjaro* (5hr) continuing to **Ferguson's Gulf** (7hr).
From **Bungoma** to:
Nairobi several per day (9–10hr);
Kisumu several per day (2–5hr);
Kitale *Mawingo* country bus at 5am, 11am, (3hr) via **Kimilili**.
From **Kakamega** to:
Nairobi several direct runs daily (7–9hr) via **Kisumu**.

Trains
Bookings can be made with *Kenya Railways* in Kisumu on ☎42211 Kisumu.
From **Kisumu** to:
Nairobi d. 6.30pm (via Nakuru, 2.10am), a 7.30am daily and "express" service d. 5pm a. 5.30am daily;
Butere d. 8.45am, a. noon daily.
From **Eldoret** to:
Nairobi d. 9pm Wed, Sat, Sun, a. 8.45am;
Malaba d. 4.10am Wed, Sat, Sun, a. 8am.
From **Malaba** to:
Nairobi d. 4pm Wed, Sat, Sun, (via Eldoret, 9pm and Nakuru 3.30am) a. 8.45am.
From **Kitale**: passenger services suspended.

Matatus
With nearly half the population of Kenya living in this region, *matatus* are widespread and most minor roads have services. Many also run on bus routes at approximately the same fare, but to even less predictable schedules.

Planes
From **Kisumu** to:
Nairobi, scheduled daily services on *Kenya Airways*. One to three flights daily (65min). Economy class fare Ksh1120.
From **Eldoret** to:
Nairobi, scheduled Tues and Fri service at 8.15am and 5pm on *Air Kenya Aviation* (75 min). Economy class fare Ksh1840.

Ferries
Kenyan lakeshore services see box on p.179.
Kisumu to Uganda service (*MV Uhuru*):
Wed d. Kisumu
Kisumu to Tanzania service (liable to suspension: enquire at the port):
Thurs d. Mwanza 2pm
　　　a. Musoma 10pm
Fri　a. Kisumu 2pm
　　　d. Kisumu 6pm
Sat　a. Musoma 7am
　　　d. Musoma 9am
　　　a. Mwanza 5pm
There are four classes; 1st, upper 2nd, lower 2nd (sitting only) and 3rd class. All cabins (including1st class) are single sex only unless married couples make a special request.

TELEPHONE AREA CODES		
Bungoma ☎0337	Kakamega ☎0331	Kisii ☎0381
Eldoret ☎0321	Kapsabet ☎03251	Kisumu ☎035
Homa Bay ☎0385	Kericho ☎0361	Kitale ☎0325

CHAPTER FIVE

THE MOMBASA ROAD AND MAJOR GAME PARKS

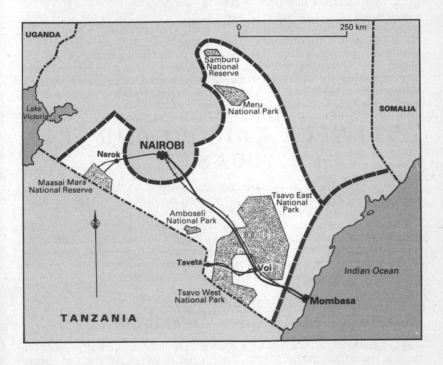

This chapter can't really be said to deal with a region. It covers the well-travelled **route from Nairobi to Mombasa** and a number of detours off it, along with five of the country's **major game parks**, all within reasonably easy reach of the capital.

The **Mombasa Highway** is Kenya's most important, though in many ways least interesting thoroughfare. The scenic interest is marginal for much of the journey and the temptation is to head straight for the coast, stopping only at the **Amboseli** or **Tsavo game parks**. But if you have time enough and the inclination to get off the main road, there are further rewarding diversions: east into **Akamba country** and the towns of **Machakos** and **Kitui**, or south towards the base of **Kilimanjaro** (which lies across the border in Tanzania) and the **Taita Hills**. Despite the trail of zebra-striped *kombi* vans towards the parks and coast, these are side roads not greatly explored.

The game parks in this chapter are, together with the Mombasa coast, the most visited parts of Kenya – and the archetypal image. This is not to take anything away from their appeal. If you travel around Kenya, it would be absurd not to visit at least one of them, for the experience is genuinely fabulous. In the 25,000 square kilometres (10,000 square miles) covered by the five parks, animals, not humans, hold sway. Their seasonal movements, most spectacularly in Maasai Mara's wildebeest migration, are the dominant plots in the drama going on all around. It's not difficult to see the wildlife but it does require patience and an element of luck that makes it exciting – and addictive.

Summaries of their individual attractions and access details to the game parks are given in the introduction on p.230. **To visit**, most people either **rent a vehicle** or join some sort of **organised safari**; sensible if expensive options, if you want to have more than a few days of wildlife viewing. With a limited budget, it is also possible, though by no means easy, to explore the parks under your own steam, **camping** at designated sites and **hitching** around with whoever you meet. More specific details are included in the sections on each park.

BETWEEN NAIROBI AND THE COAST

If you take one of the **express buses** down from Nairobi to Mombasa, you might think there's nothing worth stopping for along the way. If you take the **night train**, you won't see anything anyway.

With a little imagination and, ideally, a hired car (which will enable you to drive into and out of Tsavo National Park – see p.233,237 – at will), this stretch of the country has a great deal to offer. And any detour into the less well-known parts of **Akamba territory** or down to **Taveta** and **Kilimanjaro** should prove a worthwhile antidote to the more purple-rinse excesses of safari-land.

Machakos and Kitui – "Ukambani"

A good way to start a trip coastwards if you're in no hurry is an excursion into the heart of **Ukambani**: the land of the Akamba people. Buses, *matatus* and *Peugeot* taxis leave Nairobi's country bus station for MACHAKOS all the time, and you can be there in not much more than half an hour. At least one company also does a daily Nairobi–Mombasa service by way of the town.

Machakos

The *IBEA'S* first up-country post, established in 1889, **MACHAKOS** is ten years older than Nairobi and is a striking indication of the capital's rapid growth. "Machakos" is really a corruption of *Masaku's*, after the headquarters of a Kamba chief of the time. The name is still seen all over town.

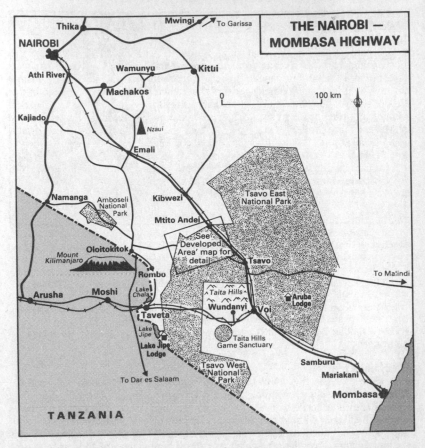

THE NAIROBI —
MOMBASA HIGHWAY

Distinctly friendly, and overwhelmingly Akamba, the town has a backdrop of green hills and a tree-shaded, relaxed atmosphere to its old buildings that is quickly endearing. The surrounding Mua Hills have lent their name to a brand of jam from the orchards which thrive on them. Sisal **basket (vyondo) weaving** is a more visible industry, though, and a major occupation for many women, either full-time or behind the vegetable stand. Machakos effervesces and it's a great place to stay for a day or two, especially on Monday and Friday, market days, and above all if you are into buying some *vyondo* (baskets). Look for (though you can scarcely miss) the truly splendid and quite venerable **mosque**.

Bed and board in Machakos

The town is rarely visited by tourists but **accommodation** and meals are easy.

Kafoca Club (Kenya Armed Forces Canteen, PO Box 695; ☎21933). Despite the uninspiring name, this is the best-run place, fairly wholesome, with its bar and TV-video lounge and a good restaurant which does filling fried platters. It's mostly a businessmen's hangout (Ksh90/120).

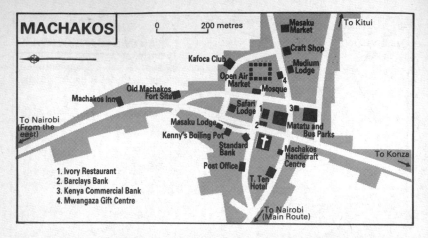

MACHAKOS

0   200 metres

To Kitui

Masaku Market
Craft Shop
Kafoca Club
Medium Lodge
Open Air Market   4
Mosque
Old Machakos Fort Site
Machakos Inn
Safari Lodge   1   3
To Nairobi (From the east)
Masaku Lodge   2   Matatu and Bus Parks
Kenny's Boiling Pot
Standard Bank
Machakos Handicraft Centre
To Konza
Post Office
T. Ten Hotel
To Nairobi (Main Route)

1. Ivory Restaurant
2. Barclays Bank
3. Kenya Commercial Bank
4. Mwangaza Gift Centre

Machakos Inn, ten minutes from the town centre. This is somewhat earthier and a good place to camp (Ksh40), with *bandas* set on a wooded slope (Ksh60/120).

T.Ten, Safari and **Masaku Motel** (PO Box 274, ☎21745) are all basic (Ksh60/120).

Five Hills Lodge, a newer place outside town on the Kitui road, is promising (PO Box 1141, ☎21482, Ksh200/300 s/c).

Ivory Restaurant is highly recommended. The menu is not unusual – chips with everything – but the chips are delicious and come with a special relish.

Kenny's Boiling Pot. Fun, with a balcony overlooking the street: at home, it would probably be a wine bar.

Machakos crafts

For **vyondo**, visit the *Machakos Handicrafts Centre* (PO Box 424, ☎21439 Machakos), a self-help women's group working in a small shop full of finished and half-finished baskets, piles of sisal, and leather straps. The finished articles are much cheaper without the strap (buy lengths of sisal braid and fit your own), and there are reductions if you want to buy several. The choice of colours here is second to none. If you like the genre, it's worth buying several and posting home a parcel. In connection, the Machakos branch of the women's *Maendeleo ya Wanawake Organisation* can be contacted at PO Box 904, Machakos ☎21600.

The *Mwangaza Gift Centre* deserves a look, too: they have some splendid wood and goatskin **drums** – the kind of thing often seen used as tables in hotel lobbies – but volume restrictions may prevent you from sending the large ones home, even if their price, and sometimes their timbre, make them irresistible. More resistible are the East African clothes-moths they often harbour – which later hatch in suitably heated living rooms – and the possibility of catching anthrax from them. Be warned that customs officers tend to impound such items on arrival. Another craft shop by the market is the cheapest of all, but their stock seems limited.

On to Kitui

Buses and *matatus* ply this route: the road passes through some attractive scenery, particularly as you wind down the hill out of Machakos, where high cliffs and chunky, maize-covered hills rise everywhere. WAMUNYU, en route, was the birthplace of the modern **Kamba carving** industry, evidence of which seems to be absent from Machakos. Akamba men who served in World War I were introduced to the techniques of wood sculpture by the Makonde ebony carvers on the Tanganyikan coast. Today, the vast majority of carvings in Kenya are produced by Akamba artists, often in workshops far from Ukambani. It's a disappointment that the serried ranks of identical antelopes and rhinos don't do justice to the tradition, even if it is a short one.

THE AKAMBA

The largely dry stretch of central Kenya from Nairobi to Tsavo Park and north as far as Meru has been the traditional homeland of the **Akamba people** (the plural is properly *Wakamba*) for at least the last five centuries. They moved here from the south in a series of vague migrations, in search, according to legend, of the life-saving baobab tree whose fruit staved off the worst famines.

With a diverse economy in better years, including mixed farming and herding as well as hunting and gathering, the Akamba slowly coalesced into a distinct tribe with one Bantu language. As they settled in the hilly parts, the population increased. But drier areas at lower altitudes couldn't sustain the expansion, so **trade** for food with the Kikuyu peoples in the fatter Highlands region became a solution to the vagaries of their generally implacable environment.

In return for farm produce, the Akamba **bartered** their own manufactured goods: medicinal charms, extra strong beer, honey, iron tools, arrowheads and a lethal and much sought-after hunting poison. In the eighteenth and nineteenth centuries, as the Swahili on the coast strengthened their ties inland, **ivory** became the most important commodity in the trade network. With it, the Akamba obtained goods from overseas to exchange for food stocks with the Highlands tribes.

Long the **intermediaries** between coast and up-country, acting as guides to Swahili and Arab caravans, leading their own expeditions and settling in small numbers in many parts of what is now East Africa. Their broad cultural base and lack of provincialism made them confident travellers and employees, and willing **soldiers and porters**. Even today, the Kenyan army has a disproportionately high Akamba contingent, while many others work as policemen and private *askaris*.

In the early years of **colonialism**, the Akamba were involved in occasional bloody incidents, but these seem to have been more often the result of misunderstandings than anything concerted. The most famous of these blew up after an ignorant official at Machakos cut down a sacred *ithembo* tree to use as a flagpole. On the whole, the Akamba's old trade links helped to ease their relations with the British. Living – and dying – with British soldiers during **World War I** gave them insights into the ways of the Europeans who now ruled them. Together with the Luo and Kikuyu, the Akamba suffered tens of thousands of casualties in these white men's wars.

Akamba **resistance to colonialism** was widespread but mostly non-violent. As early as 1911, however, a movement of total European rejection had emerged. Led by a widow named Siotune wa Kathuke, it channelled opposition to colonialism into frenetic dancing, during which teenage girls became "possessed" by an anti-European spirit and preached radical messages of non-compliance with the government. Later, in the 1930s, the *Ukamba Members Association* (one of whose leaders was **Muindi Mbingu**) was formed in order to pre-empt efforts to settle Europeans in Ukambani and reduce Akamba cattle herds by compulsory purchase. Five thousand Akamba marched in peaceful protest to Kariakor market in Nairobi – a show of collective political will that succeeded in getting their cattle returned.

Kitui town

KITUI was badly hit by the lack of rains in 1984. Children suffered from malnutrition and there were outbreaks of cholera. Despite its proximity to Nairobi, this region at the very edge of the Highlands is one of Kenya's least developed. The town is small and hasn't any outstanding features of interest, but there's a sizeable Swahili population, descendants of the traders and travellers who crisscrossed Ukambani in the nineteenth century. The town's mango trees were planted then, and the abundance of lodging houses is a reminder of the trading tradition.

Kitui was the home village of **Kivoi**, the most celebrated Akamba trader. He commanded a large following which included slaves, and it was he who met the German missionary Krapf in Mombasa and guided him back to Kitui in 1849, where the European was the first to set eyes on Mount Kenya.

Practicalities

The best places to **stay** are the *Kithomboani Hotel* (Ksh80/cube) and the newish *Gold Spot Motel* (Ksh80/double bed, Ksh100 s/c). The *Riverside Motel* on the way into town is unexceptional (Ksh80/100). A row of cheap **eateries** backs on to the Swahili quarter; a good find was *Ramrook's Place* – clean, friendly and reasonable.

Akamba, the main **bus service**, has departures to Nairobi three times daily and a night bus which calls at around 7pm on its way to Mombasa. *Mbuni* has some cheap fares (twice a day to Mombasa). Getting up to EMBU (p.130) can be a problem; public transport is scarce on this route, but short *matatu* hops, or hitching, are possible. The road to Embu via Kangonde is newly tarred, scenically dreary.

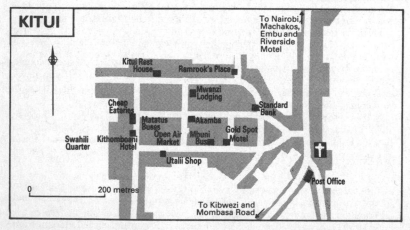

The Mombasa Highway

It's ironic that in a country overflowing with scenic beauty, the most important **highway** passes through so much monotonous landscape – not for nothing is a desolate stretch called the Taru desert. Again, the appearance of the bush depends partly on the time of year. After rains, the plains may be bursting with colour: during May and June they can be carpeted in white and blue convolvulus flowers.

This section does not cover the Amboseli or Tsavo national parks – see p.232–44.

If you travel down by bus, it's best to sit on the right of the vehicle, which gives you the best of the scenery and from which vantage you may, in clear conditions, see **Kilimanjaro**, between SULTAN HAMUD and *Hunter's Lodge*, and again south of TSAVO station. It's worth knowing there was a scare in 1989/90 about strange, bus-riding **thieves** on this route, offering their victims drugged food and drink and then melting away with their possessions while they slept. Similar rumours emanate from Colombia and Indonesia. If it happens to you, perhaps you'd write and tell us all about it.

Whichever time of year you travel down it, there are reasons to stop and detour along the Nairobi–Mombasa highway, at least if you have the luxury of your own transport and pace. But if you do drive this route yourself, **be careful**. It's fast and dangerous and road-users frequently encounter each other with deadly impact. Also be sure to drive with a full fuel tank. **Petrol stations** appear fairly regularly at the settlements between Nairobi and VOI, but supplies thereafter are not guaranteed until MARIAKANI, 120km further on, just 32km inland from Mombasa.

Nzaui

Half an hour before *Hunter's Lodge* at EMALI, a road heads off south for AMBOSELI and another turn leads north back into the Machakos Hills and the dramatic **peak of Nzaui**.

Enthusiastic reports have been received from hikers who have climbed this steep pinnacle. Without transport, you'll need a *matatu* ride from the Emali crossroads to MATILIKU, some 15km from the main road. Nzaui rears up ahead. With luck, you'll find some school-children to guide you up – it's a popular local trip. From the top of the 500-metre precipices on the south face there are sweeping views across the Kamba and Maasai plains to Mount Kilimanjaro. If you have a vehicle, there's also a lazy way up Nzaui from the north, approached from the village of NZIU, further along the same road.

NIGHT STOPS NOT FAR FROM NAIROBI

Two **overnight stops**, perhaps most useful if you're coming from Mombasa and don't fancy arriving back in Nairobi late at night.

Small World Country Club (PO Box 78, ☎239 Athi River, Ksh300/400), 37km from Nairobi, is the closest: a restaurant and motel with a racy reputation and "Traditional Dancing", open 24 hours.

Hunter's Lodge (PO Box 77 Makindu, ☎2021 Radiocall Nairobi), 160km from Nairobi. Southeast of where the road drops off the highlands, past the Machakos junction, and the Sultan Hamud junction for Amboseli, it sweeps down to **Emali**, with **Nzaui Mountain** on the left and, 30km further, *Hunter's Lodge*. This promises a lot as a place to stay, with its acacia-backed garden on the banks of the dammed **Kiboko** (Hippo) stream, peacocks, a swimming pool, peace and quiet. Rooms aren't wildly expensive (Ksh450/700), but still nothing special for the money, and the food is quite ordinary, too. But if you've just climbed Nzaui, it might seem like paradise at twice the price. Ask nicely and they'll probably allow you to camp.

Makindu

Back on the main highway, twenty minutes east of *Hunter's Lodge*, you pass the ostentatious Sikh Temple at **MAKINDU**, strung with what look like Christmas lights, and prettily unmistakable. They give a warm welcome here to travellers who want to stay, on the usual understanding. Thirteen kilometres further is the **Makindu Handicrafts Cooperative**, which has blossomed in recent years to provide work for almost fifty active members. Fifteen percent of the take goes to run the place and buy wood; the remainder is divided equally among the carvers. You can watch and photograph members at work, though it has to be said many of their carvings are fairly obnoxious, with "Maasai maidens" and similar panderings more and more prominent. Still, they know their market and the set-up obviously suits the co-op members. There are some nice pieces among the tour bus fodder, but for my money, the rejects outside the shop are better value and have more character than the polished creations inside.

Kibwezi – soursops and honey

KIBWEZI is a small Akamba trading centre off the main road at the KITUI junction. There are one or two B&Ls. The best and cleanest rooms, at the *Riverside Lodge*, come with mosquito coils, towel, soap and oil lamp (still no electricity in town) all for Ksh50 per person. The *Riverside* also runs the *New Face* hoteli, which offers good food and fantastic murals ("Hi, How are You? Not Bad. Let's have one at the NEW FACE"). Kibwezi also boasts a small **market** where you can often buy spiky green **soursops**, one of those fruits you either love or loathe. Along this stretch of the main road you'll probably also see **honey** sellers. When it's good, the honey is delicious, but try it before buying. Local custom varies – the art of beekeeping is a Kamba speciality – but the honey is best when the bees haven't been smoked out, as this taints it. Bottom price is about Ksh40 for a wine-bottle full.

Mtito Andei to Tsavo: vultures and man-eaters

The big sprawl of petrol stations and snackeries at the beginning of **Tsavo park** is somehow very Las Vegas out here in the dry country; it marks **MTITO ANDEI** (Vulture Forest), a town surrounded by stands of baobab trees. The *Tsavo Inn* here (☎18 Mtito Andei) is a pleasant retreat, and a moderately upmarket one (though it was recently closed for some time pending renovations) with a tempting pool. Camping, unfortunately, is out of the question, but you can walk from here to camp at the Tsavo West park gate (see p.233). If you want a lodging in town, try the *Okay Safari Lodge*, which is also okay for a cold beer or three. A vehicle breakdown, if you're unfortunate enough to suffer one, is best taken to the Mkamba mechanic next to the Esso station. A few words of Kikamba here work wonders (good evening – *watindata*; response – *nehsa*).

Between Mtito Andei and VOI, the only place to get anything to eat is the *Maneaters' Motel*, merely a snack bar and filling station. The most satisfied customers are clearly the baboons. The motel is right by the gulch of the Tsavo River (*Tsavo* is Kamba for "slaughter"), in the vicinity of the famous **man-eating lions** that played havoc with the building of the railway in 1898. The two lions seem to have been almost supernaturally lucky, since they eluded Colonel

Patterson's various weapons for nearly a year and ate 28 Indian labourers in that time. The *Field Museum* in Chicago has the two man-eaters stuffed and on display. Lions you won't see any more and need not fear, but along this section of the road through Tsavo Park you may well come across **elephants**. Always a brick-red colour from the soil, they used to be one of the commonest animals on the road. The latest research findings suggest further that Tsavo's 3000–4000 surviving elephants are seeking public – touristy – places where the poachers, who hide deep in the bush, can't get at them.

THE RAILWAY STATIONS

If you're desperate for water or a place to crash, the lonely little **railway stations** dotted every 15km or so along the line are usually amenable. Station masters are often helpful and glad of a break in routine – the trains don't exactly fill their days. If you're doing something uncommon like walking or cycling down to the coast (people have done so), the stations are oases.

Voi – and onwards

The only sizeable town on the road is **VOI**. It's a place you'd probably only want to stay if you were heading **into Tsavo East park** or the Taita Hills and Taveta, though if you are, it does possess several excellent **lodgings**.

Sagala View Lodge (PO Box 123, ☎2267). The most congenial, with ambitious plans beyond the B&L level and breezy upstairs rooms (Ksh200/300–550,B&B s/c).

Vuria Lodging (PO Box 29, ☎2269, Ksh70/140 with fans, mosquito nets and real toilets) is also recommended.

H.A.M's Guest House An offspring of the *Mwasungia Scenery Guest House* in Wundanyi (see p.227) and equally charming, but be careful of the electric wiring (Ksh80 per bed).

Hawaii, **Maendeleo** and **My Lodge** are all fine, too: the unappetising apparition of a man skinning a cow's head in the front yard isn't indicative of anything.

If you have time to kill at Voi, check out the **sisal factory**. You can watch the whole simple process from the crushing of the sisal spikes, through drying and combing, to the final twisting into rope.

Voi transport details

Moving on, the **train** to Mombasa pulls into Voi about 3am, the one to Nairobi at midnight. Trains to TAVETA, with connections through to **Tanzania**, leave only on Wednesday and Saturday, the market days (5am). **Buses** come in all day, mornings for Nairobi and afternoons for the coast; there are three country buses to Taveta each day, one of which continues past Lake Chala to OLOITOKITOK, 30km from Amboseli. WUNDANYI in the Taita Hills has no bus service (perhaps it's too steep) but frequent *matatus* go up there. For rides into Tsavo East, see p.237. For Taveta and the Taita Hills, see below.

The Taru Desert

After Voi, the road veers across the relentless **Taru desert**, a plateau of "wait-a-bit" thorn and occasional baobabs. The next place with food (but not much, and no petrol) is MACKINNON ROAD, distinguished by its Sayyid Baghali Shah Pir

Padree Mosque, right by the railway track. Past SAMBURU ("butterfly" in Maa; again no fuel supplies) the country is peopled mostly by members of the **Mijikenda** group, though their distinctive, droopy, thatched cottages are often replaced nowadays by more formal square ones, increasingly also whitewashed and tin-roofed in the coastal manner. The Duruma Mijikenda of this district herd cattle and grow a little sisal: there's little else they can do in such a dry region. MAJI YA CHUMVI ("salty water"), MARIAKANI ("place of the *Mariaka*", the Kamba arrows used in nineteenth-century wars against the Maasai), and Mazeras bring you closer into the coastal domain.

MAZERAS is a largely Duruma village and here **the coast** really takes over. The landscape has a quite different cast: mango trees, the lush cultivation of bananas and cassava, and (encouragement for weary travellers) the sublime sight of endless stands of **coconut palms**. For details on the route **along the ridge to the north** of Mazeras, see p.290. The main road plunges with a certain abandon down the steep scarp to the Indian Ocean.

The Taita Hills

A good option, if efforts to hitch into Tsavo prove fruitless, is to head off **west from Voi to Taveta**, a very accessible but largely unvisited region. Apart from being a route into Tanzania, the **Taveta road** has some interesting possibilities to the north and south, while for much of the time the magnificent mass of Kilimanjaro looms on the horizon.

Taita Hills Game Sanctuary

The only place attracting much tourist traffic down here is the **Taita Hills Game Sanctuary** – run by the *Hilton* chain with two of their hotels acting as bait (both plain PO Bura, ☎44 Mwatate, bookable through Hilton Reservations, PO Box 30624 Nairobi, ☎334000). The private, 110-square kilometre reserve, not actually in the hills, but south of them in a hillocky, bosky landscape, is past BURA on the south side of the road. There is virtually no chance of getting a lift into the sanctuary itself, though you could walk the half kilometre to the first hotel, *Taita Hills Lodge*, just outside, if you felt like a *Hilton* meal (Ksh330 for lunch, Ksh3070/3625 FB)). Having used the lodge facilities, you're entitled to free entry to the sanctuary (otherwise usual park fees apply), but even if you have a car this may not be worth it. Its reputation is a little overblown and, at certain times of year, the sanctuary can be virtually devoid of wildlife. Its small size is also against it – you can drive around it in an hour.

On the southern side, *Salt Lick Lodge* has to take the prize for the most bizarre **hotel architecture** in Kenya: from a distance it looks like a clump of mushrooms sprouting from the swamp. Each of its rooms is a turret on stilts, all of them linked by mock suspension bridges and there's even a drawbridge at the lobby. This camp ensemble is supposedly in keeping with the area's **World War I** battle history; most of the important Anglo-German engagements in East Africa were fought on these plains – a fact which isn't likely to divert your attention long from the price of the place (around Ksh4365/5575 FB). *Salt Lick Lodge* does, however, provide waterhole game-viewing (during the drier parts of the year) to rival the "Tree Hotels" of the Central Highlands.

THRUSH UNDER THREAT

Keen ornithologists head for the Taita Hills in search of *Turdus helleri*, the **Taita olive thrush**. This robin-like bird, the size of a European thrush, has a close relative in the ordinary olive thrush of the highlands: olive brown on top, red-breasted, red-billed. The Taita *Turdus* is distinguished by its much darker head and the fact that it appears to live only in the Taita Hills above 1600m – which gives it all of four square kilometres (1000 acres) of potential habitat. As it depends on virgin forest for its survival, the Taita olive thrush is a very rare bird indeed, and may possibly be extinct. Two or three were seen at Mbololo in 1953, and eight in the Ngangao forest in 1965. It may also survive on Ngangai. It has a bold, liquid warbling song. Good luck with the binoculars.

Wundanyi

To get a glimpse of the less ephemeral **history** of this region, go up into the **Taita Hills**. *Matatus* pitch through the fertile chasms on a switchback road to the little district capital of **WUNDANYI**. After the sultry, dry plains, you're transported into another world. The hills are amazingly precipitous and beautiful, striped with cliffs, waterfalls and dense cultivation, and highly populated. Near the peaks are patches of thick forest. There's notable prosperity up here, and a strong sense of community. Most of the people speak the Taita language, one of the coastal Bantu family related to Swahili and Mijikenda.

Wundanyi practicalities

Wundanyi's best **accommodation** is 2km out of town at the *Mwasungia Scenery Guest House*. This is a country B&L and well known throughout the hills (Ksh70/140). There's a choice of good **places to eat** in town; the *New Wundanyi Motel* is particularly recommended for tasty meals, a lively atmosphere – especially emanating from the bar – and music from an expensive-looking sound system. Big **market days** in Wundanyi are Tuesday and Friday.

Taita traditions

The Taita are welcoming and Wundanyi an attractive and enjoyable centre; the conifer trees and a genuine babbling brook running past the football field reinforce the feeling of departure from the thornbush and scrub below. This sense of suspended reality is accentuated by the **cave of skulls** outside the town, one of many ancestor shrines in the hills. Ask someone to show you the way: it's halfway to the *Mwasungia Scenery Guest House*, hidden in a banana grove just below the road. In the niche rest the skulls of 32 Taita ancestors, exhumed from their graves. The cave was a traditional advice centre where life's perplexities were resolved by consultation with the dead. Christianity has eroded some of the reverence that the Taita once had for these shrines, but the niches are left undisturbed nonetheless.

Taveta and Lakes Chala and Jipe

From the Taita Hills, the **road to Taveta** soon jumps off the tarmac and you follow the railway branch line through the southern arm of TSAVO WEST, mostly in a cloud of brilliant red dust. A number of maps mark a *Murka Lodge* along here, but it has been closed for years and Taveta is the first, and only, place worth stopping at. Still, you're almost certain to see some game on these plains, especially in the rainy season.

Taveta

Somewhat off the beaten track, **TAVETA** is situated in the rural corridor between the Tanzanian border and Tsavo West National Park. Despite its strategic significance, electricity has only just arrived and the bank near the border post is open on Monday and Friday only (and can't be relied on to change money if you've just arrived from Tanzania). The town has a mixed population of Taveta, Taita, Maasai, Akamba, Kikuyu and Luo, with strong hints of coastal influence.

The best **B&Ls** seem to be at the end of the main street, which runs to the right (north) on the other side of the level crossing as you enter the town. They are *Kuwoka Lodging House* (PO Box 51, ☎228; Ksh100/150) and *Green View Utamaduni Guest House* (much the same, making it better value at Ksh80/120), both clean, bright, and noisy, and featuring magnificent, gaudy murals in the front restaurants. The best places to eat in town, however, are the *Taveta Hotel*, between the *Green View* and the bus station, and a couple of restaurants near the bank: the *Taveta Border Hotel* (good samosas and chips) and a nameless *hoteli*, known as *Better Food For More People*, which is what it says on the wall outside. They do a mean chicken stew here. The local banana stew is also popular, though you might balk at eating eight bananas in one sitting – even if they're smothered with gravy.

To **explore the Taveta region** without wheels of your own, you'll have to rely on infrequent *matatus* and the occasional private vehicle. On market days (Wed and Sat) there's a 2pm train to VOI and more public transport.

If you are leaving Kenya at Taveta, note that there is a longer walk than you might expect to the Tanzanian side of the frontier – allow at least an hour.

Lake Chala

Transport isn't such a problem to **Lake Chala**, but you could, if necessary, walk most of the 20km there and back, and there's at least one bus a day up to Oloitokitok. A four-square kilometre crater lake north of Taveta, Chala has one shore in Kenya and the other in Tanzania. In fact, it is right by the road to Amboseli, exactly 8km from the junction outside Taveta and just a ten-minute walk up the slope. Subtly hidden in its crater, however, it is easily missed.

The lake is a deep and unbelievably transparent blue. It once had a population of harmless dwarf crocodiles (imported from Madagascar by Ewart Grogan, see below), but they are rare now and it's inhabited only by mythical monsters and paddled over by a few fishermen in dugouts. You can **camp** in a number of places on the rim and scramble easily down to the water, which is bilharzia-free. When Kilimanjaro is visible behind it, it's an exceptionally lovely scene and well worth the slight effort of getting there; you need to take supplies if you're going to stay the night. (Watch out for the luminous/psychedelic pink snake that a number of people have reported seeing inside the crater wall, on the way down to the water's edge. Although allegedly harmless, its attitude is convincingly aggressive.)

Lake Jipe

Equally interesting and totally different is **Lake Jipe**. Again, only half is in Kenya, fed by Kilimanjaro's snowmelt at its northern end as well as by streams flowing to the south from the Pare Mountains across the border. The Kenyan shore is flat and thickly carpeted in reed beds. Several villages at the northern end make a living from fishing, while Jipe's southeast shore lies inside Tsavo West National Park.

There are a number of paths down to the lakeshore from the Taveta-Voi road and finding the right one can be a problem if you're **driving**. Ask the way before leaving Taveta. The easiest is to turn right roughly 10km east of the town where a rusty and almost illegible circular sign reads "Jipe Sisal Estate". Twenty-five kilometres down this track, you reach an obscure gate for Tsavo West park, right on the lakeshore.

The only **public transport** to the lake ties in with market days in Taveta, Wednesday and Saturday. This, the *Black Rhino* bus, leaves Taveta at 6am and 3pm and returns from Jipe at 7.30am and 4.30pm. Get a place on board an hour before. Another market day alternative is to run into the *Lake Jipe Lodge* minibus buying produce in town. They are generally very helpful and will usually offer a lift down to the park gate and campsite. These vehicles apart, transport is rare indeed and your only option, and by no means an unpleasant one, would be to walk. The flat land **between the Voi road and Lake Jipe** is heavily planted under sisal, cotton fields, and even coconuts. There are also wide areas of low bush. It is an unusual part of Kenya, and rustling with bird and animal life. The *Macmillan* map, "Tsavo East and West National Parks", is a useful aid in the area.

On the lakeshore

At MUKWAJONI, the village 2km before the park gate, you'll find only the most basic provisions (apart from fish), so bring supplies from Taveta. You should be able to drink and eat at *Lake Jipe Lodge* if you don't mind relaxing budgetary controls. The lodge is new and reasonably good value relative to others (Ksh1920/3000 FB; bookings in Nairobi at PO Box 31097, Shariff House, Kimathi St, ☎227623).

There are simple *bandas* near the park gate as well as showers, toilets and **campsites**. The usual park fees are payable on arrival; there is an additional flat fee of Ksh50 per person, per night, wherever you stay. Tent or no tent, the *bandas* are recommended, as they offer shade, a place to keep food cool, and protection from some unbelievably vicious mosquitoes. Despite the attentions of these, this is a peaceful and rewarding spot, and a paradise for ornithologists. A **boat** is available to take you out on the lake for a couple of hours (Ksh80 per person). If you can persuade the ranger the outboard motor is working, you'll see more hippos and crocodiles, and of course you could cruise all the way around the lake. However, this involves accounting for the diesel fuel and issuing receipts which, when you agree to be paddled, are unnecessary.

When **exploring** the bush around the lakeshore and campsite early in the morning, beware of **hippos**. You should keep a sharp eye out, especially between the park gate and the village. A feasible target for a couple of hours' walk would be the two hills, *Vilima Viwili*, just outside the park boundary and about 2km east of the track.

Grogan's Castle

If you have wheels, **"Grogan's Castle"**, a white mansion on an isolated hill rising from the plain back near the main road, deserves a little detour. This extraordinary residence was built in the 1930s by Ewart Grogan, one of the most influential early colonists. His reputation was founded on a walk from the Cape to Cairo which he undertook in 1898, on a notorious public flogging he carried out on three of his servants (nearly killing one of them), and on his wealth: his gilt-edged reputation was such that Grogan was able to dictate terms to the governor before he even arrived in Kenya. At the peak of his prosperity, he owned over a quarter of a million hectares of land.

The "Castle" was evidently built as a kind of hacienda for the **sisal estates**. It is totally run-down these days – the only residents of the house are a large colony of rats – but it can be visited if you tip the *askari*. It's an enigmatic building, much of it stuck together with aircraft aluminium and tin roofs. There are two enormous circular living rooms with spectacular 360-degree views out towards Kilimanjaro and Lake Jipe. The huge bedrooms have mosquito-screened bed niches. On one of the landings an ostentatious cash cupboard is suitably positioned, presumably for the casual display of wealth to passing guests. It will probably end up one day as a casino or a nightclub. Judging by the comments in the visitors' book, there's no lack of interested buyers.

THE PARKS

The first realisation of where you are in these national parks – among real, uncaptured wildlife – is truly arresting. Which parks to visit can seem at first a pin-in-the-map decision: any and all of them can provide a store of amazing sight and sound impressions.

Amboseli and **Tsavo West** are the two most accessible, with ever-busy game lodges, well-worn trails, large numbers of tourists in the high seasons, and large, if brutally diminished, herds of elephant. Amboseli is perhaps least recommended of the popular parks, despite its position at the foot of Kilimanjaro: it is just too small and too well trodden. Tsavo, in contrast, is huge enough to escape company completely, except at **Mzima Springs**, for which it's worth being part of the crowd if necessary.

Maasai Mara has the most fabled reputation, with its horizons of wildlife on every side. Somewhat isolated in the west, it requires a specific visit, but it's well worth the effort (and perhaps the cost), especially during the yearly **wildebeest migration** between July and November. The Mara is also *the* place to see lions – lots of them – and, with the pounding Kenya's big pachyderms have taken from poachers in the last few years, one of the best places to see naturally constituted elephant herds.

Samburu and Meru, over on the far side of Mount Kenya, have different varieties of animals, such as northern species of giraffe, zebra, antelope and ostrich. **Samburu** – dry, thorny and split by the Ewaso Nyiro (Uaso Ngiro) River – is increasingly popular and noted for its **crocodiles** and **leopards**, albeit baited ones.

Meru, however, is perhaps the most beautiful Kenyan park, isolated, verdant and surprisingly unvisited.

Practical considerations

For some idea of their current **animal-viewing potential**, the order of enthusiasm in recent travellers' accounts places Samburu and Maasai Mara way out in front, Lake Nakuru (covered in Chapter Three) second, Amboseli and Tsavo third and fourth, and Meru last of all – though Meru's compensation is its wonderful quota of wilderness.

It's important, if you want to get as much as possible out of your visit, to have a detailed map of the park. These are often available in the park lodges or on the gates, but not always, and prices are higher than you'll pay in Nairobi. The best map for each park is mentioned in the brief details at the start of each park section.

When to visit

Climatically, the parks usually get two rainy seasons – brief in November or December, more earnest in April and May – but these can vary widely. In Maasai Mara, they merge together in one season from November to May. Meru also gets heavy rainfall, but it's more scattered. As a general rule, you will see more animals during the dry season when they are concentrated near water. After the rains break and fill the seasonal watering places, the game tends to disperse deep into the bush. Moreover, if your visit coincides with the rains, you may have to put up with some frustrating game drives, with mud and stranded vehicles. By way of compensation, in the low season (April 1–June 30 and, to a lesser extent, July 1–November 30) you'll save a fortune on bills at lodges and tented camps if your plans include such luxury accommodation. Most places reduce their tariffs by anything from a third to a half between April and June, with savings particularly spectacular for singles.

Driving

The parks in this chapter are open all year round. If you're **driving** during the rains, remember that none of the park roads are paved and unless you'd be content to keep to the main graded tracks, you will need a four-wheel drive vehicle: a night spent stuck in the mud in Maasai Mara isn't recommended. Some car hire companies will insist you have 4WD in any case. If you're driving a private vehicle – not a hired one – and can claim residence in Kenya, you can get a special six-month game park ticket which allows the car and passengers into any national park free. You can obtain this from the Parks Headquarters at Nairobi National Park main gate (information from the Wildlife Conservation and Management Department, PO Box 40241, Langata Rd, Nairobi, ☎501081). But note that this ticket does not apply to national reserves (Maasai Mara, Samburu), which are locally administered.

BABOONS: A WARNING

More serious than the occasional robbery in the parks is the continued, unstoppable damage done by those loutish hooligans, **baboons**. A locked vehicle might be safe, an unwatched tent certainly isn't. Insurance companies don't cover such contingencies.

Accommodation in the parks

Unless you have one already, consider hiring a **tent** in Nairobi (see "Nairobi directory"). Without one, Maasai Mara and Samburu are effectively off-limits for low budgets as there is no cheap *banda* accommodation at either. In any case, camping out adds to the adventure. If you're visiting the parks on a more comfortable budget and staying in **lodges** or **tented camps**, it would be wise to make **advance bookings**. Surprisingly, perhaps, such places are fairly few: Tsavo West has two, Tsavo East one, the Amboseli area five, the Samburu area five, Meru just one, and the Maasai Mara area a total of fifteen. There's a lot of pressure on beds during the peak seasons; even if your trip is delayed, a booking gives you an advantage, and you can usually phone or radio-call ahead if you're delayed or need to change your plans. Obviously if you book places in the same hotel group, these kinds of change are easier.

Animal-watching

As for **game-viewing**, it's a pursuit that soon loses its more self-conscious aspects, but it's greatly improved with a little background reading about the animals and at the very least some sort of identification guide on hand (see "Books" in *Contexts*). **Rangers** can usually be hired for the day: if you have room, someone with intimate local knowledge and a trained eye is a good companion. Knowing some Swahili animal names is a help (see p.41). Most of the lodges and tented or luxury *banda* camps have their own vehicles and run regular "game drives". These can be very worthwhile because the drivers usually know the animals and the area. Expect to pay Ksh300–500 for a two- or three-hour trip.

The usual pattern of visiting is three **"game drives"** a day, at dawn, mid-morning and late afternoon. In the middle of the day, the parks are usually left to the animals; you'll be told it's because they are all hiding. A more likely reason seems to be that the midday hours are a lousy time to take pictures. The animals are around, if sleepy, and if you can put up with the heat while most people are safely in the lodges, it can be a tranquil and satisfying time.

To see as much as possible, stop frequently to scan with **binoculars**, watch what the herds of antelope and other grazers are doing (a predator will usually be watched intently by them all), and talk to anyone you meet on your way. The best time of day is sunrise, when nocturnal animals are often still out and about and you might see that weird dictionary leader, the aardvark. Don't delay!

The Tsavo National Parks – East and West

Ksh220 per person, Ksh30 per car for each park; Ksh50 per night to camp (Wardens: Tsavo West, PO Box 71, Mtito Andei, ☎39 Mtito Andei; Tsavo East, PO Box 14 Voi, ☎2211 Voi); Maps – Macmillan Tsavo West and East National Parks at 1cm:4.2km (1988) or Survey of Kenya on separate sheets, Tsavo West SK78 and Tsavo East SK87, at 1cm:2.5km (1972).

Biggest by far of Kenyan national parks, and together one of the largest in the world, the combined areas of **Tsavo West** and **Tsavo East** sprawl across 21,000 square kilometres of dry bush country, an area the size of Wales or Massachusetts. Tsavo East is the larger portion, though all of it north of the Galana River is off-limits to the general public (write to the warden if you'd like to visit it), while south of the river the great triangle of flat wilderness with **Aruba Lodge** in the middle is not much visited. The popular part of Tsavo is a mere 1000-square kilometre **"developed area"** of **Tsavo West**, located between the Tsavo River and the Mombasa highway. Here, a combination of good access and facilities plus magnificent, well-watered volcanic and scarp landscapes attract tourists and, hopefully, animals in large numbers.

Tsavo West practical details: access and where to stay

If you are looking for a visit outside a safari tour and don't have your own car, Tsavo West is probably the easiest of the big parks to explore. From Nairobi, take a bus or hitch to MTITO ANDEI (Tsavo West park HQ and a service town for the lodges). The gate here is one of the busiest park gates in the country and your chances of getting a ride are good. If you get stuck, the rangers are usually helpful and will allow you either to camp at the site just inside, or accommodate you in a spare *banu* :. You may only be expected to pay park fees when you get a lift.

The dearth of low-budget **accommodation** – a problem that affects all the main parks to some degree – is also less of an obstacle in Tsavo West. There are six or more **campsites** dotted around the park, but the two most often used are those marked on our map: one just inside Kyulu Gate, with shower and toilet, which is conveniently close to *Kilaguni Lodge,* and the other inside the Mtito Andei Gate, where people have, in the past, been allowed to stay without their own vehicle. In addition, there are two well-equipped self-service **banda camps**, *Kitani* and *Ngulia Safari Camps*, located a few kilometres from the main **lodges**, where you can stay in considerable comfort. Bring plenty of dried food. Camping is usually Ksh50 per person and overnight stays in the double or triple *bandas* are Ksh238 per bed. The *bandas* include a kitchen, a bathroom with hot water, mosquito nets – the works. *Ngulia SC* (PO Box 42 Mtito Andei, ☎2002 Radiocall Nairobi) even has its own waterhole. Both camps are delightful places to stay, and popular with Kenyans: you might even strike up a friendship and get a lift around the park for some animal-spotting. These places both operate an irregular evening escort service for low-budget visitors who want to go to the lodges for dinner or a drink by the floodlit waterholes. Driving at night in the parks is not normally allowed. (Bookings for *Ngulia* and *Kitani* through *Let's Go Travel*, PO Box 60342 Nairobi, ☎340331).

Exploring the "developed area" of Tsavo West

Kilaguni and **Ngulia lodges** are expensive places to stay (Ksh2520/3240 FB at *Kilaguni*, a shade lower at *Ngulia*, both with large discounts from April to June). Sooner or later, whatever you do, you're bound to turn up at one or the other. And rightly so: a visit is rewarding enough just for the pleasure of sitting on the terrace with a cold beer and watching the enthralling circus going on a few yards away at the **waterholes**.

Elephants, almost orange from the dust, are Tsavo's recurring image, and they're practically resident at both lodges, drawn to *Ngulia* by the delicious top waterhole which is a sump for the lodge's laundry. A family of **leopards** has been causing a sensation here recently by showing up nightly for a meal of meat laid out on a table below the lodge. A large variety of **grazers**, such as gazelle, zebra, oryx, waterbuck and buffalo drift in and out of the picture all the time.

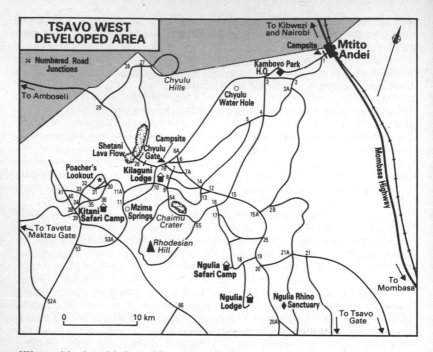

Kilaguni Lodge: birds and beasts at the bar

Kilaguni has a policy, in the high seasons, of herding casual visitors into a separate "visitor's centre", with its own bar, restaurant and information desks. Try to infiltrate the main reception area anyway, because the lodge has considerable wildlife assets in and around the bar, which is open to the panorama of the savannah and Chyulu Hills along one side. Dazzling **birds** hop everywhere, **hyrax** scamper between the tables, and **agama lizards** skim along the wall (the miniature orange and blue dragons are the males). In the grass below the terrace lives a colony of **dwarf mongooses,** while pompous **marabou storks** pace slowly up and down awaiting jettisoned bread from the dining room. At dusk, hundreds of **swallows** swoop back and forth over the drinkers to their nests in the roof; later, the **bats** take over the airways while **genets**, **jackals** and **hyenas** come for the meat scattered under the floodlights.

You can be sure that half the people in the hotel won't be paying any attention at all to this scene, but the incongruity of the whole place is brought home when dinner is called and the other half switches its attention as well.

Ngulia Lodge: ornithological highlight

The **bird enthusiasts** at *Ngulia* (PO Box 42 Mtito Andei, ☎2002 Radiocall Nairobi) in the autumn are far more earnest. The lodge is a stopover on the annual southern migration of hundreds of thousands of European birds. It seems to be situated on a narrow migration "corridor" but the reasons for its attraction for the birds – apart from its isolated lights – aren't really known. Ornithologists gather to band the birds that are trapped in mist nets, and their occasional recapture in places as far afield as Malawi, Iran and Germany slowly helps to build a picture of where the birds are moving. Perhaps not altogether surprisingly, few are ever caught at *Ngulia* again.

Mzima Springs

The biggest attraction in Tsavo West is **Mzima Springs**. This stream of crystal clear water was made famous by Alan Root's film which followed crocodiles and hippos in their underwater lives. Go very early to avoid the tour-bus atmosphere and you won't be disappointed. The luxuriant growth around the water reverberates noisily with birds and monkeys, and, with luck, some of the night's animal visitors may still be around.

There are **two large pools**, connected by a little rush of rapids and shaded by stands of date and raphia palms. The upper pool is the favoured **hippo** wallow, while the **crocodiles** have retreated to the broader expanse of water lower down. It's worth walking around this lower pool to the right where, if you're stealthy, you have a good chance of seeing them. Just make sure there's not one on the bank behind you. This word of caution applies equally to hippos, but they seem settled in their routine, content to snort and flounder at an irritating point just a little too far from the path for the visitors' satisfaction. At the side of the top pool, a circular underwater **viewing chamber** has been built at the end of a short pier. Unless you are exceptionally lucky, all you'll see is the underside of the clumps of floating papyrus and a blue swirl of perpetually revolving fish – for some reason always swimming anticlockwise.

Mzima's two **nature trails** (really tree trails) aren't of great interest unless you happen to be a botanist, but it is easy nevertheless to while away a couple of hours in the area. Try to sit for a while completely alone on the bank and you'll begin to piece together the ecological miracle of the place, as the animals and birds forget about your presence. This is where those pretentious, khaki safari outfits are actually practical.

Mzima Springs has a direct pipeline to Mombasa and is the source of most of the city's **drinking water**. Two hundred and fifty million litres of water per day gush out here, filtered to aquarium transparency by the lava of the **Chyulu range** to the north. This dark, unexplored, forested ridge creates its own rainfall: the porous rock absorbs the water like a sponge and gravity squeezes it into Mzima.

Plans were considered in 1952 to build a weir in order to raise the lower pool's level. This would have destroyed the river terrace however, and by ruining the hippos' "nursery", probably made them stop breeding. The National Parks trustees stepped in and effectively stalled development, summoning independent engineers to devise a way of taking water from beneath the lava, *above* the spring. There are one or two signs of the pipeline in the area but most are unobtrusive. Mzima has been left whole.

Lava flows

The **lava** that purifies Mzima's water can be seen in black outcrops all around this part of Tsavo. The **Shetani lava flow** is a spectacular example. Only 200 years old, the eruption that spewed it out must have been a cataclysmic event for local people and it is still the focus of stories about fire and evil spirits (*shetani* means "devil" in Swahili). There are **caves** here that despite one or two "warnings" are worthy of investigation. One of them even has a ladder and a trail of identification plaques by the bones of luckless animal victims who stumbled down. You do need a torch.

Chaimu lava flow is fun to walk over, but also a bit tricky. The lava is brittle, honeycombed and unstable, and very few plants have taken hold yet. It is possible to climb up to the volcano's crater rim, but this can be surprisingly hard work on the scree and shouldn't be attempted in the heat of the day. Be careful not to drop anything when walking (or hopping) over the lava chunks at the base of the volcano. I lost a lens cap – visible but irretrievable. And, when poking around Tsavo's caves and lava zones, you should be alert to the possibility of disturbing large **sleeping animals**. We stopped to investigate one cave and were just beginning to appreciate an unusual smell when a pair of hyenas bounded out and scampered off through the bushes. Remember, too, that Tsavo's lions have a reputation for ferocity. In the park, you should leave your vehicle at designated nature trails only, or where there's an obvious parking area. And beyond the national park boundaries you should stay on your guard – the animals aren't fenced in.

Seeking the animals

If you are eager to see particular species, *Kilaguni*'s **information centre** (usually open during the high season) should have up-to-date locations of **lion prides** and **cheetahs**, and possibly **leopard sightings**, too. But **touring around** the rest of Tsavo West is, for the most part, a question of following your inclinations.

The developed area is the hilliest sector of any of the five parks covered in this chapter, and there's an unending succession of fantastic views across volcanic plains, dotted with volcanic cones and streaked with forest at the water margins. When the animals are abundant – and their numbers fluctuate tremendously with the seasons – every turn in the track seems to bring you face to face with zebra, giraffe, huge herds of buffalo, casual prides of lions, or methodical, strolling elephants.

Among the more unusual animals to look for are the beautiful and shy **lesser kudu** antelope (always running away) and the **black rhinos**.

As recently as 1969, Tsavo had the biggest population of black rhinos in Africa – between 6000 and 9000 – and they were a common sight. By 1981, they had been poached to barely 100 individuals (the story is enlarged in the box overleaf, p.238).

The situation today has improved a little and you have some chance of seeing rhinos in Rhino Valley between *Ngulia* and *Kilaguni* (though most have been removed to the safety of the **Rhino Sanctuary** near Ngulia). The trip further on around the foot of **Rhodesian Hill** is recommended, too, and **Poacher's Lookout**, near *Kitani*, is a good place for a quiet scan with binoculars.

Tsavo East National Park

Across the highway, the railway and the apparent natural divide that separates Kenya's northern and southern environments, lies **Tsavo East**. Apart from some tumbled crags and scarps near Voi, this is an uninterrupted plain of flat bush, vast and empty, dotted with the crazed shapes of monstrous baobab trees. It is a forbiddingly enormous reserve and at times it can seem an odd folly. The northern sector – almost two-thirds of the park's area – is, due to continuing war against elephant and rhino poachers, the only part of Kenya strictly closed to the public.

Voi Gate and Voi Safari Lodge

Tsavo East has several **gates** (including Mtito Andei and Manyani) but the only one used much, and the one you should aim for if hitching, is at **VOI**, about 3km from the town. There's a peaceful and usually empty **campsite** just inside the gate where you can generally get permission to camp without a vehicle (it probably depends on how recently a lion was spotted there). Wooden cottages give some shade on their verandas; you can rent them if you want for Ksh50 per person, and get additional security and protection from baboons. There is running water. At the gate itself, there's a small educational centre (though the insects in the glass cases look as if they flew in and perished there), a short **nature trail**, plus a **staff canteen** with the usual warm beers, sodas, bread and dusty vegetables. The rangers at Voi Gate seem a helpful crowd, with sensible attitudes to lifts and hitching: you can go with them to *Voi Safari Lodge* on their 8pm staff bus (returns 3am). This lodge, a few kilometres away up the hill (Ksh1980/2640 FB; huge discounts April to June), is considerably more tranquil than its Tsavo West counterparts, with a magnificent savannah-scape plunging from the terrace to the horizon; cold drinks and nearly guaranteed game-viewing from the terrace. If you have any difficulty getting lifts into the park, you might check out the new *Lion Hill Safari Camp* – *bandas* and camping – to the left of the road between Voi and the gate.

Mtito Andei Gate and Tsavo Safari Camp

Tsavo East has another entrance at its own **Mtito Andei Gate**, but effectively this is only for access to the exclusive *Tsavo Safari Camp* for pre-booked visitors. The tented camp (bookable through *Kilimanjaro Safari Club*, PO Box 30139 Nairobi, ☎338888), is located on the other side of the Athi River – accessible only by dinghies – and you can do escorted game-viewing trips once there. It's a remote and peaceful place, with enthralling **birdlife**, and they even have a pool (around Ksh2800/3700 FB).There is no other way into the main body of Tsavo East until you get down to the **Manyani Gate** near Mudanda Rock (see p.238).

Aruba Lodge

The **best place to head for** is **Aruba Lodge**, a big, shady *banda* and campsite (PO Box 298 Voi, ☎2647 Voi; bookings in Nairobi, PO Box 14982, ☎720382). It's located by the **dam** of the same name, about 30km along the left bank of the seasonally meandering Voi River. The river's wooded margins often hide a profusion of wildlife: try the **Kanderi Swamp** at junctions 173 and 174; keep the windows up when driving through the tall grass and undergrowth. The *Aruba Lodge* vehicle goes into Voi on most days and, again, you should be able to get a ride if you're ready to relocate. *Aruba* has a shop with a few snacks, including beer, and they will put out bundles of firewood for you, but you really need to bring some food supplies into the park. Charges are the same as in Tsavo West – Ksh30 to camp and Ksh168 per person in the *bandas*. The dam lake gets visited by thousands of animals; nights can be noisy.

Tracking through the park

Tour groups don't often visit Tsavo East – indeed a number of Nairobi operators were recently acting as if the whole park was closed – allowing you the uninterrupted pleasure of exploring the wilderness, much of the time completely alone. Drive though Tsavo East around the park and you may find something special:

THE TSAVO POACHING WARS

Tsavo East was for a long time the contentious focus for **conservation issues**. The question of how to manage the **elephants** – or whether to manage them at all – is still the paramount one, in theory. The policy for years has been to hunt the **ivory poachers** and allow the elephants to reach a natural balance by starving themselves to a population their habitat could sustain. But the cycles of overpopulation and drought were too long for anyone to know if this was working out or not. Elephants, which are intelligent animals with complex kinship patterns (see box p.254), soon migrate to the increased security of national parks, often assembling in huge herds out of protective instinct.

Such questions have been submerged for several years by a gruesome crisis whose outcome may determine the elephants' very survival in Kenya. Tsavo's elephant population was over 17,000 in 1972. Today it has been poached to under 4000. Most of these survivors are young animals, poorly adjusted to the sophisticated culture of their species, with few adults to guide them. Taking account of only natural factors, orphaned infant calves are automatically doomed, while young elephants under ten years have only a fifty-fifty chance of surviving to maturity.

For a time in the early 1980s, it looked like the war against the poachers was being won. The late 1980s saw that complacency brutally shattered by an unprecedented **slaughter of elephants** in their thousands – mostly mature animals with large tusks, but including many with little ivory to offer. The poachers are no longer marginalised Akamba killing an occasional elephant with an old gun or poisoned arrows but a new breed of ivory-hunters, equipped with automatic weapons and the aim of wiping out a whole family group in a single attack.

In 1988, damning evidence emerged that the Somalian government, perhaps in collusion with Somali Kenyans and park-rangers-turned-poachers, were mounting a concerted assault on Tsavo's ivory, aiming to profit from the ten-fold increase in its value on the world market over the previous three years. Late in 1988, Somalia announced it would be exporting 8000 tusks of what it called "confiscated ivory", an incredible figure equivalent to Somalia's own entire elephant herd.

The Kenya Ministry of Tourism and Wildlife, concerned for the country's tourist image and allegedly covering up for some on its own payroll, reacted in a curiously defensive way, admitting to a tally far less than the reliable estimate of 1500 elephants killed in Tsavo in 1987–88. President Moi was said to be furious. In a style to which Kenyans are becoming increasingly accustomed, he personally ordered park rangers to shoot poachers on sight, then beefed up manpower and equipment in the Anti-Poaching Unit and deployed the paramilitary General Service Unit (or GSU, a force more commonly seen on the University campus) into the bush. Ethnic Somalis living near the boundaries of Tsavo East were summarily rounded up and trucked north to Wajir and Mandera, rekindling a bitter resentment which goes back a long way and has nothing to do with poaching.

As the news made the headlines in Kenya, some people started counting the casualties among the defending park staff, a number of whom were also killed in 1988. The spectacle unfolding – of a dirty war being fought on the plains among mutilated and unmovable elephant corpses, while the *kombi* vans followed each

it's easy to get away off the two or three beaten tracks. **Mudanda Rock** is particularly recommended at certain times of the year. Like a scaled-down version of Ayers Rock in Australia, it towers above a natural dam which, during the dry season, draws elephants in their hundreds.

other in search of the perfect picture, and tourists were advised to report seeing any poachers – was not a glamorous one.

As we go to press it's still too early to say if the elephants' slide to extinction in Kenya has really been halted. The 1989 international agreement on a five-year **ivory trade moratorium** had a remarkable effect on the numbers of elephant corpses being logged in Tsavo. Equally dramatic was the wholly unprecedented aggression with which the Kenyan parks authorities started carrying out their duties under the auspices of the bluntly pragmatic new Director of Wildlife and Conservation management, Richard Leakey, who obtained huge injections of cash and military equipment for the war. Individuals caught in the parks without authority are liable to be shot on sight, which has deterred even the most reckless poachers and raised another human rights cloud over the country. But successful or not, the difference between a flourishing population of elephants and one that has no future is hard to detect: the social structure of the herds in many districts has undoubtedly been mutilated, with many elders wiped out and too many inexperienced younger elephants unable to fend for themselves or to act in a properly mature, elephantine way.

The **black rhinos**, of course, are even further down this vicious path to near-annihilaton. Their estimated number in Kenya is about 500, that is one-eighth of the total population of the species, which remains under a serious and shocking threat of total extinction. More than 95 percent of Kenya's rhino population (most of them in Tsavo) was destroyed in the 1970s. The poaching business suddenly and dramatically escalated, when the hunters began buying automatic weapons to slaughter what are essentially quite vulnerable animals.

This escalation wasn't just the result of widespread hardship in the countryside. More significant was a radical expansion of the market for **rhino horns** – not, as is popularly supposed, in China (where minute quantities of powdered rhino horn are used for tonics and aphrodisiacs) but in the reclusive Arab country of Yemen. In North Yemen, oil money made the rhino horn dagger handle – traditionally the prerogative of the rich – suddenly within reach of thousands of Yemeni men. Many tons of horns were smuggled out of Mombasa in *dhows*. Bizarre connection, but those are the facts: *Run, Rhino, Run* by Esmond and Chryssee Bradley Martin (see "Books" in *Contexts*) follows the trail in extraordinary and depressing detail.

Yet the savage groundwork was laid long before. After World War II, the Makueni area southeast of Machakos was designated as a Wakamba resettlement area. The colonial Kenya Game Department sent in one J. A. Hunter to clear it of unwelcoming rhinos: he lived up to his name, shooting 1088 black rhinos over 50,000 acres. The Wakamba didn't take to the scheme and it fizzled out. Today, your chances of seeing black rhinos in Tsavo – or anywhere else where they are not virtually captive – are slim. They seem to exist mainly in the off-limits sector north of the Galana, where, with extinction in the air, the stakes have become terrifyingly high and there is continued armed conflict between poachers and the authorities.

At the brink of disaster, there are now concentrations of breeding black rhinos in a number of ranches and sanctuaries – notably at Nakuru, Solio, and to the north of Mount Kenya – and "saving the rhino" has become a national cause.

As recently as 1989/90, you were likely to get unforgettable glimpses of the absurd, mountainous carcasses of elephants. At the time of publication of this edition, the Anti-Poaching Unit had more or less ensured that the most you'll see are the bleached bones of a bad memory (see the "Tsavo Poaching Wars" box).

However, the desperate plight of the animals may not be immediately apparent. In a sad new twist, the elephants of Tsavo, keenly aware of the dangers they face in the bush, have taken to spending much of their time near the lodges and park roads where, shot by cameras, they are relatively safe. Herds of several hundred are not uncommon though. When you see them, you'll notice the scarcity of adults.

From Aruba, most people head up towards the **Galana River's** brown gully. There are several spots where you can park and scramble down to the sandy banks. And, while Lugard Falls seem hardly worth the naming, there are always dozens of **crocodiles** in the vicinity, extraordinarily hard to see until you get up close.

To the coast

Heading **coastwards** from Aruba, a track leads almost dead straight for 80km to the lonely Sala Gate on the banks of the Galana. *Crocodile Camp* is just outside. You can normally camp here for Ksh50, but be prepared to be directed across the airstrip and down to the river bank where camping is free – and without any facilities at all.

The thirty-odd crocs at the camp have German names and come when called, or so the predominantly *Deutschlander* tour groups who visit them are told: in fact, they emerge every evening at 7pm, German names or no. Lastly, you pass the *Galana Game Ranch*, a 6000-square kilometre private experiment in mixed cattle and game ranching and wildlife conservation. It's on the north side of the river, reached across a causeway, but was recently closed to the public by the government and its future status is unknown. Two or three hours' drive east is MALINDI.

Amboseli National Park

Ksh220, Ksh30 cars; Warden PO Box 18 Namanga, ☎2 Amboseli. Maps – Macmillan Amboseli at 1cm: 750m; Survey of Kenya SK87 at 1cm:500m (1975).

AMBOSELI is a small and very touristy park. It has obviously suffered from off-road driving and its climate makes it a bleak, shimmering plain most of the year. Scenically, however, it is totally redeemed by the stunning spectacle of **Kilimanjaro**, towering over it and (as in those clichéd safari photographs taken with telephoto lenses) appearing almost to fill the sky. Sunrise and sunset are the best times to see the mountain, especially during the rainy season when the air is much clearer. In the right light, the snowy massif, washed coral and orange, is devastatingly beautiful. Much of the time, like Mount Kenya, it's tantalisingly muffled behind thick cloud.

The erosion of the grasslands by circling *kombis* is fast destroying the park's purpose. In the dry season, most of the animals crowd into the impenetrable marshy areas and patches of acacia woodland where food plants are still available. During and shortly after the rains the picture is different, the animals more dispersed and the landscape greener. But if you have the luxury of choosing exactly which parks to visit, you might think of driving straight through Amboseli to Tsavo, or avoiding it altogether; the park certainly needs some breathing space if it's ever going to recover properly.

AMBOSELI'S HISTORY

The park has been getting smaller and smaller ever since it was created. It began as part of the Southern Maasai Reserve at the turn of the century. Tourism arrived in the 1940s and Amboseli Reserve was formed as a wildlife sanctuary. Unlike Nairobi and Tsavo National Parks, created at the same time and sparsely inhabited, Amboseli's **swamps** were used by the Maasai to water their herds and they saw no reason not to continue sharing the area with the wildlife and – if necessary – with the tourists. In 1961, the Maasai district council at Kajiado was given control of the area. But the combined destructive capacities of cattle and tourists began to tell in the 1960s; a rising water table in the following decade brought poisonous alkali to the surface and decimated huge tracts of acacia woodland. Kenyatta declared the 400-square kilometre zone around the swamps (the present day Amboseli) a **national park**, a status that utterly excluded the Maasai and their cattle. Infuriated, they all but exterminated the park's magnificent long-horned **black rhinos** over the next few years, seizing on Amboseli's tourist emblem with a vengeance. Not until a piped water supply was set up for the cattle did the Maasai finally give up the portion of land within Amboseli's boundaries. You can see their point. But the rhinos, as in so many other places, are now counted in ones and twos, and there are rarely more than a dozen in the park.

Arrivals: Nairobi to Namanga and Amboseli

The road is excellent most of the way (about four hours' drive from Nairobi) and rollingly scenic as well. Without your own transport, either take a bus down to NAMANGA from the country bus station, or get as far as ATHI RIVER on a *KBS* bus #109 or #110 and hitch from there. As usual, the best chances are with Kenyan weekenders.

Athi River

ATHI RIVER isn't interesting and pongs rather strongly from the *Kenya Meat Commission's* giant butchery, but if you get stuck hitching, the *Congress Club* (also known as *Studio 45*) is the local hot-spot and offers good self-contained **rooms** (Ksh150/250); couples can share a single, which seems to be the norm here. Food is theoretically available (probably *nyama choma*) and there's even live music at weekends. Athi River has a colonnaded colonial post office and a *Standard Bank* (open usual times).

Isinya and Kajiado

After a dull start through the Kapiti Plains, the roadside interest increases after **ISINYA**. Here, there's a **Maasai Leatherworking and Handicrafts Centre** (PO Box 24, Isinya). It is touristy, but you can find some unusual work among the beaded key-rings and "marriage necklaces". Check out the handmade shoes and massive, heavy leather bags. If your stomach is strong, you can visit the tannery, and they're happy to see you in the workshops, too. Donations from a church in Folkestone, England – of all places – help Isinya's community.

Further south, in the gentle hills where Maasai country really begins, are KAJIADO, the district capital on the Magadi railway line (see p.109) with a modernistic/Maasai-style post office, and BISSEL, where there's a roadside fruit and vegetable market each day. And, drawing close to the border – with the Tanzanian mountains a compelling lure – there are two large **tourist emporiums**, one not long before Namanga and the other in the town itself, at the big petrol station. Both are packed to overflowing with Maasai bead and leather work, as well as *Makonde* ebony carvings from southern Tanzania and, of course, Kamba animals and Kisii soapstone. They're not especially cheap but, depending on the volume of business, you can strike reasonable bargains and the choice is huge. Among all the trinketry are genuine used articles which tend to attract high prices. For these, you might do better by making offers to people you meet on the road. Bartering clothes or food often works to the benefit of both parties.

Namanga

NAMANGA sits square on the border, only 130km from ARUSHA in Tanzania. The petrol station, where the murram road leads off east to Amboseli, is probably the best place to try for a lift into the park, but if you're **staying in town**, *Namanga River Hotel* is the grandest establishment. A colonial oddity of wooden cabins set in pretty gardens, it was the halfway house on the old safari trail between Nairobi and Arusha. The era of baggy trousers and printed frocks seems just around the corner. The place has a likeable, slightly cranky atmosphere, and while it has seen better days, it's undeniably a good deal(around Ksh400/600 B&B s/c); you can also happily camp in the garden for Ksh50. In fact, failing a deluge of hotel guests, the management are quite pleased with the idea. Alternatively, cheaper beds are available at the *Five Stars Hotel* nearby (Ksh120 for s/c doubles), which has a good grocery and restaurant; and cheaper still, at *Safari Lodging* (Ksh60/100), behind the petrol station, which is at least clean and provides nets.

You may well meet a Dutch woman in Namanga, Nora Ole Sababi, who probably has as strong a claim as anyone in Kenya to being a "Mzungu Maasai". She's lived at Namanga for over a decade and employs a group of Maasai women to make tourist necklaces. The glass beads used for these are not African; they come from Czechoslovakia, which exports them to Peru and the Native American reservations as well as East Africa. And don't be misled: the expensive black and white marriage necklaces are not traditional Maasai ware. As with any art, styles change and innovations are emulated.

Amboseli National Park – accommodation options

From Namanga, a long, corrugated road – comfortable only at cowboyish high speed – takes you to the park gate. **Arriving**, as most people do, around midday, Amboseli seems a parched, unattractive place, with Kilimanjaro disappointingly hazed into oblivion. And making straight for the *Ol Tukai* park centre, with its group of lodges, *bandas*, a filling station, fences and barriers, doesn't improve first impressions by an awful lot.

Lodges and *bandas*
Reserve judgment for the late afternoon or early the next morning, however, and find your **accommodation**. Without spending too lavishly – and the lodge rooms are often fully booked in the high season, anyway – the options are limited. Most obvious is *Ol Tukai Lodge*, the **banda** site run by Kajiado district council. The

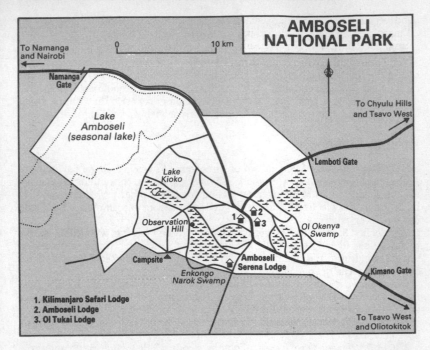

AMBOSELI NATIONAL PARK

To Namanga and Nairobi

0   10 km

Namanga Gate

Lake Amboseli (seasonal lake)

To Chyulu Hills and Tsavo West

Lemboti Gate

Lake Kioko

Observation Hill

1 ⌂2
⌂3

Ol Okenya Swamp

Campsite

Amboseli Serena Lodge

Enkongo Narok Swamp

Kimano Gate

1. Kilimanjaro Safari Lodge
2. Amboseli Lodge
3. Ol Tukai Lodge

To Tsavo West and Oliotokitok

cottages are reasonably good value, with mosquito nets and kitchens (Ksh132 worth per person or Ksh100 in the low season). Avoid forking out extra for cooking gas by using the communal firewood cooking area, which is free. *Ol Tukai's* shop has a reasonable supply of provisions. The two **tourist lodges**, *Amboseli Lodge* (☎2061 Radiocall Nairobi) and *Kilimanjaro Safari Lodge* (☎18 Amboseli; both are bookable through PO Box 30139 Nairobi, ☎227136), are both around Ksh2900/3600 FB; they're within walking distance but they're absurdly expensive to eat at. A drink by the pool (especially at the second, which is the pleasanter of the two) makes more sense, though even this is expensive, and hardly encouraged. *Amboseli Lodge* – currently showing the worst face of tourism in Kenya with rotten service and poor food – is best avoided altogether in high season.

If you're looking to unload money, *Amboseli Serena Lodge,* a half-hour drive from the *Ol Tukai* tourist sanctuary, is perhaps a more interesting and tranquil place to do it, and prices are a little lower (Ksh2540/3160 FB, bookable through *AT&H*, address on p.30)). They have made great efforts to hide the building behind a jungle of tropical plants and creepers, and this has encouraged a kind of intimate, pseudo-bush feeling accentuated by touches like a stream running through the dining room. Located by the *Enkongo Narok* swamps, there's a lot more wildlife activity here, too. Some people fall in love with it.

Camping

Real **budget accommodation** can only be had outside the park boundary at a **campsite** on Maasai land, south of *Amboseli Serena Lodge.* Apart from warm sodas, a couple of toilets are the only facilities, and even water supplies are unreliable. But it's a fine, wooded site, swarming with wildlife, so be prepared for adventures: we saw a pair of cheetahs on a kill less than a kilometre away.

If you haven't got a vehicle and get dropped off at *Ol Tukai*, a final possibility would be an unofficial bed in the drivers' *bandas*. Tour drivers pay abut Ksh40, but unless the tourist *bandas* are full, you'll have to pay a little more or chat up the right people. You can certainly eat in the drivers' canteen (good meals for Ksh30–40), make friends in their bar – a more enlivening experience than the *Ol Tukai* lodges – and you may even be able to arrange a reasonably priced game drive.

Around Amboseli

Small enough to cover easily in two or three game drives in a single day, most of Amboseli is open country with good visibility. If you take these things seriously, Amboseli lets you avoid the nagging feeling you get in other parks: that you may be in the wrong place and *that's* why you're not seeing any animals – here, you can look everywhere.

A good first stop is **Observation Hill**. Early in the morning, with Kilimanjaro a pervasive sky-filler to the south, the swamps of **Enkongo Narok**, replenished underground from the mountain top, are looped out in a brilliant emerald sash beneath. You can get out and walk around up here.

There's always a concentration of animals along the swamps and the driveable tracks which closely follow their fringes. The swamps are permanent enough to keep **hippo** here all year and there are hundreds of **elephant** and **buffalo** plus, predictably, a raucous profusion of **birdlife**. Lake Kioko at the northern end is a special oasis.

Cheetah are seen fairly frequently in the woods a little further south and there must be thousands of giraffe among the acacias. Look out, too, for the beautifully formed, rapier-horned **fringe-eared oryx** antelopes.

The open plains are scoured by **zebra** and haphazard, solitary **wildebeest**. The two species are often seen together, a good deal from the zebras' point of view because in a surprise attack the predator usually ends up with the less fleet-footed wildebeest. There are tail-flicking gazelle out here, too: the open country provides good protection against lion or cheetah ambushes.

But the biggest stretch of **arid land**, is paradoxically, Lake Amboseli – filled in with optimistic blue on so many maps, but for years on end never better than a soggy mud flat. Usually the "lake" is a vast dust bowl, and a pointless excursion. The small lakes in the north of the park tend to be disappointing misnomers as well, but **Olokenya Swamp** in the southeast is worth a slow exploration. If you're heading south out of the park it's a good dawn start to the trip.

Travel details: Oloitokitok and points onwards

Once in the park, you shouldn't have too much difficulty lining up lifts onwards. If you're **driving**, there are several routes east out of Amboseli. One heads towards the **Chyulu Hills**, then winds south to Tsavo West along the spine of the lava ridge – definitely a 4WD job unless you're feeling reckless. The Chyulus are favourite caving country with long, safe explorations possible. The *Cave Exploration Group of East Africa* found Leviathan Cave here, the longest and deepest lava tube in the world.

This route forks back at MAKUTANO, where a reasonable murram road shoots off north to EMALI and SULTAN HAMUD on the Mombasa highway.

The second main road leaves Amboseli in the southeast and branches after about 20km, one track leading directly to Tsavo West's Kyulu Gate and *Kilaguni Lodge* (see p.233). This route should be open again after **closure** in 1990 for repair work. The other fork climbs south to the Maasai country town of **Oloitokitok** with Kilimanjaro's jagged satellite peak Mawenzi dead ahead.

OLOITOKITOK (pronounced "Loytoktok") should be nothing to get excited about – just an interesting, bustling little town by the Amboseli-Tsavo circuit. But it is ignored by 99 percent of the tourist *kombis*, and it's in a fabulous position, closer to Kilimanjaro than anywhere else in Kenya and high above the plains. It is a recommended place to settle into if you're interested in finding out more about the **Maasai**, as this is their easternmost major centre. Oloitokitok is also a border crossing for the Tanzanian town of Moshi a couple of hours away, nestled behind the mountain. And you will hardly need telling it's close to Kibo Peak, twenty-five illegal kilometres as the crow flies. It's possible to find a porter/guide to take you to the top, but don't get caught in Kilimanjaro National Park, fees unpaid. The Tanzanians take the offence extremely seriously.

On the big market days (Tuesdays and Saturdays), many Maasai are in Oloitokitok and there's a fair amount of *matatu* traffic between here and TAVETA and the nearby villages. At other times, you will have to take potluck with **transport**, though there's at least one daily country bus to Nairobi, passing through TAVETA and VOI. Oloitokitok has a post office (open usual times) and a *KCB* bank (ditto) and there are a few **B&Ls**. *Mwalimu Lodge* in the lower part of town is a serious watering hole (rooms Ksh100), but there are a couple of quieter places up the hill near the market, both of which are reasonable.

Maasai Mara National Reserve

Daily charges, Ksh220 per person; Ksh50 to camp; Ksh50 per car; Ksh30 per video camera; Warden PO Box 60, Narok. Maps – Macmillan Maasai Mara at 1cm:1.25km (1988); Survey of Kenya SK86 at 1cm:1km (1975).

For a long list of reasons, **MAASAI MARA** is the best animal reserve in Kenya. The panorama sometimes resembles one of those wild animal wall charts, where groups of unlikely looking animal companions are forced into the artist's frame. You can see a dozen different species – or more – at one time: gazelle, zebra, giraffe, buffalo, topi, kongoni, wildebeest, eland, elephant, hyena, jackal, ostrich and a pride of lions waiting for a chance.

The reserve is a great wedge of undulating **grassland** nearly 2000m above sea level, watered by one of Kenya's bigger rivers, the Mara. It is in the remote, sparsely inhabited southwest part of the country, snugged up against the border and, indeed, an extension of the even bigger **Serengeti plains** in Tanzania. This is a land of short grasses, where the wind plays with the thick, green mantle after the rains and, nine months later, whips up dust devils from the baked surface.

But Maasai Mara's climate is beneficently predictable, with ample rain, and the new grass supports an annual **migration** of millions of wildebeest from the dry plains of Tanzania. To travel through the reserve in September or October, while the wildebeest are in possession, is a really staggering experience, like being caught up in the momentum of a phenomenal historic event. Whether you're watching this or a pride of lions hunting, a herd of elephants grazing in the marsh, or hyenas squabbling with vultures over the carcass of a buffalo, you are

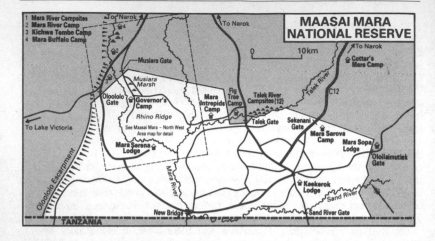

conscious all the time of being in a realm apart. There are few places on earth where animals hold such dazzling sway. It's as if you had found yourself in the New York of the natural world.

Getting to the Mara from Nairobi and Narok

Part of the reason for the Mara's fantastic spell is its isolation: a trip here is an expedition, and you might as well plan it as such. Access is most straightforward (and most expensive) by the scheduled twice-daily **air service** from Nairobi (see "travel details", p.110).

By **road**, however, rewards are greater, including the long **drive** across the Rift Valley from Nairobi sweeping across dry, stupendous vistas of range lands – the heart of the Maasai country (see box p.256). Cattle are the economic mainstay, but extensive wheatfields are pushing south. While the land often looks empty, if you stop for five minutes chances are that someone will appear – to request something or to offer a photo pose, or just to pass the time of day.

Narok

NAROK is the funnel through which almost all road transport enters the Maasai Mara. It is the last place to get petrol, a cold drink or almost anything for over 100km before you enter the reserve. First impressions aren't encouraging. A brassy atmosphere pervades the *Montorosi Café* (*Motorists' Snack Bar*) which, being the first filling station on the way into town, waylays most of the *kombis* with its big game cut-outs, reticulated sunshades and cluster of souvenir shops selling very expensive Maasai paraphernalia (the same stuff is half the price in Nairobi). Still they are good and not overly expensive mechanics, and if you're **hitching** this is probably the best point to wait and ask. If the direct approach doesn't appeal (there'll be plenty of refusals), try the bridge over the Engare Narok River on the other side of town. If you're driving, and need **petrol**, go right through Narok to the *Total* station on the far side of town, which is much the cheapest.

If you have to **spend the night** in Narok, there are a number of B&Ls near the action on the main road. Marginally the best is *Valley View B&L* (down in the town centre a little, on the right, Ksh70 a bed), so long as their notice stating *"We don't allow two men to sleep in one room – Valley View management"* doesn't put you off. Their intention, presumably, is to make work easier for the women in the bar. The *Ossobucko Hotel* isn't too bad, either – safe parking, good food, rather grubby rooms. There's a relatively good **grocery** next door. As for other mundane details, *Barclays Bank* (Mon–Fri 8.30am–1pm, Sat 8.30–11am) and the new **Post Office** are both on the main road.

Alternative routes to Narok: over the Mau escarpment

Alternative routes down to Narok reach the town **from the north**. From Lake Naivasha (on its southern shore, by the South Lake police station) and from NAKURU via NJORO, steep roads twist up over the **Mau Escarpment**. This mountain range, not as high but just as massive as the Aberdares, is little known and rarely visited. In the thin, clear air, Maasai and Nandi graze their cattle on luxuriant pastures, and large domains of thick, dark forest are still the home to Okiek (Dorobo) hunter-gatherers, though many are mixing the hunt with slightly more reliable food supplies through farming and have moved to the edge of the forest tracts and the margins of Kenya's mainstream economy.

It is enrapturing country and highly recommended for **hiking** if you have the time. As a preliminary to Maasai Mara, the Mau is a compelling alternative to the endless rolling switchback of the main Nairobi–Narok road, but you shouldn't attempt the climb – or the descent – in a saloon car, especially if it's raining. By *matatu*, the Nakuru–Narok route is a little easier than the other one; the village of EAST MAU, near the peaks, is your first destination.

Two points to note if you travel up in the Mau range. Firstly, there's little in the way of **accommodation**: ENANGIPERI, for example, midway between Njoro and Narok, has one, very basic "lodging" (more a bed in a barn) and you may find yourself asking, or being invited, to **stay with people**. This can arouse suspicions in the local authorities, who are most unused to travellers in these parts and are sensitive to the arrival of strangers because of ongoing friction between local people and immigrant farmers and landlords from other parts of Kenya. This shouldn't put you off visiting the region – it is wonderful countryside.

Into the reserve from Narok

Beyond Narok, you have to make a choice of route after about 20km. You could branch left for the fast, **mostly paved C12 road**, which is gradually building its way south towards the Sekenani gate and the eastern section of the reserve, where *Keekorok Lodge* and the reserve headquarters are the main human focuses. Or turn right, along a much more rugged road, for the western end of the reserve, the Mara River, and most of the other lodges and camps. This route can be tough and uncomfortable after rains, and isn't recommended without a 4WD vehicle.

Other routes to the Mara

You can also arrive in Maasai Mara **from Kisii** in the west (see p.191); with little difficulty from **Lake Magadi** in the east; and with no trouble at all from *Lobo Lodge* in Tanzania's **Serengeti National Park**. On this last route, you will perforce be driving a private vehicle; there's a twelve-kilometre gap between the Tanzanian formalities and the Kenya Police post at the Sand River Gate, where they'll sign you in and tell you where to go to complete formalities when you reach Nairobi. If you need to change money, *Keekorok Lodge*, 10km away, will do so for you, but sometimes imposes a small maximum of £20 or so unless you're going to stay.

Camping on a budget

Travellers on a budget aren't exactly catered to in Maasai Mara – the reserve has acquired something of an exclusive reputation on which its remoteness can capitalise. The only **accommodation option**, if you can't afford the more expensive **lodges and luxury tented camps**, is **do-it-yourself camping**.

KEEKOROK CAMPING
For camping, you are really restricted to sites outside the reserve unless you camp at the semi-official, not very wonderful, and rumoured-to-be-closing campsite near *Keekorok Lodge*: Ksh50 for toilets, water (often rationed) and a reasonably safe place to leave a tent (but beware of baboons). The staff canteen is a reliable calorie source, however, with good-value meals and a bar open until 11pm. Guides for animal-watching can often be hired here for the day to point you in the right direction. If you managed to hitch into Maasai Mara, then this is undoubtedly the most promising place to be if you intend to front up to motorised tourists in the hope of some outings in the park.

MARA SERENA CAMPING
If *Keekorok* has closed its campsite, the only other **public site inside the reserve boundaries** is next to the warden's office at *Mara Serena Lodge*. This looks like a more reliable option and, although it's an unshaded site, water is available from the office, drinks and meals are available at the lodge and you can pay to use the pool. And game is plentiful in the area.

CAMPING AT THE GATES
Driving in yourself **on a meagre budget**, you might prefer to camp at the informal **campsites at the main gates** (from west to east, Oloololo, Musiara, Sekenani, Sand River and Ololaimutiek), which charge around Ksh50 per person per night.

Musiara is one of the most popular campsites. You can camp by a little stream and while you're safe enough here, you're almost guaranteed to hear at close quarters the spine-tingling grunting roars of the Musiara lion prides. The rangers are quite happy to have campers and, if you have your own vehicle, will often be prepared to accompany you after dark for a meal at *Governor's Camp*. The *Oloololo* campsite has wonderful views of the escarpment, though *Sand River* campsite is perhaps the best, with toilets, water and a small *duka*, and it's nicely located in a spot where animals come to drink at night.

At the others, there are virtually no facilities, though drinking water may be available, and you can expect some good-natured pestering by the rangers, who will try to extract a few bob by taking you on game drives in your vehicle – sometimes with success, other times not. Naturally, if you enter the park during the day, fees have to be paid. Enterprising economies can be made by skirting the gates and avoiding payment, but spending the day watching for the rangers doesn't mix well with intensive animal viewing: it simply isn't worth it.

VICARIOUS PLEASURES

As usual, a taste of the high life can be had if you drop into a lodge for a drink (ordinary prices) or an ex-menu breakfast of tea and toast ("chai na tosti"). Tell the waiter exactly what you want, agree on a price, and don't forget to leave a tip. One or two of the lodges and camps get heavily invaded during the high seasons, *Keekorok* especially, and have begun to turn away casual visitors. Changing your clothes probably won't help – staff know exactly who's who – but discretion and some words of Swahili might. Swimming pools are usually out of bounds. Meals at the Mara camps and lodges are expensive, and you may well want to bring some food with you. The only shops are lobby gift boutiques. Most lodges and camps have their own petrol and diesel supplies, and will often sell some to non-guests, though at high prices. If you don't see any pumps or anticipate a refusal, go directly to the oiliest part of the staff compound and ask.

WILD CAMPING

There are further sites along various rivers outside the reserve. The best of these **wild campsites**, with no facilities (and nothing to keep the animals out but the strong smell of humans), are three sites on the **east bank of the Mara River**, just outside the reserve. These can be booked at the National Park Headquarters in Nairobi (Nairobi National Park's main gate; or through the warden in Narok), but in practice you can turn up and camp without making prior arrangements (Ksh50 if it's demanded). These Mara River camping places are hard to locate but better than most of the Talek River's (below), with, deep shade from the trees and fewer flies. There's another recognised camping site just west of *Mara River Camp* on the riverbank, reached by turning sharp left before you would enter the Camp grounds. There are some lively hippos here and the site has the advantage of being close to the road and nearby the Camp. You would be asking for trouble if you left your tent unguarded: either from robbery or wreckage by baboons (and probably both). Either pack up each morning or leave someone behind – perhaps a ranger if you can agree about his fee.

TALEK RIVER CAMPING

The string of twelve campsites along the north bank of the **Talek River** are particularly accessible if you arrive on the road to the eastern side of the reserve. Talek 12, the furthest west of these beyond *Fig Tree Camp*, is alluring, though it may in fact be a restricted "special campsite".

"PROFESSIONAL CAMPSITES"

The few **"professional campsites"** within the reserve – most notably *Fly*, *Paradise* and *Crocodile* – are used by film crews and the like. They have no special facilities, but they're in ideal locations and involve extravagant booking charges as well as high daily fees.

Lodges and Tented Camps

If you're considering treating yourself to a **lodge or tented camp**, either in a Maasai Mara package or independently, it is worth choosing where you stay carefully. The three lodges are all about the same price, but tented camps (or sometimes more like *bandas*) vary from expensive, to extremely expensive. There are now more than a dozen places and they vary considerably in style and price. Pressure on the thousand-odd beds can be intense, so **reserving ahead** is essential if you want to be sure of your camp or lodge. Booking addresses are given either below or in the "Hotel Bookings" box in *Basics*.

One common **additional cost**, worked into the full-board price by the most luxurious of the tented camps, covers three **game drives** per day in the camp vehicles. The camps that operate like this generally have exclusive pretensions and most of their guests arriving by air (transfers from the nearest airstrip also included). This doesn't mean they're not also attractive places to burn money. Competition, and demanding clients, keep standards high in every price range. There's nothing intrinsically cheaper about sleeping under canvas and private bathrooms, hot showers and some remarkably **good food** in the middle of the wilds naturally hoist prices sky-high.

If you're **driving in yourself**, however, it makes most sense to go to a tented camp with optional game drives. If you have poor luck with animals in your own vehicle, you can always go out on a camp game drive.These are the camps that tend to be favoured by Kenya residents.

LODGES

Olkurruk Mara Lodge (bookings through *AT&H*). The newest and smallest lodge – and slightly the cheapest – with wonderful views, somewhat isolated up on the Siria Oloololo escarpment. Individual thatched, luxury *banda*-style accommodation at Ksh3440/3660 FB, with around thirty percent low-season discount.

Keekorok Lodge (☎2178 Radiocall Nairobi). The oldest accommodation in the reserve, though quite modern, and has the best facilities, including a swimming pool. A *Block* hotel in the bush with no compromises, situated in a rather open location and perennially busy. It's also a good hour closer to Nairobi by road than its main competitor, *Mara Serena*. Balloon flights are available. Around Ksh2900/4140 FB, with substantial low-season discounts.

Mara Serena Lodge (☎3757 Radiocall Nairobi). Although the largest hotel in the park, this has, perhaps, fewer tour groups and is a touch less streamlined than *Keekorok*, its architecture more integrated into the surroundings (similar in this respect to *Amboseli Serena*, see p.243) and located in a quieter part of the reserve. The rooms are characteristically smallish *Serena* ones. Balloons again, and prices much the same as *Keekorok's*.

LUXURY TENTED CAMPS: GAME DRIVES INCLUDED

Governor's Camp (☎3745 Radiocall Nairobi; bookings through ☎331871 Nairobi). Located in the woods on a bend in the river on the site of an old hunting camp from Roosevelt days and close to the fantastic game-viewing of the Musiara marsh, *Governor's* has retained its exclusive "bush" atmosphere, with no expense spared (and all passed on to you, if you stay). The rooms are big canvas tents with solid bathrooms to the back; elephants trundle through at night; guards keep watch for more dangerous visitors and escort guests between their tents and the restaurant. Nice staff and recommended. Prices at *Governor's* for FB with three game drives per day included are around Ksh4400/6800, with some low-season reduction (but note, the Musiara area gets very soggy during, and after the rains).

Little Governor's Camp Reached by a two-kilometre drive and then a dinghy across the Mara, this is the annex from which the *Governor's* balloons fly (see p.255). Hidden in the trees by its own waterhole, with wonderful bird-watching, this is the smallest and most intimate setup in the reserve, always fully booked in advance of the main camp. It has just 27 beds, three of them double and prices are the same as the main camp.

Mara Intrepids (bookings through *Talek Limited*, PO Box 14040 Nairobi, ☎331688). Parked on a bluff overlooking the Talek River in the heart of the reserve and with a swimming pool. "Tented suites" conveys the scene here. The most expensive bed and board in the Mara, but a stylish way to dispose of your savings (around Ksh5000/7000 FB including game drives).

Mara Safari Club (Lonrho Hotels, PO Box 58581, ☎723776, Ksh4960/6595 FB including game drives). New. Opinions welcome.

MID-RANGE TENTED AND BANDA CAMPS
The following are listed in approximate ascending order of price.

Cottar's Camp (PO Box 44191 Nairobi, ☎882408 Nairobi; bookings through *Windsor Hotels*). Now renamed *Siana Springs* this is the cheapest, the most accessible, and in many ways, the best of the lot. It is some way outside the reserve boundary, but suffers no lack of wildlife for that, so you're spared park fees and also have the opportunity to walk – suitably accompanied by armed rangers – in the area. *Cottar's* has a happy lack of airs, great food and loyal repeat guests, including many Kenya residents (who get good rates). Famous features are the Leopard Lookout and night game drives. From around Ksh2000/2500 FB, cheaper low season.

Mara River Camp (PO Box 45456 Nairobi, ☎21992/3/4). On the northwest side of the reserve and in similar style to *Siana Springs* but rather less accessible and with more rustic facilities – shared bathrooms, for example. This northwest corner, centred on the Musiara swamps, is probably the best game-viewing area of all. *Mara River* is highly rated by enthusiastic naturalists and serious photographers, but it isn't the one to choose for a honeymoon. Prices similar to *Siana Springs* and, like it, with excellent low season and residents' rates – for example Ksh1245/2065 in 1991.

Mara Buffalo Camp Also in the northwest, beside the river, but not one to visit for a casual drink or meal, as all their guests are packaged by *African Safari Club* in Europe and Canada, and they no longer take bookings in Kenya. Still, if you're one of their customers, Buffalo is a pretty camp, with *banda*-roofed tents ranged along the banks of the Mara, in a good game area – often noisy at night with rowdy hyenas.

Fig Tree Camp (bookings through PO Box 40683 Nairobi, ☎220592 Nairobi). Close to the Talek Gate and just outside the boundary. Very reasonable, attractively and imaginatively laid out, with average prices and good residents' rates. As no part of the reserve is more than 40km distant from it, it's well situated for a long stay (Ksh2015/2635 FB).

Kichwa Tembo (☎3968 Radiocall Nairobi, bookings through *Windsor Hotels*). An *Abercrombie and Kent* operation and rival to nearby *Governor's Camp*. Due to the liveliness of the local fauna *Kichwa Tembo* (which means "Elephant's Head") is fenced in. Game drives are optional (prices without them Ksh3000/3900 FB, with 40 percent off in the low season).

Sarova Mara Camp (☎2263 Radiocall Nairobi, bookings through *Sarova Hotels*). The most accessible of all the Mara camps and lodges, on the main C12 entrance road, right by the Sekenani Gate and Reserve headquarters. Combining stylish lodge-like public areas with tented accommodation and a pool this aims high (Ksh3175/3900).

Mara Sopa Camp, by Ololaimutiek Gate, outside the boundary. (Bookings through *Kenya Holidays*, PO Box 72630 Nairobi, ☎336088.) Maintains a low profile in its remote corner – and relatively high prices (Ksh3250/4180 FB).

Mara Shika Camp (PO Box 10773 Nairobi, ☎225680). New. Write and tell us.

Mara Sara Camp Closed down several years ago.

Around the Reserve

Wherever you go there are **animals**. This is the one part of Kenya where the concentrations of game that existed in the last century can still be seen. The most interesting areas, scenically and zoologically, are **westwards**, signalled by the long ridge of the Siria-Oloololo escarpment. If you only have a day or two, you should spend most of your time here, near the **Mara River**. Unfortunately a large swathe of woods and grassland west of the track between *Mara Serena Lodge* and the Oloololo gate was stripped by a bushfire recently. This should recover before too long.

The reserve is crisscrossed with tracks but smooth surfaces tend to encourage off-road driving. So far this hasn't had the damaging effect it has in Amboseli – the Mara's ecosystem is far less fragile and there's more of it – but there are signs that a balance won't be maintained much longer: look at the stretch along the edge of the forest to the north of *Governor's Camp*.

Lions

Big, brunette **lions** are the best-known denizens of the reserve and there are usually several prides living around the **Musiara Swamps**, which are dry much of the year. It is sometimes possible to watch them hunt, as they take very little notice of vehicles. We accompanied one gang of adolescent lions and lionesses for a whole afternoon, just outside the boundary. After scanning a big herd of cattle across the plain for some time, they made several attempts at some impala, chased a lone hippo into the Mara River, pounced on a warthog with a broken leg but failed to catch it (to our mixed feelings of amazement and relief), and finally surrounded an elderly buffalo in the marsh and settled down to wait for darkness. The next morning, the kill was cold and they were burrowing in the old bull's carcass like bloated maggots.

Cheetahs

While lions seem to be lounging under every other bush, finding a **cheetah** is much harder. These are solitary cats – slender, unobtrusive and somewhat shy. When they move, their speed and agility are marvellous. If you are lucky enough to witness a kill (cynicism about such voyeurism is quickly dispelled when you find yourself on the spot), it is likely to take place in a cloud of dust, a kilometre from where the chase began. But cheetahs are vulnerable to too much harassment. Traditionally, they hunt at dawn and dusk (at the same times the tourists are hunting for photographs), but there is evidence that they are turning to a midday hunting pattern when the humans are shaded in the lodges – not a good time of day for the cheetah, which expends terrific energy in each chase and may have to give up if it goes on for more than thirty or forty seconds.

Leopards

Leopards are rarely seen, though there are plenty of them. You can give yourself a serious case of risen hair when you find their footprints down on the sandbanks at the edge of the Mara outside the reserve boundary. But they are largely nocturnal and prefer to remain well out of sight. You would have to crane your neck at a lot of trees to have much chance of seeing one. Their deep, grating roar at night – a grunt, repeated – is a sound which, once heard, you carry around with you.

Rhinos and other heavyweights

If you have a ranger with you, he's certain to know the current news about the **rhinos** – every calf born is a victory – though finding them is often surprisingly difficult. Check out Rhino Ridge, where a handful of the reserve's surviviving kifaru are sometimes obligingly positioned.

Maasai Mara's other heavyweights are about in abundance. The Mara River surges with **hippo**, while big families of **elephant** traipse along the forest margins and spread out into the Musiara marshes when the herbage is thick and juicy. The park is home to an estimated thousand or so elephants, with another

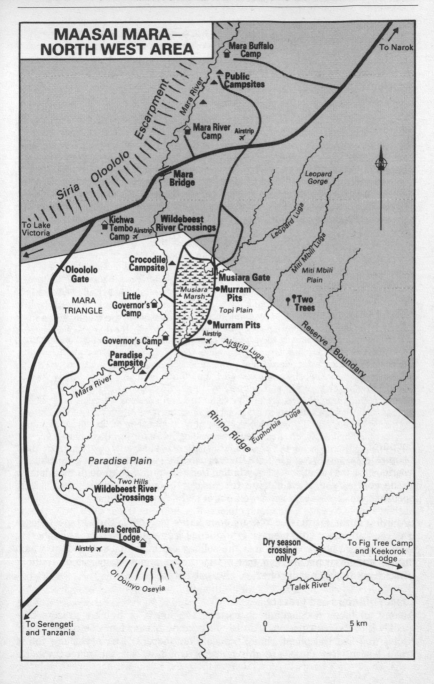

MAASAI MARA –
NORTH WEST AREA

To Narok

Mara Buffalo
Camp

Public
Campsites

Mara River

Siria   OlooIolo   Escarpment

Mara River
Camp

Airstrip

Leopard
Gorge

Leopard Luga

Mara
Bridge

To Lake
Victoria

Kichwa
Tembo
Camp

Airstrip

Wildebeest
River Crossings

Miti Mbili Luga

Miti Mbili
Plain

Olooiolo
Gate

Crocodile
Campsite

Musiara Gate

Murram
Pits

MARA
TRIANGLE

Little
Governor's
Camp

Musiara
Marsh

Topi Plain

Two
Trees

Reserve Boundary

Governor's Camp

Murram Pits

Airstrip

Paradise
Campsite

Airstrip Luga

Mara River

Rhino Ridge

Euphorbia Luga

Paradise Plain

Two Hills
Wildebeest River
Crossings

Mara Serena
Lodge

Dry season
crossing
only

To Fig Tree Camp
and Keekorok
Lodge

Airstrip

Ol Doinyo Oseyia

Talek River

To Serengeti
and Tanzania

0   5 km

NDOVU: THE ELEPHANT

Elephants are the most engaging of animals to watch, perhaps because their inter-actions, behaviour patterns and personality have so many human parallels. Like people, they lead complex, interdependent, **social lives**, growing from helpless infancy, through self-conscious adolescence, to adulthood. Babies are born with other cows in close attendance, after a twenty-two month gestation. The calves suckle for two to three years, from the mother's two breasts between her front legs.

Elephants' basic family units are composed of a group of related females, tightly protecting their babies and young and led by a venerable **matriarch**. These are the animals most likely to **bluff a charge** – though occasionally she may get carried away and tusk a vehicle or person. Bush mythology has it that elephants become embarrassed and ashamed after killing a human, covering the body with sticks and grass. They certainly pay much attention to the disposal of their own **dead rela-tives**, often dispersing the bones and spending time near the remains. Old animals die in their eighties when their last set of teeth wears out and they can no longer feed.

Seen in the flesh, elephants seem even bigger than you imagine – you'll need little persuasion from those flapping, warning ears to back off if you're too close – but they are at the same time surprisingly graceful, silent animals on their padded, carefully placed feet. In a matter of moments, a large herd can merge into the trees and disappear, their presence betrayed only by the noisy cracking of branches as they strip trees and uproot saplings.

Managing the elephant population (see "The Poaching Wars" box on p.238) leads to arcane **ecological puzzles** in which new factors keep emerging. While over-populations are usually the result of old migration routes being cut off, forcing the animals into unnatural reserves – like the Mara – the consequent foliage destruction of crowded herds also puts new life into the soil. Experiments at Hwange park in Zimbabwe showed that four times as many camel acacia seeds sprouted after being eaten and dunged by elephants than a control sample left on the ground. Dung beetles gratefully tackle the football-sized elephant droppings, break them into pellets and pull them into their burrows where the seeds germi-nate. Elephants also dig up dried-out water holes with their tusks (they're either right- or left-tusked, like human hands), providing moisture for other animals.

Yet equally convincing facts can be wheeled out to show how destructive are the massive appetites of elephants. Adults may consume up to 170kg of plant material daily – that works out at well over a hundred tons of foliage through the Mara's collective elephant gut every day.

500 living in the districts beyond its boundaries (see box). **Buffalo** are seen all over, and are not a little menacing to a small jeep surrounded by a thundering herd of several hundred tons. It is the solitary old bulls that you need to watch out for – their reputation, and that of old rhinos, is not exaggerated. Tourists' vehicles get stoved in quite often, so always back off.

Lesser grunters and grazers

Among all these outstanding characters, the herds of humble grazers fade quickly into the background. It's easy to become blasé when one of the much-hyped "big five" (elephant, rhino, buffalo, lion, leopard) isn't eyeballing you at arm's length. But those are the hunter's trophies, not the photographer's.

Warthog families like rows of dismantled Russian dolls, **zebra** and **gazelle**, odd-looking **hartebeest** and slick, purple-flanked **topi** are all scattered with abandon across the scene. The topi are peculiarly characteristic of Maasai Mara, and there's always one or two in every herd standing sentry on a tussock or an old termite mound. Topi and **giraffe** – whose dream-like, slow-motion canter is one of the reserve's most beautiful and underrated sights – are often good pointers for predators in the vicinity. And the reserve has rare herds of **roan antelope** – swaggering, horse-sized animals with sweeping, curved horns, that you'll see elsewhere only at the Shimba Hills park near Mombasa or Ruma National Park near Kisii.

The wildebeest migration

But it is the annual **wildebeest migration** that plants Maasai Mara in the imagination. With a lemming-like instinct, finally gelled into mass movement, the herds gather in their hundreds of thousands on the withering plains of Serengeti to begin the long, streaming journey northward following the scent of moisture and green grass in the Mara. They arrive in **July and August**, pouring over the Sand River and into the eastern side of the reserve around *Keekorok*, gradually munching their way westwards in a milling, unsettled mass and turning south again in October. Never the most graceful of animals, wildebeest play up to their appearance with frolicsome, unpredictable behaviour, bucking like wild horses, springing like jack-in-the-boxes, or suddenly sprinting off through the herd for no apparent reason.

The **Mara River** is their biggest obstacle and heavy rains up on the Mau Range where it rises can produce a brown flood claiming thousands of animals as they try to cross. Like huge sheep, the brainless masses swarm desperately to the banks and plunge in. Many are fatally injured on rocks and fallen branches; others are skewered by flailing legs and horns. With every surge, more bodies bob to the surface and float downstream. Heaps of bloated carcasses line the banks; injured and dying animals struggle mournfully in the mud; vultures and marabou storks squat in glazed, post-prandial stupor.

The migration's full, cacophonous impact is awesomely melodramatic – both on the plains where the multitudes graze and cavort, and at the deadly river crossings. The superabundance of meat accounts for the Mara's big lion population. And, through it all, the **spotted hyenas** scamper and loiter like psychopathic sheep dogs. Half a million wildebeest **calves** are born in January and February before the migration; two out of three to perish without returning to the Serengeti.

Balloon flights

From the ground, the migration is a compelling phenomenon, bewildering and strangely disturbing as you witness individual struggles and events. From the air, in one of the reserve's sixteen **balloons**, it resembles an ant's nest. At around Ksh6000 for the sixty- to ninety-minute flight plus breakfast (cooked on the burners) with *vin mousseux*, **balloon safaris** are the ultimate in bush chic (bookings at *Balloon Safaris Ltd*, PO Box 47557 Nairobi, ☎335807 Nairobi; or, space permitting, at one of the lodges or camps). Just watching the inflation and liftoff at dawn is a spectacular sight, especially at *Little Governor's Camp*, deep in the woods. And if irrepressible urges overtake you, this is probably the better

THE MAASAI AND THE MARA

After deep reflection on my people and culture, I have painfully come to accept that the Maasai must change to protect themselves, if not their culture. They must adapt to the realities of the modern world for the sake of their own survival. It is better to meet an enemy out in the open and to be prepared for him than for him to come upon you at home unawares.

Tepilit Ole Saitoti, *Maasai.*

When the first European hunting safaris made the Mara world famous in the early years of this century, they were ransacking a region recently deserted by the **Maasai**. Smallpox had ravaged their communities and rinderpest had torn through their herds. The wild animals had the country virtually to themselves. Traditionally, Maasai hunted only lion and, in times of famine, eland and buffalo, the "wild cattle". Only the **Dorobo** ("people without cattle" in Maa) hunted for a living. The Maasai had always lived in some harmony with the wildlife.

By 1961, the white hunters had succeeded in bringing the lion population down to nine and, to a chorus of alarm, the Maasai Mara Game Reserve was created, to be administered by the Maasai district council at Narok as a total game sanctuary – and a tourist attraction. By then, improved medicine and veterinary facilities had eased the old hardships of the Maasai way of life. They were expanding again, and land had become the biggest issue.

Of all Kenya's peoples, the Maasai have received the most attention. Often strikingly tall and slender, dressed in brilliant red cloth, beads and metal jewellery, the young men with long, ochred hairstyles, they have a reputation for ferocity pampered by an arch superiority complex. Traditionally, they lived off milk and blood (from the jugular veins of their live **cattle**), and they loved their herds more than anything else. They maintained rotating armies of spartan warriors – the *moran* – who killed lions as a test of manhood. And they opposed all interference and invasion with swift, implacable violence. Their scorn of foreigners was absolute: they called the Europeans, who came swaddled in clothing, *iloridaa enjekat* or "those who confine their farts". They derided other African peoples who cultivated, too, for digging the earth – the Maasai even left their dead unburied – while those who kept cattle were given grudging respect so long as they conceded that all the world's cattle were a gift from God to the Maasai, whose cattle-raiding was thus righteous reclamation of stolen property.

Some of this noble savagery was undoubtedly exaggerated by slave- and ivory-traders, anxious to protect their routes from the Europeans. That said, the Maasai have on the whole been stubbornly conservative, with a disinclination to change their traditional ways which has tended to mark them out as the whipping boys of Kenyan development. At the same time, something close to a cult of the Maasai has been around ever since Thomson walked *Through Maasailand* in 1883. In the early years of the colony, Delamere's obsession with the people and all things Maasai

place to get standing room in the basket – the balloon drifts serenely at around tree height above the *Mara Triangle* to the west of the river. Balloon trips are now being run by several of the larger camps and lodges, including *Serena* and *Fig Tree*. From *Keekorok*, the other balloon base, the prevailing winds tend to carry the montgolfiers westwards with a different air stream: fine for a grand view no doubt, but less satisfactory for animal watching. In order to avoid frightening the animals unduly, however, there is now a minimum height below which the balloons are not permitted to fly.

spawned a new term, "Maasai-itis", and with it a motley crop of romantic notions alluding to ancient Romans, Egyptians and even the lost tribes of Israel.

These days, the **tourist industry** has given the Maasai a major spot in its repertoire. Maasai dancing is *the* entertainment, while necklaces, gourds, spears, shields, *rungus* (knobkerries), busts (carved by Akamba carvers) and even life-sized wooden *morani* (to be shipped home in a packing case) are the stock-in-trade of the curio and souvenir shops.

For the Maasai themselves, the rewards are fairly scant. **Cattle** are still at the heart of their society; there are dozens of names for different colours and patterns, and each animal among their three million is known individually and cherished. But they are assailed on all sides: by uplands farmers expanding from the north; by eviction from the tourist/conservation areas within the reserve boundaries to the south; and by a climate of opposition to the old lifestyle from all around. Sporadically urged to grow crops, go to school, build permanent houses, and generally settle down and stop being a nuisance, they face an additional dilemma in squaring these edicts with the fickle demands of the tourist industry for traditional authenticity. Few make much of a living selling souvenirs, but enterprising *morani* can do well by just posing for photos, and even better if they hawk themselves down on the coast or in Nairobi.

Many men persevere with the status of **warriorhood**, though modern Kenya makes few concessions to it. Arrested for hunting lions, and prevented from building *manyattas* for the *eunoto* transition in which they pass into elderhood, the *morani* have kept most of the superficial marks of the warrior without being able to live the life. The ensemble of cloth tied over one shoulder, spear, sword, club and braided hair is widely seen and, after circumcision, in their early days as warriors, you can meet young men out in the bush, hunting for birds to add to their elaborate, taxidermic headdresses.

But there's considerable local frustration. When the pasture is poor, the *morani* have little compunction about driving their herds into the reserve to compete with the wildlife. All but a few of the Mara's black rhinos have been slaughtered for their horns in the last two decades. And there have even been isolated attacks on tourist vehicles.

Land is the great issue today. The Maasai have still not fully come to terms with the idea of *owning* it. "Range schemes" – plans for wheat or cattle-rearing – are common now in Maasailand, but they are just as likely to benefit newcomers from other parts of Kenya as the local Maasai. The lifestyle is changing: education, MPs and elections, new laws and new projects, jobs and cash, all impinge. The ubiquitous *ugali* is rapidly replacing the diet of curdled milk and cow's blood that now seems almost mythical. Many Maasai have taken work in the hotels and lodges while others end up as security guards in Nairobi. For the majority, who continue to live semi-nomadic lives among a welter of constraints, the future holds little promise.

Samburu-Buffalo Springs National Reserve

Daily fees: Samburu – Ksh220 per person, Ksh50 per car; Ksh50 to camp; Buffalo Springs – Ksh220 per person, Ksh50 per car; Ksh50 to camp; Warden PO Box 27, Isiolo. Map – Survey of Kenya Samburu and Buffalo Springs SK 85 at 1cm:500m.

Up in the north of the country, in the hot, arid lowlands beneath Mount Kenya, **Samburu National Reserve** was set up only twenty years ago, a tract of country

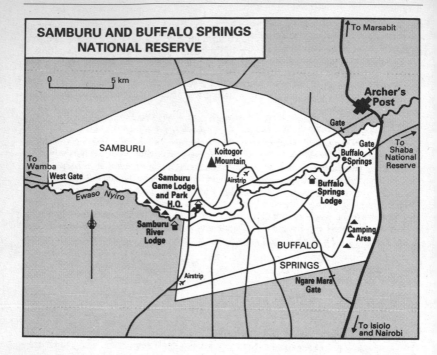

SAMBURU AND BUFFALO SPRINGS
NATIONAL RESERVE

0   5 km

To Marsabit

Archer's Post

SAMBURU

Koitogor Mountain

Gate

Gate
Buffalo Springs

To Shaba National Reserve

To Wamba

West Gate

Ewaso Nyiro

Samburu Game Lodge and Park H.Q.

Airstrip

Buffalo Springs Lodge

Samburu River Lodge

Camping Area

BUFFALO

SPRINGS

Airstrip

Ngare Mara Gate

To Isiolo and Nairobi

around the richest stretch of the Ewaso Nyiro River. In this region, the permanent water and the forest shade on the banks draws plentiful wildlife in the dry season and maintains many of the less peripatetic species year round. While the wildlife spectacle doesn't always match that of the southern parks, the scenic beauty of Samburu is unquestionable and, in the kind of mood swing which only an equatorial region can produce, the contrast with the fertile farming country of the Highlands just a few kilometres to the south couldn't be more striking. In the background, the sharp hill of Koitogor rises in the middle of Samburu Reserve, making a useful reference point. And on the horizon, thirty kilometres to the north, looms the gaunt red block of Ol Olokwe Mountain. Head up into the scratchy bush in the south of Buffalo Springs Reserve and the whole region is spread out before you.

Of the popular game parks, Samburu is usually reckoned the most remote and inaccessible. This has more to do with its location than with present practicalities. On the fringes of what is still called the "NFD" (Northern Frontier District), the combined Samburu-Buffalo Springs National Reserves were closed for many years after their creation, because of the war against Somali irredentists that flared over northern Kenya in the 1960s and early 1970s.

Practical matters

In practical terms, **access** isn't difficult. If you're circling Mount Kenya, Samburu Reserve is close at hand, a couple of hours north of NANYUKI (see p.125). Buses and *matatus* run down on to the hazy plain as far as ISIOLO (p.367) and, if you don't have wheels, this is normally as far as you can go without hitching. Arriving in time to catch a *Mwingi Highway* bus bound for Kenya's northern fastnesses, you may get a ride to Archer's Post or one of the reserve gates before it. But waiting at the Isiolo police barrier usually gets you **a lift into the reserve** itself in a few hours.

Luxury stays

Most vehicles will be heading for one of the three **lodges** – *Samburu Lodge* (☎2051 Radiocall Nairobi, bookings through *Block Hotels*) on the north bank, *Samburu Serena Lodge* (☎3900 Radiocall Nairobi, bookings through *Serena*), further upstream on the south bank, just outside the reserve, or *Buffalo Springs Lodge* (PO Box 71 Isiolo, ☎2259, bookings through *AT&H*) in the reserve of the same name. The *Samburu* lodges are both around Ksh3000/4000 FB, with the usual hefty discounts from April to June but, of the two, *Samburu Lodge* is definitely the one to go for. Despite a frenetically busy atmosphere around the riverside terraces and crocodile-viewing bars, the glorious setting of the whole place, on a broad bend of the river, reeks of atmosphere and is hard to fault. The *Serena Lodge* (used to be *Samburu River Lodge*) is strangely laid out with typically small rooms and just doesn't quite make it, while the tented/*banda* camp of *Buffalo Springs Lodge* is beginning to look rather tacky and losing its luxury credibility (if still costing Ksh1800/2280, with huge low-season savings).

At peak periods, *Buffalo Springs* is the one to head for, however, if you're looking for a **swim, a shower, a few drinks or a meal**: the other lodges are likely to give you short shrift.

West of *Samburu Lodge*, the exclusive and wonderful *Larsens Tented Camp* (bookings through *Block*) doesn't even publicise itself very hard. They don't take children under ten: they do take tons of cash and provide first class game drives and excellent food (around Ksh5500/7000 all in). There's also a new *Samburu Intrepids Club* (same booking details as *Mara Intrepids*, p.250) which charges about the same as the lodges.

Camping

There are **campsites** in Buffalo Springs Reserve, not far from the first gate, Ngere Mara; but this *Champagne Ridge* camping area has a nasty reputation for robberies. If you do stay here, you're strongly advised to take up the offer of night guards which the rangers will probably make – or insist upon. The camp is near the main road and, despite our scepticism, we were visited by intruders the night we stayed. As usual, you also face the hassle of having to pack your tent each day before setting off on the animal trail. If you don't have a vehicle, being dropped off at *Champagne Ridge* could prove painful if nobody turned up to give you a ride out again. Still, it's a pretty area among the acacias, and it abounds with giraffe and other animals.

Three other sites, without facilities, lie just west of the Ewaso Nyiro Bridge, barely a kilometre from the lodge and HQ. There are a further four "special campsites" – three along the north bank of the river in Samburu Reserve, one by the Maji ya Chumvi Stream in Buffalo Springs Reserve – which (according to the latest reports) are equipped with showers and toilets. These need to be reserved in advance (try the warden), and prices are vague and perhaps negotiable. In any event, until recently, they were only "special" because of their locations, and had no facilities at all.

Initially, the best move for the wheel-less is to get to the area of *Samburu Lodge* and **camp near the park headquarters**: not a wonderful site, no running water (and the lodge will as likely as not make you pay for that commodity), but convenient and legal. You can walk safely to the lodge's riverside bars and restaurant, sometimes flop in the pool (rather often restricted to guests, otherwise Ksh50), gloat over the crocodiles in the river below, and peer darkly through binoculars at the regular but brief evening cabaret of leopards retrieving bait from a tree on the far bank. If your finances stretch that far, you can shell out Ksh400 or so for a three-hour morning or evening game run in one of the lodge's land cruisers. Most people camping here without their own vehicles seem to manage to find the occasional ride around the reserve, if only because the opportunities exist to meet better-heeled travellers over a drink.

Note that the baboons at the campsite here are beyond being an amusement. Leave your tent and its contents only under guard. The fact that baboons regularly – and shrilly – fall victim to crocs at the water's edge seems less distressing after a day or two spent on the scene.

Around the Reserve

Except during and immediately after the rains, scrubby bush country takes up most of the reserve area, but there are some large acacia thickets, especially in the eastern part of Buffalo Springs. Here, **the springs** themselves are a welcome target; there are pools of clear if weedy water, one of which has been sanitised with concrete for the benefit of swimmers and (most of the time) the exclusion of crocodiles: it's always a good idea to check before diving in. *Buffalo Springs Lodge*, a few kilometres away, is low-key and usually good for a shower and a drink. There's a fine jungly marsh reaching nearly to the terrace, where you'll often see animals.

If Samburu's **wildlife** is occasionally disappointing, it may be fairer to say that the dry country ecosystems are prone to large variations in the animal populations as they move in search of water and pasture. Some visitors have tremendous luck here and it usually provides consistently excellent animal watching. The best areas, recently, have been along the south side of the river in Buffalo Springs Reserve, quite close to *Samburu Lodge*. Poaching has wiped out the rhino, but lions are often seen, again, most often in Buffalo Springs. Meanwhile, locally burgeoning **elephant herds** have ruined some of the riverine forest. Rarer, and localised, species compensate, though: among these, **reticulated giraffe** with their beautiful jigsaw marking, **Grevy's zebra** (the large, finely striped species with a bushy mane and outsize ears), **Somali ostrich** with blue rather than pink legs, and **gerenuk** ("camel head" in Somali), the antelope that stands on its hind legs to reach the foliage, are all common and conspicuous.

Panthera pardus

Samburu's **leopards** are a regular sight, too, at least from the terraces at the two riverside lodges, both of which have taken to baiting the trees on the opposite bank with haunches of meat. Between drinks and dinner, guests get a floodlit view of the stealthy predator reduced to giant puddy cat. The stampede for cameras doesn't encourage the leopards to stay long, so efforts are made to attach the meat firmly to the tree. It's all pathetically contrived, but only with luck or dogged persistence will you see a wild leopard except in such circumstances, and it's hard to blame the hotels for making the most of the local attractions. You should beware, at *Samburu Lodge*, of occasional excursions by the leopards across the river to the human zoo. Several recent sightings on the lodge grounds have been reported early in the evening; hence the signs warning "Do not stray beyond the lit path".

Leopards may be the most feared animals in Kenya. Intensely secretive, alert and wary, they live all across the country except in the most treeless zones. And, because they are strictly nocturnal, they often survive on the outskirts of towns and in heavily cultivated districts, carefully preying on different domestic animals to avoid a routine that could lead to their death. They tolerate nearby human habitation and rarely kill people unprovoked – though plenty of accidents do occur. Current policy is to capture rather than kill troublesome leopards and transport them to exile in Nakuru or Meru National Parks.

Recent research has shown how little is really known about these cats. For the most part, they live off any small animals that come their way, and the popular notion that they consume many baboons is apparently wrong: a baboon troop would turn on an attacking leopard instantly.

Less organised monkeys of all kinds, however, are often caught, and in Samburu (for those leopards not on the lodge gravy train), the favourite hunting grounds are the stands of forest and clumps of strange, branching doum palms by the river – these sometimes shake with monkeys. Black-faced vervet and blue monkeys are the commonest inhabitants.

Shaba National Reserve

Ksh220 per person per day, Ksh60 per car per day, Ksh50 to camp per night; Warden PO Box 27, Isiolo. No maps.

Across the rutted surface of the Marsabit road lies **Shaba National Reserve** (more fees), the third of the Samburu region reserves. *Sarova Hotels* has now fully opened their beautiful and expensive *Sarova Shaba Lodge* on the Ewaso Nyiro River (Ksh3200/4200 FB). They do good meals here and there's petrol available. Unfortunately, the alternative accommodation near the main gate – *Shaba Tented Camp* – has closed down and the reserve is otherwise blissfully undeveloped. But for animals, it's rated the equal of its two neighbours and its **springs** mean that it is better watered. If you're mobile and have a day to spare, Shaba is highly recommended. This was the area where Joy Adamson experimented with the release of hand-reared **leopards**. You may even find more wildlife here and it's certainly much less visited than Samburu-Buffalo Springs.

Meru National Park

Ksh220 per person, Ksh30 per car, Ksh50 to camp; Warden PO Box 434, ☎20613 Meru. Map – Survey of Kenya SK65 at 1cm:1km (1978).

You won't find **Meru National Park** on many safari itineraries. Of the main parks covered in this chapter, it is the least visited, the most obviously untrampled, unspoiled and pristine. Abundantly traversed by permanent **streams** flowing into the Tana River on its southern boundary, and luxuriantly rained upon, the rolling **jungle** of tall grass, riverine forest and swamp is lent a hypnotic, otherworldly quality by wonderful stands of prehistoric-looking **doum palms**; and with high cover, you never know what's going to be around the next corner*.

True, the animals aren't as much in evidence as in some parks, but the even greater absence of *kombis* and land cruisers more than compensates. After visiting some of the less bushy parks, where you can see the animals miles away, Meru's intimate, unusual landscape is quickly entrancing. Most of the time you really are alone in this surreal wilderness.

Meru is the area where the Adamsons released their lioness **Elsa** back into the wild, and where later experiments with orphaned cheetahs were cut short by Joy Adamson's murder. And, until 1988, the park's biggest wildlife attraction was its precarious herd of **white rhino**, huge appealing animals that had the full-time attention of a team of rangers to protect them.

Getting in and where to stay

Getting to Meru without your own vehicle isn't easy, but once there you'll find several cheap places to stay. From MERU town (see p.128), the last petrol and supplies before the park are in MAUA, one hour's drive into the **Nyambeni Hills** on a pretty, paved road, with steep tea terraces and plantations of *miraa*. MAUA, or rather about 3km up the hill before it at the junction, is where you'll have to wait for a lift if you are determined to try and reach the park by **hitching**. You could stand for literally days without getting one, though *matatus* do run as far as KIANGU – a third of the way between Maua and the park gate – several times a day. You could get stuck at Kiangu; it rather commits you.

A new lodge has just been built at the junction, where you might be lucky with a lift. Or, if you want to try again the next day, Maua itself (less than an hour's walk away) has the *Maua Hotel* and *Silent Lodge* – both cheap and pleasant enough.

The gate is about 30km away down a red murram road, the condition of which is sometimes diabolical, with magnificent scenery over your shoulder as you go: the Nyambenis towering above exotic *shambas* of bananas, sugar and corn, the sky, as often as not, a gaudy cloud-mural of gathering storms. Gradually, as you descend, the scene gives way to the lank grass, termite cathedrals and the scattered trees and streams that characterise the park's savannah.

Meru Mulika Lodge

If there's time left in the day, follow the signs to *Meru Mulika Lodge*, where you can soak in the pool (Ksh50) or stretch out on the terrace in front of the verdant **Mulika swamp** and watch elephants, oryx, ostriches and others. The place seems paradisial and the lodge itself is delightfully unpretentious and friendly, besides being one of the cheapest – and most hospitable – park lodges in Kenya (Ksh1340/1870 FB, bookings through *Msafiri Inns*).

---

*What you should no longer fear round the next corner are the gangs of armed Somalian poachers who, in 1988 and 1989 virtually ruled the park. During their bloody tenure, two French tourists were shot dead when they unwittingly drove into a poachers' hideout. Such was the international outcry that followed their murder, and that of George Adamson a few months later, that the Kenya government made a huge and successful effort to rout them.

Budget stays

The real **budget accommodation** is further into the park, near the park headquarters. Down here, on a stretch of open ground running down to a wooded stream, are several plain campsites, a handful of cottages/*bandas* (Ksh100-200 each one) and toilet/shower blocks. Firewood is plentiful. A third option is *Leopard Rock Safari Lodge* (bookings to PO Box 45456 Nairobi, ☎742926 Nairobi), an excellent *banda* establishment with everything you might need: electricity, hot water, mosquito nets, fully equipped bush kitchens, if all at a price (Ksh270 per person). You'd better bring some food with you because the shop at the site is rarely open or stocked. Behind the site, Leopard Rock is occasionally visited by lions, not leopards, while in front you are warned away from the foliage-entangled stream with signs that tell you it's "infested" with crocodiles – presumably small ones.

Around the Park

Meru's many tracks are mostly sandy and firm; the junctions have useful signposts (as long as you have the *Survey of Kenya* map); and the whole park is uncontaminated by tourism. It's likely you'll be required to take a ranger with you on your explorations. There are plenty of enticing areas to investigate but the **Rojewero River**, the park's largest stream, is a brilliant watercourse for exploring: densely overgrown banks flash with birds and monkeys and dark waters ripple with turtles. Large and very visible herds of **elephant, buffalo** and

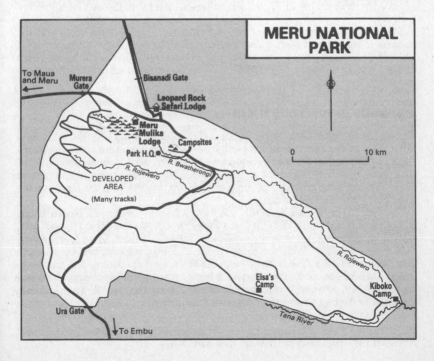

reticulated **giraffe** are common, as are, in the more open areas, gerenuk, Grevy's zebra and **ostrich**. Predators seem scarce, though they may simply be hidden in the long grass – the smaller grazers must have a nerve-wracking time of it here. Large numbers of **leopards** captured in the stock-raising lands of Laikipia have been released in the park in recent years, but as usual you have little chance of seeing them.

The rhinos' tale

Until November 1, 1988, you could always guarantee a close encounter with the **white rhinos** – close enough to see how they got the name, from the Afrikaans *weit* (meaning wide), a reference to their lugubrious grass-cropping mouths. Morning and evening, the five docile beasts were gently prodded out to graze around the park headquarters and campsites, then brought back at midday to the dust-wallow of their pen to snooze through the heat. The thousands of pounds' worth of horn that they carried on their noses ensured they could never be left unguarded.

All of this simply wasn't enough to keep them alive. Full details have never emerged of what happened, but a gang of about thirty poachers, armed with automatic rifles, stormed the rhinos' night-time paddock, killing all five, injuring several rangers and escaping with the booty of hacked-off horns.

Meru's location is dangerous; given evidence that Somalian poachers were mainly responsible for the carnage that tore through the eastern parks in the late 1980s, it seems doubtful whether Meru will be chosen for any future attempts to resettle the white rhino in Kenya. Disturbingly, several of the staff at Meru lost their jobs.

The white rhino has been extinct in Kenya since prehistoric times and the nucleus of the group at Meru came from Umfolozi Game Reserve in South Africa. Unlike black rhinos, they are remarkably good-natured animals. The head keeper of the Meru herd used to encourage visitors to pet them and even sit on them when they were lying down.

Onwards to the Tana River

If you're in the park for a couple of days, you might like to make the fairly long drive down to the **Tana River**: its confluence with the Rojewero at the southeast corner of the park is marked by waterfalls and there used to be a motorboat for river trips – worth asking about at least. Down here you are a very long way from anywhere and there are tremendous opportunities for exploring the jungle on the river banks and the wild savannah.

The four national reserves south and east of Meru – **Bisanadi**, **North Kitui**, **Rahole** and **Kora*** – are all in the Land Rover expedition category, a total of 4500 square kilometres of scrub and semi-desert, with the Tana's dense forest where they fringe the river. With the right vehicle and preparations, you could make your way, with the Tana, down to GARISSA (p.386). There are tracks to MBALAMBALA about halfway there – a highly rated place for seeing hippo and crocodile – and, beyond, a reasonable route following the river down to Garissa. If you make the trip, write and let us know how it went.

---

*Kora was the home of George Adamson (of *Born Free* fame), murdered by poachers in August 1989 when he drove through their barricade.

travel details

Between Nairobi and the Coast

Road and rail transport details for the main Nairobi–Mombasa route are given in Chapters One and Six. For **Voi**, see this chapter. **From Machakos**, *Akamba Bus* and several other companies make frequent runs to Nairobi. In the other direction, the last bus leaves Nairobi at 4pm and goes through to Kitui. **From Kitui**, most buses leave for Nairobi in the morning. Transport to Embu and the Garissa road is difficult. **Mombasa-bound**, there are buses daily through Machakos and at least one through Kitui. To **Taveta**, there are country buses on most days from Nairobi through Emali and Oloitokitok and others through **Voi**.

Summary of Parks Access

Remember to buy **maps** *for any parks you'll be visiting before setting out from Nairobi.*

TSAVO WEST: **Mtito Andei**

TSAVO EAST: **Voi**

Both towns are easily reached from Nairobi or

Mombasa by bus, *matatu*, hitching or train. Both gates are worth hitching at.

AMBOSELI: **Namanga**

Daily bus services from the Nairobi country bus station, fairly frequent *matatus*, hitching possible. Flights from Nairobi Wilson airport.

MAASAI MARA: **Narok**

Several country buses daily, some *matatus*, hitching very slow and lifts into the park rare. Flights from Nairobi Wilson airport.

SAMBURU: **Isiolo** (see p.367)

No shortage of transport to Isiolo, and lifts into the reserve from Isiolo are quite possible, even likely. Flights from Nairobi Wilson airport.

MERU: **Meru** or **Maua** (see p.129)

Lifts into the park unlikely.

Planes

For details of scheduled services to AMBOSELI, MAASAI MARA and SAMBURU, see Nairobi "travel details" (p.110).

TELEPHONE AREA CODES

Athi River ☎0150	**Voi** ☎0147	**Narok** ☎0305
Isiolo ☎0165	**Mtito Andei** ☎operator	**Namanga** ☎operator
Machakos ☎0145	exchange	exchange

CHAPTER SIX

THE COAST

Nearly everyone arrives on the coast at **Mombasa**, a considerably more enjoyable place to spend time than Nairobi. Kenya's second city, it's a tropical centre *par excellence*: steamy, lazy and scruffily dilapidated but ready, at any moment, to burst into colourful life. All around there are superb **beaches**. And, although you'll find pockets of tourist development and local crowds in the immediate city environs, this coast is not a Spanish style *costa* – yet.

Principal resort areas are **Diani Beach**; the stretch of coast north of Mombasa from **Nyali to Mtwapa**; **Watamu**; and **Malindi**. The rest is virtually untouched. For many visitors (and this is one area where you'll encounter substantial groups of package tourists) these areas of the coast represent little more than sun, sea, sand and, until recently, sex. You can, of course, have a wonderful time on the beaches doing nothing very much, but there is much more to this part of Kenya than the limited horizons of the travel brochures might have you believe and plenty of things to do if this kind of lassitude drives you nuts after a few days.

Most obviously, the beaches are the backdrop for one of the most beautiful **coral reefs** in the world, rated in the top three (with Australia's Barrier Reef and the Red Sea) by experienced divers. With even the most limited equipment, easily hired almost anywhere, you can – corny as it sounds – enter another world. With oxygen tanks and instruction, you can go a lot further. The most spectacular sections are far to the south off Wasini Island and, north, between Watamu and Malindi, each enclosed in **marine national parks**. But you can simply pull on snorkel and mask almost anywhere and swim out to discover sections of reef for yourself.

A string of **islands** – Wasini, Funzi, Chale, Mombasa itself, Lamu, Manda, Pate, Kiwaiyu – runs up the coast, all of them worth visiting and some required destinations. There are more, but this gives you some idea. And the entire coast is littered with the **ruins** of forts, mosques, tombs and even whole towns. Some – including **Fort Jesus**, **Lamu** and the ruined city of **Gedi** – are already on the tourist circuit, but there are dozens more that have hardly been cleared of bush or investigated archaeologically and they make compelling exploring. Fort Jesus Museum in Mombasa has a map of locations if you're interested.

Islam has been a major influence on the coast and you'll especially feel it in the north around **Lamu**, an idyllic island setting which you should definitely try to catch before it is lost to mass tourism. Visiting the coast during **Ramadan** might leave a slightly strange impression – of a region where everyone is on night shift perhaps – but in practical terms it makes little difference. It can sometimes be difficult to find a room during the day, if only because everything appears to be shut, but you can usually find a lax restaurant serving food, and you'll do most of your eating after dark in any case. During *Id ul Fitr*, at the end of Ramadan, and *Maulidi al Nebi*, the holiday for the prophet's birthday, lodgings often fill up early.

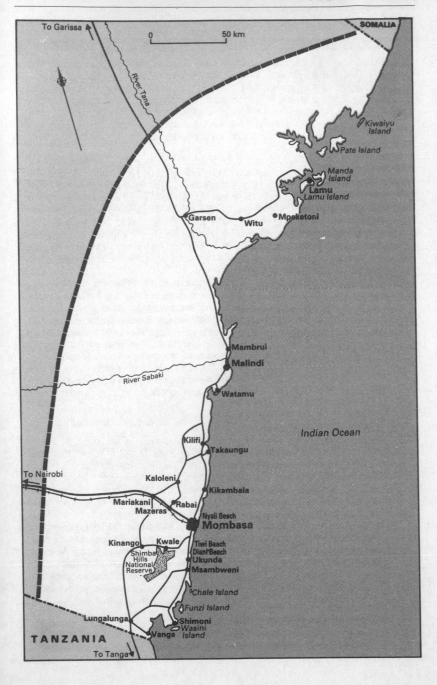

COASTAL CULTURE: SWAHILI AND MIJIKENDA

The coast is where East Africa meets the classical world. Partly through the intermediary of **Islam**, with its direct and simple tenets, foreign ideas have shaped the society, language, literature and architecture. Apart from the pragmatic Portuguese, whose interests seem to have been entirely mercenary, immigrants and traders from Arabia and Asia – once or twice even China – have been a subtle and gradual influence on the coast. They arrived each year in March or April on the northeast **monsoon**, the dry *kaskazi* wind, and returned in September on the southerly monsoon or *kusi*.

Some, by choice or mishap, would be left behind. Through intermarriage from the earliest times (and these must have been before Islam appeared on the scene in the seventh century), a distinct ancient civilisation called **Swahili** emerged. Swahili, which is thought to derive from the same Arabic root as *sahel*, meaning edge or coast, is also a language, known to its speakers as **ki-Swahili**. It is one of the more mainstream of the Bantu languages, spoken throughout much of Africa south of the equator. Like all old languages used by trading peoples, it contains strong clues about whom they mixed with. Swahili isn't based on Arabic any more than English is based on Latin, but it is full of words derived from Arabic and peppered with others of Indian, Portuguese and English origin.

The Swahili are not a "tribe" in any definable sense. **Who the Swahili are** should emerge throughout this chapter. No less than, say, the English, they are the result of the mixed heritage reflected in their language. Questions of family background and status in the community have traditionally loomed large: families that trace their roots – not always very plausibly – to foreign shores in the distant past tend to claim superior social status. Nor, predictably, was skin colour ignored. Essentially Muslim, the Swahili interpretation of the religion varies from place to place and according to circumstance: rigidity of form is an alien concept in Swahili culture. Essentially coastal, not all Swahili trade, nor do they all fish – some Swahili groups even avoid eating fish. Coconuts, mixed farming, cattle and goats are all vitally important.

THE TOWNS

Like the language, it was long thought that the **towns** of the coast began as implants, that is, as Arab, or even Persian, trading forts. It is now known that most were already in existence before any of the great post-Islamic wars and migrations took place in the Middle East. Mombasa, Malindi, Lamu and a host of lesser-known settlements are essentially ancient African towns that have always tolerated and even encouraged peaceful immigration from overseas. In fact, the Swahili style has always been to welcome the new and the sophisticated.

With few exceptions, however, any attempt to compromise the independence of these towns was met with violent resistance. The Portuguese were least successful. When they arrived at the end of the fifteenth century, memories of the Moorish occupation of their own country were still fresh. Accommodation to Islam, or to dark-skinned strangers, was not on their agenda and, despite a long acquaintance with the coast, they never established an enduring colonial presence, as they did in Goa on the south Indian coast, further along the same trading route.

THE SLAVE INHERITANCE

Slavery on the coast was originally less a black and white moral issue than is commonly assumed. In the past, it was not unusual for people in need to lend a member of the family to others in exchange for goods or services. The **Mijikenda** peoples, for example, maintained close links with the coastal towns, trading their produce, providing armed forces when the towns were under threat, and being supplied in return with overseas trade goods, especially cloth and tools. As traders, the Swahili sometimes accumulated surpluses of grain on the coast at times of severe drought inland. In exchange for food, Mijikenda children would be taken to the towns by their relatives and fostered with Swahili families with whom they had links – to become, in effect, slaves. Later, they intermarried, or paid off the debt and returned, though a small number were probably sold overseas. But when slavery itself became a major aspect of commerce, and the available foreign goods irresistible (cloth, firearms, and liquor from Holland, France, England and America), then any trace of trust in the old arrangement vanished. The weak and defenceless were captured and sold to slavers from the coast, often to end up on Dutch or French plantations around the Indian Ocean or in Arabian households. And, with the domination of the **Sultan of Oman** on the coast in the early nineteenth century, and the large-scale emigration of Arabs to East Africa, slaves from the far interior were increasingly set to work on their truly colonial coastal farms and plantations. When the British formally freed the slaves in 1907, they became part of Swahili society.

THE MIJIKENDA PEOPLES

The other principal people of the coastal region are the **Mijikenda** (Nine Tribes), a loose grouping whose Bantu languages are to a large extent mutually intelligible and closely related to Swahili. They are believed to have arrived in their present homelands in the sixteenth or seventeenth century from a quasi-historical state called Shungwaya. This centre was probably located somewhere in the Lamu hinterland or in the southwest corner of present-day Somalia. According to oral tradition, the people who left it were the Giriama, the Digo, the Rabai, the Ribe, the Duruma, the Chonyi, the Jibana, the Kauma and the Kambe (as distinct from the Kamba of the interior). All these "tribes" now live in the coastal hinterland, with the **Giriama** and **Digo** the largest and best-known groups. They share a degree of common cultural heritage, each tribe having a *kaya* central settlement, a fortified village in the forest some kilometres from the coast, usually built on raised ground. The *kayas* still exist and, although most are run-down, some are still inhabited by one or two elders. They each contain a *fingo*, a charm said to derive from the ancestral home of Shungwaya. It is possible to visit some of the *kayas* but they are by no means tourist attractions: sincerity and some tact will be needed.

Like so many other Kenyan peoples, the Mijikenda had age-set systems that helped cut across the divisive groupings of clan and subclan to bind communities together. Much of this tradition has been lost during this century; the installation of a new ruling elders' age-set, for example, required the killing and castration of a stranger.

Economically, the Mijikenda were, and still are, diverse. They were cultivators, herders (especially the Duruma and, at one time, the Giriama), long-distance traders with the interior, makers of palm wine (a Digo speciality now diffused all over Mijikenda-land), hunters and fishermen. They have successfully maintained their cultural identity, warring with the British in 1914 over the imposition of taxes and the demand for porters for World War I, and preserving a vigorous conservative tradition of adherence to their old beliefs in spirits and the power of ancestors. Many Mijikenda, however, have found conversion to Islam a helpful religious switch in their dealings with coastal merchants and businessmen. Perhaps this is the latest development in the growth of Swahili society.

Nature and wildlife

The hundreds of kilometres of sandy beach that fringe the low-lying coastal strip are backed by dunes and coconut palms, traversed by scores of streams and rivers. Flowing off the plateaus through tumbling jungle, these waterways meander across a narrow, fertile plain to the sea. In sheltered creeks, forests of **mangrove** trees cover vast areas and create a distinctive ecological zone of tidal mud flats, hopeless for beaches or swimming, but a bird-watcher's paradise.

Wildlife on the coast seems in keeping with its lusher, more intimate feel. The big game of up-country Kenya is more or less absent (though you could try **Shimba Hills National Park** near Mombasa), but smaller creatures are abundant. Monkeys are especially common, birdlife is prolific, snakes – brilliant disguise artists – are rarely seen but lizards skitter everywhere, including upside down on the ceiling at night, and chameleons waver across the road. So do giant millipedes, up to a foot long, harmless scavengers of rotten fruit. Insects, including some fierce mosquitoes, are here in full force, but most are attractive participants in the coast's gaudy show.

Some pre-coast practicalities

The coast is the part of Kenya most affected by the **seasons**. April to June are much less busy, and much cheaper, than the rest of the year. While the beaches tend to be damp and the weather muggy and overcast, you can make savings of more than fifty percent at some hotels.

Nairobi–Mombasa railway

For getting to the coast, the **train journey** between Nairobi and Mombasa is one of the highlights of Kenyan travel: even if you usually drive, you should try to make at least one journey between capital and coast with *Kenya Railways*. Nowhere can the institution of leisured rail travel be better preserved than here; with just two services a day in each direction, the cars (mostly ancient British-

---

SWAHILI PROVERBS AND SAYINGS

The Swahili are renowned for the imagery, rhythm and complexity of their proverbs. The first of these few – an admonishment to be patient – is the one you will most often hear.

Haraka, haraka: haina baraka – Haste, haste: there's no blessing in it.

Nyumba njema si mlango – A good house isn't (judged by) its door [ie, don't judge by appearances].

Mahaba ni haba, akili ni mali – Love counts for little, intelligence is wealth.

Faida yako ni hasara yangu – Your gain is my loss.

Haba na haba kujaza kibaba – Little by little fills the pint measure.

Kuku anakula sawa na mdomo wake – A chicken eats according to her beak [interpretations invited . . .].

Mungu alitolandika, haliwezi kufutika – What God has written cannot be erased.

Heri shuka isiyo kitushi, kama shali njema ya mauwa – Better an honest loincloth than a fancy cloak (of shame).

Mke ni nguo, mgomba kupalilia – A wife means clothes (like) a banana plant means weeding.

built ones) are spotless and the service impeccable. Take the early (all stations) train for more time to gaze out of the windows by daylight: from Nairobi, you'll see the Nairobi National Park and game on the Athi Plains; from Mombasa, the steep climb from jungly coast to arid semi-desert. Remember that couples may only share a first-class compartment, as the four-berth second-class compartments are single sex. Remember, too, to get up in time for breakfast, especially if you didn't treat yourself to dinner. On which subject, it's worth noting that the first "sitting" for dinner has to vacate rather swiftly for the second. Vegetarians are well catered for: mention it when you buy your ticket. See the section on trains in *Basics*.

Buses to the coast
Buses to Mombasa are a small saving on the train and go by day as well as night, but most of the road is dull and the experience not as much fun as the train. For coverage of the route, see p.222–26.

Flights
You can also **fly** to Mombasa, Malindi or Lamu from Nairobi. Flying to Lamu from Nairobi makes sense if you have the cash (about £50; see Nairobi "travel details") and not much time, as you avoid retracing your steps between Lamu and Mombasa, but it's not an interesting flight. If you'd like to fly for the fun of it, the Lamu–Malindi hop is inexpensive and has stunning views over jungle and reef.

Accommodation
On **accommodation**, an alternative to hotels is **self-catering villas and cottages**. There's a good selection along the beaches north of Mombasa, at Malindi and at Diani beach and it's a very sound financial proposition for families or groups. *Kenya Villas*, PO Box 57046, Westminster House, Kenyatta Ave, Nairobi (☎338072) act as agents for many holiday home-owners. Large houses, to sleep eight for example, can be had for under Ksh1000/night.

One word of warning for the coast. Tempting as it can be, **sleeping out**, except on the most deserted of beaches, is very unwise. Anywhere near Mombasa or Malindi, it's asking for trouble, although the reputation of some of these beaches for daylight snatchings and more grievous assaults is unfairly exaggerated. In general, you will have to find a room, or at least a recognised campsite.

MOMBASA AND NEARBY

Arriving in **Mombasa** by train in the morning, there's ample time, if the heat doesn't fell you, to head straight out to the beaches, either south to Diani or north towards Malindi. But you should consider spending a few days in Mombasa itself, tuning in to the coast, catching the cadences of *"Kiswahili safi"* (pure Swahili) and looking around Kenya's most historic city. If you have time, there are two worthwhile trips you can make inland to areas which are much less known: **Shimba Hills National Reserve** to the southwest and, well off the beaten path to the northwest, the **Mijikenda country** between Mazeras and Kaloleni. If you would rather take this latter detour before reaching the coast proper – and it's a pleasant introduction to the region – buses or the early (all stations) train from Nairobi will drop you at **Mazeras**, a simple hitching or bus trip away from Mombasa.

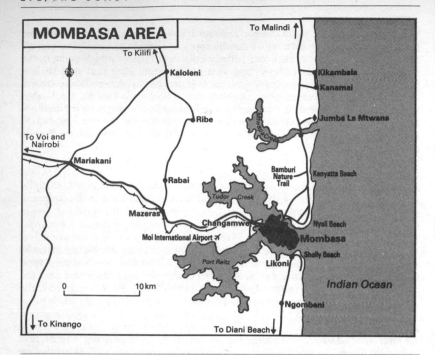

MOMBASA AREA

To Malindi
To Kilifi
Kaloleni
Kikambala
Kanamai
Ribe
Jumba La Mtwana
To Voi and Nairobi
Mariakani
Bamburi Nature Trail
Kenyatta Beach
Rabai
Tudor Creek
Mazeras
Changamwe
Nyali Beach
Moi International Airport
Mombasa
Shelly Beach
Port Reitz
Likoni
Indian Ocean
0   10 km
Ngombeni
To Kinango
To Diani Beach

Mombasa

Kenya's second city can come as a revelation. There's a depth of history here, and a sense of community which the capital lacks. Steamy, sleazy, hot – you're always thirsty – and physically *tropical* in a way that could hardly be more different from Nairobi, **MOMBASA** is the slightly indolent hub of the coast – a faded, flaking, charming city that still, despite its gentle sprawl, feels like a small town that was once great.

Actually an island, Mombasa is now connected to the mainland to the west by causeways, to the north by a bridge, but on the south, still, by a ferry; it is intricate and its streets wriggle deceptively. At its most appealing heart is the **Old Town**, a lattice of lanes, mosques and cramped, elderly houses sloping gently down to the once-busy dhow harbour. **Fort Jesus**, an impressive reminder of Mombasa's complicated, bloody past, still overlooks the Old Town from where it once guarded the harbour entrance. It is now a national monument and museum.

Within easy walking distance, and clustered all around, is the whole of downtown, twentieth-century Mombasa: wide streets, a refreshing lack of high-rises, and a surprising number of open spaces. Even here, in the commercial centre of one of Africa's busiest ports, the atmosphere is relaxed and congenial. Rush hours, urgency and paranoia seem to be Nairobi's problems (as everyone will tell you), not Mombasa's. And the gaping, marginal slums that one expects to find outside African cities hardly exist here. True, Likoni and (especially) Changamwe on the mainland are burgeoning suburbs which the municipality has difficulty keeping up with, but the brutalising conditions of Mathare Valley or Kibera are absent.

Despite the palms, the sunshine and the happy languor, all is not bliss and perfection: **street crime**, though it hardly approaches Nairobi's level, is a serious problem, and you should be wary of displaying your valuables or accepting invitations to walk down dark alleys. But, as a general rule, Mombasa is a far less neurotic city than Nairobi. There's nowhere in the centre that could be considered a no-go area. One indication of this is that the city stays awake much later. Climatic encouragement may be part of it, but at an hour when central Nairobi is empty but for taxis and *askaris*, Mombasans are strolling in the warm night, old men are conversing on the benches lining Digo Road, and many shops remain open: the small-town freedoms are still healthy here. All this adds up to a city that is richly satisfying and rewarding to stay in.

Ethnically, Mombasa is perhaps even more diverse than Nairobi. Asian and Arab influence is particularly pervasive, with fifty mosques and dozens of Hindu and Sikh temples lending a strongly oriental flavour. Still, the largest contingent speaks Swahili as a first language and it is the **Swahili civilisation** that, more than any other, accounts for Mombasa's distinctive character. You'll see women in head-to-foot *bui-buis* or brilliant *kanga* outfits, men in *kanzu* gowns and hip-slung *kikoi* wraps. The smaller community of settlers and European expatriates figures less prominently here than in Nairobi, but it continues to wield disproportionate economic and social clout. For up-country settlers, Mombasa and the coast have long represented "sea level and sanity" – a holiday break from the grind of making a living in the Highlands.

As a tourist town, Mombasa doesn't go out of its way; indeed, its best quality is its lack of pretension. It is principally a port (**Kilindini**, with a harbour recently dredged by Americans, takes up most of the western side of the island) and, increasingly, an industrial city with a major oil refinery (on your right as you arrive by train). In short, it is **not a resort**. Visiting sailors are as important to its tourist economy as bona fide tourists, and (a grievous shortcoming) the island has no real beaches. Even the biggest hotels are relatively modest. The vast majority of the obvious tourists in town are here only on a shopping trip from their north or south coast beach hotels. You may not be able to resist the lure of the beaches for long, but the seedily romantic port city deserves time unless you are in a big hurry; there are few places in the country with such a strong sense of identity.

Arrivals

Arriving on the night **train** is the best way; it loops down the steep scarp to the ocean as you wake up to the rustle of starched waiters and the clatter of shiny teapots. When you walk out of the station into the glare of the morning sun Haile Selassie Road is directly ahead, leading in one straight kilometre to the city's main north–south thoroughfare, **Digo Road**. The **Old Town** begins on the far side of Digo. To the left of Haile Selassie are markets and bus stations; to the right, a concentration of hotels; then, parallel to it, **Moi Avenue** – the tourist strip. If you elect to pick a taxi out of the swarm awaiting the train's arrival, Ksh40 is the going rate to be taken to any town centre hotel.

Arriving by **bus or car**, you come over Makupa Causeway with the railway, diverging on the island to head 4km straight down **Kenyatta Avenue**, through low-income suburbs that become increasingly commercial as you approach the centre. Kenyatta joins with **Mwembe Tayari** in a sprawling bus station and snack food district. If you get out here, walk on down Kenyatta Avenue to Digo Road.

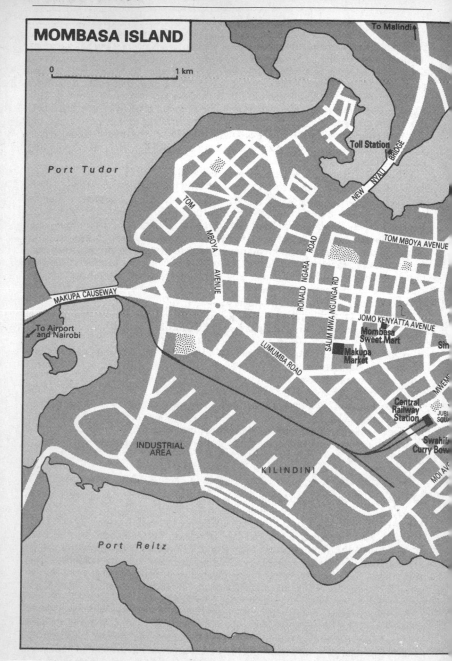

MOMBASA ISLAND

0   1 km

To Malindi

Toll Station

Port Tudor

NEW NYALI BRIDGE

TOM MBOYA AVENUE

TOM MBOYA AVENUE

RONALD NGARA ROAD

SALIM MWA NGUNGA RD

MAKUPA CAUSEWAY

To Airport
and Nairobi

JOMO KENYATTA AVENUE

Mombasa
Sweet Mart

Sin

LUMUMBA ROAD

Makupa
Market

MWEMB

Central
Railway
Station

JUBI
SQU

Swahili
Curry Bow

INDUSTRIAL
AREA

KILINDINI

MOI AVE

Port Reitz

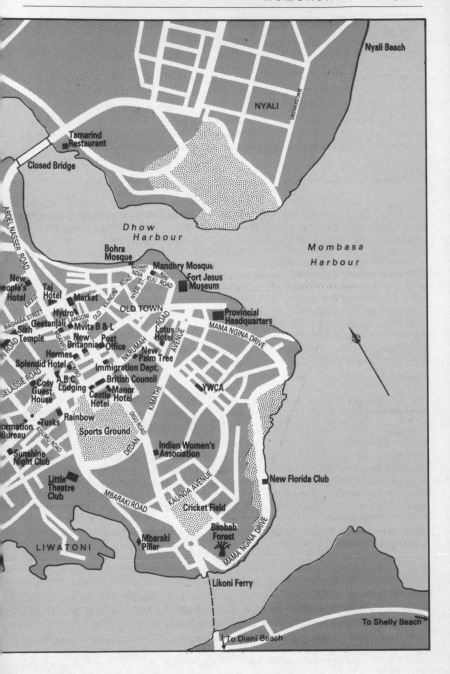

Nyali Beach

NYALI

GREENWOOD DRIVE

Tamarind
Restaurant

Closed Bridge

Dhow
Harbour

Mombasa
Harbour

Bohra
Mosque

BACHAWY

NDIA
KUU ROAD

Mandhry Mosque

Fort Jesus
Museum

New
People's
Hotel

Taj
Hotel

KWANI

Market

NYERI ST

OLD KILINDINI ROAD

ROAD

OLD TOWN

Provincial
Headquarters

MAMA NGINA DRIVE

Hydro

BIASHARA STREET

Geetanjali

LANGONI

Mvita B & L

Lotus
Hotel

Sikh
Temple

ROAD

MSHINI

New
Britannia

NKRUMAH

New
Palm Tree

AVENUE

ROAD

Hermes

KIBO

Post
Office

Splendid Hotel

Immigration Dept.

SELASSIE ROAD

A.B.C.
Lodging

British Council

KIMATHI

YWCA

Cosy
Guest
House

Castle
Hotel

Manor
Hotel

DIGO ROAD

Rainbow

Tusks

Sports Ground

DELAN

Indian Women's
Association

Information
Bureau

KISUMU ROAD

Sunshine
Night Club

Little
Theatre
Club

MBARAKI ROAD

KAUNDA AVENUE

New Florida Club

Cricket Field

MAMA NGINA DRIVE

Mbaraki
Pillar

Baobab
Forest

LIWATONI

Likoni Ferry

To Shelly Beach

To Diani Beach

By air, you arrive some 12km from the city centre at Moi International Airport on the mainland near Port Reitz. As in Nairobi, taxis (Ksh150 is the going rate), the *Kenya Airways* bus and the *KBS* bus provide a three-tier service into town. If you can handle a few kilometres' walk, the road to the Nairobi highway (where you'll quickly pick up buses and *matatus*) is not unpleasant and along it, on the left, is an enormous Kamba woodcarvers' "village". It isn't a place you're likely to bother visiting unless you are out here anyway – where the art of woodcarving has been reduced to not much more than a human conveyor belt. There are no special reductions should you want to buy; it's just a good education in a lowly sector of the tourist industry and, that said, quite entertaining.

Lodgings

You might reasonably expect to find a concentration of **cheap lodgings** in the Old Town. Curiously enough, this isn't the case, though most of them cluster in the streets just to the west.

Hydro (PO Box 85360, ☎23784), corner of Digo and Langoni Rds. The cheapest place in town, often full. No singles, and only one double room, and security in the shared rooms is none too hot. Still, it's an old standby, perfect for groups of three or four, and usefully located (Ksh50 per bed and even cheaper on the roof, or Ksh75/150 s/c).

New People's Hotel (PO Box 85342, ☎312831), Abdel Nasser Rd. Big undistinguished block, handy if you're bussing up to Lamu in the morning and not at all bad, though single rooms arc cube-like (Ksh84/169).

New Britannia (PO Box 83535, ☎312038), Gusii St. A US Peace Corps hangout with a noisy bar but decent rooms, some with fans (Ksh115/140).

Mvita Boarding and Lodging, corner of Hospital St and Turkana St, near Digo Rd. Clean doubles with fan for Ksh120.

Balgis (PO Box 80445, ☎25558), Digo Rd across from the junction with Old Kilindini Rd. Similar to the *Mvita* and also well priced, but lacks a bar downstairs – to the advantage of light sleepers.

Cosy Guest House (PO Box 83011, ☎313064), Haile Selassie Rd Convenient if you've just arrived by train. Character it lacks, but large rooms, fans and balconies (in the doubles only) compensate (Ksh90/140) making it currently the most popular lodging in town. Try to get a first- or second-floor room to overcome the low water pressure.

ABC Lodge (PO Box 84935, ☎313340), Kwa Shibu Rd. A shade brighter than the *Cosy*, but otherwise similar – so the rates seem a little high (Ksh100/200).

Fortuna Hostel Annexe (not on map), Haile Selassie Rd. Basic but good with fans and reasonable shower (Ksh160 double).

Sports View Hotel, Ronald Ngala Ave. A new place – modern, clean, quiet and good value (under Ksh300/double).

Taj Hotel (PO Box 82923, ☎23198), Digo Road. Better kept than most but still a little expensive at this level (Ksh160/300).

Pricier hotels

In a **higher price bracket**, you will generally find comfortable, old-fashioned hotels with **self-contained rooms**, fans or air conditioning and **breakfast included**. Compared with Nairobi, they tend to be good value.

New Palm Tree (PO Box 90013, ☎311756), Nkrumah Rd. With its sunny, first-floor courtyard a likeable joint, but, in common with a number of places in Mombasa, has problems with its water – and none that's hot (Ksh320/450 s/c B&B).

Hotel Splendid (PO Box 90482, ☎20967) Msanifu Kombo St. Perhaps slightly less appeal-ing than the *New Palm Tree*, but popular for its fifth-floor roof garden bar/restaurant. Room 42 is the best of several larger-than-average rooms, with balconies and fans (from Ksh212/ 382).

Manor (PO Box 84851, ☎21821), Nyerere Ave. One of the town centre's top two hotels (from Ksh450/900; sister hotel of Nairobi's *Fairview*). Grand style atmosphere and all the mod cons you could desire.

Castle (PO Box 84231, ☎23403), Moi Avenue. Considering the alternatives, the *Castle* is way overpriced (Ksh780/1200), though it carries the cachet of Mombasa's downtown rendezvous point.

Lotus Hotel (PO Box 90193, ☎313207/313234, telex 21105), corner of Mvita and Cathedral Rds. Located on a quiet corner not far from Fort Jesus, the *Lotus* – which exudes a wonderful Maugham-ish ambience – is the best bet in Mombasa and often full, but emphatically worth checking (from around Ksh600/900).

Long stays and shoestring accommodation

For **long stays** in Mombasa, you might like to consider the **YW/YMCA** (PO Box 85744, ☎20632) on the corner of Kaunda and Margaret avenues. It charges around Ksh7000/9000 FB per month.

Sikh Temple Complex, Mwembe Tayari. This is another possibility – people have stayed here in the past, but perhaps made themselves unwelcome as enquiries produced no enthusiasm.

Sunrise High School/Arya Nursery School guesthouse. Three gates further up the street from the Sikh temple, in the compound, there's a low-cost guesthouse (Ksh40 per bed).

Eating, drinking, nightlife

Mombasa is well supplied with good, **cheap restaurants**. If you're newly arrived from "up-country", they are one of the city's chief delights, as a discernible cuisine involving coconut, fish, chicken, rice and beans, incorporating spicy Asian flavours, begins to make an impression on your palate.

Recoda Hotel, Nyeri Street. Perhaps mombasa's best restaurant for **Swahili food**. Open only in the evening, a good excuse to throw off lingering misgivings and plunge into the Old Town after dark. Sitting at pavement tables, you eat from a limited but very cheap list of deli-cious fish, creamed beans, cassava, plantain, *mahamri* and *mushkaki* with salad. If you're not prepared to pick your portion, they'll just bring you a never-ending selection judged suitable. Go early as by 8pm, they're running out of favourites. There's another, similar place just a few doors away. Ksh70 would see anyone incapacitated, though you can eat pretty well for half that.

Swahili Curry Bowl (☎311084), Tangana Rd close to the station. Again, one hundred percent authentic Swahili cooking. Here the menu's more extensive but prices are still low – a great spot for a meal before the train trip back to Nairobi.

Hydro Hotel, corner of Digo and Langoni Rds. The restaurant usually serves good food, with curries and *pilau* the staples and *biriani* a twice-weekly special.

New Chetna, Haile Selassie Ave, near the *Cosy Guest House*. Traditional Indian food at low prices (hot).

Geetanjali's (☎26260), Msanifu Kombo St. Just one of a whole range of places specialising in all-you-can-eat meals with a strong **Asian** accent (Ksh60–90 range). Particularly recom-mended for vegetarian food, and blissfully air-conditioned (closes at 9pm).

Bashur, Langoni Rd. Very good, cheap meals.

Singh's (☎493283), Mwembe Tayari. Good curries.

Splendid View Restaurant (tucked behind the *Hotel Splendid*). Try the *Faluda* for an extraordinary gastronomic experience. Unfortunately they've no alcohol licence.

Chinese restaurants. Several places on Moi Ave – *Chinese Overseas* is good.

Hamburger House, Kisumu Road, just near the Tusks on Moi Avenue. Well above average with an extensive menu (Ksh70–90).

Castle Hotel Reasonably good pizzas for only Ksh50.

Tamarind Restaurant (☎471747) Out of Mombasa over Nyali Bridge; go right at the traffic lights by Frere-town bell tower, then follow the signs. If you're in the mood for expensive **seafood** in a plush, jet-setting atmosphere, this is the place. In a stupendous position, with Mombasa spread out panoramically across the creek, this is considered to be one of the best eating-houses in Kenya. If you're going to do it, you might as well dive in at the deep end with a Ksh500 seafood platter.

Snacks and juice bars

For **snacking**, and the **drinks** you'll probably want to consume ceaselessly, there are corner cafés, hole-in-the-wall juice bars, and confectionery shops all over town:

Pistachio, Chembe Rd. Hard to beat for its ice cream and various kinds of coffee, but not particularly cheap. Their breakfast is good value however.

Anglo-Swiss Bakery, Chembe Rd. The best in Mombasa, and the place to buy something to eat with your coffee at the next venue. . .

Kenya Coffee Board, Moi Ave. The KCB do their own exquisite "pineapple pies" and rather resent coffee drinkers smuggling in cakes.

Chuck Norris' Juice Bar, Makadara Rd, near the Lido cinema. Cheap and delicious – positively astral avocado juice.

Cosy Tea Room, Nkrumah Road (closed weekends). Rather more authentically Mombasan, with first-class meat pies.

Taheri Cold House, Nkrumah Road (again, closed weekends). Excellent juices and they used to do delicious, filling dishes of *Chana Bateta* (it seems another establishment 100m down the street may have it now).

Mombasa Sweet Mart, a twenty-minute walk up Kenyatta Ave on the left. Must be the cheapest place anywhere for toothsome indulgence, with an eye-popping variety of **Indian sweetmeats**.

Pan shops

Also highly characteristic of Mombasa are the Indian **pan shops**, often doubling as tobacconists and corner shops. You have to try *pan* at least once It's essentially a mildly narcotic dessert, chewed and sucked but not swallowed, consisting of your choice of sweet spices, chopped nuts and vegetable matter, syrup, and white lime, from a display of dishes, all wrapped in a hot-sweet, dark green *betel* leaf. Pop the parcel in your mouth and munch – it tastes as exotic and unlikely as it sounds – then spit out the pith when you're finished.

Bars

The **Castle Hotel's** patio is Mombasa's answer to the *Thorn Tree Café*, the place where everyone arranges to meet. Despite renovations which have given it a prettier face, the *Castle's* public image is still shackled to a reputation as the biggest open-air pick-up joint in Mombasa. Sailors favour it, early in the evening. The "Garden Bar" (side entrance) is not as frenetic, though usually just as crowded.

Across the street, the **Istanbul** draws a large local crowd to a lively pavement terrace, but increasingly, the prostitues gather here too. They can be a pain – or a laugh – depending on your mood. The food here (barbecues for the most part) is inexpensive.

The **Lotus Hotel**, corner of Mvita and Cathedral Rds, is really nice for a civilised beer.

Nightlife-low life

The tourist hotels are outside town and so are the flashiest discos, most of them attached to hotels. That leaves Mombasa itself depleted of high-tech action, and few bands find it worthwhile to play on the island when the resorts pay more. Mombasa has a clutch of less self-conscious **nightspots** you wouldn't take the family to, they're mostly down at the more disreputable end of Moi Avenue, where it fades into the docks district of Kilindini.

Rainbow, Mnazi Moja Rd, just off Moi Ave. The cheap and cheerful approach here typifies most of the clubs.

Sunshine, Moi Avenue.

Kasbah, over the chemist in Digo Road.

Birds, next to the *Bristol Hotel*, behind the Post Office.

Istanbul, Moi Ave. Sometimes has live bands on Sunday afternoons.

New Florida (☎313127), Mama Ngina Drive overlooking the ocean. Attempts a slicker, more expensive scene, with a choreographed floor show and lots of glitter. In the essentials however – thumping disco, grinding hookers – it doesn't differ noticeably from its Nairobi namesake. A two-kilometre walk, so it's preferable to take a taxi here, or at least back.

Midland Hotel A long-established gay rendezvous.

Kestrel Club Also attracts a gay crowd.

If you don't want to join the throngs in the clubs but don't feel inclined to stay in your room either, **walking after dark** is generally safe in the Old Town and along the main thoroughfares. Around the Old Town, you'll still come across one or two coffee-sellers selling their thick black *kahawa* from traditional highspouted jugs. Like the men who used to sell glasses of water, their trade has almost died out. And at the corner of Langoni and Old Kilindini roads, there's a very good *halwa* shop, normally open late: a hundred grams of fragrantly perfumed almond *halwa* is a fine accompaniment to coffee.

Mombasa in the past

Mombasa is one of East Africa's oldest settlements. The island has had a town on it, located somewhere between the present "Old Town" and Nyali Bridge, for at least **700 years** and there are enough documentary snippets from earlier times to guess that some kind of settlement has existed since BC, though probably under a different name. Mombasa's own optimistic claim (frequently repeated in the tourist literature) to be 2500 years old comes from Roman and Egyptian adventure stories.

Early tales

Precisely what was going on before the Portuguese arrived is still barely discernible. An armchair traveller, Al-Idrisi, compiled the following in the early twelfth century about a place called *Manfasa* in roughly the right location:

> *This is a small place and a dependency of the Zanj [coastal people]. Its inhabitants work in the iron mines and hunt tigers. They have red coloured dogs which fight every kind of wild beast and even lions.*

This sounds most unlikely, but then the history of Mombasa is a series of unlikely episodes. **Ibn Battuta**, the roving fourteenth-century Moroccan, spent a relatively quiet night here in 1332 and declared the people of the town "devout, chaste and virtuous . . . their mosques . . . strongly constructed of wood . . . the greater part of their diet . . . bananas and fish". But another Arab writer of 100 years later found a less ordered society:

> *Monkeys have become the rulers of Mombasa since about 800 AH [1400 AD]. They even come and take the food from the dishes, attack men in their own homes and take away what they can find. The master of the house chases the thieving monkey and does not cease cajoling him until the animal, having eaten the food, gives back the dish or vessel. When the monkeys enter a house and find a woman they hold congress with her. The monkeys divide into bands each with its own chief and march behind him in an orderly manner. The people have much to put up with.*

Vasco de Gama and other Portuguese visitors

Apocryphal story or not, Mombasa had considerably worse depredations to put up with after **Vasco da Gama's** expedition, steaming with mercenary zeal, dropped anchor on Easter Saturday 1498. After courtesy gifts had been exchanged, relations suddenly soured, the fleet was prevented from entering the port, and a few days later, richer by only one sheep and "large quantities of oranges, lemons and sugar cane", da Gama went off to try his primitive diplomacy at Malindi, and found his first and lasting ally on the coast.

Mombasa was visited again in 1505 by a fourteen-strong fleet. This time, the king of Mombasa had enlisted 1500 archers from the mainland and stored arsenals of stone missiles on the rooftops in preparation for the expected **invasion** through the town's narrow alleys. The attack, pitching firearms against spears, poisoned arrows and stones, was decisive and brutal. The town was squeezed on all sides and the king's palace (of which no trace remains) was seized. The king and most of the survivors slipped out of town into the palm groves which then covered the island, but 1513 Mombasans had been killed – and five Portuguese.

At this point, the king suggested he might save Mombasa by agreeing to become a vassal of Portugal, but he was too late and the request was turned down: it would have compromised the freedom of the Portuguese to **loot** the abandoned town if they had just entered into an accord. They took their time, picking over the bodies in the courtyards and breaking down the strongroom doors, until the ships at anchor were almost overladen. Then, as a parting shot, they fired the town. The narrow streets and the cattle stalls between the thatched houses produced a conflagration that must have razed Mombasa to the ground.

Yet in 1528, the Portuguese returned to wreck and plunder anew the city which had grown on the ashes of the old. In the 1580s, it happened twice more; on the last occasion, in 1589, there was a frenzied **massacre** at the hands of the Portuguese and – coincidentally – a marauding tribe of nomads called the *Zimba* (about whom little is known except their cannibalistic notoriety). The Zimba's unholy alliance with the Europeans came to an abrupt end at Malindi shortly afterwards, when the Portuguese, together with the townsfolk and 3000 Segeju archers, wiped them out.

By now, Mombasa would seem to have been devastated beyond recovery. Yet remarkably, only two years after this last catastrophe, it launched a major land expedition of its own against its old enemy, Malindi. It had finally met a decisive match. The party was ambushed on the way by Malindi's Segeju allies, who themselves stormed and took Mombasa, later handing over the town (in which they had little interest) to the Portuguese at Malindi. The Malindi corps transferred to Mombasa, the Malindi sheikh was grandly installed as sultan of the whole region, and the Portuguese set to work on **Fort Jesus**, dedicated in 1593.

Fort Jesus . . .

Once completed, the fort became the focus of everything that mattered in Mombasa, changing hands a total of nine times between 1631 and 1875. The history of the town during this time is largely the history of the fort.

The first takeover happened in 1631, a **popular revolt** by the town that resulted in the killing of every Portuguese. But the Sultan, lacking support from any of the other towns under Portuguese domination, eventually had to desert the fort: the Portuguese, waiting in Zanzibar, reoccupied it. For the rest of the seventeenth century, they continued to hold Mombasa and, at first, consolidated their control of the Indian Ocean trade.

Meanwhile, however, the **Omani Arabs** were becoming increasingly powerful. When Dutch, English and French ships started to appear on the horizon, time was clearly running out for the Portuguese trading monopoly. Efforts to bring settlers to their East African possessions fell through, and they retreated more and more behind the massive walls of Fort Jesus. Portugal's East African "empire" was under siege, and in 1696–98, Fort Jesus itself was isolated and besieged into submission by the Omanis who, with support from Pate and Lamu, had already taken the rest of the town. After 33 months, almost all the defenders – the Portuguese corps and some 1500 Swahili loyalists – had died of starvation or plague.

. . . in Arab hands

Disenchantment with the new Arab rulers was soon being fomented, spilling over in 1728 into a mutiny among the fort's African soldiers. The Portuguese were invited back – for a year. Then the fort was again besieged and this time the Portuguese gave up quickly. They were allowed their freedom, and a number are said to have married and stayed in the town. But Portuguese power on the coast was shattered for ever.

The new Omani rulers were the **Mazrui** family. Soon after the return of some kind of normality in Mombasa, they declared themselves independent of Oman, a direct challenge to the **Busaidi** family who had just seized power in the Arabian homeland. Civil war in Oman prevented the Busaidis from doing much about their wayward overseas agents: with the **Nabahani** family in Pate no longer paying much allegiance either, any effort to control what were fast reverting to independent states was increasingly difficult. As usual, the lack of unity on the coast prevented any lasting independence.

Intrigue in the Lamu archipelago led to the Battle of Shela (p.223) and Lamu's unwittingly disastrous invitation to the **Sultan of Oman, Seyyid Said**, to occupy its own fort. From here, and by now with British backing, the Busaidis went on to attack Mazrui Mombasa repeatedly in the 1820s.

There was a hiccup in 1824 when a British officer, Captain Owen, fired with enthusiasm for defeating the slave trade, extended British protection to Mombasa on his own account, despite official British support for the slave-trading Busaidis. Owen's "Protectorate" was a diplomatic embarrassment and – no surprise – did not last long. The Busaidi government was only installed when the Swahili "twelve tribes" of Mombasa, the traditional inhabitants of the immediate hinterland, fell into a dispute over the Mazrui succession and, alienated from their rulers, called in Seyyid Said, the Busaidi leader. In 1840, he moved his capital from Oman to Zanzibar and, with Mombasa firmly garrisoned, most of the coast was soon in his domain.

Surviving members of the Mazrui family went to Takaungu near Malindi and Gazi, south of Mombasa. British influence was sharpened after their guns quelled the mutiny in 1875 of *"al-Akida"*, "an ambitious, unbalanced and not over-clever" commandant of the Fort. Once British hegemony was established, they leased the **coastal strip** from the Sultan of Zanzibar and Fort Jesus became Mombasa's prison, which it remained until 1958.

Fort Jesus

Open daily 8.30am–6pm, Ksh100; Warden, PO Box 82412, ☎312839.

Today **Fort Jesus** is a quietly studious museum-monument, surprisingly spacious and tree-shaded inside its giant walls, and retaining most of its original and (over the centuries) repaired character. The curious angular construction was the design of an Italian architect and ensures that assailants trying to scale the walls would always be under crossfire from one of the bastions. It is a classic European fortress of its age.

The best time to visit is probably first thing in the morning; the guide book on sale is an interesting store of information. Look especially for the restored **Omani House**, in the far right corner as you enter the fort. Avoiding head contact with the lintel, climb up to the flat roof for a wonderful view over Mombasa. Interesting in their own way, too, are the uncomfortable-looking, wall-mounted **latrines**, which would presumably have been closed in with mats. It is immediately obvious that Fort Jesus was not so much a building as a small, resolutely fortified town in its own right. The ruins of a church, storerooms, and possibly even shops are up at this end and, to judge by some accounts, the main courtyard has at times been a warren of simple dwellings. Captain Owen described it in 1824 as being:

> . . . .*a mass of indiscriminate ruins, huts and hovels, many of them built wherever space could be found but generally formed from parts of the ruins, matted over for roofs.*

Most of the archaeological interest is at the seaward end of the fort, where you'll find the **Hall of the Mazrui** with its beautiful stone benches and eighteenth-century inscription – and a sad quantity of twentieth-century graffiti as well. A nearby room has been dedicated entirely to the display of a huge plaster panel of older **graffiti**, scribbled and etched onto the wall by bored Portuguese sentries. Their subjects are fascinating: ships, figures in armour (including caricatures of the Captain of the Fort wielding his baton), fish, a chameleon and various motifs. Illiteracy precluded much writing but oddly enough, there's nothing obscene either (or has it been erased?). The small **café** up here has been serving first-class lime juice for years.

Fort Jesus museum

The **museum**, on the eastern side of the fort where the main soldiers' barracks block used to be, is small, but it manages to convey a good idea of the age of Swahili civilisation and of its breadth. Most of the displays are of pottery, indigenous or imported, some from as far afield as China and some of it over 1000 years old. A number of private collections have contributed pieces and there's probably still a wealth of material in private hands. Look out for the big carved door taken from the Mazrui house in Gazi (p.299) and also the extraordinary whale vertebra used as a stool. The museum has a good exhibit on the long-term project to recover as much as possible from the wreck of the *Santo Antonio de Tanna*, which sank in 1697 while trying to break the prolonged siege of the fort. Some 7000 objects have already been brought to the surface, but the bulk of the ship itself remains nine fathoms deep in the harbour.

Around town

From Fort Jesus, the **Old Town** is an easy objective. The first impression – of a quarter entirely devoted to gift and **curio shops** – is none too encouraging. But this turns out to be purely the result of Fort Jesus' adjacent car park and touristic appeal, and the shops don't extend far into the Old Town. They are especially ostentatious down at the end of Ndia Kuu Road, where several emporiums are overwhelmingly luxuriant in their displays and multilingual enticements. One or two provide free coffee, which alone is nice. Many of them, it has to be said, are selling a lot of worthless junk. Some deal in shells, including shell lamp stands, ornaments, etc, a trade which operates on the fringes of the law in Kenya. Further west, away from the fort, they are smaller, and correspondingly cheaper and less pretentious. *Utamaduni*, just down Ndia Kuu from the crafts corner, has some interesting bits and pieces worth looking over.

Mosques and architecture

The Old Town is not in fact that old. Most buildings date from the nineteenth century, and though there may be foundations and even walls which go back many centuries, you'll get a clearer guide to the age of the town from its twenty-odd **mosques**.

The Mandhry Mosque on Bachawy Road, founded in 1570, is officially the oldest; rarely open to visitors, it has a striking minaret. The Basheikh Mosque on Old Kilindini Road, recently repainted in fresh cream and white, is acknowledged also to be very old, "about 1300" they'll tell you, though this may be exaggerated. Entering the mosques – as long as they aren't locked – is usually all right for men who arrive properly covered and barefoot. Sometimes you may be expected to wash hands and feet as well. Women, however modest, will as often as not be politely refused.

Much of the other **architecture** in the Old Town is profoundly influenced by the Indian-style Zanzibari tastes of Busaidi occupation during the nineteenth century. This is particularly noticeable in the elegant fretwork balconies and shutters still maintained on a few houses, notably on Ndia Kuu. For older relics, you'll have to poke around more conscientiously. There are a number of quite ancient tombs along the seafront, especially towards the northern end of the Old Town, some of which have pillars; this is the part of Mombasa considered to be "medieval", or in other words pre-Portuguese.

Returning south along the twisting **seafront road** ("seafront" although the harbour can only be glimpsed), you come to a gigantic new mosque of the Bohra Muslims: "Burhani Masjid for Dawoodi Bohra Community", says the sign. In the unassuming setting of the Old Town, it is an imposingly massive edifice.

The dhow harbour

The **dhow harbour** is wildly overrated. There are usually a few boats in port but you can no longer expect to see dozens, let alone hundreds, of dhows, even at the end of the northeast monsoon in April, traditionally the peak time for arrivals. Seasonal variations are less important now that the big *jahazis* have engines. Nor are you likely to have the opportunity to go aboard one of these exotic vessels – a tourist tradition, with coffee and souvenirs, that has died out as port officials have become more officious. Instead, try to imagine how it must once have looked, chat to the many policemen standing around and don't, whatever you do, raise your camera. Attempting to travel by dhow from Mombasa is, regrettably, an equally discouraging story. Lamu holds more promise (see "travel details").

The Jain Temple

Heading up towards Digo Road, you might enjoy stopping by at the **Jain Temple**, whose entry is in Langoni Road. This sublime creation – intricate icing sugar outside, scrupulously clean and scented interior, decorated in dozens of pastel shades – was only built in 1963. Jainism is a Hindu religion closely related to Buddhism, which prohibits the eating of any kind of animal food; in its extreme form, even root vegetables are taboo. The temple interior is ornamentally and substantially magnificent: the painted figurines of deities in their niches are each provided with a drain so they can be easily showered down, while around the ceiling, exquisitely stylised pictures portray scenes from life, including a familiar snake temptation in a garden.

For a return to earth, visit Mombasa's municipal marketplace, **Mackinnon Market**, which has a splendid abundance of tropical fruit, including such exotics as jackfruit (too big for most people at around 10kg) and soursops (a taste you'll either love or hate). Behind the market is a row of stores devoted to spices, coffee and tea – good for bulk turmeric or what-have-you – and several good dessert shops.

Cloth and hardware

Mombasa is also a cheap place to buy the **fabrics** the coast is famous for. Check out the latest *kanga* designs in **Biashara Street**, probably the most with-it fashion centre in Kenya. Some of the home-produced patterns are so good they are beginning to make an impact abroad as well: unusual combinations of brilliant fast colours are used to startling effect. It is worth pricing several shops before buying, and perhaps going with company so you can bargain for several lots at once. In the high season, Biashara Street swarms with tourists looking for "the real Mombasa", so you'll need all your haggling skills; it's actually quite difficult to budge prices more than the token five shillings for the sake of politeness: business is just too good.

Beyond Kwavi Road, Biashara Street shifts from textiles to a less gaudy section of household goods – winnowing trays, coconut graters, palm bags, mats, spoons, furniture: more mundane, but just as interesting to browse.

Strolling on

For the most part, the rest of Mombasa's pleasures derive from just being here.* Strolling, with plenty of cold-drink stops, is a time-honoured Mombasan diversion.

You will probably want to see that immortal double pair of elephant **tusks** on Moi Avenue. To get to them, you have to run the gantlet of curio booths that have almost hidden the cool hideaway of Uhuru Gardens on the right, with its Africa-shaped fountain. And when you get there, you may regret your determination to view the tusks close up: they are revealed as grubby aluminum.

More rewarding, if you have time and the inclination for **a long walk**, is the circuit which takes off around the breezy, seaward side of the island down **Mama Ngina Drive**: a fine morning or afternoon's walk, with lots of places to sit and watch the waves pounding the coral cliffs through the break in the reef. Come down here in the early evening and you'll find half of Mombasa doing the same. At the end of Mama Ngina is an extensive and surprising forest of enormous **baobab trees**, frequently associated with ancient settlements on the coast. And just across the Likoni Ferry roundabout is a huge pillar tomb, the **Mbaraki Pillar**. Supposedly the burial place of a seventeenth-century mainland sheikh, chief of one of the "twelve tribes", it's some eight metres high, but even so is dwarfed by the nearby towers of a molasses refinery.

Directory

American Express c/o *ETCO Mombasa*, PO Box 90631, Nkrumah Rd (☎312461).

Area code ☎011.

Banks Barclay's Bank (PO Box 90183, ☎26520), bureau de change on Moi Ave, is open Mon–Sat 8.30am–12.30pm, 2–4.30pm.

Beaches Nearest are **Shelly Beach** (*matatu* or bus from Jomo Kenyatta Ave to Likoni Ferry, then turn left and walk/hitch 2–3km) and **Nyali Beach** (matatu or bus from Abdel Nasser Rd to Nyali Bridge, then turn right and go 4km). Shelly is more peaceful but relatively uninteresting and narrow, the reef close. Nyali is pretty good, crowded, the reef further out. *Nyali Beach Hotel* is large, very expensive, and handles fancy tour groups. *Mombasa Beach Hotel*, 2km further north, is marginally cheaper and has a recommended water slide. Most of the time, hotels will not mind if you use their beaches, bars and restaurants. More coverage on p.288 and 290.

Bookshops Mombasa has few compared with Nairobi, so don't rely on finding maps here. *Bahari Book Centre*, on Moi Ave opposite the *Castle*, has the best selection of books, maps and foreign papers.

British Council City House, PO Box 905904, Nyerere Ave (☎23076), has the usual good, air-conditioned, library with recent editions of British papers. You can buy your own at the stand at the bottom of the stairs.

Car hire This tends to be cheaper in Mombasa than in Nairobi, but not by much. You'll find the majority of outlets on Moi Ave and Nkrumah Rd. Mini-mokes are also available (for coast cruising but nothing more adventurous) and are the cheapest option. Try *Lofty Safaris*, 1st Floor, Hassanali Building, Nkrumah Rd (☎20241) or *Glory Car Hire* PO Box 85527, Trans-Ocean House, Moi Ave (☎21159 or 313561 or 493179), who have been getting good notices lately.

---

* People have spent hours searching for the **Ivory Room** where poachers' hoards were once displayed. Like the demolished **Kilindini Mosque**, it no longer exists.

Consulates include the following representatives:

Austria Mr T. Gaal, PO Box 84045, 3rd Floor, Ralli House, Nyerere Ave (☎313386 or 312687 – ☎485550 residence);

Belgium Capt. J. Stallaeri, PO Box 90141, Mitchell Cotts & Co. Building, Moi Ave (☎20231 or 311030 – ☎471315 residence);

Denmark Mr J. Nielsen, PO Box 99543, Liwatoni Bay (☎316051 – ☎471616 residence);

Finland Capt. K. Trayner, PO Box 99543, Comarco, Liwatoni Rd (☎3160651 – ☎471786 residence);

West Germany PO Box 90171, Canon Towers, Moi Ave (☎24938, ☎23848);

Greece Mr P. Samoilys, PO Box 99211, Dar-es-Salaam Rd (☎315563 – ☎471511 residence);

India PO Box 90614, Bank of India Building, Nkrumah Rd (☎24433 or 311051);

Italy Mr A. Santagati, PO Box 48958, Ambalal House, Nkrumah Rd (☎311932 – ☎471573 residence);

Netherlands PO Box 90230, ABN Bank, Hassanali Building, Nkrumah Rd (☎25241);

Norway Mrs A. Sondhi, PO Box 83058, Reef Hotel, Nyali (☎471771);

Rwanda PO Box 87676, Karim House, Moi Ave (☎20466);

Sweden PO Box 86108, Southern House, Moi Ave (☎20085);

Switzerland Mr F. Schumacher, PO Box 85722, Ambalal House, Nkrumah Rd (☎316684 – ☎485314 residence);

UK Mr J. Walters, PO Box 84105, Greenwood Dr, Nyali (☎471768);

USA PO Box 88079, Palli House, Nyerere Ave (☎315101).

Crocodiles Billboards around town yell about *Mamba* (crocodile) *Village* in Nyali. Entry is a hefty Ksh80 to the "crocodile trail" and croc film show. A series of semi-natural pools, created in a disused quarry, house many hundreds of crocs at all stages of growth. But the overall effect – with "croco-burgers" in the snack bar and unlimited saurian souvenirs – is tacky, and the crocodile trail sits uneasily with the skin-farming half of the operation which is not on show.

Dhows to Lamu See "travel details" on p.346.

Groceries *Omee's* on Moi Ave, opposite the *Istanbul* and *Ebrahim's*, first right after the tusks, is recommended.

Immigration Visas and visitors' passes should be dealt with in Nairobi, but you can get visitor's pass extensions at the Provincial Headquarters off Mama Ngina Dr, (☎311745). Or check at the *Immigration and Information Department* on the corner of Nkrumah and Digo roads.

Maps The *Survey of Kenya* town plan of *Mombasa Island and Environs* is useful but it pre-dates the new Nyali Bridge and many recent street name changes.

Markets Apart from the Mackinnon and the big street market off Mwembe Tayari, there's **Makupa market** in the heart of Majengo, the island's low-income housing district. A colourful, multipurpose market with a busy, rural atmosphere, it's well worth a visit. Go 1.5km up Jomo Kenyatta Ave, then left at Salim Mwa Ngunga Rd.

Cinemas Not much choice. The *Regal*, Digo Rd, and the *Kenya*, Nkrumah Rd, often show American films.

Post office and telephones Digo Rd is the General Post Office for poste restante and main services. Mon–Fri 8am–4.30pm; Sat 8am–noon; (Sun & public holidays 9–10am, limited service only). There are card phones here.

Railway ticket office Open daily 8am–noon & 2–6.30pm only, in the station (☎312221).

Safaris A number of possibilities apart from Shimba Hills (see p.292). Expect to pay Ksh1500–2000 for a one day safari (5am start) to Tsavo, including lunch at *Voi Safari Lodge*. *Ketty Tours*, PO Box 82391, Moi Ave (☎315178/312204) are recommended.

Swimming pool At the Indian Women's Association, Nyerere Ave, halfway to the Likoni Ferry, a good pool open during school terms on weekdays 5–7.30pm; otherwise, 9–noon, 2–6.30pm, Ksh20.

Theatre The *Little Theatre Club* (PO Box 81143, ☎312101) on Mnazi Moja Rd is a sometime venue for the *Shangari Players*, who put on works by African playwrights. *LTC Players* occasionally put on African productions, but on the whole they're an outlet for amateur dramatics in the expat/settler community. Seats are Ksh50 for non-members.

Tide tables Can be very useful, especially in the Lamu archipelago; available in bookshops.

Tototo This is the *National Christian Council of Kenya (NCCK)* retail shop in Msanifu Kombo St. Good for sisal and grass-woven bags. More expensive than the street but you can browse unhassled.

Tourist Information Bureau (PO Box 99596, ☎25428) on Moi Ave near the tusks. Open Mon–Fri 8am–noon, 2–4.30pm; Sat 8am–noon. Bafflingly unhelpful staff, but they do have a number of leaflets as well as maps for sale.

Travel agents *Farways Safaricentre*, Moi Ave (PO Box 87815, ☎23307/9, telex 21016) opposite the *Castle Hotel*, is helpful for flight, train and hotel bookings, though beware you are not being surcharged an "agent's commission", which should be paid to the agent by the hotel or transport company, not by you.

Vaccinations The Public Health Department in Msanifu Kombo St gives yellow fever and cholera jabs Wed am and Fri pm; typhoid Wed pm. For women only: yellow fever and cholera Tues pm, typhoid Mon am.

North of Mombasa: suburban attractions

It's easy to **get out of Mombasa for the day** to explore the nearby north coast. If it's busier, brasher, and generally less pastoral than the south coast (see p.293), there are also more targets for a day trip up here, with correspondingly less allure if you simply want to stretch out on the beach. There is ample transport from Abdel Nasser Rd bus and *matatu* area near the *New People's Hotel*. Alternatively walk out to the other side of the new bridge and wait for a public or private lift. You won't wait long. For travel to Kilifi, Watamu, Malindi and beyond, see p.303.

Bombolulu
Open Mon–Fri 8am–12.30pm & 2–5pm; free (PO Box 83988 Mombasa, ☎471704 Mombasa).

On the main road just 3km from Nyali Bridge, **Bombolulu** is a jewellery-making centre and farm training school that employs 100-odd disabled people (mostly polio victims) from Coast Province. The **jewellery workshop** is the programme's biggest money-spinner, with hundreds of original designs in metal and local materials (old coins, seeds) now being exported to the USA and Europe – you'll come across them in charity gift catalogues. **Bombolulu Gardens** produces fruit, vegetables and garden plants, all for sale in the shop; trainees spend two years here, learning skills to improve productivity on their own *shambas* or to give them a better chance in the job market. The gardens and jewellery workshops are well worth a visit: prices aren't high and the success of the programme is self-evident.

Bamburi Nature Trail
Open daily 2–5pm, Ksh50.

Five kilometres beyond Bombolulu, the **Bamburi Nature Trail** is an unusual example of a wholehearted attempt to rehabilitate a giant quarry. The Bamburi Cement Factory (whose kilns are visible for miles around) has been scouring the land for limestone here since 1954, at the rate of 35 hectares each year. In 1971, they began a concentrated programme of tree planting in an effort to rescue the disfigured landscape. More recently, as the project gained momentum, fish-breeding was established, and large numbers of animals and birds introduced, including the baby **hippo**, Sally, now adult but still bottle-fed for visitors – she has become the nature trail's rather precious symbol. The hippo used to belong to film-maker Alan Root, but she damaged a VW and he brought her here; she now mows the lawn and provides fertiliser for the fish ponds. There are plenty of **crocodiles**, too, in a setting devoid of *Mamba Village's* landscaped excesses.

You'll have the opportunity to get close to a number of other animals, including pelicans, crowned cranes and various antelopes, mostly in simple enclosures beside the trail, several of which have access for walking among evidently happy occupants. The trail's family of **serval cats** will probably be your only chance in Kenya to see this beautiful, long-limbed feline.

You walk mostly through a dense forest of casuarina, a tree known for its ability to withstand a harsh environment, across ground which is mostly below sea level, permanently moist with salty water percolating through the coral limestone bedrock. The fish-farming side of the operation experiments with different races of *tilapia*, a freshwater fish highly tolerant of brackish conditions, 35 tons of which now reach shops and restaurants every year. With beehives in the trees by the main road to complete the picture, the Bamburi Trail is a serious bid to put the small-is-beautiful principle into conservation practice: a modest contribution in a land of vast wildlife parks, but a terrific success. The trail is open throughout daylight hours but feeding time is at 4pm. *KBS* bus #31 (from Abdel Nasser Rd, beyond the Malindi buses area), will drop you at the Nature Trail bus stop; don't catch a *Bamburi* bus – you want *Bamburi Cement Factory*.

Suburban beaches: up to Kikambala

Between Bamburi Quarry and Mtwapa Creek, more than a dozen beach hotels throng the six-kilometre shoreline. The #31 comes along this way. **Shanzu Beach**, where the coast curves gently east to meet the entrance of Mtwapa Creek, is reputedly the best on this stretch, with swimming possible even at low tide.

Just past the nature trail is **Kenyatta Municipal Beach,** unquestionably public and, unfortunately, not very interesting. As there's nowhere cheap to stay, you should – unless you're returning to Mombasa – forge on to the altogether more appealing beach and budget accommodation in KIKAMBALA on the other side of Mtwapa Creek (see below).

If you're out for the day, there should be little difficulty in visiting any of the hotels and using their beach fronts. Drift into one of them in "smart-casual" attire and avail yourself of facilities. If you're nabbed, you may pay up to Ksh200 non-resident's fee so, alternatively, be comfortable and pay upfront. Either way, *Whitesands* is perhaps the nicest hotel along this stretch.

Jumba la Mtwana
Open daily, Ksh30.

Mtwapa Creek marks the edge of Greater Mombasa, and tropical suburbia – with its scattered villas, supermarkets, clubs and restaurants – is more or less left behind. From here on, the road heads more determinedly, with fewer distractions, up to Kilifi, Watamu and Malindi. But one site worth pausing for (and worth a day out of town in its own right) is **JUMBA LA MTWANA**. This national monument, one of three between Mombasa and Malindi, is the ruined centre of a wealthy four-

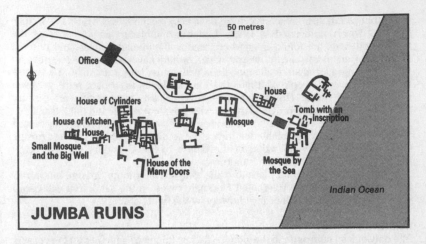

Office

House of Cylinders

House of Kitchen House
Small Mosque
and the Big Well

House of the
Many Doors

House

Mosque

Tomb with an
Inscription

Mosque by
the Sea

0   50 metres

Indian Ocean

JUMBA RUINS

teenth- or fifteenth-century Swahili community. If you are dropped off at the sign about a kilometre past Mtwapa Bridge, it's 3km down to the site (directly on the beach), but you have a good chance of getting a lift before you arrive there.

Jumba la Mtwana means "Mansion of the Slave", but it has been deserted for some 500 years and probably had a different name in the past. It's a small site in an enchanting setting among baobabs and lawns above the beach. This seems a strange place for a town, right on an open shore, with no harbour, and it's possible the inhabitants were pushed here by raiding parties from inland groups, relying on Mtwapa Creek as a safe anchorage for the overseas traders who visited yearly. Jumba is fortunate in having good water. But why it was deserted, and by whom, remains a mystery.

Compared with Gedi, further north, Jumba's layout is simple. Though it lacks the eerie splendour of that much larger town, it must once have been a sizeable settlement; there were three mosques within the site and a fourth just outside. Most of the population would have lived in mud-and-thatch houses which have long since disintegrated. In Swahili culture, building in stone (in fact coral "rag" of different densities) has traditionally been the preserve of certain privileged people, principally the long-settled inhabitants of a town; newcomers would almost always build in less durable materials appropriate to their shorter-term stake in the community. It is also believed that building in stone required legal sanction, as it was the material for mosques.

The best of Jumba's mosques is **The Mosque by the Sea** (a helpful little guidebook is sometimes available at the ticket office – much of this account has been culled from it), which shows evidence of a separate room for women, something which is only nowadays becoming acceptable again in modern mosques. The cistern where worshippers washed is still intact, with coral foot-scrapers set nearby and a jumble of tombs behind the north wall facing Mecca. One of these has a Koranic inscription carved in coral on a panel facing the sea and must have been the grave of an important person:

Every soul shall taste death. You will simply be paid your wages in full on the Day of Resurrection. He who is removed from the fire and made to enter heaven, it is he who has won the victory. The earthly life is only delusion.

The **people of Jumba** seem to have been very religious and hygienic – virtues that are closely associated in Islam. Cisterns and water jars, or at least the remains of them, are found everywhere among the ruined houses, and in most cases there are coral blocks nearby which would have been used to squat on while washing. Latrines are all stone-lined with long-drops. Of course, it is possible that the poorer people of Jumba lived in squalor in their mud huts, yet even the **House of Many Doors**, which seems to have been a fifteenth-century "boarding and lodging", provided guests with private washing and toilet facilities.

Look out for the two **smaller mosques**, each with its well-preserved, carved coral *mihrab* (the arched niche that indicates the direction of Mecca), and for the strange chinks in several walls (in the House of the Cylinders and the Small Mosque), the purpose of which is unknown.

Jumba Beach is a good place to while away an afternoon. Strange but attractive screw pines grow, aerial-rooted like mangroves, in the sand. You can **camp** here as well; there are toilets and showers by the ticket office.

Kikambala

The only official **campsite** in the vicinity is a few kilometres further up the coast at **KIKAMBALA**: *Kanamai Conference and Holiday Centre*, or *"Kanamai Youth Hostel"* (PO Box 46 Kikambala, ☎2046 Kikambala). This is about as far as you'd want to come on a day trip out of Mombasa, but it makes a good stop-over and is the first low-budget beach spot to the north (the beach itself is a three-kilometre walk from the highway). *Kanamai* is a big, sprawling place under the coconuts, run by the *NCCK*, with dorm (Ksh40/bed) and double room (Ksh50/room) accommodation, or camping for only Ksh40. The site is pretty as the whole coastal strip here is thickly forested and the beach itself a glorious white expanse. The only drawback is that swimming at low tide is nearly impossible, so if you're coming for the day from Mombasa, consult a tide table before setting off. A half-hour stroll along the sandy lane through the emerald woods brings you to *Whispering Palms Hotel* (PO Box 5, Kikambala, ☎2004 Kikambala). Here, if you feel so moved, you can join a largely German crowd in all the usual holiday pursuits, day and night. Just that little bit further from Mombasa, its prices are slightly lower than most equivalents (Ksh1920/2580 FB). *Kanamai* itself provides basic meals in the dining room (Ksh40–50) and has a shop with a few provisions, but for a stay of several days you should bring supplies. The centre's van can take you up to the Kikambala *dukas* on the main road most mornings and, once or twice a week, if you chip in for petrol, into Mombasa. You are not utterly marooned.

Note: if you're **continuing north**, beyond Kikambala, see p.303.

Inland from Mombasa: Mijikenda Country

Coming from Nairobi, **MAZERAS** marks the end of the long vistas of scrub; it's perched right on the edge of the steep scarp, amid bananas and coconuts. If you are travelling by road, it isn't a bad idea to break your journey here and savour the new atmosphere; city buses between Mazeras and Mombasa, about 30 minutes away. The *hotelis* serve good, flavourful, coastal *chai* and, for the travel-weary, Mazeras has delightful **botanical gardens** – bamboo, ponds and green lawns for a snooze in the shade – just a couple of hundred metres towards Mombasa. Across the road and up the hill a little way is a **mission** and its century-old church, signs of an evangelical presence in the hills behind Mombasa that goes back, remarkably, nearly 150 years.

For historians of Methodism and the Church Missionary Society or (more likely) connoisseurs of palm wine, the fine **road to KALOLENI**, 22km north of Mazeras, is a required sidetrack. It is a beautiful trip in its own right: wonderfully scenic, looping through lush vales with a wide panorama down to the coast on the right and millions of **coconut trees** all around. There's at least one bus every hour from Mombasa, which makes this an easy day trip away from the coast and especially appealing in the high season if your sense of adventure has become numbed by the influx of tropical paradise-seekers.

Rabai

RABAI is the first village you come to, capital of the **Wa-rabai** Mijikenda and site of the first mission established in East Africa. A German pastor, the Reverend Krapf, came here in 1846 and left his mark on the community when, 33 years later, a very imposing **church**, now blue and white, was erected to preach down at the wayward coconut palms. The centre of the village and the church, surrounded by schoolrooms and sports fields, lie half a kilometre off the main road on the right. The original church is now used as a schoolroom, as is the cottage of Rebmann, Krapf's proselytising partner. Between them, the two missionaries managed to explore a great deal of what is now Kenya without the demonstrations of firepower so many of their successors thought necessary. Krapf's own house has recently been renovated and is now a private home. For all its significance, and despite the presence of the *Krapf Memorial Secondary School*, Rabai "centre" has, in all truth, hardly anything to offer.

Ribe

RIBE (the **Wa-ribe** village) is more substantial but harder to get to. Seven kilometres from Rabai, an unmarked track snakes up to the right from a deep valley floor: the village is one-and-a-half kilometres along it. It consists of a few small shops and the *Nuru Bar*, a shady courtyard with much-needed cold sodas, and there should also be rooms ready by now.

Fifteen minutes' walk away, through *shambas* and dense undergrowth, is a tiny, neglected **cemetery** near the site of Ribe's Methodist mission, itself crumbled to its foundations and overgrown. It isn't hard to find, and it's worth a look for the pathetic graves of the few missionaries who struggled here before succumbing in what must have been nearly impossible conditions. They were often young: the Reverend Butterworth died in 1864, aged 23. It isn't surprising that the cemetery faces out to sea; to Mombasa, supplies, the mail and new companions.

Kaloleni: tembo town

The paved road ends at **KALOLENI**. On the way, you pass through dense coconut groves where many of the trees have been initialled to avoid ownership disputes. **Palm wine** (*tembo*) tapping, banned by the government, is still widely practised here, with the **Giriama** section of the Mijikenda leading the field. They call palm wine "the mother of the coconut", since tapping the trees for juice hinders formation of the nuts.

Tapping is done by cutting off the flower stem, binding it tightly and allowing the sap that would have produced new coconuts to collect in a container – usually a baobab pod – tied to the end. Here it ferments rapidly and has to be collected regularly. Variations in the local market for *tembo*, which is most often drunk at community gatherings like weddings and funerals, and in the coastal market for copra (the dried coconut flesh used in soap and oil manufacture), tend to influence the owners of trees in their decision whether to tap or to grow copra. You will often see trees that have been notched to enable the tappers to reach the top but the step-notches sometimes terminate several yards below the crown, indicating that a tree has been left a number of years to develop coconuts.

Palm wine is locally available up and down the coast. In Kaloleni a beer bottle-full costs Ksh5. It is best when cold, but rarely is, and you drink it (discreetly) through a reed straw with a coconut-fibre filter.

The best place to stay in Kaloleni is *Kaloleni Central Restaurant* (PO Box 34, ☎64) in the town centre, opposite the main bus stop. Clean and friendly, rooms there cost Ksh50.

Shimba Hills National Reserve

Ksh220, student reductions, cars Ksh30; Warden, PO Box 16030, Kwale; Map – Survey of Kenya SK93 at 2.5cm:1km (1980).

Probably Kenya's most underrated wildlife refuge, **Shimba Hills** is less than an hour from Mombasa and, at 500m above sea level, a real refresher after the humidity down below. The hilly reserve of scattered jungle and grassland is comparatively little visited which is all to the good: it has a quite wonderful game-veiwing lodge and one of the best situated camping and *banda* sites anywhere.

Kwale and access to the reserve

From Mombasa (Likoni ferry bus park), there are hourly *KBS* buses to **KWALE**, and there are fairly frequent country buses, too. The reserve's **main gate** is some 5km beyond Kwale along an elephant-dunged murram road. Here, you can try for **a lift** around the park. Since your best bet is with Mombasans, Sundays and public holidays are the easiest times. If you have no luck, you can always **catch the next bus** going on to KINANGO. There are often elephants on this stretch of the road, which actually passes through a corner of the reserve. A third alternative, on Sunday and Wednesday afternoons, would be to enquire about **a lift with the reserve vehicle**, which usually goes to Kidongo Gate on the southeast side of the reserve to collect gate money. You should be able to get a ride, though people will want *chai*. Ask at the warden's house and offices just outside Kwale. Lastly, if you're car-less and none of these options appeal, you can always opt for a straightforward **half-day safari from Mombasa** (tickets from most coast hotels and travel agents – about Ksh700). If you come up to Kwale on the bus, the last one back to Mombasa is the *KBS* at 8pm. In case of need, there are two decent B&Ls in town, both Ksh100 a double.

Shimba Tree-hotel

Latest development is a new **game-viewing lodge** called *Shimba*, a kind of coastal *Treetops*. From about Ksh1800/2500 HB with some low-season reductions it's cheaper than the highlands tree-hotels and a highly recommended outlay.

There's a lot of forest all around and **leopards** regularly emerge after dark to take bait. *Visacard* was so taken with the place they sent Alan Whicker there for an advert, to perform with a cheetah along the walkway from the lodge. This is an exciting little elevated walk through the boughs to another glade.

The resident naturalist, old Kenya hand John Arkle, is exceptionally helpful and well informed. Most days he takes out groups on escorted walks and usually locates the sable antelope for which the reserve is famous.

You can also get a transfer from Mombasa virtually free when you reserve a room: check with any travel agent or with a north or south coast hotel.

Around the park

Predators are rarely seen in Shimba Hills but you may well see elephant, buffalo and giraffe. The reserve is best known for its herds of **sable antelope**, magnificent-looking animals as big as a horse – it's their only habitat in Kenya. The even bigger roan antelope, which have been relocated from other parts of Kenya, look similar but have tufted ears. You are unlikely to see any: rangers say they have "died out", or maybe they were good eating.

The status of the sable antelope seems uncertain, too. They are supposed to be on the increase, but the rangers believe that many are poached for meat. You are almost certain to see groups of chestnut-coloured females but the territorial, jet-black males are solitary and harder to find. If you have a guide he'll know, but they're most commonly seen in the area overlooking the ocean, between the campsite and Giriama Point.

Staying cheaply

What Shimba Hills lacks in wildlife spectacle it more than makes up for with enchanting views in every direction, especially seawards. Haze tends to blot out Mombasa itself but the fringe of Diani beach is always visible. The **camping and banda site** (Ksh40 to camp, Ksh100 per person in *bandas*) is located at one of the best vantage points in the reserve, about 3km from the main gate. The *bandas* here are adequate (though the bedding, lamps, shower and nearby toilet, and kitchen tents can't be relied on) but the setting is sublime: a thickly forested bluff hundreds of metres above the coconut-crowded coastal plain. It is well worth spending the night up here just for the sunrise. If you do, you'll probably have the place to yourself.

THE SOUTH COAST

The coast south from Mombasa to the Tanzanian border is on the whole quieter than the north, with just one highly developed resort at **Diani Beach**. Beyond this, the coast is little known and, in most tour operators' minds at least, nobody stops until they reach **Shimoni**. This is great news if you have the time to go searching out untrodden beaches by car, bicycle or motorbike (all available to hire), or on foot using good public transport – the road runs close enough to the shore most of the way to make walking down to the beach practical.

Most of the people who live along the coastal strip here are **Digo** and their neat, rectangular houses, made of dried mud and coral on a framework of wood, are a distinctive part of the lush roadside scene. Although they belong to the

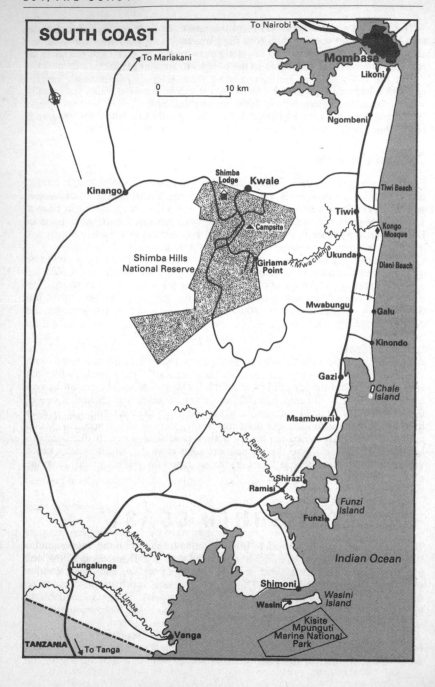

SOUTH COAST

To Nairobi

To Mariakani

0   10 km

Mombasa

Likoni

Ngombeni

Shimba Lodge

Kwale

Tiwi Beach

Kinango

Tiwi

Kongo Mosque

Campsite

Ukunda

Diani Beach

Shimba Hills National Reserve

Giriama Point

Mwachema

Mwabungu

Galu

Kinondo

Gazi

Chale Island

Msambweni

R. Ramisi

Shirazi

Ramisi

Funzi Island

Funzi

Indian Ocean

R. Mwena

Lungalunga

R. Limba

Shimoni

Wasini Island

Wasini

Kisite Mpunguti Marine National Park

TANZANIA

To Tanga

Vanga

Mijikenda group of peoples, the Digo are unusual in being matrilineal: they traditionally traced descent through the female line, so that a man would, on his death, pass his property on to his sister's sons rather than his own. It is an unusual system with interesting implications for the state of the family and the position of women.

However, the joint assault of Islamic and Western values over the last century has shifted the emphasis back towards the male line, and in many respects women in modern Digo society have less freedom and autonomy than they had at the turn of the century.

Down to Tiwi and Diani

The Likoni ferry makes all the difference. The sense of separation from Mombasa is immediate. More pragmatically, the lack of a bridge may have deterred developers and contributed to the south coast's fairly late arrival in the tour brochures. *Matatus* down to the ferry go from the Post Office.

Likoni and Shelly Beach

LIKONI itself is nothing special; it's a typical seaside suburb and there's not much to hold you. A beach road runs off around the headland to the east, but the beach is narrow and tends to be strewn with seaweed. Unless you want to check out *Shelly Beach Hotel* (PO Box 96030, Mombasa, ☎45100 Mombasa), which is a convenient 3km from the ferry and has surprisingly reasonable rates (Ksh605/ 980 HB), just hop on a bus – any bus – and make for Tiwi or Diani.

Tiwi beach

A continuous strip of beach runs between Likoni and Msambweni, backed by palms and broken once or twice by small rivers. The first magnet is **TIWI BEACH.** Popular among travellers more for **Twiga Lodge** than the beach itself, it nevertheless rates as genuine tropical paradise material. *Twiga Lodge* is reached down a three-kilometre dirt road, signposted along with a clump of others, on the main road. You are advised to heed the notice about not walking: it seems incredible but many robberies at *panga*-point have taken place on the lonely path. Wait for a ride. This shouldn't be a huge problem as a local resident has set up a taxi service.

Twiga Lodge (PO Box 80820, ☎4061 Kwale) is one place on the south coast where overlanders and budget travellers are made to feel completely at home. The place has been going for years and has a good shady lawn for camping (Ksh40/person), just above the beach. There are also double rooms and a number of *bandas* available; prices vary according to mood, season and how long you want to stay – May and June, if damp, can be a bargain. The bar/restaurant does some good food and often gets lively in the evenings when it fills with interesting expatriate characters. Despite the *askaris*, there were recently serious security problems at *Twiga Lodge* but it seems they have now been resolved. Check the situation with the boss on arrival.

If you don't find what you're looking for at *Twiga Lodge*, investigate the *Minilets* tented *bandas* next door (around Ksh200–450 for twin beds depending on season – servants' services included!) which are also popular.

Diani beach

In the dry season, it is normally possible to wade across the Tiwi River from *Twiga Lodge* to Diani beach. Here, surrounded by venerable baobabs, at the usually deserted northern end of the beach, is the disconcerting **Kongo Mosque**. Also known as *Diani Persian Mosque*, the building is enigmatic. It is too complete to be considered a ruin, and, judging by what looked to me like the remains of several chicken sacrifices, the site, if not the mosque itself, still has some ritual significance. Named after the Kongo Forest, the mosque is thought to be fifteenth-century and the one remaining building – maybe the only stone one – of a Wa-shirazi settlement here (see p.300). The river mouth was the first safe anchorage south of Mombasa. There's an electric atmosphere hereabouts; the mosque broods like a huge tomb under the trees. Not all of its five heavy wooden doors are secure but you may not feel like slipping inside, especially if you're alone. Continuing, you could walk on down Diani beach.

Most people arrive by road on the hourly *KBS* service from Mombasa. It leaves the coast highway at UKUNDA and does a loop of the Diani beach road end to end, which means you can stay anywhere without needing your own transport.

Diani fulfills everyone's dreams about the archetypal palm-fringed beach; it is simply fantastic. The sand is soft and brilliantly white, the sea is crystal-clear turquoise, the reef a safe, twenty-minute swim away. Arching out overhead, the palms keep up a perpetual slow sway as the breeze rustles through the fronds. Competition for space along this paradise is about all that mars it, but even this is rarely a nuisance as the hotels are well spread out and many group customers tend, strangely enough, to prefer the pool.

Running several hundred metres behind the beach, Diani Road can seem like Kenya's number one strip in the high season. Fortunately, thick jungle comes between it and the peaceful shore, though more of the **Jadini Forest** disappears every year as one new plot after another is cleared.

Down to earth: "budget" accommodation

Budget accommodation along the beach is sparse and none of the hotels will entertain campers in their gardens. The only really **cheap place to stay** is **Dan Trench's** – a kind of coastal *Mrs Roche's*. Trench, an indomitable survivor of the development around him, is the son of the people who once owned much of the land down here. His garden is a clutter of luxuriant foliage, deteriorating whitewashed *bandas* and tents (Ksh40 for bed space, some private rooms, Ksh50 per tent, plus tents for rent for Ksh50 each). It used to be all the impoverished traveller could ask and is still worth checking out, but for the present this is probably only a place to come to if you're broke or have no possessions you'd regret losing. The landlord isn't able to keep up with tropical rates of decay and there's no real security to the place. Dan Trench's house is on the landward side of the *Trade Winds Hotel*, the first you come to on the Diani beach road after turning right at the junction from Ukunda. If you install yourself there, give your valuables to the landlord for safekeeping.

A better bet these days is **Larry Peacock's**, just around the corner from *Trade Winds* and 300m further along, which is secure and comfortable, if a little eccentric in the landlord department. The three rooms in his garden are about Ksh400 each. The beach is yours and *Trade Winds Hotel* generally welcoming if you just want to use their bars and restaurants. Saidi Hamisi Kitindi, the bicycle fruit-seller, arrives unfailingly every morning as he has for years with bananas, papayas, mangoes, mandarins and exceptional grapefruit.

If you have a little more cash, the cheapest nearby option is the self-catering (or rather servant-catering) complex of *Warandale Cottages* (PO Box 11, Ukunda, ☎2083 Diani Beach), highly regarded by Kenyan residents and just to the north of the Ukunda junction (Ksh1200 for two beds, Ksh1750 for four). *Trade Winds* itself is good value off-season. See the next section. Nearer the south end of the strip, *Nomad Beach Hotel* (PO Box 1, Ukunda, via Mombasa, ☎2155 or 2099 Diani Beach, closed in May) attracts some travellers to its lovely wooded site with fine stands of forest behind. At Ksh1050/1470 and Ksh1800 for four (s/c luxury *bandas*, B&B), it's about the cheapest better-than-average accommodation on the beach, and there's a good restaurant.

When you've passed all the touristy alternatives, there are one or two good options at the end of the Diani beach road. Beyond the end of the tarmac road is *Diani Beachalets* (PO Box 26, Ukunda, ☎2180 Diani Beach), a secluded cluster of English-style beach chalets aimed at self-catering families and three or four *bandas* (Ksh348 a night for two with all facilities). A great place to get away to and evidently secure. If the accommodation is full, they may let you camp. There is a *mzungu*-run *duka* nearby at the end of the paved road.

In the same area, *Four Twenty South* (PO Box 90270, Mombasa, ☎312449 Mombasa) is another cottage set-up (four degrees and twenty minutes south of the equator) with prices from around Ksh780/1020 .

Higher living

The **tourist hotels** on the beach are all, by Kenyan standards, expensive. Coming straight from abroad they seem a little more reasonable and, if you can handle the hordes of other guests, you'll find the standards very high. Most offer low-season reductions, but during the high season few will leave change from Ksh3000 for a twin room with full board. Generally, the more interesting and money-worthy abodes are to the south of the Ukunda junction – an area which also retains some flicker of pre-hotel times. To the north, the scene is brasher and more despoiled. As the briefest of guides, the following are the cheaper mainstream establishments along the strip.

Trade Winds (PO Box 8, Ukunda, ☎2016 or 2116, bookings through *AT&H*), which is very convenient and modestly low-key (and good value in the low season – Ksh1050/2100 FB as compared with Ksh1980/2640 high season).

Two Fishes, further south (PO Ukunda, ☎2101 or 2037 Diani Beach, wonderful pool, similar prices, also *AT&H*).

Jadini Beach (PO Box 84616, Mombasa, ☎2021–5 Diani Beach),

Africana Sea Lodge (also PO Box 84616, ☎2051 Diani Beach) and

Safari Beach (PO Box 90690, ☎2088 Diani Beach). All three are pleasant *Alliance* establishments, more expensive than *Trade Winds* and *Two Fishes* but with impressive low-season and residents' discounts. They are close neighbours, sharing each other's facilities on south Diani beach.

Eating and getting supplies on Diani Beach

Finding food in Diani is not difficult, and there's an increasingly heavy scattering of shops along the strip. The *Sports Recreation Club* near *Trade Winds* sells cheap and good quality food and drink and there's a *Barclays* **bureau de change** (Mon–Fri 10am–1pm) nearby. For anyone staying at *Dan Trench's* or *Larry Peacock's*, more down-to-earth eats can be had at James and Angelina's *hoteli* by the *Trade Winds* entrance. You can order in advance here and the price will come down as the number of diners increases, so go in a group. If you're staying at the *Beachalets*, there are limited provisions at the nearby *duka*.

Most of the hotels have snack menus, salad bars and all the rest; if you choose carefully and avoid the dubious temptation of Ksh100 fruit juice cocktails, you can depart satisfied. Breakfast at *Robinson Baobab* is reckoned to be the best on the coast. *Nomad's* is good value, especially at weekends, when they go in for all-you-can-eat meals.

Lastly, and highly recommended if you're feeling financially flush, is *Ali Barbour's* (evenings only, closed Sun, ☎2033 Diani), a place with a lavish French and seafood menu, bizarrely built inside a deep coral cave. Even if you have no intention of disposing of Ksh1000 for two (with wine), it's worth dropping in just to have a look. The bats have been evacuated but, despite the big hole in the roof to let in the starlight, they haven't quite eradicated the subterranean smell. There's a good daytime beach bar.

If you're **buying your own food**, the ambient fish and fruit sellers can often give really good deals to supplement what you buy in the shops, especially if you're around for a few days.

Ukunda

You can hitch, bus or walk into **UKUNDA** on the main highway. This is Diani's town, with a bank (Mon–Fri 10am–1pm), post office (Mon–Fri 8am–12.30pm & 2–5pm), various *dukas* and the locally notorious *Farmers' Day & Night Club* – a raucous disco and bar. There's a pleasant walk to Ukunda through the bush past the airstrip, down the two-kilometre track that begins directly opposite *Trade Winds* entrance. This takes you past a truly gigantic baobab tree (girth 22m) which has been given presidential protection "for the enjoyment of the people of Kenya and their children". Ukunda suffers its own limitations as far as supplies are concerned. You might not spend all that much more time away from the beach if you just take the *KBS* bus straight up to Mombasa.

Days on Diani

Filling the day isn't difficult. You can rent goggle and mask (Ksh50–60/day) and float across the lagoon to the reef. Diani is also ideal for **windsurfing** (from Ksh150/hour) and there's plenty of opportunity for more dramatic activity – water-skiing and parascending, for example. When you tire of this, or of just lying under the palm trees, you could **rent a bike** and go off exploring. Bicycles seem to be about Ksh200/day (bargain hard). An outfit across the road rents motorbikes (unlimited mileage) for little more than twice as much, which has to be a better deal. Mini-mokes work out at about Ksh800/day.

Unless you're hunting souvenirs (north past the Ukunda turnoff are *one hundred* souvenir stalls – they're numbered – in a seemingly endless trail flanking the road past several opulent hotels) or aiming for Kongo Mosque (20 minutes' walk beyond the north end of the road), it is more interesting to head south along Diani Road. Here there are more hotels, of course, but also, approaching the end of the paving, some wonderful patches of jungle: the dwindling **Jadini Forest**. *Cobra Camp* is a pitiful collection of forest animals penned up in foul-smelling cages. If you'd like to look for some of them in the wild rather than supporting this miserable venture, any of the tracks leading off to the right will take you

straight into magnificent stands of hardwood trees, alive with birds and butterflies, and rocking with colobus and vervet monkeys. You will be told the forest is
the haunt of leopards. Come down here at night and you will see eyes in the dark
(they're probably bushbabies) but it's hard to believe that even leopards would
put up with so violent a destruction of their habitat.

After dark

Diani by night mostly revolves around the hotels' fairly sterile **discos**. It seems
only the *Trade Winds'* bar retains a hint of a pub-like atmosphere from pre-
tourism days. There's also **Giriama dancing**; not something to go out of your
way for, but fun if you happen upon it: a couple of professional troupes work the
hotels, performing acrobatically to the accompaniment of superb drumming. Or
you might try the *Bushbaby*, an open-air nightclub opposite *Two Fishes Hotel*,
which attracts hotel staff as well as intrepid hotel guests in search of local colour
(or the equivalent in German). It's free for *Two Fishes* guests, otherwise not
expensive to get in and, while slightly sleazy it's fun for a bop and they serve tasty
kebabs.

To get around Diani Beach at night, without your own vehicle, you'll have to
rely on getting rides or walking (the last *KBS* bus leaves for Mombasa about
7pm). Hitching up and down the Diani road is safe and not too difficult; and, while
hotels issue warnings about walking on the beach at night (and there are *askaris*
in number to underline them), under a full moon, it's a pleasure that's hard to
resist.

Southwards to Shimoni

Heading further south, you have to return to Ukunda first unless you want a long
walk, or have a mountain bike or motorbike; Diani's road peters out in the scrub
although a trail does keep on going, eventually rejoining the **main road**. Shimoni
is the main attraction but there are several worthwhile stops en route if you have
the time, and no shortage of beaches that deserve investigation.

The first of these is KINONDO (turn left about 10km south of Ukunda), where
you can walk a couple of kilometres down the coast to a forested peninsula that
points out to sea. Here the jungle comes right to the beach. At the end of the
peninsula is **CHALE ISLAND**, an uninhabited beauty just 600m long, usually
visited by boat from *Nomad's* on Diani.

Gazi

GAZI is next, a sleepy little village just off the road. It was once the headquarters
of the Mazrui leader **Sheikh Mbaruk ("Baruku") bin Rashid**, who acquired a
reputation for torturing prisoners after half suffocating them in the fumes of burning chillis. The story was perhaps intended to discredit him, as he was the principal figure behind the Mazrui Rebellion in 1895, an uprising against British
authority that saw Mbaruk flying a German flag at his house and supplying his
men with arms donated by the Germans. The British were forced to send for
troops from India; even so, fighting continued for nine months before an Omani
puppet regime was re-established and the rebels crushed. Mbaruk died in exile in
German Tanganyika.

His mansion is now a primary school, which you can look around out of school hours. More than 150 years old, it was obviously once a very grand place – the heavy ceiling timbers show that it once had an upper storey – but it is now sadly neglected. Fort Jesus Museum has plundered its fine front door and unfortunately left an ugly scar. To know where to stop for Gazi, you'll have to ask, as there isn't a sign on the highway. The village itself is on a deep, mangrove-filled bay and has no beach to speak of. "Gazi beach", about 2km south of the village, is more promising.

Msambweni

Continuing down the road, **MSAMBWENI** is a sizeable village with a famous leprosarium. The road down to the beach goes right through the village, following the coast for several kilometres before turning back to the highway. This stretch is currently being developed, but so far in a very low-key fashion, with only a few cottages and one or two quasi-exclusive clubs: the *Beachcomber Club* (bookings through *Let's Go Travel* in Nairobi, Ksh750/1200) and the *Black Marlin Hotel* (PO Box 80 Msambweni, ☎90, Ksh1150/1800 FB) however, are practically bargains in this part of the world. The beach is lovely – low cliffs and less uniformity than Diani – and Msambweni looks like a possibility for camping out; you might also find a room in the village.

Funzi Island

If instead of returning to the main road, you followed the coastline (either on the rough track or the beach), you would eventually reach **FUNZI ISLAND**, separated from the mainland by a narrow channel which you can walk across at low tide. You could easily camp on the island if equipped for a fair amount of self-sufficiency. Funzi village is at the southern end, about 6km from the mainland, and there are beaches and sections of reef scattered close to the forested shore on both sides of the island. The new and exclusive *Funzi Island Fishing Club* – a tented camp in a grove of mango trees (around Ksh6000 per person FB including all extras; game-fishing not obligatory; bookable through *Abercrombie and Kent*) – looks like a place to dream about.

Shirazi/Kifunzi

The coast highway meanwhile passes through verdant regions of parkland, with borassus, doum and coconut palms (borassus are the ones with a bulge in the trunk) interspersed with swampy dells, before the landscape is firmly established as rolling fields of sugar cane, culminating in RAMISI, the coast's main sugar-producing area.

On the shore, just before you reach Ramisi, is the tiny and very old settlement of **SHIRAZI**, also known as Kifunzi (which means "Little Funzi"). Any of the tracks through the sugar fields on the left of the road will take you to the hamlet – a scattering of houses in the jungle and a small harbour among mangroves. The people of Shirazi call themselves **Wa-shirazi** and are the descendants of a once-important group of the Swahili-speaking people. During the fifteenth and sixteenth centuries, they ruled the coast from Tiwi to Tanga (Tanzania) from their eight settlements on the shore. Around 1620, these towns were captured by the Wa-vumba, another Swahili group. The Wa-shirazi, now scattered in pockets along the coast, speak a distinctive dialect of Swahili. Historians used to think they originally emigrated from Shiraz, in Persia, but it now seems more likely that very few of them have any Persian ancestry and the name was adopted for political reasons. Shirazi/Kifunzi, which may be one of the original eight villages, is an important *Wa-shirazi* centre.

Shirazi, like many villages on the coast, is a backwater in every sense. The people cut a small quantity of *boriti* (mangrove poles), much less than formerly; they fish and they grow some produce in their garden plots, which are continually being raided by monkeys. But the setting is memorably exotic and worth the short walk from the main road. They don't have sodas at Shirazi, but they do have coconuts and tranquillity.

There are some unspectacular ruins of walls and a disused well amid tangled foliage just a hundred metres or so to the south of the village. On the north side is the more interesting hulk of a Friday Mosque, its mihrab still standing. Elders here describe how earlier inhabitants were routed by the Maasai and fled to the Comoros Islands. They remember when the mosque was intact, though by the turn of the century it had already been abandoned.

Shimoni

The turn for **SHIMONI** is indicated by a cluster of tourist signs and more will surely sprout up unless the United States gets the naval base that it wants at Wasini. This would be a far worse calamity for this remarkable area than the reach of another tentacle of tourism. It seems the USA may have acquired Manda Island up north, which is hardly a better result. For the present, Shimoni and the rocky sliver of Wasini Island remain both idyllic and fascinating – a rare combination.

Shimoni practicalities
There are three *KBS* buses and several *matatus* arriving each day from Mombasa, and, although Shimoni is small, the demand for accommodation by big-spending game-fishermen has brought two hotels. The *Pemba Channel Fishing Club* (PO Box 44, Msambweni, ☎5Y2 Msambweni) is for serious anglers only and closes for three months at the end of the fishing season in March. *Shimoni Reef Fishing Lodge* (PO Box 82234, Mombasa, ☎471771 Msambweni) is open to all, year-round, but while it's pleasant enough and has a public bar, it is certainly not budget accommodation (Ksh1320/2320 FB). There don't seem to be any lodgings in Shimoni, but since Wasini Island is an alluring ten-minute boat ride away, there's no compelling reason to spend the night on the mainland.

The caves of Shimoni
While you are in Shimoni, however, you should visit the **caves** after which it was named (*shimo* in Swahili). Shimoni's caves have achieved fame in Kenya, if not much further afield, through Roger Whittaker's melodramatic warblings. Whether they were actually used for storing slaves prior to shipment, or whether (as the alternative version has it) they were a secret refuge from Maasai and other raiders, are questions you can ponder as you pick your way around the piles of bat droppings and stinging creepers (beware!) on the floor. The path to the caves winds into the jungle from a point directly opposite the jetty. Stamp the ground and you'll notice it's hollow in places. These are coral caves and you descend a ladder through a jagged hole in the ground to reach them. Once down, shafts of sunlight pierce through holes in the forest floor to illuminate the

stalactites and dangling lianas quite beautifully. Recent explorations show that the cave system extends some 20km underground.

With more time, there are some ruined buildings in Shimoni (the *IBEAC* – see p.396 – used to have its headquarters here), including a large two-storey house in the heart of the village near the fish auction house, which might be worth a look. The auctions are also interesting – there's one every morning – though exciting exhibits like marlin and shark are rarely on the slab.

Wasini island

WASINI is easily reached. Between July and April, when *Wasini Island Restaurant* (☎2331 Diani Beach) is open, there's a boat to speed lunchers across the channel for Ksh100 a load, and this is the going rate for other motorboat operators. Local people use *jahazi* sailing boat *"matatus"* which – notwithstanding the resentment of the diesel men – you should be able to use, too (Ksh10 each way). This is certainly more fun but you'll need to haggle determinedly.

Only five kilometres long and one across, Wasini is delightfully adrift from the mainstream of coastal life. There are no cars, nor any need of them: you can walk all the way around it in a couple of hours on the narrow footpaths through the bush. With something of Lamu's cast about it, the island is completely undeveloped, and the village of Wasini, an old *Wa-vumba* settlement, is built in and around its own ruins. It is a fascinating place to wander and there's even a small pillar tomb which still has its complement of inset Chinese porcelain. The **beach** in front of the village is littered with shells, but don't assume anything: a lot of them have been collected from the reef and dumped here, and people will try to sell them to you, so it wouldn't be wise to treat them as legitimate beachcombings. Nevertheless, the wealth of interesting items on the shores of Wasini – not just shells but shards of pottery, pieces of glass, scrap metal – add up to a beachcomber's paradise you could explore for hours.

Behind the village is a bizarre village green, an area of long-dead **coral gardens** now raised out of the sea but still periodically flooded at spring tides. It is covered in a short swathe of "lemon grass" – reputedly a good vegetable. Walking through the coral grottoes with birds and butterflies in the air leaves a surreal impression of snorkelling on dry land.

For real **snorkelling**, Wasini has ideal conditions in the limpid water all around. The couple who run the tourist restaurant to the right of the village organise snorkelling trips in a large dhow to the reefs around Kisite Island, part of **Kisite-Mpunguti Marine National Park**, which has indisputably the best goggling in Kenya. The trip is not cheap (Ksh950) but the price includes an endless seafood lunch. *Nomad*'s in Diani Beach can tell you departure times from Shimoni jetty; they vary with the tides. The same dhow based at Wasini can be chartered for private trips to almost anywhere. If you can afford it (Ksh8000 per day, full board, up to six people), the whole Swahili coast – even Zanzibar – can be yours.

Accommodation in Wasini is very limited (more by the island's total reliance on rainwater than by anything else), but there are usually houses for rent for under Ksh100 per day in either the ancient village of Wasini itself or the newer settlement at the other end of the island, Mwkwiro. Since 1988, there has also been a **banda and camping site** known as *Mpunguti Lodge*, run by the same local man who started the *Wasini Island Restaurant* (Masoud Abdullah Muhemba, PO Box 89, Ukunda). Bed and breakfast is around Ksh150 per person, and magnificent Swahili cooking (competition for *Thorn Tree Safaris*) around Ksh200 a meal. Camping is only Ksh40 but try to bring food (including fruit) and as much drinking water as possible with you, particularly out of season.

Vanga

Kenya's southernmost town, **VANGA** is also the largest of the coastal settlements to have been left alone by the tourist industry. The seventeen-kilometre murram road to Vanga begins, curiously, midway through the Kenyan border post at LUNGALUNGA (a couple of lodgings there but nothing of interest). It skims the Tanzanian border through *shambas* and, as it nears the sea, tunnels through glorious jungle in greenhouse gloom. Vanga itself is in the **mangroves**, approached through the swamp down a causeway which is regularly flooded by spring tides.

It is a largish village with a main street, a number of stores and *hotelis*, and a centrepiece coffee and soft drinks bar, a circular meeting place where men come in the evening to chew *miraa* and reflect on the community's isolation. "We have no employment" is a common complaint; the fishing co-operative is the only local provider of a cash income but it isn't always able to buy the entire catch and members are not supposed to sell to anyone else. Many people sell garden produce in Mombasa, which explains the series of *matatu* departures through the night to ensure early arrival at the markets.

Hotel tourists are not likely to be attracted to Vanga as there really isn't anything for them to do or anywhere to stay. For the less fastidious, dugout canoes can be hired very cheaply for wobbly punting trips through the mangroves, and there are some serene little beaches nearby. Locals are more than willing to accommodate visitors – I was plied with the best **palm wine** I've tasted – and Vanga is a sure antidote to a surfeit of Diani and Malindi.

THE NORTH COAST: KILIFI TO MALINDI

From Mtwapa Creek up to **Malindi**, the landscape is a diverse collage: from rolling baobab country and sisal plantations as you near **Kilifi** to groves of cashew trees after it; thick, jungly forest and swamp around Mida Creek, then a more compact, populated zone of *shambas* and thicket as you approach Malindi. **Kilifi and Takaungu creeks** are stunning – the clash of blue water and green cliffs almost unnatural.

There is wide scope for **beach-hunting** along this part of the coast. Malindi and, to some extent, Watamu have been developed, but Kilifi functions largely as a Giriama market-centre and district capital, while Takaungu seems virtually unknown, a throwback to pre-colonial days. There's also superb **snorkelling** at Watamu and Malindi **Marine National Parks**. And the ruined town of **Gedi**, deep in the jungle near Watamu, is one of the most impressive archaeological sites in East Africa.

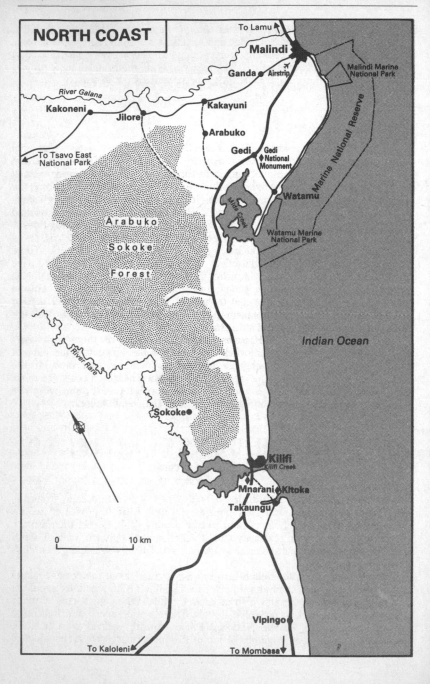

NORTH COAST

To Lamu

Malindi

Ganda • Airstrip

Malindi Marine
National Park

River Galana

Kakoneni •

Jilore •

Kakayuni •

To Tsavo East
National Park

Arabuko •

Gedi • Gedi
National
Monument

Marine National Reserve

Watamu

Mida Creek

Watamu Marine
National Park

A r a b u k o

S o k o k e

F o r e s t

River Rare

Indian Ocean

Sokoke •

Kilifi
Kilifi Creek

Mnarani • Kitoka

Takaungu

0   10 km

Vipingo •

To Kaloleni

To Mombasa

Kilifi and environs

Between Kikambala and Kilifi lies a major **sisal-growing** area, focusing around the small town of VIPINGO (one or two *dukas* and *hotelis*, not much else). Across thousands of acres, plumb-straight rows of fleshy-leafed sisal plants stretch in every direction, the surviving **baobab trees** standing out bizarrely.

Baobab stories

The baobab's strange appearance has a number of explanations in **mythology**. The most common one relates how the first baobab planted by God was an ordinary looking tree, but it refused to stay in one place and wandered round the countryside. As a punishment, God planted it back again – upside down – and immobilised it. Baobabs may live well over 2000 years, making them among the longest-living organisms. During a severe drought, their large green pods can be cracked open and the nuts made into a kind of flour. The resulting "Hungry bread" is part of the common culture of the region. Towards Kilifi, the road bucks through a hilly area and the baobabs grow more profusely amid the scrub.

Takaungu

Ten kilometres before you reach Kilifi, there's a turn-off to the right to **TAKAUNGU**. Although there are two *matatus* most days from Mombasa to Takaungu, the chances of a lift are relatively slim if you get dropped off at the turn. But it is not a long walk (5km) and it gives you time to shed the highway and "The Coast" from your mind. Takaungu is enchanting – a quiet, composed village of whitewashed Swahili houses situated on a high bluff above **Takaungu Creek**. There are three mosques and one or two small shops and *hotelis*, but no formal lodgings; if you want to stay and you speak a little Swahili, people will put you up for a very reasonable price. Food supplies are variable; women will prepare food if you ask, and especially if you supply the ingredients. There's no produce market, but a small fish market by the creek. Be there when the catch arrives to get the tasty ones. Go easy: Takaungu is a place that repays time spent getting to know it. If you just want to kick back and rest up, pass it by and head on to Lamu.

There's a small seaside **beach**, 1km east, through the secondary school. **Takaungu Creek** is startlingly beautiful, the colour of blue Curaçao, and absolutely transparent. The small swimming beach on the stream is under water at high tide, but you can still dive from the rocks. Upstream, the creek disappears between flanks of dense jungle. When you're ready to move on, the tiny, council-operated rowing boat provides a slow and almost free service across the creek to the Kilifi side; from there, it's a ninety-minute (5km) walk through the sisal fields to the Kilifi ferry.

Kilifi and the creek

Kenya's coastline has been submerged in the recent geological past and the result has been the creation of the islands and drowned river valleys – the creeks – of today. **KILIFI**, a small but animated place, is, again, on a creek. When the Portuguese knew it, Kilifi's centre was on the south side of the creek and called **MNARANI**. Together with KITOKA on the north side of Takaungu Creek, and a settlement on the site of the present town of Kilifi, these three constituted the

In recent decades, as the **Giriama** have expanded, Kilifi has become one of their most important towns. Giriama women are quickly noticed by everyone for their unusual dress. Traditionally a kind of kilt of grass or leaves, it is now made of *kanga* cloth with hips and buttocks accentuated by a bustle of coir fibre stuffed underneath. Older women still go topless but younger women usually cover up, at least in town. The Mijikenda peoples, and the Giriama especially, are remembered as great sorcerers and practitioners of witchcraft, and Kilifi is still the frequent scene of accusations that sometimes reach the press.

"state" of Kilifi. Mnarani's few **ruins** (Ksh30) sit under the trees high above Kilifi Creek to the west of the road. There's not a lot to see here apart from a very tall pillar tomb supported by iron props, a couple of mosques and a precipitous well that plummets right down to creek level. The site is archaeologically famous mainly for the large number of inscriptions found on its masonry, all in a difficult, and so far untranslated, form of monumental Arabic. Truthfully, however, for the non-buff Mnarani's most memorable aspect is its superlative position overlooking the creek, the toing and froing of the ferry, and the less attractive work going on to build the road bridge which may by now be finished. The visit fills time well if you are **waiting for the ferry** (which, if you're heading south to Mombasa to make an onward connection, you should know can easily delay you for an hour or two).

Other distractions of the south side of the creek include a **serpentarium** that is one of the coast's better-kept snake parks, with tame, wrap-around pythons and knowledgeable staff, and, on the seaward side of the road, the *Mnarani Club* (PO Box 81443, Mombasa, ☎2318 Kilifi) – a quasi-exclusive, mostly German, tour centre and venue of game fishing competitions (Ksh1708/2318). There's more heart in the row of bars and *hotelis* before you reach it. And there's a fair amount of life on the ferry dock itself, with green coconuts (*madafu*) and **cashew nuts** the main attractions. Kilifi's biggest employer is the 1500-person cashew nut factory on the other side.

Kilifi town

Kilifi is draped along the north side of the creek to the east of the main road. Even if most travellers merely see it from the inside of a bus while more fares are being picked up, staying the night is not an unpleasant prospect, if only to drink endlessly of the *Kilifi Hotel's* wonderful, fresh, cold fruit juices (right by the bus station). **Accommodation** is surprisingly thin on the ground: *Toplife B&L* on the cliff-top road is a good place to have a drink or eat outside, overlooking the creek, but the Ksh60 cubes are basic and a couple of others aren't much better. Best in town is the brand new *Tushauriane B&L*, directly behind the bus station, which has spotlessly clean and comfortable rooms with mosquito nets (Ksh80/120). Top ranker outside the tour circuit is the newish *Mkuajoni Motel* (back on the main road behind the *Agip* station), offering good, clean rooms with mosquito nets and a very continental open-air bar and restaurant (Ksh200/380 s/c); there's the attractive, added prospect of manic Friday and Saturday night discos. Food-wise, Kilifi's best eatery at the moment is *Jay's Coffee House,* on the main street opposite the *KCB*, with a slight emphasis on healthy eating, but all the greasy-spoon standards to fall back on.

Kilifi's not inconsiderable seaside–settler/yachtie community tends to hover around the bar of the *Seahorse Hotel* (☎2513 Kilifi), a twenty-minute walk landward of the main road, on the sheltered north side of the creek. This, informally, is Kenya's **sailing centre;** if you're on the lookout for onward **passages to points east,** or if you'd simply like to do some crewing, you might get lucky at the *Seahorse*. You can spend a much more eccentric evening at the *Kilifi Club* which, far from being the bridge-and-*Daily Telegraph* place you might expect, is nowadays a *nyama choma* bar with suggestive rondavels, and Kilifi's hottest spot at weekends. It faces the *Mnarani Club* across the creek.

The **beaches** around Kilifi are mostly accessible only through private property, and the best are up on the open coast to the northeast of the town, a full 3km from the centre. So if you have time on your hands, you could enquire at the **cashew factory** (PO Box 49, Kilifi, ☎2411 Kilifi) about a visit, which is said to be possible and interesting. The nuts are expensive because there are so few of them on the small trees: each one hangs, in an unlikely fashion, from a juicy, pear-shaped, yellow-and-orange fruit, refreshing to suck but inedible. The nut shells are processed to extract an oil used for making preservatives, for waterproofing and even for brake linings.

Cashew trees line both sides of the road north of Kilifi, but they soon give way to great tracts of jungle where monkeys scatter across the road and hornbills plunge into the cover of the trees as you approach. This is the **Arabuko-Sokoke Forest**, the largest patch of lowland jungle left in Kenya. At one time it would have covered most of the coastal hinterland behind the shoreline settlements. If you have a car or a few days for some walking, there are over 500 square kilometres to explore. Much of it has been penetrated and cut as the sawmills you'll come across testify, but several good-sized areas of untouched hardwood forest and stands of rubber trees remain. And, although this isn't the Amazon jungle, a degree of preparation is wise if you plan on venturing far down any of the tracks leading off the main road. *Survey of Kenya* maps would be useful (the "Kenya Coast" tourist map at the very least), though new tracks are constantly being cut and old ones allowed to over-grow. A **compass** is helpful. For details on the forest near Malindi, see p.318.

The forest is home to a brilliant variety of butterflies and many unusual species of birds. A tiny, and shy, antelope, the **Zanzibar duiker**, only 35cm high, is also found here, usually in pairs. But, like the extraordinary **golden-rumped elephant shrew**, you're more likely to see these rare animals around Gedi, where the thump and smell of tourists no longer disturbs them as much.

Gedi ruins

Open 7am–6pm daily, Ksh50. Gedi is approached down the road to Watamu, turning left at modern Gedi (1km from the Mombasa-Malindi highway) and following the track; Warden ☎32065 Watamu.

The Arabuko-Sokoke Forest may partly explain the enigma of **GEDI**. This large, thirteenth- to seventeenth-century Swahili town was apparently unknown to the Portuguese despite the fact that, for nearly 100 years, they maintained a strong presence in Malindi only 15km away, at a time when Gedi is judged to have been at the peak of its prosperity. It is not mentioned (at least by the name of *Gedi*) in any Arabic or Swahili writings either, and it has to be assumed that, set back from the sea and deep in the forest, it was never noticed – a baffling assumption.

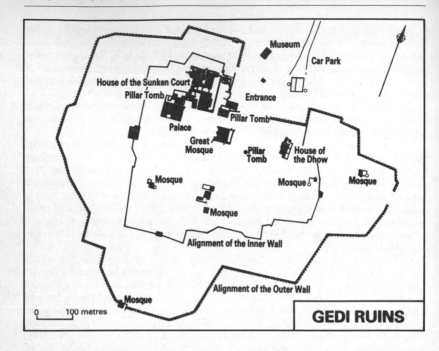

GEDI RUINS

The **ruins** are confusing, eerie, and in the late afternoon hauntingly beautiful. Even if you are resolutely uninterested in seeing any of the other sites on the coast, don't miss this one. Forest has invaded the town over the three centuries since it was deserted, and baobabs and magnificent buttress-rooted trees tower over the dimly lit walls and arches. Gedi has a sinister reputation and local people have always been uneasy about it; it has collected an unhealthy share of **ghost stories** and tales of inexplicable happenings since 1948, when it was opened as a national park and tourists started to visit it.

Some of this cultural memory may derive from the supposed occupation of the ruins in the eighteenth century by the **Galla**, a tribe of irrepressible expansionists whose violent and unsettled lifestyle was long a major threat to the coastal communities. The Galla, it's believed, were the original cause of Gedi's desertion by its inhabitants. James Kirkman, the archaeologist who first worked at Gedi, remembers:

> . . .*when I first started to work at Gedi I had the feeling that something or somebody was looking out from behind the walls, neither hostile nor friendly but waiting for what he knew was going to happen.*

Gedi tingles spines easily, even today, particularly if you are on your own. James Kirkman's booklet, which is usually available at the entrance gate, has a lot of interesting details as well as a plan of the site, which we've reproduced, above. Its directions, however, tend to lead you in circles; it's better just to follow your nose.

Exploring Gedi

The town seems fairly typical of medieval Swahili settlements. It was walled, and originally covered some 45 acres. The majority of its estimated 2500 citizens – or at least inhabitants – probably lived in mud and thatch huts, long overwhelmed and dissolved by jungle, on the southern, poorer side of town, away from Mecca. The palace and the "Stone Town" were in the north. When the site was re-occupied at the end of the sixteenth century, after a hiatus of fifty or so years, a new inner wall was built, enclosing just this prestigious zone.

The Palace

The **Palace**, with its striking entrance porch, sunken courts and honeycomb of little rooms, is the most impressive single building. The concentration of **houses** to its right is where most of Gedi's interesting finds were made and they are named accordingly: House of the Scissors, House of the Ivory Box, House of the Dhow (with a picture of a dhow on the wall). If you have already been to Lamu, the tight layout of buildings and streets will be familiar, although in Gedi all the houses were single storey. As usual, sanitary arrangements are much in evidence. Gedi's toilets are all of identical design, and superior to many long-drops you find in Kenya today. While many of the houses have been modified over the centuries, these bathrooms seem original, almost as if the town was purpose-built, like a housing estate. Look out for the **House of the Sunken Court**, one of the most elaborate, with its self-conscious emulation of the palace's courtyards.

The Great Mosque

Gedi's **Great Mosque**, one of seven on the site, was its Friday Mosque, the mosque of the whole town.

Compared with other ruined mosques on the coast, this one is very large and had a *minbar*, or pulpit, of three steps in stone, rather than the usual wood construction. Perhaps an inkling of the kind of people who worshipped here – and they were men *and* women – and the style of their Islam, comes from the carving of a broad-bladed **spearhead** above the arch of the mosque's northeast doorway. Whoever they were, they were clearly not the "colonial Arabs" beloved of European classical scholars, who were once thought to have been the people of Gedi: it's hard to believe that Arabs would have used this spear symbol of East African pastoralists.

Tombs

Nearby is a good example of a **pillar tomb**. These are found at sites all along the coast and are associated with men of importance – chiefs, sheikhs and senior elders of the community. The fact that this kind of grave is utterly alien to the rest of the Islamic world is further indication that Islam on the coast was distinctly African for a long time. Such tombs aren't constructed any more, though there's a nineteenth-century one in Malindi. It looks very much as if the more recent waves of Arab immigration to the coast have tended to discourage what must have seemed to them an eccentric, even a barbaric, style. The **Dated Tomb** next door gives an idea of Gedi's age. Its epitaph reads 802 AH – or AD 1399.

Gedi's mystery

The longer you stay here, the further you seem from an answer to Gedi's anomalies. The display in the small **museum** shows that the town must have been actively trading with overseas merchants, yet it is 5km from the sea and 2km from Mida Creek; the sea level has probably moved inland over the centuries, so it might have been further even than this. Then, at times of supposed Galla aggression, sailing into Mida Creek would have been like entering a lobster pot. The reasons for Gedi's location remain thoroughly obscure and its absence from historical records grows more inexplicable the more you think about it.

Natural mysteries

It is easy to spend hours here and rewarding to walk down some of the well-swept paths through the thick jungle away from the main ruins. In the undergrowth, you catch spooky glimpses of other buildings still unexcavated. And with patience you'll see a **golden-rumped elephant shrew**. A bizarre animal the size of a small cat, it resembles a giant mouse with an elongated nose, running on stilts. In one of those mysteriously evolved animal relationships, it consorts with a small bird, the **red-capped robin chat**, and your best chance of seeing the shrew is to look for its fluttering companion among the tangle of branches – the shrew will be close by. Gedi also has monkeys, bushbabies, tiny duiker antelope and, according to local belief, a huge, mournful, sheep-like animal that follows you like a shadow down the paths.

Watch out, incidentally, for the savagely physical *siafu* **ants** that have colonised many of the ruins. They form thick brown columns massing from one hole to another and sometimes gather in enormous clumps. Be careful where you put your feet when stepping over walls. And try not to stand on the walls themselves: they are fragile, and the freedom to walk around Kenya's ruins without restriction isn't likely to continue if they suffer as a result.

When Gedi has sufficient visitors, the **Giriama village** up by the main entrance and car park often reverberates with drumming and dancing. Whether it's good or not depends at least as much on the audience as on the performers.

Watamu

After Gedi, **WATAMU** seems fairly superficial. More than anything else, it's a purpose-built resort, an agglomeration of four hotels, a strip of beach-front private homes, a compact coconut village of *hotelis* and curio stands and the **beach**. The beach, and the coral offshore, are really the only justification for visiting Watamu. Fortunately, they are justification enough: this is an exceptional shoreline. The crags of coral gardens out in Watamu Marine National Park are – despite all the visits in glass-bottom boats – as vivid and magically perfect as they must have been for millennia.

The road from Gedi runs dead straight for 6km, passes Watamu's post office and telephone, then hits the Watamu beach road. *Matatus* scud up and down here all the time. Turn left for *Watamu Beach Hotel*, Watamu **village** and a branch of *Barclay's bank* (Mon, Wed, Fri mornings only). Also down here is a superb little **snake park**, privately owned, fascinating and lovingly kept on the strength of donations. Turn right for three more hotels – *Ocean Sports*, *Hemingways* (ex-*Seafarers*) and *Turtle Bay* – twenty or thirty private homes and, at the end of the narrow bar down which the road runs, the Marine Park ticket office. And that's Watamu.

Practical Watamu

Accommodation can be a problem. Off-season (April, possibly May), the hotels sometimes offer rooms at rates that even people on low budgets might start to consider. *Ocean Sports* is a small place with only forty beds, and it's relatively good value even in high season. At the *Seventh Day Adventist Church "Youth Site"*, just to the left of the junction, there's a forlorn patch for **camping** and the possibility (if it has been renovated) of hostel accommodation. Don't rely on this, however: the place has been dilapidated and barely functioning for some time, and British soldiers take it over for their own R&R arrangements for months on end.

At all events, Watamu village itself has some accommodation. The *Mushroom Club* (located strategically close to the *African Safari Club's Watamu Beach Hotel*) has rooms (Ksh200 s/c double), but they aren't necessarily intended for sleeping and you'll find it a noisy place to stay. Better to try the *Villa Veronika Mwikali Lodge* (Ksh300): charming, spotless and secure (PO Box 57, Watamu, ☎83 Watamu). A top-value new place is *Dante's Hotel and Restaurant*, offering s/c double rooms with fans from Ksh250 a night – and iced tea.

Tourist Hotels
Watamu Beach Hotel (☎32001 Watamu, bookings ☎225228 Nairobi).
Ocean Sports Ksh1000/1200 HB (PO Box 340, Malindi, ☎32008 Watamu).
Hemingways Ksh650/1250 (bookings through *Bookings Ltd* ☎225255 Nairobi).
Turtle Bay Ksh605/1210 (PO Box 22309, ☎221143 Nairobi).

Watamu village
Watamu village is a weird mixture of unhurried fishing community and frenzied Germanophile souvenir centre. The traditional rubs elbows with the pseudo-hip. Samburu and Maasai *morani* in full ochred splendour stand around waiting for photographers – and potential female customers. The mosque has a notice which says "All Muslims are Welcome for Prayers. No Trespass. By Management". The *Mushroom Club*'s **strip shows** cross the line drawn by the hotels and attract staff as well as more adventurous guests.

Underwater Watamu

The creation of the marine park's **total exclusion zone** for fishermen has not been greeted with rhapsody all the way around. On the other hand, tourists come in larger numbers every year and Watamu evidently hasn't gone far wrong in identifying their needs.

For **visits to the park**, check out *Ocean Sports Hotel* and possibly *Turtle Bay*. Expect to pay Ksh200 including park entrance fee. The spectacle can be breathtakingly stupendous if you've never swum in a shoal of coral fish before: every conceivable combination of colour and shape – and a few inconceivable ones – is represented. It seems impossible that fish should be such colours. The ostentatious dazzle of some of them, especially the absurd parrot fish, can be simply hilarious.

Usual destination of most trips are the **"coral gardens"**, a kilometre or two offshore, where the boat drifts, suspended in five or six metres of scintillatingly clear water. Here, over a group of giant coral heads, where fish naturally congregate and where offerings of bread have obviously further encouraged them, you enter the unusual park.

If you can **dive to the sea floor**, you'll get an intense experience of sharing the under-sea world with the fish and the coral. Watch out for the small, and harmless, octopuses which stay motionless until disturbed and then jet themselves across the seabed. Above, the boat's hull creates a deep shadow which, associated with food from the passengers, attracts thousands of fish. As you return to the surface, they move out of the way in mysterious unison, each one avoiding all the others in a kind of natural lightshow of fantastic beauty. If such adventures aren't your forte, the glass bottoms of the boats provide an alternative view – but it's often a rather murky and narrow one.

Great cod

At the entrance to Mida Creek is a famous group of caves. Known as the **"Big Three Caves"**, these are the meeting place of a school of **giant groupers**, or rock cod, that once numbered only three but are now many more. Up to two metres long and weighing over 300 kilos, they are placid, stationary monsters – thankfully for anyone intrepid enough to dive down for an eyeballing. There are boat trips here as well.

Malindi and around

When Vasco da Gama's fleet arrived at **MALINDI** in 1498, they were met with an unexpectedly warm welcome. The king of Malindi had presumably heard of Mombasa's attempts to sabotage the Portuguese fleet a few days earlier and, no friend of Mombasa himself, he was swift to ally himself with the powerful – and dangerous – Portuguese. Until they finally subdued Mombasa nearly 100 years later, Malindi was the centre of operations for the Portuguese on the coast. Once they had built Fort Jesus, Malindi's ruling family was invited to transfer their power base there, which they did, and for many years Malindi was virtually a ghost town as its aristocrats lived it up in Mombasa under Portuguese protection.

Malindi's reputation for **hospitality** to strangers has stuck and so has the suggestion of **sell-out**. As a steadily growing, rock-solid development area for the cultivation of, principally, *deutschmarks* and *lire*, the town is slipping towards cultural anonymity: it can't seem to make up its mind whether to be like Mombasa or Lamu. It does retain a Swahili atmosphere, which Mombasa has partly lost in urban development, but it utterly lacks Lamu's self-contained tranquillity. Here is one town in Kenya that would go into precipitate decline were the crutch of tourism removed.

Consequently, whether you enjoy it or not depends, at least in part, on how highly you rate the unsophisticated parts of Kenya, and whether you appreciate a fully fledged **resort town** for its facilities or loathe it for its tackiness. And of course it depends on when you're here. During the summer holiday season, as well as in December and January, Malindi can be nightmarish. Everything African about the town seems to recede behind the swarms of window-shopping tourists and mini-mokes. Even so, Malindi at its worst in still relatively placid compared with, say, the Mediterranean, and off-season (reduced here to the long rains only – April to June) can seem positively subdued, as if exhausted. Though often damp and grey at this time of year, Malindi occasionally has the air of a Bournemouth or Bognor about it; the faded muddle of an ageing resort garnished with tropical plants. It was opened as a settlers' seaside escape in the 1930s (in Kenyan terms a very long time ago) and the last of the sun-wrinkled generation of a bygone era can still be seen walking on Lamu Road.

Fortunately, Malindi has some important saving graces in this mixed bag of characteristics. Number one is the **coral reef**. The combined Malindi/Watamu Marine National Parks and Reserve enclose some of the best stretches on the coast. Kisite/Mpunguti on the south coast is reckoned by connoisseurs to be even better, but the Malindi fish have seen many more strange faces in masks and have become so used to humans that they swarm in front of you like a kaleidoscopic snowstorm. Malindi is a **game-fishing** centre with regular competitions and a bit of a **surfing** resort, too. Good-sized rollers steam into the bay through the long break in the reef during July and August, whipped up by the southerly monsoon winds.

Despite the heavy reliance on tourism, Malindi remains a thriving and ancient **town**. An interesting old Swahili quarter, one or two "ruins", a busy market, shops, *hotelis* and plenty of lodgings, all compensate for the tourist boutiques, beauty salons and estate agents, and they do give Malindi a certain advantage as a beach resort over Diani or the places north of Mombasa – especially if you have no transport of your own.

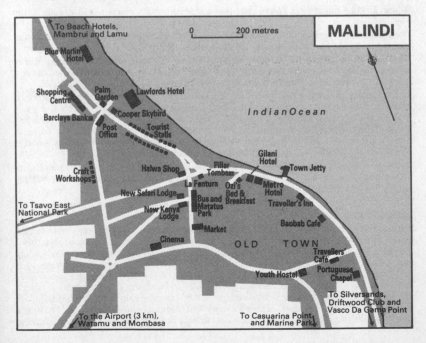

Arrival, sleeping and eating

In the practical things of life, Malindi is uncomplicated. **Buses** and *matatus* arrive in the town centre, either by the market or on the messy high street between the cheapest of the B&Ls. Arriving **by air**, the Ksh100 taxi ride into town from the airstrip, 3km south, seems wildly expensive: walking, with a good chance of a free lift, is a realistic alternative.

Rooms

Accommodation is no problem, though over Christmas (in the beach spots), and during *Maulidi* and at the end of *Ramadan* (in the town lodgings), the choices may be restricted; the tourist and traveller haunts vary seasonally in price by up to fifty percent.

New Safari Lodge Cheap and noisy, but okay if you're just looking for a place to drop your gear and crash. Energetic ground-floor restaurant.

La Fantura (PO Box 361, ☎20400). Bastardised Swahili house with plywood room dividers. Not as noisy as the *New Safari*.

New Lamu Hotel (not on map). Best value in town with comfortable doubles for under Ksh100, big mosquito nets, serious showers and cheap and reasonable food downstairs.

Tana Hotel (PO Box 766, ☎20657; formerly the *New Kenya* as marked on map). Much improved, and more expensive, since its previous incarnation (Ksh300/double).

Metro Hotel The faded quasi-colonial image – walls festooned with stuffed fish and nameless marine curios – is more promising than the rooms (Ksh59/118), but the seafood menu and bar are agreeable, and the new manager is making a name for herself as a helpful and generous organiser.

Gilani Hotel Unappealing rooms but reasonable value for couples and groups (from Ksh180/260).

Traveller's Inn Offspring of the *New Safari*. One of the most popular – low-key, friendly and traveller-oriented – but much cheaper for two or three (Ksh160/240 B&B). No fans or nets.

Ozi's Bed & Breakfast (PO Box 60, ☎20218). Top in the current popularity ratings despite being a little more expensive than most. Really good breakfasts with fresh fruit and the rest and worth the 4am awakening by the mosque nearby (around Ksh250/500 B&B s/c).

Youth Hostel Although much moved around, closed and reopened, now seems established in the location marked on the map. Off-season a rather staid and possibly lonely bed space (Ksh50), though the comments and stories in the visitor's book are always worth perusing. When Malindi is hopping, however, the good bathrooms and beds, clean and airy common areas, a fridge, and a fine rooftop represent excellent value and the hostel seems a haven of near-sanity and security – if you can get a bed. YHA membership isn't required.

Lutheran Church Guest House North side of town. More hostel-type accommodation with a good garden and clean, mosquito-netted rooms with fans (PO Box 409, ☎21098; Ksh65/130, Ksh100/200 s/c).

Camping and *bandas*

Silversands Campsite (PO Box 422, ☎20412). 2km from town. If you're prepared to forgo a little security to be **on the beach** (in the high season you'll have lots of company) then this is the place. Despite the nuisance of being some distance from town and unable to leave a tent unguarded with confidence, this beach is the obvious choice for anything more than an overnight stay in Malindi. *Banda*-type huts at Ksh155–290 (room for two people, sometimes discounted over longer stays but seasonally variable) and camping fees of Ksh40 per person per night. But showers here are saltwater (pay a day's membership at the *Driftwood*, below, and you can have real, hot ones). There's a snack and cold drinks store on the site. For beach-lounging only, this isn't a bad place. The major drawback is the millions of microscopic ants, the destruction of which is sure to tax your inventiveness. Try *Doom* or *It*. Beware that solo travellers walking between town and Silversands beach have several times been the victims of muggings in recent years.

Driftwood Club, further south along Silversands beach (PO Box 63, ☎20155), various prices for B&B from around Ksh600/800 for basic rooms to Ksh1000/1200 with AC). Snack bar and reasonable à la carte menu that's not too over-priced. Discos on Wednesdays and Saturdays, windsurfers for rent, and even an inexpensive squash court.

Upmarket Malindi

Over a dozen hotels, villa complexes and "clubs" provide for the swarms of high season visitors though, surprisingly, only five of them are large hotels.

Blue Marlin (PO Box 20, ☎20441). Much renovated, this is where Ernest Hemingway once contemplated game-fishing but stayed in the bar instead. Rooms (Ksh975/1300 HB) are a touch cheaper than the norm and, in May and June, genuine bargains are sometimes on offer. All are located on the north side of town.

Lawford's (PO Box 20, ☎20440). Seems reasonable value (Ksh900/1200 HB) with really nice rooms but only a mediocre restaurant and hordes of *Deutschlanders* consuming their annual holidays.

Scorpio Villas (PO Box 368, ☎20194). An exceptionally well-laid out and well-run self-catering development south of the town on Silversands Beach. Prices for a four-bed villa (with eight hours of servant attendance per day) start at about Ksh1600.

Kingfisher Lodge (PO Box 29, ☎20123, fax 21168). Unusual, small, pretty, family-run *banda* lodge, with a pool, located about 2km inland. Transport locally – to the beach, to town – is included in the tariff (around Ksh1500/2000 FB). Remote area safaris can be arranged at the lodge. Recommmneded for a tension-free (and pretension-free) splurge.

Meals, snacks

You're presented with two basic options for **eating** in Malindi. The first is ordinary *hoteli* fare supplemented by a scattering of Indian-style juice and samosa bars; the second is a much higher price bracket that includes the big hotels and a number of more lavish restaurants. If you're buying your own food, you'll find **Malindi market** is celebrated for fruit and vegetables, second only to Mombasa's on the coast.

Baobab, down on the waterfront. Alhough it may not be "the coolest café on the coast" this catches *Silversands* campers on the way back from town with tasty snacks, friendly service and a bar next door.

Abbas's Eating Place, just south of the *Baobab*. A fine discovery, Abbas serves snacks, ginger coffee and tea and, with advance notice in the morning and a small deposit, delicious Swahili meals under the stars at the end of the day.

Travellers' Café Run by a group of women and really popular with youth hostellers for its cold beers and large portions of tasty food.

I Love Pizza, also on the seafront. Flashy and recommended for everything but its dried-up cardboard pizza – and if you don't mind spending what you might at home. Good atmosphere.

The Metro Formerly reliable, its recently opened restaurant is so far untested.

Palm Garden Provides escape from Lamu Road's gauntlet of souvenir stalls – a convenient rendezvous that's primarily a bar, serving inexpensive curries and seafood.

Eddie's Ngowe Rd (☎20283), beyond the *Eden Roc Hotel*, in north Malindi. The best place for a splurge. Glorious seafood blow-outs round the pool for around Ksh500.

Bawaly and Sons Halwa Shop Highly deserving of a mention, a long-established spot to try several varieties of the gooey jelly (of which "Turkish Delight" is a dull relation). Tiny cups of spiced *kahawa* come free.

Filling the day

Not unexpectedly, **snorkelling and watersports** are Malindi's touristic *raison d'être*. Windsurfing, water-skiing, diving and deep-sea fishing are all slightly cheaper here than at the resorts around Mombasa. It's the main wave-surfing, stretch with boards available from all the hotels. Unfortunately, all are marred somewhat by the Sabaki River's annual outpouring of thousands of tons of prime red topsoil from the up-country plateaus. The cloudy water prevents the growth of coral as far south as Vasco da Gama point and, ironically, Malindi Bay and the tour-group hotels dotted along it face out to a muddy-brown seascape for much of the year. Murky as it is, this water is not unpleasant to swim in.

Marine park trips

Trips out to the **marine park** further south can be arranged with the boat trip salesmen who make their rounds of *Silversands* (and elsewhere) most mornings. You should find a little room for discussion but won't be able to knock prices down much below the current standard of Ksh150 (includng park fees), especially at peak times and your outing may be curtailed if you bargain too ruthlessly. *Sharif's Boats* (☎20374 Malindi) is said to be a decent operator. Try to check the condition of masks and snorkels, and insist on a set for each member of the party. Flippers aren't likely to be up to much (that's assuming they fit you). With your own or hired gear, of course, you could swim to the reef a few hundred metres off the beach. Even so, the six square kilometres of the **national park** (normal hours but only Ksh80 entrance fee at the ticket office past Casuarina Point) takes in the loveliest areas of coral garden. The trip a few kilometres offshore – usually in a glass bottom boat – is worth every shilling. If you have scuba qualifications, you can also **dive**. The going rate is about Ksh700 per dive with all equipment provided. Lorenz Riedl (PO Box 160, Watamu) is recommended.

Around town: gossip, monuments, snake parks and nightlife

Other than the beach and the sea, **strolling around town** is the occupation of most of Malindi's temporary residents, and not without its idiosyncratic rewards. The old part of Malindi is a half-hour diversion: interesting enough even though there's nothing specific to see and few of the buildings date from before the second half of the nineteenth century. But the juxtaposition of the earnest and ordinary business of the old town with the near-hysterical *mzungu*-mania only a couple of minutes' walk away on Lamu Road produces a bizarre, schizophrenic atmosphere that is characteristic of Malindi and not noticeable to the same extent anywhere else on the coast.

The town has an amazingly salacious reputation which is not entirely home-grown: some European tour operators have in the past been quite inventive in their every-comfort-provided marketing strategies. With a massive recent slump in German tourists (now why should that be?), perhaps the era of the sex safari is really over. The Italians are now in the ascendant (even Italian football results are posted in one restaurant window) and a spate of gossipy stories in the press about financial wickedness – or cleverness – among the Italian community, which has invested heavily in the area, resurrected the shaggy dog of "Mafia connections" – until President Moi publicly declared the issue closed.

Archaeologically, Malindi's offerings are scant. The two pillar tombs in front of the Friday Mosque on the waterfront are fine, upstanding examples of the genre, though the shorter one is only nineteenth-century. This being Malindi, its appearance is always described as "circumcised". Islamic scholars on the coast tend to disagree with the automatic phallic label applied by foreigners. Malindi's other monuments are Portuguese. **Vasco da Gama's Cross** down on the point of the same name makes a good excuse for a stroll: the **church**, whose foundations were laid in the sixteenth century, is an undistinguished, whitewashed cube, the site of a Portuguese burial on which a chapel was built. The most recent Portuguese bequest is the 1959 **Vasco da Gama Monument** near the town square.

If you're drawn to **wildlife**, you could visit one of Malindi's **snake parks** – the best is supposed to be the one at Casuarina Point (Wednesday and Friday at 4pm are feeding times) – or the rather sad **falconry** in town, on Lamu Road, but it's tempting to recommend avoiding such places entirely.

For **action at night**, Malindi's northern half buzzes through the high season. The discos are rarely a big deal but they are for the most part affordable. You may even find live music.

Malindi directory
Area code ☎0123.

Banks *Barclay's* (PO Box 100, ☎20036 Malindi), *Standard Bank*, and the *KCB* open Mon–Fri 8.30am–1pm, Sat 8.30–11am. *Barclay's* is also open Mon–Fri 2.30–5pm for foreign exchange only.

Bicycle hire Everybody's doing it. *Silversands Campsite* are old hands, but reportedly not happy if you want to take their machines far from Malindi. Two other places – the travel agents next to *I Love Pizza* and *Travellers' Café* near the Youth Hostel – may have better bikes, but prices are a little higher (around Ksh100/day). *Silversands'* bikes come with gyroscopic pedals and unusually shaped wheels for Ksh70/day or Ksh400/week.

Car hire *Glory Car Hire* PO Box 994, Ngala Building, Lamu Rd (☎20065), maintains a high profile on the coast and you can leave the vehicle in Nairobi or Mombasa for a supplement. A limited number of motorbikes are available.

Flights *Eagle Aviation*, *Equator* and *Air Kenya Aviation* connect Malindi with Nairobi, Mombasa and Lamu.

Game-fishing The Malindi Festival happens in October and the "Billfish Tournament" in January, but if you're into it, you can go hunting big fish from September to April. In 1980 they caught a marlin that weighed over one third of a ton. It will cost you from Ksh5000–10,000 a day for the boat and the gear.

Kangas Cheaper here than in Biashara St in Mombasa, but a poorer choice.

Post office Mon–Fri 8am–4.30pm, Sat 8am–noon. Good poste restante.

Safaris Try to avoid taking a safari to Tsavo out of Malindi. They tend to be more expensive than similar trips departing from Mombasa.

Safe deposit *Lawford's Hotel* rents boxes to non-residents.

Train tickets *Bunson Travel* make bookings for *Kenya Railways*.

Out of Malindi: Mambrui, the Arabuko-Sokoke Forest and Hell's Kitchen

The best way to get around town and its environs is **by bicycle**. Several places rent out bikes (see above). If you've been relying for some time on public transport, cycling gives a tremendous lift, enabling you to go virtually anywhere. The flat countryside around Malindi is ideal and Gedi (90 minutes) or Watamu (2 hours) are easy objectives, with the guarantee that you'll be wind-blown either there or back, depending on the time of year.

Mambrui

You might be tempted to cycle north to what one piece of tourist literature describes as "the Arabian Nights town of **Mambrui**". True, there's a pretty mosque and the unusual spectacle of cows on the beach, but the very ruinous pillar tomb certainly isn't worth the dust-blown journey and the village itself could hardly be less exciting.

The Arabuko-Sokoke Forest

For immersion in raw nature, pedal for an hour on the road out of Malindi towards Tsavo East National Park and, as you near the banks of the Sabaki (or Galana) River, you'll enter the **Arabuko-Sokoke Forest**. To make the most of the day, try setting out early by *matatu*, with your bike on the roof rack. There are several *matatus* daily, and one country bus service, but departure times are unpredictable.

The places to aim for are KAKAYUNI (12km) and JILORE (some 20km inland from Malindi). Kakayuni is the larger of the two and offers a forest road of 10km or so, leading via ARABUKO, to the main coast highway. Mostly, however, this path goes through marginal forest lands. Continuing to Jilore is more promising. Jilore is a tiny centre, with a scattered collection of huts and one nominal *duka*. The village's position, though, on a high ridge overlooking a bend in the Sabaki/Galana River, is an impressive contrast to the depths of the forest into which you now plunge.

About 3km from Jilore you come to the new forest station and from a cross-roads nearby a good trail leads back 13km in a southerly direction to the main Kilifi–Malindi coast road. If you're doing this trip by car, the track is driveable, and it's also clear enough for walkers to follow without getting lost. But a bicycle is the best option and quiet enough to give you good animal-viewing and bird-watching opportunities. The track is seldom used by motorists and you're not likely to see other people. Plenty of side turnings can also be explored – again, most confidently on a bike – but the main route is pleasant enough. Around the track's halfway mark, the soil changes from red murram to a light grey, coral sand, signalling the transition back to the coast. Your emergence onto the main highway, five or six kilometres south of GEDI (see p.307), is sudden. You could wait for a short time for a *matatu* straight back to Malindi or, if the day is still young and your energy unsapped, turn inland again a couple of kilometres north up the road, where another track should lead to Arabuko and Kakayuni.

The Marafa Depression: Hell's Kitchen

Northwest of Malindi, the **Marafa Depression** is the remains of a large sandstone ridge, now reduced by wind, rain and floodwater to a series of gorges, where steep gullies and narrow *arrêtes* alternately eat into or jut from the main ridge wall. The colours of the exposed sandstone range from off-white through pale pinks and oranges to deep crimson, all capped by the rich tawny topsoil. It's particularly dramatic at sunset.

"Hell's Kitchen" is the common moniker for this pretty spectacle, though the locals call it *Nyari* – "the place broken by itself" – and tell numerous moralising **stories** about its dark origins. The village which once stood here was favoured by God with the news of a forthcoming miracle, delivered to the inhabitants by an angel. They were commanded to move on, and all did so, except one old woman who refused to believe such nonsense. The village (and the old lady) disappeared soon after, leaving *Nyari*. Whether that was the miracle is not reported, but it's intcresting to note how the story varies according to the teller – in Islamic circles, "God talked through an angel", while among traditionalists, "the gods informed a wise woman".

In Marafa, fork right at the end of the village, and the canyon is about half a kilometre down that road on the left, invisible until you're right on the edge. At the lip of the gorge the first signs of commercialism – a small car park and a couple of seasonal souvenir stands – don't detract much from the site. It's easy to descend the steep path to the bottom and you can count on spending an hour or two exploring the natural architecture of what looks like an early *Star Trek* set.

With a vehicle, you might sensibly combine the Arabuko-Sokoke Forest with a visit to this "mini Grand Canyon" (Bryce Canyon in Utah is a lot more like it) by crossing the Galana/Sabaki River – if the bridge across the river at Jilore (marked on some maps) actually existed. In its absence, take the road out of Malindi heading north (which involves a left turn on the other side of the Sabaki bridge) and thence go via MARIKEBUNI and MAGARINI. You're looking at a round trip of about 80km, one which – given the vagaries of **public transport** – only drivers or the most energetic cyclists would manage in a day. The daily bus to MARAFA leaves Malindi in the afternoon, "sleeps" in Marafa village and returns to the coast the next morning. Buses to MBAINI (leaving Malindi in the morning) and DIKATCHAL (departing in the afternoon) also pass through Marafa but nothing arrives there in time to catch a ride back again the same day. In season, you might just hitch a lift back. Otherwise, with a scattering of *dukas* and *hotelis* among its whitewashed, thatched houses, but **no lodgings**, a tent and some pleasantries down at the police station seem in order.

Onwards to Lamu

The **flight to Lamu** is an experience not to be missed if you have a little spare cash, but the **bus journey** is a bit of an adventure in its own right and repays you with more than just a cheaper ticket. It can also be diabolically uncomfortable: buy a ticket as early as possible and insist on your right to a seat. *Tana River Bus* (office and depot behind the *Kobil* station in Malindi, PO Box 181, ☎20116) run one or two services around 7.30 or 8.30am daily. If you wait for the Mombasa buses to arrive mid-morning, they're generally full. If you're standing in the aisle, the next six hours isn't amusing.

Installed by a window, on the other hand (ideally on the left to avoid the sun), you can fully appreciate the flat, gentle, dull landscape, sometimes brown and arid but more usually grey-green and swampy, which opens out as Malindi's low hills are left behind. When the scenery palls totally, the trip is enlivened by the other passengers, by stops at fly-blown GARSEN and little WITU for *chai* and a bite to eat, and by occasional flashes of colour: the sky-blue cloaks of **Orma** herders or the red, black and white of shawled **Somali** women. Wonderful **bird-life** and **wild animals** are evident, too: giraffe and antelope, notably waterbuck; even the odd elephant if you look hard enough. And impeccable sources attest to having recently seen **lions** between Garsen and Mokowe. Again, animals are most likely to be seen out of the left side of the bus.

The Chinese-built New Garsen Causeway now spans the Tana outside Garsen with a bridge and provides a flood-proof highway. In the past, **during the rains**, bus services were often disrupted, either because the buses were stuck in the mud or because the Tana River was too high for the primitive, **hand-hauled car ferry** to operate. In that case they used to ferry people across the Tana by dugout canoe and, *inshallah*, there'd be another bus waiting on the other side. Of the several bus operators on the Lamu route, *Tana River* is usually more reliable, *Tawakal* less so. The road is increasingly dotted with tarmac stretches.

THE LAMU ARCHIPELAGO

A cluster of hot, low-lying desert islands tucked into the coast near the Somalian border, **Lamu** and its neighbours have a special appeal which no one seems able to resist. While each town or village has its own distinct character, together they epitomise a separate spectrum of Swahili culture. For although the whole coast is – broadly – "Swahili", there's a world of difference between these islands and the coconut beaches of Mombasa and Malindi.

To a great extent they are anachronisms. Electricity arrived less than twenty years ago; there are still no motor vehicles; life moves at the pace of a donkey or a dhow. Yet there have been considerable internal changes over the centuries and Lamu itself is now changing faster than ever. Because of its special position in the Islamic world (see p.333), Saudi Arabian direct aid has poured into the island: the hospital, schools and religious centres are all supported by it. At the same time, there are efforts to open Lamu beyond its present tourist market which so far has encompassed only low-budgeters or stylish air safaris. Rich foreign sponsors are eagerly sought and several lodging houses have been set up with what is bluntly called "white girl money". Islanders are ambivalent about the future. A string of hotels along the beach? A bridge to the mainland? Tarmac to Malindi? A new port and naval base on Manda? It all seems possible, eventually (the tarmac is certainly coming and the latter project is rather likely), and it would all contribute to the destruction of Lamu's timeless character. Some of the up-country officials working here might not disapprove: the town, with its one bar, is not a popular posting.

But the damage that would be done goes further than spoiling the tranquillity. The Lamu archipelago is one of the most important sources for knowledge about pre-colonial Africa. **Archaeological sites** indicate that towns have been built on these islands for at least 1200 years. The dunes behind Lamu beach, for example,

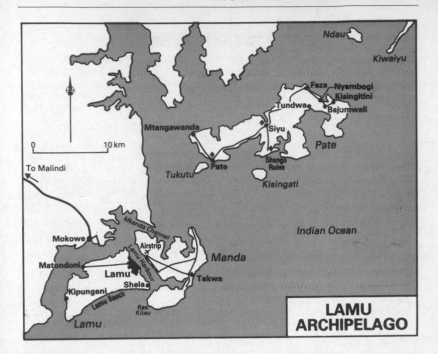

are said to conceal the remains of long-deserted settlements. And somewhere
close by on the mainland, archaeologists expect to uncover the ruins of
Shungwaya, the town which so many coastal peoples claim as their ancestral
home. The whole region is an academic's delight, a source of endless confusion
and controversy, a place where there is still real continuity between modern life
and history.

For the present, at least, the islands survive. Lamu, most people's destination,
still has plenty to recommend it. **Manda**, right opposite, is little visited in its own
right and seems doomed to be overtaken by slightly mysterious new developments (see p.337). **Pate Island** makes a fascinating excursion if you have a week
or more in the area (p.338). And **Kiwaiyu**, not quite within the archipelago but
exotic and alluring enough to be worth the effort if you have time, is a wisp of a
beach island 9km long and barely 500m across, lying to the northeast of the other
islands (p.344). Those who visit Kiwaiyu normally arrive by private plane, but you
can feasibly reach it by boat from Faza or by grouping together to charter a dhow
in Lamu.

Lamu

Perhaps best left to the end of your stay in Kenya, **LAMU** may otherwise precipitate a change in your plans as you're lulled into a slow rhythm in which days and
weeks can pass by unheeded and other objectives get forgotten. For many,
Lamu's deliciously lazy atmosphere is the best worst-kept secret on the coast.

The undeniably **Arab** flavour of Lamu is not nearly as old as the town itself. It derives from the later nineteenth century when the **Omanis**, and to some extent the Hadhramis from what is now **Yemen**, held political and cultural sway in the town. The first British representatives found themselves among pale-skinned slave-owning Arab rulers. The cultural and racial stereotypes which were subsequently propagated have never completely disappeared.

Lamu was established on its present site by the fourteenth century but there have been people living on the island for very much longer than that. The fresh water supplies beneath Shela made the island very attractive to **refugees from the mainland** and people have been escaping here for 2000 years or more – most recently in the 1960s when Somali secessionists and cattle raiders caused havoc. It was also one of the earliest places on the coast to attract settlers from the Persian Gulf; there were probably people from Arabia and southwest Asia living and inter-marrying here even before the foundation of Islam.

In 1505, Lamu was visited by a heavily armed **Portuguese** man-of-war and her king quickly agreed to pay the first of many cash tributes as protection money. The alternative was the sacking of the town. For the next 180 years Lamu was, nominally, under Portuguese rule, though the Portuguese favoured Pate as a place to live. In the 1580s, the Turkish fleet of Amir Ali Bey temporarily threatened Portuguese dominance, but superior firepower and relentless savagery kept the Muslims out and Lamu, with little in the way of an arsenal, had no choice but to bend with the wind – losing a king now and then to the Portuguese executioners – until the Omanis arrived on the scene with fast ships and a serious bid for lasting control.

By the end of the seventeenth century, Lamu's Portuguese predators were vanquished and for nearly a century and a half it had a revitalising breathing space. This was its **Golden Age**. Lamu became a republic ruled over by the *Yumbe*, a council of elders who deliberated in the palace (now a ruined plot in the centre of town), with only the loosest control imposed by their Omani overlords. This was the period when most of the big houses were built and when Lamu's classic archi-tectural style found its greatest expression. Arts and crafts flourished and business along the waterfront made the town a magnet throughout the Indian Ocean. Huge

Eyes, ears, tongue and nose get a comprehensive work-out here, so that actually *doing* anything is sometimes a problem – like walking through treacle. Hours can be blissfully spent on a roof or a verandah just watching the town go by, swinging effortlessly from one of the day's five prayer calls to the next, from tide to tide, and from dawn to dusk.

Lamu is something of a **myth** factory – classical as well as popular. Conventionally labelled "an old Arab trading town", it is actually one of the last viable remnants of the **Swahili civilisation** that was the dominant cultural force all along the coast until the arrival of the British. In the late 1960s and early 1970s, Lamu's unique blend of beaches, gentle Islamic ambience, funky old town and population well used to strangers was a recipe which took over where Marrakesh left off. It acquired a reputation as Kenya's Kathmandu: the end of the (African) hippie trail and a stop-over on the way to India. Shaggy foreigners were only allowed to visit on condition they stayed in lodgings and didn't camp on the beach. A sign of those times still intimidates the odd freak arriving at the jetty with its order for "all visitors to report to the police".

ocean-going dhows rested half the year in the harbour, taking on ivory, rhino horn, mangrove poles and cereals. There was time to compose long poems and argue about language, the Koran and local politics. Women did well, too, though ironically the best known, poet **Mwana Kupona**, is famous for her "Advice on the Wifely Duty" given to her daughter. The house where she lived for a while is up behind the fort. Lamu became the northern coast's **literary and scholastic focus**, a distinction inherited from Pate.

In fact for a brief time Lamu's star was in the ascendant in all fields. There was even a famous victory at the **Battle of Shela** in 1812. A combined Pate-Mazrui* force landed at Shela with the simple plan of capturing Lamu – not known for its resolve in battle – and finishing the construction of **the fort** which the Nabahanis from Pate had begun a few years earlier. To everyone's surprise, particularly the Lamu defenders, the tide had gone out and the invaders were massacred as they tried to push their boats off the beach. Appalled at the overkill and expecting a swift response from the Mazruis in Mombasa, Lamu sent to Oman itself for **Busaidi** protection and threw away independence forever. Had the eventual outcome of this panicky request been foreseen, the Lamu *Yumbe* might have reconsidered. Seyyid Said, Sultan of Oman, was more than happy to send a garrison to complete and occupy Lamu's fort – and from this toehold in Africa, he went on to smash the Mazrui traitors in Mombasa, taking the entire coast and moving his own Sultanate to Zanzibar.

A stepping-stone in the plans of the mighty, Lamu gradually sank into economic collapse towards the end of the nineteenth century as Zanzibar and Mombasa grew in importance. In a sense, it has been stagnating ever since. The building of the Uganda railway from Mombasa and the banning of slavery did nothing to improve matters for Lamu in purely economic terms, and it seems that decline has kept up with the shrinking population. However, the new **resettlement programme** on the mainland at Lake Kenyatta (*Mpeketoni*) is already spinning off new faces to Lamu and a revived commercialism from up-country has taken root in the market square. *Petley's Inn*, the town's only bar, runs out of beer more often than it used to.

* The Mazrui were the Omani family who had set themselves up independently in Mombasa and incurred the wrath of the Busaidi rulers back in Oman.

This is no longer necessary; nor, it seems, does anyone want to camp out these days. The proliferation of good, reasonably priced lodgings in the heart of the town encourages an ethos more interactive than hippie-escapist. Every other traveller you've met along the way seems to end up here, in an ever recycling community. Happily, travellers and locals cross paths enough to avoid any tedium – though for women travelling without men, this can itself become tedious (see p.335).

Arrivals and disorientation

The **bus trip** ends at MOKOWE on the mainland, where a chugging *mtaboti* (motorboat) takes you out around the creek for a thirty-minute ride to the town.

If you **drive** to Lamu yourself, you'll have to leave your vehicle in the car park where it will, by all accounts, be safe: tipping the *askari* beforehand may improve security further. Don't be misled by boys who try to sell you a *mtaboti* charter for Ksh100. Wait instead for the next bus to arrive and take the public *mtaboti* with everyone else.

Flying up, planes land on Manda Island directly opposite the town across the harbour; if you approach from here, the short boat trip gives a wonderful, spreading panorama of Lamu's nineteenth-century waterfront.

Whichever way you arrive, when you climb up the steps of the jetty you'll be met by a **guide** or three, offering "the best room in Lamu". Much as you might prefer to wander unguided, soaking it all in, and tracking down a room yourself, you probably won't escape; unless you've already made a booking, your first hour or so is likely to be full of milling confusion as you're led from one suggested lodging to another through a baffling maze of streets. In the long run, and with discretion, it's better not to fight this little hustler's ritual: carrying bags gives you away as newly arrived. Nobody's going to lead you up an alley and rob you – the town is really too small for that – and once you've settled on a room and argued the toss with the landlord over who's going to pay the hustler his **tip**, you'll be left in peace.

When discovering Lamu for yourself, you shouldn't get lost too easily if you remember that **Harambee Avenue** – the *Usita wa Mui* or *Njia Kuu* – runs parallel to and 50m behind the waterfront, and that streets leading into town all climb slightly uphill. Many of the places mentioned in this section are keyed by number or letter on the map. But getting lost is anyway rather terrific.

Lodgings in Lamu town

The better **lodgings** are generally those on the waterfront or those with a height advantage: places along the *Usita wa Mui* tend to be suffocatingly hot. Best known is *Petley's Inn* (PO Box 4, ☎3107) but having the only bar in town has grossly inflated its reputation and they've even been known to charge an entrance fee for non-guests who want to drink the warm beer, or else restrict public drinking to Saturday night. (For the lowdown on beer, see the "Lamu directory" on p.334). *Petley's* accommodation is shameful and exorbitant, and if you happen to be put here on a short package from Malindi or Mombasa, you should still look for a lodging elsewhere, even paying the modest extra from your own pocket. *Petley's* is no place to spend time in Lamu. *Peponi Hotel*, out on the beach at Shela (and covered on p.336), is much more expensive and altogether a different prospect.

BANANA SYNDROME

Three of the lodgings marked on the map (overleaf) have acquired notoriety for minor theft from rooms and hassles from the owner/manager, especially for women. Specifically, one "chain" of three lodgings, to which many people are taken – one not far from the post office, one south of the Jumaa mosque and one in the north of Mkomani on the waterfront – are consistently cited. None of these is included in the listings that follow. Keep your **ear to the ground** when moving around: the gossip is part of the town's appeal.

Seasons and prices

In December, January, July and August, and particularly during *Maulidi*, **rooms availability** can be tight. It's a good idea to book ahead if you can. We've given PO Box and telephone numbers where available and would appreciate more addresses for the next edition. You can also try writing to the lodging, just using the address PO Lamu, Coast Province, Kenya.

WATER IN LAMU

Before you settle in, try to ascertain the quality of the **lodging's water supply**. You'll soon appreciate the critical problem here: a handful of lodgings seem to have overcome it and advertise 24-hour water as a feature. Lamu is one place where it's quite common to catch hepatitis – an unpleasant and lasting souvenir usually associated with drinking infected water. You should check where the water comes from. If the lodging has a long-drop toilet and an open drinking-water cistern in the same bathroom, move on. It only takes one cockroach falling in the water to contaminate it.

Prices vary dramatically. You can pay up to three times as much, in the same lodging, in the high season months, as in April or May, the cheapest period. And another trend in recent years has been the "gentrification" of a number of erstwhile hippie hangouts – and attendant price increases that outstrip the rest of the country. Because of the huge seasonal variations and the fact that prices are open to negotiation we have not given prices for the cheaper Lamu lodgings. If you like the place, aim to agree a rate for the duration of your stay, paying every day. You may find, at peak times, that some lodge owners insist their prices are fixed – simply a rather unfair bargaining position when rooms are scarce. As a very rough price guide for the cheap places, expect to pay from Ksh50/100 minimum to Ksh200/300 maximum, depending on lodging and season.

It is quickly obvious that everyone in Lamu has their **favourite lodging houses**, almost always determined as much by the owners and staff as by the walls and whitewash. The following listings are personal favourites and establishments that travellers regularly recommend in feedback to *Rough Guides*.

CHEAP LODGINGS (KEYED ON MAP)

Full Moon Guest House (10) Large rooms and the town's prime location with a wonderful veranda above where it's all happening. First lodging to try on arrival.

Beautiful House/Mama Nawili's (3) A lapsed old favourite but still the very cheapest establishment, with a fine elevated position.

Castle Lodge (4) (PO Box 10, ☎3123/3132). "Renovated and remodelled" according to the owners, this long-established place by the Fort may now need skillful bargaining to get the nicer rooms at budget rates. Excellent roof terrace and especially good upstairs rooms.

Kenya Lodging (14) Comes highly recommended, with laid-back staff, clean and secure rooms, and genuine 24-hour, hand-hauled water. It can be stuffy, however, so choose your room carefully.

Rainbow Lodge (5) Frequently praised.

Kandara's Lodge (1) Clean, secure and cheap.

Paradise Guest House (16) A new conversion in *Hal-Udy* style, with 24-hour water, brought by electric pump from the well (when there's current).

Casuarina Rest House (24) (PO Box 10, ☎132) Self-contained, self-catering apartments in a really good waterfront position. Don't be put off by the police station underneath.

CHEAP LODGINGS (NOT KEYED)

Jambo Guest House Behind the Jumaa mosque in Mkomani. With fans, mosquito nets and a near perfect roof-top, this newish place is one of the best value lodgings in town.

Karibuni Guest House Next to the *Jambo Guest House*. Clean and quiet.

New Shamauty Lodge Next to the *Full Moon*. Good water supply and fair prices.

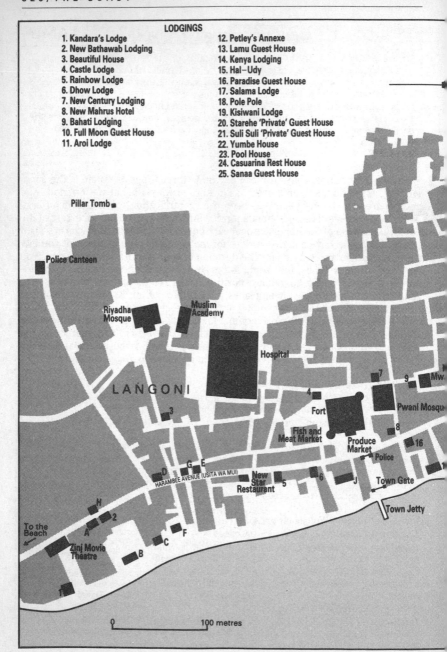

LODGINGS

1. Kandara's Lodge
2. New Bathawab Lodging
3. Beautiful House
4. Castle Lodge
5. Rainbow Lodge
6. Dhow Lodge
7. New Century Lodging
8. New Mahrus Hotel
9. Bahati Lodging
10. Full Moon Guest House
11. Aroi Lodge
12. Petley's Annexe
13. Lamu Guest House
14. Kenya Lodging
15. Hal–Udy
16. Paradise Guest House
17. Salama Lodge
18. Pole Pole
19. Kisiwani Lodge
20. Starehe 'Private' Guest House
21. Suli Suli 'Private' Guest House
22. Yumbe House
23. Pool House
24. Casuarina Rest House
25. Sanaa Guest House

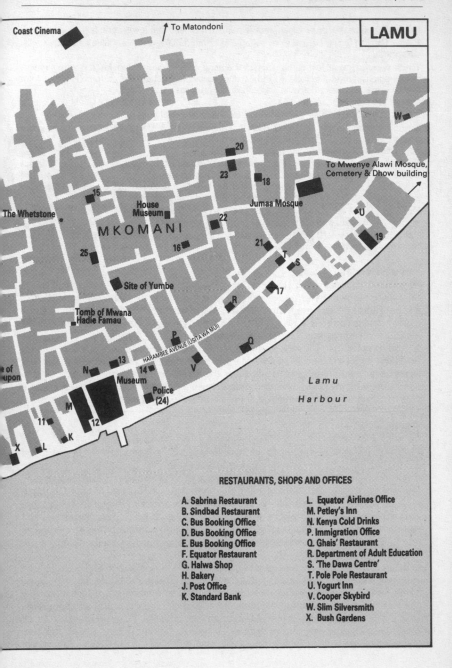

LAMU

Coast Cinema

↑ To Matondoni

To Mwenye Alawi Mosque, Cemetery & Dhow building

20

23

18

W

House Museum

Jumaa Mosque

15

The Whetstone

M K O M A N I

22

U

25

16

21

19

T

S

Site of Yumbe

17

R

Tomb of Mwana Hadie Famau

P

Q

e of upon

13

HARAMBEE AVENUE (USITA WA MUI)

V

N

14

Museum

Police (24)

Lamu

Harbour

M

11

12

X

L

K

RESTAURANTS, SHOPS AND OFFICES

A. Sabrina Restaurant
B. Sindbad Restaurant
C. Bus Booking Office
D. Bus Booking Office
E. Bus Booking Office
F. Equator Restaurant
G. Halwa Shop
H. Bakery
J. Post Office
K. Standard Bank

L. Equator Airlines Office
M. Petley's Inn
N. Kenya Cold Drinks
P. Immigration Office
Q. Ghais' Restaurant
R. Department of Adult Education
S. 'The Dawa Centre'
T. Pole Pole Restaurant
U. Yogurt Inn
V. Cooper Skybird
W. Slim Silversmith
X. Bush Gardens

Palm View Guest House Clean, with a kitchen, nice staff and lowish prices.

Peace Guest House Behind town, signposted from the *Yoghurt Inn*. Clean and cheap, with a big garden – camping possible.

Tini's Guest House Just off our map to the north beyond *Slim Silversmith*. A very popular, newer place, scrupulously clean, with a fine verandah, kitchen and fridge. Only the loud mosque right next door detracts. Top end of the price range.

MORE EXPENSIVE LODGINGS AND HOTELS (KEYED)

Yumbe Guest House (22) (PO Box 81, Lamu ☎3101). A lovely recent conversion and a positive alternative to *Petley's* if you want some *real* comfort and style, with guaranteed 24-hour water (s/c rooms with fan Ksh450/750 B&B).

New Mahrus Hotel (8) (PO Box 25, ☎3001). Prices have gone through the roof (from Ksh350/400 to Ksh500/600 s/c B&B), inexplicably, because there's nothing special offered beyond modern bathrooms and fans. One of the least "Lamu-esque" places, it's a comfortable and ordinary Kenyan hotel, attractive only to the odd Lamu-phobe.

Hal-Udy (15) A cut above all the others in this range (Ksh400/600 s/c B&B). Hidden away at the back of town, with exotic furniture and four beautiful rooms.

Pool House Hotel (23) An extraordinary creation and it does have a swimming pool (prices as low as Ksh300/night, low season).

Private Houses

In addition to these establishments we've sketched – or if the lodgings all prove full (some of the cheaper places will give you roof space for Ksh40–50 until there's a spare room) – there are many "private" **self-catering guest houses** that can be a good deal if you're in a group. These offer a degree of home comfort few of the lodgings can supply and they are usually superb old Swahili houses.

A third possibility is to ask around for an **empty house** whose caretaker would be willing to let you stay for a reasonable fee. This can work out cheaper than any other arrangement but bear in mind that the caretaker is sticking his neck out.

Finding a private house can seem an impossibility at first, but persist in putting your requirements about and you shouldn't have to wait more than a few days.

Eating

There are enough **restaurants** and passable *hotelis* in Lamu to enable you to eat out twice a day for a week before going back to your first port of call. Not only are there lots, but they serve a wonderful range of food. Nowhere else in Kenya is there such a concentration of eating places with an overwhelmingly budget-traveller clientele. Unfortunately, the rock-bottom prices of only a few years ago are rising fast and some places are already expensive by Kenyan standards. It's still possible to eat for as little as Ksh20–30, but you can easily pay ten times as much in some of the waterfront eating houses. Again, prices really rocket in the peak visitors' seasons.

A fine balance has been achieved between what is demanded and what can be supplied: yoghurt, fruit salad, pancakes, muesli and milkshakes have become Lamu specialities. Superb lobster and crab dishes, oysters, swordfish and delicious shark are also on many menus, and it's a nice change to find a fishing town where you can actually eat seafood relatively cheaply. A number of ordinary *hotelis* serving the up-country staples – beans, curries, pilau, steak, chicken, chips, eggs, even *ugali* and *karanga* – crowd along Harambee Ave, particularly down in Langoni.

Bush Gardens (not keyed), On the waterfront. A seafood and kebab place with a popular following and a balmy proprietor who's too busy showing off to remember the food – but who cares. When it comes, it's first-rate (especially that "Zanzibar sauce") and not as costly as you might expect. Worth patronising for the garlic bread alone.

Café Delicious (not keyed), Harambee Ave. Run by a welcoming up-country woman whose Saturday night all-you-can-eat buffets pull in enthusiastic crowds.

Coconut Juice Garden (not keyed) On the way out of town in the south of Langoni. Best juices on Lamu – orgasmic coconut and date mix.

Coral Reef – formerly Yoghurt Inn (U) Recently renamed and now under new management this is a Lamu institution renowned for breakfasts to set you up for the day. A big travellers' hangout, with an unlimited variety of taped music (including some you thought you'd never hear again) to supplement the usually first-rate food. In the high seasons they do a different "special" every night and there's always something vegetarian on offer. Open 7am–2pm, 4–9.30pm, closed Fri.

Equator (F) Despite lavish attention to service and the kitsch Swahili interior like a circus big top, not outstandingly more expensive than several other places. Cordial comments and help with cracking your crab are part of the show, though the elderly co-owner and poet-manqué, Ron Partridge, who gave it much of its flavour, has now died. The food remains eminently up to scratch and there's wine available. Great ice cream.

Ghai's Restaurant (Q) Rather variable, though it does have a firm reputation for seafood. Trouble is the sewer right next door provides about the only atmosphere.

Hapa Hapa (10), below the *Full Moon Guest House*. Popular rendezvous with an ambitious menu, good pancakes and some of the best shakes in town, but meals tend to be on the small si⁻¹e. Service is yawningly slow, even for Lamu.

Jambo Cafe (not keyed) Harambee Ave, north of the Dept. of Adult Education (closed Sundays). A fine place for breakfast with wonderful porridge.

Kenya Cold Drinks (N) Simple, spotless café with an irresistible line in Indian sweetmeats and cakes and very good, expensive milkshakes (closed Fri and evenings).

Labanda (off the map to the south, left of the *Olympic*). A new and very good restaurant, with fantastic "Lobster Vasco da Gama" well out of the ordinary – prices not.

Masri Hotel (not keyed), opposite the *New Mahrus*. Best and cheapest yoghurt in town.

New Mahrus Hotel (8) Roof-top restaurant that should be good at the price but isn't particularly.

New Olympic (B) (formerly the"Sindbad" as on the map; and previously the "Olympic"). The restaurant with an identity crisis still does good seafood and pancakes and is sometimes a popular post-beach rendezvous.

New Star (labelled) Recommended – one of the cheapest places in town –especially for breakfast before an early morning walk to the beach. It opens at 5.30am – a marvellous time of day. Don't order any of their three varieties of identical-tasting and disgusting ice cream.

New Swahili Dishes (not keyed), Market Square near the fort. Simple and cheap Indian and local dishes cooked well.

Petley's Inn (M) Nothing special, though said to do decent kebabs at lunchtime.

Sabrina (A) Busy and inexpensive *hoteli* with lots of reliable and calorific menu items. The ginger coffee stall outside in the evenings does aromatic two-shilling cuplets.

Lamu eating can be too much of a good thing and it's easy to slip into the habit of always eating out. But if you find it too expensive and if you have a camp stove or charcoal-burning *jiko* at your disposal (note that several lodgings have kitchens you can use), a whole new world starts to open up. Try, for example, **cooking** fish in coconut. Any restaurant will show you how to grate out the flesh and strain off the cream that's used as a basis for sauces, using a conical coconut basket, but get to the **fish market** early to pick up the best buys. Tamarind is another good complement to fish. The **fruit and vegetable market** in front of the fort – run for the most part by up-country women – has all the rest you'll need. Lamu has wonderful fruit and is famous for its enormous, aromatic **mangoes,** but you should also try the unusually sweet and juicy **grapefruit.**

Seeing the town

Perhaps surprisingly for so laid-back a corner of Kenya, there's no shortage of things to do in Lamu. The **town** itself is unendingly fascinating to stroll through, with few monuments but hundreds of ancient houses, arresting street scenes and cool corners to sit and rest. And the **museum** is exceptional, outshining all Kenya's others bar the National Museum in Nairobi. It is difficult to construct a guided tour of Lamu – serendipity comes to everyone here, and in any event, you're better off exploring in snatches, wandering around whenever you have a spare hour or two – but the following ideas are worth pursuing whenever you lack the energy for the beach.

Architecture and town planning

Initially confusing, Lamu is not the random clutter of houses and alleys it appears. Very few towns in Africa have kept their original **town plan** so intact (Timbuctoo in West Africa is another) and Lamu's history is sufficiently documented, and its architecture well enough preserved, to give you a good idea of how the town developed.

The basic division is between the **waterfront** buildings and the town behind, separated by the **Usita wa Mui**, now called Harambee Avenue. Until around 1830, this main street was itself the waterfront, but the pile of accumulated rubbish in the harbour had become large enough by the time the fort was finished to consider reclaiming it; gradually, those who could afford to, built on it. The **fort** lost its pre-eminent position and Lamu, from the sea, took on a different aspect, which included Indian styles such as arches, verandas and shuttered windows.

Behind the new waterfront, the **old town** retained a second division between **Mkomani** district, to the north of the fort, and **Langoni** to the south. These locations are important as they distinguish the town's long-established quarter (Mkomani) from the still-expanding district (Langoni) where, traditionally, newcomers have built their houses, often of mud and thatch rather than stone or modern materials. This north/south division is found in most Swahili towns and reflects the importance of Mecca, due north.

Lamu is divided further into over forty *mitaa* or **"wards"**, roughly corresponding to blocks. The names of these suggest a great deal about how the town once looked: they're all listed in *Lamu Town A Guide* by James Allen, an excellent book if you can find it. *Kinooni* ward (Whetstone Corner) boasts to this day a heavy block of stone on the street corner for sharpening swords, reputedly imported from Oman. And *Utakuni* ward (Main Market) still has a row of shops, even though most of this north side of town is now purely residential.

In this, one of the least spoiled parts of Lamu, the museum has restored an eighteenth-century house (the **House Museum**) to approximately its original appearance (times and admission as for the main museum).

The stone houses: design for living

Lamu's **stone houses** are unique, perfectly constructed examples of architecture appropriate to its setting. The basic design is of an open, topless box enclosing a large courtyard, around which are set inward-facing rooms on two or three floors. These rooms are thus long and narrow, their ceilings supported by close-set timbers or mangrove poles (*boriti*). Most had exquisite carved doors at one time, though in all but a few dozen homes these have been sold off to pay for upkeep. Many also had *zidaka*, plaster-work niches in the walls to give an illusion of extended space, which are now just as rare. Toilet arrangements are ingenious, with fish kept in the large water cisterns to eat the mosquito larvae. On the top floor, a *makuti* roof shades one side. In parts of Lamu these old houses are built so close together you could step across the street from one roof to another.

The private space inside Lamu's houses is inseparable and barely distinguishable from the public space outside: the noises of the town – donkeys, mosques, cats (Lamu is a veritable cat's Calcutta) – percolate into the interiors, encouraged by the constant flow of air created by the narrow coolness of the dark streets and the heat which accumulates on upper surfaces exposed to the sun. There's an excellent display of Lamu's architecture at the museum in Nairobi.

The fort

As for specific buildings and monuments to seek out, they're few. The **fort**, dating from 1821, seems oddly stranded in its new position, deprived of its role as defender of the waterfront or, currently, of any other role. It has recently become a national monument and there are rumours that it will open as a museum, but at the time of writing it is simply closed. At least you need no longer worry about accidentally getting it in your camera viewfinder, as was the case until a few years ago, when it served as a prison.

Tombs high and low

The other national monument in Lamu (though you may not believe it when you see it) is the fluted **pillar tomb** behind Riyadha Mosque. This may date from as far back as the fourteenth century and the occasional visit by a tourist might persuade the families in the neighbourhood that it's worth preserving; it can only be a matter of time before it leans too far and collapses on a passing *mtoto*. In the middle of town by a betel plantation is another tomb, that of **Mwana Hadie Famau**, a local woman of the fifteenth or sixteenth century. This has been walled up and lost the porcelain-embedded pillars which would have stood at each corner.

The donkey sanctuary

Up along the waterfront, just north of *Ghai's restaurant*, you won't miss the **donkey sanctuary**. Lamu district has over 3000 donkeys and the "International Donkey Protection Trust", a Devon-based charity, has put considerable energy and resources into setting up and maintaining this rest home for old and lame beasts that would otherwise perish of exhaustion or end up in a stew. It's not a tourist attraction, but they do rely considerably on donations from visitors and the staff are welcoming. If you call in, don't forget to shut the gate behind you!

The northern fringes: dumps and dhow-builders' haunts

Heading out of town to the north, through *Tundani* ward (Fruit-Picking Place) and *Weyoni* ward (Donkey Racetrack), you reach the **cemetery**, goal of many religious processions and an interesting short walk. Past the suburbs, you come out to the slaughterhouse and rubbish dumps, populated by marabou storks. In the inlet behind them, several large **dhows** and a number of smaller boats are moored. Many are rotting, one or two are quite new, even unfitted. Tradition notwithstanding, Lamu, rather than Matondoni (see below), seems to be the island's main boat-building centre. If you have dreams of owning a dhow (they make great houseboats), a representative price for a forty-foot hull is £4000. The price depends entirely on the time the *fundis* take to build it – two years isn't unusual.

Lamu Museum: exhibits and implications

Open daily 8am–6pm, Ksh100; Curator, PO Box 48, Lamu, ☎3073.

The one specific visit which you should definitely count on devoting a few hours to is **Lamu Museum**. Don't weigh up the cost (£2 isn't much) because, of Kenya's five regional museums, Lamu's is the only one that fully lives up to its name. There's no need to fill spare rooms here with game trophies and miscellaneous trivia; the region's history provides more than enough material.

As you enter, there's a large aerial photo of the town to give a fascinating bird's-eye insight. Elsewhere, exhibitions of **Swahili culture** – architecture, boats and boat-building, domestic life and life cycle – are all absorbingly displayed.

There are also several rooms devoted to the non-Swahili peoples of the mainland: farmers like the **Pokomo**, **Orma** cattle herdsmen and **Boni** hunters. Two magnificent ceremonial **siwa horns**, one in ivory from Pate, the other from Lamu itself in brass, are the prize exhibits – probably the oldest surviving musical instruments in black Africa. The Pate *siwa*, slightly more ancient, dates from the mid-seventeenth century. Wooden imitations are on sale all around town.

Tradition and morality in Lamu

A number of **old photographs** are also displayed in the museum, giving the lie to pat pronouncements about "unchanging Lamu". The women's cover-all **buibui**, for example, turns out to be a fashion innovation introduced comparatively recently from southern Arabia. It wasn't worn in Lamu much before the 1930s when, ironically, a degree of emancipation encouraged women of all classes to adopt the high-status styles of **purdah**. In earlier times, high-born women would appear in public entirely hidden inside a tent-like canopy called a *shiraa*, which had to be supported by slaves; the abolition of slavery at the beginning of this century marked the demise of this odd fashion. Outsiders have tended to get the wrong end of the stick about Swahili seclusion. While women are undoubtedly heavily restricted in their public lives, in private they have considerable freedom. The notion of **romantic love** runs deep in Swahili culture. Love affairs, divorces and remarriage are the norm, and the *buibui* is perhaps as useful to women in disguising their liaisons as it is to their husbands in preventing them. Which gives a slightly different timbre to the attentions shown by Lamu men to unattached *wazungu* women. Frustration isn't always the reason.

All this comes into focus a little when walking the backstreets. You may even bump into some of Lamu's **transvestite** community – cross-dressing men whose community is accepted and long-established and derives from Oman. In fact, the more you explore, the more you realise that the town's conventional image is like the walls of its houses – a severe facade concealing an unrestrained interior.

ISLAM IN LAMU

Even when you start checking out some of Lamu's twenty three **mosques**, the tone of rigid conformity you might expect is still lacking. Most are simple, spacious buildings, as much refuge-cum-men's club as place of prayer. There's no special need to enter them: their doors are always open and there's little to see. Male visitors, covered up and humble, are normally allowed inside; women are generally excluded. But you might enquire about the **Mwenye Alawi Mosque** at the north end of town. This used to be Lamu's one exclusively female mosque. I asked a woman outside the locked building, however, and was told that men have taken over – women must now pray at home.

The oldest known mosque is the **Pwani Mosque**, by the fort, parts of which date back to the fourteenth century. At one time, it would have been the place of worship on a Friday for the whole of Mkomani quarter. Lamu's present Friday mosque is the **Jumaa Mosque**, the big one in *Pangahari* ward (Sword-Sharpening Place) near the *Yoghurt Inn*.

The star of Lamu's mosques, as well as being one of the youngest, is the sumptuous **Riyadha Mosque** down in Langoni, well to the back of town. It was built at the turn of the century and has brought about a radical shift in Lamu's style of Islam, and indeed in the status of Lamu in the Islamic world. It was founded by a descendant of the prophet, or Sharif, called Habib Saleh, who came from the Hadramaut (Yemen) to settle in Lamu in the mid-nineteenth century. He and his group introduced a new freedom to the five-times-daily prayers with singing, tambourines, and spontaneous readings from the Koran. They attracted a large following, particularly from the slave and ex-slave community, but gradually from all social spheres, even the aristocratic families with long Lamu pedigrees. Some of the other mosques adopted the style but the Riyadha, apart from being Lamu's largest, is still the one most closely associated with this kind of inspirational worship. Non-Muslim men who visit while they're in session are likely to be invited in and encouraged to sit cross-legged with the rest of the assembly. Any sense of stale ritual is far removed. The atmosphere is light and the music infectious. More than one *mzungu* has converted to Islam here.

The Riyadha is also famous as the spiritual home of Lamu's annual **Maulidi**, a week-long celebration of Muhammad's birth which, with processions and dances, involves the whole town, drawing in pilgrims from all over East Africa and the Indian Ocean. For faithful participants, the Lamu *Maulidi* is so laden with *baraka* (blessings) that some say two trips to Lamu are worth one to Mecca in the eyes of God. If you can possibly arrange it, this occasion is the time to be in Lamu; but unless you make bookings, you'll need to arrive at least a week in advance to have any hope of getting a room. Starting dates for the next three years are roughly 3 Oct 1991, 23 Sep 1992 and 12 Sep 1993.

Next to the Riyadha is the big, square **Muslim Academy** – like the Riyadha itself, and so much else in Lamu, heavily under Saudi patronage. Men and women are both allowed to have a look around but there's very little to see. More interesting is the chance to talk to some of the foreign students: I had an unlikely conversation in French with three Swahili boys from the Comoros Islands.

Lamu directory

Area Code ☎0121.

Bank *Standard Bank* (PO Box 100, ☎3265).Opening hours are Mon–Fri 8.30am–1pm, Sat 8.30–11am.

Beer Two options are available if *Petley's* has "run out": first the *Kenya Breweries* depot by the bank during the day, preferably by the crate; and second the *Police Canteen* out in the sandy parts beyond the Riyadha Mosque if you're caught without a *Tusker* after dark. The deal there is basically buying one bottle for the policemen for every (negotiable) number of bottles for yourself. It's still a bargain. Slightly less of a bargain is ruse number three: ordering "ice cold tea" at one or two of the otherwise non-alcohol-serving seafront restaurants.

Betel One of Lamu's traditional exports, betel is the green vine you see trailing out of all the empty plots in town. The sweet-hot tasting leaves are wrapped around other ingredients, including white lime and betel nut, which stains the teeth red, to make *pan*.

Buses and planes Buy bus tickets (offices C, D and E) as early as possible, especially during the rainy season when some services may be cancelled. The same applies to air tickets, with the catch that you'll save a little money if you risk waiting for a standby. Cancelling plane tickets you've already got from Mombasa, Malindi or Nairobi is a big pain, as refunds are usually only available from the issuing agent.

Camping gas Small cylinders can be bought at the first shop south of the produce market.

Cinemas Lamu has two. The *Zinj* seems to be closed. The open-air *Coast Cinema* is best anyway.

Clothes and tailors Concentrated in Langoni. They will run up clothes in a day or so very cheaply. The easiest way to end up with something that fits is to provide a model garment. For really original T-shirts try the Rasta artists in the shack behind the *Sabrina* (A) who do some inventive air-brush designs.

Dhows to Mombasa See "travel details" on p.346.

Discos There's usually a disco on the last Friday of the month at the *Civil Servants' Club* on the hill just south of town.

Fax *Eagle Aviation* has a fax machine – Ksh 500 for international missives.

Food shopping If you want to buy **fresh fish or shellfish** to cook yourself, get to the fish market very early. By 9am all the interesting watery denizens have been sold. The **halwa shop** (G) and the **bakery** (H) – lovely bread – are both in Langoni. The **Dawa Centre** (S) is a delightful little herb, spice and traditional medicine shop full of weird and wonderful smells.

Health Be more than ordinarily careful about the provenance of the water you drink. Malaria can also be a problem. If a fever doesn't subside after a 24-hour cure, go straight to the hospital. For your teeth, you can buy toothbrush sticks (*msuake*) from the old man outside the *New Star*.

Library The museum has quite a good library on the top floor which you can ask to use (closed weekends, public holidays); books only, no foreign papers.

Police The days of hassle are long gone. Don't fail to stand still, however, if you're on the waterfront when the national flag is lowered at 6pm, or you'll find yourself "discussing" with them. Lamu is also a favourite place to trap *wazungu* who have failed to extend their visitor's permit. Go to the Immigration Office (P) in plenty of time.

Post Office Mon–Fri 8am–12.30pm & 2–5pm; Sat 9am–noon. Poste restante available.

Safe Deposit At the bank, boxes cost Ksh50 for 6 months with a charge of Ksh25 for each removal.

Woodcarving and jewellery Woodcarving shops are mostly found along the Njia Kuu in Mkomani. Model dhows, chests, furniture and. *siwa* horns are attractive but bulky. Beautifully hand-carved safari chairs are also a hassle to carry but worth the effort at under Ksh600. Some of the shops selling jewellery and trinkets have some genuinely old and interesting pieces. Look out for tiny lime caskets in silver buffalo horn, or silver earlobe plugs and old coins. A recommended **silversmith** is *Slim Silversmith* (W) up at the north end of town. They'll make jewellery for you; bargain well.

Swahili lessons Lamu is a good place to learn but as yet nothing is organised. Get in touch with the Dept of Adult Education (R) on Harambee Ave, and see if they can help.

Windsurfing At *Peponi* in Shela. About Ksh200/hour, Ksh600 half day.

Around the island: beaches and beyond

The one place everyone goes on Lamu is, of course, the **beach** – and fair enough; it more than repays the slight effort of getting there and the walk is enlivened by **Shela** and its mosque on the way. **Dhow trips** with a beach barbecue are the stock-in-trade of the waterfront hustlers, and as such hard to avoid even if you wanted to; always fun, they also give you the chance to see the ruins of Takwa on **Manda Island**.

Fewer people see the interior of Lamu Island itself, which is a pity as it's a pretty if rather inhospitable reminder of how remarkable it is that a town exists here at all. Much of it is patched into *shambas* with the herds of cattle, coconut palms, mango and citrus trees that still provide the bulk of Lamu's wealth.

Matondoni and Kipungani

MATONDONI is the most talked-of destination: a fine walk if you make an early start, with a hot return made more bearable by the prospect of a cold drink at the end of it – the soft sand track isn't much fun in blazing sunshine. A sane and enjoyable alternative is to go **by donkey**: fix up a beast at *Pole Pole Lodge*. In truth, Matondoni itself is not wildly exciting and its fame as the district's principle dhow-building centre seems misplaced. A recent serious fire has brought hardship, and people may be impatient if you don't show any signs of spending mo ney.

Kipungani

If you really want to look **around the whole island**, proceed from here to KIPUNGANI, a half-hour walk from the end of the beach. This is the halfway mark on the circum-island walk; the whole trip needs eight or nine hours. It is useful to know the state of the tides for the stretch from Matondoni to Kipungani as it can be done by a direct route through the mangroves at low tide.

The beach

A deserted twelve-kilometre sickle of white sand, splashed by bath-warm sea and backed by empty **sand dunes**, Lamu's **beach** is the real thing; you half expect Robinson Crusoe to come striding out of the heat haze. Unprotected by a reef, the sea here has some motion to it for once: it is one of the few places on the coast where, at certain times of the year, you can bodysurf (August is probably best). Beyond *Peponi Hotel*, it's also a beach where, on your private square kilometre, you can dispense with swimming costume.

Nudity is something you should be sensitive about, however. While few local people would go out of their way just to be offended, it can be construed as provocative. Women may find that wanderers along the beach can be a nuisance or – very occasionally – a serious threat. Stay in shouting distance, at least, of other sunbathers and preferably go to the beach in company. A spate of incidents several years ago explains the forbidding sign at *Peponi's* beach suggesting you go no further; in the company of others, this can safely be ignored.

Do beware the **sun**, the more likely assailant. There's absolutely no cover and you'll usually find that the cooling breeze is too strong to erect a sunshade. You'll need to take something to drink or fruit from the market and protection for your skin. Coconut oil, on sale in town, is favoured by some people to avoid drying out, but you need a tan to begin with otherwise it fries your skin. It's good for jellyfish stings. . . Ordinary factor type sun-cream is available in town, too. Lastly, and perhaps obviously, if you walk for miles along the beach in the early morning, you'll have to do it back again in the heat of the day.

Getting there

Getting to the beach, you can either walk the pleasant shoreline from Lamu's harbour down to Shela (about 40 minutes) and then head as far down the sands as you like, or you can take a motorboat or dhow (still only Ksh10) to *Peponi's*. The third option you might be tempted to try, striking out across the *shambas* behind town and heading direct for the middle of the beach, is actually a time-consuming and exhausting shortcut that involves a lot of wading through deep sand.

Shela

SHELA, once a thriving settlement, is now in limbo, midway between rural decline and tourist boom. Its people, who trace their ancestry back to Manda Island and speak a dialect of Swahili quite distinct from Lamu town's, are gradually leaving the village, many for Malindi; a number of fine old houses have been bought by foreigners and converted into ravishing holiday homes, decked in bougainvillea and empty most of the year (some can be rented, if you ask around).

Largely deserted, Shela's only sight is the strange, much-photographed **Friday Mosque**, built in 1829, which stands out for its rocket-shaped minaret, unusual in East Africa. If you're suitably dressed and bare-footed, ask politely to go up to the top.

Peponi

After the mosque, the focus is the **Peponi Hotel** (PO Box 24, ☎3029/3154, telex 21471), where everyone stops in for a cold drink. It is fabulously situated and, if you can afford it (Ksh3600/4900 FB, closed May and June), you won't want for much – though to feel right, you need to be on honeymoon at least (best rooms are the high numbers, from #21). And while it's an utterly hedonistic place to lounge away a few days, you won't have the thrill of staying among the mosques and street life of Lamu town itself.

The gaggle of beach boys playing football at low tide or loafing around the hotel terrace sizing up the latest speedboat tourist arrivals from Manda airstrip are part of the limited **gay scene**. The atmosphere of an embryonic Key West is beginning to pervade Lamu and *Peponi* ("Heaven"), its only international-class hotel, is the natural venue.

Shela bed and board

If you seriously want to spend all your time on the beach, however, the *Shela Rest House* (☎3091) would be considerably gentler on the pocket. A beautiful eighteenth-century mansion, it has rooms and apartments with kitchens; prices are negotiable, around Ksh250–300 per bed, Ksh1000-plus for a five- or six- room apartment. The *Samahani* (Ksh350/400) is a little more reasonable. For **cheap eats**, there's a café down on the shore just before *Peponi*, an offspring of the *New Star* in town and, like its mother restaurant, an ideal breakfast target if you've made an early start for the beach from town.

Dhow trips

Lamu hustlers must be the least disagreeable in the world. That said, where the hotel guides left off after you settled in, the dhow-ride men take up the challenge. You'll be persistently hassled until you agree to go on a trip and then, as if the word's gone out, you'll be left alone. Truth is, your face quickly becomes familiar to anyone whose livelihood depends upon *wazungu*.

In fact the **dhow trips** are usually a lot of fun and, all things considered, very good value. The simplicity of Swahili sailing is delightful, using a single lateen sail that can be set in virtually any position and never seems to obstruct the view of passengers. Slopping past the **mangroves**, with their primaeval-looking tangle of roots now at eye level, hearing any number of squeaks aand splashes from the small animals and birds which live among them, is quite a serene pleasure.

Basically, the price will depend on where you want to go, for how long, and how much hard work it's going to be for the crew. Agree on that beforehand (a full day with lunch for less than Ksh250 is unlikely, but on the other hand out of season, you might get a couple of hours for Ksh100) then gather as large a group as is practicable and pay afterwards. Agree also on who's supplying food and drink apart from any fish you might catch. Sailing trips to Matondoni tend to end up being over-organised when you get there, so aren't especially recommended.

A couple of pertinent **practical points**: cameras of the more expensive kind are easily damaged on dhow trips; wrap them up well in a plastic bag. And take the clothes and liquid you'd need for a 24-hour spell in the Sahara – you'll burn up and dry out otherwise. Dhow crews think it's all very amusing.

Dhow trip variations

The cheapest trip is a slow sail across Lamu harbour and up Takwa "river", fishing as you go, followed by a barbecue on the beach at **Manda Island**, then back to town. This might commence with some squelching around in the mud under the mangroves digging for huge bait-worms. If the trip is timed properly against the tides, you can include a visit to **Takwa ruins**, or, for rather more money, you can stay the night on the beach behind the ruins and come back the next day. Few sailors are prepared to venture out into the ocean, so Takwa has to be approached from the landward side up the creek, and this can only be done at high tide – and if misjudged can mean a long wait at Takwa before you can set off again.

A further variation has you sailing south down Lamu harbour, past the headland at Shela and out towards the ocean for some snorkelling over the reefs on the southwest corner of Manda. Snorkel and mask are normally provided.

Manda

Practically within shouting distance of Lamu town, **Manda** is almost uninhabited and, apart from being the site of the main airstrip on the islands, and the location of the old ruined town of Takwa – favourite destination of the dhow trip operators – it is not much visited. Water supplies are tenuous and elephants often trudge across the narrow Mkanda Channel from the mainland, destroying any crops. Significant archaeologically for the ruins of Takwa and Manda, this island is also the location of two hotels – the exclusive *Manda Island Village* (formerly the *Ras Kitau Beach Hotel*, PO Box 99 Lamu, ☎3206, around Ksh3000/4000, closed May–

July) and the *Blue Safari Camp* (PO Box 3205, ☎3791 Radiocall Nairobi; bookings through PO Box 41759, Nairobi, ☎338838), a more or less private establishment catering for heads of state and similar clients (Ksh11,000/double FB . . .). Neither welcomes strays.

That said, the island is crisscrossed with paths through the jungle, should you be taken by the urge to spend a day there. And go soon. **Rumours** have been flying around the archipelago as fast as in the days of the old sheikhdoms that either an **American naval facility**, or a **new seaport** for northeast Kenya, or a **gas terminal** for the finds around Garissa is going to be built on Manda. The hoteliers and farmers have been given notice to leave and the latter will be accommodated in bush country on the mainland further north. The dredgers have already started clearing the channels. Meanwhile **motorboats** frequently make the crossing from Lamu town to the Manda **airstrip jetty** – where they sell "duty-free mangoes" in the "departure lounge" – and there's nothing to stop you using them.

Takwa ruins

Whether you make a flying visit to **TAKWA** or sleep out on the beach behind it (there are some shelters), the site is well worth seeing. It is a national monument, so it has been properly cleared and there's an entrance fee of Ksh50.

A flourishing town in the sixteenth and seventeenth centuries and deserted, as usual, for no one knows what reason, Takwa is in many respects reminiscent of Gedi. As at other sites, toilets and bathrooms figure prominently in the architecture. In Islam, cleanliness is so close to godliness as to almost signify it – the Takwans must have been a devout community. The doors of all the houses face north towards Mecca, as does the main street with the **mosque** at the end of it. The mosque is interesting for the pillar at one end which suggests it was built on a tomb site (a founder of the town perhaps?), and, for the simple lines of its mihrab, so different from the ornate curlicues of later designs. Another impressive **pillar tomb** stands alone, just outside the town walls, its date translating to about 1683. It has a very ancient significance and still occasionally attracts pilgrims from Shela (some of whom claim descent from Takwa) who come to pray for rain.

Takwa has been thoroughly cleared but, in order to preserve it for the future, hardly excavated at all. What has been found, however, suggests an industrious, healthy, well-balanced community. They lived in an easily defensible position with a wall all around the town, the ocean on one side behind the dunes and mangroves on the other. Despite this, they appear to have left in a panic and, as usual, there's ample room for conjecture about why. In this sense, most of Kenya's ruined towns are very different from those of the classical world, although they were influenced by it. Part of their great appeal lies in the open debate that still continues about who, precisely, their builders and citizens were and why they so often left in such evident haste. And there's always the fascinating possibility that old Swahili manuscripts will turn up to explain it all.

Pate Island

Only two hours by boat from Lamu, totally unaffected by tourism, and rarely visited, **Pate Island** has some of the most impressive ruins anywhere on the coast and a clutch of old Swahili settlements which, at different times, have been as important as Lamu or more so. There are few places on the coast as memorable.

Pate is mostly low-lying and almost surrounded by mangrove swamps; no two maps of it ever agree (the one on p.321 shows only the permanent dry land), so getting on and off requires deft use of the tides. This apparent remoteness coupled with a lack of information must have deterred travellers, for in truth Pate is not a difficult destination and, in purely physical terms, it's an easier island to walk around than Lamu, with none of the exhausting soft sand.

A *matatu* **motorboat** (one of three plying the route) leaves daily from the municipal jetty at Lamu. You pass the one making the return trip in the **Mkanda Channel**; this is navigable only at high tide, and even then can be a close shave when the boat is overloaded, as it usually is. On Pate, the boats call at **Mtangawanda** (the dock for Pate town; journey time about two hours) and **Faza** (a total of up to four hours) at the northern end of the island. The obvious plan is to start in Pate Town and walk through **Siyu** to Faza, returning to Lamu from there. You could also do this in reverse, of course, but there is a major drawback, in that the boat might not pick you up at Mtangawanda on its return if, as often happens, it's full. The walk itself can be done in a day if the tides force an early start, but you may well find yourself wanting to stay longer.

Practical points

The daily motorboat leaves Lamu in time to catch a high tide in the Mkanda Channel about an hour later. **Tide tables** could be useful here, but don't be dissuaded by hustlers who insist the service doesn't operate and offer their dhow. Keep asking – it sometimes seems there's a conspiracy of silence on this one.

Accommodation on Pate island is rarely a problem but, with no proper lodgings, a **tent** is a useful backup. Normally, you'll be invited to stay by someone almost as soon as you arrive in a village. It is wise to take **water** with you (five litres if possible) as Pate's supplies are unpredictable and it's often very briney. As for **food**, most people live on home-produced food and staples brought from Lamu; although there are a few small shops on the island, it's a good idea to have some emergency provisions. These make helpful gifts as well. **Mosquitoes** on Pate are a serious menace. The shops sell mosquito coils but, during the day, you may be glad of repellent, even if you don't usually bother with it.

If you plan on spending several days on Pate, and you're interested in the archaelogy of the region, you should ask for **advice and contact names** from Lamu museum.

Pate town

From the dock at Mtangawanda, a narrow **footpath** leads to Pate through thick bush; ask for the *ndia ya Pate*, the "path to Pate". Once on the trail it's easy to follow. You cross a broad, tidal "desert", pockmarked with fiddler crab holes, then climb a slight rise to drop through thicker bush, and arrive after an hour on the edge of town.

Small as it is, you would hardly describe **PATE** as a village. After Lamu it comes as a series of surprises. The town plan is much the same – a maze of narrow streets and high-walled houses – but here the streets are earth, and the houses are of coral and dried mud, unplastered and somehow forbidding. The overall layout is confusing, with no slope, as in Lamu, to guide direction. But the most striking difference is the *Wa-pate* – the **people**, and notably the women. Brilliant, determined women with short, bushy hair and rows of gold earrings,

HISTORY OF PATE

According to its own **history**, the *Pate Chronicle*, the town was founded in the early years of Islam with the arrival of Arabian immigrants. This statelet is supposed to have lasted until the thirteenth century, when another group of dispossessed Arab rulers – the **Nabahani** – arrived to inject new blood into Pate. The story may have been embellished by time but archaeological evidence does support the existence of a flourishing port on the present site of Pate as early as the ninth century; probably by the fifteenth century the town exerted a considerable influence on most of the quasi-autonomous settlements along the coast, including Lamu. As usual, the claims of the royal line to be of overseas extraction were by now more political than biological in nature.

The first **Portuguese** visitors were friendly: they traded with the Pateans for the multicoloured silk cloth that the town had become famous for, and during the sixteenth century, a number of Portuguese merchants settled and married in Pate. The Portuguese also introduced gunpowder, which enabled wells to be easily excavated, a fact which must have played a part in Pate's rising fortunes. But as Portugal tightened its grip and imposed taxes, relations quickly deteriorated. There were repeated uprisings and reprisals until, by the mid-seventeenth century, the Portuguese had withdrawn to the security of Fort Jesus in Mombasa. Even today, though, several families in Pate are said to be *Wa-reno* (from the Portuguese *reino*: kingdom), meaning Portuguese or of partly Portuguese descent.

During the late seventeenth and eighteenth centuries, having thrown out the old rulers and avoided domination by new invaders like the Omani Arabs, Pate underwent a **cultural rebirth** and a flood of creative activity similar to Lamu's. The two towns had a lively relationship, and were frequently in a state of war. At some time during the Portuguese period, Pate's harbour silted up and the town began to use Lamu's, which alone must have caused difficulties. In addition, Pate was ruled by a Nabahani king who considered Lamu part of his realm. The disastrous Battle of Shela (p.323) in 1812 marked the end of Lamu's political allegiance to Pate and the end of Pate as a city-state.

stare out directly, unhidden by *buibuis*. Some wear nineteenth-century American gold dollars or half-dollars, though these reminders of the great Yankee trading expeditions of the last century have become so valuable that many have been sold. Big silver, gold or buffalo-horn **earlobe plugs** can also be seen, as well as nose-rings. If you speak any Swahili you're likely to find the dialect here unrecognisable. *Wazungu* are rare, and, after Lamu's studied repose, Pate is arrestingly upfront.

Free hospitality does not seem to be the custom and you may find yourself in the sticky position of bargaining with a family for **bed and board**, an unusual situation with not much room for manoeuvre. At night, the town resounds with the chimes of dozens of big old **wall clocks**, further reminders of American trade here in the last century; juxtaposed with the muezzins' calls to prayer, they sound thoroughly bizarre.

Pate **today** is a shadow of its former self, reduced to the status of sub-location: its only link with government an assistant chief, its sole provision a primary school. But at least its inhabitants are said to remain the richest on the island thanks to their cash crop, **tobacco**, possibly introduced by the Portuguese and certainly grown here longer than anywhere else on the coast.

The Nabahani ruins

More layers are peeled off Pate's enigmatic exterior when you start to explore the ruins of the **Nabahani** town just outside the modern one. The acres of walls, roofless buildings, tombs, mosques and unidentifiable structures are fascinating, the more so perhaps because this isn't an "archaeological site" in the commonly expected mould. Tobacco farmers work in the stoney fields between the walls.

Boys will guide you around the ruins for a small payment. Most impressive are the **Mosque with Two Mihrabs** (one for men and one for women?), a nearby house that still has a facing of beautiful *zidaka* (niches) on one wall, and the remains of a sizeable mansion. This last building, you'll be told, is a **Portuguese house**. Certainly, the worn-down stumps of bottle glass projecting from the top of one of its walls do lend it a curiously European flavour and in the plaster on another wall are scratched two very obvious galleons. Its ceiling slots are square for timbers rather than round for *boriti* as elsewhere in the ruins.

Shards of pottery and household objects lie in the rubble everywhere but many of the interiors of the buildings are so clogged with tangled roots and vegetation that getting in is almost impossible. It is worth persevering, however: the sense of personal discovery is exciting and immensely satisfying if you can ignore the mosquitoes that silently home in on bare legs when you walk through the weeds.

Many of the walls and buildings have already been demolished to obtain lime for tobacco cultivation. Without weighty financial backing, it's hard to see how the Lamu Museum could ever preserve the remains of old Pate as well as compensate the farmers. Gradually, tragically, it is all returning to the soil. In the meantime, see it – and photograph it – while you still can.

Siyu

The **path from Pate to Siyu** is a slightly tricky eight kilometres. Having set off in the right direction, the first half-hour is fairly straightforward; if in doubt, bear right. You come to a crossroads (easily missed unless you look backwards) and turn right. This narrow red dirt path soon broadens into a track known as the *barabara ya gari* (the "motor highway" – there was once a car); it takes you to a normally dry tidal inlet where you veer left a little before continuing straight on through thick bush for another hour to reach Siyu.

Wherever the bush on either side is high enough you may come across gigantic **spiderwebs** strung across the path. The matching spiders are brightly coloured, non-hairy, and merely waiting for insects, but they are nevertheless intimidating enough to remind you of where you are. Fortunately they have the sense to build their webs well out of reach.

Siyu town

SIYU is less documented than Pate. Even less accessible by sea, the town was a flourishing and unsuspected centre of Islamic scholarship from the seventeenth to the nineteenth centuries and apparently something of a **sanctuary** for Muslim intellectuals and craftsmen. While Lamu, Pate and other trading towns were engaged in political rivalry and physical skirmishing, Siyu never had its heart in commerce or maritime activities, and never attracted much Portuguese attention. Instead, there was enormous devotion to **Koran-copying, book-making, text illumination** and cottage industries like the **woodcarving** and **leatherwork** for which it's still famous locally. Siyu **sandals** are said to be absolutely the best, though plastic flip-flops have forced almost all the makers out of business. Siyu **carved doors** are among the most beautiful of all Swahili doors, with distinctive guilloche patterns and inlays of ground shell.

The sources of wealth and stability for Siyu's florescence are a little mysterious, but the town's agricultural base obviously supported it well and it was probably the largest settlement on the island in the early nineteenth century, with up to 30,000 inhabitants. The British Vice Consul in Zanzibar described it in 1873 as still "the pulse of the whole district".

These days you wouldn't know it. Less than 4000 people live here, and signs of the old brilliance are hard to find. Siyu lost its independence and presumably much of its artistic flair when the sultan of Zanzibar's Omani troops first occupied **Siyu Fort** in 1847 – though it was twenty years before the Omanis were able to hold it for more than a brief spell.

Built in the early nineteenth century (no one knows for sure by whom), the fort is Siyu's most striking building and indeed, in purely monumental terms, it's the most imposing building on the island. Substantially renovated, it is almost the only surviving trace of the glory days. Most of Siyu's houses today conform to the "open-box" plan typical of the Kenyan coast: yellowish mud with a ridged *makuti* roof, open at each end. These houses stand, each on its own, with no real streets to connect them, so although it's larger than Pate, Siyu feels far more like a village.

The cultural isolation of these communities from each other, which continues to this day, is easily appreciated after arriving in Siyu from Pate. There are still few *buibuis* here but there's much less jewellery in evidence and the atmosphere is altogether less severe.

For help with **accommodation**, go to see Bakari Maalim if possible. He's employed by Lamu Museum and sometimes hosts visitors who have applied there to see the archaeological sites on the island. He has three bicycles with which he escorts people to the ruins at Pate and he'll be happy to see you in Siyu.

Shanga ruins

You'll need Bakari Maalim's help if you hope to visit the ruins of **SHANGA**, a large Swahili town at least 1000 years old, which would be almost impossible to find unaided. Expect to pay around Ksh80 for a guide. Shanga is on the south coast of the island, about an hour's walk from Siyu. You have to fight your way, literally, through the undergrowth when you arrive at the site. The most impressive sight is the white pillar tomb, eminently phallic, which you come to first. The very large Friday Mosque nearby and a second mosque nearer the sea are only the most obvious of innumerable other remains in every direction.

In 1980, Shanga was largely cleared, and partly excavated, by a team from Kenya National Museums, with Cambridge University archaeologists and *Operation Drake* participating. More recently, London University has been excavating the site – against some stiff resistance from Kenya National Museums. What they have found is a walled site of thirteen acres, with five access gates and a cemetery outside the walls containing 340 stone tombs. There was even a sea wall. Inside the town, 130 houses were surveyed, together with what looks to have been a palace similar in some respects to the one at Gedi. Shanga is believed to have been occupied from the ninth to the fourteenth centuries and, like Gedi, no very convincing reasons have been found for why it should have been abandoned, nor why it was never mentioned by travellers and traders of the time.

Limited work has been done here to restore some of the plaster in a set of wall niches and on the fluted pillar tomb, but on the whole the clearing and excavating only seems to have encouraged the jungle. Getting from one ruin to the next isn't easy. Dangerously camouflaged **wells** and **snakes**, both common, add further to the Shanga experience. If you walk on down to the sea – and assuming you have a certain capacity for hardship in paradise – there's said to be a beautiful **beach** and some ideal camping spots.

Faza

Siyu to **FAZA** is a shorter walk than from Pate to Siyu and more interesting, as it twists and turns through waist-high grass, fertile *shambas* and several sections of bush. It should take about two hours, but you'll need guidance at least as far as the airstrip the island inherited from an oil-prospecting venture several years ago. From there it's straightforward: an hour or so out of Siyu, you reach the first of Faza's *shambas*. There are usually people around on the narrow path; if you catch up with someone from behind, announce your presence before trying to pass. Strangers are unusual and you could give someone – especially an old person – quite a fright.

On a coast of islands, it's not so surprising to find that Faza itself is virtually an island, surrounded by tidal flats and mangroves. A secondary school, health centre, police station (with nothing to do) and even a recently opened post office and telephone exchange have made Faza the most important settlement on Pate Island. There used to be a small lodging in Faza, too, but the dearth of visitors forced the owner to close up shop. **Private accommodation**, though, is easy to find. Fishing is the commonest occupation, with much of the catch going to a steam-powered cold room at Kisingitini, from where it's shipped to Mombasa.

Faza's history and archaeology
Archaeologically Faza has less to offer than its neighbours. Of Swahili towns, it was one of the most defiant to any attempts to usurp its independence; it was razed by the Pate army after a dispute over water rights in the fifteenth century, and again by the Portuguese in 1586 after collaborating with the Turkish fleet of Amir Ali Bey. On this occasion the entire population was massacred and the king of Faza's head was taken to Goa in a barrel of salt to be paraded triumphantly in the streets. Faza's unfortunate history may partly account for its relative lack of ruins, but one success is commemorated in the **tomb** of Seyyid Hamed bin Ahmed al-Busaidy (also known as *Amir Hamad*), commander-in-chief of the sultan of Zanzibar's forces, who met his death in 1844 under a hail of arrows. He was on an expedition against Siyu and Pate, and retreating to the relative safety of Faza when he was ambushed by a party of Siyu bowmen. His grave (*kaburi*), with a long epitaph, lies just outside Faza.

The ruins of the **Kunjanja Mosque** also merit a visit. Now theoretically protected by the Ministry of Tourism and Wildlife, the mosque – barring its *mihrab* – is just a pile of rubble; the *mihrab*, however, turns out to incorporate exquisite and unusual heart motifs, including the *shahada* (the Islamic creed) inscribed within a heart.

As a contemporary Kenyan rural centre, Faza makes an interesting place to walk around and you're almost certain to have plenty of time to fill before the boat leaves. One part of the village is devoted entirely to cattle stalls but goats run everywhere, ruining the efforts of the primary school principal to prevent soil erosion on the badly rutted and sloping football field. A fine evening stroll takes you across the mud on a rickety wooden causeway to the thickets on the "mainland" where the island's new and expanding secondary school is located.

From Faza you could, if you wanted, walk on to the **other villages** on the island, all fairly modern and bunched together within forty minutes of Faza: Kisingitini, Bajumwali, Tundwa (Chundwa), and the closest, Nyambogi.

Onwards: Kiwaiyu

From Faza you're also within striking distance of the paradisial pop stars' retreat of **Kiwaiyu Island**, about two hours away by *mtaboti*, if you can find one. Check out the situation in Faza, but it seems likely that a group dhow charter in Lamu would be a cheaper way to visit Kiwaiyu. For around Ksh1000 a day, you can charter a small dhow for three or four days, including breakfast and dinner, snorkelling and fishing gear, and plenty of fresh water. Split this price among five or six people and it's very reasonable. The best advice is to form an enthusiastic group around the lodgings in Lamu, then start negotiations, as soon as possible, directly with whoever is going to be running the show. Too often, arrangements are made with dhow hustlers which owners and crew can't or won't honour.

You can expect to spend 24 to 36 hours on the journey in each direction depending on wind, tides and the skill of the crew – though with the wind behind you, it's possible to get up to Kiwaiyu in under eight hours. The snorkelling around the **Kiunga Marine National Reserve** is nice enough, though not as consistently good as Malindi-Watamu, but the sailing experience, the nights under stars, and the acquaintance of the Swahili crew is altogether highly recommended.

On Kiwaiyu, **budget travellers** stay at the very reasonable camping and *banda* site, near the beach on the inshore coast of the island. The boss tells every visitor all about the film he made with Omar Sharif. Most people just drag one of the cane beds down onto the beach and sleep under the stars. With the right companions it's heaven.

Luxury lodges
The two **luxury lodges** at Kiwaiyu, *Kiwaiyu Mlango Wa Chanu Lodge* (bookings PO Box 55343, Nairobi, ☎503030) and, opposite it on the mainland, *Kiwaiyu Safari Village* (bookings PO Box 48217, Nairobi, ☎331878, telex 22678; best rooms #1–15) are virtually the only supply points, and they don't get many unexpected visitors (prices around Ksh5200/7200 including FB and extras). There are daily flights from Nairobi.

Kenya's northeastern corner

There is nothing to keep you from visiting the **far northeastern coastal region** by land if you're determined. You could *matatu*-hop from the jetty at Mokowe to HINDI, then leave the Malindi to Mombasa route and head for the Somalian border at DAR-ES-SALAAM/SHAKANI. On the way, you pass the sweetly named

Mundane Hills, but back on the coast things should improve. There are plenty of Swahili ruins, including the **walled city of Ishakani,** and a reportedly pretty coastal road leading back south to the headland opposite Kiwaiyu – every reason to think there's as much here for determined travellers as in the rest of the coast put together. In the dry season it's certainly worth slogging up here with a *Suzuki*. Again, if you go, let us know.

travel details

Buses
From Mombasa (corner of Mwembe Tayari and Jomo Kenyatta Ave) **to Nairobi:**
Akamba (PO Box 99020, ☎316770); *Goldline* (PO Box 83542, ☎20027); *Coast Bus* (PO Box 82414, ☎20916); *Malindi Taxis* (PO Box 83857, ☎25441) at least one day (6-7hr) and one night (8hr) service each; *RVP* (PO Box 86305, ☎26194), corner of Haile Selassie and Kwa Shibu Rds, dep. 8am, 3pm, (7hr). NB. The night journey can be cold: have warm clothes handy.

From Mombasa to Dar-es-Salaam
Various companies, several services daily, 14hr.

From Mombasa (Abdel Nasser Rd) to Malindi
Frequent, on the hour; 90min–4hr depending on Kilifi Creek crossing.

From Mombasa (Abdel Nasser Rd) to Garissa
Early departure daily on *Mbuni* (☎25441), *Tana River* (☎25053), or *Garissa Bus Service*. buses can be picked up mid-morning in Malindi, midday in Garsen.

From Mombasa (from Abdel Nasser Rd) to Lamu
Garissa Express daily 7.30am; *Lamu Bus* Wed, Sat 7am; *Tawakal Bus* Mon, Tues, Thurs, Fri, 7.30am; *Tana River* daily 6am, journey time 8–10hr with occasional seasonal delays.

From Malindi to Lamu
Tana River Bus at least daily (7.30am, 8.30am, 6–8 hr).

From Lamu to Garsen, Malindi and Mombasa
All services return, in principle, the following day.

From Lamu to Nairobi
Garissa Express runs three times weekly out of **Mpeketoni** (near Witu, 40km south of Mokowe) dep. Tues, Thurs, Sat at 6am, arr. Garissa 12.30pm, arr. Nairobi 7pm. Connection **from Lamu to Mpeketoni** must be made the day before by local *matatu*.

Matatus
Frequent services between various points on the **main coast road** (Malindi–Vanga). Limited services north of Malindi.

Peugeot Taxis
Frequent **Mombasa–Malindi** services at roughly twice the bus fare and at least twice the speed.

Trains
Bookings details: see Mombasa and Malindi "directories".
From Mombasa to **Nairobi** daily at 5pm (arr. 8am) and 7pm (arr. 8.30am).

Planes
Prestige Airways and *Kenya Airways* are recommended over *Equator Airlines*. Other names operating include *Air Kenya Aviation, Eagle Aviation* and *Skyways Airlines*.

From Mombasa to Nairobi 6–8 times daily on *Kenya Airways* (50–145min according to routing and aircraft), one or two flights daily via **Malindi** (30min).

From Mombasa to Lamu twice daily (60min) **via Malindi**

ECONOMY CLASS FARES
Mombasa to Nairobi Ksh1250
Mombasa to Malindi Ksh650
Mombasa to Lamu Ksh1650
Malindi to Lamu Ksh1000

From Malindi to Nairobi Three times daily on *Kenya Airways* nonstop (80min).

From Malindi to Mombasa Up to five daily (30min).

ECONOMY CLASS FARES
Malindi to Nairobi Ksh1250

From Lamu to Mombasa At least twice daily (60min) via **Malindi** (30min).

From Lamu to Nairobi At least twice daily (90–105min).

From Kiwaiyu to Nairobi via Lamu on *Air Kenya Aviation* daily at 3.15pm (140min).

ECONOMY CLASS FARES
Lamu to Malindi Ksh1000
Lamu to Mombasa Ksh1650
Lamu to Nairobi Ksh3000
Kiwaiyu to Nairobi Ksh4400.

Hitching

Mombasa–Malindi and **Likoni–Diani beach** Straightforward enough.

Mombasa–Nairobi Take a *KBS* bus to Mazeras; hitch from there.

Malindi–Lamu Difficult and not worthwhile.

Sea Travel

Mombasa to Tanzania

New twice-weekly, high-speed ferry service from Mombasa to Tanga, Zanzibar, Dar-es-Salaam dep. Mombasa Tues and Fri 8am, arr. Dar 4pm. (fares: Tanga Ksh750, Zanzibar Ksh1000, Dar-es-Salaam Ksh1150).

Mombasa to Zanzibar

Twice-weekly passenger boat (50–80 passengers) 16hr, Ksh370.

Mombasa to Europe

Ask around the ship's captains at Kilindini – a tough nut to crack. The *Mediterranean Shipping Company*'s monthly service through the Suez canal to Livorno and the UK is available if you have the money (see p.11).

Indian Ocean voyages

Check *Mombasa Yacht Club* or, more likely, *Seahorse Hotel* in Kilifi for crewing. There are no passenger services to Asia.

Dhows from Mombasa to Lamu

Dhows to Lamu, or beyond, from Mombasa, are notoriously difficult to find these days. Passengers *are* sometimes taken but there are no hard and fast rules for getting a passage. The stumbling block – at least the first one – is that dhows have no passenger insurance so any passage is effectively illegal and a proportion of the fee you negotiate will be needed for official "*chai*".

Dhows from Lamu to Mombasa

Relatively straightforward, once you've found an agreeable captain and assuming it's the right time of year – December to March. There's protocol: first you should go to the District Commissioner's secretary's office (first floor on the right, opposite the town jetty) for a form absolving the captain and the government of all responsibility in the case of mishap. Then take one copy to him, which he'll present to Customs, on the first floor across the courtyard, when he files his crew and passenger manifest. They'll tell you it's a 36-hour trip to Mombasa but count on some doldrums and allow up to 3–4 days. Bring fruit and anything else you anticipate needing to break the monotony of unvarying fish and *ugali* meals. You should get a passage for less than Ksh300, which covers everything. Compared to the bus, this is a comfortable and laid-back voyage.

TELEPHONE AREA CODES			
Diani beach ☎01261	Kilifi ☎01252	Lamu ☎0121	Mombasa ☎011
Kikambala ☎01251	Kwale ☎0127	Malindi ☎0123	Watamu ☎0122

CHAPTER SEVEN

THE NORTH

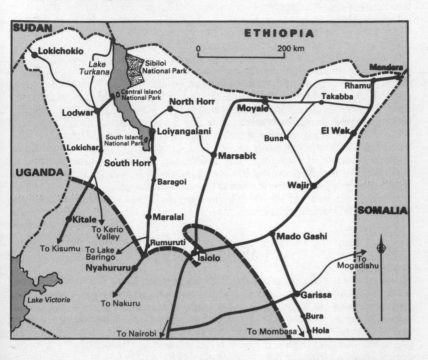

There is one half of Kenya about which the other half knows nothing and seems to care even less.

Negley Farson, *Last Chance in Africa*

Kenya is rarely thought of in terms of desert, but **the North** – over half the country in area – is exclusively arid land, burned out for more than ten months of the year. The old Northern Frontier District (and still called NFD by many) remains one of the most exciting and adventurous parts of Africa for independent travel: a vast tract of territory, crisscrossed by ancient migration routes, and still tramped by the nomadic Samburu, Rendille, Gabbra, Turkana, and Somali herders.

The target for most travellers is the wonderful jade splash of **Lake Turkana**, very remote in feel and highly unpredictable in nature (when British sailors first ventured out on it, they reckoned it could turn "rougher than the North Sea"). To get to Turkana, you have the option of organised camping safaris, as well as buses and lorries up from the hub of Highlands Kenya. Elsewhere in the north travelling can be harder going, usually by gut-shaking lorries, with heat and dust constant, the water often briny and useless for washing. But the **desert towns** have their own rewards, not least in the bewilderment of arriving and finding places so little known yet so important to an enormous compass of countryside and population.

Because of the layout of the **roads and tracks** that radiate north from the central highlands, you'll need to make a decision about which "spokes" to cover: there are few east–west routes. Don't be over-ambitious. Buses, lorries, and hitching can work out in northern Kenya but they are exhausting. If you're driving, water and mechanical know-how should be your priorities since you'll need to be almost self-sufficient.

A **seasonal** factor in the Islamic eastern parts of the region is **Ramadan** (see p.38): during the month of fasting you'll find many *hotelis* closed during the day – which, with the efforts of daytime travel, can be hard to handle. And, of course, there are the annual **rains**. Though the landscape is parched for most of the year, when the rains do come (usually some time around May), they can have dramatic effect, bringing torrents of water along the ravines, tearing away fords and bridges, and sweeping over the plains to leave an ooze of mud and new shoots. In these conditions, you can easily be stranded – even along the paved road up to Lodwar. However, if your plans are flexible, it's an exciting time to explore. Several of the Turkana camping trip operators run their vehicles throughout the year, adding mud and river crossings to the usual challenges.

Driving your own vehicle at this time of year is not recommended unless you've got 4WD and experience.

TURKANA

Straddled at its northern end by the Ethiopian border, **Lake Turkana** stretches south for 250km through Kenya's arid lands, bisecting the rocky deserts like a turquoise sickle. It is hemmed in by sandy wastes and by black and brown volcanic ranges, and the lake scene changes constantly. The water, a glassy, milky blue one minute, can become slate-grey and choppy or a glaring emerald green, sometimes even jade, the next. It feels remote and hallucinatory – an unexpected departure from the natural order of things.

The lake was discovered for the rest of the world as late as 1888 by the Austrians **Teleki** and **von Hohnel**, who named it "Rudolf" after their archduke and patron. Later, it became eulogised as the "Jade Sea" in John Hillaby's book about his camel trek. The name "Turkana" only came into being during the wholesale Kenyanisation of place names in the 1970s. By then, it had also been dubbed the "Cradle of Mankind", the site of revelatory fossil discoveries in the field of human evolution. And it was becoming something of a spiritual mecca for atavists, an excuse for a week of riotous assembly in a safari lorry or a dignified weekend in a *Cessna* and a lakeshore lodge.

But to depict Lake Turkana as "Kenya's latest touristic discovery" as one or two glossies would have you believe is, thankfully, a monstrous piece of hype: there are two lodges, one on each shore, catering for perhaps two dozen people between them at any one time. Otherwise there are one or two windy campsites and that's it. As yet, the only **asphalt** – that certain sign of imminent change – is the crooked finger that reaches north from **Kitale** to **Lodwar** and on to **Kalokol** on the western shore.

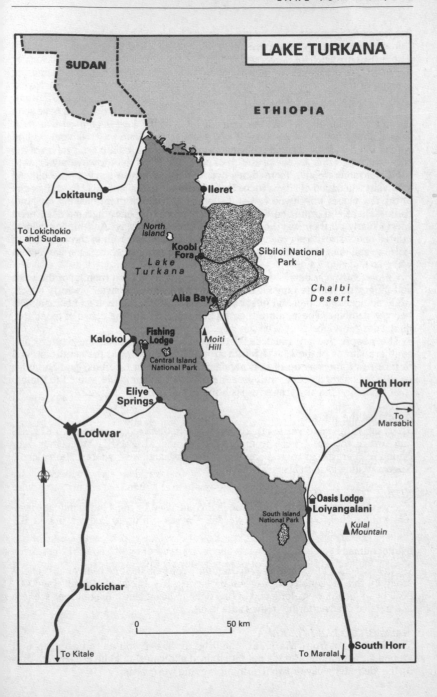

Ecology and climate

Lake Turkana is the biggest permanent desert lake in the world, with a shoreline longer than the whole of Kenya's sea coast. Yet today it's a mere sliver of its former expanse. Like a gigantic sump, with rivers flowing in but no outlet, a staggering average of three metres' depth of water **evaporates** from its surface each year (nearly a centimetre a day). As a result, it is alkaline, though not inimical to water life. Recent drought years, and irrigation projects in southern Ethiopia, have seen the inflow drying up, so that the water level is at the lowest point in living (or passed down) memory. Less than 10,000 years ago the lake was 150m deeper and spread south as far as Baringo; this mammoth inland sea fed the headwaters of the Nile, which accounts for the presence of **Nile perch** but not for why they grow to such enormous weights (sometimes over 100kg). It is also home to the biggest surviving population of **Nile crocodiles** – between 10,000 and 22,000 – and is one of the few places where you can still see great stacks of them basking on sand-banks. There is a profusion of birdlife, including European migrants seen most spectacularly on their way home between March and May. And hippos, widely hunted and starved from many of their former lakeshore haunts through lack of grazing, still hang on in fairly large numbers, though you won't see many unless you go out of your way.

Climatically, Turkana is devastatingly hot and dry for ten months of the year, and muggy during the rains. It is notorious for its strong easterly **winds** which, while not incessant, puff and gust energetically most of the time and occasionally become demonic. These, more than hippos or crocs, are the cause of most acci-dental deaths of local people on the lake.

The **people** you are most likely to meet are **Turkana** on the western and southern shores of the lake, **Elmolo** around Loiyangalani in the southeast, and **Samburu** on the way up to Loiyangalani. The Turkana (see box) and Samburu (p.361) are pastoral people with great reverence for their cattle, while the Elmolo (p.364) are traditionally property-less hunters and fishers.

A note on the routes

There are **three road routes** to Turkana: one to the western shore from KITALE and two to the east shore from MARALAL and MARSABIT (the latter very remote). There is no route connecting the east and west shores: the volcanic **Suguta Valley** forms a blazing hot barrier.

KITALE TO LAKE TURKANA

The **western approach from Kitale** is the one used by most independent travel-lers without their own vehicles. Two daily **buses** run up to Lodwar, one or the other of them continuing to Kalokol.

MARALAL TO LAKE TURKANA

On the east side, the **Maralal–Loiyangalani route** is the one used almost exclu-sively by the Turkana **camping safari** lorries. If you can afford the Ksh6000–9000 or so for the week-long trip, it has definite advantages: magnificent scenery and a sense of adventuring in the route itself.

MARSABIT TO LAKE TURKANA

The third route, **from Marsabit**, could be feasible if you are prepared to wait around for a lift there. But it's not much used and you should be prepared to give up the idea after a day or two if nothing is going westwards.

THE TURKANA

The Turkana, the main people of the **western shore of the lake**, have had very little contact with the outside world, or even with the Republic of Kenya. Linguistically, they are related to the Maa-speaking Samburu and Maasai. Indeed, along the northwest shore of the lake, the people are probably an old mixture of Turkana and Samburu, although like the Luo (also distantly related by language), the Turkana did not traditionally practise circumcision. They moved east from their old homeland on the borders of Sudan and Uganda in the seventeenth century. The desolate region between the lake and the Ugandan border which they now occupy is barely habitable land, and their daily struggle for existence has profoundly influenced the shape of their society and, inevitably, helped create the funnel into modern Kenya which Lodwar, with its new road, has become.

The Turkana are more individualistic than most Kenyan peoples and they show a disregard for the ties of clan and family that must have emerged through repeated famines and wars. Although essentially **pastoralists**, always on the move to the next spot of grazing, they do grow crops when they can get seed and when the rains are sufficient. Often the rains fail, but in 1985 and again in 1988, they were the best they had been for decades; this will hopefully have revived a situation that was looking desperate and which took a terrible toll of children in the early 1980s. With characteristic pragmatism, the Turkana have scorned the taboo against fish so prevalent among herders, and **fishing** is a viable option that is increasingly popular. More and more people are migrating to the lakeshore – with their herds, of course – hoping to make good.

Turkana **bellicosity** is infamous in Kenya (Turkana migrants to the towns of the south are frequently employed as *askaris* – security guards). Relations with their neighbours, especially the Merille to the north of the lake, have often been openly aggressive. British forces were engaged in the gradual conquest of the Turkana – the usual killings, livestock raids, and property destruction – and they succeeded, at some cost, in eventually disarming them of their guns in the 1920s. But the Merille, meanwhile, were obtaining arms from Abyssinia's imperial government, and they took savage advantage of the Turkana's defenceless position. When war was declared by Italian-held Abyssinia in 1940, the British re-armed the Turkana, who swiftly exacted their revenge on the Merille. They were later disarmed again.

Violence is no longer in the air – certainly not down at **Ferguson's Gulf** – though you might see older Turkana men with scars on their arms and chests to indicate who they've killed: females on the left upper arm and chest, males on the right.

But while the killing is largely a thing of the past, Turkana directness is unmistakable in all their dealings with *wazungu*. They are, for example, resolute and stubborn bargainers (even if you're not interested in buying), while offers of relatively large sums for photos often leave them stone cold – not necessarily from any mystical fear of the camera, but because of a shrewd estimation of what the market will stand, and hence, presumably, of their own reputation. Unlike the Maa-speaking warriors, the Turkana rarely pose for a living.

AIR SAFARIS

A last option is **flying**. In principle, there are three flights a week from Nairobi's Wilson Airport (see Nairobi "travel details" p.110). **Air safaris** (around Ksh12,000 for three days) destroy much of the sense of the lake's isolation, and they don't give enough time to explore either, but the flight itself – between the Aberdares and Mount Kenya – is sublime. See "travel details" p.390.

North to Lodwar

At least two **buses** a day leave from KITALE to LODWAR, both at around 8am. The price varies from Ksh100 to 140, and you should bargain hard. *JM* tends to be cheaper than *Kilimanjaro Success*, with a particularly crowded vehicle said to account for the higher than usual fares, the explanation accepted by all with resignation being that the tyres wear out faster . . . It's worth taking some water for this trip.

The best part of the **eight-hour journey** is the beginning, as you pass **Saiwa Swamp National Park** (see p.203) then go through the green valleys of **Trans-Nzoia** towards KAPENGURIA, site of the trial of Kenyatta and five colleagues in 1953. This inaccessible town was deliberately chosen to hinder the work of the defence lawyers – "a maze of rascalities", one of them called it. All six defendants were found guilty of belonging to *Mau Mau* and sentenced to seven years in jail with hard labor. Beyond Kapenguria (or rather the turnoff for it at Makutano, since the highway itself bypasses the town by two or three kilometres), the road scales a neck of the Cherangani Hills, then plunges headily along their northern slopes, following a tributary of the Turkwel River before slipping through the defiles of the **Marich Pass** and down on to the southern Turkana plains.

The last petrol station and bank before Lodwar are at Makutano. From **the plains** on, it's hard to extract much of scenic interest, though if you're driving there is a possible detour to the **Turkwel Gorge** (signposted on the left). This route drops several hundred metres into the heat – a steep, rough, winding road with plunging precipices and spectacular views prevailing all round. At the small centre of KONGOLAI you meet the sizeable **Suam River** (which rises on Mount Elgon and flows into the Turkwel) which represented the Ugandan border until 1970. The bridge, which you cross to continue to the Turkwel Gorge, is dominated by a dramatic and towering tooth-like rock outcrop.

The main A1 Lodwar road simply extends through the thorny wilderness between the Nasalot and South Turkana national reserves, neither distinctive.

Lodwar: the town

For most Kenyans, mention of **LODWAR** conjures up remote and outlandish images of the badlands, an aberrant place where anything could befall you. And the Turkana District capital is, to put it mildly, a wild town: unformed, loud, and somehow incongruous in this searing wilderness. It is currently Kenya's desert boom town; the lake's fishing, the possibility of oil discoveries and merely the new road from Kitale all encouraging emigration.

While **Turkana people** predominate, **Luo** and **Luyia** have also arrived in search of opportunities. As the exhaustion of farming country in the south drives people further and further afield in the quest for land and work, Lodwar and the area around it is becoming increasingly attractive to pioneers and cowboys of all sorts. The distinct and lasting impression is of a town with a high population of men – and a certain impatience. Shortly after I arrived, a Land Rover collided, absurdly, with a motorbike at a sandy corner. No damage was done, the two vehicles drove away, but the crowd that had gathered was clearly disappointed at the anticlimax. Newspapers arrive with the bus each afternoon, eight hours after the rest of the country have received theirs. All around the shady trees in the centre of town, men sit reading them, discussing the daily stories, trying to reduce the **isolation** felt here. It is said that when news of the August 1982 "coup" came through, the police in Lodwar immediately freed all the prisoners and relaxed with beer for the rest of the day. It's that sort of town.

The Turkana have been able to go south more easily with the buses on the new road, though elders who don't speak English or Swahili tend to get pushed around and ripped off. Coming north, there has been a lot of overpriced fruit and vegetables from Kitale (shrivelled apples and oranges in the grocery stores) and all the little signs of affluence – radios, bicycles, stereos, factory furniture – that draw in the people from the boondocks. Whispers about **oil** somewhere to the north have increased the atmosphere of restless anticipation. Canadian oil workers come and go, helicopters buzz the town. And then there's us: the tourists. Hand-me-down trinkets are suddenly worth a day's wages – or a week's, with the right customer – and wrist knives are worth making again, even if they'll probably never be used in earnest. Lodwar is changing fast – and, increasingly, doing so to the beat of its own drum.

Practicalities

Lodwar is an incredibly hot, dusty town most of the year, but for a day or two you may find the rough, frontier atmosphere exhilarating, especially after the faintly parochial airs of the Highlands (or "down-country", as it's known here in the far north). There's a *KCB* bank and a post office (open Mon–Fri) and at least three **places to stay**. Most presentable of these is the *Turkwel Lodge* (PO Box 14, Lodwar, ☎21201 Lodwar; Ksh150/200, cottages Ksh300 B&B), fairly clean, with the very definite luxury of fans in each room, a good restaurant and a rowdy bar. This is where officials, aid workers, and oil men stay. The sign in the rooms says, "We hope your stay with us will be quite nice"; it's certainly quite noisy, with Lingala tunes thumping out from a new system until the early hours. Considerably cheaper and less salubrious are the *New Mombasa B&L* (Ksh60 a bed) and the *Ngonda*, where the bus drops you. The new *New Lodwar Lodge* looks promising, with its two s/c *bandas* (prices negotiable).

For **food**, there are one or two okay *hotelis* but I found public eating here an uncomfortable experience. While Boy George warbled on the ghetto-blaster in the background, I was watched intently by three pairs of eyes; and when I'd finished, a little shadow dashed in and scooped my scraps into his dish almost before I stood up. The *Delicious Hotel*, *Kasarani Hotel* and *Sunshine Lodge* – all down the same street as the *Turkwel* – offer clean, fast service and big piles of local food, or chips as a standby if nothing else appeals. There's even a twenty-four hour *chai na mandaazi* joint.

Apart from just hanging around and taking in the scene, though, there's not a lot to do here and you'll probably want to move down to the lakeside after a night. If you have the time and some spare energy, though, maybe **take a hike up one of the hills** behind the town. Lodwar's canopy of acacias makes it surprisingly invisible below, but the view stretches for miles. Lodwar's **market** is worth checking out, too, particularly if you're into weaving or want to buy baskets – there's always a crowd of women making them. Also worth investigating is the *Diocesan Crafts Shop*, which has a big selection of baskets, trays, and mats marketed by the Catholic mission.

The lake

To get to the **lakeshore** sometimes requires a little perseverance. ELIYE SPRINGS used to be *the* place for travellers but recent reports suggest that the *bandas* there are run-down and facilities virtually nonexistent. It is certainly difficult to get to without your own vehicle but, if you make it, the springs themselves, bubbling up warm from beneath a cover of palm trees, are said to be exceptional.

Ferguson's Gulf is a more reliable destination. The village you want initially is called KALOKOL (formerly known as Lokwar Kangole). Most days there will be several vehicles making the trip there: ask around or wait by the ford across the (seasonal) Turkwel River outside town. You can also jump on the bus when it comes up from Kitale at the end of the afternoon. If you're heading straight through to the lake from Kitale you simply have a one- to three-hour wait while the bus refills with passengers in Lodwar.

Kalokol

Kalokol has a pair of **lodgings**. The popular *Oyavo's Hotel* (Ksh50 a bed) is a very pleasant place to stay which should fulfill all your expectations about African lodgings. Built of palm logs and palm leaf thatch, George Oyavo's lodging contains an animated fauna in the rafters. They provide paraffin lamps, but you should bring a padlock for your door. The major deficiency is its notoriously cockroachy long-drops. *Skyways*, across the street, boasts slightly cheaper rooms, better sanitary arrangements and, most significantly, a really wonderful old pop music collection.

While food supplies have improved a little in the last year or two with the opening of a few *dukas*, Kalokol doesn't have a lot in this line and it's not a bad idea to bring some fruit, at least, with you from Kitale or Lodwar. There's a decent *hoteli* next to *Skyways* and *Oyavo's* does excellent broiled fish if you order far enough in advance. You can also do your own cooking.

The village is especially good for buying **Turkana crafts** and souvenirs: wonderful (and far too big) baskets, sharp wrist knives and finger knives, rich-smelling, oiled head stools, ostrich shell necklaces, and a whole array of snuff and tobacco horns made of cowhorn (traditionally) or pieces of plastic piping.

If you are ready to leave Kalokol for Kitale, you'll need to be up at around 4am to catch one of the buses, which then spend the early part of the day in Lodwar, hunting for passengers.

By the lake

To **visit the lake**, you might do well to pay something to one of the children in the village as a guide, though it's easy to find your way there. The walk also depends on the water level in Ferguson's Gulf (it has been virtually dry since 1985).

The lodge and Longech

It's about 5km through palm groves to *Lake Turkana Fishing Lodge* (PO Box 509, Kitale, ☎2142 Radiocall Nairobi, bookings through *Ivory Safaris*, see "travel details" p.390). Ferguson's Gulf itself has no more than a narrow, knee-deep channel of water, easily forded. Rather an inevitable target, the lodge is perched at the end of a sandy spit, offering shade and expensive cold drinks, shelter from the fan-heater wind and a beautiful view over the bay. It is surprisingly spartan (its

A FISHY STORY

A few years back **Kalokol** acquired a big Norwegian-aided fish filleting and freezing plant and many Turkana came to the co-operative there looking for a livelihood. As many as 20,000 Turkana homed in on the lake's fishing opportunities in the early 1980s. Many were persuaded to give up their herds, but thousands of animals were driven down to the lakeshore while their owners looked for work, bringing ecological disaster to the area around Kalokol and Lodwar. Firewood gathering and over-grazing are the main causes. The project was a failure almost from the beginning. The plant's electricity requirements could not possibly be met with the local supply; it ran its cold rooms for just two days. Then the trawler sank. And as these major setbacks were contemplated, the diversion for irrigation of water from the Omo River in Ethiopia began to decrease the lake's supply, leaving the Norwegian jetty high and dry hundreds of metres from the shore. The project now has to cope with severe under-employment as the lake's fish stocks have plummeted, too.

chalets are described as "basic-luxury") but not outrageously overpriced, allowing for its location (Ksh1100/1950 FB). It caters mostly to weekend visitors who arrive by air. Midweek it's often empty; you can sometimes **camp** nearby and use the bar and water supply, though with the amount of hassle you can expect from local kids this isn't likely to appeal for very long. In low season, you might negotiate a cheap, midweek **stay in the lodge**. Alternatively, people will give you **bed space in Longech**, the village that stretches a couple of kilometres down the shore, for Ksh30 or so, or for an exchange: "What have you?" Fresh or dried fish is usually available but the only other food is the lodge's steep set menu.

Being here: birds, friends, dances
Simply **being by the lake** fills the time, with the constantly mutating background of the western shore across the bay, as well as the closer prospect of Turkana fishermen, hundreds of species of birds, and the occasional glimpse of crocodile or hippo on the water surface. From a distance, the activity at the water's edge seems silent since the wind whips the sound away westwards, lending the whole scene a bizarre, dream-like quality. Down on the shore you can talk with the children who follow you everywhere and often speak good English. If you make friends, you can be taken looking for snakes (be careful), to see *changaa* brewing (always by women), or, if you're lucky, to a wedding dance. Ordinary teenagers' and children's dances happen several times a week, but are best when there's a full moon: the boys tie cans of stones to their ankles and pretend to ignore the girls' flirting.

Swimming
Swimming is generally fine, and while the crocodiles are often big, they seldom attack. They are not rated as man-eaters, since they haven't been widely hunted. This is apparently because their skins aren't up to standard due to the alkaline water – though the line of skins that the local game warden had outside his house seemed to contradict this. Hippos are certainly much more to be feared, as are the lake's peculiarities of climate.

The tales surrounding the two human skulls that lay, unaccountably (and may still lie), in the sand below the lodge are varied, but they are probably the result of drowning accidents on the remote eastern coastline. One of them was certainly far from ancient. They're a very effective reminder of the precariousness of life here.

Game-fishing

When you're tired of wandering around Longech, being mobbed by toddlers, watching the fishermen paddling out on their waterlogged rafts, and the pied kingfishers hover and plunge over the shallows, there are a few active things to do. If you're feeling rich and macho, you can rent **fishing** rods and the lodge's boat and, with luck, land several hundred pounds of Nile perch: the game-fishing is rated as some of the most exciting and rewarding in the world. By all accounts, though, the perch don't play properly and almost line up to be landed. Fishermen rate the tiger fish as more of a fighter. The lodge will cook your catch for you (or some of it) and you can add your mark to the fishermen's tales on the walls of the bar.

Central Island National Park

An ordinarily less boisterous trip to **Central Island National Park** is highly recommended. This is one of two island national parks in the lake (the other is the less accessible South Island). Central Island is a unique triple volcano poking gauntly out of the water; the island covers just five square kilometres, most of which is taken up by the three crater lakes hidden behind its rocky shores. This is the nesting ground for big colonies of water birds but, like some African Galapagos, the island really belongs to the reptiles. Crocodiles breed here in the largest concentration in Africa and at the right time of year (usually April–May), you can witness the newly hatched croclets breaking out of the nests and sprinting with loud squeaks down to the crater lake where they'll pass their first season. The vegetation is scant, but some of the sheltered lees are overgrown with thick grass and bushes for a short period each year, and the nests are dug beneath this foliage.

Boat trips from the lodge cost the better part of Ksh3200 for a nine passenger vessel and Ksh1400 for a boat that takes up to four only. The only option is to walk south, down the lakeshore in front of Longech and try to hire a fishing boat for the trip. It's worth knowing that the park game warden, who accompanies the lodge's boat trips, will normally want to intervene at this point and generally makes it impossible to make the trip privately – in fact the most recent reports suggest the villagers aren't interested. A National Parks entry fee of Ksh88 each (possibly now Ksh220) is liable to be demanded, which, in view of the activities of some of the National Parks staff in the area, leaves a very bitter taste. If you find a boat the best plan is to go immediately rather than make arrangements in advance. Do be sure, however, that it is thoroughly lake-worthy and the crew know what they are doing: vicious squalls can blow up fast and it's at least 10km to the island. A compass can be useful – as we found out when dense, purple clouds descended around us and the waves started thrashing up to two metres or more.

Onwards from Lodwar

Onwards? It's possible, but by no means easy, to explore the region of Turkana **north of Ferguson's Gulf and Lodwar**. A road, due to be paved, turns left across the Turkwel River outside town and goes up to LOKITAUNG, branching left after about 60km for LOKICHOKIO and the Sudanese border. This is part of the new transcontinental highway that will link Juba in Sudan with Nairobi, but until the conflict in southern Sudan is resolved the border is likely to remain closed. Ask around in Lodwar for the latest news.

Maralal, Loiyangalani and the east shore

This is the exciting route to **Lake Turkana**. Anyone who has been up to Loiyangalani will talk your ear off telling you about the adventures they had on the way. It is one of the most exhilarating and remote journeys you can make.

Driving
From Nairobi, the distance is a good deal shorter than to the west coast but even full tilt on the rough roads it's a two-day **drive**. Saloon cars can make it as often as not, though vicious bedrock greets many a sump, and the car hire companies aren't enthusiastic, but to be sure of arriving you'll need 4WD (a Suzuki jeep is ideal). Even then, if you go during the rainy season, you could be held up for 24 hours or more at several points.

Turkana camping safaris
The obvious solution is a **camping safari**, though, as with any group travel, this has its limitations. Still, a week isn't long enough for irritations to detract from the experience and most people thoroughly enjoy these trips, coming back loaded with amazing souvenirs and photographs, and stories of weird and wonderful encounters. A major drawback is the brevity of organised trips and the fact that they therefore run to a rough timetable. The oldest, and many think the best, outfit is the *Safari Camp Services'* **"Turkana Bus"**, which runs every other Saturday throughout the year. They have loads of experience – and with the ancient Bedford lorries they use, they need it. The Turkana Bus has participants sitting outwards, which is preferable to a back-to-front-facing seating arrangement. Look out for this when making bookings. Other companies are *Gametrackers, Zirkuli* and, longer than most (ten days) and excellent value, *Special Camping Safaris*. Addresses are given in the "Nairobi Directory" on p.89. You can reserve in advance from abroad or they'll refer you to local agents in your own country (see the operators and agents on p.8 for example).

On your own two feet
If your budget is tight, but you have time and a flexible attitude, and don't want a spoon-fed adventure, the maximum exposure to Turkana and the north comes from **travelling completely independently**. This may require some patience, especially at MARALAL, the terminus of public transport, where you'll have to line up a lift. It also puts the onus on you to part company from the driver when you want to and not necessarily go the whole way to LOIYANGALANI in one ride.

The Routes to Maralal

Three roads lead to **Maralal**, the Samburu district town at the end of the first stage of the trip north.

Nyahururu to Maralal: C77
The easiest route – the C77 – rolls up from NYAHURURU via Rumuruti. Each morning at least one **bus** and sometimes a *matatu* or three leave Nyahururu. The C77 bounds over the ranching and cereal country of **Laikipia**, settled after World War I by British soldiers, but once a Maasai stronghold. Most of the settlers have

left, and it's a bleak, somewhat forlorn region. **RUMURUTI** (onomatopoeic Maa for "mosquito") is hardly noticeable any more; it merely marks the end of the paved road. The road to Rumuruti was built in the early 1980s for a minister who lives there and needed to be able to get to and from Nairobi without using a tractor. Maralal was connected with electricity at the same time, because, say the cynics, it would have been too obvious if the lines had only gone to his house. *Let's Go Travel* in Nairobi has a reasonably priced cottage here, suitable for groups, and there's some very good game country in the vicinity. For **night stops** in Rumuruti you might also check out the *Tumaini Country Restaurant* which has rooms and claims, "We are famous for making people happy". Equally inviting is the dilapidated *Laikipia Club* with its improbable efforts to preserve those old values.

The road follows the **Ewaso Narok River** for some way beyond Rumuruti before climbing, broad and stoney, towards Maralal's plateau. On the way, the two roads referred to above join it.

Lake Baringo to Maralal: D370
The first of these is the lonely but well-constructed and recently regraded **murram road from the Rift Valley**, which, in its earlier stages has breathtaking views back over Lake Baringo and some fascinating Pokot villages on the way. It's only a D road, but don't be discouraged from driving it. There are no buses, though, and you'd be lucky to find a *matatu*. For the best chances of **hitching** success, ask at *Lake Baringo Club* or wait at the KAMPI YA SAMAKI junction (p.162).

Isiolo to Maralal: A2 and C79
The other route (the maddeningly corrugated A2) comes up from ISIOLO past ARCHER'S POST, then heads off left as the C79 past the turn for WAMBA where it becomes the C78. Despite a continuation of the A2's washboard surface, scenically the C79/78 also has everything to recommend it, including some magnificent desert buttes. Again, there is very little public transport, but a bus does now run this route, Isiolo–Maralal, three times each week, usually packed full of Samburu warriors. Your best chances of **hitching a ride** are at the Samburu lodges or the Isiolo police barrier (p.370).

Maralal

Some of the settlers would have dearly liked to set themselves up around the cool, conifer-draped highlands of **MARALAL**. But even before British administrators made this the district capital, Maralal had been a spiritual focus for the **Samburu people** and, despite some dithering, the colonial administrators didn't accede to the settlers' demands.

Maralal is a peculiar town, spread with exaggerated spaciousness around a depression in the hills. Samburu crowd its two dusty streets, with a brilliant collage of skins, blankets, beads, brass, and iron, and a special smell, too – of sour milk, fat, and cattle. The main hotel is called *Buffalo House*; the bank is a blue, wooden construction open Tuesday and Thursday for two hours (note: they won't change travellers' cheques here). The place sets itself up for Wild West comparisons and even the climate is appropriate – unbelievably dusty, almost always windy, and, at 2220m, sharp enough at night for log fires and braziers. All it needs are wolves, and even there hyenas fill the role.

Of course, the regular arrival of safari lorries means that Maralal has plenty of persistent **souvenir salesmen**. Yet despite this (or perhaps because of it – very few *wazungu* stay more than a few hours), it's a good place to get to know Samburu people and especially worthwhile on Christian holidays. Many Samburu around the town have become Catholics and the colourful procession on Palm Sunday – mostly women in their thousands, waving branches and leaves – is riveting.

Practicalities and pleasures: the town and the wildlife sanctuary

The people far outshine their disappointing town: most of the **lodgings** are rudimentary. *Kariara Lodging* is okay at Ksh60/100 (but you need a padlock); the *Green Bar* is even cheaper; *Lokudishu*, next to the *Starlight Bar*, is friendly but not remarkably clean; *Jamuhuri* is much the same. The biggest, *Buffalo House* (PO Box 28, ☎2228), is decent enough but more expensive than usual (Ksh150/250). The Somali-run *Pop Inn* is recommended for pancakes.

There are alternatives, like a fullblown **lodge** and a couple of **campsites**, but none are very satisfactory without a vehicle. *Maralal Safari Lodge* (PO Box 70, ☎2060, bookings through *Thorn Tree Safaris*, p.30), signposted two or three kilometres out of town on the Lake Turkana road (Ksh1400/2190 FB, Kenya residents half-price and frequent special offers), is very attractive with its huge wooden chalet-style rooms, comfortable and undersubscribed. Your patronage is therefore welcome in the bar and restaurant, and you can sit on the terrace to watch the animals from the surrounding **Maralal National Sanctuary** (zebra, baboon, impala, eland, warthog, buffalo, and hyena) filing up the hill to the concrete waterhole a few metres away. The lodge's water is the only permanent source in the district. And if you simply must see a wild **leopard** in Kenya, a baited hide half a kilometre away is guaranteed to lure one for your camera every afternoon – on payment of Ksh100 or your money back. The forest seems extraordinarily scanty to harbour such a secretive animal. But the leopard may, in truth, be the only one and the latest reports suggest it hasn't been seen for a while.

To reach the **public campsite**, you'll really need a ride past the lodge and branching left from the Turkana road to the *Samburu Rural Development Centre*. The site (Ksh50) is just behind it on a fine but exposed hillside with erratic water supplies. It was closed for a while in 1988 and its future seems uncertain.

While you're waiting to move on, Maralal offers a fair range of diversions. A number of "guides" can escort you to local **Samburu witch doctors and blacksmiths** and a nearby **Turkana village**. Ask around at *Buffalo House* but don't be surprised to find some wily con-artists at work around town. And remember, of course, that a guide is paid for guiding: if the people you are taken to see want paying as well, that's all extra. Prepare yourself with several packs of *Sportsman* and a couple of "kilos" of *miraa*.

After dark, there's a **disco** most evenings and always at weekends; or you could sit through *Delta Force* or *King Solomon's Mines* in the *Buffalo House* **video bar** with a crowd who know them frame by frame; and the cinema across from the *Starlight* usually gets in some genuine celluloid on Saturdays. Maralal has its moments but serious beer drinkers appreciate it most.

Lastly, if you forget to visit the liberally signposted **"Kenyatta House"**, don't fret. The fact that Kenyatta was detained here in 1961 before his final release doesn't really improve the interest of this unexceptional and empty bungalow. It seems a pity it's a national monument and not some family's home. Maralal's most famous contemporary resident is the travel writer and Arabist **Wilfred Thesiger**.

Yare Safaris and Camel trek centre

If you're bent on camping out, there's a fairly recent campsite–safari centre developed by *Yare Safaris*, located three kilometres south of town off the Nyahururu road. *Bandas* are Ksh300/470 B&B, camping Ksh50 (bookings through their Nairobi office PO Box 63006, ☎725610). *Yare* seems to be at the forefront of adventure travel in the north; from this base they run safaris by **4WD vehicle**, with **camels** and **on foot** into the surrounding Samburuland. Prices are keen, and it's possible to book in advance and link up at Maralal, or simply to turn up at the site and hope there's a departure with space. They have also recently been involved in trying to initiate and promote an annual **camel race** at Maralal – bringing in visitors and raising interest in nomadic pastoralism at the same time.

Moving on from Maralal

You may find a source of **rides onward** at a campsite or the lodge, but you're more likely to catch vehicles by staying in town and spreading the word at the petrol stations, only one of which normally has fuel. Let it be known you are willing to travel in the back of a lorry; many people will assume you're not. Supply lorries do go up to Loiyangalani and your chances of eventually scoring a lift are good.

Heading on north on the other hand, Maralal is the last place where you can **change money** (at the bank, where they don't like travellers' cheques, or at the lodge, where they don't have much cash), where there's a **post office** (Mon–Fri 8am–1pm, 2–5pm), and where you can be sure of getting **petrol** if you're driving. And if **beer** is important to you (and it can assume great importance up in the desert), then stock up on that, too, before following the route below.

Finally, if your next destination happens to be **the coast**, the *Mwingi Highway* bus to ISIOLO is scheduled to depart every Monday, Wednesday, and Friday. From Isiolo, you could bus on to MADO GASHI, GARISSA, and down to the coast – a journey that avoids Nairobi – but you do need time.

North into Samburuland

The first stretch of the road **north from Maralal** climbs higher into the **podocarpus forests** of the national sanctuary. Twenty kilometres from the lodge, a detour to the left takes you through the village of POROR, past a large wheat-farming project and, after 6km, to the dramatic scimitar edge of the **Losiolo Escarpment**. The Rift Valley is, by its nature, bordered from end to end by vertiginous escarpments and each one seems more impressive than the last. But Losiolo is not just an escarpment, it's a colossal amphitheatre dropping down to Suguta Valley, 2000m below. Try to get here very early in the morning – it is awesome.

From Poror, the road north is increasingly rough and hot. Settlements are few but evenly scattered: MARTI, BARAGOI, and South Horr each have basic *chai* kiosks, one or two Somali-run *dukas*, a mission, and a police station.

South Horr and Kurungu camp

BARAGOI marks the end of the forbidding El Barta Plains, as the road now climbs into ravine and mountain country, fantastically green if there's been rain.

There's a positive jungle all year round at the oasis of **SOUTH HORR**, wedged tightly between the Nyiru and Ol Doinyo Mara mountains. There is good, dirt-cheap camping at the *Forest Department Campsite*, located up a rough trail to the left of the road a kilometre before the negligible village of South Horr. Facilities

THE SAMBURU

The Samburu are historically close to the Maasai. Their languages are nearly the same (both *Maa*) and culturally they are virtually indistinguishable to an outsider. Both came from the region around northwest Turkana in the seventeenth century: the Samburu turned east, establishing themselves in the mountain pastures and spreading on to the plains; the Maasai continued south.

Improvements in health and in veterinary care over the last century have swelled the Samburu population and the size of their **herds**. Many in the driest areas of their range in the northeast have turned to **camel herding** as a better insurance against drought than cattle. Since livestock is the basis of relations between in-laws (through the giving of "bridewealth" from the husband to his wife's family), having camel herds has disrupted patterns of marriage and initiation into new generations because camel herds increase more slowly than cattle herds. And the reality on the ground is all about twice as confusing as it sounds on paper. Memories, recording every transaction over successive generations, are phenomenal (the Samburu have only just begun to acquire writing).

The Samburu **age-set system**, like many others in Africa, is a complicated arrangement to which a number of anthropologists have devoted lifetimes of investigation. Essentially it's a gerontocracy (rule by old men) and the elders are assured, by the system they manipulate, of having the first choice of young women to marry. The promiscuous and jingoistic – but, by Samburu reckoning, still juvenile – warriors are forced to wait, sometimes into their thirties, before initiation into elderhood, marriage and children bring them a measure of real respect. In turn, they perpetuate the system on their own sons, who have everything to gain by falling in line and much to lose if they withdraw their stake in the tradition, perhaps by going to Isiolo or Nairobi to look for work.

For **women** the situation is very different. They are married at fifteen or sixteen, immediately after their clitoridectomy and before they have much chance to rebel. But they may continue affairs with their *morani* boyfriends, the unmarried juniors of their new, much older husbands. They spend more of their lives married than their male peers, which accounts for how most men have more than one wife. This **polygamy** in itself seems to be an important motivating force for the whole generation system. For the warriors and their girlfriends, there's a special young people's language – a vocabulary of conspiratorial songs and idioms – which has to be modified with the initiation of every age-set, so that it's kept secret from the elders.

This highly intricate system is now beginning to collapse in many areas, with a widespread **disruption of pre-colonial ways**; even the circumcision initiation of boys to warriorhood is less of a mass ceremony. While herds are still the principal criterion of wealth, people in some areas are turning to agriculture: after the rains you can see planting holes at the roadside in certain places, with corn the main crop. There are enormous problems for such initiatives, especially when there's no aid or government support, but they do show that the standard stereotypes don't always fit. As for the *morani* warriors, opportunities for cattle-raiding and lion-killing have diminished with more efficient policing of their territories. For some, tourist hunting has taken over. You can even see *morani* in full rig striding past the hotels on the Indian Ocean beaches.

consist of long-drops, an *askari*, and a river for drinking water, bathing, and washing the dust out of your clothes. This site, a short walk from South Horr village, where most vehicles stop, is a good base for meeting up with supply or mission vehicles in hopes of a lift north.

For a place to bump into motorised tourists, the delightful **Kurungu Camp** is preferable, a half-dozen kilometres past the village along the sandy, vegetation-festooned track to Loiyangalani. This is a well looked after **campsite** operated by *Safari Camp Services*, surrounded by flowering bushes and shaded by distinguished old trees. The status of the furnished *bandas* is uncertain at present – they were recently closed – and supplies of cold drinks can't be relied on either, but there are bucket showers. Camping out here (Ksh50) is fabulous anyway.

It is worth spending a couple of nights at Kurungu and exploring the **mountain forest** around you – it hides lots of wildlife, including elephants and buffalo, and it bursts with birds and butterflies. You can be guided by Samburu up the lower slopes or, more ambitiously, on the stiff hike up to **Nyiru Peak**, which has stunning views over Lake Turkana. If you entertain thoughts of any more daring expeditions in the region, know that **camel hire** should cost in the region of Ksh150–200 per beast per day. Be careful if you're embarking on anything way off the beaten track. Many men who will sell themselves as guides have led surprisingly sheltered lives; they don't know the desert like the backs of their hands any more than you do. Real knowledge and experience are sought after and more expensive.

At Kurungu, you are also likely to have the (mixed) pleasure of **Samburu dancing**, especially if you're on an organised safari. For about Ksh60, you are allowed into the arena to take as many pictures of the dancers as you want. Scepticism is briefly swamped by the hour-long jamboree that follows. A troupe of *morani* go through an informal dance programme, flirtatiously threatening their audience with whoops and pounces. Young women and little girls join in – sometimes with the evident disapproval of older Samburu onlookers – to be propositioned with whisks of the men's ochred hairdos. Meanwhile, there's the constant offering of necklaces, trinkets, spears, pouches, stools, and more photo poses, to be negotiated individually with those who are too old or too young to dance.

The *morani* dance and dance and no one feels the money was badly spent. But is it authentic? Does it mean anything? What do *they* think? It's extremely difficult to disentangle motives from relations, and better to forget about the fleeting illusion of "authenticity" on these occasions, accepting them for what they are: vivid, funny, dynamic entertainment.

Down to the lake

After South Horr, the track opens onto featureless plains of black lava with the massif of Kulal dominating the northern horizon. The lava is hard and jagged – a vicious test for tyres – and the track itself, pummelled to a fine dust, can become a quagmire after a rainstorm. The numerous stone circles and cairns around here are probably the remains of ancient settlements and burial sites.

The **lake** appears – just when you were beginning to wonder – as the road drops away in front: a stunning vista of shot blues and greens, with the black, castellate silhouette of South Island hanging as if suspended between lake and sky. Descending a little further, there are safe bays for swimming, and, an hour or so later, you reach Loiyangalani.

Loiyangalani and the lakeshore

It isn't much of a place, **LOIYANGALANI**. "The place of the trees" is a vague agglomeration of grass huts, mud huts, tin shacks, a police station, a school, a pair of campsites, "the mission" and "the lodge". It's a small community far from metropolitan Kenya, without newspapers and often without beer (a real measure of its isolation!). The land around is mostly barren and stoney, with palm trees and acacias clustered around the settlement's life source, a **spring** of fresh water.

The village came into being in the early 1960s with the *Oasis Lodge* and the Italian mission to the Elmolo people, a small group who live by hunting and fishing on the southeastern lakeshore. Somali raiders ransacked both establishments in 1965, but since then the two institutions have been left alone. The **mission** is now starting to thrive and its net of influence has reached most of Loiyangalani's more permanent inhabitants, especially the children who come to the school. The **lodge** (around Ksh2200/3000 FB, bookings through *Muthaiga Connection*, see "travel details" p.390) tries to be exclusive, often charging a Ksh100 entrance fee to casual visitors to discourage the safari campers from drinking the entire stock of beer.

If you want to visit **South Island National Park**, you should ask about a trip at the lodge first, but spread the word and you may find a much cheaper means of getting there. It's a thirty-kilometre return so the weather needs to be fair.

On dry land, you could make a stab at climbing **Kulal**, if you have the energy. There are two summits, joined by a narrow and dicey ridge. The climb itself, once you're on the right track, is straightforward enough, but talk to some gem-hunters who may guide you up. And note that, although Kulal seems to tower over Loiyangalani, two days is barely enough to walk to the base and back: you really will need transport unless you're very determined and suitably equipped. The views from the top are said to be fabulous and bird-watchers have the added incentive of a rare species of **white-eye** peculiar to the mountain.

In Loiyangalani

There are two budget oriented places to camp or stay reasonably cheaply in Loiyangalani. *El Molo Lodge* (bookings through PO Box 34710 Nairobi, ☎723177) has well set-up *bandas* from around Ksh400/500, camping for Ksh50 and a swimming pool – that campers have to pay extra to use. The *bandas* at *Sunset Strip* are less comfortable than *El Molo*'s (around Ksh400) but the *Strip* offers pretty enough camping sites between the palms (again, Ksh50), which give some shelter from the wind lashing down from the fortress bulk of Kulal, and it's marred only by the high wire perimeter fence – built to allow you to leave your gear with some confidence. *Sunset Strip* has showers, toilets and a kitchen-bar-terrace with variable supplies of sodas and beer that are always twice the usual price.

Loiyangalani has no real B&L, though there are one or two minimal *hotelis* and *dukas*. The misnamed *Cold Drink Hotel* is supposed to have a couple of rooms at the back and certainly boasts some interesting murals – but drinks are cheaper and colder from the blue shop opposite.

The **village**, for all its apparent drabness, isn't dull. When you've had enough of haggling through the campsite fence for artefacts and fantastic quartz, onyx, amethyst, and other semi-precious stones collected from Kulal, you can wander over to the springs and the very together looking school. You'll inevitably pick up a cluster of teenagers – Turkana, Elmolo, Samburu, Rendille – eager to practise their English. Swahili has never made much impact up here and English is the usual teaching medium.

Loiyangalani's **"beach"** is a grubby strip a couple of kilometres down the road. People do swim, but the dingy water is hardly enticing. Many of the loose stones on the shore also shelter scorpions (not serious) and carpet vipers (very serious), both of which seem to be absent from the campsite.

THE ELMOLO

The people of Loiyangalani with the best claim to be the original inhabitants are the **Elmolo**, about which much has been written and little said. In Kenya, they're famous for being famous. Dubbed "the smallest tribe in the world" (in number, not size), they are the only hunter-gatherer community in the country who can be visited quite easily and who don't resent the intrusion.

The Elmolo call themselves *el-Des*: their usual name comes from the Samburu *loo molo onsikirri*, "the people who eat fish". They once inhabited South Island and, until recently, a small island in Elmolo Bay, but their main settlement now is a gathering of grass huts on the torrid shore 8km north of Loiyangalani. Most of the 400-strong community live here, partly by **fishing** and the occasional heroic crocodile or hippo hunt, partly by **cash receipts** from tourist visitors.

The Elmolo are enigmatic. At the time of Teleki's discovery of the lake, they spoke a **Cushitic** language, the family to which Somali and Rendille belong. Recent linguistic research on historical migrations points to their having arrived on the shores of Lake Turkana at a very early time – perhaps over 2000 years ago. They seem to have no tradition of livestock-herding which might have been kept up if they had turned, like the Turkana, to fishing as a supplement. Today they speak **Samburu** and have started to intermarry with them. This, as well as the mission's influence, has been quite significant in raising their numbers (from less than 200 twenty years ago) and also in diluting their cultural identity: once strictly monogamous, polygamy isn't uncommon now; they send some children to the school in Loiyangalani as weekly boarders; they've bought a motorboat to take tourists across the bay to a small island. And on the slope, right behind the village, a new Catholic church looms ominously.

All this signals the final curtain for a culture and history that has been largely ignored or refuted. The conventional wisdom about hunter-gatherers in Kenya is that they are often the descendants of pastoralists who lost their herds. But if the Elmolo are, as some say, pastoral Rendille who took to fishing in order to survive, then it's strange that they have never tried to replace their herds. For without herds, they could never hope to pay bridewealth for wives from their non-fishing neighbours in the traditional way. A better explanation, and one favoured by the Elmolo themselves, is that their people have always been fishermen and hunters, and, until very recently, pressures from other tribes, particularly the Turkana, had pushed them almost to the point of annihilation.

At the end of the twentieth century, the Elmolo fishing culture is beginning to rub off on other ethnic groups and even the Samburu have started to eat fish. As long as twenty years ago, Peter Matthiessen could write:

> *The Samburu and Turkana may linger for weeks at a time as guests of the Llo-molo, who have plenty of fish and cannot bear to eat with all these strangers hanging around looking so hungry. Other tribes, the Llo-molo say, know how to eat fish better than they know how to catch them. . . "We have to feed them," one Llo-molo says, "so that they will feel strong enough to go away."*

> Peter Matthiessen,
> *The Tree Where Man was Born*

The Elmolo are charming, hospitable people, though how they survive in their chosen environment is almost beyond belief. Outwardly similar in dress and appearance to the other people of the area, they are slightly smaller, but the bowed legs which are supposed to be the characteristic result of their diet seem to be confined to the older people – I'd have thought all that fish would give them strong bones.

In the evenings, **dances** often take place around Loiyangalani: informal, energetic, pogo-ing performances for fun, always worth checking out. Track them down by the booming sound of collective larynges.

Anthropo-tourism

At **Elmolo bay**, 8km north of Loiyangalani, lives the last viable community of **Elmolo people** (see box). To visit them, you generally pay Ksh80–100 each (depending on the size of your party) to the headman to be given the freedom of the village, including the right to take photos and a trip to the island opposite the bay to look for **crocodiles**. Impromptu dances start, little hands are slipped engagingly into yours for a walk around the low, grass huts. Older people stare rather blankly from the entrances. The ground is a litter of fishbones, string, shreds of cloth. Someone sets up a stall of beadwork and gourds – apparently identical to what you could find up and down the Rift Valley. It's a novel, disturbing experience which contrives to be stage-managed and voyeuristic at the same time.

Over on the island – which, because of Lake Turkana's lowering, you can now reach by a slightly roundabout route on dry land – you should see **crocodiles** if you walk softly and approach the far shore cautiously. On the island's stern, rocky beaches, the remains of Elmolo fish picnics and old camps are everywhere. I found a marvellous, nearly fossilised hippo tusk from some long-ago feast. Today, a hippo hunt has to be organised discreetly (strictly speaking, hunting hippos is illegal) and usually takes place further north on the marshier shores below Moiti Hill. Hippos have gone from Loiyangalani.

Further north: Sibiloi National Park

Sibiloi National Park (usual fees) provides a powerful temptation to go further north – even for jumping ship if you came up to Turkana by safari tour. The park is in theory accessible even by saloon, but you shouldn't risk it without careful enquiries. If you're looking for a lift at Loiyangalani, a steady trickle of sturdier vehicles does pass through, heading for the park, and you shouldn't have too much difficulty returning south again.

Discoveries in human prehistory

Sibiloi was created to protect the sites of numerous remarkable **hominid fossil** finds made since 1968 by Richard Leakey's team from the University of Nairobi. The park, 1600 square kilometres of rock desert and arid bush, is an exceptional source because many of the fossils are found on the surface, blown clean by the never-ending wind. The finds set back the dates of intelligent, cooperative, tool-making behaviour among hominids further and further all the time, but most of the species concerned are assumed to have died out. The crucial discoveries that will link humankind to our pre-human ancestors have yet to be made. One striking find made at Sibiloi in 1972 was "1470", the skull of a *Homo habilis* over two million years old, believed to be a direct ancestor of modern *H. sapiens*. As more and more discoveries are made, here and in southern Ethiopia and Tanzania, evolutionary theories are beginning to flesh out. The most important current site is in the north of the park at Koobi Fora.

Practicalities
The so-called **museum** at the "expedition" headquarters in Alia Bay, where some of the fossils (including part of a 1.5-million-year-old elephant) are supposedly displayed *in situ* isn't easily traced: all that was found recently were empty ranger buildings and unhelpful staff. There are no real facilities for visitors and, apart from water supplies, you need to be self-sufficient.

Animal life
At times, though, Sibiloi has a surprising wealth of **wildlife**. Indeed, until the 1930s, there were large numbers of elephant living here. Rainless years, ivory hunters, and especially the increase in the herds of livestock, contributed to their demise. But lion, cheetah, hyena, both kinds of zebra (the ordinary Grant's and the finer-striped, taller Grevy's), giraffe, ostrich, Grant's gazelle, and gerenuk all occur here, though there's no guarantee you'll see much. Because of the protection from hunters, hippo and crocodile are numerous. The tree cover is minimal. The closest you're likely to come to finding trees is the petrified forest of stone trunks, reminders of the lush vegetation of the lakeshore in prehistoric times.

THE NORTHEAST

Northeastern Kenya has a single and limited travel circuit: up through **Isiolo** to **Marsabit Mountain and National Park**. It's well worth doing. But so is some of the rest of this vast **wilderness region**, even though Kenyans themselves will try to imply you are deluded to consider the idea.

Beyond, or east of Marsabit the few towns – Moyale, Mandera, WAJIR, and Garissa – are considered remote administrative outposts, controlling land essentially peripheral to the onward thrust of development and change. Few travellers (and no tour groups) ever make it up here and the rewards if you venture out into these districts are hard to pin down. Savagely hot, rebarbative wastelands unfold for hours on end as you bus or truck your way along interminable dirt roads to towns that can at first seem devastatingly anticlimactic. But there is, as ever, fascination in the regional population: the Somalis, Rendille, and Boran who live by herding their camels and cattle, moving from well to well, crisscrossing the deserts on old migration routes. Being among them is a reward in itself. They tend to be stern and indifferent until you break the ice, and then the kindness and hospitality they show are astonishing. The dusty, flyblown towns, too, take on distinctive characters as you get to know them; they owe little in atmosphere to down-country Kenya.

Travel throughout the northeast has a special quality. The normal stimuli of passing scenery, animals, people, and events fleetingly witnessed is replaced with a massive open sky, a shimmering greenish-brown earth, and just occasionally a speck of movement – some camels, a pair of ostriches, a family moving on with their donkeys. It is a sparse, selective, absorbingly simple landscape. And not the least of its attractions is its restful absence of hassle and shove, and a solitude that can hardly be found anywhere else.

But, except for the Marsabit run, this is travel almost entirely for its own sake. If you decide to go all the way to **Moyale** or **Mandera** (the two towns at the end of the route "spokes"), the greatest reward is in getting there. Retracing the journey in the opposite direction is a more dubious pleasure. However, the towns do also offer the possibility of brief sorties into **Ethiopia** and **Somalia**, with full permission. There are generally no special conditions attached to crossing the borders for a few hours to wander around. For me these glimpses were provocative enough reasons in themselves for venturing up here.

Isiolo

ISIOLO is the hub for travel to Marsabit, Moyale, Wajir, and Mandera, and the northeast's most important town. Located at the end of the paved road, there's no problem getting here from the Mount Kenya region (see p.127).

Southernmost of the "Northern Frontier" towns, Isiolo is on the border between two different worlds – the desert and the fertile Highlands. The terrific **Somali influence** here is something you'll notice everywhere you travel in the northeast. Isiolo is one of their most important towns in Kenya because it was here that many veteran Somali soldiers from World War I were settled. Recruited in Aden and Kismayu, they gave up their nomadic lifestyle to become livestock and retail traders, the "town Somali".

But **the town** is really a cultural kaleidoscope, with Boran, Meru, Samburu, and Turkana inhabitants as well as the Somalis. To someone newly arrived from Nanyuki or Meru, the upland towns seem ordinary in comparison. Women from the irrigated *shambas* around Isiolo sell cabbages, tomatoes, and carrots in the busy market. Cattle owners and merchants exchange greetings and the latest news from Nairobi and Moyale. Goats scamper through the alleys. Hawkers stroll along the road raising their Somali swords and strings of bangles to the minibuses heading up to Samburu National Reserve (see Chapter Five). And, in the shade, energetic *miraa*-chewing and hanging around are the major occupations. *Miraa* has a long history in Somali culture and the Nyambeni Hills, where most of the Kenyan crop is grown, are just 30km away.

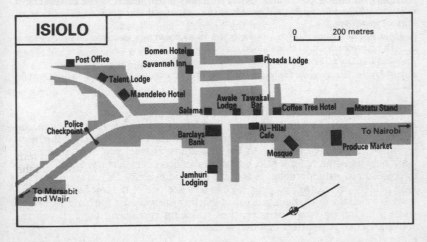

Staying in Isiolo

Arriving here is particularly exotic at night. The 9pm *OTC* bus from Nairobi doesn't get in till about 2am, and the town can be seen glittering out on the plain far below for an hour or more beforehand. During Ramadan, lanterns glow along the pavements for the *miraa* sellers and most of the shops are still open. You can find a B&L or crash on the bus until dawn.

Lodgings

Isiolo boasts one reasonably good hotel. Of the more humble **lodgings** all are cheap, and several surprisingly above average.

Bomen Tourist Class Hotel (PO Box 67, Isiolo, ☎2225). The best in town and fairly new with rooms (around Ksh350/450 s/c B&B) that far outshine anything else.

Jamhuri Lodging Clean, courteous, and mellow – currently the most popular cheap place.

Silent Inn Past the *Jamhuri* to the west. Spotless, and the luxury of morning hot water (Ksh60/90 s/c single).

Posada Lodge Also worth looking into. Quiet, with cheap meals.

Silver Bells Hotel (not marked on map) Between the *Bomen* and *Posada*. Clean and quiet.

Nanyuki Guest House (not on map) Big rooms, warm water of a morning, and dead cheap.

Savannah Inn This is on the whole a good place, run by a Meru family, with decent rooms around a pleasant, shady coutyard. But, while the beer is cold and the food above average, too (including the likes of toasted sandwiches), the place is so noisy at night that few people get much sleep here – the boss will keep you and anyone else in conversation for hours with opinions on everything. Irritating shortages of change and water aren't endearing either.

Food and drink

Somali *hotelis* provide excellent **food**, day and night. Now that you're in the north-east, you'll see pasta (usually spaghetti) appearing quite prominently on menus – one of the better Italian bequests to the Somalis.

Coffee Tree Hotel Down-to-earth eats.

Salama Restaurant The best in town – especially for an early breakfast.

Frontier Green Café (fomerly the *Awale Lodge*) Has a brilliant, tree-filled garden restaurant with disco, flourescent spider's webs (!) and UV tubes – in outlandish contrast with the rest of the town. Long popular for its good spiced *chai* for next to nothing a glass. *Akamba* bus bookings are made here.

Al-Hilal Also pretty good, especially noted for its samosas and pancakes, and it has some ultra-cheap accommodation (Ksh40/80).

Tawakal Bar Open 24 hours a day and doubles as the *OTC* ticket office.

Talent Lodge The most worthwhile move on a hot afternoon, for a cold beer on their rooftop terrace.

Crafts, salesmen and other distractions

Isiolo is one of the best places to buy **bracelets** of copper, brass, and aluminium. Prices are generally around Ksh15 for the simple ones, up to Ksh60 for the heavier, more complicated designs. In the tourist low season, you may present the day's only opportunity for a sale, so prices can drop even further. Short "Somali swords" in red leather scabbards are also much in evidence. If you are interested (and politely persuasive), you can be taken to see one of the few blacksmiths in town to watch the fascinating process of twisting the wires for the bangles. Profits come from buying rough bangles, then polishing and selling them. If you go, you're generally expected to make a purchase.

While the bangle and knife salesmen throng as soon as you sit down for a *chai*, their approach is rarely aggressive. Women offer small, woven dolls, and one boy furtively suggested I should buy "one treetop of mercury". I couldn't figure this out until he explained he'd been illegally buying drops of pure mercury from Samburu who collect the stuff in the hills, and he now had an orange squash bottle full. It seemed unlikely enough to be true.

If you're at a loose end in the evening, the *Comix Cinema*, up near the *Posada*, is a **video screen** with an endless mix of movies you'd forgotten about plus more up-to-date war, ninja and kung-fu rubbish.

Waiting in Isiolo: transport connections

This is a great town for passing the time of day. Memorable conversations are one of its strong points. And, when you're **heading north**, waiting in Isiolo is a predictable part of the trip.

Mwingi Highway – an intrepid **bus service** and virtually the only public transport over a quarter of a million square kilometres – does fairly scheduled runs to the four towns of the far north. The booking office is at the junction near the *Maendeleo Hotel*.

Departures

Buses leave Monday, Wednesday, and Friday for **Marsabit** (arriving the same day) and **Moyale** (arriving the following day). They leave Wednesday, Friday, and Sunday for **Wajir** (arrival the same day) and **Mandera** (the next day). There's also a service from Isiolo to **Maralal** leaving Sunday, Tuesday, and Thursday. Departure times depend on how quickly the bus fills up. Journey times are about five to six hours to Maralal and Marsabit, at least eight hours from Marsabit to Moyale, while Wajir and Mandera are about nine hours each stage, all assuming no hold-ups (climatic, mechanical or human).

Fares and booking

The **fare stages** are fixed for each sector (Isiolo–Maralal, Isiolo–Marsabit–Moyale and Isiolo–Wajir–Mandera) with the price from Ksh120 to Ksh200 depending on the length and severity of the stretch in question. You won't be overcharged for your seat, but you may have to knock the price down for

---

A NOTE ON SECURITY AND ROADBLOCKS

For fear of rebellion among the Somali population, and because of occasional highway robberies, the **military presence** in the northeast is pervasive: roadblocks, vehicle searches and armed escorts are part of everyday life. Illegal immigrants (refugees) from war-torn Somalia are one reason for this. You should be sure your passport is in order for the duration of your trip up north. Other frustrations are caused by *miraa* sales, both from and to the bus or truck you're travelling in; they can add hours to a journey.

Yet the incidents that Kenyans fear are rare and usually attributed to "bandits" without political motives. Don't let down-country misconceptions deter you. The lack of traffic probably makes travelling up here safer. And foreign travellers are a welcome sight in a region which is frustrated to be eddying in the margins of Kenya's mainstream.

luggage. The buses quite often leave a day late or, when out of sync, a day early. Make every effort to **get a ticket as soon as you can**. Buying one on the day of departure is often impossible, though buses do travel with miserable, standing passengers, who you should at all costs avoid joining. Try hard, too, to get a seat at the front of the bus as knee-room is short.

Alternatively, you can usually find a lift in the back of a lorry for somewhat less than the bus fare by asking around. It is worth exploring all the possibilities for a comfortable ride: the fullest lorries are the most satisfactory, if also the slowest. And, lastly, you can walk to the **police barrier** and wait for a lift where drivers sign their vehicles out of town. The police can be quite helpful and lifts to Marsabit and Wajir don't seem uncommon, though Maralal is a harder prospect from this angle.

Isiolo shortlist

Bank *Barclay's* distinguished-looking Foreign Legion fortress is probably functional as well as extravagant, open Mon–Fri 8.30am–1pm, Sat 8.30–11am (Note: there is no bank in Moyale, though branches of the *KCB* have recently opened in Wajir and Mandera).

Post office Mon–Fri 8am–1pm, 2–5pm.

Samburu National Reserve Isiolo is Samburu's supply town and there are reasonable hitching prospects at the police barrier (see p.259 and p.265).

To Marsabit – and North Horr

If the bus is travelling at a good speed the trip from Isiolo isn't uncomfortable, despite corrugations that shake smaller vehicles to breaking point. Passing over the usually dry Ewaso Nyiro River, and through the row of *dukas* which is ARCHER'S POST, the road veers northwest and for half an hour the great mesa of **Ol Olokwe Mountain** spreads massively across the horizon in front of you. If you are travelling independently with a vehicle, it can be climbed.

For several hours beyond Ol Olokwe you roar across the flat **Kaisut Desert**. LAISAMIS isn't much of a break and the Losai National Reserve – which you have just crossed – isn't any different from the rest of the scenery. The **approach to Marsabit**, though, is unmistakeable. The road begins to climb and suddenly you're on a hilly island in the desert, a region of volcanic craters, lush meadows, and forest. The branches of the trees on the steep slopes are disguised by swathes of Spanish moss, looking at first glance like algae-covered rocks in shades of grey and green.

Marsabit town

MARSABIT is a surprise: it's hard to prepare yourself, after the flat dustlands, for this fascinating hill oasis, in the desert but not of it. Rising a thousand metres above the surrounding plains, it is permanently green, well watered by the clouds which form and disperse over it in a daily cycle. The high forest is usually mist-covered until late morning, the trees a characteristic tangle of foliage and lianas.

The town is the capital of the largest administrative district in the country, as well as a major meat and livestock trading centre. It is small in size and intimate in feel; walking around you're always bumping into familiar faces. The lively

PEOPLES OF THE NORTHEAST

Identities in Marsabit can be confusing. The **Boran** and the **Gabbra** are closely related in language and custom, both part of the **"Galla peoples"**, a migrating drift of pastoralists who arrived in northern Kenya several hundred years ago from the Horn of Africa. At the time, they caused havoc in the region, only to be themselves pressured by the ensuing expansion of **Muslim Somalis** from the east. Many Boran and Gabbra, especially those who have adopted a more sedentary life, are now Muslims and have taken on Somali styles in dress and culture. The **Rendille** look and act like Samburu, with whom they are frequently allied: they speak a language close to Somali but have non-Muslim religious beliefs. They normally herd camels rather than cattle and, to a great extent, they continue to roam the deserts, facing the prospect of settling down without any enthusiasm at all and visiting Marsabit only for vital needs or a brief holiday.

These days, however, distinctions other than superficial ones are increasingly hard to apply as more and more children are sent to school and down-country ideas percolate up the road. The concept of "tribe", which in many regions has never been very relevant, seems more useless than ever. Still, language and religious beliefs remain significant in deciding who does what and with whom. Gabbra and Boran for example, traditionally scathing about trade, have begun to change through their long association with groups of trading Somalis.

cultural mix in the main market area is the biggest buzz: transient **Gabbra** herdsmen and **Boran** with their prized shorthorn cattle, the women in the printed shawls and chiffon wraps of **Somali** costume, rubbing elbows with ochred **Rendille** wearing skins, high stacks of beads and wire, and fantastic braided hairstyles (see box above). There are government workers here, too, from other parts of Kenya, and a scattering of **Ethiopian immigrants** and refugees.

Boarding and Lodgings

Lodgings are a simple detail. If *Kenya Lodge and Hotel* wasn't so outstanding, there would be no need to mention the others; but it's likely to be full and you're

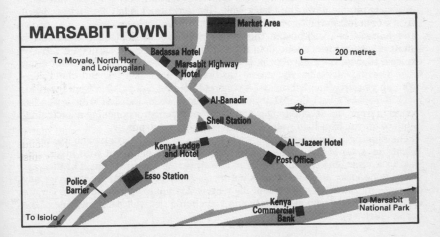

recommended to make a beeline for it as soon as you arrive – it's a gem – clean, modern, cosy, and fantastic value (Ksh70/100). The restaurant no longer serves Ethiopian fare, just the usual staples; still, the Ethiopian family who run it (notice the Amharic writing over the door) are sympathetic and helpful. The three other places in town are the big *Marsabit Hotel* (PO Box 110, ☎2210), with the town's main **bar** and night-time focus, a bakery below (fresh bread every afternoon), and some self-contained rooms with double beds (Ksh80/160 s/c); the *Badassa Hotel*, an unexceptional B&L with a decent *hoteli*; and the *Al-Jazeera*, which offers extremely cheap and peaceful accommodation and, if you happen to be driving, very safe parking. Whichever you choose, ask about **hot water** before moving in: night temperatures can drop very low (*Marsabit* means "place of cold") and luke-warm showers are no fun. Recent water problems have cut off piped water completely in the dry season, so forget about any showers then. New boreholes should solve this.

Walks out of town

There's a number of **trips you can make on foot** from Marsabit in a few hours or less – particularly good restoratives if you failed to get into the park without your own vehicle.

The easiest is the short walk up to the big wind-powered **generator** on a hill just west of the town. Turn left just before the police barrier and simply follow the path. There are rewarding views from it.

A longer excursion takes you up to the **VOK transmitter** up behind the town, an excellent morning or afternoon hike through lush forest with magnificent panoramas of the whole district from the top. There are wells up here, too (see below). During the rainy season, everything is tremendously green and you walk over flowering meadows through clouds of butterflies – pure therapy.

From there, you should be able to see the closest sizeable crater, **Gof Redo**, about 5km north of the town in the fork of the roads to MOYALE and NORTH HORR. Follow either road from where they fork for about 3km, then turn left or right accordingly for a one-kilometre cross-country walk. The crater is quite a favoured hideout for greater kudu and there's a population of cheetah around here too, not infrequently seen from a vehicle (but likely to flee if you're on foot). You can scramble down the crater wall. Gof Redo can't really be missed, but a friend from town would be reassuring.

Even easier is a walk to the **"Singing Wells"** at Ulanula (called Hulahula by some). These are less exotic than they sound, but they're still a good excuse to explore. Ulanula is a conical peak to the right of the Isiolo road, about 6km from town. Leaving Marsabit, you cross two bridges, then turn left and climb 200–300m up a narrow, tangled ravine. A concrete holding tank, visible from the road, gives the place away. Behind it are two natural wells, the first with a wooden trough in front, the second longer and apparently deeper, containing a fluctuating depth of brown, frog-filled water. A silent pumphouse stands by.

The **singing** is done not by the wells but by the Boran herders who use them. When the water is low, human chains are formed to get it out with luxuriantly leaking leather buckets: singing helps the work. At the driest times of the year you may be lucky and witness this but try to get here early. Animals are usually driven to the wells after dawn and it's a brisk 75-minute walk from town. Go out there in the late afternoon, though, and you should get a lift back with one of the day's vehicles up from Isiolo.

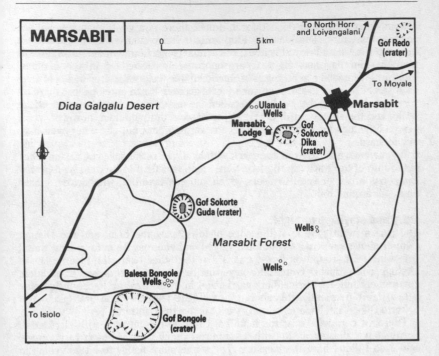

Marsabit directory

Bank Kenya Commercial Bank Mon–Fri 8.30am–1pm, Sat 8.30–11am.

Books For some Marsabit background, try *The Hills are Falling* by Mude Dae Mude, a novel widely available in Kenya and perhaps in Marsabit.

Food For Ethiopian food and a varied menu of Kenyan food, visit the *Al-Banadir Restaurant*. The *Al-Jazeera* serves edible meals, too. If you order their yogurt, the curious taste is of wood smoke used to sterilise the gourd it was kept in. Or simply head for the market. There is very cheap food in a lively atmosphere at any time of day from the *hotelis*: hefty two-bob pancakes, *githeri*, *mandaazi* and *nyama choma*. The *hotelis* double as butchers so you can select your own slab for roasting from the carcasses hanging up.

Post office Mon–Fri 8am–1pm, 2–5pm.

Onward travel details out of Marsabit

Buses *Mwingi Highway* runs services to Moyale on Tuesday, Thursday and Saturday and to Isiolo on Tuesday, Thurday and Sunday.

Petrol Supplies are usually available. Ask around the petrol stations if you are trying to hitch a lift to **Loiyangalani**; your first target is North Horr.

Marsabit National Park

Dawn to dusk, Ksh220, student reductions available, Ksh30 cars, preferably 4WD; Map –
Survey of Kenya Marsabit National Reserve SK 84 at 1cm:1km.

Having made the long journey to Marsabit, you will certainly want to get into the **park**. The forest is wild and dense, its two crater lakes idyllically beautiful.

Except during the long rains (March–June), there is a good chance you'll see some of the long-tusked Marsabit **elephants**, relatives of the famous Ahmed – a big tusker to whom Kenyatta gave "presidential protection", with elephant guards tracking him day and night (now replicated in fibreglass in the National Museum). Marsabit's new king is Mohammed, his tusks estimated at a cool 45kg each side. The park is also renowned for its **greater kudu** antelope and there's a very wide range of other wildlife. Between the nearly impenetrable forests of the peaks and the stoney scrub desert at the base of the mountain, however, you'll need a little luck for sightings. This is a rewarding park but one where you have to look hard.

If you venture to **drive in the park** without 4WD, make sure you can get back out. Some of the tracks in the forest are steep and tend to be muddy. *Marsabit Lodge* has a pair of Land Cruisers which you can take out, with driver – three hours for around Ksh700.

Entry and staying overnight

The park's **main gate** is at the edge of town, past the bank and the District Commissioner's office. It is not often visited and you may be in for a long wait if you want a lift around its forest tracks. On the other hand, the inverse law of hitching will probably come into play when a vehicle does arrive. In addition, government officers and soldiers garrisoned in town drive up to the **lodge** (see below) fairly frequently; this short trip, with the view over the first lake – Gof Sokorte Dika – and its forested rim, is a lot better than nothing.

There's a **campsite** near the main gate, said to be "infested with elephants". Fortunately I did get a lift (with a Rumuruti rancher in Marsabit to purchase cattle) so I didn't have the pleasure. The rangers are happy to let you camp in their compound anyway, and they have showers and toilets.

Marsabit Lodge (PO Box 45, ☎2044 Marsabit, bookings through *Msafiri Inns*, p.30), about 3km from the gate, has a fantastic location but zero ambience. In purely relative terms, it isn't over-expensive (Ksh955/1520 FB, much cheaper for Kenya residents) but it is perhaps superfluous: as the best in Marsabit, its function as official accommodation has largely overtaken its touristic *raison d'être*. Ahmed died the year it opened. If you'd like to stay, they might come and get you from the gate, but the staff often walk between the lodge and town, and you should be able to accompany them. It's a wonderful walk through the forest, with clouds of butterflies and the occasional mouth-drying encounter with buffalo or elephant.

Marsabit's fauna

Your animal count in the park will very much depend on the season of your visit. Good rains can encourage the grazers off the mountain and out into the temporarily lush desert, and the predators (always far fewer) will follow. **Elephants** especially are tremendous wanderers, sometimes strolling into town, causing pandemonium. More problematically, the people of Marsabit have been encouraged to cultivate around the base of the mountain, at the same time creating a barrier to the elephants' free movement and unintentionally providing them with free lunches.

The **birdlife** in the park is amazing: almost 400 species have been recorded, including 52 different birds of prey. Very rare **lammergeiers** (bearded vultures) are thought to nest on the sheer cliffs of Gof Bongole, the largest crater, which has a driveable track around its ten-kilometre rim.

Marsabit is also something of a **snake** sanctuary. We noticed frequent rustles and slithers, and almost drove over a very large cobra. This stood its ground when we went back to look, climbing into the bush and spreading its hood. Clearly this isn't a place to go barefoot or in sandals.

There are several **places to camp**, but Gof Sokorte Guda (Lake Paradise), a stunning, dark pool a kilometre across for much of the year, has wonderful sites on its crater rim, where a night would be chilly and thrillingly spent – lion, leopard and the rare and shaggy striped hyena are all seen and heard from time to time. Official fees for this *Lake Paradise Special Campsite*, however, run to over Ksh1000 – which includes the obligatory accompanying ranger – apparently not a negotiable figure.

North Horr

Reaching **NORTH HORR** from Marsabit is getting easier all the time, though continuing the logical next step down to Lake Turkana and Loiyangalani is still very difficult. There is a more or less regular passenger lorry which leaves Marsabit "often", as well as mission, Education Department, commercial, and oil industry vehicles. You'll be better off thinking in terms of camping out at North Horr because there aren't any lodgings. Missions there seem affable – for as long as they're not abused.

To Moyale

From Marsabit, the **journey to Moyale** takes between five and nine hours depending on the vehicle. For the first three of these you descend from the mountain's greenery past spectacular craters – Gof Choba is the whopper on the left – to the forbidding black moonscape of the **Dida Galgalu Desert**. Dida Galgalu means "Plains of Darkness" according to one Boran story. Another account derives it from Galgalu, a woman buried here after she died of thirst trying to cross it. The road arrows north for endless miles, then cuts east across watercourses and through bushier country beneath high crags on the Ethiopian frontier. There are some magnificent, spiring **termite mounds** up here, a sight that seems quintessentially African, yet one which can be quickly taken for granted, like leafless trees in a northern winter.

As the distances roll away, 250km is resolved as just a few bends, a couple of scenery changes. Over spaces that would take days to cover on foot you can see where you have been and where you are going – the pastoralists' conservatism hallowed by the landscape. The road bends north and winds up through the settlements of Burji farmers – Boran who have given up the nomadic herding life – past their beautifully sculpted houses and sparse fields to Moyale.

Moyale

Straddling the Ethiopian border, **MOYALE** makes Marsabit look like a metropolis. Though the town is growing rapidly, and was recently supplied with electricity, the centre is small enough to walk around in fifteen minutes. You'll find several sandy streets, a pretty mosque, a few *dukas*, a bar, a camel-tethering ground, two petrol stations (one of which occasionally belies its defunct appearance), a big police station, a fairly large market area, no bank and an incredibly slow post office – five weeks to Europe. Not much to write home about in fact, and not a lot to do except wander around, perhaps steel yourself to try some camel milk (very rich and creamy) and pass the time of day with everyone else.

The most interesting aspect of Moyale is its **architecture** – at least, the good number of traditionally built houses which are still standing. The Boran build in several styles, including circular mud and thatch huts, but in town the houses are rectangular, of mud and dung on a wood frame, with a flat or slightly tilted roof projecting a metre or two to form a porch, supported by sturdy posts and tree trunks. The roof is up to half a metre thick, a fantastic accretion of dried mud, sticks, scrap, and vegetation. Chickens and goats get up there, improving the roof's fertility, and every time it rains another layer of insulating herbage springs up. As a result, the houses are cool while the outside temperature hovers above 30°C most of the year. July and August are cooler.

Practicalities in Moyale

Accommodation is very limited. The most established B&L is *Barissah Hotel*, which shares frontage with the bar. The *Barissah* has a dozen dark cubes around an earth compound (Ksh50 each), and, while it's hardly clean, it is friendly enough. The restaurant has *karanga* and *chapatis* every evening, 24-hour *malayas*, and a permanent supply of warm tea. You need to bring a padlock, and "showers" (a basin of water) have to be ordered. The water can be briny at times and if you have the means, it's worth bringing a few litres of drinking water up from Marsabit. You can obtain **clean water** in Moyale from the Ministry of Water. Can't say fairer than that.

A second lodging, where family and guests share the same roof, is *Bismillahi B&L*, across the way from the *Barissah* behind the Esso pumps. It's Ksh50 a bed and facilities here don't match the *Barissah*'s, but food here is good. *Silent Lodge* has clean, three-bedded rooms at about Ksh40/bed. There are other B&Ls on the main street, past the mosque.

Into Ethiopia

The most enticing prospect in Moyale is to cross the valley into **Ethiopia** and spend a few hours, or even a night, there. For Kenyans and Ethiopians, the border is an open one. For foreigners there used to be just a few formalities, and, until recently, crossing was still remarkably easy considering the normal restrictions on tourists' movements in Ethiopia. The latest travellers' reports suggest this may no longer be the case, but the account of the visit (see box opposite) holds good for about one in two who try it. Doubtless it depends much on the latest directives from Nairobi and Addis, and on relations between the two governments, which have generally been good. You can increase your chances by ensuring your Kenyan visa (if you have one) is a multiple entry type, thus allowing you back in again. Naturally, an Ethiopian visa wouldn't hinder your progress either, though the embassy in Nairobi is not likely to concede that entry through Moyale would be permitted (by the rule book, tourists go into Ethiopia only by air through Addis Ababa). Kenya is building a big new border crossing post at Moyale, presumably anticipating increased trade and communications.

A FEW HOURS IN SOUTHERN ETHIOPIA

First you visit the Kenyan police sentry box down the hill, where you may be told that, strictly speaking, your intentions are unlawful and if their senior officer got to hear of it . . . The usual arrangement applies, so have some small notes with you. From here the road up the hill to Ethiopia is wide and invitingly tarred, though used almost exclusively by pedestrians and livestock. At the Ethiopian post they will ask you if you have an entry visa and, if you have, your passage should be straight-forward – though you may simply not be allowed to travel overland to Addis Ababa. Otherwise, explain you're just visiting briefly and go to see the customs and immigration officials at the office on the right as you go up the hill. After they've made one of two phone calls you should be allowed in. On no account go on up the hill if you haven't seen the immigration officer. You may well be given permission to stay the night, but note that customs searches are thorough and cameras must be left in the office. Probably the best plan is to take a room in Kenya and leave your gear there.

Ethiopian Moyale is larger than its Kenyan counterpart and noticeably more prosperous – a result, it seems, of the paved road to Addis, some piped water, and a long-established electricity supply. There are several bars, a hotel that wouldn't look out of place in a small town in Greece, lots of simple stores, and plenty of eating places. The market buzzes colourfully with camels and goats, piles of spices, flour, and vegetables.

Otherwise, apart from the optimistic slogans in English that line – and bridge – the road, and the slightly fantastic caricatures of Marx, Engels, and Lenin on the wall, life here seems much the same as over the border but easier. As a back-door view of Ethiopia, however, it may be no more representative than the other side of town is of Kenya.

But never mind that; there are some **new tastes** to try. A good place to eat *njera* and *wat*, the Ethiopian equivalent of *karanga na chapati*, is the *Negussie Hotel* (up the hill, take the first left past the wooden slogan "bridge", then the first right). *Njera* is soft, unleavened millet bread, with an uncanny resemblance to a dish rag, sometimes delicious, other times not. *Wat* is a spicy stew that can be made of any kind of meat or vegetables. The *Negussie* also has a bar serving Ethiopian beer or white wine from *Awash Wineries*, not for sensitive palates but cheap enough. You can pay for everything in Kenya shillings; Ethiopian currency is the *birr*.

If you are **staying the night**, head for the state-chain *Bekele Molla Hotel PLC*, about 2km from the border. The bar here appears to be the focus of night-time action for hundreds of kilometres and the rooms are clean and nominally self-contained. *Zibib*, on sale in the bar, is Ethiopian *ouzo* and easily drunk. If your bill seems pre-dated, that's because the Amharic calendar is eight years behind the Gregorian one.

English will serve you much better than Swahili, which is spoken by very few people. The people in this part of Ethiopia are mainly **Boran** and **Konso**, not Amhara, but an Amharic word worth remembering is thank you – *amaser-genalehu*.

Onward travel – the next step

Unless you were lucky enough to have a visa and be given clearance to travel overland to Addis Ababa, you'll probably be thinking about **returning to Marsabit and Isiolo** on the next bus or, if your thirst for adventure is still not quenched, getting to WAJIR and MANDERA. You can also find occasional food aid transport trucks heading straight down to **Mombasa**.

Moyale to Wajir

The track from **Moyale to Wajir** is infrequently used and often impossible after rain, while the one **along the border to Mandera** was virtually abandoned until recently. Nevertheless, both routes are now served by small, undaunted bus companies. On alternate days, the ironically named *Mandera Express* runs, in eight to twelve hours, to Wajir (Ksh180), not Mandera. The route is through the pretty, northern borderlands (much woodland, lots of wildlife) towards TAKABBA, cutting back south before it reaches that village and passing through BUNA; from there, Wajir is monotonously and uneventfully reached in a few hours.

Moyale to Mandera

The other bus, *Mandera Quick Service*, is a kind of giant *matatu* that plies roughly six times a month from Moyale to Mandera (Ksh300), taking two days to cover the severe track, with a night stop in the small centre of Takabba. Vehicles that use the track along the border, rather than via Takabba (mostly lorries), are driving illegally, and your comfort tends to be ignored: it gets cold in the back at night and there are no food supplies of any kind between Moyale and RHAMU.

In Moyale, the police are very helpful and will let you know if any *GKs* (government vehicles) are going your way. Only GK vehicles can travel when they like. Others have to go in escorted convoy. One quite likely possibility is hitching a ride to BUNA (about half way to Wajir), where there is a mission, and then finding another vehicle to Wajir. Assuming *Mandera Express* and *Mandera Quick* are operating, you have the option of waiting for their next run. Otherwise, you'll have to go back to Marsabit and Isiolo on *Mwingi Highway* – setting off Monday, Wednesday, and Friday.

From Isiolo to Wajir. . .

Undoubtedly the hottest, wildest, most remote route in the country, Kenya seems all but left behind when you set off from Isiolo for **Wajir and Mandera**. The journey unfolds, predictably enough, with the bus running full tilt for hours on end in a cloud of dust across a sizzling pancake of sand, gravel, and meagre scrub. The road stretches, empty in both directions, to indiscernible melting points on the horizon.

Mado Gashi and Habaswein

Often enough, a late departure means a night stop at **MADO GASHI**, a witheringly unappealing Somali and "Somali-ised" Boran village which is a crossroads for coast, northeast, and central highlands traffic. People aren't unfriendly but the long stares here, more than at most places, can be a little intimidating. I went out for a walk at dusk in a wrap-around, coastal *kikoi*, not dissimilar from what most men were wearing, and met with looks of utter disbelief (not surprisingly, you might say).

Sleep in, or on top of, the bus if you like. While there are numerous **lodgings**, the village has no electricity or running water, so they're spartan and generally dirty (about Ksh40 a bed). Marginally preferable is *Mount Kenya Lodge* at the

Isiolo end of town, which is fresher and quite passable. If you're exceptionally lucky, Mado Gashi's "cinema" will be showing something: one of the *chai* shops has a generator and a projector, and a small killing is made whenever the owner gets some reels. The impact of such entertainment on a community like this has to be seen to be believed.

The only settlement of any size between here and Wajir is HABASWEIN. This is located on the edge of the Lorian "swamp", a seasonal flood plain where the Ewaso Nyiro River sheds the rain that falls on the north and east sides of Mount Kenya.

Wajir

First impressions of **WAJIR** are of its size, a fair amount of construction going on, a "Centre for the Disabled", whitewashed, blue, and yellow buildings, and a feeling of Araby in the air which genuinely reflects the town's considerable Arab population. The place has a real gravity of its own, electricity and running water, and the "legionary" castellated fortress for which it's famous.

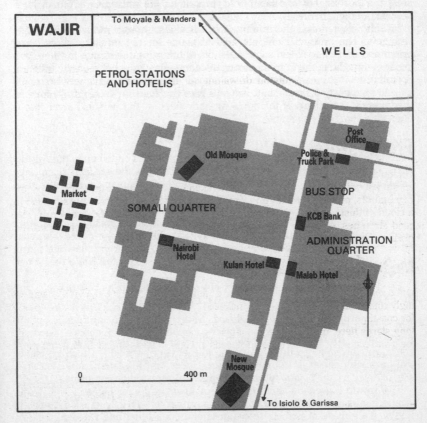

Some background: an incident

Like most of the major settlements in the northeast, Wajir's significance comes largely from its **wells**. More than a hundred of them are scattered across seventy square kilometres of desert, providing the basis of a livelihood for the **Somali** people of the region through their milk camels. The wells have always been bitterly fought over and jealously protected. Conflict between Somali clans and clan sections over water rights is probably as old as the clans themselves. Feuds are never forgotten: vengeance and blood money are traditional elements in the struggle for survival in this inimical environment.

Early in 1984, tensions were running higher than usual and parliamentary balance had gone awry with some sections feeling unrepresented by the town's two Somali MPs. Amid accusations of atrocities between rival clans, the regional administration announced an amnesty for those Somalis who surrendered their guns. Wajir's recent notoriety stems from this point, when thousands of men and boys of the Degodia clan were rounded up and interned by the authorities in a fenced military airstrip at Wagala, west of the town, for refusing to comply. Hundreds subsequently died of exposure or dehydration or were killed trying to escape. A local tragedy of catastrophic proportions, the **massacre** left many families without their menfolk.

Visiting Wajir today, the trauma is still obvious, though rarely spoken of to strangers. The provincial officials held to blame for the massacre were transferred and there have been some attempts to bring improvements to the town's services. But the problem remains one of communication – between the different Somali clans, between Somali and non-Somali, and between Wajir and metropolitan, down-country Kenya. The town will give you food for thought. Despite all this, there's a measure of tolerance on both sides at the personal level that is often little short of remarkable.

Time in Wajir

Finding **somewhere to stay** in the town is no problem. I ended up in the *Nairobi Hotel*, desperate for shade, a cold drink or ten, food, a shower, and sleep: they had it all (Ksh50/100). There are a number of other lodgings; the *Kulan* is good value (Ksh50/bed inside or out) with decent, rather basic food. And the *Malab*, right by the bus stop, is reportedly excellent, with fans as well as mosquito nets.

Because of Wajir's very high **water table** (only 10m below ground), mosquitoes are a terrible menace here, and you should come adequately prepared with your favourite repellent. For the same geological reason, long-drop toilets are not in use, but there's not much you can do to prepare yourself for the *kimbo* tins. Avoid the water if you can.

Food is good in Wajir, with many places offering pasta, pilau rice (*mchele*) and the distinctive black, spiced, delicious tea of the northeast called, aptly, *strungi*.

Around Wajir

And **what is there to do**? The main pastime seems to be chewing *miraa*, but you'll probably soon get tired of that (or at least your jaws will). There are one or two **bars** with cheap *AFCO* (armed forces) beer on the eastern, administrative, side of town: try the *Soweto* for mixed Somali/Administration company.

The **market area** on the west side of town is fascinating and well worth wandering around. Quite different from any market you'll have seen before in Kenya, it's a maze of Somali *herio* (grass and stick huts) and wooden shelters.

There's a wide assortment of locally made domestic odds and ends including beautiful and simple pottery incense burners for scenting clothing. Fruit and vegetables are in short supply and fairly uninteresting: you'll usually find oranges and sometimes slashes of brilliant red watermelon, though often on the main street between the *Nairobi* and the *Kulan* hotels rather than in the market itself. On the next street up you'll find **tailors** sitting under the trees at their treadle machines in a scene duplicated in thousands of towns across Africa. There is said to be a **craftsmen's quarter** of metal workers and other artisans around the big new mosque on the way out to Isiolo.

If you'd like to visit some **wells**, the closest are just a little north of town past a flurry of street activity, a part-time petrol station, the administrative departments, and the post office. Obviously the activity around the wells depends on the condition of the pasture in the region and for much of the year the big herds of camels are out in the desert on clan grazing grounds. But when they are here at the wells the scene is memorable.

Lastly, and somewhat bizarrely, there's also said to be a **squash club** in town, surely one of the least likely places to find one. If you ask, you should also find the **"Royal Wajir Yacht Club"** – now known as the *Gamia* (Camel) *Club* – and certainly worth asking about at the very least. It may, in fact, be the squash club. It was named thus to bring a bit of a smile to the faces of the British officials posted here in the 1940s and 1950s. Wajir, otherwise, isn't exactly a bundle of laughs.

Wajir directory

Buses From the *Kulan Hotel*, to Mandera Sun, Wed, Fri 8am; To Nairobi Sun, Tues, Thur 5.30am.
Trucks To Mandera, from outside the police station, cheaper than the bus.
Kenya Commercial Bank Mon–Fri 8.30am–1pm, Sat 9–11.
Post and telephone office Mon–Fri 8am–1pm, 2–5pm, Sat 8am–1pm.

. . . and Mandera

Once in Wajir, why stop there? While it's not a journey for sybarites or weak bladders (vehicles roll for hours on end), the final desperate kick **up to Mandera** takes you as far from Nairobi as you can get, which is not an altogether unattractive proposition sometimes, and it gives you the chance to cross the border for a peek at Somalia.

El Wak and Rhamu

About halfway from Wajir to Mandera is **EL WAK** (The Wells of God) and a scramble of people eager to buy whatever *miraa* the bus travellers have for sale. There used to be a Camel Corps here, but the police today seem to have abandoned the dromedary as a way of getting around. Should you end up spending the night here – and, travelling by bus and lorry, it is amazing how many unscheduled night stops you'll make in the northeast – the bed and board on offer at the only **lodging** is pretty insalubrious.

Another possible overnighter is **RHAMU** (confusingly, often pronounced "Lamu"). Renowned for its mosquitoes, it is right on the Ethiopian border by the seasonal Daua River. There's an *NCCK* centre here where you can stay and a garrison of numbingly bored soldiers to talk to.

From Rhamu, the **paved road** which has been an on-and-off affair since El Wak is continuous to Mandera but in a very sorry state indeed. There is fairly frequent transport and a daily *matatu* run in the evening. The road is straight and largely empty, with the barren fastnesses of Ethiopia rising up remotely on the left, but it's one of the most dangerous in Kenya as it crosses, unperplexed, a series of steep north–south ridges with a broadside lack of regard for gradient. Shattered hulks of vehicles litter the slopes, having stalled and rolled backwards. If you are in the back of a heavily laden lorry, it is worth at least finding a suitable position for leaping off. It's scary. Some of the slopes have been circumvented by zigzags and the latest news is that the worst of them are being levelled. There's ample compensation for an unpredictable journey in the startling quantities of wildlife that's often to be seen along this way – ostriches, warthogs, giraffes, gazelle; you name it.

If your vehicle makes the Wajir–Mandera connection by way of the Somalian border route, you you veer to the right, after El Wak, and make straight for Mandera via the village of ARABIA (and why it's called that we'd like to know for the next edition).

Mandera: market forces

More than a thousand kilometres from Nairobi and only half that to Mogadishu (capital of Somalia), **MANDERA** nestles at the tip of a much disputed salient of Kenyan territory wedged uncomfortably between Ethiopia and Somalia. The town, more even than Wajir, has only the most tenuous lifeline to Nairobi – and this thanks mainly to *Equator Airlines*, which flies in a daily shipment of *miraa* in a twin-engine *Cessna*. The same plane collects and delivers mail, messages (Mandera has telephones but only just) and government workers.

Because of the difficulties of land communication with Nairobi, the town relies heavily and uneasily on food supplies from Somalia. As at Moyale, the **border** here is virtually an open one for local people. But, unlike the Ethiopian border town, Mandera's economy depends on this fact; Somalian currency is used widely here and is openly on sale. Rice, sugar, milk powder, and flour – much of it originally foreign aid to Somalia – are carried across no-man's-land to Mandera, while tea, soap powder, a plethora of household utensils and *miraa* are taken back to Somalia.

The miraa trade

The import of **miraa** ("*qat*" or "*gatty*") into Somalia was banned by the Somalian government in 1984. It is one half of an extensive black market trade in luxuries operating alongside the one in vital commodities. In the opposite direction, into Kenya, everything from cassette players to cameras to thermos flasks, all imported into Somalia from the duty-free enclaves along the Persian Gulf, find their way into Mandera, down the gauntlet of police checks along the road to Isiolo and out into the markets of Kenya.

The ramifications of all this traffic, both illegal and quasi-legal, are hard to follow, but the immediate results are noticeable as soon as you visit a *hoteli* and discover that samosas are "fifty shillings" apiece and a *chai* is "thirty shillings". Food is in fact generally cheap, but such is the demand for Kenyan shillings by Somalians that most "local" prices are quoted in their **Somali shilling** equivalents. On the black market the Kenya shilling is worth up to 28 Somalian shillings. The key to the cross-border trade is *miraa* and its importance can be judged from the fact that Somalia banned it only under pressure from the World Bank, which pointed out that the Somali shilling was being undervalued because of the demand for Kenyan shillings to buy *miraa*. Not surprisingly, the effect seems to have been to make *miraa* even more valuable – and Somalia's currency as soft as a bunch of the stuff after the three-day journey from Meru. A Mandera branch of the *Kenya Commercial Bank* has recently opened (Mon–Fri 8.30–1pm, Sat 8.30–11am), but so far it doesn't seem to have set off the sweeping changes in the region you might expect. (Whether you're changing money or not, though, the air conditioning makes it a fine place to hang out.)

Mandera is not the Kenya you've come to know. And if you've just entered from Somalia it could hardly be a less typical introduction. But, for sheer novelty value, it's worth every bump and ounce of sweat expended in getting here. If you hate it, the *miraa* plane can take you (assuming a spare seat) back to the banalities of Nairobi in two hours.

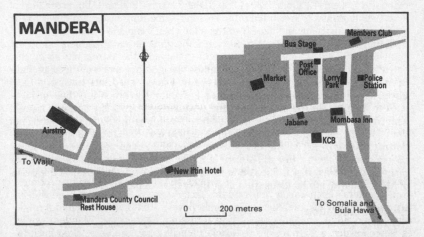

Mandera practicalities

The town itself lacks the established atmosphere of Wajir and, like Moyale with Marsabit, makes its southerly neighbour look positively urbane. The Girls' Secondary School, for example, is the only one in the entire district (25,000 sq km) and it has just 22 students. Mandera consists of a cluster of Somali *bula* (hamlets) interspersed with the usual scattering of administrative buildings. As a place to stroll around, it is filled with interest and revelation, and I had no difficulty passing a couple of days here while waiting for transport south. The fairly tense atmosphere of Wajir is replaced by something lighter, although there is always the possibility that one of the rockets that sometimes swoop over the town in the sporadic conflict between Ethiopia and Somalia might deflect towards Mandera itself.

Lodgings and food

There are very few **lodgings**. The only decent ones are the *Jabane*, which is close to the middle of things, offers fans, showers and towels (Ksh50/bed), and does the best food, and the *Mombasa Inn*, next door, which is a little more basic and not as comfortable (Ksh40/bed). The *Mandera County Council Resthouse* is a third option, a surprise with its neat, self-contained rooms, fans, and clean water (take note); it's hard to resist after the journey. For anything from Ksh150–300 B&B per person you may think it's worth it, but you'll score better on conversation and local immersion down at the cheaper places: the *Resthouse* is just a bit far from the town centre. The *New Iftin* and the *Mombasa Inn* both have restaurants – scruffy, rapid-turnover joints swirling with old chits and face-stuffing patrons.

Market and miraa

Mandera's **market** is the town's focus and, like Wajir's, a bustling maze of huts and shelters – liveliest around 9 or 10am after the *miraa* arrives – with small stores and *hotelis* all around. For a beer, try the *Members' Club*, the only licence holder in town and open after 4pm, which occasionally comes up with a few crates. To post letters from this far corner of Kenya, you can use the post office (Mon–Fri 7.30am–12.30pm, 2.30–4.30pm, Sat 7.30am–12.30pm), but post takes at least four days just to reach Nairobi. To send something faster, go down to the airstrip in the morning and hand it to the pilot when the plane comes in.

Getting on the **plane** to return to Nairobi is quite an entertainment: amid the confusion of activity centering around the pilot and the *miraa* big shots, the potential passengers vie for seats – or rather places, since some of the seats have been removed. The big bales of *miraa* are off-loaded, sped into town in a Land Rover and exchanged for huge volumes of banknotes which are then brought back to the pilot for the purchase of the next consignment. The scene is fraught with confusion but if there's a seat you'll be offered it by the Somali charterer, not the pilot. The usual price falls between Ksh1000 and Ksh2000 (it can drop right down to Ksh700–800 in the dry season when the roads are better and fewer people want to fly; try to estimate the number of planes arriving, sometimes as many as *eight* every day!). The two-to-three hour flight, which clips past the peaks of Mount Kenya, is a fabulous treat after those days of hard travelling.

Helpful information

It's **worth knowing** that the *KCB* bank is as helpful as possible, but they have to radio Nairobi for the day's rates and the transaction can take hours (which can be spent watching the *miraa* barons come and go with their colossal wads). Mandera has critical water problems outside of the rainiest months of the year, December and April. All the town's water is supplied by the Daua River. If you can choose a time to visit the town, however, come in August for the annual *ASK* show, when Mandera gets a rare chance to blow its own trumpet. It's also worth knowing that you're strongly advised not to try to visit Ethiopia from here: there's no official crossing, and no bridge.

Into Somalia

The **Kenya-Somalia border** is fairly open to local people, with a constant stream of loaded pedestrians moving goods in both directions – the experience is less than relaxed. There doesn't appear to be a formal Kenyan border post, nor any advantage in looking for one, though apparently the Kenyans are setting up a big new crossing. The Somalian post is usually chaotic and you'll probably be directed on to the police station before you look around the Somalian border town of Bula Hawa. There's no need for a visa, but you need your passport. Some officials may point out you should have a visa and insist on keeping your passport. Get a receipt or a name; there won't be a problem. You should leave baggage and anything that might excite suspicion (cameras or notebooks, for example) behind in Mandera. And you may well be shadowed by a pair of flared trousers in dark glasses and moustache, and asked at some point to explain your movements. It's all absurdly filmic.

Bula Hawa

BULA HAWA (Eve's Village) is a sad little town that acts as a staging post for the Somalian half of the cross-border trade. Its main "strip" is a street lined with open booths of precisely the Arabian Nights style you never expect to see in real life. Languid merchants stretch across their brilliant carpets sipping tea and displaying an astonishing assortment of luxuries from kitsch to high-tech – the original duty-free bazaar. There are perfumes, cameras, walkmans, TVs, gigantic ghetto-blasters, textiles packed in Indonesian canned fruit cartons, as well as cut glass, cosmetics from Taiwan, T-shirts made from recycled food aid sacks and a mass of trinkets and gadgetry. Coming across all of this after the wilderness of the desert is outrageous. The dusty lanes are roamed by camels and goats; the walls are bullet-pocked; there are one or two small eating places. If you have a visa – and feel safe given whatever the latest BBC World Service news is from Somalia – there's a daily bus to MOGADISHU.

Prices in Bula Hawa's shopping centre are very low by Kenyan standards (Ksh1500 for a personal stereo, for example), but you'd be very unwise to buy anything openly with Kenyan currency until you thoroughly knew the score.

Leaving Mandera

Apart from the **plane** out (a daily service that's often increased to two or three flights, and sometimes a whole flock, before public holidays, especially during Ramadan when lots of *miraa* is chewed), there are two **bus** services back to the hub of Kenyan life.

Buses to Wajir and beyond

In theory, *Mwingi Highway* sets off for **Wajir and Isiolo** on Wednesday, Friday, and Sunday at 9am, arriving Wajir the same evening, and crawling into Isiolo some time late the next day. The *Garissa Express* goes to **Wajir** on Tuesday, Thursday, and Saturday, and continues to **Garissa** at dawn the next morning, with connecting services on to Nairobi, Malindi, and Mombasa at around noon that day.

Transport to Moyale and other points

If you want to travel west from Mandera, rather than south, the *Mandera Quick Service* bus offers unpredictable two-day jaunts through the north to Moyale for the price of a typical London taxi ride (see the Moyale section p.375).

For even less money – and sometimes more speed and comfort – you could also try your luck to almost anywhere with the **lorries** around the big tree by the police station.

Garissa

GARISSA, North Eastern Province's capital, is the least interesting of the desert towns, relatively close to Nairobi and Mombasa, and visibly influenced by both. Still, though emphatically not worth a special visit, it has its ethnic interest: a large Somali contingent that lives more harmoniously with their non-Somali neighbours, many of whom are coastal Muslims. Physically, Garissa is (for the present) the lowest bridging point across the **Tana River**. While the Tana is not mighty, the view of the loop of brownish-red water where it flows under the new bridge just outside town is quite impressive, especially after rain: a sullen reminder of Kenya's water and erosion problems – you suddenly realise this is the biggest river you've seen in the country.

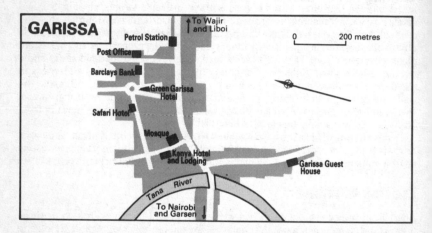

Bed and board

The town itself is dull, its streets recently asphalted. There are plenty of **bars**, a **bank** (Mon–Fri 8.30am–noon, Sat 8.30–11am, until a year or two ago the only one in the whole province) and **petrol stations**. It hovers uncertainly between coast, up-country and desert. It was recently in the news several times as the site of various serpentine encounters – a large python was found in the District Commissioner's office and a cobra in a school toilet. They were probably fleeing the heat; this is Kenya's hottest town and often unflaggingly humid as well. During the day the thermometer rarely leaves the 32–37°C zone.

So, having formed an idyllic picture, you'll want to know where to retreat from Garissa's charms. The best **lodging** is *Safari Hotel* (PO Box 56), a clean B&L with running water (Ksh80/120) and a good restaurant doing *mkate mayai* each evening. The *Green Garissa Hotel* is very basic, without running water (Ksh60/100), while the cut-price beer and gloomy, self-contained rooms at the *Garissa Guest House* (PO Box 55 ☎2019) aren't worth the longish walk or the price (Ksh180 B&B per person). *Kenya Hotel and Lodging* has a busy restaurant but its rooms are unappetising.

Passing the time

You'll probably want the first transport out of Garissa, but if you have some time to kill, stroll down to the **Tana Bridge** in the late afternoon and watch Kenya's precious topsoil flowing to the ocean. You can sometimes see hippo from here and even crocodile (Garissa District has a high incidence of death by *mamba*), and there are signs warning you about the banks where they lurk. Just over the bridge on the right is a row of *hotelis* and bars that come alive in the evenings.

Lastly, in case you were interested, Garissa Boys' Town, which used to be worth a visit, is no longer encouraging tourists. While they are still producing fine melons and other vegetables with the help of orphans, the tourist guesthouse and swimming pool are no more.

Getting out of Garissa

The *Garissa Express* sets off north on Tuesday, Thursday, and Saturday, arriving in Wajir (Ksh200) the same day and Mandera (Ksh320) the following evening. To LIBOI (the most direct crossing point into Somalia from Nairobi), there are departures from Garissa on Thursday and Saturday only at 9.30am. Nairobi has several daily connections with Garissa. Buses arrive at and depart from a spot opposite the *KBS* terminus in Eastleigh.

To MOMBASA and MALINDI, *Garissa Express*, *Mbuni*, and *Tana River* buses share the route with 6am departures (Ksh200 to Mombasa, Ksh170 to Malindi) from the *Kobil* station, or from outside the *Safari Hotel*. *Garissa Express* runs a daily 12.30pm service as well. Catch an early bus, though, and you can connect at Garsen with a Lamu-bound coastal route vehicle. If you're in Garissa on Monday, Wednesday or Friday you can also catch *Garissa Express* to the resettlement zone of MPEKETONI near Witu (departs 1pm), which is a forty-kilometre *matatu* hop from Mokowe and the hedonistic pull of Lamu.

Down the Tana to Garsen

The route down to the coast runs through Orma and Pokomo country – low-lying, flat, and densely bush-covered. The Orma **cattle herders** of this region are invariably swathed in brilliant, distinctive deep blue cloth, a much-favoured colour which was being imported along the coast over 1000 years ago. Don't expect much of the Tana's remaining pockets of **riverine forest** to grace the scene, however, much less the river itself, as for most of the way the newly gravelled road isn't close. The bus calls at **BURA**, a desolate resettlement area, with the oddly sited *Bura Country Club* a sure target for motorists or others moving under their own steam (Ksh100 per bed in the *bandas* or half that to camp). Next comes **HOLA**, which, with its coastal-style houses and animated main street, is a nice place to spend a day or two – and it's not far from the river. Try the *Safari Hotel* for a clean, quiet, friendly stay and good cakes. While here, you can (like everyone else) get a free ride across the Tana in a Pokomo dugout. And there's evening entertainment, too: the *Riverway Cinema* shows American and Indian films on a tiny screen under the stars.

For LAMU, leave the bus at **GARSEN** and pick up another in the afternoon or the following day. Garsen isn't anyone's favourite place but there are **lodgings** and no shortage of *hotelis*. Try the *3-in-1 Lodging and Restaurant*, which lacks some basic amenities but is reasonably clean, with a good restaurant. In season incidentally, Garsen's **mangoes** are reckoned to be some of the best and cheapest in Kenya.

Tana River Primate National Reserve

Ksh88 (likely to increase to Ksh220); Ksh30 for vehicles.

Getting to the **Tana River Primate National Reserve** doesn't look easy without your own vehicle. In fact, with only a small degree of perseverance (assuming you don't actually mind walking narrow trails through tall forest), you can find your way to the river, the research headquarters and a new campsite. **MNAZINI** is the easiest place to head for if you're without wheels: the 6am bus from Garissa makes the side-trip down to the village itself; the midday bus will only drop you at the junction, an easy, six-kilometre walk away.

Mnazini is a fine, coastal-style village beneath mango trees; no lodgings but *hotelis* will take you in for the night once you've cleared it with the sub-chief and the headman. One of the **village shops** also has most of what you're likely to need for a few days' stay in the reserve. Beyond Mnazini, there's nothing in the way of food but occasional fruit and garden vegetables.

Nobody knows Tana River Primate National Reserve by that name. Locals all refer to **Mchelelo**, the site of the primate research headquarters. The twelve-kilometre walk to get there involves two river crossings over the Tana's meanders, and there's no way you'd find the **route** through the **bush and gallery forest** unguided. Pokomo guides are happy to help and not hustling. At the first river crossing, Pokomos cross for free, Somalis pay Ksh25 and *wazungu* wait and see. The second crossing is more egalitarian: Ksh15 a head.

In the reserve

Mchelelo campsite (Ksh50) is small, secluded, and ravishingly pretty, with a shower and long-drop. Primatologists occupy campsites nearby and make visitors very welcome. The reserve's protected inhabitants include **Tana River red colobus** and **Tana River crested mangabey** monkeys, both extremely rare and vulnerable if the tourists don't turn up to keep the reserve functioning. At present, it survives with international help under the auspices of the *National Museums of Kenya*. In the immediate short term, continued encroachment on the forest threatens both species of monkey; the colobus very rarely leaves the trees.

In terms of **animal-watching**, your chances of seeing groups of both monkeys are really good. The forest areas are fairly restricted, even within the reserve, and it's not difficult to find them in a day or two. Other wildlife in the area includes blue monkeys, baboons, various squirrels and even elephants, lions, giraffe, and buffalo. At one time it was possible to make raft and boat trips on the sluggish river, dodging large numbers of hippos and crocodiles, but such adventures haven't operated as commercial safaris for several years. You're likely to find local people willing to take you.

If you're **driving**, the Baomo or Mchelelo tracks to the river are the ones to use, though the latter doesn't seem to be signposted from the road. The track to Baomo is indicated on the road, but *Baomo Lodge* itself, while it still appears on some maps, is assuredly abandoned.

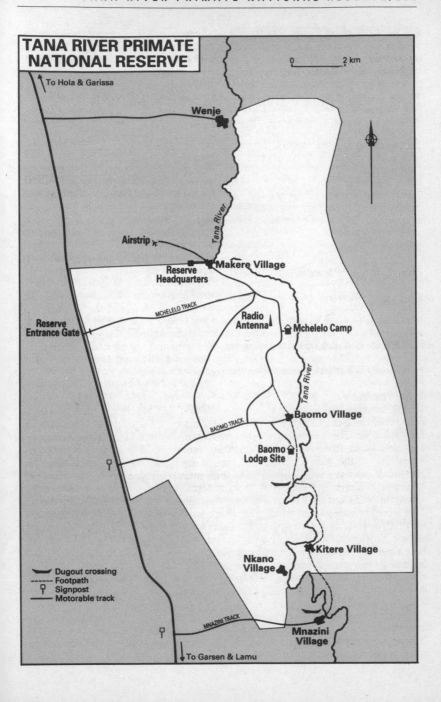

TANA RIVER PRIMATE NATIONAL RESERVE

0   2 km

To Hola & Garissa

Wenje

Tana River

Airstrip

Makere Village

Reserve
Headquarters

MCHELELO TRACK

Radio
Antenna

Mchelelo Camp

Reserve
Entrance Gate

Tana River

BAOMO TRACK

Baomo Village

Baomo
Lodge Site

Kitere Village

Nkano
Village

Dugout crossing
Footpath
Signpost
Motorable track

MNAZINI TRACK

Mnazini
Village

To Garsen & Lamu

Generalities

Because of their importance, particulars about **road transport** are given throughout the chapter. On the main axes – **Kitale–Lodwar**, **Nyahururu–Loiyangalani**, **Isiolo–Moyale**, **Isiolo–Wajir–Mandera**, and **Nairobi–Garissa** – you will rarely be stuck for a ride too long. Least frequented is the route up to Loiyangalani and this is the only one with no bus service.

Buses: a summary

This indicates the minimum service you can expect in the north. The reverse service applies on each route with the same frequency. Arrival times are not guaranteed.

From Kitale to Lodwar 2 daily, one continuing to **Kalokol** arriving same day;
From Nyahururu to Maralal 1 daily arriving same day;
From Isiolo to Maralal 3 weekly arriving same day;
From Isiolo to Marsabit 3 weekly, continuing to **Moyale** the following day;
From Moyale to Wajir 3 weekly, arriving same day;
From Moyale to Mandera 6 every month, arriving the following day;
From Isiolo to Wajir 3 weekly, continuing to **Mandera** the following day;
From Garissa to Wajir 3 weekly, continuing to **Mandera** the next day;

From Garissa to Nairobi 3 daily;
From Garissa to Liboi (for Mogadishu) 2 weekly;
From Garissa to Mombasa and Malindi 2 daily;
From Garissa to Mpeketoni (for Lamu) 3 weekly.

Planes

Hitching a lift on *Equator*'s daily charter to Mandera is harder than getting a lift back again because *miraa* is a more profitable cargo than passengers.

Flights to Lake Turkana are usually part of inclusive weekend packages at around Ksh12,000 per person:
***Lake Turkana Fishing Lodge* and the west shore:**
Ivory Safaris Tours (PO Box 74609, Nairobi, ☎226623), Salama House, Mama Ngina St, Nairobi.
***Oasis Lodge* at Loiyangalani**:
Muthaiga Connection (PO Box 34464, Nairobi, ☎25255).

There is also a flight-only service to any or all of the **Turkana airfields** (Lodwar, Kalokol, and Loiyangalani) with *Air Kenya* – full information in Chapter One, Nairobi, "travel details". Air hops **across the lake** are possible but depend on the number and departure or arrival points of passengers paying the full fare from Nairobi.

TELEPHONE AREA CODES

Garisssa ☎0131
Isiolo ☎0165
Lodwar ☎0293

Loiyangalani (operator exchange)
Mandera ☎0192

Maralal ☎03681
Moyale ☎0185
Wajir ☎0136

PART THREE

THE
CONTEXTS

THE HISTORICAL FRAMEWORK

The picture of Kenya's past that the first Europeans formed – a multitude of primitive peoples with no appreciable history – has, of course, been brushed aside in this century. Techniques have been found for tracing past events and migrations by combining oral traditions and comparing languages. Nevertheless, Kenya's precolonial past is still the subject of endless conjecture and, up-country, it's difficult for the traveller to keep much sense of it – especially since the physical record in ancient architecture is virtually nonexistent. On the coast, settlement ruins, old documents and the Islamic tradition help considerably to retain the feeling of a long past. What follows, up to the colonial period, is a simplified and much condensed overview, intended to pull together the historical accounts of individual peoples that are given throughout the guide. More emphasis here is given to the firmer history of the last hundred years or so.

THE CRADLE OF MANKIND – PREHISTORY

Kenya could be the place where human beings first evolved. The oldest remains belonging indisputably to **ancestral hominids** have been found on the shores of Lake Turkana. But it's hard to say whether this is conclusive proof: older finds made elsewhere could suddenly turn the theory upside down.

The East African **Rift Valley**, however, is ideal territory for the search for human origins: volcanic eruptions have repeatedly showered thick layers of ash and cinders over fossil beds, building up strata that can be reliably used to compare ages. The **Leakey** family have been instrumental in much of the work that has been done. Olduvai Gorge, in Tanzania, was the first major site to disclose evidence of human prehistory, and Louis Leakey and his wife, Mary, worked there from the 1930s. Their son, Richard, went on to explore the Turkana region

and found even older fossils, putting Kenya in the spotlight of scientific attention. A suggestion in support of the "Cradle of Mankind" idea is that the Rift Valley's very formation – a major event on the earth's crust, which began some twenty million years ago – may have been the environmental spark that catalysed human evolution.

At any rate, while current research pushes the dates back further and further, it hasn't answered the biggest question: if this is the cradle, who were the parents? The search for an **evolutionary line** linking humans directly with more primitive primates is still the number-one priority. **Theories** change so fast that books published in the 1960s and early 1970s contain ideas that today have been completely overturned. The **"ape-men"** *australopithecines* are no longer regarded as ancestors of *Homo sapiens* and it is now known that our own ancestors shared evolutionary time with them in East Africa. The fossil skull *1470* (its catalogue number), discovered by **Bernard Ngeneo** in 1972 and now in the National Museum in Nairobi, is evidence of this. Between two and three million years old, it's an example of *Homo habilis*, "handy man", a direct human ancestor.

Until Ngeneo's discovery, it was thought that while the massive, plant-munching *Australopithecus boisei* did eventually die out, its slighter, higher-brow neighbour *A. africanus* survived, adapting and evolving into the *Homo* line. Now it's believed all three species lived on the savannah and forest margins at the same time. A recent flood of discoveries of *Homo* fossils shows that the evolutionary line that eventually led to human beings was already established as long as five million years ago. Most spectacular in recent years has been the discovery of the nearly complete 1.5 million-year-old skeleton of a twelve-year-old boy of the species *Homo erectus*, our immediate ancestor. It was *erectus* ("upright" man – in fact the *australopithecines* probably spent most of their time upright, too) who developed **speech**, discovered how to make **fire** and improved enormously on the **tool-making** efforts of *Homo habilis*. **Olorgasailie** and **Kariandusi** are two "hand axe" sites, probably belonging to *Homo erectus*, which have been used within the last 500 thousand years. And it was *erectus* who, if the "cradle" theory is right, spread the humanoid gene pool to Asia, Europe and the rest of Africa, where, over the next few hundred thousand years, *Homo sapiens* emerged on the scene.

Fascinating and revealing as all this is, it's a remote kind of history. There is not necessarily any special connection between the evolutionary story in Kenya and the historical story of the last two thousand years or so.

EARLY INHABITANTS

Real history begins with the **hunter-gatherers**. Numbering probably fewer than a hundred thousand, living in small units of several families, and either staying in one place for generations or moving through the country according to the dictates of the seasons, these **earliest human inhabitants** may have been related to the ancestors of present-day Pygmy and Bushman peoples, and probably spoke "click" languages similar to those spoken by the Bushmen today (*Khoi* and *San*). Remnant hunter-gatherer groups still live in remote parts of Kenya – the **Boni** on the mainland north of Lamu, the **Sanye** along the Tana River and the **Okiek** and **Dorobo** in parts of the Highlands – but their languages are mostly adoptive ones from neighbouring peoples. The hunting and gathering way of life is one that has persisted in the cultural memories of most Kenyan peoples and some of the groups who still practise it may have veered away from farming or herding societies in times of hardship.

The earliest distinct migration to Kenya was of **Cushitic**-speaking people from the Ethiopian Highlands. Occasional hunters and gatherers themselves, they were also livestock herders and farmers; over the centuries, they filled the areas that were too dry for a purely subsistence way of life. They also absorbed many of the previous inhabitants through inter-marriage. Having herds and cultivating land brought up questions of ownership, inheritance and water rights, and an elaboration of social institutions and customs to deal with them. The Cushites left evidence of their settlements in burial cairns and living sites at places like **Hyrax Hill**, near Nakuru. Stone cairns and hollow depressions in the ground are found all over the Kenya Highlands and in the Rift Valley, especially out in the dry areas towards Lake

Turkana. The same people may have built the **irrigation works** still used today along the Elgeyo escarpment, west of Lake Baringo. They had a strong material culture, using stone, particularly obsidian, to produce beautiful arrowheads, knives and axes, and they made a whole range of pottery utensils as well.

The **Somali** and **Rendille** of the northeast are the main groups still speaking Cushitic languages, though their arrival in Kenya was more recent. Today, only the **Boni** still speak a language related to the Southern Cushitic of the first farmers and herders, although the Boni themselves are hunter-gatherers. For the most part, the earliest Cushites were absorbed by peoples who came later and they adopted new languages and customs. The changes were not all one-sided, however: **circumcision** and **clitoridectomy**, practised by the early Cushites, became important cultural rituals for many of the peoples who succeeded and absorbed them.

For present-day Kenya, the most important arrivals began to reach the country in the first few centuries AD. From the northwest and the headwaters of the Nile came the **Nilotic**-speaking ancestors of the **Kalenjin**; from the west and the south came speakers of **Bantu** languages, forebears of today's **Kikuyu**, **Gusii**, **Akamba** and **Mijikenda**, among others. (*Bantu*, a word coined by twentieth-century linguists, derives from the common stem for "person" – *ntu* – and the plural prefix *ba*. The word is not found in any of the 600 contemporary Bantu languages, spread across the continent, but it may have been the one used for "people" in the original proto-language before it diversified.)

The new arrivals brought not just themselves and their languages, but also new technologies, including iron-working. **Iron** had enabled the Bantu to spread from the Nigeria/Cameroon area across central Africa, clearing the virgin forests and hoeing the ground for their crops. Eastwards, they encountered new Asian food crops – bananas, yams and rice – which had arrived in East Africa by way of the Indonesian colonisation of Madagascar. This new diversity of foods helped people to settle permanently in chosen regions. The Kalenjin consolidated in the Western Highlands. But the Bantu were particularly successful and, as their broad economic base took hold across the southern half of Kenya, their languages quickly spread. Herding, hunting, fishing and gathering were important supplements to the agricultural mainstay, while trade conducted with their exclusively pastoral or hunter-gatherer neighbours, especially in iron tools, carried their influence further.

By **about 1000 AD**, Kenya's Stone Age technology had been largely replaced by an Iron Age one, and as human domination of the country increased, the beginnings of real specialisation in agriculture and herding set in among the peoples.

Down on **the coast**, Bantu immigrants mixed, over several hundred years, with the longer-established Cushitic-speaking inhabitants and with a continuous trickle of settlers from Arabia and the Persian Gulf. With the advent of Islam, this melange gradually gave rise to a distinct culture and civilisation – **Swahili** – speaking a Bantu language laced with foreign vocabulary. The Swahili were Kenya's link with the rest of the world, trading animal skins, ivory, agricultural produce and slaves for cloth, metals, ceramics, grain, ghee and sugar, with ships from the Middle East, India and even China. The Swahili were the first Kenyans to acquire firearms. They were also the first to write their language (in the Arabic script) and the first to develop complex, stratified communities based on town and countryside. Swahili history is covered in more depth in Chapter Five.

LATER ARRIVALS

New **American crops** – corn, cassava and tobacco – spread through Kenya after the Portuguese arrived at the beginning of the sixteenth century. They undoubtedly increased the country's population capacity, while enabling a greater degree of permanent settlement and providing new trade goods.

At about this time, a pastoral **Nilotic**-speaking people, distantly related to the earlier Kalenjin arrivals, began a migration from the northwest. These were the first **Luo**-speakers who, some generations earlier, had left their homeland (around Wau in southern Sudan) for reasons that were probably largely economic. In the alternately flooded and parched flatlands around the Nile, unusual conditions could be catastrophic. The Luo ancestors were always

on the move, herding, planting, hunting or fishing. Politically, they had a fairly complex organisation, as for months on end, while the Nile flooded, communities would be stranded in concentration along the low ridges. Several good years might be followed by drought, and population pressure then forced less dominant groups to go off in search of water and pasture. The overall trend was southwards. Groups of migrants picked up other, non-Luo-speakers on the way, gradually assimilating them through intermarriage and language change, always drawing attention with the impressive regalia and social standing of their **ruoth** – the Luo kings.

On the shores of Lake Victoria, where they finally settled, sleeping sickness is thought to have wiped out many of the Luo herds. But they were pragmatic, resourceful people, whose background of mixed farming and herding during the era of migration supported them. They turned to agriculture and, increasingly, to fishing.

Towards the end of the seventeenth century, another Nilotic, pastoral people, the **Turkana**, appeared in Kenya. Linguistically closer to the Maasai Nilotes, they seem to have shared the Luo resilience to economic hardship and they, too, have (recently) turned to fishing. Also like the Luo, and almost unique among Kenyan peoples, they have never practised circumcision.

The *Maa*-speakers – **Maasai** and **Samburu** – were the last group to arrive in Kenya, and their rise and fall had far-reaching effects on neighbouring peoples. Moving southwards from the beginning of the seventeenth century, their nomadic pastoral lifestyle enabled them to expand swiftly and, in a few generations, they were transformed from an obscure group into a dominant force in the region. Culturally, they borrowed extensively from their neighbours, especially the **Kalenjin**. Kalenjin words and cultural values were adopted, including circumcision, the age-set system and some ancient (originally, probably Cushitic) taboos against eating fish and certain wild animals. It is likely that much of the "traditional" Maasai appearance also owes something to these contacts. The Maasai migration was no slow spread. Their cattle were periodically herded south and other peoples were raided en route to enlarge the herds; by 1800, they were widely established in the Rift Valley and on the plains, everywhere between Lake Turkana and Kilimanjaro. In response to Maasai dominance, many of the Bantu peoples adopted their styles and customs. Initiation by genital mutilation, probably already practised by most Bantu-speakers, was imbued with a new significance – especially for the Kikuyu – by intermarriage and close, if not always peaceable, relations with the Maasai.

Severe **droughts** in the nineteenth century pushed the Maasai further and further afield in search of new pastures, bringing them into conflict, and trade, with other peoples. Drought, disease and rinderpest epidemics (which killed off their cattle) were also responsible for a series of civil wars between different Maasai sections in the second half of the nineteenth century.

These **Maasai civil wars** disrupted the **trading networks** which had been set up between the coast and the interior, mainly by Swahili, Mijikenda, Akamba and Kikuyu. Dutch, English and French goods were finding their way up-country, and American interests were already being served nearly two centuries ago, as white calico cloth (still called *amerikani* today) became a major item of profit. From western Kenya and Uganda, **slaves** were being exported in exchange for foreign commerce in the last throes of the slave trade's existence. Largely in response to slavery and widespread fighting, the first **missionaries** installed themselves up-country (the earliest went inland from Mombasa in 1846). Throughout this period, the Maasai disrupted movements through their territories and attacked Swahili slavers, Bantu traders and explorer-missionaries alike. The Maasai *morani* were specifically trained for raiding – a kind of guerrilla warfare – but, while their reputation lived on, they were bitterly divided among themselves and not organised on anything like a tribal scale.

By the time Europe had partitioned the map of Africa, the Maasai, who could have been the imperialists' most intractable enemies, were unable to retaliate effectively. The Kalenjin-speaking **Nandi** of the western highlands, who had begun to take the Maasai's place as Kenya's most feared adversaries, put up the stiffest resistance. They were organised

to the extent of having a single spiritual leader, the *orkoiyot*, who ruled what was in effect a theocracy. Their war of attrition against the British delayed advances for a number of years. But the Nandi did not have the territorial advantage that would have helped the Maasai, and the murder of their *orkoiyot*, **Koitalel**, by the British, destroyed their military organisation.

THE INVASION: 1885–1902

All Kenya's peoples resisted colonial domination to some degree. In the first twenty years of British attempts to rule, tens of thousands were killed in ugly massacres and manhunts, and many more were made homeless. Administrators – whose memoirs (see "Books") are the most revealing background for that period – all differed in their ideas of the ultimate purpose of their work and the best means of imposing British authority.

British interests in East Africa at the close of the last century had sprung from the European power struggle and the "scramble for Africa". The 1885 Berlin Conference chopped the continent into arbitrary spheres of influence. Germany was awarded what was to become Tanganyika; Britain got Kenya and Uganda. In 1886, formal agreements were drawn up and Kilimanjaro was ceded to Victoria's grandson, the Kaiser, giving each monarch a snowcapped equatorial mountain.

But rivalry wasn't far beneath the red tape and Germany clearly had Uganda earmarked. Sir William Mackinnon, who for a decade had been pressing for a licence to start trading, was now given permission to start commercial operations with his *Imperial British East Africa Company* (*IBEAC*) in 1888. The company officers – mostly young and totally inexperienced English clerks – established a series of trading forts at fifty-mile intervals in a line connected by a rough ox-track leading from Mombasa into Uganda. Machakos, Murang'a and Mumias all began as *IBEAC* stations. **Uganda** was the focus of interest, since Kenya – decimated by drought, locusts, rinderpest and civil war – seemed largely a deserted wasteland. And Uganda was strategically important for **control of the Nile** – which had long been a British preoccupation. Conspiring foreign powers were mentioned darkly in the House of Lords.

Britain's claim was in danger of lapsing if Uganda could not be properly garrisoned and supplied. It was also a centre for the **slave trade** that Britain, in need not of slaves but of new markets, was committed to wiping out. And in the back of many minds was the kind of sentiment expressed by the London *Times* in 1873:

There seems no reason not to believe that one of the finest parts of the world's surface is going to waste under the shroud of malaria which surrounds it, and under the barbarous anarchy with which it is cursed. The idea dawns upon some of us that some better destiny is yet in store for a region so blessed by nature, and the development of Africa is a step yet to come in the development of the world.

In the end, the practicability of developing "some better destiny" for Uganda proved out of reach.

With the bankruptcy of the *IBEAC* and its failure to establish any kind of administration, the British government formally stepped into the breach in 1885 and declared a **Protectorate** over Uganda and Kenya. Having acquired the country in a haphazard lottery, the government was now forced to do something with it. A useful gesture was required, one that had been moot in parliament for years. Her Majesty's government decided to build a **railway**. This classic, valedictory piece of Victorian engineering took six years to complete and cost the lives of hundreds of Indian labourers. Financially, it was a commitment which grew out of all proportion to the likely returns and continued to grow long after the last rail was laid. But its completion transformed the future of East Africa. From now on, the supply lines were secure and the interior only a month's journey from Europe by ship and rail. Suddenly the prospects for developing the cool, fertile Kenya Highlands looked much more attractive than the distant unknowns of Uganda and its powerful kingdoms.

More immediately, the railway physically divided the **Maasai** at a time when they were already disunified and moving into alliances with the British. Their grazing lands, together with the regions of the **Kalenjin** and **Kikuyu** on the lower slopes of the Highlands, were to become the heartland of white settlerdom.

THE KENYA COLONY

While the government, typically, dragged its feet, the story circulated that Kenya might be a land of opportunity: a new New Zealand, or even a Jewish homeland. A party of Zionists was in fact escorted around Kenya but declined the offer. It was Sir Charles Eliot, the Protectorate's second governor, who was the main mover behind the settlement scheme. While there was an undercurrent of consideration for "the rights of natives" (which shouldn't be forgotten; many blind eyes were turned on what took place in Kenya ninety years ago), the growing clamour of voices claiming the support of British taxpayers – who had met the bill for the railway – outweighed any altruism. Eliot's extravagant reports on the potential of BEA (British East Africa) were published and, willy-nilly, government policy was directed towards getting the settlers in and making the railway pay. Landless aristocrats, middle-class adventurers, big-game hunters, ex-servicemen and Afrikaners (the farming land was also advertised in South Africa) began to trickle up the line. Using ox-wagons to get to the tracts of bush they had leased, they started their farms from scratch. Lord Delamere, governor himself for a time, was their biggest champion. In the years leading up to World War I, the trickle of settlers became a flood and by 1916 the area "alienated" to Europeans had risen to 15,000 square kilometres of the best land. Imported livestock was hybridised with hardy, local breeds; coffee, tea, sisal and pineapples were introduced and thrived; European crops flourished in superabundance and cereals soon covered thousands of hectares.

Nearly half the land worth farming was now in the hands of settlers, but it had rapidly become clear that it was far from empty of local inhabitants. Colonial invasion had occurred at a low point in the fortunes of Kenya's peoples and, unprepared for the scale of the incursion, they were swiftly pushed aside into "Native Reserves" or became "squatters" without rights. As populations recovered, serious land shortages set in. The British appointment of "chiefs" – whose main task was to collect a tax on every hut – had the effect of diverting grievances against colonial policy on to these early collaborators and laying the foundations of a class structure in

Kenyan society. Without a money economy, employment was the only means available to pay taxes and, effectively, a system of forced labour had been created. The whole apparatus quickly became entrenched in a series of **land and labour laws**. A poll tax was added to the hut tax; all African men were compelled to register to facilitate labour recruitment; squatters on alienated land were required to pay rent, through labour; and cash cropping on African plots was discouraged or banned (coffee licences, for example, were restricted to white farmers). The Highlands were strictly reserved for white settlement, while land not owned by Europeans became Crown Land, its African occupants "tenants at will" of the Crown and liable to summary eviction.

Asians, too, were excluded from the Highlands. While the leader of Kenya's Indians, **A. M. Jeevanjee**, had called for the transformation of Kenya into the "America of the Hindu", the proposal never came near consideration by the British. Barred from farming on any scale – except in the far west, where they developed sugar cane as an important crop – Indians concentrated on the middle ground, setting up general stores (*dukas*) across the country, investing in small industries and handling services.

WORLD WAR I

World War I, although there were comparatively few battles in Kenya itself, had a number of profound effects. Some 200,000 African porters and soldiers were conscripted and sent to Tanganyika (German East Africa), where one in four of them died. Those who returned were deeply influenced by the experience. They had seen European tribes at war with each other, they had experienced European fallibility, and witnessed the kind of organisation used to overcome it.

General von Lettow Vorbeck, the German commander, waged a dogged campaign against British forces despite the fact that his own were vastly outnumbered, with the aim of engaging as much manpower as possible and taking the heat off German forces in Europe. He earned a respectable place in the history books as a result. Nevertheless, the Germans lost the war – and Tanganyika – to the British, and the Crown's commitments in East Africa were suddenly multiplied.

Sir Edward Northey, governor of Kenya at the time of armistice, pushed his **Soldier Settlement Scheme** through without difficulty. Its aim, to double the settler population in Kenya to 9000 and increase revenue, seemed promising enough to a government sapped by war. But the Soldier Settlement Scheme was bitterly resented by Africans, particularly those who had fought beside the soldiers and were now excluded from their gains.

EARLY NATIONALISM AND REACTION

Political associations sprang up among mission-educated and ex-servicemen: the *Kikuyu Association*, the *Young Kikuyu Association*, and the *Young Kavirondo Association*. **Harry Thuku,** secretary of the *Young Kikuyu Association*, realised its potential and reformed it as the *East Africa Association* in order to recruit on a nationwide basis. The hated registration law by which every African was obliged to carry a pass – the *kipande* – was a prime grievance, but tax reduction, introduction of land title deeds and wage increases were demanded as well. Alliances were built up with embittered Indian associations and 1921 saw a year of **protests** and rallies. These culminated in Thuku's detention, **violent suppression** and the shooting by police of 25 demonstrators at a mass rally calling for Thuku's release. He remained in detention for eleven years.

The Indian constituency eventually secured two nominated seats (not elected) on the Legislative Council. Africans meanwhile remained voiceless, landless, disenfranchised and segregated by the colour bar.

As the settlers became established, they began to contribute appreciably to the income of **the colony** (which Kenya had officially become in 1920). Most of them seem to have believed that they were in at the beginning of a long and glorious pageant of **white dominion.** Indeed, settler self-government, along Canadian or South African lines, was a declared aim. African demands were hardly heeded by the authorities, but the Colonial Office was in a difficult position over the **Indians,** who were already British subjects and whose demands for equal rights they had trouble in refuting. Tentative proposals to give them voting rights, allow unrestricted immigration from India and abolish segregation caused alarm and indignation among the settlers. Their *Convention of Associations*, already arguing the case for White Home Rule, formed a "Vigilance Committee", which worked out detailed military plans for rebellion, including the kidnapping of the governor and the deportation of the Indians. Sensing a crisis, the Colonial Office drew up a white paper and a grudging settlement was reached that allowed five Indians and one Arab to be elected to the Legislative Council (the colony's local government), as opposed to eleven Europeans.

The primacy of African "interests", admirably reiterated yet again in the *Devonshire Declaration*, was still denied any real expression, least of all by Africans themselves. A system of *de facto* **apartheid** was being practised. It was in this climate in the 1920s and 1930s that, floating above their economic troubles, the settlers had their heyday – the Happy **Valley life** so appallingly and fascinatingly depicted in *White Mischief* and other books.

EDUCATION, KENYATTA AND THE KIKUYU

The opportunities available to Africans came almost entirely through **mission schools** at first. Again, there was conflict between government and settlers on the question of **education**. The Colonial Office was committed, on paper at least, to the general development of the country for all its inhabitants, while the white farmers were on the whole adamant that raising educational standards could only lead to trouble. A crude form of Swahili had become the language of communication between Africans and Europeans. But the teaching of English was a controversial issue that hardliners foresaw eventually rebounding on government and settlers alike. In frustration, self-help **Kikuyu independent schools** were set up in the 1930s, primarily in order to teach their own children English.

Whether barring access to English education would ultimately have made any difference is debatable, but by the late 1930s there were already enough educated Africans to pose the beginnings of a serious challenge to white supremacy. One of these was **Jomo Kenyatta***. After Thuku's imprisonment and the subsequent bloodshed at Nairobi in 1922, the *East African Association* was dissolved. It was succeeded by the **Kikuyu Central Association (KCA)**, which Kenyatta joined in

1928. The *KCA* was the spearhead of **nationalism** and lobbied hard for a return of alienated land, the lowering of taxes and for elected African representatives on the Legislative Council. It also protested against missionary efforts to outlaw "**female circumcision**" on the grounds that the church was attempting to undermine Kikuyu culture. This last conflict led to a leadership crisis in the *KCA* and for a number of years threatened to swamp other issues. But Kenyatta spent most of the period between 1931 and 1946 in Britain, campaigning for the *KCA*, studying anthropology under Malinowski at the London School of Economics and writing his homage to the Kikuyu people, *Facing Mount Kenya*.

Kenya survived the 1929 stock market crash and the resulting world **trade slump** as the colonial government became increasingly committed to the struggling settlers it was now bailing out. Exports fell catastrophically, coffee planting by non-whites was still prohibited and the tax burden continued to be placed squarely on Africans. Faced with this crisis, even some of the settlers began to accept that large-scale changes were in order. Just as awareness was growing that the economy could not survive indefinitely unless Africans were given more of a chance to participate in it, Kenya was thrown into World War II.

WORLD WAR II . . . AND MAU MAU

Perhaps not surprisingly, soldiers were easily recruited into the **King's African Rifles** when Italian-held Ethiopia (then Abyssinia) declared war on Kenya. By a combination of carrot and stick, thousands of young men were drafted. Volunteers wanted money, education and a chance to see the world; conscripts, filling the quotas assigned to their chiefs, faced a life at home or on the reserve that was no better. Propaganda immediately succeeded in casting Hitler's image as the embodiment of all racist evil. Some Africans thought the war, once won,

---

* Kenyatta, born in the late 1890s, went to a mission school and was baptised a Christian. He had also been circumcised and initiated into Kikuyu adulthood. His name was adopted from the shop he ran in Nairobi, *Kenyatta Stores*, after the traditional beaded belt he always wore.

would improve their position in Kenya. They were partly right. Military campaigns in Ethiopia and Burma owed much of their success to African troops and during the war their efforts were glowingly praised by Allied commanders.

On the soldiers' return, a new awareness, similar to that felt by the returning porters and *askaris* of World War I, but more profound, had crept up on them. The white tribes of Europe had fought the war on the issue of self-determination: the message wasn't lost on Africans. Yet still, in almost every other sphere of life, they were demeaned and humiliated. The *KCA* had been banned at the outbreak of war, allegedly for supporting the Italian fascists, and African political life was subdued. Real change, for 99 percent of the population, was still a dream.

Kenya's food-exporting economy had done well out of the war and it was clear the colony could make a major contribution to Britain's recovery. The post-war Labour government encouraged economic expansion without going far to include Africans among the beneficiaries of the investment. Industrialisation gathered momentum and there was a rapid growth of towns. There was also further promotion of **white immigration** – a new influx of European settlers arrived soon after the war – and greater power was given to the settlers on the Legislative and Executive Councils. Population growth and intense **pressure on land** in the rural areas were leading to severe disruptions of traditional community life as people were shunted into the reserves or else left their villages to search for work in the towns. On the political front, militant **trade unionism**, dominated by ex-servicemen, gradually usurped the positions of those African leaders who had been prepared to work with the government.

POST-WAR AFRICAN POLITICS

A single African member, Eliud Mathu, was appointed to the Legislative Council in 1944. More significant, however, was the formation of the *Kenya African Union (KAU)*, a consultative group of leaders and spokesmen set up with the governor's approval to be a liaison with Mathu. The *KAU*'s first president was Harry Thuku but it was **Kenyatta**'s return from England in 1946, to an unexpectedly tumultuous hero's welcome, that signalled a real

departure for African political rights and the birth of a new current of nationalism. *KAU* was transformed into an active political party – and ran straight into conflict with itself. The **radicals** within the party wanted sweeping changes in land ownership, equal voting rights and abolition of the pass law. The **moderates** were for negotiation, educational improvement, multi-racial progress and a gradual shift of power. Nor were the moderates convinced that their own best interests lay in confronting the British head on: they had all achieved considerable ambitions within the settler economy. Kenyatta was ambitious himself but the Europeans mistrusted his intentions and rumour-mongered about his communist connections, his visit to Russia during his time abroad and his personal life.

Despite Kenyatta's efforts to steer a middle course, *KAU* became increasingly radical and Kikuyu-dominated. While he angled to give the party a multi-tribal profile to appease the settlers, he also managed to sacrifice some moderates in the leadership for the sake of party unity. But there were defections as well. Several radicals, including **Dedan Kimathi**, joined an underground movement and took **oaths** of allegiance against the British. Betrayal of the movement was punished by execution and collaborators with the government faced the same threat. Oathing groups emerged secretly all around the Highlands and, by 1952, a central committee was organised to coordinate activities.

THE MAU MAU REBELLION

The question of how much the *KAU* leadership was involved in what came to be known as **Mau Mau** (from *Muma*, a traditional Kikuyu oath) is one that reappeared time after time in the years leading to and after independence. Certainly *Mau Mau* attracted large numbers of young men from the rural periphery of towns like Nyeri, Fort Hall and Nairobi, and they used Kenyatta's name in their propaganda. Many members had taken part in strikes in the late 1940s: they were mobilised into violent action by the shortage of land on the reserves and the contrast with the new-found success of the settlers. There was a burning desire to oust the Europeans from the "White Highlands". The *Mau Mau* oath-takers called themselves the

Land and Freedom Army*.* **Ex-soldiers** who had fought for the British, many of whom had learned guerrilla warfare in Burma, were crucial to their military effort.

Kenyatta played a delicate political game, condemning strikes and even oath-taking but ready to seize on any chance to exploit the situation. In 1952, incensed by simmering African nationalism and random outbursts of violence on white farms, the settlers pressured the government into declaring a **state of emergency**. *Mau Mau* was banned and all African nationalist organisations were proscribed. Kenyatta and other *KAU* leaders were arrested, convicted of founding and managing *Mau Mau* – on the flimsiest evidence – and sent into internal exile. For the next four years, while "The Emergency" blazed and African political life was brought, once again, to a virtual standstill, the full weight of British military muscle was brought to bear against the revolt, barely forty years since the era of "punitive expeditions".

Thousands of **British troops** were sent to Kenya. To them, every African was a potential terrorist, every homestead a *Mau Mau* hideout. As the troops moved in, the hard-core guerrillas fled into the forest and lived off the jungle for months on end, launching surprise attacks at night. They relied on considerable support from the Kikuyu homesteads for supplies, intelligence reports and stolen weapons. Under emergency powers, a policy of "villagisation" was enforced and tens of thousands of Kikuyu were relocated to "secure villages" or detained in barbed-wire concentration camps: at one point, one-third of the entire male Kikuyu population was being held in detention.

The **end of the revolt** came with the British capture and execution of **Dedan Kimathi**, the *Land and Freedom Army's* commander-in-chief. Helicopters and defoliant were brought in to flush out the last pockets of resistance, but in any case morale was low. The Western press made much of *Mau Mau* atrocities, though a total of just 32 European civilians and about fifty troops were killed in the struggle. For Africans, the figure was around 13,000 men, women and children, mainly Kikuyu. Many of these, uncommitted to *Mau Mau,* yet living in key locations as far as the British were concerned, were caught, sometimes literally, in the crossfire.

The authorities described *Mau Mau* as a tribal uprising, a meaningless explosion of tension. Paranoid settlers perceived an external communist threat in the uprising. Some observers, more critically, went so far as to call it a Kikuyu civil war between those established on the reserves and others – the guerrillas – newly displaced from European farms. And while Akamba, Maasai, Luo, Meru and Embu did join the *Land and Freedom Army*, its membership was overwhelmingly Kikuyu-speaking. As a focus for nationalism, the revolt served as a political barometer: the tension between the loyalists and the rebels and their sympathisers was the fulcrum on which Kenyan politics was to swing in the years leading up to and after independence. Jomo Kenyatta was in many ways lucky to have been forced to sit out the period, on the fence, in detention.

INDEPENDENCE – UHURU

With the emergency over, the *KAU* leaders still at liberty set about exploiting the European fear of a repeat episode. Anything that now delayed the fulfillment of African nationalist aspirations could be seen as fuel for another revolt. There was no longer any question of a Rhodesia-style, white-dominated independence. Settlers, mindful of the **preparations for independence** taking place in other African countries, began rallying to the cry of multi-racialism in a vain attempt to secure what looked like a very shaky future.

At the 1960 Lancaster House Conference in London, African representatives won a convincing victory by pushing through measures to give them majorities in the Legislative Council and the Council of Ministers. Members, all nominated by the colonial authorities, included **Tom Mboya**, the prominent and charismatic Luo trade unionist, and the radical politician **Oginga Odinga** (another Luo), as well as **Daniel Arap Moi** and the Mijikenda leader **Ronald Ngala**. A new constitution was drawn up and eventual access to the White Highlands was accepted. The declaration promised that "Kenya was to be an African country": the path to independence was guaranteed. **Macmillan** was saying as much in his "Wind of Change" speech given to the South African Parliament at the time the Lancaster House Conference was meeting. The settlers perceived a "calamitous betrayal", with universal franchise and African-dominated independence expected within ten years. (In fact, it happened earlier than anticipated.) Minority tribal associations meanwhile foresaw troubles ahead if the **Kikuyu-Luo elite** achieved independence for Kenya at the cost of the smaller constituencies. In 1960, the *Kenya African National Union (KANU)* was formed. Soon after, a second, more moderate party, the *Kenya African Democratic Union (KADU)*, was created, to federate the minority, largely rural-based, political associations in a broad defensive alliance against Kikuyu-Luo domination.

Elections were held in 1961 and *KANU* emerged with nineteen seats against *KADU*'s eleven. But *KANU* refused to form a government until Kenyatta was released. Settlers began to leave the country, selling their farms and evacuating before the predicted collapse of European privilege – or even holocaust – that some feared if the "leader unto darkness and death" were set free.

A temporary coalition government was formed, composed of *KADU*, European and Asian members. Kenyatta was duly released and, six months later, a member resigned his seat, making room for him on the Legislative Council. In 1962, Kenyatta became Minister for Constitutional Affairs and Economic Planning – a wide portfolio – in a new coalition government formed out of the *KADU* alliance and *KANU*. Despite a second London conference to try to reach an agreement about the federal constitution demanded by *KADU*, the question was left in the air. Independence elections the following year (though the Somalis of the northeast, who had no wish to be in Kenya, boycotted them) seemed to answer the constitutional question. *KANU* emerged with an even greater lead and a mandate for a non-federal structure. On June 1 – Madaraka Day – Kenyatta became Kenya's first prime minister. And on December 12, 1963, control of foreign affairs was handed over and Kenya became formally **independent**.

THE KENYATTA YEARS – HARAMBEE

It was barely sixty years since the pioneer settlers had arrived. Many of them – those who hadn't panicked and sold out – were now determined to stay and risk the future under an **African government**. Despite his unjust seven years in detention, Kenyatta turned out to have more consideration for their interests than could have been foreseen. He held successful meetings with settlers in his home village; his bearded, genial image and conciliatory speeches assuring them of their rights and security quickly earned him the respected title *Mzee* and wide international support. Many Europeans retained important positions in administration and the judiciary.

Milton Obote and Julius Nyerere, leaders of newly independent Uganda and Tanzania, held talks with Kenyatta on setting up an **East African Community** to share railways, aviation, postal services and telecommunications, and customs and excise. This was formally inaugurated in 1967. There was a mood of optimism: it looked very much as if Kenya had succeeded against all the odds.

But there were urgent issues to contend with. **Land reform** and the rehabilitation of freedom fighters and detainees were the most pressing. Large tracts of European land were bought up and a programme to provide small plots to landless peasants was rapidly instigated. Political questions loomed large as well. On December 12, 1964, Kenya became a republic, its head of state no longer the Queen, but rather President Kenyatta. *KADU* was dissolved "in the interests of national unity", its leaders absorbed into the ruling *KANU* party. There was, it seemed, no longer any need for an opposition: everyone was on the same side and Kenya was henceforth a *de facto* one-party state. For the sake of "national security", British troops were kept on, initially to quell a revolt of ethnic Somalis in the northeast and an army mutiny in Nairobi. A defence treaty has kept a British force at Nanyuki ever since.

There was heavy emphasis on cooperation and unity. The spirit of *Harambee* (pulling together) was endorsed by Kenyatta at all his public appearances. *Harambee* meetings became a unique national institution, fundraising events at which – in a not untraditional way – donations were made by local notables and politicians towards self-help health-care and educational programmes. During the 1960s and 1970s, hundreds of *Harambee* schools were built and equipped in this way. But the ostentatious gifts, and particularly the guaranteed press coverage the next day with donors listed in order of value, sometimes reduced the

Harambee vision of community development to an exercise in patronage and competitive status seeking.

On the **economic front**, the first decade of independence saw remarkable changes and rapid growth. Although only a quarter of the country gets enough rainfall to make it agriculturally reliable, the settlers' fairly broad-based crop-exporting economy was a powerful springboard for development; one, moreover, that wasn't difficult to transfer to predominantly African control. While many large landholdings were sold *en bloc* to African investors, smaller farmers did begin to contribute significantly to export earnings through coffee, tea, pyrethrum and fruit.

Industrialisation proceeded at a slower pace. Kenya's mineral resources are very limited and the country relies heavily on oil imports. **Foreign investment** wasn't especially beneficial as investors were given wide freedoms to import equipment and technical skills and to re-export much of the profit.

Growth, rather than a radical redistribution of wealth, was the government's main concern. Although by 1970 more than two-thirds of the European mixed farming lands were occupied by some 50,000 Africans, and the overall standard of living had improved considerably, income disparities were greater than ever. And 16,000 square kilometres of ranch lands and plantations remained largely in foreign hands.

From the outset, it was clear that the **fruits of independence** were not going to be shared fairly. Kikuyu-Luo domination – but particularly Kikuyu – was irksome and strongly resented by other groups. It was perhaps inevitable that the people who had lost most and suffered most under British rule should expect to receive the most benefits from independence. However, many Kikuyu had also been able to take advantage, as far as it was possible, of the settler economy by earning wages, setting up businesses and sending their children to school.

The resettlement programme was abandoned in 1966, its objectives "largely attained". But many peasants, having been squatters on European farms, were now "illegal squatters" on private African land. Thousands migrated to the towns where unemployment was already a serious problem. Kenya was becoming a class-divided society.

POLITICAL OPPOSITION... AND REACTION

It was in this climate that *KANU*'s leadership split. **Oginga Odinga**, the party vice-president, resigned in 1966 to form the socialist **Kenya People's Union (KPU)** and 29 MPs joined him. The ex-guerrilla Bildad Kaggia became deputy head of the *KPU* and a vocal agitator for poorer Kikuyu. Kenyatta and Mboya closed ranks in *KANU* and prepared for political conflict. *KPU* was anti-capitalist and claimed to speak on behalf of the masses, who it maintained had been betrayed by *Uhuru*. On foreign affairs it was firmly non-aligned. Denouncing the opposition, *KANU* – led in this respect by Tom Mboya – stressed the need for close ties with the West, for commercial enterprise and foreign investment, and for economic conditions that would attract foreign aid. Ideologically, *KANU* talked of "African socialism". *KPU*'s stand was claimed to be divisive: the country should be pulling together to fight the triple evils of poverty, ignorance and disease.

KPU was barely tolerated for three years, its members harassed and detained by the security forces, its activities obstructed by new legislation and constitutional amendments. Odinga was succeeded, briefly, in the post of vice-president by Joseph Murumbi and then Daniel Arap Moi.

Odinga had strong, grassroots support in the Luo and Gusii districts of western Kenya. But **Tom Mboya**'s supporters came from an even broader base, including many poor Kikuyu. By the end of the 1960s, speculation was mounting about whether he would be able to take over the presidency on Kenyatta's death. As the *Mzee*'s right-hand man he was widely tipped to succeed – a possibility that alarmed Kenyatta's Kikuyu supporters. The republic's second political **assassination*** decided the matter: Mboya was gunned down by a Kikuyu assassin in central Nairobi on July 5, 1969. No high-level complicity in the murder was ever brought to light, but Mboya's death was a devastating blow to Kenya's fragile stability, setting off shock waves along both class and tribal divisions. There was widespread fighting

---

* The first was that of Pia Gama Pinto, an outspoken Goan communist politician who was killed in 1965.

and rioting between Kikuyu and Luo, fuelled by years of rivalry and growing feelings of Luo exclusion from government. During a visit by Kenyatta to Kisumu – where he attended a public meeting at which Odinga and his supporters were present – hostility against his entourage was so great that police opened fire, killing at least ten demonstrators.

The *KPU* was immediately banned and Odinga detained without trial. Although the constitution continued to guarantee the right to form opposition parties, non-*KANU* nominations to parliament were, in practice, forbidden. There was a resurgence of oath-taking among Kikuyu, Meru and Embu, pledging to maintain the Kikuyu hold on power. The Kikuyu contingent in the army was strengthened and a new force of shock troops, the *General Service Unit (GSU)*, was recruited under Kikuyu officers: independent of police and army, it was to act as an internal security force. In the early 1970s, Kikuyu control – of the government, the administration, business interests and land – gripped tighter and tighter.

Internationally, however, Kenya was seen as one of the safest African investments – a model of stability and democracy only too happy to allow the multinational corporations access to its resources and markets. The development of the tourist industry helped give the country a bright and positive profile. And, in comparison with most other African countries, some still fighting for independence and others beset by civil war or paralysed by drought, Kenya's future looked healthy enough.

But in achieving record economic growth, foreign interests often seemed to crush indigenous ones. An elite of rich profiteers – nicknamed the **Wabenzi** after the Mercedes they favoured – extracted enormous private gains out of transactions with foreign companies. Nepotism was blatant and Kenyatta himself was rumoured to be one of the richest men in the world. For the mass of Kenyan people, life was hardly any better than before independence. Graduates poured out of the secondary schools with few prospects of using their qualifications; population increase was (and remains) the highest in the world; and most damaging of all, land distribution was still grossly unfair in a society where land was the basic means of making a living for nearly all.

In 1975, in the first ever explicit public attack on the Kikuyu monopoly of power, the radical populist MP **J. M. Kariuki** warned that Kenya could become a country of "ten millionaires and ten million beggars". He was arrested for his pains, then, some weeks later, was found murdered in the Ngong Hills. Reaction was stunned and a massive turnout at his funeral was followed by angry **student demonstrations**. Kariuki's appeal had derived from unimpeachable honesty and forthrightness and a stubborn perseverance in addressing the issues of economic and social justice. He riled his opponents by his sincerity and his refusal to espouse any easily shot-down ideology. Although a Kikuyu himself, from a non-ruling northern clan, a former *Mau Mau* detainee and at one time a close associate of Kenyatta, he was unquestionably a threat to the Kikuyu power base. A parliamentary report on his death had two prominent names deleted at Kenyatta's demand. "Kariuki's death," wrote the then outspoken *Weekly Review*, "instills in the minds of the public the fear of dissidence, the fear to criticise, the fear to stand out and take an unconventional public stance." Kenyatta and the Kikuyu clique meant business. In the following years, a number of other MPs were detained. The burning issue of landlessness was no longer one many people were prepared to shout about.

As criticism at home was suffocated, foreign criticism of the direction Kenya was taking began to grow. Early in 1975, a series of bomb explosions in Nairobi – attributed to a "poor people's" liberation group – drew attention to the country: the foreign press carried reports of entrenched **corruption** from the president and his family down. Kariuki's murder and, later, a parliamentary row over ivory smuggling in which Kenyatta was heavily implicated, refocused attention on Kenya. But the government was far from inviting serious condemnation from the West. Kenya was seen, despite its formal non-alignment, as a staunchly anti-communist ally of Britain and America, and a recipient of massive grants and loans (for which, in return, foreign investors were allowed to reap handsome profits). And as was rightly pointed out, there was no clear successor to the president nor any effective opposition worth cultivating.

Kenyatta had retreated into dictatorial seclusion, propped up by close Kikuyu cronies, among them Chief Koinange and Charles Njonjo, who ten years later was to cause a political storm. As parliament, and even the cabinet, took an increasingly passive role in decision-making, the pronouncements from the *Mzee*'s "court" began to be accompanied by vague suggestions of threats to his government from unspecified foreign powers. By 1977, the **East African Community** had ceased to function. Its structure had always favoured Kenya as the strongest member, and it was wracked by mistrust between Kenya and Tanzania, then further torn by Idi Amin's 1971 coup in Uganda. Kenya finally seized the lion's share of community assets, mostly ships and rolling stock in the territory at the time. Hostility towards Tanzania's socialist policies, delayed elections, further detentions and growing allegations of corruption formed the sullen backdrop to **Kenyatta's death**, in bed, on August 28, 1978.

KENYA IN THE 1980S – NYAYO

The passing of the *Mzee* took Kenya by surprise. There was a nationwide outpouring of grief and shock. Mourners filed past the coffin for days. For many, however, there was also a profound sense of relief and anticipation. An era was over and the future might better reflect the ideas of twenty years earlier.

Fears about the succession proved unfounded as vice-president **Daniel Arap Moi** smoothly assumed power with the help of Mwai Kibaki and Charles Njonjo. He quickly gathered popular support with moves against corruption in the civil service (where the mass of Kenyans felt it most), his stand against tribal nepotism (he himself comes from a minority group, the Kalenjin), and the release of all Kenyatta's political prisoners. The press, too, traditionally circumspect and conservative, relaxed a little. Moi assured Kenya and the world that, while he would not be making radical departures from Kenyatta's policies, the more blatant iniquities of the old guard's paternalistic system would be ironed out.

But the honeymoon was short. Odinga and other ex-*KPU* MPs were prevented from standing in the general elections of 1979. **Student protests**, focusing on the anniversary of

Kariuki's murder, began again: the closing of the university became an annual event. On the international scene, the whole Indian Ocean region became strategically important with the fall of the Shah of Iran and the Soviet invasion of Afghanistan. Kenya developed significantly closer ties with the **United States**, extending military facilities to American vessels in exchange for gifts of grain after a failure of the harvest in 1983. Ironically, the country's own surplus had been exported the previous year.

In the early years of his presidency, Moi's **Nyayo** (footsteps) philosophy of "peace, love and unity" in the wake of Kenyatta found wide appeal, and his apparent honesty and outspoken attacks against tribalism impressed many, making him friends abroad, too. But the failure to make any adjustments in economic policy in favour of the rural and urban poor resulted in strong, if muted, criticism at home. The propertied elite is no longer dominated so heavily by Kikuyu, but it continues to thrive. Corruption, meanwhile, has re-emerged as a national woe.

THE AUGUST COUP ATTEMPT

Two major events have rocked the government in the last decade. On Sunday, August 1, 1982 – three months after constitutional amendments were pushed through by Njonjo to make Kenya officially a one-party state – sections of the Kenya Air Force attempted a **military coup**. Kenyans woke to the sound of continuous Bob Marley on the radio, a repeated coup broadcast and, in Nairobi at least, sporadic gunfire. There was widespread confusion for several hours. The *People's Redemption Council*, who had taken the radio station, were unknown: there had been no lead-up. Most of the army was on military exercise in the north, and at first the air force rebels were in control. During the course of the day, hundreds of shops, especially in Nairobi, were looted, mostly by civilians. Asians, particularly, suffered huge losses: a number of Asian women were raped and many Asian homes ransacked.

By the end of the day, the "coup" had disintegrated into a free-for-all but, as it became clear that pre-arranged support among other armed forces had not been organised, the army and the *GSU* consolidated against the *KAF*, shooting hundreds of men, raping and killing women and patrolling the streets on the look-out for rebels. Dozens of students were killed. The government announced 159 deaths, but witnesses claim to have seen more bodies on a single street.

In the immediate aftermath of the coup attempt, thousands of airmen were arrested and the service itself was disbanded. The university, believed to be a "breeding ground for subversion", was dissolved. Fourteen airmen were sentenced to death though only two, who had fled to asylum in Tanzania, were eventually executed when handed back to Kenya. There had been considerable Luo involvement in the attempt to seize power and Oginga Odinga was once again placed under house arrest.

THE NJONJO AFFAIR AND AFTER

Foreign investors held their breath and tourist bookings slumped, but postmortems of the uprising faded as the country was distracted by a new political drama – the "**Njonjo affair**". In May 1983, Moi announced to an astonished parliament that he had evidence that a foreign power was grooming a politician to take over as president. The charges were unspecific but the Attorney General **Charles Njonjo**'s name was mentioned and he rapidly fell from grace. A member of the Kikuyu elite who had shored up Kenyatta, Njonjo was a skilled politician with a wide circle of influence outside Kenya. His name was often linked with South Africa and Israel; during the judicial enquiry into his activities it was alleged that he had embezzled *KANU* money, that he was privy to the coup attempt and also to another in the Seychelles. More crucially, there was intense rivalry between Njonjo and Mwai Kibaki, the sober and respected vice-president, over the question of succession.

The case, which filled the papers for over a year, was brought to a close with the purge from *KANU* of Njonjo's associates. He himself was ordered to pay back misappropriated funds, but was eventually granted a pardon by the president on Independence Day 1984, with the understanding that his political life was terminated.

Whatever lay behind it – most likely Njonjo's designs on the presidency – the Njonjo affair succeeded in easing away the volatility engendered by the coup attempt.

Odinga and a number of other political detainees were released. More broadly, provincial administration was increasingly "de-tribalised", with officials working away from their home areas. And, on another front, a complete restructuring of the educational curriculum put new emphasis on technical and vocational studies. For university candidates, a new quasi-military *National Youth Service* programme was launched, with students engaged in public works across the country. **Student unrest** continued, however. Twelve students were killed in February 1985 when the *GSU* broke up a meeting on the campus, ostensibly about canteen food, but considered subversive by the authorities. On the other side of the political fence, *KANU* "youth wingers" began taking the law into their own hands, forming vigilante groups to attack criminal suspects and those suspected of "causing disunity".

REGIONAL AFFAIRS

Relations with **Uganda** reached an all-time low in the late 1980s, with that country regarded by the government as Kenya's worst enemy. Hundreds of Ugandan residents of Kenya were expelled early in 1987, accused of fomenting dissent, and later in the year there were unexplained border skirmishes in which a number of soldiers and police died on both sides. In March 1989, an unexplained bombing raid on the northwestern outpost of Lokichokio was blamed on Uganda – though anti-government forces in southern Sudan are more likely culprits.

In other foreign affairs, Moi has maintained a high profile: signing a defence treaty with **Ethiopia** and improving relations with **Somalia**; taking the chair in the *Organisation for African Unity (OAU)* for 1981–82; and re-opening diplomatic ties – and the border – with **Tanzania**.

Moi's *rapprochement* with Somalia seems to have resolved the status of **northeastern Kenya**. In this Somali region, grievances against decisions taken at the Lancaster House talks in 1960 led to the "shifta wars" of the 1960s and early 1970s. Many Somali clans favoured unification with Somalia and there was bitter resentment of the control of the region by metropolitan Kenya. Isolated attacks on transport and villagers still occur, but

Somalis are now represented in the cabinet and it was a Somali general in the army who was instrumental in the crushing of the August coup. Northeastern Kenya remains heavily under military control, however. In 1984, there were reports from the isolated town of Wajir of an army massacre of up to 1200 Somali civilians during an arms round-up. An official statement responded to questions in parliament with the claim that 57 men had been killed during an army intervention in inter-clan fighting. But the details — smothered by a highly embarrassed government — were never allowed to emerge.

KENYA TODAY: INTO THE 1990S

Economically, Kenya has come a long way since independence. But with the population today standing at about three times what it was thirty years ago (8 million then; around 24 million today), the rate of improvement in standards of living is levelling off, and by some indexes has actually declined since 1980.

Politically, there's less room for doubt. Despite an enduringly positive reputation overseas, Kenya has suffered a steady decline in democratic practices, the rule of law and human rights in general.

THE ECONOMY 1985–90

While imports continue to outstrip exports, servicing the national debt costs Kenya a far smaller proportion of export earnings than many poor countries have to surrender. But **development** is deeply dependent on foreign aid grants and loans: few African countries receive as much. And behind the fairly optimistic figures for economic growth there are persistent spectres: a fresh half-million school graduates each year competing for barely 100,000 new jobs in the swelling towns, an unwieldy, obstructive bureaucracy, minimum wage rises that trail behind accelerating inflation, and agricultural cooperatives and marketing boards in the rural areas that are notoriously corrupt and inefficient.

Natural factors, too, have been important in trimming development. The savage **drought** of 1984 resulted in near-famine conditions in many parts of the north and east. While that has been countered by bumper crops following several good rainy seasons, there's a continuing chronic shortage of **storage facilities** and little guarantee that similar disasters won't recur.

Kenya is still heavily reliant on the fortunes of **coffee** and **tea** on the world markets, and also has to import three-quarters of its energy requirements.

In the **tourist industry** — now the biggest earner of foreign exchange — foreign tour operators were unnerved by the attention given to Kenya's **AIDS** problem. Highlighted by the British Army's temporary ban on some coastal resorts for soldiers on leave, and the rumour that the virus could be spread by mosquitoes, the scare caused bookings, particularly from Germany, to plummet.

Further adverse publicity damaged the industry in Britain as the case of **Julie Ward**, whose murder in the Maasai Mara was at first clumsily covered up, unfolded for week after week. The inquest that was finally held delivered a verdict of murder, but the perpetrators were still unknown. Scotland Yard detectives were called in. On top of the murder of naturalist **George Adamson** in Kora and several other attacks and murders of tourists in 1989–90, even the tabloid reputation of the country abroad was being sullied.

Bad news from the parks continued, however, with shocking levels of **elephant poaching** disastrously polluting Kenya's glossy safari image. While the ivory scandals which smeared Kenyatta's family have not been repeated under Moi's presidency — and indeed Moi is known to take poaching very seriously, issuing orders to shoot poachers on sight — internal corruption was partly responsible for the scale of the slaughter that far exceeded anything during Kenyatta's rule.

In June 1989 Kenya announced a major **offensive on ivory smuggling** and succeeded in persuading most importing countries, including the USA, Britain, Hong Kong and (remarkably) Japan to place a blanket ban on any further consignments. The Wildlife Service, under the new directorship of **Richard Leakey**, has taken stern control of the situation and largely through force of arms — hunting down poachers — has stemmed a holocaust that, for a few months, looked close to burning itself out as the elephants in some areas were poached near to extinction.

THE POLITICAL CLIMATE 1987–89

Domestic **political developments**, too, have had economic repercussions in recent years. An *Amnesty International* report in 1987 condemned Kenya's human rights record, and an American congressional delegation was "stunned" by the mistreatment of political detainees and the fears expressed by Kenyans – as well as by its own abrupt treatment at the hands of the Kenyan Special Branch. While the USA does not want to jeopardise its agreement to use the recently upgraded naval facilities at Mombasa, nor to upset its chances of a welcome at the new north Kenyan port being planned on Manda Island, there has been a clear cooling-off of relations between Washington and Nairobi. The question of America's **aid commitment** to Kenya is now an issue in Congress and Moi cut short his American visit in March 1987 after State Department criticism of human rights abuses. His proposed trip to Norway and Sweden, where many political refugees live, was abandoned after a lashing in the press in Scandinavia, and many Western aid donors are rethinking their Kenya programmes in light of recent events.

During the last three years of Margaret Thatcher's premiership, however, Britain's aid commitment was stepped up. Kenya is the largest recipient of British aid in Africa. The two leaders exchanged visits in 1987, and confirmed their warm relations, discreetly assuming a diplomatic trade-off over the human rights issue in Kenya and Thatcher's stand against South African sanctions.

Until the end of the 1980s, Moi appeared firmly in control and it was never clear why opposition of any kind was dealt with so harshly. Despite efforts to throttle all **dissent**, the ground swell of resentment continued to grow and, to a large extent, attitudes were polarised less along tribal lines than in the past. An opposition group, **Mwakenya** (a Swahili acronym for *Union of Nationalists to Liberate Kenya*), one of several shadowy organisations mounting anti-government campaigns, attracted attention through its pamphlets, calling for the replacement of the Moi government, a return to democracy and an end to corruption and Western influence. While such groups barely identified themselves and didn't appear to pose any united threat to the government, hundreds of people were arrested in the late 1980s. Their defence lawyers tended to get arrested themselves. As reported by *Amnesty*, a number of detainees died in custody and prisoners have reportedly been tortured and kept in waterlogged cells beneath Nyayo House in Nairobi.

The **university** continues to be the target of much of the new order in Kenya. There is a growing anti-intellectualism at the highest levels of government that seriously jeopardises the viability of higher education. For the future of the country, this is at least as dangerous as the blunt police violence that in November 1987 resulted in serious injury to foreign journalists visiting the campus.

In June 1989, President Moi announced the release of a number of Kenyans detained without trial. But this appears to have been only a temporary respite, for within a year the cells were filling again.

ROOTS OF THE NEW OPPOSITION 1989–90

The development of an underground **opposition** in Kenya isn't surprising. For a long time now, public meetings of more than five people have been subject to police approval. Dissent, even within the sole party, *KANU*, has been crushed, and further illiberal measures were adopted by the government, including the power to dismiss judges (rescinded after the *KANU* constitutional congress in December 1990) and the change from secret balloting at elections to a public be-seen-and-counted "queue-voting" system, in which voters line up behind the candidate of their choice. As the independence of the judiciary has been eroded, so the power of the party has consolidated.

Measures intended ostensibly to ensure ethnic balance in the **cabinet** have meant a lack of security of tenure for most ministers, whom the president frequently shifts around or dismisses if their power base begins to assume threatening proportions. Under these circumstances, the effectiveness of ministries is greatly reduced. Such ephemerality extends to the vice-president. Josephat Karanja emerged from relative obscurity to hold the deputy position for just a year, before being forced to resign in April 1989 over a mass of unsubstantiated accusations. The smear campaign (which faintly echoes the "Njonjo affair") split Kikuyu opinion and gave Moi his first opportunity to appoint a non-Kikuyu as his vice-president – the Maasai finance minister George Saitoti.

A trend noted in recent years has been the apparent subtle infiltration of **Kalenjin** people into high civil service posts and the assertion that the country is being run by the civil service over and above Moi's ministers. It's a hard notion to disprove, especially in view of the mistrust with which the Kikuyu are viewed by the current regime. But the reality of a Kalenjin "shadow government" is seriously open to question. The very term *Kalenjin* is an invention of the colonial era (see p.145), while lists of Kalenjin appointments are easily misinterpreted by recourse to shallow, tribalist notions of loyalty, especially when various other Nilotic-speaking officials are added for good measure.

The factors that more seriously undermine the government's credibility are its dogged refusal to countenance any change of direction from the narrow path of **single-party domination** and the total vacuum beneath President Moi, which leaves foreign governments no choice but to deal with, and thus support, the incumbent.

As power is increasingly concentrated in fewer hands – and whose hands becomes a topic for rumour – only the **church** and a few powerfully connected politicians have dared to question the government. President Moi is a regular church-goer and is unlikely to risk a head-on collision with senior clergy.

The grisly **murder of Robert Ouko**, the Luo Foreign Minister, in February 1990 at his farm near Kisumu, sparked off the first explosion of **civil unrest** in a rolling crisis that beset the government throughout most of 1990. Scotland Yard was, once again, called in to investigate the murder and their report was delivered to President Moi in July, but never made public. Ouko, a stout supporter of President Moi who enjoyed excellent personal relations with governments in both Britain and the USA, was widely viewed as a potential successor to the presidency, and was backed by Britain for the vice-presidency in 1988.

A week of **rioting** (most violently in his home town of Kisumu) and intense rumour-mongering shook the country. It is widely believed that Ouko's murder was the work of government agents exceeding their briefs, though there is no plausible explanation for why they should have been set upon him. An alternative account may simply be that personal, rather than political, motives were involved.

Ouko's murder was followed, in August, by the gravely embarrassing death in a road accident of the outspoken **Bishop Alexander Muge** on his return from a visit to Western Kenya. It was a visit against which he had been warned in the most menacing terms by the Minister for Labour, who subsequently resigned from the cabinet.

Although the riots of February had dismayed the government, July 1990 saw highland towns in **violent tumult** as public opposition to the government mounted in the wake of demands for a multi-party system by three heavyweight public figures. The former cabinet minister **Kenneth Matiba**, **Raila Odinga** (son of the veteran politician Oginga Odinga) and the ex-mayor of Nairobi, **Charles Rubia**, all declared themselves for a multi-party system and denounced the violent mass evictions that had recently taken place in the Nairobi slum of **Muoroto**: they were subsequently detained without charge. Several human rights and pro-democracy lawyers were also arrested and one, **Gibson Kamau Kuria**, who escaped arrest, was given refuge in the US embassy. A Nairobi **pro-democracy rally** (banned by the government) degenerated into attacks on buildings and security forces and there were dozens of deaths in street battles with police, who were using guns. President Moi blamed "hooligans and drug addicts" for the explosion.

In reality these combined challenges represent possibly the fiercest threat yet to Moi's regime, even counting the failed coup attempt of 1982. Ngugi wa Thiongo has been named (not surprisingly) as one of Mwakenya's leaders and claims there is wide support for a coalition of opposition forces. But government officials claim that the opposition is largely drawn from Kikuyu-speaking areas and that the talk of multi-partyism is a cover for a Kikuyu takeover.

In the increasingly hostile climate, the government has come down hard on **journalists**, virtually stifling local newspapers and accusing the foreign press and even the **BBC** in Nairobi of mischief-making. The corporation is the latest in a notorious line-up of divergent – and diversionary – enemies of Kenya, including the Ku Klux Klan and Colonel Gaddafi.

PROSPECTS

Throughout the middle of 1990, a **constitutional review commission** toured Kenya, under the chairmanship of vice-president George Saitoti, gathering grassroots political opinion – the first and only frank attempt to move in a popular direction. The results surprised the body, which drafted a (confidential) report covering a wide range of hitherto barely voiced criticisms of government and political life in Kenya. Queue-voting came in for particular hostility. Having unleashed a high level of expectation, however, there are few if any signs that the government is prepared to meet it.

On the contrary: the **December 1990 KANU conference** resoundingly rejected any move away from the one-party state. Most of the July and August **detainees** are still in jail. Several political prisoners have been charged with treason after complicated coup plots were unearthed and pinned on them. One opposition lawyer, returning in secret to Kenya (and arrest) from **Norway**, led Kenya to break off diplomatic relations with Oslo. The move can only hurt Kenya as Norway has been one of the country's best and most sensitive friends in the aid community, providing it with countless aid packages and development projects. Meanwhile, the murder of **Robert Ouko** remains unsolved and the **truck driver** whose vehicle smashed head-on into Bishop Muge's car was sentenced to a seven-year jail term.

Part of the difficulty of incidents like the murder of Robert Ouko and the death of Bishop Muge lies in the way they have been handled. The government's incapacity to deal with crises tend to stigmatise it, even before it might be shown to have absolutely no involvement – and even when, as in the Muge case, such a suggestion seems fanciful in the extreme.

And of course whatever its political climate, there is no doubt that Kenya is one of the best places in Africa in which to work as a foreign correspondent. The large community of journalists is duty-bound to seek out the dirt, putting Kenya, more than most African countries, under international scrutiny.

But even without the flocks of reporters picking over its problems, Kenya is beginning to look tragically isolated, under siege to events and opinion, at home and abroad. The political demise of Margaret Thatcher caused the leadership some unease, while relations with the United States are beginning to look very strained – even despite America's high regard for the county in geo-political terms and its importance during the Gulf crisis.

On the broader horizon, meanwhile, Kenya's uneasy slide into economic dependency on the rich countries looks set to continue, giving the government little room to manoeuvre against foreign interests on behalf of national ones. Whether it has much choice – as political dissenters insist it does – and how far a nationalist stand would go to resolving the problems of landlessness, unemployment and poverty – the root causes of political opposition – must remain the biggest questions for the second quarter-century of independence.

BOOKS

There is a substantial volume of reading matter on Kenya, though much of the European output has been fairly lightweight and the more scholarly works tend to be indigestible. For pre-departure reading, the growing body of Kenyan literature provides a good foretaste. Some of the following titles may be most easily available in Kenya (or try the importers *Leishman & Taussig* on ☎/fax 0636 813774). It's worth visiting libraries and second-hand bookshops to find those titles which are out of print (o/p). The inter-library loan system can find you most books, given time. Or try one of the advertisers at the back of the book or the addresses on p.20–21.

TRAVEL AND GENERAL ACCOUNTS

Negley Farson, *Behind God's Back* (Zenith, o/p). An American journalist's account of his long overland journey across Africa on the eve of World War II. A lively book if you can stomach the alarming shifts between criticism of the colonial world and participation in its worst prejudices.

John Hillaby, *Journey to the Jade Sea* (Grafton, £3.50). An obvious one to read before a trip to Lake Turkana; Hillaby's account of his walk in the early 1960s is dated and not always very informative – an adventure, as he writes, "for the hell of it", with sprinklings of tall stories and descriptions of loony incompetence.

Patrick Marnham, *Fantastic Invasion: Dispatches from Africa* (Penguin, o/p). Although more than a decade old, nothing has since

matched this withering and devastatingly sharp collection of journalism, which includes several essays on Kenya. Tunnels beneath the mountain of dross written about Africa.

David Lamb, *The Africans* (1984; Mandarin, 1989). There's really no contest between Marnham and Lamb, a *Los Angeles Times* hack, for a contemporary view of the continent. *The Africans* has been almost a best-seller, but Lamb's fly-in, fly-out technique is a muddled, statistical rant, couched in cold war rhetoric and, even when ostensibly uncovering a pearl of wisdom, he can be rebarbatively offensive.

Peter Matthiessen, *The Tree Where Man was Born* (Pan, £4.99). Wanderings and musings of the Zen-thinking polymath in Kenya and northern Tanzania. Enthralling for its detail on nature, society, culture and prehistory, and beautifully written, this is a gentle, appetising introduction to the land and its people.

Shiva Naipaul, *North of South* (Penguin, £4.99). A fine but caustic account of the late Naipaul's travels in Kenya, Tanganyika and Zambia. Always readable and sometimes hilarious; the insights make up for the occasionally angst-ridden social commentary and some passages that widely miss the mark.

Evelyn Waugh, *A Tourist in Africa* (Mandarin, £3.99). First published in 1960, Waugh's diary of a short trip to Kenya, Tanganyika and Rhodesia is determinedly arrogant and uninformed, but funny, too – and brief enough to consume at a single sitting.

EXPLORERS' ACCOUNTS

You might also try to have a look at some of the explorer's books; the following deal largely with Kenya and make for interesting pre-departure reading.

Joseph Thomson, *Through Maasailand: To the Central African Lakes and Back* (1885, 2 vols, o/p).

Rev. J L Krapf, *Travel and Missionary Labors in Africa* (1860, o/p).

C H Stigand, *The Land of Zinj* (1912, o/p).

COLONIAL WRITERS: AUTOBIOGRAPHY

Not surprisingly perhaps, settler society produced few notable authors. Karen Blixen was the literary prima donna.

Isak Dinesen (Karen Blixen), *Out of Africa* (Penguin, £3.99). This has become something of a cult book, particularly in the wake of the movie. First published in 1937, it describes her life on her Ngong Hills coffee farm between the wars. Read today, it seems to hover uncertainly between contemporary literature and historical document. It's an intense read – lyrical, introspective, sometimes obnoxiously and intricately racist, but worth pursuing and never superficial, unlike the film. Dinesen's own *Letters from Africa* (Picador, o/p) gives posthumous insights.

Judith Thurman, *The Life of Isak Dinesen* (Penguin, o/p). A biography that sets the record straighter and was the source of much of the material for the *Out of Africa* film, which the original book left out.

Peter Beard, *Kamante's Tales from Out of Africa* (Harcourt, Brace Jovanovich, o/p). Fascinating photos of Blixen and friends, as well as an unnecessarily condescending handwritten text by the grandsons of Kamante (her houseboy in Kenya), transcribing the memories of one of the principal characters in *Out of Africa*.

OTHER WORKS OF THE COLONIAL ERA

Beryl Markham, *West with the Night* (Virago, £5.99). Markham made the first east–west solo flight across the Atlantic. This is a first and last book about her life in the inter-war Kenya colony, drawing together adventures, landscapes and contemporary figures. Not great literature but highly evocative.

Elspeth Huxley, *The Flame Trees of Thika* (Penguin, £4.99); *The Mottled Lizard* (Penguin, £4.99). Bland entertainments, based on her own childhood, from a prolific author who has also written numerous works on colonial history and society, including *White Man's Country* (o/p), a biography of the settlers' doyen, Lord Delamere. Her latest in a long line of reminiscences – *Out in the Midday Sun: My Kenya* (Penguin, £4.99) – is as readable (if also predictable) as any. Her most recent book is *Nine Faces of Kenya* (Collins Harvill, 1990, £16), a dewy-eyed anthology of East African ephemera. More interesting is the collection of her mother's letters, *Nellie's Story* (Weidenfeld & Nicholson, o/p), which includes some compelling coverage of the Mau Mau years from the pen of a likeably eccentric settler.

Richard Meinertzhagen, *Kenya Diary (1902–1906)* (Eland). The haunting day-to-day narrative of a young British officer in the protectorate. Meinertzhagen's brutal descriptions of "punitive expeditions" are chillingly matter-of-fact and make the endless tally of his wildlife slaughter pale inoffensively in comparison. As a reminder of the savagery that accompanied the British intrusion, and a stark insight into the complex mind of one of its perpetrators, this is disturbing, highly recommended, reading. Good photos, too.

Harry Hook, *The Kitchen Toto* (Faber and Faber, £3.95). By way of an antidote to a surfeit of settlers' yarns, this screenplay tells the story of Mwangi, a Kikuyu houseboy caught up in the early stages of the Mau Mau rebellion. Writer-director Hook's **movie** is as keen as a country *panga* and draws masterful performances from a largely unknown cast.

KENYA IN MODERN WESTERN FICTION

Kenya has been the setting for the work of several recent writers, most noticeably three women.

Toril Brekke, *The Jacaranda Flower* (Methuen). A dozen brief stories compiled after a stay in 1985, mostly touching on the lives of women – some moving, some ironic. Supposed to "bridge the gap between Western understanding and African women's lives", the gap remains, but it's clearly illuminated.

Martha Gellhorn, *The Weather in Africa* (Eland, o/p). Three absorbing novellas, each dealing with aspects of the Europe-Africa relationship, set on the slopes of Kilimanjaro, in the White Highlands of Kenya and on the tourist coast north of Mombasa. Highly recommended.

Maria Thomas, *Come to Africa and Save Your Marriage* (Serpent's Tail, £7.95). Most of these stories are set in Kenya or Tanzania. Thomas's characters are solid but the stories leave a wearying aftertaste as if there were nothing positive to be had from the expatriate experience. Her first novel, *Antonia Saw the Oryx First*, is painfully detailed – a good antidote to *Out of Africa*.

HISTORY AND PEOPLES

There's a good range of background reading on Kenyan history and a large number of anthropological works on different peoples. Few of the latter are mentioned here. The best source for specialist ethnographic titles is probably the School of Oriental and African Studies Library in London. See p.21.

KENYA IN AFRICAN HISTORY

Roland Oliver and J D Fage, *A Short History of Africa* (Penguin, £5.99). Dated but still the standard paperback introduction.

Basil Davidson, *Africa in Modern History* (Penguin, £6.95). Lucidly argued and very readable summary of nineteenth- and twentieth-century events.

Alan Moorehead, *The White Nile* (Penguin, £9.99). Moving closer to Kenya, this is a riveting account of the search for the source and European rivalries for control in the region.

Christopher Hibbert, *Africa Explored: Europeans in the Dark Continent 1769–1889* (Penguin, 1984). Entertaining read, devoted in large part to the "discovery" of East and Central Africa.

KENYA IN GENERAL

William R Ochieng, *A History of Kenya* (Macmillan, Kenya). Somewhat pedestrian but the best general overview from prehistory to 1980, with useful maps and photos to show the way. *A Modern History of Kenya 1895–1980* (Evans, £9.95) covers the twentieth century in eight chapters – solid enough up to the middle of Kenyatta's reign.

William R Ochieng, ed, *Themes in Kenyan History* (James Currey, 1990, £9.95). A brand new collection of writings by historians and other academics, all teaching in Kenyan universities.

Fedders and Salvadori, *People and Cultures of Kenya* (Transafrica and Rex Collings, o/p). A useful tribe-by-tribe introduction. Cynthia Salvadori's *Through Open Doors: A View of Asian Cultures in Kenya* (Kenway Publications, o/p) combines a stack of lively and readable erudition with fascinating marginal notes and sketches – superlative.

Kenya's People (series of ten pamphlets, Evans, Kenya). Simple and reliable background on ten of Kenya's peoples. Aimed at Kenyan secondary schools, they're pitched just right for culturally uninitiated visitors.

Jomo Kenyatta, *Facing Mount Kenya* (Heinemann, o/p). A traditional, functionalist, anthropological monograph, but written by a member of the society in question – in this case, the Kikuyu – under the supervision of Bronislaw Malinowski at the London School of Economics, shortly before World War II. One of the few scholarly works ever written on traditional Kikuyu culture, this is as interesting for the insights if offers on its author as for its quite readable content. Interesting Kikuyu glossary.

Bethwell A Ogot, *Historical Dictionary of Kenya* (Scarecrow Press, Metuchen, New Jersey, USA, libraries). From a reliable series that covers nearly every African country, this is an A to Z of Kenya's history to 1979 written by one of the country's leading historians. Includes an extensive bibliography.

COASTAL HISTORY

G S P Freeman-Grenville, *The East African Coast* (1962, Oxford University Press, o/p). If you're heading for the coast, this is fascinating: a series of accounts from the first century to the nineteenth century – vivid and often extraordinary.

Sarah Mirza and Margaret Strobel, *Three Swahili Women* (Indiana, £8.95). Three histories of ritual, three women's lives. Born between 1890 and 1920 into different social backgrounds, these biographies document enormous changes from the most important of neglected viewpoints.

James de Vere Allen, *Swahili Origins: Swahili Culture and the Shungwaya Phenomenon* (James Currey, forthcoming spring 1992, £11.95). The life work of a challenging and readable scholar, bound to raise a fascinating field of study to new prominence.

PROTECTORATE AND COLONIAL KENYA

Errol Trzebinski, *The Kenya Pioneers* (Heinemann, o/p). Despite academic pretensions, this is something of a paean to the early settlers.

Charles Miller, *The Lunatic Express* (o/p). The story of that railway. Miller narrates the drama of one of the great feats of Victorian engineering – as bizarre and as madly magnificent as any Wild West epic – adding weight with a broad historical background of East Africa from the year dot. The same author's *The Battle for the Bundu* (Macmillan, o/p) follows a little-known corner of World War I, as fought out on the plains of Tsavo between British Kenya and German Tanganyika – immensely readable.

James Fox, *White Mischief* (Penguin, £4.50). Investigative romp through the events surrounding the notorious unsolved murder of Lord Errol, one of Kenya's most aristocratic settlers, at Karen in 1941. Well told and highly revealing of British Kenyan society of the time. Michael Radford's 1987 **film version** is equally enjoyable, and a good deal more stimulating than the *Out of Africa* movie.

THE MAU MAU REBELLION

Bruce Berman, *Control and Crisis in Modern Kenya* (James Currey, £11.95). A study of the growth of state control, from the 1890s through to inter-war crisis and post-war disintegration.

Tabitha Kanogo, *Squatters and the Roots of Mau Mau 1905–63* (James Currey, £8.95). Delves into the early years of the "White Highlands" to show how resistance, and the conditions for revolt, were built into the relations between the settler land-grabbers and the peasant farmers and herders ("squatters") they usurped. Strong on the role of women in the Mau Mau movement.

David Throup, *Economic and Social Origins of Mau Mau* (James Currey, £9.95). Looks at the story from the end of World War II, examining the colonial mentality and differences in efficiency between peasant cash-cropping and more wasteful plantation agriculture.

Frank Furedi, *The Mau Mau War in Perspective* (James Currey, £9.95). The Land and Freedom Army had two aims. Furedi analyses, using new archival sources, the continued struggle for land redistribution once the struggle for independence had been won.

R G Edgerton, *Mau Mau: an African Crucible* (I B Tauris, £14.95). An account of the revolt based on guerillas' testimonies. Includes explorations of the role of women and class-formation in modern Kenya.

J M Kariuki, *Mau Mau Detainee: The Account by a Kenya African of His Experience in Detention Camps* (Oxford University Press, o/p). A remarkably forbearing account of life and death in the detention camps. Kariuki's vision for the future of Kenya and his loyalty to Kenyatta have a special irony after his assassination in 1975. Recommended.

Donald L Barnett and Karari Njama, *Mau Mau from Within: Autobiography and Analysis of Kenya's Peasant Revolt* (Monthy Review Press, o/p). An account based on personal recollections.

AFTER INDEPENDENCE

Anthony Howarth, *Kenyatta: A Photographic Biography* (East African Publishing House, libraries) is a roughly hewn biography composed of an amalgam of black and white photographs, news clippings and quotations. It doesn't pretend to be exhaustive, but manages to capture the spirit of the leader and the struggle for independence.

Jeremy Murray Brown, *Kenyatta* (o/p), and **David Goldsworthy**, *Tom Mboya: The Man Who Kenya Wanted to Forget* (o/p) are the two big biographies: both weighty and deeply researched.

Oginga Odinga, *Not yet Uhuru* (Heinemann, o/p). The classic critique of Kenya's direction at the time it was written.

Tom Mboya, *The Challenge of Nationhood* (Heinemann, £4.95). The vision of Kenya's best-loved statesman – and a Luo – assassinated in 1969 for looking like a clear successor to Kenyatta.

Ngugi wa Thiong'o, *Detained – A Writer's Prison Diary* (Heinemann, £5.50). A retrospective of Kenya's history up to 1978, woven into the daily routine of political detention during Kenyatta's last year. Ngugi discourses widely and, while his reflections are occasionally pedantic or obscure and sometimes written with almost religious fervour, he hits home often. His *Barrel of a Pen: Resistance to Repression in Neo-Colonial Kenya* (New Beacon, £6.95) hones some of his points sharply. See the box opposite.

Guy Arnold, *Modern Kenya* (Longman, o/p). A digestible look at Kenyan politics, economy and society. A concise, if somewhat guarded, survey, but meatier than it might appear.

NGUGI WA THIONG'O

The dominant figure of modern Kenyan literature currently lives in exile in Britain: although most of his books in English are not banned in Kenya, his political sympathies are.

Ngugi's work is art serving the revolution — didactic, brusque, graphic and unsentimental. His novels, especially the later ones, are unforgiving: the touch of humour that would leaven the polemic rarely comes to the rescue. Powerful themes — exploitation, betrayal, cultural oppression, the imposition of Christianity, loss of and search for identity — drive the stories along urgently. Characters deal with real events and the changes of their time, struggling to come to terms with the influences at work on their lives. Ngugi's style is heady, idealistic, and undaunted, never teasing or capricious. Disillusioned with English ("Whom do I write for?"), his first work in Kikuyu, in collaboration with Ngugi wa Mirii, was the play *Ngahiika Ndeenda (I will Marry When Want)*, and its public performance by illiterate peasants at the *Kamiriithu Cultural Centre* in Limuru got him detained for a year. He'd found his mark. Ngugi's work in the Kikuyu language is now banned, or rarely available, in Kenya.

Most of Ngugi's writings in English are published in the Heinemann paperback *African Writers* series. Try *Secret Lives* for short stories, *Weep not Child* for a brief but glowing early novel, or, for the mature Ngugi, *Petals of Blood* – a richly satisfying detective story that is at the same time a saga of wretchedness and struggle (see p.421 for an excerpt). Others include *The River Between*, on the old Kikuyu society and the coming of the Europeans, *A Grain of Wheat*, about the eve of independence, *Devil on the Cross* (written in detention on scraps of toilet paper), and his latest, *Matigari* ("The Patriots"). *Matigari*, first published in Kikuyu by Heinemann in 1986, had a remarkable effect in the Central Highlands. Rumours circulated that a man, Matigari, was spreading militant propaganda against the government: the police even tried to track him down, before realising their mistake and confiscating all copies of the book.

Ngugi has also written two other plays: *The Black Hermit* and *The Trial of Dedan Kimathi* (with Micere Mugo). His contribution to Kenyan literature – and liberation literature – is enormous; delving in is rewarding, if not always easy.

Anonymous, *In Dependent Kenya* (Zed Books, £14.95). Published in 1982, a book that pulls no punches, fully and bitterly condemning the status quo and Kenya's paralysis in the neo-colonial web. Remorseless, trenchant and to the point; read it for instruction but don't take it with you.

UMOJA, *Moi's Reign of Terror* (£3.50). Another one to leave at home, documenting the dark side of modern Kenya.

Jean Davison, *Voices from Mutira: Lives of rural Gikuyu Women* (L Rienner, £12.95). Covering the period from the 1950s to the present, this is particularly interesting for the attitudes it documents on brideprice and genital mutilation.

Frank Willett, *African Art* (Thames and Hudson, 1988). An accessible volume; good value, with a generous illustrations/text ratio.

Geoffrey Williams, *African Designs From Traditional Sources* (Dover, 1971). A designer's and enthusiast's sourcebook, from the copyright-free publishers.

Roy Braverman, *Islam and Tribal Art* (Cambridge UP, 1974). A useful paperback text for the dedicated.

Jane Barbour & Simiyu Wandibba, *Kenyan Pots and Potters* (Oxford University Press, £5.95). This comprehensive description of pot-making communities includes techniques, training, marketing and sociological perspectives.

ARTS

Most works dealing with the arts cover the whole continent. For books covering Kenya's music, see the box on p.435.

Susan Denyer, *African Traditional Architecture* (Heinemann, 1982). Useful and interesting, with hundreds of photos (though most of them old) and detailed line drawings.

KENYAN FICTION IN ENGLISH

Although a number of authors have written in the older languages of Kenya, English still predominates as the medium for artistic expression, a situation which creates dilemmas for writers struggling both to reach a readership at home and to find viable channels for publication.

Ngugi wa Thiongo, *Decolonising the Mind: The Politics of Language in African Literature* (James Currey, £4.95). Ngugi has long been closely associated with attempts to move Kenyan literature and African literature in general towards expression in the readers' mother tongues. See the box above.

PROSE COLLECTIONS

African Short Stories, edited by Chinua Achebe and C. L. Innes (Heinemann, £4.95). A collection which treats its material geographically, including Kenyan stories from **Jomo Kenyatta**, **Grace Ogot**, **Ngugi** and a spooky offering (*The Spider's Web*) from **Leonard Kibera**, brother of Sam Kahiga.

Unwinding Threads – Writing by Women in Africa, edited by Charlotte H. Bruner (Heinemann). Also geographical, with succinct introductions to each region. East Africa features Kenyan writers **Charity Waciuma** and the excellent **Grace Ogot**, whose *The Rain Came* is a bewitching mystery myth, pulling traditional Luo tales together with her personal fiction in a perplexingly "Western" form.

Two Centuries of African English, edited by Lalage Bown (Heinemann, o/p). Includes non-fiction extracts from the work of **J M Kariuki** (*Mau Mau Detainee*), **Ali Mazrui** on intellectuals and revolution, **Githende Mockerie** and **R Mugo Gatheru** recounting their childhoods, and **Tom Mboya** on Julius Nyerere, first president of Tanzania.

NOVELS AND SHORT STORIES

Meja Mwangi, *Going Down River Road; Carcase for Hounds; Kill Me Quick* (all in Heinemann's *African Writers Series*); *The Cockroach Dance* (Longman). Mwangi is lighter and more accessible than Ngugi, his fiction infused with the absurdities of urban (Nairobi) slum life. *Going Down River Road* is the best known: convincing scenes, chaotic action and sharp dialogue (though it's never clear whether the English/American street-cool is meant to be real, or an effort to render the Swahili-Kikuyu "Sheng" slang of the slums). Great *in situ* reading.

Thomas Akare, *The Slums* (Heinemann, £4.50). A bleaker read than Mwangi, but also more humane. Without quotation marks, the dialogue melds seamlessly into the narrative;

no doubts about the authentic rhythms of Kenyan English here. But much is assumed to be understood and there's much that won't be unless you're sitting under a 25-watt light bulb in a River Road Boarding & Lodging.

Sam Kahiga, *Flight to Juba – Short Stories* (Longman, Kenya); *The Girl from Abroad* (Heinemann). Vital, exasperating, obnoxious and plain crazy – a writer to love to hate (see excerpted story, p.425).

Ali Mazrui, *The Trial of Christopher Okigbo* (Heinemann, £4.50). A clever "novel of ideas" from the US-based political scientist, who always succeeds in infuriating both critics of Kenya and its supporters. His latest book, *Cultural Forces in World Politics* (James Currey, £9.95) is a survey of cultural and political ideas which also addresses the issues surrounding Salman Rushdie's *Satanic Verses*.

Marjorie Oludhe Macgoye, *Coming to Birth* (Virago, £3.95). A novel putting a woman's view on life in Kenya from one of the country's few published women writers.

Bramwell Lusweti, *The Way to the Town Hall* (Macmillan, o/p). Enjoyable satire aimed at small-town politicians and businessmen. A Swahili dictionary (to translate the characters' names!) is a help.

David Mulwa, *Master and Servant* (Longman, £4.50). Growing up in colonial Kenya. A funny and affecting string of episodes.

Mude Dae Mude, *The Hills are Falling* (Kenya Literature Bureau, £4.20). Life from Marsabit to Nairobi.

Kenneth Watene, *Sunset on the Manyatta* (East African Publishing House, £4.95). A Maasai man in Germany.

KENYAN POETRY

The oldest form of written poetry in Kenya is from the coast. Inland, poetry in the sense of written verse is a recent form. But oral folk literature was often relayed in the context of music, rhythm and dance.

SWAHILI POETRY

Swahili poetry reads beautifully even if you don't understand the words. Written for at least 300 years, and sung for a good deal longer, it's one of Kenya's most enduring art forms. An *Anthology of Swahili Poetry* is currently available, compiled and rather woodenly translated by **Ali A Jahadmy** (Heinemann). Some of Swahili's best-known classical compositions from the Lamu archipelago are included, with pertinent background.

There's a more enjoyable anthology of romantic and erotic verse, *A Choice of Flowers*, with **Jan Knappert**'s idiosyncratic translations and interpretations (Heinemann), and the same linguist's *Four Centuries of Swahili Verse* (Heinemann) which expounds and creatively interprets at much greater length. A translation of an exquisite poem from the latter is included on p.429.

KENYAN POETRY IN ENGLISH

Poems of Black Africa, edited by Wole Soyinka (Heinemann, £4.50). A hefty and catholic selection. From Kenya, it includes the work of **Abangira**, **Jared Angira**, **Jonathan Kariara** and **Amin Kassam**.

Heinemann Book of African Poetry (Heinemann, £5.95). A new volume, which includes the work of Kenyan poet Marjorie Oludhe Macgoye.

WILDLIFE, MOUNTAIN AND CAMPING GUIDES

Having a field guide, especially to the hundreds of species of birds that will pass your way, makes a huge difference to travelling on safari. For more rugged outdoor activities, several specialist guidebooks are now available. See also the Mount Kenya "Maps and Guides" section on p.120.

John Williams, *A Field Guide to the National Parks of East Africa* (Harper Collins, £12.99). Covers parks, reserves, animals and birds, but there's too much space devoted to long lists of fauna and the practical details for the parks are dated. Williams's *Field Guide to the Birds of East and Central Africa* (Harper Collins, £12.99) is the standard spotter's tome. His *Field Guide to the Butterflies of Africa* (Collins, o/p) is exotic and useful if you can get hold of a copy.

T Haltenorth and H Diller, *The Collins Guide to the Mammals of Africa* (Harper Collins, £12.99). With excellent illustrations, distribution maps and a superabundance of detail, this has superseded Williams's mammal guide.

Michael Blundell, *A Field Guide to the Wild Flowers of East Africa* (Harper Collins, £12.99) is the new botanical companion in the series.

Ray Moore, *Where to Watch Birds in Kenya* (Transafrica Press, 1982, available in Kenya and sometimes in the UK). Invaluable tips and background for the devoted birder.

Mountains of Kenya (Mountain Club of Kenya, 1989). A detailed and practical guide, comprehensively updated since its earlier incarnation and well worth buying if you plan to do any Kenyan hiking.

Guide Book to Mount Kenya and Kilimanjaro (MCK). For fully equipped alpinism, this is indispensable.

Andrew Wielochowski, *East Africa International Mountain Guide* (West Col Productions). Fairly up-to-date for Mount Kenya and other, more obscure ascents.

David Else, *Mountain Walking in Kenya* (McCarta, 1991, £11.95). A new title in an established series of walking guides, useful if you intend to do a lot of hill walking or climbing.

David Else and Jill Bitten, *Camping Guide to Kenya* (Bradt, 1989, £7.95). The only book of its kind, exclusively for compulsive campers. Comprehensive campsite listings make it helpful for long stays in the country – there's some good weekenders' material here.

COFFEE TABLE BOOKS

John Schmid, *The Kenya Magic* (Beachwood Publications, o/p). A light introduction to the country and the best by far of the general coffee table offerings, including some perceptive commentary to accompany the travelogue. The photos, on 35mm format, are superb and refreshingly simple.

Mohamed Amin, *Cradle of Mankind* (Camerapix, o/p). Stunning photographs but a balefully inadequate text. Covers the Lake Turkana region.

Tepilit Ole Saitoti and Carol Beckwith, *Maasai* (Elm Tree Books, o/p). *The* Maasai coffee table book; some photos are too much to take at reading distance. Exquisite but largely staged portraits of a vanishing culture (and even Beckwith's camera can't disguise the tourist souvenirs in the background). Variably interesting, chauvinistic text, which plays the cult value of the Maasai for all it's worth.

David Keith Jones, *Shepherds of the Desert* (Elm Tree, o/p). Brilliant photos (many in black and white), with a text more lucid and less superficial than most glossies; this book concerns itself only with northern Kenya.

Brian Jackman and Jonathan Scott, *The Marsh Lions* (Elm Tree, o/p). Beautifully produced and painstakingly researched study of the lions and other animals around the Musiara Marsh in Maasai Mara. To come across a lion you *recognise* in an animal book (she with the missing tail-tip) is different, anyway.

Esmond and Chrysee Bradley Martin, *Run Rhino Run* (Chatto & Windus, o/p). Carefully researched, this is a serious book that knocks over the myths about the rhino horn trade and shows just how close to the brink the world's five species are.

Mitsuaki Iwago, *Serengeti* (Thames and Hudson, £14.95). Stunning scenes and portraits from Serengeti (the Tanzanian continuation of the Maasai Mara) from a master photographer. Simply the best volume of wildlife photography ever assembled, this makes most glossies look feeble. If you're trying to persuade someone to visit East Africa – or if any purely aesthetic argument were needed to preserve the parks and the animals – this is the book to use.

WRITING FROM KENYA

Very little Kenyan literature appeared in print before World War II. But while East Africa has tended to lag behind the rest of the continent in modern forms – the novel, short stories, drama and modern poetry – there's a rich tradition of oral literature and a specifically coastal Swahili verse culture that put African stories into writing as long as three hundred years ago.

THE ORAL TRADITION IN PRINT

With the exception of the coast, precolonial Kenyan literature was entirely oral and stories were passed – and modified – from generation to generation. These **folktales**, *commonly told by the leaders of the community to the children, were very often "trickster" tales about animals. While they frequently contained a moral, their main purpose was to entertain.*

THE HARE'S PRACTICAL JOKE

A long, long time ago, there were two people who were very good friends. One was Mr. Hare and the other Mr. Hyena. They used to visit each other and on each of these visits, the Hare used to carry in his bag some honey and sweetened meat. He used to put his little finger in the bag and give his friend to lick. Said the Hare: "Brother, I have something very, very sweet in my bag here. Take it and see for yourself." The Hyena liked it very much.

"Hi, Hi, Brother Hare, give me some more, more I say. It is very, very . . ".

"No, no, this is a sweetness that you must have a little at a time."

And the same thing happened day after day for many days. One day, the Hare came on as usual and said:

"Brother Hyena, may I give you something very, very sweet, sweeter than sweetness itself?"

"Yes, my good friend, I'd love some very, very much." And the Hare gave his sweetened finger to the Hyena to lick.

"Oh, Hare, my very good friend do give me more."

"No, no, old man, you cannot eat much of this sweetness. It is a sweetness that must be eaten sparingly".

"But brother, where do you get much much sweetness?"

"I get it from those mountains you see above our heads," pointing at the white clouds. "Once you eat this sweetness you should never pass piss or shit because then the sweetness gets lost."

"Then what do people do so that they do not pass out piss or shit after they have eaten this sweetness?"

"Ah, Mr. Hyena, that is very simple, they have their bottoms sewn up and if you want, I can do the sewing up for you."

"Yes, yes, do sew it up for me." And the Hare sewed the Hyena's bottom.

They took three bags each and the Hare led the way to the sweetness that never passes. Now the Hyena ate the honey, the honeycombs and the dead bees. Then the Hare said: "Now that we have filled our stomachs and our bags let us go home." Now when they were on the way, the Hyena went down to the stream to drink some water. And when he drank he just dropped down like a stump of a tree. He stayed and stayed and stayed there; his eyes popping out like sweet potatoes. He stayed there for so many days, until he thought he was going to die.

One day he saw the Eagle coming down to drink some water – said he:

"Good Brother Eagle, help me."

"Hi, brother, how shall I help you?"

"Come round behind me at my bottom end. You will see a string going right through it, prick it and pull carefully because I feel pain. I was sewn up by the Hare and he did a very bad thing."

Now as soon as the Eagle touched this string a flood of piss and shit rushed out and covered the Eagle and the piss was like a mountain with the Eagle as the core.

One day there was a heavy rain which washed away the piss and shit, slowly by slowly until the Eagle emerged with a scratch on the neck. He flew away swearing revenge on the Hyena. For many days he and the Hyena played hide and seek until one day the Hyena, being the foolish person, forgot that he was the sworn enemy of the Eagle. The Eagle being clever did not want a physical contact with the Hyena. He knew very well that the Hyena was stronger than him. Now he started to show the Hyena the choice pieces of meat that he carried in his bag and every day he gave a little to the Hyena saying: "Brother, I carry this kind of meat, have a bite" and the Hyena said: "Brother Eagle, these delicacies, this choice meat you give me, where does it come from?"

"Now, Brother Hyena, these delicacies, the choice meats are very, very many. If you like, I can take you where they come from. But," continued the Eagle, "it is impossible to get that meat alone. You must come too. Now go and collect all your people. Let them bring bags, tins and drums. Then we shall bring as much meat as will last for three years."

The Hyena was very happy and he ran to collect all his people. Panting: "Do you see all that meat above? My friend brings it to me every day. Now this friend has told me to collect all my people so that we can go and fetch this meat. Let each one of you bring tins, bags or drums and I, with your permission, will ask the Eagle to mention the day on which we can go".

Said all Hyenas: "Hi, we also would like to eat the white choice meat."

All the Hyenas of that country had gathered together and when they saw the Eagle coming towards them they said: "Now, Brother Eagle, let us go to get this meat. Tell us when we can go".

The Eagle said, "We shall go on the third day from today. Be ready."

On that day the Hyena gathered and the Eagle arranged them in a line according to age, the smallest one being put at the back. The Eagle was right in front. He said to the Hyena behind him: "Now, Brother, hold tight to the feathers of my tail," and the Hyena held tight. "Everybody hold each other's tail," he shouted and then he flew up, up, up, and heading to the choice meats in the sky. Now when they had gone very high, the Eagle asked:

"Are you all clear off the ground?"

"No, no, some are still touching the ground." He flew, flew and flew.

"Can you see the earth?"

"Yes, yes, we can see it." The Eagle was waiting to hear that all the Hyenas could no longer see the earth.

"Can you see the earth?"

"We see it dimly now." The Eagle flew and flew.

"Do you still see the earth?"

"We see only black, black darkness, we cannot tell where the earth is."

The Eagle knew then that the distance from the earth was very, very great. Then he said to the Hyena behind him:

"Hi, hi, my friend, a scratch, a scratch on my back wing," and the Hyena behind let go the tail feathers of the Eagle. Suddenly the whole line of Hyenas went tumbling down. Kuru Kuru Kuru like the sound of thunder. Some Hyenas crushed their limbs, their bones and died instantly. Some died before they reached the earth. Only the last Hyena was left, but she acquired a limp in the leg which she carries to this day.

Reprinted from Kikuyu Folktales, *edited and translated by Rose Gecau. By permission of Kenya Literature Bureau.*

HARE AND HORNBILL

Hare and Hornbill were great friends. One day Hare said: "My friend, we have looked for girls all over this land, and there are none that are good enough for you and me. Let us go up to Skyland, perhaps we will find some suitable ones."

Hornbill replied: "I know it is getting a bit late for us to get married, but you know my problem, you know I have this terrible thing!"

"You mean your chronic diarrhoea? But that is nothing to worry about." Hare produced a cork of the right size and blocked up Hornbill's anus.

The two friends made preparations for the journey, and after saying good-bye to their families, Hare got on Hornbill's back and they flew up through the clouds into Skyland. There was a big marriage dance. Hare and Hornbill put on their dancing costumes and went straight into the arena. Hornbill danced gracefully, touching the ground lightly and moving his wings up and down to the rhythm of the drums. His neck swayed this way and that way, and his eyes sparkled with love. Hare danced as best he could, but he could not follow the rhythm of the dance, and sang out of tune; moreover, his big ears looked funny. Beautiful girls fought to dance before Hornbill, but none came anywhere near Hare; and when he approached the girls they ran away from him. That night Hornbill slept with a very pretty girl. Hare slept cold.

The next day Hornbill won two girls; Hare again slept cold. The next night when Hornbill was asleep, resting beside his fourth lover, Hare tip-toed into the house and unhooked the cork. Three days' accumulation of diarrhoea spewed out and flooded the entire house. The stench rose like smoke and the dancers fled from the arena, and Hornbill woke up, and in great shame flew down through the clouds, leaving Hare behind.

There was much commotion as the Skylanders tried to find out what had happened. Hare denied all knowledge of the cause of the trouble.

"But where is your handsome friend?" they asked.

"I am also looking for him," said Hare, adding, "I must find him otherwise it will be a bit difficult to return to earth."

When they failed to find Hornbill the Skylanders decided to get rid of Hare by lowering him down to earth on a rope of plaited grass. The girls cut many heaps of grass. They made the rope and tied one end around Hare's waist and continued to plait the other end as Hare was lowered downwards. The Skylanders gave Hare a drum and told him, "As soon as you reach the earth beat this drum very hard so that the girls may stop plaiting the rope." Hare thanked the Skylanders, said good-bye and began his homeward journey.

Hare descended slowly through the clouds, but on seeing the faint tips of the highest mountain he hit the drum very hard. The skylanders stopped plaiting and dropped the rope. Hare came hurtling down like a falling stone. But just before hitting the ground he cried to the smallest black ants, "Collect me! Collect me! Collect..".

Hare hit the ground and broke up into many many very small pieces. The smallest black ants collected the pieces and put them together again, and Hare became alive. But today when Hare is running you hear his chest making crackling sounds, because the bones of his chest were not put together properly.

Reprinted from Hare and Hornbill, *a collection of folktales edited and translated by Okot p'Bitek. By permission of Heinemann Educational Books.*

PETALS OF BLOOD

Ngugi wa Thiongo *is Kenya's best-known writer and one of the country's most consistently outspoken critics. The following extract from the satirical* Petals of Blood *has been taken from the middle of the book. The people of Ilmorog, a village in the Rift Valley, are beginning to appreciate the power and influence of the New Kenya.*

CHANGES COME TO ILMOROG

Munira folded the newspaper and went to Wanja's place to break the news. He felt for her and Nyakinyua. He did not expect favours. He just wanted to take her the news. And to find out more about it. She was not at her Theng'eta premises. Abdulla told him that she had gone to Nyakinyua's hut. Munira walked there and found other people. News of the threatened sale must have reached them too. They had come to commiserate with her and others similarly affected, to weep with one another. They looked baffled: how could a bank sell their land? A bank was not a government: from whence then, its powers? Or maybe it was the government, an invisible government, some others suggested. They turned to Munira. But he could not answer their question. He only talked about a piece of paper, they had surrendered to the bank. But he could not answer, put to sleep, the bitter scepticism in their voices and looks. What kind of monster was this bank that was a power unto itself, that could uproot lives of a thousand years?

He went back and tried to drink Theng'eta, but it did not have the taste. He remembered that recently he had seen Wambui carting stones to earn bread for the day and he wondered what would happen to the old woman. She was too old to sell her labour and sweat in a market.

"The old woman? Nyakinyua?" Munira echoed Karega's question, slowly. "She died! She is dead!" he added quickly, almost aggressively, waking up from his memories.

Karega's face seemed to move.

Nyakinyua, the old woman, tried to fight back. She tramped from hut to hut calling upon the peasants of Ilmorog to get together and fight it out. They looked at her and they shook their heads: whom would they fight now? The

Government? The Banks? KCO? The Party Nderi? Yes who would they really fight? But she tried to convince them that all these were one and that she would fight them. Her land would never be settled by strangers. There was something grand, and defiant in the woman's action – she with her failing health and flesh trying to organise the dispossessed of Ilmorog into a protest. But there was pathos in the exercise. Those whose land had not yet been taken looked nervously aloof and distant. One or two even made disparaging remarks about an old woman not quite right in the head. Others genuinely not seeing the point of a march to Ruwaini or to the big City restrained her. She could not walk all the way, they told her. But she said: "I'll go alone . . . my man fought the white man. He paid for it with his blood . . . I'll struggle against these black oppressors . . . alone . . . alone . . ."

What would happen to her, Munira wondered.

He need not have worried about her. Nyakinyua died peacefully in her sleep a few days after the news of the bank threat. Rumour went that she had told Wanja about the impending journey: she had said that she could not even think of being buried in somebody else's land: for what would her man say to her when she met him on the other side? People waited for the bank to come and sell her land. But on the day of the sale Wanja redeemed the land and became the heroine of the new and the old Ilmorog.

Later Munira was to know.

But at that time only Abdulla really knew the cost: Wanja had offered to sell him her rights to their jointly owned New Building. He did not have the money and it was he who suggested that they sell the whole building to a third person and divide the income between them.

So Wanja was back to her beginnings.

And Mzigo was the new proud owner of the business premises in Ilmorog.

Wanja was not quite the same after her recent loss. For a time, she continued the proud proprietor of the old Theng'eta place. Her place still remained the meat-roasting centre. Dance steps in the hall could still raise dust to the roof, especially when people were moving to their favourite tunes:

How beautiful you are, my love!
How soft your round eyes are, my honey!
What a pleasant thing you are,
Lying here
Shaded by this cedar bush!
But oh, darling,
What poison you carry between your legs!

But Wanja's heart was not in it. She started building a huge wooden bungalow at the lower end of her shamba, some distance from the shanty town that was growing up around Abdulla's shop, the lodgings and the meat-roasting centre, almost as a natural growth complement to the more elegant new Ilmorog. People said that she was wise to invest in a building the money remaining after redeeming her grandmother's shamba: but what was it for? She already had a hut further up the shamba, hidden from the noise and inquisitive eyes of the New Ilmorog by a thick natural hedge. She went about her work without taking anybody into her confidence. But it was obvious that it was built in the style of a living house with several spacious rooms. Later she moved in: she planted flower gardens all around and had electric lights fixed there. It was beautiful: it was a brave effort so soon after her double loss, people said.

One night the band struck up a song they had composed on their first arrival. As they played, the tune and the words seemed to grow fresher and fresher and the audience clapped and whistled and shouted encouragement. The band added innovations and their voices seemed possessed of a wicked carefree devil.

This shamba girl
Was my darling
Told me she loved my sight.
I broke bank vaults for her,
I went to jail for her,
But when I came back
I found her a lady,
Kept by a wealthy roundbelly daddy,
And she told me,
This shamba-lady girl told me,
No, Gosh!
Sikujui
Serikali imebadilishwa
Coup d'état!

They stopped to thunderous handclaps and feet pounding on the floor. Wanja suddenly stood up and asked them to play it again. She started dancing to it, alone, in the arena. People were surprised. They watched the gyrations of her body, speaking pleasure and pain, memories and hopes, loss and gain, unfulfilled longing and desire. The band, responding to the many beating hearts, played with sad maddening intensity as if it were reaching out to her loneliness and solitary struggle. She danced slowly and deliberately toward Munira and he was remembering that time he had seen her dancing to a juke-box at Safari Bar in Kamiritho. As suddenly as she had started, she stopped. She walked to the stage at the bandstand. The "house" was hushed. The customers knew that something big was in the air.

"I am sorry, dear customers, to have to announce the end of the old Ilmorog Bar and meat-roasting centres, and the end of Ilmorog Bar's own Sunshine Band. Chiri County Council says we have to close."

She would not say more. And now they watched her as she walked across the dusty floor toward where Munira was sitting. She stopped, whirled back, and screamed at the band. "Play! Play! Play on. Every body dance – Daaance!" And she sat down beside Munira.

"Munira, wouldn't you like to come and see my new place tomorrow night?"

Munira could hardly contain himself. So at long last. So the years of waiting were over. It was just like the old days before Karega and the roads and the changes had come to disturb the steamy peaceful rhythm in Ilmorog, when he was the teacher.

The next day he could not teach. He could not talk. He could hardly sit or stand still in one place. And when the time came, he walked to her place with tremulous hands and beating heart. He had not been inside the new house and he felt it an honour that she had chosen him out of all those faces.

He knocked at the door. She was in. She stood in the middle of the room lit by a blue light. For a second he thought himself in the wrong place with the wrong person.

She had on a miniskirt which revealed just about everything, and he felt his manhood rise of itself. On her lips was smudgy red lipstick: her eyebrows were pencilled and painted a luminous blue. What was the game, he wondered? He thought of one of the many advertisements he had earlier collected: Be a platinum blonde: be a whole new you in 100% imported hand-made human hair. Wanja was a really new her.

"You look surprised, Mwalimu. I thought you always wanted me," she said, with a false seductive blur in her voice. Then in a slightly changed voice, more natural, which he could recognise, she added: "That's why you had him dismissed, not so16 ßpok now. They have even taken away my right, well, our right to brew. The County Council says our licence was sold away with the New Building. They also say our present premises are in any case unhygienic! There's going to be a tourist centre and such places might drive visitors away. Do you know the new owner of our Theng'eta breweries? Do you know the owner of the New Ilmorog Utamaduni Centre? Never mind!" She had, once again, changed her voice: "But come: what are you waiting for?" She walked backwards: he followed her and they went into another room – with a double bed and a reddish light. He was hypnotised. He was angry with himself for being tongue-tied and yet he was propelled toward her by the engine-power of his risen body and the drums in the heart. Yet below it all, deep inside, he felt a sensation of shame and disgust at his helplessness.

She removed everything, systematically, piece by piece, and then jumped into bed.

"Come, come, my darling!" she cooed from inside the sheets.

He was about to jump into bed beside her and clasp her to himself, when she suddenly turned cold and chilly, and her voice was menacing.

"No, Mwalimu. No free things in Kenya. A hundred shillings on the table if you want high-class treatment."

He thought she was joking, but as he was about to touch her she added more coldly.

"This is New Kenya. You want it, you pay for it, for the bed and the light and my time and the drink that I shall later give you and the breakfast tomorrow. And all for a hundred shillings. For you. Because of old times. For others it will be more expensive."

He was taken aback, felt the wound of this unexpected humiliation. But now he could not retreat. Her thighs called out to him.

He took out a hundred shillings and handed it to her. He watched her count it and put the money under the mattress. Now panic seized him. His thing had shrivelled. He stood there and tried to fix his mind on the old Wanja, on the one who had danced pain and ecstasy, on the one who had once cried under watchful moonbeams stealing into a hut. She watched him, coldly, with menace, and then suddenly she broke out in her put-on, blurred, seductive voice.

"Come, darling. I'll keep you warm. You are tonight a guest at *Sunshine Lodge*."

There was something pathetic, sad, painful in the tone. But Munira's thing obeyed her voice. Slowly he removed his clothes and joined her in bed. Even as the fire and thirst and hunger in his body were being quenched, the pathetic strain in her voice lingered in the air, in him, in the room everywhere.

It was New Kenya. It was New Ilmorog. Nothing was free. But for a long time, for years to come, he was not to forget the shock and the humiliation of the hour. It was almost like that first time, long ago, when he was only a boy.

Indeed, changes did come to Ilmorog, changes that drove the old one away and ushered a new era in our lives. And nobody could tell, really tell, how it had happened, except that it had happened. With a year or so of the new Ilmorog shopping centre being completed, wheatfields and ranches had sprung up all around the plains: the herdsmen had died or had been driven further afield into the drier parts, but a few had become workers on the wheatfields and ranches on the earth upon which they once roamed freely. The new owners, master-servants of bank power, money and cunning came over at weekends and drove in Landrovers or Range Rovers, depending on the current car fashion, around the farms whose running they had otherwise entrusted to paid managers. The peasants of Ilmorog had also changed. Some had somehow survived the onslaught. They could employ one or two hands on their small farms. Most of the others had joined the army of workers who had added to the growing population of the New Ilmorog. But which New Ilmorog?

There were several Ilmorogs. One was the residential area of the farm managers, County Council officials, public service officers, the managers of Barclays, Standard and African Economic Banks, and other servants of state and money power. This was called Cape Town. The other — called New Jerusalem — was a shanty town of migrant and floating workers, the unemployed, the prostitutes and small traders in tin and scrap metal. Between the New Jerusalem and Cape Town, not far from where Mwathi had once lived guarding the secrets of iron works and native medicine, was All Saints church, now led by Rev. Jerrod Brown. Also somewhere between the two areas was Wanja's *Sunshine Lodge*, almost as famous as the church.

The shopping and business centre was dominated by two features. Just outside it was a tourist cultural (Utamaduni) village owned by Nderi wa Riera and a West German concern, appropriately called Ilmorog African Diamond Cultural and Educational Tours. Many tourists came for a cultural fiesta. A few hippies also came to look for the Theng'eta Breweries which, starting on the premises owned by Mzingo, had now grown into a huge factory employing six hundred workers with a number of research scientists and chemical engineers. The factory also owned an estate in the plains where they experimented with different types of Theng'eta plants and wheat. They brewed a variety of Theng'eta drinks: from the pure gin for export to cheap but potent drinks for workers and the unemployed. They put some in small plastic bags in different measures of one, two and five shillings' worth so that these bagfuls of poison could easily be carried in people's pockets. Most of the containers, whether plastic or glass bottles, carried the famous ad, now popularised in most parts of the country through their sales vans, newspapers and handbills: POTENCY — Theng'a Theng'a with Theng'eta. P=3T.

The breweries were owned by an Anglo-American international combine but of course with African directors and even shareholders. Three of the four leading local personalities were Mzigo, Chui and Kimeria.

Long live New Ilmorog! Long live Partnership in Trade and Progress!

Reprinted from Petals of Blood. *By permission of Heinemann Educational Books.*

Short stories are immensely popular in Kenya and you'll find stacks of well-thumbed, short romantic novels at any second-hand bookstall. **Sam Kahiga**'s *energetic, exasperatingly racy style, sprinkled with a combination of British and American idioms, is strange at first, but his stories are revealing about the values of modern, urban Kenya.*

A HIGH VOLTAGE AFFAIR

At school I was afflicted by that chronic laziness that is often the lot of young students who think they are especially clever and can pass any exam through sheer genius. After getting my "O" levels with nine points and no sweat at all, I went to Strathmore College for "A" levels. I remember my goal then – to be a nuclear physicist. And if that was too advanced for the Third World then I'd compromise gracefully, step down, and just be a bloody good research scientist. The Third World could do with some of those.

Well my "A" levels were a disaster. What could I blame it on? Girls, booze or drugs? I blame it on the lot – plus the sort of risky confidence that comes after you've been top of the class too many times. Of my days in Strathmore I remember the movies and the parties rather than what happened in the labs. Except for jokingly trying to invent a drug that could give one a trip I hardly applied myself. And when the final results came out I realised that I was on a bad trip that just wouldn't end up in the university. It was bad, shocking, in fact.

Guys whose IQs were nowhere near as high as mine got called up to the university. As for me I was bad news in academic circles. Trying to save face I applied feverishly to foreign universities. My daddy could afford to send me to one. But no foreign university seemed interested. I kept trying until my daddy casually let me know that if I was intending to go abroad I would have to get the dough myself. That's what is known as fatherly affection.

Let me explain his attitude, for I understood it perfectly. My daddy (his friends and enemies call him GM) was no kid-spoiler. Although he could afford to send me round the world seven times he wasn't going to help because I had proved I was a failure. If I had failed at home I would not succeed abroad. I realised for his acid comments that he knew about the kind of life I had led at Strathmore – girls, booze, drugs. Could he then seriously think of sending me to America, that modern Babylon and hippy headquarters.

"Go on your own," said GM. He had turned a blind eye to my mischief until I let him down and failed to make it to the university. And GM is not the kind of man you let down and get away with it. He himself had never failed. Where he couldn't work his way out smoothly he bulldozed. If the front door was closed he tried the back door. That was the way he made his millions in the construction business.

Sons of poor men were going to university, so why not GM's first-born? He felt betrayed. What was it that he had not done for me? My pocket money had been two hundred and fifty bob a month. And he had told me to buy any book that I wanted. So why had I not gone to university?

GM had never even been to high school because he had been born too many years before the fruit of independence ripened. When independence came he was just a mason grade three. We lived at Shauri Moyo. GM grabbed his share of the fruit and we moved off to Lavington where I had my own motor-cycle and a couple of rooms to myself which were a mess of wires, novels and beat music that made my mother ill. The smell of my strange "cigarettes" made her ill too, but mothers are like that. You have to be patient with them.

I agree that GM spoilt me. But all the money and stuff he showered on me was on the understanding that I would live up to his expectations, which I did until those hazy "A" levels. In fact I did more. For instance at seventeen I was the maintenance man around the place, the little genie who knew what was wrong with the TV, the fridge or even his car. GM couldn't even change his own spark plugs. He trusted me to tune and service his car and considered me the last word in wiring. Now you can begin to understand about the two hundred and fifty bob pocket money. I spent most of it on cocaine.

After I had failed GM didn't want to see me around. He is a very unforgiving man. He had dug up my Strathmore background and it had shocked him so much that he didn't want me to even touch his car.

What finally broke up our relationship was when the disciplinarian daddy in him came to the surface and he thought he could teach me a physical lesson just because my room smelt of something strange. He sniffed and realised that it was grass.

The rest is embarrassing. Let's just say that there was yet another side of me that he hadn't known. I had a panther's reflexes that had come from picking up all that one needs to know about judo and karate. I didn't hurt him at all but he stared at me from the floor with great surprise. Through his gaping mouth I saw a little film of blood on his small white teeth — nothing serious.

After that there was nothing else to do except pack. The mansion at Lavington was a bit too small for both of us.

Somehow I feel that this background is important before I tell the story that follows. When I went to the Power Institute to train as a technician for the Power Company I went on my own ticket. The exams accompanying the interview were tough and gruelling to most of the boys but I sailed through, although I was half-starving. They accepted me at the Power Institute on my own merit, not a millionaire's influential word. It is important that this is understood.

Every young boy carries in his heart the soft-focus image of a woman he could love, serve and die for. I'm still not sure whether she eventually turns up, this ever youthful, totally compliant dream girl whom you want to set on a pedestal and worship. She is mutable, changing with your fancy and experience, but something remains constant about her, whether you are twelve or forty.

This constancy I guess is the subservience to your ego. She will love you no matter what happens, no matter who else is there. She loves you when you are vomiting into the toilet bowl and sticks by your side as you piss into a dark alley. She will be petite and cuddlesome when you are in a gentle mood and you want her to be like that. She will have an Afro hairdo if that's what you want. She's a virgin, nobody ever touched her before. Sometimes her breasts are small, sometimes her breasts are large. Sometimes she's innocent, sometimes she's master of the Kama Sutra, a deep well of erotic knowledge.

The first time she came to me in the flesh (or was it her more mundane twin sister?) was at the Power Institute at the beginning of the second year. My thoughts were hardly on love but on electro-magnetic forces, watts, ohms and coulombs. Instead of breasts I was thinking of turbines and transformers and the only kick I ever got during those sober, sombre months was the flow of electrons through me whenever I was fool enough to step on a live wire. In short, I was immersed in electricity, my biggest love since childhood. I hadn't seen anybody for a year — nobody mattered. For companions I had watts, coils and ohm's law. If I needed a drink, coke was enough, thanks. The hostel supplied the grub. There wasn't much else I felt I needed.

Then during Easter we had a dance at the hostel and this chick came along with one of the boys. I remember I was pretty lonesome hanging around the stuffy room with my coke and yet expecting nothing from all the bull-shit. To make things worse it was raining badly outside and I couldn't walk back to the hostel even if I had wanted to.

What is dancing? I asked myself. Some hangover from some primitive era. Some sort of savage convolution totally outside the realm of scientific discipline. I wanted to go home but the damn rain was falling. When I looked out of the window the world was suddenly lit up by the taut gnarled roots of a devilish lightning flash. "Jupiter's thunder-bolt." "God's footstep." To scientists: atmospheric electric phenomena. I wanted to go to bed.

She was very pretty but couldn't have been with a worse man. Mbote was rude, coarse and argumentative. He was a slum child and he was proud of the fact. No efforts at all to be a gentleman. The girl he was with was a lady from the toe up to the rich mass of black hair. And if I wasn't wrong she was trying to catch my eye.

I put my ginger ale on the ledge of a window (tired of cokes by now). I singled her out from the rest of the clumsy humanity, forgave her for imperfections and danced with her to a slow number.

"What's your label?" I asked.

"I beg your pardon?"

"The name. What's your name?"

"Esther."

"Esther what?"

"Mbacia."

Esther Mbacia. I was a bit annoyed with her for looking like my dream girl while going around with a guy like Mbote. My dream girls are supposed to be my own. They shouldn't be wandering around among crude wolves. They might get eaten. I wouldn't have been surprised if she ended up in Mbote's cubicle.

"You didn't tell me your name, but I know you," she said. "You are GM's son, aren't you?"

"So?" I asked coldly.

"I used to see you when you were in Strathmore. I was then in Kenya High. You know, when you had that motor-cycle." I couldn't help grinning.

"Your girl-friend was my classmate, Edith." Edith, a grass addict.

"Mbacia," I said. "Is your father the Mbacia? Mbacia Enterprises?"

"Happens to be," she said.

"Oh." ·

"Oh, what?"

"Nothing."

We laughed together. And then I saw the livid angry eyes of Mbote staring at me over the rim of his glass of alcoholic poison. He was mixing everything, the only way he could get drunk cheaply. He had drunk changaa ever since he was a small boy in Majengo slums, so beer to him was mere water.

"Your boyfriend looks angry and dangerous," I said.

"He's not my boyfriend," said Mbacia's daughter.

There might have been a fight that night had I been just any other boy. But my reputation was good. They knew my reflexes. Mbote was a dreaded street fighter who bullied almost everybody else but he knew I could paralyse him by just touching a nerve. Neatly, with no glasses being broken. He didn't want that. I didn't want to be unfair so I gave her a date and went to bed.

So that's how the tragic triangle started. Poor slum boy grabs a rich girl, wants to make her happy in his own rude way. Rich boy comes along with polished karate and his father's millions behind him and poor boy has no chance. The fact that I was broke most of the time didn't worry her one bit. In fact it seemed to add to my attraction. GM's son, but always broke. How funny!

I liked serious movies but also liked seeing Chinese movies to improve on my karate. She liked ice-cream, chewing gum and I'm not quite sure what else. I liked her. A girl doesn't have to have a line of interest to be liked. I still don't know her line of interest. She doesn't share my passion for turbines and transformers but so what? So nothing. She was high voltage. There were electrostatic forces in her breasts. When she smiled at me the electrons flowed. She was my cathode and I was her anode.

She was Mbote's heartbreak. Poor slum boy, son of a Majengo prostitute, he had never had any love in his life. He thought he had found it in Esther. Esther thought she had found it in me. The eternal triangle.

He came to me one night when I was reading and knocked on the door of my cubicle. He was totally drunk. I threw him out. I threw him out because he called me a hybrid.

"Just because you are a hybrid and she's a hybrid you feel you must cross-breed. To keep the millions in one family."

"Get the hell out," I said. But I had to remove him physically.

What I think shattered him was my bringing Esther to the end of term dance. At first he was vulgar and insulting, though not talking to us directly. I heard the words "hybrid" and "cross-breeding" and tried to take no notice. Then I saw that he was staring at us silently, no longer speaking. The jilted lover: why not just find a girl? Why let this thing play on his complexes? I wished I could give him the girl but I was already in love with her. Or maybe there was this vacuum in my soul that she very conveniently filled. Sometimes it's difficult to distinguish love from the flight from loneliness.

The following morning was Sunday and that was when the nightmare began. Most of the boys had already gone home and the hostel was almost deserted.

With a towel around my loins I went into the shower room. Mbote who was waiting for that move came and locked the door with a key. Standing outside the door he told me a lot of things. How he had loved and how I had ruined his chances.

"What's the point of locking the door?"

"I want to kill you."

The shower was running, the warm water caressing my skin. He was going to kill me. He must be joking. And yet I knew how reckless he was, the kind of strange practical jokes he used to play on people. Better watch out.

"Look Mbote, Esther is mine," I said, wearily.

"You snatched her. You rich people think you can snatch everything. You think you are smart. You'll pay for it."

"How?"

"I want to make you dance. You like dancing I'll make you dance."

"Look, open the door and stop being stupid. What are you up to?"

"When you come out of there you won't be alive."

"Why?"

"The shower room is wired. I'm just about to give you a thousand volts." I got the idea. I broke into a sweat. I stared at the wet floor of my death cell. The water would conduct the electricity from wherever the terminals were.

"Open the door and don't be stupid," I cried and that was the last thing I said before the current shot up through my bare feet and shot me up to the ceiling. I screamed, then hit the floor unconscious.

Hospital. The first week was a blank. The next one I began to recognise people – chaps from the Power Institute, GM, Esther.

The third week I was fine and that was when they told me that Mbote had electro-cuted himself when I was in a coma. The cops

had come for him and rather than face the law he had taped electric wires to his head. He had turned on the switch, died instantly and made headlines for the first and last time.

I try to look on it all to see why and how it happened but I'm still not strong enough to sort out little psychological details. Or perhaps my mind just refuses to work. I saw a picture of Mbote's mother in the papers and she was wailing, saying he was a good boy. I take my own refuge behind public opinion for that's all I can do. Public opinion has it that Mbote was crazy to try and electrocute GM's son. He was quite right to electrocute himself, though. But he shouldn't go round trying to electrocute heirs to millions. (GM wants to know if I need bodyguards.)

It all depresses me. When my heart is really low I call up Esther on the phone.

"Doctor says I need lots of therapy, girl, and only you can give it to me. So come over quick."

She always does. I told you she's high volt-age – if you see what I mean. Maybe she really *is* hybrid.

Reprinted from the collection Flight to Juba *by permission of Longman Kenya.*

SWAHILI POETRY

Swahili poetry is Kenya's oldest written literature, recorded in Arabic script since the seventeenth century and in the Roman alphabet since the turn of this century. The oldest poems are praise and wedding songs from the oral tradition and narrative epics relating the early years of Islam. There's a wide variety of forms but the rhythms and rhymes are not too unfamiliar to Western ears. Swahili, with its infinite capacity for allusion and imagery, has produced some beautiful verse. **Shaaban Robert**, who died in 1962, is probably the greatest twentieth-century Swahili poet. This lament for his wife was written in the shairi metre of sixteen syllables to the line.

AMINA

Amina unmejitenga, kufa umetangulia,

Amina, you have withdrawn yourself, you led the way in dying,

Kama ua umefunga, baada ya kuchanua,
Nukuombea mwanga, peponi kukubaliwa.

Like a flower you have closed, after having opened first,
I pray for you, my light, that you may be welcomed in paradise.

Mapenzi tuliyofunga, hapana wa kufungua.

The love we made between us, no one ever will undo it.

. . . .

Nilitaka unyanyuke, kwa kukuombea dua,
Sikupenda ushindike, maradhi kukuchukua,

I had hoped that you would rise again, and I prayed for you,
I did not want you to be defeated, and be carried away by the disease,

Ila kwa rehema yake, Mungu amekuchagua.
Mapenzi tuliyofunga, hapana wa kufungua.

But by His mercy, God has chosen you.
The love we made between us, no one ever will undo it.

. . . .

Majonzi hayaneneki, kila nikikumbukia,
Nawaza kile na hiki, naona kama ruia,

My grief is indescribable, every moment I remember,
I keep thinking this and yonder I see things as if I were dreaming,

Mauti siyasadiki kuwa, mwisho wa dunia.

I did not believe in death first, that it was the end of the world, this life.

Mapenzi tuliyofunga, hapana wa kufungua.

The love we made between us, no one ever will undo it.

. . . .

Nasadiki haziozi, roho hazitapotea,
Twafuata wokozi, kwa mauti kutujia,

I believe that souls don't perish, they cannot be lost forever,
We pursue salvation's pathway, when death's angel comes to meet us,

Nawe wangu mpenzi, Peponi utaingia.

And you, my beloved partner, you will enter heaven's gateway.

Mapenzi tuliyofunga, hapana wa kufungua.

The love we made between us, no one ever will undo it.

. . . .

Jambo moja nakumbuka, sahihi ninalijua,
Kuwa sasa umefika, ta'bu isikosumbua,

Just one thing I do remember, one I know for sure and truly,
That you have now reached the place where no suffering can plague you,

Kwayo nimefurahika, nyuma nilikobakia.

Therefore do I still feel gladdened, here where I am left behind.

Mapenzi tuliyofunga, hapana wa kufungua.

The love we made between us, no one ever will undo it.

. . . .

Ninamaliza kutunga, kwa kukuombea dua,
Vumbi tena likiunga, roho likirudishiwa,

I have finished my composing, while for you I pray,
When dust is rejoined together, when the soul returns into it,

Mauti yakijitenga, mapenzi yatarejea.

While the power of death retires, then our love will be returning.

Mapenzi tuliyofunga, hapana wa kufungua.

The love we made between us, no one ever will undo it.

Translated by Jan Knappert, 1979. Reprinted from *Four Centuries of Swahili Verse* (Heinemann), by permission of the translator.

MUSIC IN KENYA

Kenya doesn't have the home-grown musical vitality of some African countries, and you can speculate on the reasons why. Its colonial peculiarities haven't helped, nor, in the same connection, has the Anglo-Americanisation of musical culture and the domination of the big mainstream record labels. Still, as the personal accounts below show, the sounds are here if you listen.

A SHORT HISTORY OF KENYAN MUSIC

You can hardly ignore the multiplicity of musical **sounds** emanating from Nairobi's teeming streets. At midday, you can hear the rap of the amplified preachers in Jeevanjee Gardens or, a little further down Moi Avenue, buskers accompanying themselves on home-made instruments. Wandering into the River Road area on the east side of town, you're barraged by the sounds of singles blasting forth from scores of mini music shops and street sellers with stalls set up on the pavement. Out in the suburbs on a Sunday afternoon you can sample any number of different forms of live music, from the drumming and singing of the many indigenous churches to recreational music at bars and hotels, ranging from the traditional Luo *nyatiti* (lyre) through middle-of-the-road lounge acts to African pop dance music. This enormous variety has evolved out of a number of separate strands.

NGOMA – THE DRUMS

Kenya's oldest musical tradition is **ngoma**, still the central term used to describe all the facets of a musical performance, including the accompanying dances. *Ngoma* in most Bantu languages of Kenya refers to a specific kind of **drum** and a related dance, but more broadly the term means drums in general and a genre of music using drums as its main instruments.

Although an inter-ethnic *ngoma* called *beni* (band) emerged on the coast around the turn of the century and spread inland (you can still witness this anachronistic, marching band form on special occasions in Lamu), *ngoma* music today is essentially ethnic, related to a specific language group and using the respective vernacular and local dance rhythms. *Ngoma* also provides most of the music used during the life-cycle festivities (birth, initiation and circumcision, marriage and death), whether in the town or the country. You can buy *ngoma* music on singles. Look out for recordings by Luyia **sukuti** groups: the *sukuti* is the central drum of these ensembles.

GUITARS AND GUITAR STYLES

From the early 1950s on, with society rapidly changing, the coming of recording and broadcasting, and the introduction of new instruments, especially the **guitar**, an acoustic guitar-based music developed as accompaniment to songs sung in **Swahili**. A basis for Swahili-language popular music had already been laid by the *beni* groups flourishing in East African towns during the first half of the century. *Beni* songs, as well as the new guitar songs, featured the strong and critical social commentary so beloved of Kenyans. The songs are usually in the form of a short story and may comment on an actual political or social topic, or perhaps recount a personal experience of the musician. Romantic songs are almost nonexistent, even in songs dealing with men and women.

The guitar styles themselves developed out of different instrumental techniques and musical perceptions, but they were influenced by the records available at the time, mainly from other parts of Africa. Kenyan musicians of the period cite **Jean Bosco Mwenda** and **Losta Abelo**, both from Katanga (today, Shaba Province, Zaire) and **George Sibanda**, from Bulawayo in Zimbabwe, as important inspirations. From this period, the notables of Kenya's acoustic guitar styles are **John Mwale**, **George Mukabi** (directly out of the Luyia *sukuti* tradition) and **Isaya Mwinamo**, to name a few.

The 1960s saw the introduction of **electric guitars** as well as larger groups (of three to four guitars). *Kwela* and **twist** were the rage, coming from or via Southern Africa. These were the days of the **Equator Sound Band** (Equator being the main record label), featuring the songs of **Daudi Kabaka**, **Fadhili William**, **Nashil Pichen** and **Peter Tsotsi**.

Developments in the popular music of Kenya ought to be seen in a larger regional frame including Tanzania and Zaire. In fact, Swahili-language music has been dominated by **Tanzanian musicians** for a long time, and Tanzanians record and perform in Kenya. The late Tanzanian guitarist, vocalist, songwriter and band leader, **Mbaraka Mwinshehe**, was even proclaimed "Soloist National" in Kenya. **Simba Wanyika**, **Les Wanyika** and **Issa Juma** (Super Wanyika Stars), all with their origins in Tanzania, were among the most popular musicians in the 1970s and early 1980s, all of them still performing today in and around Nairobi.

Zairean music has kept an unmistakable presence both in records and live music, with groups like **Prince Lessa Lassen's Popolipo**, **Samba Mampangala's Orchestra Virunga** and **Orchestra Zaiken** dominating the Nairobi club scene. But with perennial work permit problems, their status is never secure. The popular band **Vundumuna**'s stay at *The Carnivore* was abruptly terminated at the height of their popularity when they were unable to extend their work permits. After more than ten years as one of Nairobi's most popular bands, **Les Mangalepa** are (for the moment) quiet.

Meanwhile, the current favourites are the recently rejuvenated **Virunga**, **Les Wanyika**, **Orchestra Zaiken** and the **Pressmen Band** – poppy new MOR darlings.

THE VERNACULAR REVIVAL

In the 1970s, a strong resurgence of bands and musicians singing in **vernacular languages** and featuring locally derived dance styles hit the Kenyan scene. Most important among these guitar bands were the **Luo *benga*** groups from the area of western Kenya bordering on Lake Victoria. Characteristic of the *benga* style is the fast beat, rhythm guitar-playing with strong roots in the tradition of the *nyatiti* harp, and a punchy, up-front bass line. In the 1970s and early 1980s, *bonga* was the craze and large crowds of mostly young men used to gather in front of record shops such as *Victoria Music Store* on Sheikh Karume Road in Nairobi to listen to the latest *benga* hits around lunchtime. In recent years, the excitement has diminished, a reflection of the economic recession in the larger music and recording scene. But despite problems in the music business, *benga* looks set to stay. Variants of the *benga* beat have been adopted by groups singing in other Kenyan languages. Among the better known Luo *benga* bands are **D O Misiani's Shirati Jazz** and **Victoria "B" and "C" Kings**. Another Luo band, **Sega Matata**, have recently gained a wider Kenya audience through a series of topical songs in Swahili that were among the top-selling records of the mid-1980s.

In Nairobi and the Central Highlands, **Joseph Kamaru** is the doyen of **Kikuyu** music; he and **Councillor D K (Daniel Kamau)** are renowned for their strong social and political commentary and their poetic use and knowledge of the Kikuyu language. The recent death of Kakai Kilonzo, leader of the **Kilimambogo Brothers Band**, has deprived Kenyans of one of their most innovative and interesting musicians. Although ethnically identified as a **Kamba** musician, Kilonzo's Swahili lyrics made his music readily accessible to other groups, extending his popularity well beyond his own Kamba people. Other fine Kamba musicians such as **Peter Muambi**, **Onesmas Musyioki (Kalambya Boys)** and **Ngoleni Brothers** have yet to extend their following beyond their local audiences.

It is difficult to characterise and distinguish the music of these bands with different ethnic backgrounds. Beats like *benga* are freely borrowed, while Luo and Luyia guitarists have a long history of playing in predominantly Kikuyu and Kamba bands, further complicating the mix. But, while it may be difficult to sort out precisely what clustering of characteristics makes Luo bands sound Luo and Kamba bands sound Kamba, it's unlikely you would have much difficulty in distinguishing the end results. Certainly, the differences in the sounds of the languages are a help and the melody, harmonies and rhythms give further clues.

TARABU MUSIC

Tarabu, the main popular music of the coastal **Swahili** people, deserves special mention. It could be lumped in with the above-mentioned *ngoma* and vernacular guitar bands, as it has a long tradition in the festive life of the Swahili and is also the general music of entertainment of the coastal communities. But the music has strong Arabic-Islamic overtones in instrumentation, especially in the haunting vocals. Earlier *tarabu* (*taarab*, *tarab*) groups used the full Arabic orchestra, including the lute-like *oud* and violins. Today the main instruments are mandolin or guitar and either an Indian harmonium or a small electronic organ/piano, plus a variety of local, Arabic or Indian drums. Indian movies, with their strong musical component, are very popular among the coastal people and under their influence many features of Indian music have entered *tarabu*. From as early as the 1940s *tarabu* has been sung not only in Swahili but also in Urdu/Hindi. Many of the lead singers and bandleaders of *tarabu* groups are women, almost unique in Kenyan traditional music. The focus of *tarabu* is intricately rhythmic poetry and, in this, **Juma Balo** is one of its masters. Leading female voices are **Malika** and **Zuhura**, while mixed-sex vocals are the feature of the **Black Star** and **Lucky Star Musical Clubs**, originally from Tanzania.

Werner Graebner

Like most African countries, Kenya has a rich cultural heritage of **traditional music**, and it also has the potential for a thriving popular music industry. You'll probably be disappointed, however, at the selection of available albums. Although there are adequate studios and dozens of bands making (or wanting to make) records, the pop scene is dominated by 45rpm singles. Many of the albums available are collections of recent hit singles, although there's a small number of LPs which can stand with the best of any from Africa. As international productions of one sort or another, some of these can be found in record stores in Europe and America, but their availability, even in Kenya, can't be guaranteed.

African music styles heard in Kenya include the classically inspired Swahili **tarab** music, which has a pronounced Islamic flavour and a

kind of spiritual, old-world charm, and **Swahili guitar band music**, which reached its peak in the 1960s and 1970s by combining elements of Congolese with South African *kwela* and local indigenous music. The main influence since the 1970s, however, has been from Zairean (or Congolese) music. A near-invasion by Zairean nationals led to the formation of several top-ranking dance bands at the expense of indigenous pop styles. These local sounds were often decried by local enthusiasts for being "vernacular" and therefore appealing only to one tribal group. Visa restrictions recently imposed on Zairean nationals, the overseas tours of **Shirati Jazz** and a bubbling interest in other indigenous Kenyan guitar bands, indicate hope for a commercial resurgence of Kenyan pop.

COMPILATION ALBUMS

Tribal Songs of Kenya (POLP 316). Disregard the title: this is a compilation of hot vernacular pop in the language of "Kenya's great tribes". Includes Maroon Commandos, Orchestra Intuma Jazz, The Lula Band, Historia Kumbuka Band and six other groups.

The Best Songs of 1984 (ASLP 406). A typical compilation of Zairean studio hits, with one number by Nguashi Timbo, who wrote the Kenyan classic song "Shauri Yako".

The Nairobi Beat – Kenyan Pop Music Today (Rounder 5030). Great 1989 cross-section of Kenyan vernacular and Swahili pop, with tracks from Shirati Jazz, Maroon Commandos, Bana Likasi (Lovy), Super Bunyore Band (Shem Tube), Mbiri Stars, Kalambya Sisters and Wafula Hamisi.

Guitar Paradise of East Africa (Virgin Earthworks). A stunning seventy-minute CD, with tracks in Luo, Swahili, Lingala, Luyia, Kamba and Kikuyu by Sukuma Bin Ongaro, H O Kabaselleh, Les Mangalepa, Simba Wanyika, Super Mazembe, Peter Mwambi, Kilimambogo Brothers, the Famous Nyahururu Boys and Daniel Kamau. The songs by the latter two lift you right off the floor.

Djalenga (SWAH 001). A UK-released mini-album with tracks from Super Wanyika, Prince Lessa Lassen and Super Lovy.

SWAHILI LANGUAGE ARTISTS

Simba Wanyika Original, *Kenya Volume I* (AMG 0003). Probably the most popular Swahili band in the region, they have released several Soukous-style albums since the late 1970s, but this is one of the few still available. A new album, released in Nairobi, is *Mapenzi ni Damu* (POLP 572).

Les Wanyika, *Nilipi La Ajabu* (POLP 582). The veteran Swahili language ensemble had a smash hit with this in Nairobi in 1989–90. Their latest, *Les Les Non Stop* (Polydor again), is another chart-topper.

Mavalo Kings, *Heshima Kidogo* (POLP 581). A new album available in Kenya, from the "cousins" of Les Wanyika.

Issa Juma and the Super Wanyika Stars, *Sigalame II* (Discafrique). Re-release of a 1983 classic. Exhilarating Tanzanian guitar work.

Orchestra Makassy, *Agwaya* (V 2236). Old and wonderful album of Swahili, Shona and Lingala songs by a big group of mostly Tanzanian artists. The brilliant "Kufilisika sio Kilema" makes a fine Swahili lesson for *tembo* parties.

Les Kilimambogo Brothers, *Simba Africa* (PAM 003). Akamba-style benga, sung in Swahili for greater reach and repackaged on the German African music label.

Maroon Commandos, *Usiniambie Unaenda* ("Don't tell me you're going" – LZE 68). A few years old, but one of the finest of the 7th Battalion Kenya Army band's LPs. Their urban Swahili sound provides an interesting contrast to the Kenyan-based Zairean groups and pervasive *benga*. A new album should be just out.

Them Mushrooms, *New Horizon* (POLP 548). A popular band who mix reggae numbers with straight ahead *benga*, this album is only a limited sample of their work. Their current live shows are packing the dance floors. There's a new Nairobi-released album: *Going Places* (POLP 573).

Pressmen Band, *Musenangu* (CBS). First vinyl effort of the former tourist circuit combo. A mix of coastal folk songs and rhythms with Kenyan urban and international influences. A big hit with the younger city crowd in Nairobi.

ZAIRE CONNECTION

Samba Mapangala & Orchestra Virunga, *Virunga Volcano* (Virgin Earthworks). A British-licensed version of one of Kenya's greatest (Zairean) pop hits. This classic session album includes some real gems, with "Ahmed Sabit" the most sweetly distinctive track. The Virungas' most recent release in Kenya (on CBS) is called *Vunja Mifupa* ("Break the bones").

Baba Gaston, *Revival* (ASLP 1004). One of the godfathers of Kenyan pop, this Zairean bandleader opened up the country to Lingala language (Zairean) music in the early 1970s.

Les Mangalepa, *Greatest Hits* (JJLP 005). Typical of the East African variant of Zairean music from a band now newly incarnate in Harare. *Lisapo* (Phillips) has intricate soukous arrangements. *Madina* (ASLP 413), their last Kenyan recording, has mostly English lyrics on more Kenyan rhythms. *Safari* (ASLP 988) can be found occasionally in Europe.

Super Mazembe, *Maloba d'Amor* (AFRI 007). Another top Zairean band, Mazembe have dissolved, but may be reforming on the coast. Discafrique has reissued some of their old tunes, on what seems to be a re-release of the *Kaivaska* album made with Virgin in 1983.

Orchestra Super Lovy, *Super Lovy 2* (LOVILP 411). One of the most prolific Lingala groups in Kenya, they also appear on several compilations.

KENYAN LANGUAGE GROUPS

Shirati Jazz, *Benga Beat* (WCB 003). Following their debut visit to Britain and the recording of this big-selling LP, Shirati are now thought of as the top *benga* group, even though the leader, Owino Misiani, was absent – which shows. The punchier *Benga Blast* (Virgin Earthworks) speaks this particular musical language much better. Globestyle's Shirati production is *Piny Ose Mer* ("World Upside Down"), a brutally minimalist *benga* selection recorded in Nairobi. On Discafrique, there's also the wonderfully top-heavy *My Life and Loves*, with D O noisily in charge (AFRILP004), and, if you can track it down (possibly on the "Jicco" label), a newly released collection of old Shirati songs called *Long Life to Mary* (JCLP022). In Kenya, you may also find copies of the recently released *Rose Atieno* (POLP 580).

Kalambya Sisters, *Katalina* (ZSS 07). A 12-inch single licensed in Germany, the songs of these "schoolgirls on speed" have a unique charm and energy. You'll be lucky to find this, but seek the Sisters out on the new *Rounder* compilation (above).

Shem Tube, Justo Osala and Ende Okola, *Abana Ba Nasery* ("Nursery kids") (Globestyle). Classic 1960s recordings from western Kenya in the Luyia *omutibo* style, including some Fanta top percussion.

Bungoma Success (Songa, see "Music Magazines" box). Licensed by Diploma Music House, the first compilation of Bukusu language recordings in the UK from the likes of Wasike wa Musungu, Jack Musee and Wesley Barasa Marani with the BP Sunday National Jazz Band. A nice taster.

Luo Roots: **Kapere Jazz Band, Paddy J Onono, Ogwanglelo Okoth, Orchestra Nyanza Success** (Globestyle). Pretty and peculiar pickings from the persistently exploratory label. More evidence of Kenya's hidden musical riches.

TARABU MUSIC

Songs the Swahili Sing (OMA 103). This collection of scratchy "oldies" is a good introduction to the coastal region's *tarab* sounds .

Maulidi and Musical Party, *Mombasa Wedding Special* (ORB 58). One of Kenya's leading *tarabu* group in a 1989 recording by the Globestyle "expedition".

Black Star and Lucky Star Musical Clubs, *Nyota* (Globestyle). Mombasa sounds from veterans of the *tarabu* scene.

The Music of Zanzibar 1 and 2 (ORBD 032 and ORBD 033). More *tarabu* sounds on Globestyle from the island which nurtured the style's roots. Both albums contain substantial sleeve notes; the first is mostly instrumental.

Phil Bunce, Graeme Ewens, Doug Paterson and Richard Trillo

SELECTED AFRICAN MUSIC STOCKISTS

Bangor: *Cob Records*, 320 High Street, Bangor (☎0248 353 020).

Bath: *Soul Survival*, 6 River St Place, Julian Road, Bath BA1.

Belfast: *Caroline Music*, 10 Ann Street, Belfast (☎0232 231 108).

Brighton: *Brighton Records*, 13 East Street, Brighton BN1 1HP (☎0273 25884).

Bristol: *Biashara*, 84 Colston Street, Bristol BS1 (☎0272 260 902); *Joliba*, 44 Picton Street, Bristol, BS6 5QA (☎0272 49303); *Tony's*, 58 Park Street, Bristol BS1 (☎0272 214 659).

Cardiff: *Spillers*, 36 The Hayes, Cardiff (☎0222 224 905).

Carlisle: *Calabash Records*, Irthing House, Irthington, Carlisle CA6 4NS (☎06977 3742).

Crewe: *World Roots Music*, 66 Edleston Road, Crewe CW2 7HD (☎0270 257 138).

Edinburgh: *Virgin*, 131 Princes Street, Edinburgh (☎031 225 4583).

Glasgow: *A1 Sounds*, 98 Renfield Street, Glasgow 2 (☎041 332 9657); *Iona Records*, 155 Stockwell Street, Glasgow G1 4LR (☎041 552 0969).

Hebden Bridge: *System*, 48 Market Street, Hebden Bridge, West Yorkshire (☎0422 843 056).

Hove: *Replay*, 143 Dyke Road, Hove (☎0273 733368).

Keighley: *The Den*, Basement, 38 Cavendish Street, Keighley BD21 3RG (☎0535 606 086).

Leeds: *Jumbo Records*, 102 Merrion Centre, Leeds, LS2 8PJ (☎0532 455570).

Liverpool: *Probe*, 8-12 Rainford Gardens, Liverpool 2 (☎051 227 5646).

London: *Stern's African Record Centre*, 116 Whitfield Street, London W1P 5RW (☎071 387 5550).

Manchester: *Decoy Records* 30 Deansgate, Manchester M3 1RH (☎061 832 0183).

Newcastle: *J.G. Windows*, 1-7 Central Arcade, Newcastle-upon-Tyne NE1 5BP (☎091 232 1356).

Norwich: *Backs*, 31 Swan Lane, Norwich NR2 1HZ (☎0603 625 658).

Nottingham: *Selectadisc*, 19 Bridlesmith Gate, Nottingham (☎0602 580 437).

Sheffield: *Record Collector*, 235 Fullwood Road, Broomhill, Sheffield S10 (☎0742 668 493).

Winchester: *Tubes*, 14 Stockbridge Road, Winchester;

York: *Red Rhino*, 73 Goodramgate, York YO1 2LF (☎0904 36499).

MUSIC BOOKS

Ronnie Graham, *Storn's Guide to Contemporary African Music* (Pluto Press, 1989). An invaluable, country-by-country survey of styles, artists and releases. New edition on the way.

Chris May and Chris Stapleton, *African All Stars: the Pop Music of a Continent* (Paladin, 1989). An indispensable, highly readable account of the development of African music's many strands.

MUSIC MAGAZINES

Worldbeat Glossy and effusive global world music coverage from surely the loudest pages ever seen on a news stand. Good journalism and strongly tipped to survive.

Take Cover A more modest approach, in black and white, serving specifically African, Latin and Caribbean interests and without any mad media mogul backing. Sadly, went straight into hibernation in 1990 after Issue No. 1.

Folk Roots The main organ of the publisher of *Take Cover*, this is long-established, widely available, and worth a look for limited African coverage.

Straight No Chaser (4 Lordship Park, London N16 5UD). Stylish quarterly dedicated to jazz and anything else that takes their catholic fancies. Lots of interesting contributors.

Songa A Kenyan pop fanzine which shows all too clearly the effects of Kenyan music starvation on rural communities in West Sussex. The highly recommended first issue (£2.50 from 104 High St, Billingshurst, W. Sussex RH14 9QS) comes with a cassette of tracks from Bungoma and lots of pithy views. Don't even ask if there'll be a No. 2. There might. (Stop press: there is.)

ONWARDS: AFRICAN TRAVEL OPTIONS

Many travellers start African journeys in Kenya. And even if you don't intend to cross the continent, Kenya gives multiple options for onward travel, though currently the only very practical directions are south or west. The following pieces are intended as brief introductory notes. For relevant embassies in Nairobi, see the "Nairobi Directory" section in Chapter One.

GUIDEBOOKS

For travels south of Kenya into **Zimbabwe and Botswana**, the comprehensive and stimulating new guide *Zimbabwe and Botswana: the Rough Guide* (Harrap Columbus) is the obvious choice. And if you're heading for **West Africa**, again, the new *West Africa: the Rough Guide* covers all seventeen countries with unprecedented attention to detail and a wealth of background and maps unavailable in any other publication. Both books are usually on sale at the *Nation Bookshop* in Nairobi.

The only guide that covers the whole continent is *Africa on a Shoestring* (Geoff Crowther, Lonely Planet, last revised 1989), but it's never sufficiently up-to-date to offer more than predeparture background. Most of the countries highlighted below (but not Sudan, Ethiopia or Somalia) are covered in the more useful *East Africa – A Travel Survival Kit* (Geoff Crowther, Lonely Planet, 1987), though it, too, is beginning to look very historical. There are fewer travel details but no shortage of appetising outdoor recommendations in *Backpacker's Africa* (Bradt Publications, 1989), which skims through all the accessible countries from Kenya southwards in search of mountains to hike and trails to backpack.

TANZANIA

Entry requirements: British and most other Commonwealth passport-holders are issued free visitors' cards; US citizens need visas. Travellers with South African stamps in their passports are prohibited, as are travellers who may have been to South Africa and cannot prove otherwise. Israeli stamps in your passport can also cause problems. If you have a "single entry visa" to Kenya, you can still enter Tanzania (but only Tanzania) and return again to Kenya within its validity. Health advice follows Kenya's. It's worth writing to the Tanzanian Tourist Corporation, Azikwe, PO Box 2458, Dar-es-Salaam, or visiting a tourist office – often much more informative than Kenya's.

A visit to **TANZANIA** is an obvious extension to Kenyan travel. Arusha, the country's safari capital, makes a good base for exploring the **northern game parks** and is an easy day's bus journey from Nairobi. The **Serengeti**, a continuation of the Maasai Mara but a dozen times bigger; **Ngorongoro Crater**, where a complete ecosystem is contained inside an extinct volcano; **Lake Manyara**, with its tree-climbing lions; and the twin-peaked massif of **Kilimanjaro** all add up to an enticing circuit. Despite its popularity, it rarely feels like a milk-run. Northern Tanzania's wildlife and scenery are rated equal or superior to any in Kenya, and the much lower key tourist development is quite a contrast.

The coast, too, is alluring – twice the length of Kenya's and strewn with the sizeable islands of Zanzibar, Pemba and Mafia. **Bagamoyo**, on the mainland, and **Kilwa**, far to the south, are pretty hideaways, too. **Zanzibar** itself shares Lamu's appeal, but it has a hinterland region and there's plenty of scope for lazy exploration (the five-times-weekly direct flights from Mombasa to Zanzibar aren't outrageously expensive and there's a new Mombasa–Tanzania high-speed ferry service). The **bureaucracy** of Zanzibar (which retains the trappings of a separate country, united with the mainland) can be a tedious introduction, but the human **welcome** is a wonderful palliative.

For the most part, the **rest of the country** is a vast dry plateau, desperately poor, and is tough travelling. Worth the long journey and fairly high cost, though, is a visit to the **Gombe Stream National Park** on the hilly shoreline of **Lake Tanganyika**. This famous chimpanzee reserve is one of the very few places left to see them in the wild.

Tanzania's socialist economy has been in dire straits for many years, due to a host of indigenous problems and a lack of international support – particularly in the wake of the costly invasion of Uganda and the overthrow of Idi Amin. In practical terms, this means that while petrol and food supplies have improved and **shortages** of basic supplies are now rare, anything luxury (from toilet paper on up) may be scarce and expensive. Come prepared.

You'll have to accept the necessity of black market **money** changing if you want to avoid a very expensive stay (the black market rate, to which many prices have adjusted, is at least twice the bank rate). The currency declaration form is taken seriously these days: yours is liable to be spot-checked almost anywhere, but especially in tourist regions. Form forging and all sorts of other illegal wheezes have mostly been eradicated. It is important to make sure you change at least some convincing sums of money in the banks. Apart from that, the government is increasingly allowing foreign currency to be accepted in payment for all but minor items, with change given in Tsh, which means you have no choice but to accept the official rate.

These detractions needn't prevent Tanzania from being an attractive country to travel in. Trains and buses are the main means of **transport**. Trains run from Dar-es-Salaam to Tanga and up to Moshi and Arusha, west to the new capital, Dodoma, and Tabora, then further west to Kigoma on Lake Tanganyika and Mwanza on Lake Victoria. The most important line is the **Tazara railway**, twice a week, to the Zambian border. Train bookings need to be made far in advance. Bus journeys are on poor roads – lots of potholes and breakdowns – and there are occasional police checks. Carry food and water. Ferries operate on the lakes and on the coast.

Dar-es-Salaam is not a compelling city and cheap **accommodation** with rooms available somewhat hard to find. As everywhere, electricity and water may be erratic. Most towns do have cheap lodgings, but a tent is a very useful asset.

The **parks**, though magnificent, are more expensive attractions than in Kenya: US$10 entry fee plus a combined daily fee and camp-ing charge of US$15 per person, payable only in hard currency. Arusha has some camping safari operators who make the costs just about bearable, but you'll usually have to find companions to fill the seats, and four is about the minimum worthwhile number. Driving in yourself is prohibitive. If you're put off climbing Kilimanjaro by the cost (totals around $400) and general commercialism, be consoled by the words of one traveller: "This is the most boring mountain I have ever climbed in my life." The ascent of Mount Kenya is certainly more satis-fying, even if it is less splendid to look at from the ground.

You should be careful where you point your **camera** in Tanzania. Outside the parks, suspi-cions may be innocently aroused. English is spoken much less widely than in Kenya and a smattering of the national **language**, Swahili, will help enormously. **Women** travelling alone, or with other women, may find Tanzania a more relaxed country to travel in than Kenya.

UGANDA

Entry requirements for Uganda are hard to pin down. The official line seems to be that visas are needed by all, except for nationals of Eire, Italy, Spain, the Scandinavian countries and West Germany. In the past, British and other Commonwealth citizens have usually been issued with tourist passes at the border, but it's not a bad idea to visit a Uganda Embassy or High Commission, whatever your nationality, just to check. The border with Kenya has occasionally been closed in a low-level war of accusa-tions between the two governments. Yellow fever vaccination certificates are mandatory and you're advised to have others, too. There's a new drive to develop Uganda's tourist potential and the newly created Uganda Tourist Development Corporation has a PR company working on its behalf at 29 Hatton Garden, London EC1N 8DA (☎071 831 3342) – leaflets and information.

UGANDA's reputation has suffered nearly as much as its people over the last twenty years, though with the wide support being given now to President Museveni's *National Resistance*

Movement (at least in the south and west), things may at last improve. Amnesty International, however, have recently cited serious cases of violent, clumsy repression and the intimidation and mass execution of detractors, especially in the districts around Soroti, though these atrocities would appear to be the result of army indiscipline, rather than murderous government policy. Such events are unlikely to impinge on your visit, but the region is best avoided. As has long been the case, it's wise to talk to someone who's just been in the country because conditions change rapidly. The latest upset in Uganda has been the invasion of Rwanda by Ugandan-based rebels and the fact that Museveni must have known of their plans.

Nearly all travellers find their worst fears appeased by exceptionally friendly people: and tourists are usually treated politely by officials. English is very widely spoken. Ugandan **currency** is very shaky and the black market offers at least twice the official rate of exchange. But make sure you get a currency declaration form. The requirement to change hard currency ($150 on entry and $30 per day of your stay) has been rescinded. Still, some costs have to be met in hard currency – fancier hotels, for example. Currency forms aren't always carefully scrutinised when departing through land borders.

Uganda is considerably smaller than Kenya. Flat plains splashed with rivers and swamps rise westwards to **lakes Edward and Albert**, the **White Nile**, the snow-streaked **Ruwenzoris** (the "Mountains of the Moon") and the high border with Zaire. This western part holds the country's major attractions, including the newly reopened and far from empty **Muchison Falls National Park**. It's a stunning landscape and, out here, it is easy to see how Uganda could once have been called "The Pearl of Africa". The northeast half of Uganda, however (roughly northeast of a line from Tororo to Arua), is barely under Kampala's control, and sporadic fighting and uprisings still occur. Even if you could slip past the checkpoints, this is dangerous territory.

The **mountains** offer superb hiking and bush-walking amid equatorial montane vegetation. In the southwest, a clutch of parks (some dense jungle) are still just about functioning. This should be a good region to track **mountain gorillas** but, though cheaper

and less organised than the Rwanda gorilla industry (see below), it's also less certain you'll find them. Recent international efforts to preserve the remaining gorillas have also led to a clampdown on visitors. Moreover the even more recent rebel invasion of Rwanda was launched from this part of Uganda, which may make it currently off-limits.

Transport and **accommodation** have been hit-and-miss for a long time, but things have greatly improved since the late 1980s. Church centres and mission stations need no longer figure very prominently in your travels: there are now cheap **hotels** everywhere, much like Kenya's, and perhaps offering higher standards. Transport is much improved as well and roadblocks are gradually being removed. The **railway** still runs through from the Kenya border via Kampala to Kasese near the Zaire border and offers cheap if uncomfortably slow travel. The border with Sudan in the north is currently closed. **Food** isn't likely to be a problem. Bananas are big in the south.

Uganda needs stability for some years before it can be recommended unreservedly. But for adventurous travellers prepared to reserve judgement on the bad press, it's a stimulating trip. Increasing numbers of people are visiting from Kenya and the country is trying to gear itself up for tourism in quite a big way. If you want to fix up something organised in advance, try contacting *Hot Ice*, PO Box 151, Kampala (☎010 256 41 243800, fax 244779), who offer various safaris.

RWANDA AND BURUNDI

Entry requirements: most nationalities require visas for Rwanda and Burundi although Rwanda exempts West Germans. There has been a Burundi consulate in Kigoma (Tanzania) for some years and you can get Rwanda visas in Bujumbura, but it's much better to get visas for both countries in Dar or Nairobi.

West from Kenya into central Africa are **RWANDA** and **BURUNDI**, two of the continent's smallest countries. Ex-Belgian colonies little known outside the region, their societies reflect the old feudal traditions of cattle-herding fiefdoms with rigid tribal distinctions. After the Belgians left – having further divided the peoples – both countries experienced waves of revolt and counter-revolt, which, in Burundi culminated in the slaughter of the Hutu peasantry by the ruling Tutsi. Some stability was imposed by military governments, but in Burundi there was major conflict again in 1988. Tens of thousands of Hutu fled to Hutu-ruled Rwanda after a full-scale terror of massacres. Then, in October 1990, an invasion of Rwanda by exiled Tutsi rebels based in Uganda was only put down after fierce fighting in several Rwandan towns.

For the future, it's clear that Tutsi-dominated Burundi and Hutu-dominated Rwanda need a joint approach to their domestic problems. The Tutsi government of Burundi has, since 1987, started an effort at power-sharing with the country's Hutu.

Set in a highlands region on the western arm of the Rift Valley system, Rwanda and Burundi are mountainous, heavily cultivated, highly populated, poor, francophone and expensive. Kigali and Bujumbura – their respective capitals – are difficult for low budgets. Before the recent invasion, Rwanda had established an embryonic tourist industry for transiting overlanders, and its **mountain gorillas** are a magnetic draw in their own right. Tour operators in Kigali would set you up with a visit to one of the gorilla family groups. The country won't be receiving many visitors, however, until some sort of stability is achieved once again.

ZAIRE

Entry requirements: Zaire's borders close now and again so you need to be flexible. Visa requirements, too, are notoriously changeable. Non-Africans, without exception, need visas, but the cost and validity vary considerably depending on your passport and which Zaire embassy you visit. If you can use it before it expires, find out about getting a visa from your home embassy. Otherwise, the embassy in Nairobi probably makes the least fuss. You'll normally need a letter of recommendation from your own embassy. To enter Zaire, cholera and yellow fever vaccination certificates have to be shown, and you're advised, as a health precaution, to have the full range of shots.

You can easily make a side trip from Kenya to **ZAIRE**, though most travellers take in the country as part of a trans-African journey. Unpredictable in the purest sense, Zaire is far too big to come to terms with. Once in, you tend to enter a kind of dream state. How the country functions at all is a miracle – and says a lot for the common sense, patience and civility of ordinary people. Much of the **northern rain forest** region is enclosed by the trailing tributaries of the Zaire River. This is where most overlanding travellers pass and it is, essentially, anarchic. The government in Kinshasa has very few agents out here and society and economy are left to manage as best they can: teachers and civil servants are forgotten; roads and bridges collapse for weeks on end. Everything is expensive. Here you'll find torsos of roast monkey for sale in the markets, pygmy hunters melting into the forest, Greek and Portuguese plantation barons, narrow gauge railways, steamboats teeming with passengers and jungle in every direction.

Along the **Ruwenzoris** in the east, the towns rely on East Africa, and especially Mombasa, for their relative prosperity and sophistication. Swahili will help in eastern Zaire and French is indispensable for the rest of the country.

Major **attractions** are the climbable volcanoes (one still active), and gorillas and other wildlife in the Virunga and Kahuzi-Biega National Parks. **Goma**, on the rugged shore of Lake Kivu at the border with Rwanda, and **Bukavu**, at the southern end of the lake on the Burundi border, are the main centres for hiking trips, with permits, porters and guides.

Deep in the rain forest further north, especially around **Epulu**, you'll come across commercial overland expeditions "seeing the pygmies". If you'd like to meet and spend some time with these people without feeling like a complete monster in their forest home, allow plenty of time, make friends and wait for invitations: the experience is unforgettable. Keeping your predatory camera out of sight will help relations. Many "pygmies" (the different groups have their own names, but all speak Bantu languages, having long ago lost their own) live on the road much of the time these days, working on Bantu farms and foreign-owned plantations. But the forest is still, exclusively, their real home.

Travel is slow in Zaire and there are virtually no buses; use lorries, ferries, one or two train services and, above all, your legs.

Concerning **bed and board**, the missions are increasingly loath to put up travellers, but sometimes you'll have to do your best to persuade – a tent is a big help. Hotels, like food and restaurants when you can find them, are *très chers*. Again in this respect, things are easier in the string of towns along the eastern highlands and the few large towns in the interior.

Officials in Zaire may be highly sensitive about *sécurité* – be extremely cautious with your camera. Similarly, be wise to the **currency** situation. Banks are few, the official exchange rate is lousy and the black market flourishes. But be prepared to produce your currency declaration form to the various brands of police and security officials. If it shows you haven't changed any money in a bank, you're in for tedious wrangling and bribery.

SUDAN

For entry into Sudan visas are required by all, and South African or Israeli stamps in your passport will prevent your getting one. Travellers who have arrived in Egypt via Israel, stamp or no stamp, are likely to be denied a visa at the embassy in Cairo. Yellow fever and cholera certificates necessary.

North of Kenya, onward land travel possibilities are limited. Until the early 1980s **SUDAN**, like Zaire, was a giant expanse of Africa with limitless potential for resourceful travellers, despite the endless bureaucracy of travel permits. But with the downfall of Numeiri, the south has openly risen up against Muslim rule from Khartoum and much of **southern Sudan is off-limits** to travellers. This includes the whole of the region bordering Uganda and Kenya, making overland travel out of the question. The once-popular **Nile route** is closed and even *Sudan Airways* has stopped flying between Nairobi and Khartoum. Until the military coup in June 1989 it was still just about possible to travel overland to or from Khartoum through the Central African Republic and the western border. At the time of writing, as the country writhes in the grip of a brutal dictatorship

which allies itself with Saddam's Iraq, the prospects for travel anywhere in Sudan are bleak. With the further spectre of **mass famine** looming after the failure of the harvest in 1990, prospects for the immediate future of Sudan look grim indeed.

In the event of the border with Kenya reopening, there's a new route being ploughed through the bush to connect Lodwar with Juba in Sudan.

ETHIOPIA

Ethiopian entry requirements include "sufficient funds" (as much as $50 per day) and an air ticket out of the country. Only nationals of Kenya are exempt from visas. Yellow fever and cholera certificates are mandatory. Try writing in advance to the Ethiopian Tourism and Hotel Commission, PO Box 2183, Addis Ababa, for information.

ETHIOPIA is one of the most compelling countries in Africa – an ancient mountain kingdom considerably expanded in the last two hundred years but Christian at its Amharic heart since the fourth century. Colonialism affected it only briefly when the Italians usurped its independence from 1936 to 1941. Revolution in 1974 deposed the Emperor **Haile Selassie** and plunged the country from feudal misery into chaos, eventually resolved by a Soviet-backed military dictatorship. Somalia declared war over its claim to the Ogaden region, while secessionist movements in Tigre and Eritrea have kept the Ethiopian government fully occupied throughout the catastrophic drought of the early 1980s. By 1990 the regime was barely holding together and under severe pressure from the north by rebel groups which threaten to sever links with the country's Red Sea ports. After the widespread failure of the harvest in 1990, a new famine was set to pitch Ethiopia into further distress in 1991.

Although it may still be possible to cross the border into Ethiopia from Kenya for a few hours (see the section on Moyale, p.377), official entry can only be made by air into Addis Ababa (about $200 from Nairobi). Once in the country, your movements are restricted to the environs of the capital and one or two nearby towns. Longer trips – to visit **seventeenth-century** castles, rock-hewn churches, the **Semyen Mountains** and **Bale Mountains National Park** and a string of jewel-like **lakes** in the Ethiopian Rift Valley – can only be arranged through tour operators in Addis, and they're very costly. You need **travel permits** and there are restrictions on the use of public transport and non-government hotels. Camera paranoia and general xenophobia are predictably high among officials.

All of this is disappointing, because Ethiopia is undoubtedly fascinating and rewarding. The country isn't likely to open up in the foreseeable future. If you decide to fly into Addis, or in the unlikely event you're given permission for overland entry via Moyale in Kenya, visas are issued without too much fuss in Nairobi.

SOMALIA AND BEYOND

Getting visas for Somalia (required by all) is protracted – allow a month – and by no means easy. Enquire about getting a Somalian Travel Permit from the Somalian Immigration Office in Nairobi – supposed to be presented to the Ministry of Tourism in Mogadishu. Somalia's borders are closed on Fridays. Cholera and yellow fever certificates are needed. For details of buses to Liboi and the Somalian border, see the section on Garissa, p.387.

In the past, **SOMALIA** has provoked widely divergent responses from travellers. There's considerable mistrust of foreigners – especially in the towns – and a state security apparatus that seems to percolate every fibre of society. Women travelling alone tend to be well treated and chaperoned everywhere. Male travellers can expect endless questions from men and boys claiming to be "security agents", as they often are. Photography is out of the question.

One of the few countries in Africa with a largely homogeneous culture – Somali – the country has kept its powerful clan divisions within the unity of one language (Somali) and one religion (Islam). Somalia has switched **foreign protectors** three times: from the United States to the Soviet Union and, as the war with Ethiopia ground on, back to America again (a peace agreement with Ethiopia was signed in 1987). Up to 700,000 refugees have flooded into Somalia from Ethiopia, creating a

critical national problem. Despite early achievements, the state-controlled, doctrinaire Marxist economy gradually withered and free market principles, under IMF and World Bank tutelage, have been asserted. Most of Somalia is dry and barren, and pockets with agricultural potential are now the focus of much development aid.

Since 1987, a savage genocidal **war** has been fought against Issaqi nomads in the north who are partly united under the banner of the Somali National Movement. Hundreds of thousands have been displaced and thousands more killed in bombing raids (led by Zimbabwe-recruited mercenaries) that reached a peak of ferocity early in 1989. The towns of Hargeisa and Burao have been largely destroyed. Bans on journalists and a Ministry of Disinformation working full tilt mean it's hard to unravel the present situation. The latest news indicates that the government in Mogadishu is under siege to a host of temporarily united rebel forces. There have been reports of widespread massacres and extra-judicial executions as well as political detentions and torture on a mass scale.

Assuming a) you get a visa, b) you can handle relations and c) the country is not actually tearing itself apart at the time, Somalia is an extraordinary and often welcoming land. There's always someone to help you out and show you the way. There's little writing in English – most people read and write Somali as well as speak it – but the remnants of British and Italian colonial influence are still evident in that people are eager to practise European languages. The only large towns – **Kismayu**, the capital **Mogadishu**, and **Berbera** (location of an American military base) – are on the coast and travel and other practicalities are much as you'll have come to expect from travel in north-east Kenya – only perhaps more so. In theory, there are also two flights a week between Nairobi and Mogadishu (about $130).

Travelling through Somalia (assuming the current conflict doesn't prevent it) just about makes possible an unusual and recommended overland route into (or out of) Africa through **DJIBOUTI** and **NORTH YEMEN** – though you'll have to fly into or out of North Yemen's capital, **Sana'a**. This is an adventurous journey – almost certainly foolhardy at present – and, for a good part of the way, United Nations personnel and their vehicles may figure prominently. It may also still be possible to find a dhow down to Lamu from Mogadishu or Kismayu – or, with lots of luck and a fair dose of courage, vice versa.

THE INDIAN OCEAN

Lastly, natural onward steps from Kenya would appear to be **India** or the Indian Ocean islands – the **Seychelles**, the **Comoros**, **Mauritius** and **Madagascar**. Flights to Bombay run as low as Ksh5000 at Nairobi travel agents (see Nairobi "Listings"). The islands are somewhat expensive targets and expensive, too, once you've arrived.

SEYCHELLES

Entry to the **SEYCHELLES**, however, is simple – just arrive with your cholera certificate; no visa is required for any nationality – and the archipelago is a delightful place for a holiday. You can help keep the costs down with **guest houses** (especially off-season), hired **bicycles** and inter-island ferries (rather than flights). For getting there: *Kenya Airways* flies from Nairobi to Mahe twice a week (excursion fares from Ksh8000).

COMOROS

The French- and Swahili-speaking **COMOROS** are equally amenable, and very little known – tourists are rare here. Visas are available on arrival at Moroni, the capital. There are two flights a week on *Air France* and one on *Air Mauritius* (one-ways to the Comoros – no excursions – are about Ksh5000).

MAURITIUS

Tourists flock to **MAURITIUS** of course – the majority of them South African – and the hilly, wooded interior and fabulous beaches are spectacular assets. Visas are not required for British or Commonwealth nationals, or citizens of the European Community, the Scandinavian countries, Israel, Japan or South Africa. Americans need them. You'll have to show an onward ticket on arrival. There are two flights a week from Nairobi on *Air Mauritius* (21-day excursion fares about Ksh11,000).

MADAGASCAR

MADAGASCAR is worth making an ultimate goal for your travels: for its diverse scenery, unique wildlife, the distinctive Malgache people and language, and overall unusual mixture of African and southeast Asian cultures. You'll need some French. You may also need persistence to get a seat on the plane from Nairobi or Dar-es-Salaam, but it's worth any amount of hassle if you can afford the fare; two flights weekly from Nairobi (21-day excursion fares about Ksh7000). Visas for Madagascar are required for all nationalities – obtainable in Nairobi from *Air Madagascar*'s office at the *Hilton*.

A BEGINNER'S GUIDE TO SWAHILI

Surprisingly, perhaps, Swahili is one of the easiest languages to learn. It's pronounced exactly as it's written, with the stress nearly always on the penultimate syllable. And it's satisfyingly regular, so even with limited knowledge you can make yourself understood and construct simple sentences.

In Kenya, you'd rarely be stuck without Swahili, but it makes a huge difference to your perceptions if you try. People are delighted if you make the effort (though they'll also tend to assume you understand more than you do). Don't forget, that for many Kenyans, Swahili is another foreign language they get by in, like English. For travels further afield in East Africa, and especially in Tanzania, some knowledge of Swahili is a very useful backup.

The language has spread widely from its coastal origins to become the *lingua franca* of East Africa and it has tended to lose its richness and complexity as a result. Up-country, it is often spoken as a second language with a minimum of grammar. On the coast, you'll hear it spoken with tremendous panache: oratorial skills and punning (to which it lends itself with great facility) are much appreciated. Swahili is a Bantu language (in fact one of the more mainstream of the family), but it has incorporated thousands of foreign words, the majority of them Arabic. Far more of this Arabic inheritance and borrowing is preserved on the coast. The "standard" dialect is derived from Zanzibar Swahili, which the early missionaries learned and first transcribed into the Roman alphabet. **Written Swahili** is still not uniform and you'll come across slight variations in spelling, particularly on menus.

PRONUNCIATION

Once you get the hang of *voicing every syllable*, **pronunciation** is easy. Each vowel is syllabic. Odd-looking combinations of consonants are often pronounced as one syllable too. *Mzee* for example, is pronounced "mz-ay-ay" (rhyming with "hey!") and *shauri* (troubles, problem) is pronounced "sha-oor-i". Nothing is silent.

You'll often come across an "**m**" where it looks out of place: this letter can precede any other. It's almost always pronounced as one syllable with the letter(s) that follow It: eg *mnyama* – animal; *mbwa* – dog; *mboga* – vegetables. Just add a bit of an "m" sound at the beginning; "mmmb-oga". Don't say "erm-bwa" or "mer-boga"– you'll be misunderstood. The letter "n" can precede a number of others and gives a nasal quality.

For memorising, it often helps to ignore the first letter or syllable. Thousands of nouns, for example, start with "ki" (singular) and "vy" (plural), and they're all in the same noun class.

A as in **A**rthur
B as in **b**ed
C doesn't exist on its own
CH as in **ch**urch, but often sounds like a "t", a "dj", or a "ky"
D as in **d**onkey
DJ as in py**j**amas
DH like a cross between **dh**ow and **th**ou
E between the "e" in **E**dward and "ai" in **ai**ling
F as in **f**an
G as in **g**ood
GH at the back of the throat, like a growl; nearly an "r"
H as in **h**armless, sometimes contracted from KH as in lo**ch**
I like the "e" in **e**vil
J as in **j**ug
K as in **k**iosk, sometimes like soft "t" or "ch"
KH a "k" but breathier
L as in **l**ullaby, but often pronounced "r"
M as in **M**artian
MN one syllable, eg *mnazi* (coconut), "mna-zi"
N as in **n**onsense
NG as in wro**ng**, but sometimes pronounced with no "g" sound at all
O as in **o**range, never as in "open" or "do"
P as in **p**enguin
Q doesn't exist (except in early Romanised texts; now "k")
R as in **r**apid, or rolled as in the French *rapide*
S as in **S**amson
T as in **t**iny
TH as in **th**anks, never like the "th" in them
U as in l**u**te
V as in **v**ictory
W as in **w**obble
X doesn't exist
Y as in **y**ou
Z as in **z**ero

ELEMENTARY GRAMMAR

Noun classes put people off Swahili. They are something like the genders in French or Latin in that you alter each adjective according to the class of noun. In Swahili you add a prefix to the word. Each class covers certain areas of meaning and usually has a prefix letter associated with most of its nouns. For example, words beginning "ki" or "ch" (singular), and "vi" or "vy" (plural) are in the general class of "things", notably smallish things (eg, *kitoto* – small child, infant). Words beginning "m" in the singular and "wa" in the plural are people (eg, *mtu/watu* – person/people; *mtalii/ watalii* – tourist/s). Words beginning "m" (singular) and "mi" (plural) are often trees and plants (eg, *mti, miti* – tree/s), or have connections with life.

Most abstract nouns begin with "u" (eg, *uhuru* – freedom, *utoto* – childhood). There are seven or eight classes (and plurals for each) but this gives you some idea.

Prefixes get added to adjectives, so you get *kiti kizuri* – a good chair; *mtu mzuri* – a good person; *miti mizuri* – lovely trees. Really correct Swahili, with everything agreeing, isn't much spoken except on the coast, and you can get away with murder. But once you've grasped the essential building blocks – the root meanings and the prefixes, suffixes and infixes of one or two letters which turn them into words – it becomes a very creative language to learn.

VERBS

There are a few exceptions and irregularities but the **verb system** is basically straightforward and makes conversational Swahili a realistic goal even for convinced non-linguists.

to want	*ku-taka*	to look	*ku-tazama*
to come	*kuja* irregular; the infinitive "ku" part stays with the root	to hear	*ku-sikia*
		to buy	*ku-nunua*
to go	*kwenda*, ie ku-enda but, again, *usually* keeps the "ku" part	to know	*ku-jua*
		to think	*ku-fikiri*
to eat	*ku-la*	to like/love	*ku-penda*
to drink	*ku-nywa*	to be able (can)	*ku-weza*
to sleep	*ku-lala*	to give	*ku-pa*
to be tired	*ku-choka*	to bring	*ku-leta*
to stay	*ku-kaa*	to be/become	*ku-wa*
to say, speak	*ku-sema*	to come from	*ku-toka*
to see, to meet	*ku-ona, ku-onana*	to have	*ku-wa na* (lit. "to be with")

PRONOUNS

Me, I	*Mimi, Ni*	She/he	*A*	You (pl.)	*Ninyi, M*
You	*Wewe, U*	Us, We	*Sisi, Tu*	Them, They	*Wao, Wa*
Him/her	*Yeye,*				

TENSES

present tense	*-na-*	future tense	*-ta-*
past tense	*-li-*	just past, or still going on	*-me-*

EXAMPLES OF PRONOUNS, VERBS AND TENSES

she wanted	*a-li-taka*	have they gone?	*wa-me-kwenda?*
I'm tired	*ni-me-choka*	she said...	*a-li-sema*
we will sleep	*tu-ta-lala*	can I...?	*ni-na-weza?*
did you hear?	*u-li-sikia?*	I will bring	*ni-ta-leta*
they like...	*wa-na-penda*	we are staying (at/in)...	*tu-na-kaa...*
are you (pl.) going?	*m-na-enda?*	I know	*ni-na-jua*
has he come?	*a-me-kuja?*		

For the present tense of "to have", you can say *mimi nina gari* ("I am with a car"/"I have a car") or just *nina gari, una gari, ana gari*, etc.

WORDS AND PHRASES

The words and phrases listed here are all in common usage but Swahili (like English) is far from being a homogeneous language, so don't be surprised if you sometimes get some funny looks. And for lack of space for explanation, there are a number of apparent inconsistencies; just ignore them unless you intend to learn the language seriously. These phrases should make you understood at least.

USEFUL GREETINGS

Jambo/Hujambo	Hello, good day, how are you? (multi-purpose greeting, means "Problems?")	*Kwaheri/ni*	Goodbye to one/many
		Asante/ni	Thank you to one/many
		sana	very (a common emphasis)
Jambo/Sijambo	(the response) No problems	*Bwana*	Mister, the equivalent of *Monsieur* in French
Habari?	How are things? (literally "News?")		
		Mama	like the French *Madame* or *Mademoiselle*, for adult women
Nzuri	Fine, good, terrible		
Hodi!	Hello? Anyone in? (said on knocking or entering)	*Kijana*	youth, teenager (pl. *vijana*)
		Mtoto	child, kid (pl. *watoto*)
Karibu	Come in, enter, welcome (also said on offering something)	*Jina lako nani?/ Unaitwaje?*	What's your name?/What are you called?

BASICS

My name is/I am called	*Jina langu/Nina itwa...*	I don't know	*Sijui*
Where are you from?	*Unatoka wapi?*	where (is)?	*wapi?*
		here	*hapa*
Where are you staying?	*Unakaa wapi?*	when?	*lini?*
		now	*sasa*
I am from...	*Ninatoka...*	soon	*sasa hivi*
I am staying (at/in)...	*Ninakaa...*	why?	*kwa nini?*
		because...	*kwa sababu...*
See you!	*Tutaonana!* (lit. "We shall meet")	who?	*nani?*
		what?	*nini?*
yes	*Ndiyo* (lit. "it is so")	which?	*gani?*
no	*hapana* (a general negative); *la* (Arabic – heard mostly on the coast)	true	*kweli*
		and/with	*na*
		or	*au*
I don't understand	*Sifahamu/Sielewi*	(it) is/(they) are	*ni* (a useful little connector when you can't think of an alternative eg. *njia ni nzuri* – the road is good)
I don't speak Swahili, but...	*Sisemi kiswahili, lakini...*		
How do you say in Swahili?	*Unasemaje kwa kiswahili...?*	isn't it?	*siyo?* (equivalent of French *n'est ce pas?*)
Could you repeat that?	*Sema tena* (lit. "speak again")	I'm British, American German, French, Italian	*Mimi Mwingereza, Mwamerika, Mdachi, Mfaransa, Mwitalia.*
Speak slowly	*Sema pole pole*		

DAILY NEEDS

Where can I stay?	*Naweza kukaa wapi?*	washing water	*maji ya kuosha*
Can I stay here?	*Naweza kukaa hapa?*	hot/cold water	*maji moto/baridi*
room/s	*chumba/vyumba*	I'm hungry	*Nina njaa*
bed/s	*kitanda/vitanda*	I'm thirsty	*Nina kiu*
chair/s	*kiti/viti*	Is there any...?	*Iko...? Kuna...?*
table/s	*meza*	Yes there is...	*Iko..., Kuna...*
toilet, bathroom	*choo, bafu*	No there isn't any	*Haiko..., Hakuna...*

DAILY NEEDS

How much?	Ngapi?	Reduce the price, come down a little!	Punguza kidogo!
money	Pesa		
What price...?	Bei gani...?	shop	duka
How much is...?	Pesa ngapi...?	bank	benki
I want...	Nataka...	post office	posta
I don't want...	Sitaki...	café, restaurant	hoteli
Give me/bring me (can I have?)	Nipe/niletee	telephone	simu
		cigarettes	sigara
again/more	tena	I'm ill	Mimi mgonjwa
enough	tosha/basi	doctor	daktari
expensive	ghali sana	hospital	hospitali
cheap (also "easy")	rahisi	police	polisi
Fifty cents	sumni	tip, bribe	"chai"

TRAVEL AND DIRECTIONS

Bus/es	bas, basi/mabasi	Stop!	Simama!
car/s, vehicle/s	gari/magari	Where are you going?	Unaenda wapi?
taxi	teksi	To where?	Mpaka wapi?
bicycle	baiskeli	From where?	Kutoka wapi?
train	treni	How many kilometres?	kilometa ngapi?
plane	ndege	I'm going to...	Nenda...
boat/ship	chombo/meli	Move along, squeeze up a little	Songa!/songa kidogo!
petrol	petroli		
road, path	njia/ndia	Let's go, Carry on	Twende, endelea
highway	barabara	straight ahead	Moja kwa moja
on foot/walking	kwa miguu	right	kulia
When does it leave?	Inaondoka lini?	left	kushoto
When will we arrive?	Tutafika lini?	up	juu
slowly	pole pole	down	chini
fast, quickly	haraka	I want to get off here	Nataka kushuka hapa
Wait!/hang on a moment!	Ngoja!/ngoja kidogo!	The car has broken down	Gari imevunjika

TIME, CALENDAR AND NUMBERS

What time is it?	Saa ngapi?	this month	mwezi huu	9	tisa
"four o'clock"	saa nne	(lit. "moon")		10	kumi
quarter past	na robo	Monday	jumatatu	11	kumi na moja
half past	na nusu	Tuesday	jumanne	12	kumi na mbili
quarter to	kasa robo	Wednesday	jumatano	20	ishirini
minutes	dakika	Thursday	alhamisi	21	ishirini na moja
early	mapema	Friday	ijumaa	30	thelathini
yesterday	jana	Saturday	jumamosi	40	arobaini
today	leo	Sunday	jumapili	50	hamsini
tomorrow	kesho	1	moja	60	sitini
daytime	mchana	2	mbili	70	sabini
night time	usiku	3	tatu	80	themanini
dawn	alfajiri	4	nne	90	tisini
morning	asubuhi	5	tano	100	mia moja
last/this/next week	wiki iliopita/hii/ ijayo	6	sita	121	mia moja na ishirini na moja
this year	mwaka huu	7	saba	1000	elfu
		8	nane		

SIGNS

Danger	*Hatari!*	Fierce dog!	*Mbwa mkali!*
Warning	*Angalia!/Onyo!*	No entry!	*Hakuna njia!*

WORDS WORTH KNOWING

good	*-zuri* (with a prefix at the front)	problems, hassles	*wasiwasi, matata*
		no problem	*hakuna wasiwasi/ hakuna matata*
bad	*-baya* (ditto)		
big	*-kubwa*	friend	*rafiki*
small	*-dogo*	Sorry, pardon	*Samahani*
a lot of	*-ingi*	It's nothing	*Si kitu*
other/another	*-ingine*	Excuse me (let me through)	*Hebu*
not bad	*si mbaya*		
okay, right, fine	*sawa*	What's up?	*Namna gani?*
fine, cool	*safi*	If God wills it	*Inshallah* (heard often on the coast)
completely	*kabisa*		
just, only	*tu (kitanda kimoja tu* – just one bed)	Please	*Tafadhali* (rare up-country and not heard much on the coast either)
thing/s	*kitu/vitu*		

And two phrases you're more likely to hear than to ever say:

Take a picture of me!	*Piga picha mimi!*	Help the poor!	*Saidia maskini!*

BOOKS AND COURSES

There are a number of published teach-yourself **courses** around. "*Swahili Grammar*" by E O Ashton (Longman) is very turgid and unchanged since 1947. *Teach Yourself Swahili* by D V Perrrot (Teach Yourself Books) isn't a lot better. For the analytical approach, the best book is probably *Simplified Swahili* by Peter M Wilson (Longman, 1985). *Kiswahili kwa Kitendo* ("Swahili by Action"; Harper & Row, 1972) is good if grammar appals you, but it's bulky and expensive. A new course by Joan Maw, *Twende!* (Oxford University Press), looks promising and Lonely Planet puts out a small, useful pocket guide. The Berlitz phrasebook is good for laughs, but of little use on the ground. As for dictionaries, the *Swahili Dictionary* from Teach Yourself Books suffers amazing gaps (it's the kind of dictionary that would lead you to ask the waiter for "some puree of oranges and sugar" when you wanted marmalade) but it's cheap and about all there is.

OTHER LANGUAGES

The following brief lists are intended only for introductions and as a springboard for communication. If you'll be spending time in a particular linguistic region, you may be surprised at how difficult it is to track down usable primers

and phrasebooks for these languages. Very little material exists for non-native speakers of African languages, though you can make some progress if you're prepared to struggle (with a dictionary) with short novels or the Bible and the like. Try the sources on p.20–21 for further ideas. However, even the library of the School of African and Oriental Studies is rather bereft of user-friendly material.

LUO (LAKE VICTORIA)

How do you do?	*Iriyo nade?*	3	*Adek*	8	*Aboro*
Response:	*Ariyo maber!*	4	*Angwen*	9	*Ochiko*
Thank you	*Erokamano*	5	*Abich*	10	*Apar*
1	*Achiel*	6	*Auchiely*		
2	*Ariyo*	7	*Abiriyo*		

MAA (MAASAI)

Greetings to a man:	*Lo murrani! Supa!*	3	*Okuni*
Response:	*Ipa!*	4	*Oonguan*
Greetings to a woman:	*Na kitok! Takuenya!*	5	*Imiet*
Response:	*Iko!*	6	*Ile*
Thank you (very much!)	*Ashe (naleng!)*	7	*Oopishana*
Goodbye!	*Sere!*	8	*Isiet*
1	*Obo*	9	*Ooudo*
2	*Aare*	10	*Tomon*

KIKUYU (CENTRAL HIGHLANDS

How are things?	*Kweruo atia?*	1	*Imwe*
Fine!	*Ni kwega!*	2	*Igiri*
How are you?	*Waigua atia?*	3	*Ithatu*
Are you well? (plural)	*Wi mwega/Muri ega?*	4	*Inya*
Response: ("nothing wrong")	*Asha, ndi mwega*	5	*Ithano*
		6	*Ithathatu*
Goodbye (when you're leaving)	*Tigwo na wega*	7	*Mugwanja*
		8	*Inyanya*
Goodbye (when you're staying)	*Thii na wega*	9	*Kenda*
		10	*Ikumi*

KENYAN TERMS: A GLOSSARY

These words are all in common usage. Remember, however, that plural forms often have different beginnings.

AFCO Armed Forces Catering Odnance

ASK Agricultural Society of Kenya

ASKARI policeman, security guard

BANDA any kind of hut, usually round and thatched

BARABARA main road

BOMA a fort or defensive stockade, sometimes meaning village

BORITI mangrove poles, used on the coast for building and exported to the Gulf states for the same purpose

BUIBUI the black cover-all cloak and scarf of Swahili women

BWANA mister, a common term of address

CHAI not just tea, but also the common term for a tip, or more often a small bribe or persuasion

CHOO toilet (pronounced *cho*)

DUKA shop, store

DUKA LA DAWA chemist

FUNDI mechanic, craftsman, expert

GARI car

GK Government of Kenya

HARAMBEE "pull together" – the ideology of peaceable community development espoused by Kenyatta. Harambee meetings are local fund-raising gatherings – for schools, clinics, etc – but they've come in for some criticism in recent years as politicians vie to contribute the most money

HOTELI small restaurant, *chai* shop, café

JUA KALI "hot sun" – open-air car repairer's yard or small workshop

KANGA printed cotton sheet used as a wrap, often incorporating a motto

KANISA church

KANU Kenya African National Union, Kenya's sole political party

KBC Kenya Broadcasting Corporation

KIKOI brightly coloured woven cloth

MAENDELEO progress, development

MAGENDO corruption, bribery, abuse of power

MAKONDE beautifully worked Tanzanian wood carving, typically in ebony and representing entwined spirit families – much copied in the tourist markets

MAKUTI palm leaf roof common on the coast

MALAIKA angel

MALAYA prostitute

MAMA common term of address for married women

MANAMBA *matatu* tout, "turnboy"

MANYATTA temporary cattle camp (Maasai)

MASKINI the poor, beggars (*Saidia maskini!* – "Help the poor!")

MATATU pick-up taxi, usually full to overflowing

MKENYA Kenyan citizen (pl. *wakenya*)

MORAN man in the warrior age group of Maasai or Samburu (pl. *morani*)

MSIKITI mosque

MTALI tourist (pl. *watali*)

MUNGU God

MURRAM red or black clay soil, usually referring to a road

MWANANCHI person, peasant, worker (pl. *wananchi*, the people)

MZEE old man: "*the* Mzee" is Kenyatta

MZUNGU white person (pl. *wazungu*)

NCCK National Christian Council of Kenya

NGOMA dancing, drumming, party, celebration

NJIA road, path

NYAYO "footsteps" – the follow-in-his-footsteps philosophy of post-Kenyatta Kenya propounded by President Moi

PANGA multi-purpose short machete carried everywhere in the countryside

SAFARI journey of any kind

SHAMBA small farm, plot

UHURU freedom, independence

ULAYA Europe

INDEX

Italicised entries indicate topics, animal names or places to stay. Capitalised italics are reserved for the names of ethnic groups or languages. Bold entries are generally major headings in the guide.

MAP INDEX

REGIONS AND PARKS

TOWN AND SITE PLANS

HELP US UPDATE

We've gone to great lengths to ensure that this third edition of **Kenya: the Rough Guide** is as up-to-date and accurate as possible. It's been completely overhauled and hugely expanded with new maps and a mass of fresh practical information – more than 100 extra pages. Much of the credit for this is due to the many readers – opposite – who sent letters, cards and even dog-eared, annotated copies of the *Rough Guide*, for which we're always immensely grateful. But Kenya changes fast and if you feel there are places we've overrated or under-praised, or find we've missed something or covered something which has gone, then please write. The lowdown on your favourite nightclub, hotel or restaurant is as interesting as letters about obscure routes through the bush. Please locate places as accurately as possible (sketch maps are a help). We'll acknowledge all information used in the next edition and will send a free copy, or any other *Rough Guide* if you prefer, for the most useful (and legible!) feedback.

Richard Trillo, Africa Editor (Kenya 4th Edition), The Rough Guides, 149 Kennington Lane, London SE11 4EZ

THOSE WHO HELPED UPDATE

This edition owes an enormous debt to the readers and users of the second edition who wrote in with opinions and information. My thanks to everyone.

Simon and Sue Addinall, Peter Beck, Jackie Beecham, CW Benjamin, Roderick H Blackburn, Guilain Boudreau, Philip Breeze, Phiip Briggs, Andrew Brown, Linda Brown, Jane Bryce, Anja Buijsen, Justin Busbridge, Ronald Cameron, Jean Clements, Stephen Crocker, Tony Davis, Hans van der Deune, Saartje Drijver, Richard Dunn, Jonathan Elms, Graham Essex, Reinhard Ehli, Peter and Gill Flegg, Stephen Foster, JJ and R Gainford, Ken Garfinkel, Jonathan Gibson, Pauline Ginsberg, Karl Gittings, Rosalind Greig, Chinch Gryniewicz, Iain Hardy, Barbara Hogenboom, Thomas Hoskins, Michelle Howley, ML Hubbard, Susie Irvine, Mike and Harriet Kendrick, Graham Kenyon, Julian Kilker, Ingrid Kosterink, Tony Lane, Dave Leffman, Eugenio Llorente, Michéle and Paul Losse, Anne Magill, Helen Matthews, Peter McEachran, Mike Mead, Julie Meech, Frankie Meehan, TC Millington, NJ Mitchell, Alan Moorcroft, Hilary Moore, Grant Morton, Ilse Mwanza, Kala Nobbs, Ina M Numan, Rosemary Obuyu, David O'Brien, John Oldale, Charlie Pascoe, Matthew Prager, Jenny Prudden, Dev Rana, Peggy Redmond, Linda Reeder, Keithe Sales, Valerie Salisbury, Yukiko Sato, Tessa van der Schoot, Rob Schouten, George and Lorna Sether, John Speyer, Rosalind Sutton, Tony Sutton, Catherine Tattersfield, Margaret Taylor, John Thorne, Arnoud Thuss, RL Tucker, Annemarie Visagie, Dave Warne, Jean Watters, Pam Wear, Paul Weeks, Sandra Whittington, Robert Wilkinson, Peter Womack and Be Yeo.

MEDITERRANEAN WILDLIFE

THE ROUGH GUIDE

MEDITERRANEAN WILDLIFE: THE ROUGH GUIDE is an
essential companion for anyone interested in the fauna and flora
of the Mediterranean region, featuring detailed
country-by-country wildlife site guides to France, Greece, Italy,
Morocco, Portugal, Spain, Tunisia, Turkey and Yugoslavia, with
practical details on how to get to the sites and where to stay
nearby. Introductory sections provide a keynote guide to the
plant and animal species, while background articles analyse the
environmental issues facing the Mediterranean in the 1990s.

Written and researched by Pete Raine, with a team of
international wildlife contributors. Illustrated throughout with
line drawings by Tessa Lovat-Smith.

Published by Harrap Columbus, price £7.99

ROUGH GUIDES – THE FULL LIST

- Amsterdam
- Berlin
- Brazil
- Brittany and Normandy
- California and West Coast USA
- Crete
- Czechoslovakia
- Eastern Europe
- Egypt
- France
- Germany
- Greece
- Guatemala and Belize
- Holland, Belgium and Luxembourg
- Hong Kong
- Hungary
- Ireland
- Israel and the Occupied Territories
- Italy
- Kenya
- Mexico
- Morocco
- Nepal
- New York
- Paris

- Peru
- Poland
- Portugal
- Provence and the Cote d'Azur
- The Pyrenees
- San Francisco
- Scandinavia
- Sicily
- Spain
- Tunisia
- Turkey
- Venice
- West Africa
- Yugoslavia
- Zimbabwe and Botswana

Forthcoming:
- ❏ Tuscany and Umbria
- ❏ Romania
- ❏ Florida
- ❏ United States
- ❏ Canada
- ❏ Thailand
- ❏ Europe

ROUGH GUIDE SPECIALS

- Mediterranean Wildlife
- Women Travel: Adventures, Advice & Experience
- Nothing Ventured: Disabled People Travel the World

Forthcoming:
- ❏ World Music

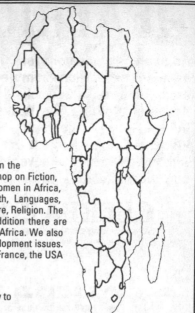